John Wilmot, second Earl of Rochester, is still commonly regarded as 'the wicked Earl', and his reputation as a rake has imparted an air of dilettantism to his poetry. By contrast, *Rochester: The Poems in Context* emphasises the poet's sharp, restless intellect, a more powerful driving force in his poems than the sensual appetites stressed by previous critics. Marianne Thormählen uncovers his familiarity with, and sly allusions to, events and leading characters in Restoration politics; his awareness of trends in science, theology and philosophy; his acute representations of contemporary mores; and his commitment to high standards in literary craftsmanship. As a result, a more complex picture of Rochester emerges – that of a serious artist who tackled major issues during a particularly turbulent period in English history.

While Rochester's texts are always at the focus of the discussion, the book has much to offer readers whose main interest is in late seventeenth-century culture and civilisation rather than in Restoration literature. Among the issues reflected in Rochester's poems and addressed by the author are religious discord in seventeenth-century England, the position of women scholars and poets, military matters, statecraft and foreign affairs under Charles II, and developments in philosophy and science.

ROCHESTER
The poems in context

ROCHESTER

The poems in context

MARIANNE
THORMÄHLEN

CAMBRIDGE
UNIVERSITY PRESS

Published by the Press Syndicate of the University of Cambridge
The Pitt Building, Trumpington Street, Cambridge CB2 1RP
40 West 20th Street, New York, NY 10011-4211, USA
10 Stamford Road, Oakleigh, Melbourne 3166, Australia

First published 1993

Printed in Great Britain at the University Press, Cambridge

A catalogue record for this book is available from the British Library

Library of Congress cataloguing in publication data
Thormählen, Marianne, 1949–
Rochester: the poems in context / Marianne Thormählen.
p.   cm.
Includes bibliographical references and index.
ISBN 0 521 44042 4
1. Rochester, John Wilmot, Earl of, 1647–1680–Criticism and interpretation.   1. Title.
PR3669.R2T47   1993
821'.4–dc20 92–34379 CIP

ISBN 44042 4 hardback

Cambridge University Press gratefully acknowledges publication assistance from the Swedish
Council for Research in the Humanities and Social Sciences

To Claes Schaar

E come sare' io sanza lui corso?
Chi m'avrìa tratto su per la montagna?

Purgatorio III.5–6

Contents

Acknowledgements   *page* xi

Introduction   1

CUPID AND BACCHUS
1 *Cupid and Bacchus*   9

MEN AND WOMEN
2 *The love lyrics*   29
3 *'The Imperfect Enjoyment' and 'A Ramble in Saint James's
   Parke'*   84
4 *'A Letter from Artemiza in the Towne to Chloe in the
   Countrey'*   104

PRIDE AND PHILOSOPHY
5 *Upon Nothing*   141
6 *'A Satyr against Reason and Mankind': the context*   162
7 *'A Satyr against Reason and Mankind': the argumentation*   190

COURT AND SOCIAL
8 *'Tunbridge Wells'*   241
9 *'Timon'*   266
10 *Court satires and lampoons*   285

CRAFT AND ART

11 *'An Allusion to Horace'*   309
12 *The poems on Mulgrave and Scroope*   337

    Epilogue   357

    Select bibliography   366
    Index   373

Acknowledgements

———◆◆◆◆———

A British Council Fellowship enabled me to spend the spring of 1987 in Oxford, where the facilities and staff of the Bodleian Library were instrumental in establishing a basis for my research on Rochester. My home university of Lund made a vital contribution by reducing my teaching load for two years. Subsequent visits to the Bodleian were possible thanks to travel grants from the Elisabeth Rausing Memorial Fund (on two occasions), the New Society of Letters (*Vetenskaps-societeten*) at Lund, and the Wenner-Gren Foundation. I would have had to spend much more time there, and in other international research libraries, had I not enjoyed the magnificent support of the Lund University Library. Its efficient staff have processed thousands of inter-library loans for me in the past two decades and still greet me with a smile. I am also greatly indebted to the Swedish Council for Research in the Humanities and Social Sciences for a generous contribution to printing costs. A further obligation I am glad to acknowledge is to Dr Keith Walker, editor of the scholarly old-spelling edition of *The Poems of John Wilmot, Earl of Rochester* (1984), and to his publisher Basil Blackwell; quotations from Rochester's poems were taken from this edition.

Among the organisations and institutions whose assistance I recall with gratitude, one played a very special role. Most scholars in the Humanities are thankful for the opportunity to do research on a full-time basis for one year; the Alexander von Humboldt Foundation in Bonn gave me two, proving a constant source of munificent, amicable and blessedly unbureaucratic help. For a native of egalitarian Sweden, contacts with this unashamedly élitist organisation were peculiarly instructive. In Hamburg, where I spent my two years as a Humboldt Fellow, Professor Dr Rudolf Haas received me with the greatest kindness and courtesy, creating an ideal working climate for me. Sadly, my home from home at the *Seminar für Englische Sprache und Kultur*, the Department Secretary's office, now no longer houses Frau Christa Jöhnke, whose conversation was as tangy and invigorating as her coffee.

The families of wandering scholars have unique opportunities to show their mettle. My husband Axel, our two daughters and my gallant mother responded to every challenge with characteristic magnanimity and good humour, enabling me not only to work, but to work happily. Perhaps their greatest gift was the feeling that I was entitled to expect it from them.

What I never had any right to expect was that my former tutor and supervisor, Professor Claes Schaar, would continue to extend the same self-effacing but universal helpfulness to the junior colleague that he gave the student. For over twenty years, even after his retirement as Head of the English Department at Lund in 1986, his unstinting encouragement, fruitful advice and stringent criticisms have aided my every step.

Introduction

Even today, many people regard John Wilmot, the second Earl of Rochester, as a poet whose work is dominated by an 'overwhelming desire for sexual pleasure'.[1] Critical comments on the urgency with which Rochester's verse articulates a painful lack of inner assurance[2] have not dispelled the traditional image of him as a man and poet impelled by sensual appetite. A rake's reputation is particularly hard to live down, and that image has had a remarkable staying power, misleading as it is. In fact, nobody who did not know what sexual desire is like would be any the wiser after perusing the Rochester canon.[3] While few of his poems lack an erotic dimension, they have virtually nothing to say about the nature of sexual appetite and gratification.

This realisation is no novelty, nor is the contention that Rochester possessed an unusually keen intelligence. What this study attempts to do is to emphasise the way in which mental and physical experience are brought together in his work. Previous Rochester critics have tended to stress the poet's search for firm beliefs and a stable identity. While the absence of rest and quiet is strongly felt in his poetry, I do not think that this feature is due to a fruitless hankering for secure convictions. It seems to me that Reba Wilcoxon is quite right when maintaining that Rochester's ethic is based on sensual pleasure as the highest good.[4] The trouble is that it is not good enough.

Arguing such a case would not call for hundreds of pages. The reason

---

[1] An expression used, with reference to Rochester, by Harold Weber in *The Restoration Rake-Hero: Transformations in Sexual Understanding in Seventeenth-Century England* (Madison, 1986), p. 3.

[2] See, for instance, Dustin H. Griffin, *Satires Against Man: The Poems of Rochester* (Berkeley, Los Angeles and London, 1973), pp. 10–20, and Reba Wilcoxon, 'Rochester's Philosophical Premises: A Case for Consistency', *Eighteenth-Century Studies* 8 (Winter 1974–5), 198.

[3] See pp. 29 and 82–3 below.   [4] 'Rochester's Philosophical Premises', 200.

I

why this book has acquired such ample proportions has to do with another aspect of its approach to Rochester: the wish to study the poems in their historical context.

This is the third published critical full-length study of Rochester's poetry. While its predecessors[5] contributed a wealth of information on the seventeenth-century background, they focused on literary connexions and influences. Valuable as these analyses are, Rochester's poetry repays efforts to contemplate it in the light of Restoration events, developments and personalities in the fields of national and international politics, religion, philosophy and social life.

It has often been suggested[6] that Rochester was not interested in politics, and that his poetry is largely unaffected by the major events of his time. On the contrary, his satires contain a number of passages where history is transmuted into poetry, to borrow George deF. Lord's phrase.[7] Besides, a great many details from Rochester's poems gain freshness and poignancy when related to contemporary conditions. The disorders afflicting the various sufferers at Tunbridge Wells, the culinary predilections adumbrated in *Timon*, and the faiths and infidelities of the ladies satirised in *Signior Dildo* may serve as examples of such phenomena. Lines and phrases that seemed to be of a general nature, perhaps even somewhat platitudinous, are suddenly seen to embody sly allusions to notable figures in Restoration society.

It would indeed have been odd if a man of Rochester's brains and perspicacity had remained unaffected by the way of the Restoration world. Burnet stresses his love of gossip, and his poems and letters[8] testify to this inclination. A much-quoted letter to Henry Savile[9] states that Rochester and his addressee had both dabbled in, and proved useless at, 'Polliticks'. The expression may merely be taken to refer to Court intrigue, or to Rochester's occasional appearance in the House of Lords; but it hardly implies indifference to affairs of state. The marvellous Bendo Bill[10] shows with what mastery Rochester was able to imitate, and even enhance, the highly specialised jargon of seventeenth-century

---

[5] Griffin's *Satires Against Man* and David Farley-Hills, *Rochester's Poetry* (London, 1978).

[6] Cf. Griffin's essay 'Rochester and the "Holiday Writers"' in Dustin Griffin and David M. Vieth, eds., *Rochester and Court Poetry: Papers Presented at a Clark Library Seminar 11 May 1985* (Los Angeles, 1988), p. 38.

[7] From his preface to the first volume (New Haven and London, 1963) of the *Poems on Affairs of State: Augustan Satirical Verse, 1660–1714*, p. lv.

[8] Jeremy Treglown's edition of *The Letters of John Wilmot Earl of Rochester* (Oxford, 1980) is an invaluable aid to the Rochester critic. Quite apart from the letters themselves, Treglown's annotation is a source of vital infor mation throughout.

[9] P. 67 in Treglown's edition of the *Letters*. [10] See p. 249 below.

quacks. The speaker of the *Satyr against Reason and Mankind* moves sure-footed among the philosophical and religious tenets of the late seventeenth century. And, finally, the *Allusion to Horace* is the work of a critical intelligence of a high order. Rochester was not a great or in any way original thinker; but he was, as James Sutherland has said, 'the most brilliant person at the Court of Charles II'.[11]

Not only did Rochester possess first-class brains; they contributed to the mental make-up of a detached observer who took nothing on trust. The word 'sceptic' has been applied to him,[12] and with good reason: nowhere has Rochester articulated a sober belief in a circumstance or phenomenon beyond his own direct experience. In a crucial passage from his conversations with Burnet, he averred that 'he was sure *Religion* was either a mere Contrivance, or the most important thing that could be'. For a man who 'was not master of his own Belief', and who regarded believing as, at best, 'but a probable Opinion',[13] it was not permissible to move with assurance beyond the evidence of his senses.

These reflections have not made any distinctions between views expressed in Rochester's letters, in his discussions with Burnet and in his verse. The problem of how to draw such distinctions cannot be evaded, however. Rochester's reputation as a poet has certainly suffered in consequence of his personal notoriety. Even his contemporaries were aware that licentious works from other, and less able, pens were imputed to him. Thanks to the pioneering efforts of twentieth-century editors, above all David M. Vieth, Rochester's *œuvre* has been shorn of such spurious pieces. Even so, a peculiar reluctance to avoid letting the wicked-Earl image colour analyses of the canonical poems is – as was pointed out above – still with us.

A new and thoroughly researched biography of Rochester, viewed as a representative of his time, would no doubt divert attention from his dissipations, such as they were, and direct it towards his cultural *milieu*. Among the issues which await scholarly clarification are the extent of Rochester's learning and his development (if any) as *homo politicus*; the religious currents and developments in his household; and the conse-

---

[11] *English Literature of the Late Seventeenth Century* (Oxford, 1969), vol. VI of the *Oxford History of English Literature*, ed. Bonamy Dobrée and Norman Davis, p. 171.

[12] Cf. Griffin, *Satires Against Man*, ch. I ('The Mind of a Skeptic').

[13] Gilbert Burnet's *Some Passages of the Life and Death of John Earl of Rochester* (1680) has been published in many editions. For the modern Rochester student, it is most conveniently consulted in Farley-Hills, ed., *Rochester: The Critical Heritage* (New York, 1972). The relevant passages occur on pp. 77 and 66.

quences of his long sojourns in France. Did Rochester study Stilling-fleet's *Origines Sacrae*, Descartes, Browne's *Religio Medici*, and the works of Henry More, Walter Charleton, Joseph Glanvill and Gassendi?[14] Did he actively embrace Whig ideology towards the end of the 1670s, or were his views on political events, personages and so on chiefly conditioned by personal tastes and distastes from first to last? Did he persuade his wife to become a Catholic, as Burnet would have us believe, and if so, when and why? (Developments during the mid- and late 1670s might make it seem prudent to have a practising Catholic in the family.) How did Rochester spend his months in France? What *salons* did he frequent, what plays did he see and what people did he meet? It is hard to believe that a young English courtier with literary aspirations and a sceptical mind, who spent many weeks in France with plenty of time on his hands, would never have any contacts with the intellectual high-society set there. It is surely natural to imagine that Rochester, who had lived in France as a child and knew several highly placed people at the Court of Louis XIV, would soon seek out a congenial social and literary atmosphere. Investigations of such matters lie outside the scope of this study of Rochester's poems; but there is no doubt that they would provide valuable guidance for critics analysing his verse.

Quite apart from considerations of this kind, the problem of voice, of identity, is one that every student of Rochester's poems has to face. Despite the historical bias of this book, the biographical dimension is not, on the whole, much to the fore in it. There are two reasons for my unwillingness to call the 'I' of the various poems 'Rochester'. One is the poet's mastery of disguise, so well brought out in Anne Righter's (now Anne Barton) seminal lecture on Rochester.[15] Several of Rochester's best poems are demonstrably dramatic monologues, among them *A Letter from Artemiza in the Towne to Chloe in the Countrey* and the *Song of a Young Lady to her Ancient Lover*.[16] Even where a speaker utters

---

[14] These works are commended in William Ram(e)sey's *The Gentlemans Companion, or, a Character of True Nobility, and Gentility In the way of Essay* (London, 1672), p. 128. We know that Rochester was familiar with one of Ramesey's choices; 'for a Diversion, you may read *Hudebras* [*sic*]' (p. 129).

[15] It was printed as 'John Wilmot, Earl of Rochester' in the *Proceedings of the British Academy* 53, 1967 (1968), 47–69. A recent reminder to this effect was supplied by D. K. Alsop in '"An Epistolary Essay from M. G. to O. B. upon Their Mutual Poems" and the Problem of the Persona in Rochester's Poetry', *Restoration: Studies in English Literary Culture 1660–1700*, 12.2 (Fall 1988), 66–7 ('The difficulty of discovering the "real" Rochester is compounded by his particular enjoyment of mask, imitation, and self-parody', 66).

[16] Eric Rothstein's *Restoration and Early Eighteenth-Century Poetry*, vol. III of *The Routledge History of English Poetry* (Boston, London and Henley, 1981), makes several important observations

opinions which sound very like the Rochester we know from traditional sources, there are obstacles in the way of identification. The other
reason is the peculiar lack of stability, of poise, that characterises the
poet's work. Even where the argumentation is both persuasive and
coherent, one senses the irritable movement of an unquiet mind behind
it.

Rochester's verse shows us a mind which constantly demands that the
body supply evidence of true worth. Despite its yearning for fixity, for
the moment when the senses provide complete and immutable
satisfaction, that mind has the strength to refuse to be taken in by tainted
ware. Where Rochester's contemporaries are balanced, even complacent, hitting their targets squarely, his poetry is always on the move.
I think that Rochester's mind was the most interesting thing about him,
and that the way in which that mind tackled great existential issues in a
particularly turbulent historical period was the most interesting thing
about it.

Textual difficulties and problems of authorship caused much confusion
during the early decades of twentieth-century Rochester criticism.
Worthy pioneering contributions like Johannes Prinz's *John Wilmot Earl
of Rochester: His Life and Writings*, published in 1927,[17] have suffered in
the eyes of later generations as a result of quantities of argumentation
built on poems that were not in fact written by Rochester.[18] Vivian de
Sola Pinto, the second great name in early-twentieth-century Rochester
scholarship, contributed a biography which, despite its virtues, has long
cried out for a successor.[19] His Muses' Library edition of Rochester's
poetry, first published in 1953, represented a great advance at the time
but has now been superseded.

Where Rochester's poetry is concerned, one name towers above all
others in respect of textual scholarship. David M. Vieth's *Attribution in*

---

regarding Rochester's speakers, applying the term 'dramatic monologues' to his poetry; see
pp. 31–2. [17] In Leipzig; it is no. 154 in the Palaestra series.

[18] Still, Vieth's tribute to this predecessor in his *Rochester Studies 1925–1982: An Annotated
Bibliography* (New York, 1984), p. 134, is satisfyingly generous. Another early work of
Rochester criticism, albeit on a much more modest scale, whose usefulness is marred by such
inaccuracies is Fredelle Bruser's still intriguing 'Disproportion: A Study in the Work of John
Wilmot, Earl of Rochester', *University of Toronto Quarterly* 15 (July 1946), 384–96. The same
goes for two biographical works that retain their fascination: Graham Greene's *Lord Rochester's
Monkey: Being the Life of John Wilmot, Second Earl of Rochester* (London and New York, 1974);
and Charles Williams' *Rochester* (London, 1935).

[19] The first version was published as *Rochester: Portrait of a Restoration Poet* (London, 1935); the
revised biography, *Enthusiast in Wit: A Portrait of John Wilmot Earl of Rochester, 1647–1680*,
appeared in 1962 (Lincoln and London).

Restoration Poetry[20] constituted a tremendous achievement when it appeared in 1963 and still does. In it, Vieth proposed a Rochester canon to which subsequent decades have only seen marginal amendments. In 1968, Vieth's edition of *The Complete Poems of John Wilmot, Earl of Rochester* laid a solid foundation for, and did much to inspire, modern Rochester criticism.

Vieth's *Complete Poems* consists of modernised texts. The editor explained his decision to modernise by maintaining that 'there is virtually no basis for an old-spelling text of Rochester's poems' (p. xlv). It is true that there is no single authoritative seventeenth-century text, and very few of the poems exist in Rochester's holograph. Even so, Vieth's modernisation, while no doubt helpful in winning a wide audience for Rochester in the 1960s, has often been felt to be too radical (see below). In 1984, Keith Walker published an old-spelling edition of *The Poems of John Wilmot Earl of Rochester*.[21] Quotations in this study are taken from that edition.

The decision to use Walker's texts rather than Vieth's was by no means a foregone conclusion. As several reviewers have noted, there are errors and omissions in the newer edition. A more fundamental objection was summed up by Ken Robinson:

For the vast majority of poems [Walker] cannot claim to represent Rochester's spelling or punctuation. At best we are given versions close to those read by contemporaries. It is difficult to see the wisdom of preferring the spelling, capitalization, and accidentals of a variety of scribes and compositors to the judgement of an editor.[22]

Walker clearly felt that there was no need to impose a regularising editorial element on the texts and refrained from aiming higher than presenting versions read in Rochester's lifetime (Introduction, p. xv). Freely admitting to being 'everywhere indebted' to Vieth (p. xiv), he has applied the labours of others as well as his own scholarship and judgement to give us an old-spelling edition, the first ever with collations, which takes stock of present-day Rochester scholarship and criticism. As such, it is a vital contribution to research on Rochester.

Walker also gives an important answer to the question of why an old-spelling edition should be desirable in the first place:

---

[20] The full title is *Attribution in Restoration Poetry: A Study of Rochester's Poems of 1680* (New Haven and London).

[21] Oxford (Blackwell). A paperback edition, with some corrections, has subsequently appeared.

[22] Review of Walker in *The Modern Language Review* 81.4 (October 1986), 989. See also Paul Hammond's review of Walker's edition in *The Review of English Studies* 37.146 (May 1986), 263.

A great many of Rochester's words are 'slightly different' [the reference is to a quotation from Vieth regarding the respective meanings of 'satyr' and 'satire'] in connotation from their modern equivalents, and it may serve some purpose to be reminded of this. (p. xv)

Indeed they are, and indeed it does. Practically every line in Rochester's poems should send an attentive reader to the *OED*. Some words are explained by editors; but how many readers – even when acquainted with Restoration English – realise that 'duty' in line 13 of *The Fall* refers to a vassal's tribute, and that 'Baffl'd' in line 5 of *My Lord All-Pride* means 'disgraced, dishonoured'? Vieth's radical modernisation entailed blunting his readers' awareness of the all-important fact that words we automatically assume we understand do not always mean what we think they do.

Other reactions to Vieth's over-modernisation[23] have expressed further grounds for unhappiness with his editorial policy in this respect. In a seminal essay on Rochester, Barbara Everett pointed out that 'the primary need in presenting a poet is not to obscure his tone',[24] referring to Vieth's text as 'able but toneless'. Margaret Anne Doody has seconded this view.[25]

As Dustin Griffin concluded in a review of Walker's and Hammond's[26] Rochester editions, 'specialists will probably want to have both [Vieth's and Walker's] editions'.[27] The latter cannot, as Robinson says, properly be said to have superseded the former, and neither is definitive. In view of the situation a few decades ago, however, present-day Rochester readers are indeed fortunate in having them both.

This study of Rochester's poetry adds very little to the labours of textual scholars. A few altered readings and datings are suggested, but they are of no great importance. Nor are any substantial advances made with regard to the order in which the poems were written. The chronology is a vexed issue; the spectacle of editorial struggles with it has left me with no ambition to map out Rochester's poetic development stage by stage. In any case, I do not think that the matter of Rochester's development is itself of overriding importance. Certainly, it is not, in my view, sufficiently interesting to be set up as the fundamental

---

[23] A term applied to Vieth in Robinson's review, 989.

[24] 'The Sense of Nothing', in Treglown, ed., *Spirit of Wit: Reconsiderations of Rochester* (Oxford, 1982), p. 15.

[25] See *The Daring Muse: Augustan Poetry Reconsidered* (Cambridge, 1985), p. 268, n.2.

[26] *John Wilmot Earl of Rochester: Selected Poems* (Bristol, 1982).

[27] *The Scriblerian* 18 (1985), 73.

organising principle of a study of his poetry. Consequently, the structural outline of the book has been determined by other concerns. It has seemed most natural and expedient to start with Rochester's lyrics on sensual/erotic topics. The satirical works are best considered in succession, and in view of the wealth of secondary material drawn into those analyses, beginning with them would have resulted in a decidedly top-heavy structure. The book is divided into five sections. To some degree, each of them draws on the preceding one(s). However, many readers will only be interested in one or two works and will not wish to be burdened with the necessity of ploughing through a great number of pages looking for scattered references to them. With their needs in mind, I have tried to make it possible to read every section – and, as far as possible, each chapter within every section – as a self-contained unit.

The present study is the outcome of an obstinate feeling that there was more 'to' John Wilmot than people seemed willing to admit. The air of dilettantism that still clung to his verse, despite much admirable work by twentieth-century scholars,[28] seemed inconsistent with what came across to me as the records of an exceedingly sensitive, acute and essentially incorruptible mind, records transmitted by way of the expert craftsman's cold eye and painstaking hand. I may have failed in my ambition to present Rochester's poetry as the work of a complex and serious artist; but I would be glad if this book went some way towards erasing the stubborn remains of the wicked-Earl-who-wrote-with-ease image.

---

[28] One of them, Rachel Trickett, supplied a thoughtful and balanced view of Rochester's stature as an artist in *The Honest Muse: A Study in Augustan Verse* (Oxford, 1967), p. 89.

CUPID AND BACCHUS

I

Cupid and Bacchus

The section entitled 'Love Poems' in Keith Walker's edition of
Rochester's poetry contains a handful of poems where 'love' in terms of
heterosexual relations, with or without an emotional element, is not the
main issue. The *Song* beginning 'Love a *Woman*! y'are an *Ass*' is
virtually a negation of conventional love lyrics. For various reasons, the
poem *Grecian KINDNESS. A SONG* ('The utmost Grace the *Greeks*
could show') does not fit in readily with the designation 'Love Poem'
either, and nor does the Anacreontic poem called *Upon his Drinking a
Bowl*. Like *Grecian Kindness*, the latter fuses the deities of love and wine;
but the joys of love are typified by 'Two lovely *Boys*', and the greater
part of the poem is devoted to the splendours of the ideal 'Cup'.

The three versions of the poem called *To A Lady, in A Letter*[1] form a
somewhat different case. This lyric consists of the epistolary address of
a lover to his mistress, and sexual pursuits play a vital part in it. It thus
has a better claim to the 'Love Poem' label than the three lyrics whose
main accent is on drinking. Still, it does constitute an *apologia* for that
very pursuit; and it has seemed more natural to discuss it along with
them.

One of Rochester's best-known poems, *The Disabled Debauchee*,
makes up the fifth member of the Cupid-and-Bacchus category. Placed
by Walker among the 'Satires and Lampoons', it is a poem in which the
two occupations of drinking and sexual activity are combined, again
with an unmistakable reference to pederasty.

The ensuing discussion focuses on four main topics: the attractions,
and effects, of drinking; Rochester's indebtedness to the Anacreontic
conventions that flourished in seventeenth-century England; pederasty,

---

[1] This is the title given to the last versions published by Vieth (who includes two) and Walker
(whose edition contains three).

or paedophilia; and the inferiority of the female sex. On all these points, Rochester's poems recall a number of classical loci. Much in the way of classical influence had of course been handed down by the poet's predecessors in France as well as in England; this is especially true of the Anacreontic elements. Still, the poems in this category seem to testify to that 'very good grounding in Latin' which Vivian de Sola Pinto believed Rochester to have acquired as a boy.[2]

FOLLOWING THE GOD OF WINE

In his letter[3] of 22 June 1671(?) to Henry Savile, Rochester asserts, 'that second bottle Harry is the sincerest, wisest, & most impartiall downright freind we have, tells us truth of our selves, & forces us to speake truths of others'.[4] The core of the eulogy on the second bottle expresses a central concern in the poet's works. Rochester hated insincerity as much as he detested folly and presumptuousness. Hence, his subscription to the *in vino veritas* dictum implies an exalted opinion of the properties of wine.

In the poems, however, this effect of alcohol is not expressly mentioned; other reasons for imbibing are emphasised instead. Thus, for instance, wine is a natural companion of 'mirth', and enjoying it in the company of a cheerful friend is simply pleasurable in itself. However, convivial drinking may also be conducive to loftier attainments by affording potent stimulation to the mind. In 'Love a *Woman*! y'are an *Ass*', drinking 'engender[s] *Wit*'; and the second version of *To A Lady, in A Letter* (in Walker's edition) extols the ability of wine to 'raise / Our thoughts', affording 'Idea's fitt to praise / What wee thinke fitt to Love'.

A succession of classical poets had acclaimed the same virtue (cf., for instance, Horace's *Epistle* I.19 and *Ode* III.25); as Robert Herrick put it in *His fare-well to Sack* (lines 31–2), '*Horace, Anacreon* both had lost their

---

[2] Albeit, naturally, on the basis of very different texts. See *Enthusiast in Wit*, p. 5. Cf. the dissimilar views on Rochester's classical attainments offered by Burnet and Thomas Hearne, easily accessible in Farley-Hills' *Critical Heritage* volume, pp. 48 and 170n. On the familiarity of Restoration readers with classical works, including indecent ones, see Roger Thompson, *Unfit for Modest Ears: A Study of Pornographic, Obscene and Bawdy Works Written and Published in England in the Second Half of the Seventeenth Century* (London, 1979), pp. 3–4.

[3] The – as far as I am aware – only extant critical discussion of any length to deal with drinking in Rochester's verse gives detailed consideration to this letter; see John D. Patterson, 'Rochester's Second Bottle: Attitudes to Drink and Drinking in the Works of John Wilmot, Earl of Rochester', *Restoration* 5.1 (Spring 1981), 6–15.

[4] P.67 in Treglown's edition of Rochester's *Letters*.

fame, / Had'st thou not fill'd them with thy fire and flame.' The conviction that mental pressures and impulses are of greater importance in Rochester's poetry than physical ones is fundamental to this book, and I think it is characteristic of Rochester that his poetry goes beyond mere celebration of the unsophisticated pleasures of inebriety.

Seventeenth-century English poems on the benefits of wine offer several examples of the alliterative monosyllabic pair 'wine' and 'wit'; Henry Vaughan's *A Rhapsodie* supplies a vigorous instance. Among Rochester's contemporaries, though, another classical virtue of the grape is usually more in evidence: that of dispelling care and sorrow. The poetry of antiquity testifies to the same powers, from the fiftieth lyric in the *Anacreontea*[5] to Horace's *Odes* (see, for instance, I.18 and IV.12) and Propertius' *Elegy* III .17.

When the speaker in Rochester's *Upon his Drinking a Bowl* states that he uses wine to dispel his anxiety, he joins this aspect of drinking with another, equally celebrated by poets ancient and modern:

> *Cupid*, and *Bacchus*, my Saints are,
>   May drink, and Love, still reign,
> With *Wine*, I wash away my cares,
>   And then to *Cunt* again.

This is an unusually blunt[6] rendering of the classical tenet according to which Venus and Bacchus form a natural pair. Again, examples can be found in virtually all the Greek and Roman poets known to seventeenth-century Englishmen, and the two deities are combined in large quantities of French and English Renaissance and Baroque verse, much to the disgust of moral writers.[7]

In the poem *Grecian Kindness*, Rochester joined Cupid and Bacchus in a somewhat subtler way than he had done in the stanza from *Upon his Drinking a Bowl*:

---

[5] Varying practices in the numbering of the *Anacreontea* have caused a certain measure of confusion in respect of Rochester's debt to them; see p. 17n. below. I have adopted the order usually employed in twentieth-century editions.

[6] Cf. Everett, 'The Sense of Nothing', p. 26.

[7] See, for instance, Matthew Scrivener's *A Treatise Against Drunkennesse: Described In its Nature, Kindes [,] Effects and Causes, especially that of Drinking of Healths* (London, 1685?), pp. 44–5. Another contemporary who warned his readers not to drink to excess was Richard Allestree. In the 1671 edition of his *The Whole Duty of Man* (originally published in 1660), he disposes, one by one, of what he calls the 'False Ends of drinking', all of which can be studied in contemporary verse, such as 'Good-fellowship', 'the maintaining of friendship and kindness amongst men', 'the chearing of their spirits', 'the putting away of cares' and 'the bare pleasure of the drink' (pp. 170–6).

besides the famous second-bottle letter, including a revealing one which Treglown places in 1673–4. In it, Rochester begs his friend to send him some good wine, as he is in 'imminent peril of sobriety'.[9] The letter represents a valiant effort to impart a bantering tone to what is, with painful obviousness, an urgent plea. Its well-turned phrases and attempted light-heartedness cannot conceal the desperation of the habitual drinker threatened by the distress of involuntary abstinence.

Biographical evidence hence suggests that Rochester was more than a 'social drinker', though Burnet's report of his five-year spell of drunkenness may be an exaggeration. Even so, those poems of Rochester's where drinking is much to the fore are not entirely without intimations of disenchantment.

The Disabled Debauchee can be taken to suggest a darker side to inebriety. First of all, it proceeds from the certainty that drinking is ruinous to one's health in the long run:

> So when my *Days* of impotence approach,
> And I'm by *Pox*, and *Wines* unlucky chance,
> Forc'd from the pleasing *Billows* of debauch,
> On the dull *Shore* of lazy temperance...

True, the man who envisages his future disabilities maintains that 'Past joys have more than paid what I endure.' But how credible are his asseverations? Several critics have recorded their uncertainty regarding his status and values;[10] but I have little doubt that the rake foreseeing his disreputable old age is deliberately satirised by the poet.

There are two main reasons for this belief. To begin with, there is the formal aspect. As Pinto has pointed out,[11] the heroic stanza employed in

---

[9] Pp. 91–2 in Treglown's edition of Rochester's *Letters*.

[10] See, for instance, Farley-Hills, *Rochester's Poetry*, p. 116. Ronald W. Johnson, commenting on Rochester's 'ability to create the ambivalent persona', called the speaker of *The Disabled Debauchee* 'oddly proud and pathetic'; see 'Rhetoric and Drama in Rochester's "Satyr Against Reason and Mankind"', *Studies in English Literature 1500–1900* 15.3 (Summer 1975), 371. David Vieth mentions *The Disabled Debauchee* as an example of 'divided consciousness' in the Restoration; see his 'Divided Consciousness: The Trauma and Triumph of Restoration Culture', *Tennessee Studies in Literature* 22 (1977), 52–3. Eric Rothstein's description of the third 'central voice' of satire, 'the self-deluder, who is at once the central intelligence of the satire and its butt' (*Restoration and Early Eighteenth-Century Poetry*, pp. 20–1), seems highly appropriate for the speaker of *The Disabled Debauchee*.

[11] In 'John Wilmot, Earl of Rochester, and the Right Veine of Satire', *Essays and Studies* (London, 1953), pp. 56–70. The essay has been reprinted in William R. Keast, ed., *Seventeenth-Century English Poetry: Modern Essays in Criticism* (Oxford, 1962; I have used the revised edition of 1971, where the relevant remarks are found on pp. 482–3).

The Disabled Debauchee is that of *Gondibert* and *Annus Mirabilis*.
Applying this stanza – immediately recognisable, to a Restoration
audience, as a borrowing from the stately works of Davenant and
Dryden – is a powerful mock-heroic device. Dustin Griffin has suggested that the initial stanza in *The Disabled Debauchee* is indebted to
Dryden's 'old admiral' in the sixty-first stanza of *Annus Mirabilis*.[12] This
seems perfectly likely, and if there is a deliberate reference here, it is a
better joke than Griffin appears to have realised. The 'old admiral' in
question is none other than the redoubtable George Monck, Duke of
Albemarle, and the stanza quoted by Griffin contains a covert allusion to
a wound he sustained in the Three Days Battle. The 'dreaded Admiral'
'sees below his scatter'd leaves' – a tactful reference to Monck's
breeches, shot away in a Dutch volley which left him with a wounded
buttock.[13] Rochester's contemporaries will have felt the full impact of
these mock-heroic elements and been ready to view the speaker of the
poem as a satirical creation.

The moment when the satirical perspective comes into play is at the
beginning of the fourth stanza. The three introductory ones have
demonstrated the ease with which Rochester handled the language and
style of heroic verse. The piling-up of words such as 'brave, courage,
wise, daring, fight, bold, glory, delight, fierce, rage' and so on creates
a formidable show of military heroism. It all crashes to the ground with
the bathos of lines 13–16 (quoted above).

The force of this contrast will have been more keenly appreciated by
Restoration readers, who were thoroughly familiar with poetic praises
of martial exploits, than it can be today. The poet's skill in retaining and
manipulating military terminology throughout the poem, after the
radical change of perspective in the fourth stanza, is proof of his fine
craftsmanship. While *The Disabled Debauchee* has been commended by
many Rochester critics, the edge of its satire has not, I think, been fully
appreciated.

That may be due to an element of prejudice on the part of well-
informed readers, who naturally expect any poem by the notorious
Rochester to defend debauchery. Judged on its own terms, however,
The Disabled Debauchee paints a forbidding picture of the pursuit, and
the consequences, of riotous living. The very idea of cautious youths
and moralists being persuaded to intemperance by a decrepit old man,

[12] *Satires Against Man*, pp. 50–1. Griffin notes that a near-contemporary of the poet's, Thomas
Rymer, saw the poem as a parody of Restoration heroic verse (p. 48).
[13] See p. xlv in Lord's *Poems on Affairs of State* volume.

marked by venereal disease, is ridiculous.[14] The list of his achievements is singularly uninspiring, not to say downright paltry, too:

> I'll tell of *Whores* attacqu'd, their Lords at home,
> *Bawds Quarters* beaten up, and *Fortress* won,
> *Windows* demolisht, *Watches* overcome,
> And handsome ills, by my contrivance done.

These lines contain details reminiscent of the disgraceful Epsom brawl, which is also alluded to in *To the Post Boy*.[15] Some Rochester admirers have refused to believe that such a stinging attack on Rochester as the latter poem could have been written by himself, but Vieth has defended its authenticity in vigorous and unanswerable terms.[16] It seems likely to me that *The Disabled Debauchee* was born out of a similar impulse. One of the few complimentary things one can say about Rochester is that he was not a hypocrite. Nobody will have known better than he that the actions described in lines 33–6 of *The Disabled Debauchee* were anything but 'handsome ills'.

A passage from Etherege's *The Comical Revenge; or, Love in a Tub* – a successful play, well known to the Court Wits (it was dedicated to Dorset, then Lord Buckhurst) – lends added weight to the assumption that such deeds were hardly praiseworthy. Sir Frederick Frollick has described how, in his cups, he was refused admission to a lady's house, 'whereupon a harsh word or two flew out, "Whore", I think, or something to that purpose'. The pert maid Jenny replies,

These were not all your heroic actions. Pray tell the consequence, how you marched bravely at the rear of an army of linkboys; upon the sudden, how you gave defiance, and then waged a bloody war with the constable; and having vanquished that dreadful enemy, how you committed a general massacre on the glass-windows. Are not these the most honourable achievements … ? (I.ii)

At a later point in the same play, the revolting Sir Nicholas Cully (see below p. 245), also drunk, draws his sword and demands, 'Shall I break the windows?', at which the gamester Wheedle replies, 'Hold, hold, you are not in a house of evil reputation' (IV.iii). Consequently, the exploits recounted in lines 33–6 of *The Disabled Debauchee* were on

---

[14] An entirely different reading of the poem can be consulted in Ian Donaldson's 'The Argument of "The Disabled Debauchee"', *Modern Language Review* 82 (1987), 30–4.

[15] For a brief account of this incident, see Vivian de Sola Pinto, *Enthusiast in Wit*, pp. 162–3. Cf. also pp. 357ff. below.   [16] See *Attribution*, pp. 201–3.

record, in Rochester's circle, as representing the kind of loutish behaviour to which drunkards are prone.

The penultimate stanza moves from petty pranks to heinous villainy:

> With Tales like these, I will such thoughts inspire,
> As to important mischief shall incline.
> I'll make him long some *Antient Church* to fire,
> And fear no lewdness he's called to by *Wine*.

It is hard to imagine that even Rochester's most rabid detractors would have expected him to advocate literally herostratic atrocities. However, it must be admitted that the speaker of John Oldham's *Aude aliquid. Ode* (commonly known as *A Satyr Against Vertue*) does just that (section 8, lines 185–206). Oldham's poem was 'Suppos'd to be spoken by a Court-Hector at Breaking of the Dial in Privy-Garden' – an obvious reference to one of Rochester's misdeeds. According to Harold F. Brooks, 'Oldham's "Ode" purports to be Rochester's rant on the occasion.'[17] Still, Oldham's poem is undoubtedly a *Satyr* and should be regarded as such, not as a realistic rendering of Rochester's beliefs. Rochester would hardly have signified his approval of Oldham's work if he had thought it possible that its pseudo-glorification of Herostratus and Nero – also a feature in Oldham's *Satyrs upon the Jesuits* – would be taken seriously. Consequently, the similarity between the disabled debauchee and Oldham's 'Court-Hector' reinforces rather than weakens the satirical flavour of Rochester's line on the '*Antient Church*'.

The last stanza of *The Disabled Debauchee* again emphasises the ludicrous contrast between the figure of the old soldier (the term '*Statesman*-like' lending some support to the Albemarle connexion), 'prest with courage still', and the – also fictional – creation of the old rake, 'safe' and 'Shelter'd' in impotence.

In Rochester's poetry, Bacchus – by and large – comes off rather better than Cupid. Even so, the former 'saint's' realm is not without its defects, and the worship expressed in Rochester's verse is not unreservedly devout. For all the favourable qualities of wine, it is as unable to provide lasting contentment as its counterpart, love.

ROCHESTER AND THE ANACREONTIC TRADITION

Rochester's place in the Anacreontic tradition is a complex issue. In addition to *Upon his Drinking a Bowl*, admitted to the canon by both

---

[17] P. 400 in Harold F. Brooks and Raman Selden, eds., *The Poems of John Oldham* (Oxford, 1987). The relevant passage from Oldham's poem is found on pp. 63–4.

Walker and Vieth,[18] Walker includes a lyric called *Anacreontic* among the 'Poems Possibly by Rochester'.[19] To deal with this minor matter first, its last four lines substantiate Vieth's disapproval of its 'clumsy syntax' and 'imprecise diction' and make Rochester's authorship, at least of the last lines, unlikely.[20] Whoever wrote this lyric, it reflects the growing coarseness of Anacreontic poetry in England from the late seventeenth century onwards.[21]

So does Charles Cotton's version of the twenty-first lyric in the *Anacreontea* (with expressions like 'Of Liquor spuing full'). Cowley's rendition is more genteel, but not to the extent that the possibly-by-Rochester *Anacreontic* can be said to 'parody' it.[22] The Greek original is much shorter and terser than these English imitations, and so is one of the first French translations, Rémy Belleau's ode *Qu'il faut boire par necessité*.

While *Upon his Drinking a Bowl* may well have been influenced by Ronsard, it is hardly an 'imitation', as Walker calls it, and definitely not a 'translation' (Curt A. Zimansky's term, quoted by Vieth in his headnote to the poem). In fact, Belleau's translation of the Anacreontic lyric concerned ('Vvlcan fay moy d'argent fin', p. 12 in the 1578 edition of Belleau's *Les Odes d'Anacreon Teien*) bears the same kind of loose similarity to Rochester's poem as Ronsard's version.

Ronsard's rendering of *Anacreontea* No. 4[23] contains several elements and many details that are completely lacking in *Upon his Drinking a Bowl*. Conversely, important lines in Rochester's poem have no counterpart in Ronsard's. There is, for example, nothing corresponding to the second stanza in Ronsard's version. Two other differences are more striking, though: the topicality of stanzas three and four, and the reference to amorous and alluring boys:

[18] With reservations ('Probably Rochester') in the latter's *Attribution*, p. 405.
[19] Walker refers to an unpublished D.Phil dissertation by Michael Hilton (University of Oxford, presented in 1980), where it is suggested that this might be an authentic Rochester poem. Michael Baumann, anticipating Walker, says that it is 'möglicherweise von Rochester'; see *Die Anakreonteen in englischen Übersetzungen* (Heidelberg, 1974), p. 81.
[20] See p. 233 in Vieth's edition of Rochester's poetry.
[21] See Baumann, *Die Anakreonteen*, pp. 81–2. The conclusion of Oldham's *The Cup* ('An Ode of Anacreon, Paraphras'd') also illustrates this tendency.
[22] A claim made by Walker; see p. 308 in his edition.
[23] Walker prints the *Meslanges* (1555) text (pp. 246–7). In most current editions of the *Anacreontea*, the poem with the closest resemblance to Rochester's is the fourth, not the seventeenth (and eighteenth), as Zimansky and Vieth maintained (headnote in Vieth's edition). This, however, is not – as Baumann has suggested – due to any oversight on their part but to the re-ordering of the *Anacreontea* which took place in the nineteenth century. Before these operations began, the order adopted by the French editor who made these texts available to a wide audience in 1554 – Henricus Stephanus, or Henri Estienne – had been observed.

> Engrave no *Battail* on his Cheek,
>   With *War*, I've nought to do;
> I'm none of those that took *Mastrich*,
>   Nor *Yarmouth Leager* knew.
>
> Let it no name of *Planets* tell,
>   Fixt *Stars*, or *Constellations*;
> For I am no Sir *Sydrophell*,
>   Nor none of his *Relations*.
>
> But carve thereon a spreading *Vine*,
>   Then add Two lovely *Boys*;
> Their Limbs in Amorous folds intwine,
>   The *Type* of future joys.

Unlike Belleau and Ronsard, whose translations Rochester probably knew,[24] Robert Herrick and Thomas Stanley, whose Anacreontic verses/translations he might have known,[25] and Cowley, whose *Anacreontiques* he must have known, Rochester steps out of Arcadia and grafts the classical poem on to his own country and time. The references to the siege of Maastricht and the camp at Yarmouth have given scholars a *terminus a quo* for the poem; they are connected with the Third Dutch War. Another specific reference to late-Restoration England is the sneer at astrology and its practitioners in the 'Sir *Sydrophell*' line.[26]

The refusal to have wars and constellations decorate the superb cup commissioned from the master craftsman is present in the original *Anacreontea* poem, as well as in Ronsard's and Belleau's versions of it. Rochester is not content with reproducing this dual dismissal; he imparts a note of burlesque to it. That note is admittedly faint in stanza three, where the only comic element resides in the allusions to the costly and unlucky Dutch War. In the ensuing stanza, though, contemptuous

---

[24] In respect of Belleau, this assumption is supported by what seem to be borrowings from his *Impuissance* in Rochester's *The Imperfect Enjoyment* (see p. 93 below). They were noted and discussed by Richard E. Quaintance Jr in his 1962 Yale dissertation, 'Passion and Reason in Restoration Love Poetry', pp. 208–13.

[25] Baumann emphasises the lack of appreciation that these two men's work met with (*Die Anakreonteen*, pp. 53–7). Herrick's *Hesperides* had been published in 1648, but the volume failed to make an impression on his time. Stanley, however, knew it. In 1651, he published the first complete English translation of the *Anacreontea*. One reason why Rochester might conceivably have seen Stanley's work is that the latter, a fine classical scholar, was also a staunch Royalist who supported others during the Protectorate years. He also knew Italian, Spanish and French poetry and translated Théophile de Viau and Ronsard as well as the *Anacreontea*. Taken altogether, he and Rochester had enough in common for some sort of connexion to be possible. Incidentally, Stanley's *History of Philosophy* has been suggested as a potential purveyor of 'popularized Epicureanism' to Rochester; see Griffin, *Satires Against Man*, p. 15.

[26] This gentleman, as Rochester's editors have pointed out, belongs to Butler's *Hudibras*, part 2.

irony is apparent. The reference to Butler's ridiculous astrologer robs the Anacreontic stars of any serious significance they may have had for previous poets.

In Rochester's day, poking gentle fun at one's country's military efforts, however unfortunate, was not of course good manners, although many satirical lines were written on the Third Dutch War. Nor was astrology a subject to be treated with disdain. True, Butler and Rochester were by no means the only people who mocked it in their time; but the general view was that the stars did exercise some influence on the lives and fortunes of human beings.[27]

When Rochester placed his Anacreontic poem in a late-seventeenth-century context, he created a break in the Anacreontic tradition, and he did it with characteristic irreverence. More than a hint of 'low', topical satire seeps into the celebration of Cupid and Bacchus. The last two stanzas to some extent restore the classical Anacreontic *milieu*, complete with pretty boys; but the last line throws the poem off balance again.

The coarseness of 'And then to *Cunt* again', coming after three highly conventional and rather insipid lines, is surely a calculated effect. If Rochester indirectly desecrated the classical pastoral landscape by means of the topical allusions in stanzas three and four, the final lines do not paint a very lofty picture of the way in which the two saints are worshipped. According to K. E. Robinson, the conclusion of the poem '[reduces] wine to an anaesthetic in the endless rut of drinking and whoring'.[28]

In this respect, too, Rochester's *Upon his Drinking a Bowl* constitutes a break with Anacreontic conventions. Gone are the effervescence, the sprightliness and the good-humoured physicalness of his predecessors in the genre. Herrick, for instance, could write the odd 'naughty' poem in this vein; Ronsard could weave delicate indecencies into his eulogies on love; and Cowley was no stranger to *risqué* innuendoes. But their Anacreontic verse, regardless of all the individual differences, is suffused with joy, a glory in sensual delights which is also there in the original *Anacreontea*. There are traces of it in *Upon his Drinking a Bowl*, especially in stanzas two and five, but the end of the poem swears at it. Rochester frequently subverts poetical conventions; on this occasion, he comes close to murdering one.

---

[27] See Douglas Bush, 'Science and Literature', in Hedley Howell Rhys, ed., *Seventeenth Century Science and the Arts* (Princeton, 1961), pp. 36–7.

[28] 'The Disenchanted Lyric in the Restoration Period', *The Durham University Journal* 73.1 (1980), 72. Cf. also Patterson, 'Rochester's Second Bottle', 11.

WOMAN OR BOY

The *Anacreontea* praise paedophiliac as well as heterosexual love, the seventeenth poem describing the beautiful boy Bathyllus (Bathyllon) in all his youthful glory. This element is toned down somewhat in the French Anacreontic verse which inspired so many poets in other European countries, and in England the paedophiliac component virtually disappears. Even Thomas Stanley, a translator rather than a paraphraser, keeps Bathyllus out of the picture, and Herrick and Cowley steer clear of all references to the love of a man for a boy. Consequently, Stanley's version of the fourth poem in the *Anacreontea* (XVII according to his numbering) does not contain the original's concluding mention of the beloved Bathyllus.

Whether or not Rochester had read the Greek originals – his knowledge of Greek is a dubious matter –, the fifth stanza in *Upon his Drinking a Bowl* portrays the joys of love in an unmistakably classical manner.[29] This divergence from those English Anacreontics that he (may have) read forms another departure from a domestic tradition.

It also raises the issue of Rochester's alleged 'bisexuality' or 'homosexuality'. He may have had homosexual relationships; there is no proof for or against this. Paedophilia is a different matter.[30] Both in ancient times and today, it is at least as common among basically heterosexual men as it is among homosexuals.[31] In ancient Greece, paedophilia and heterosexuality were associated. In Greek literature, '"Boy or woman" ... sometimes occurs as if difference of orientation in the sexual appetite were not important.'[32] Several ancient poets, Roman as well as Greek, are on record as finding sexual relations with boys over eighteen, or when facial and pubic hair had begun to appear, inadmissible.

One Roman poet who, like the author(s) of the *Anacreontea*, saw nothing unnatural in the love of boys as well as of women was Martial.

---

[29] Henri Estienne's Latin translations removed the necessity of studying the *Anacreontea* in the original language, and Rochester could have come across them or other renderings in Latin.

[30] Most Rochester scholars fail to distinguish between paedophilia and homosexuality. One exception is Jeremy Treglown, who finds no conclusive evidence of homosexual relations with one man Rochester seems really to have loved – Henry Savile – but points out that 'they had a common interest in boys'. See Treglown's Introduction to Rochester's *Letters*, p. 25.

[31] See, for instance, the fifth chapter in Edward Brongersma's *Das verfemte Geschlecht: Dokumentation über Knabenliebe* (Munich, 1970; this book is a German translation of the author's *Pedofilie*, which was published in Amsterdam in 1961). Cf. also Glenn D. Wilson and David N. Cox, *The Child-Lovers: A Study of Paedophiles in Society* (London and Boston, 1983), pp. 123–6.   [32] K. J. Dover, *Greek Homosexuality* (London, 1978), p. 65.

His epigrams were well known among the Court Wits; Sedley translated some of them. The forty-ninth is one example among many:

> Uxorem nolo Telesinam ducere: quare?
> moecha est. sed pueris dat Telesina. volo.[33]

Against this background, Vieth's attempt to weaken the case for Rochester's 'homosexuality' by referring to his 'unusually happy marriage' is somewhat naive.[34]

In the Rochester poems, the only locus that can be quoted as evidence of homosexuality (as distinct from pederasty) is lines 41–3 in *The Imperfect Enjoyment*, where the speaker discourses on the lack of discrimination shown by his penis:

> Stiffly resolv'd, twou'd carelesly invade,
> *Woman* or *Man*, nor ought its fury staid,
> Where e're it pierc'd, a *Cunt* it found or made.

Somewhat surprisingly, however, both Vieth and Walker have departed from their copy-text at this point, substituting the '*Man*' found in the extant manuscripts for the '*Boy*' of the text they both selected as being the best. In view of the overt references to paedophilia in three other canonical poems, and the lack of evidence of homosexuality, I think the reading '*Boy*' should be reinstated in line 42.

The three poems where sexual relations with boys are held up as being desirable present such relations in very different ways. In 'Love a *Woman*! y'are an *Ass*', the speaker is referring to the deft services of a hireling, which prevent an intermittently stirring physical urge from interfering with the pleasures of drinking:

> Then give me *Health*, *Wealth*, *Mirth*, and *Wine*,
> And if busie *Love*, intrenches,
> There's a sweet soft *Page*, of mine,
> Does the trick worth *Forty Wenches*.

The relevant stanza in *The Disabled Debauchee* describes quite a different situation:

> Nor shall our *Love-fits Cloris* be forgot,
> When each the well-look'd *Link-Boy*, strove t'enjoy,

[33] The Loeb translation runs, 'I will not take Telesina to wife: why? she is an adulteress. But Telesina is kindly to boys. I will.' Cf. also Horace's *Satire* I.ii.116–18, where it is suggested that a servant girl ('ancilla') or a boy ('puer') could easily soothe the fever of the blood. Ovid, however, claimed to prefer girls to boys because he wanted pleasure to be mutual (*Ars Amatoria* II.683–4). [34] See p. xxii in the Introduction to his edition of Rochester's poetry.

> And the best Kiss, was the deciding *Lot*,
> Whether the *Boy* fuck'd you, or I the *Boy*.

The arbiter in the kissing competition is clearly the linkboy, whose
decision may mean that the speaker does not enjoy much of a '*Love-fit*'
after all – another indication of the essential fallibility and inferiority of
the 'pleasures' he extols.[35] This boy, unlike the 'sweet soft *Page*' in
'Love a *Woman*', thus has the upper hand, and the man who desires him
must face the possibility of rejection. Despite this major difference, the
two passages have one thing in common: the absence both of
sensuousness and of emotion.

The latter is also lacking in the fifth stanza of *Upon his Drinking a Bowl*
(naturally enough, as the relevant locus is a description of a suitable
decoration for an artefact); but certainly not the former. Rochester
wrote surprisingly few lines that can be said to be downright sensual;
but 'Their Limbs in Amorous folds intwine' is definitely one of them.
It might be argued that one boy with Bathyllean qualities would have
sufficed; but such a motif would not have been so erotically stimulating.
It is the encounter of two perfect young bodies ('Limbs...intwine',
'Amorous folds') that makes the desired picture a titillating one.

The word 'future' in line 20 is (as Patterson has suggested) a
noteworthy one. Of course, it could be held to be quite natural in the
context, which after all involves the ordering of a work of art; but the
present tense is employed in line 19, as if the customer were momentarily
carried away by his vision. The poet could easily have used some other
disyllabic expression; 'future' has every appearance of being a deliberate
choice.

Most of the delights, of any kind, outlined in Rochester's poetry are
'future joys'. Actual sexual satisfaction as a result of heterosexual
intercourse is only described in one of Rochester's love lyrics, the *Song*
whose first line runs, 'As *Chloris* full of harmless thought'. None of
Rochester's first-person poems ever celebrates the experience of
heterosexual consummation; this is a vital point about his love poetry,

---

[35] Cf. Reba Wilcoxon, 'Rochester's Sexual Politics', *Studies in Eighteenth-Century Culture* 8 (1979;
ed. Roseann Runte), 138, and Carole Fabricant, 'Rochester's World of Imperfect Enjoyment',
Journal of English and Germanic Philology 73 (1974), 342. Fabricant is one of the few Rochester
critics to have commented on the prevalence of physical failure and frustration at any length;
she has, for example, observed that 'Rochester's writings deal less with orgasm than with its
obstruction; less with sexuality than with the *failure* of sexuality' (339). While I do not share
her basic view of the reasons for this aspect of Rochester's work ('an underlying repulsion
against all worldly and sensual things', 350), her article stresses an essential feature in
Rochester's poetry which is too often overlooked.

and it is repeated more than once in the 'Men and Women' section of this book (see below). In the pro-pederasty poems, too, the pleasure is conditional or unrealised; 'if busie *Love*, intrenches'; 'Whether the *Boy* fuck'd you, or I the *Boy*'; 'The *Type* of future joys'.

Like Ovid, the speaker of *The Disabled Debauchee* proceeds from the conviction that old men are past the pleasures of love, as well as the exploits of war.[36] That glum prospect is not compensated for by glowing accounts of present raptures. Taken altogether, Rochester's poems offer a rather bleak outlook for erotic delights, regardless of whether partners are represented as women or boys.

FAREWELL WOMAN

The homoeroticism of ancient Greece and Rome is often related to the inferior status of women in these societies. The love of a beautiful boy, physical passion being accompanied by profound personal devotion, was held to be a much finer thing than being infatuated with a woman. It should be borne in mind, though, that upper-class Athenian young men had little or no opportunity to indulge in erotic pursuits with girls or women of their own class; to them prostitutes were the only women readily available.[37]

The situation in Restoration England was not altogether different. Respect for the intellectual attainments and moral qualities of women was at a low ebb (see pp. 124ff. below). At the same time, attractive unmarried girls of good family, however teasing and flirtatious they might be, had to remain chaste – or at least appear to be so.[38] For the men of Rochester's circle, the usual female sexual partners were married women, kept women, actresses and prostitutes, category boundaries being indeterminate. It is not perhaps so surprising that these ladies, to whom material advantage was usually paramount, did not inspire much chivalrous devotion.

The explosive contempt for the female sex which erupts in lines 1–8 of Rochester's 'Love a *Woman*! y'are an *Ass*' is too sustained and violent to be overlooked. It constitutes a complication for those who wish to

---

[36] Cf. *Amores* i.ix.4. The poet(s) of the *Anacreontea*, however, did not feel that grey hair was an impediment to amorous pursuits.

[37] See, for instance, Dover, *Greek Homosexuality*, pp. 88–90 and 149. Cf. also James Grantham Turner, *One Flesh: Paradisal Marriage and Sexual Relations in the Age of Milton* (Oxford, 1987), pp. 131–2.

[38] Cf. D. R. M. Wilkinson, *The Comedy of Habit: An Essay on the Use of Courtesy Literature in a Study of Restoration Comic Drama* (Leyden, 1964), p. 92.

represent Rochester as being in favour of the equality of the sexes, or at least as a man who liked and understood women. The animus is clearly directed against *all* women, virtuous wives included. The second stanza reflects the characteristic Restoration-rake revolt against family pressures and obligations. As for reproduction, the speaker leaves that to the servants – 'dirty *Slaves*' who have to rely on their offspring in their old age. As a rule, mid- and late-seventeenth-century gentlemen were not philoprogenitive. Wilkinson quotes a passage from Francis Osborne's *Advice to a Son*, where this presumably affectionate father denigrates the institution of marriage, one consequence of which is that married women

alter their shapes, and embase their celestial Beauties, when by discharging their Husbands of the venom of Love, they swell themselves with the bulk and dangers of Childbearing.[39]

Osborne warns his son against the peril of worshipping 'a silly Creature' and refers to the man who marries for love as one who performs 'the basest of Drudgeries without wages'. The sentiments expressed in Rochester's poem were hence in no way original.

This rejection of women has been explained in various ways. Katharine M. Rogers suggests that Rochester's 'glutted sensuality' made him feel 'sexual disgust'[40] – in which case the relevant passage would be the record of simple surfeit. Reba Wilcoxon tries, unsuccessfully, to reduce 'Love a *Woman*!' to a rejection of indiscriminate sexual activity.[41] Griffin, who unaccountably refers to the opening stanza of 'Love a *Woman*!' as 'conventional anacreontic', believes that Rochester's anti-woman songs may 'reflect Rochester's utter disillusionment with sex and with women'.[42]

The arrogance of the first stanza and the revulsion of the second do not agree with the idea of someone turning his back on something he has had to excess. There is not a hint of weariness in these lines, no suggestion of satiety, as in – for instance – Byron's *So We'll Go No More A-Roving*. It is a diatribe, apparently triggered – like Juvenal's

---

[39] See Wilkinson, *The Comedy of Habit*, p. 41. The two parts of Osborne's *Advice* were originally published in 1656 and 1658; a new edition came out in 1673. The *Advice* was extremely popular in contemporary England; see John E. Mason, *Gentlefolk in the Making: Studies in the History of English Courtesy Literature and Related Topics from 1531 to 1774* (Philadelphia, 1935), p. 69.

[40] *The Troublesome Helpmate: A History of Misogyny in Literature* (Seattle and London, 1966), p. 162.   [41] 'Rochester's Sexual Politics', 138–9.

[42] *Satires Against Man*, p. 90. To Griffin, the first four lines of this poem do not belong to that category; they are merely 'light banter'.

famous sixth satire – by hearing someone speak of his love for a woman. Besides, the speaker in this lyric does not merely reject heterosexual activity; he despises women in a general sense, too.

Such virulence often betrays the speaker's own vulnerability. In a much-quoted passage from his letters, Rochester admitted to Savile that he, like his friend, had turned out to be hopelessly inept (an 'Errant fumbler') at two of the three 'Buisnisses of this Age', namely 'Woemen' and 'Polliticks', and that the only 'exercise' where he had not disgraced himself was 'drinking'.[43] I see no reason why this remarkable statement should not be taken seriously, like the other communications to Savile. Otherwise, the inclusion of the addressee in the not very flattering reckoning would be a gratuitous insult.

Attempts have been made to view 'Love a *Woman!*' as atypical, an isolated instance of no great significance. Yet it is also possible to go too far in the other direction, regarding it as an altogether sincere personal confession on Rochester's part. What this poem seems to me to express is a kind of loathing that originates in a feeling of inadequacy. The speaker severs *all* intercourse with women, retiring to all-male company. Such a radical measure suggests something different from mere disillusionment or an overdose of female sexuality. It could be argued that female society is painful for him because it reminds him of his own hurtful experiences, and to a proud man like the speaker, nothing can hurt like personal failure. This approach would provide a link with the 'Errant fumbler' admission and impart some auto-biographical relevance to the poem; but it must be admitted that it is, essentially, as speculative as the opinions quoted above.

To A Lady, in A Letter also raises issues which are difficult to resolve with certainty.[44] On the face of it, the gentleman letter-writer is proposing a settlement, Restoration-proviso-style, geared to the mutual satisfaction of the parties. If the lady will stop marring their amorous encounters by her 'Jealiousy', and accept her lover's absences due to drink, he will put up with her infidelity during those absences. A balance of 'pleasures' is set up: hers consists in sexual intercourse with potent sparks; he 'pursues' his in wine.

This superficial equilibrium is undermined by several factors. First of all, we do not know how the recipient will react to the proposal; all we

---

[43] P. 67 in the *Letters*; this is the 'second-bottle' letter referred to above (p. 10).

[44] An awareness of complexity beneath the surface of this poem is displayed by Doody (*The Daring Muse*, p. 60) and by Sarah Wintle in 'Libertinism and Sexual Politics', in Treglown, ed., *Spirit of Wit*, pp. 150–3.

do know is that it was her jealousy that prompted it (the first two versions printed by Walker state this clearly). Why should a woman with her alleged inclinations be jealous of her partner's drinking sessions (stanza three in the third version implies that she knows what he is doing when he is not with her)? Second, a disproportionate part of versions 1 and 3 is devoted to a description of her kind of 'pleasure', indiscriminating, insatiable sexual activity. The joys he derives from wine – whose nature one would expect him to want to explain to her, to make her see that she has no grounds for disapproving of them – are sketched in the last stanza of the second version but hardly given any space in the other two. Third – and this is the darkest undercurrent of all – the second stanza establishes that the rationale for the outlined scheme is 'witt'. In other words, the speaker appeals to her good sense and judgement, crediting her as well as himself with some intelligence. In fact, it is the only bit of common ground for the two parties that the poem establishes. Again, mental capacity is shown to be more profoundly significant than physical activity. It is the more disturbing that Chloris' 'pleasure' is not only unrelated to cerebral pursuits; it even forms an offence against 'witt' since her partners are emphatically said to be deficient in that respect. By contrast, the man claims (albeit only in the last stanza of the second version) to derive mental benefits from his particular 'passion/pleasure'.

A continuation of the relationship is implied; indeed, the jealousy problem being disposed of, it should be 'perfect Blisse'. Still, the poem ends on a note of separateness – you do this and I do that, and 'whole nights', too. The argumentation which set out from the wish for perfect mutual 'Enjoyment' has lost sight of it at the end. Beneath the specious persuasiveness, the picture emerges of a man whose main desire is to escape from the society of a woman whom he actually despises.

Both *To A Lady, in A Letter* and the 'Love a *Woman!*' *Song* thus seem to testify to the inferiority of women, the repulsiveness of female sexuality and the virtues of wine. One of the benefits of the latter is that women are excluded from it. (On this point, incidentally, the poet diverges from the Anacreontic tradition, where female revellers imbibe with the males.)

A passage from Shadwell's *Epsom Wells* shows that this was not necessarily the attitude of every Restoration libertine. Rains and Bevil enjoy convivial drinking for precisely the reasons suggested in Rochester's Cupid-and-Bacchus poems, but it is not the ultimate pleasure:

LUC. Are not you angry in your heart to be kept from your belov'd Bottles?

RAINS. The Devil take me, I love you so, that I could be content to abjure Wine for ever, and drink nothing but Almond-milk for your sake.

BEV. We never meet like Country-Sots to drink only, but to enjoy one another, and then Wine steals upon us unawares, as late hours do some times upon your selves at Cards.

RAINS. And it makes your dull Fools sit hickupping, sneezing, drivelling, and belching, with their eyes set in their heads, while it raises men of heat and vigour to mirth, and sometimes to extravagance.[45]

The contrast between Rains' first-quoted heroic speech and the attitudes expressed, and implied, in the poems discussed above is patent. Clearly, not all the witty protagonists created by Restoration writers placed Bacchus before Cupid; but the Rochester speakers do, both explicitly and implicitly. This ranking is accompanied by an appreciation of the pleasures afforded by 'lovely *Boys*'. The denigration of women seen in 'Love a *Woman*!' and suggested in *To A Lady, in A Letter* is not only associated with distaste for female sexuality, but also with contempt for the female intellect.

[45] v.i; p. 170 in Montague Summers' edition of *The Complete Works of Thomas Shadwell* (London, 1927), vol. II.

MEN AND WOMEN

---◆◦◦◦◆---

2

The love lyrics

The reader of Rochester's love poems confronts a writer who rarely contemplates aspects of love other than the purely physical, but who has little if anything to say about the glories of sexual fulfilment. The women addressed in these poems have few personal attributes beyond the conventional conquering eyes and resistless charms found in so many seventeenth-century lyrics, and the means by which some of them are to be 'persuaded to enjoy' are ratiocinative rather than seductive.[1] The poems where the lyrist's pessimism and restlessness push him beyond Restoration conventions which he knew well, and handled expertly, belong to the finest love lyrics of the century. When, for instance, the pulse of an unquiet heart and the pressing fancies of an irritable intellect jointly prompt the realisation that consummated love with a complaisant partner is not enough, great poems result: *The Fall*, 'Absent from thee' and *The Mistress*. A few other lyrics attain high excellence without appearing to owe their success to the poet's peculiar dissatisfaction with what many men desire (*Love and Life*, for instance, sometimes held to be Rochester's best short poem).

If Rochester only wrote about half a dozen love lyrics that deserve to rank with the finest lyrical efforts of his time, it may seem extravagant to pay as much attention to the others as this chapter does. However, reviews of the minor poems contribute to an awareness of the patterns and traditions Rochester employs *and* departs from. Besides, attentive study of lyrics that might seem if not undistinguished, then at least undistinguishable from run-of-the-mill Restoration efforts at a first reading may reveal unexpected complexities.

Consequently, some consideration is given to virtually all the lyrics in

[1] On the element of cool rationality in Rochester's love poetry, see John Harold Wilson, *The Court Wits of the Restoration: An Introduction* (Princeton, 1948), p. 78.

29

Walker's 'Love Poems' section. The ones whose main concern is bibulous rather than amorous are, of course, dealt with in the previous chapter; and *The Imperfect Enjoyment* shares a subsequent one with *A Ramble in Saint James's Parke*.

Anyone who wishes to discuss Rochester's love poems in bulk, and at length, has to face a formidable problem of classification. Chronology can be dismissed at once. Vieth's and Walker's editions testify to the impossibility of establishing consensus on this point. Even if this were not the case, the rationale of a chronological organising principle – that of charting a line of development – would, as was pointed out above (p. 7), be difficult to apply to Rochester.

Previous Rochester scholars have dealt with the problem in very different ways. In David Farley-Hills' study, an extensive attempt is made to fit the lyrics into a scheme consisting of 'platonic', 'anti-platonic' and 'libertine' categories. Farley-Hills' model and his readings often clash, though, and the resulting confusion defeats the ambitious purpose.

One reason for that confusion is that Farley-Hills has to a great extent concentrated on the question of where the argumentation of a poem is heading. In Rochester's love poems, however, inconsistencies and contradictions abound. Many of them are not so much concerned with driving home a point as with exploiting the various facets of a situation.[2] Even a reader familiar with Rochester's poetry may well find himself/herself surprised by the variety of attitudes in – and often *within* – the love poems. It is not easy to make any one statement about Rochester's love poetry that is not contradicted, in part at least, somewhere in his verse.

The complexity of Rochester's love poetry as a whole also becomes apparent when a set of concepts designating different kinds of love is tested on the poems. Jean H. Hagstrum has shown that the English Renaissance and Restoration do not allow for a dividing line between 'amour-désir' and 'amour-tendresse',[3] and it definitely would not operate where Rochester is concerned. Other terms employed by French seventeenth-century scholars turn out to be inapplicable as well.[4]

---

[2] This point is well expressed in Righter's 'John Wilmot', 62. See also Vieth, '"Pleased with the Contradiction and the Sin": The Perverse Artistry of Rochester's Lyrics', *Tennessee Studies in Literature* 25 (1980), 50.

[3] *Sex and Sensibility: Ideal and Erotic Love from Milton to Mozart* (Chicago, 1980), p. 75.

[4] I have found Jean-Michel Pelous' *Amour précieux: Amour galant (1654–1675)* (Paris, 1980) very helpful in grasping the essential conceptions of love in seventeenth-century France. Further assistance was supplied by Claude Dulong, *L'Amour au XVIIème siècle* (Paris, 1969); Renate

Before contemplation of the obstacles to classification becomes too paralysing, it is best to stake out the common ground of the great majority of Rochester's love poems. Fulfilment by way of sexual intercourse is a feature in nearly all of them, but it is viewed in a variety of ways: active desire, vain adoration and anger at obstacles (non-fulfilment); anticipated physical union (fulfilment expected); satisfying sexual climaxes narrated (fulfilment achieved); advocacy of certain modes of behaviour which are supposed to yield more pleasure than mere sexual intercourse (beyond fulfilment); and the fear of losing what one has gained and/or dissatisfaction with it (a state which might be called post-fulfilment).

These categories, in that order, supply the structural framework of this long chapter. The reason why such an arrangement has seemed expedient does not lie in any inherent interest that those categories might possess; they are little more than organisational instruments and should not be taken too seriously. Rather, it is hoped that the reader who comes to the final category – post-fulfilment – after reviewing the others will find it easier to appreciate the distinctive qualities of the poems that belong to it. Also, this arrangement allows Rochester's variety to manifest itself freely. Finally, the grouping of his lyrics around this central concern gradually reveals the restlessness and anxieties associated with that concern in most of Rochester's love poetry.

PERSUASION, ADORATION AND FRUSTRATION: NON-FULFILMENT

The Advice constitutes an assembly of compliment and argument whose elegance is not marred by its traditional components. The idea of the fair lady whose eyes would have made a slave of Cupid had he been able to see is found in a number of poems by Rochester's predecessors and contemporaries. Military metaphors are commonplace, too; the poetry of Suckling and Lovelace, for instance, offers plenty of examples. The notion that 'Universal Nature does enjoyn' surrender to the reign of Love is one that Théophile de Viau and his successors in France helped give conventional status in the seventeenth century. As for the assertion that 'even streams have desires', it is anticipated not only in Donne's

Elegy 'Oh let mee not serve so',[5] but also in Ovid's *Amores*, III.vi.24 ('flumina senserunt ipsa, quid esset amor'). Even so, the mixture of elaborate flattery and thinly veiled threat lends a certain inner tension to the poem.

The assurance that

> All things submit themselves to your command,
> Fair *Celia*, when it does not Love withstand

establishes three hierarchical levels. It is true that the lady's wishes reduce all other mortals to slavish obedience – but only when compliant with those of the real tyrant, Love. She is in fact as totally at Love's mercy as her would-be lover is at hers. Her beauty is merely Love's instrument, a circumstance which is given rather brutal expression in the couplet

> Beauty's no more but the dead Soyl which Love
> Mannures, and does by wise Commerce improve

which is followed by an overstrained metaphor,

> Sayling by Sighes through Seas of tears, he sends,
> Courtship from Forraign hearts ...

The first, heavily alliterative line contributes to the impression that this is the work of a very young poet.

The Rochester poems in the persuasion-to-enjoy genre are not numerous. Even if we include the lines beginning 'Leave this gawdy guilded Stage' (see below), it only contains three items in addition to that dubious candidate – *The Advice*, the *Song* beginning '*Phillis*, be gentler I advice', and *Verses put into a Lady's Prayer-book*. In all of them, ardent desire for the favours of a particular woman is far less in evidence than grim suggestions that she stands to lose much more by non-compliance than the man who addresses her.

In lines 31–4 ('Submit then *Celia*', etc.), the 'voluntary' surrender of Love's citadel[6] is seen as the sole alternative to violent conquest followed by indignity. If the implications of lines 31–2 are formidable, the menace embodied in the conclusion of *The Advice* is rather milder than the penalties envisaged in other poems belonging to the persuasion-to-enjoy category:

---

[5] A debt to Donne is proposed by Walker, p. 232 in his edition of Rochester's poems.

[6] Keith Walker retains the plural form 'Citadels' in his rendering of his copy-text. Vieth decided that the plural 's' was a misprint, and it seems highly likely. Apart from the fact that citadels do not usually come in bunches, the idea of the lady splitting herself into several fortifications is a somewhat complicated one.

> For your own ends
> Cherish the Trade; for as with *Indians* we
> Get Gold and Jewels for our Trumpery,
> So to each other for their useless Toyes,
> Lovers afford whole Magazins of Joyes:
> But if youe're fond of Bawbles, be, and starve,
> Your Gugaw Reputation preserve;
> Live upon Modesty and empty Fame,
> Forgoing Sense, for a Fantastick Name.

The exchange of 'Bawbles' is a mere token procedure heralding the mutual opening of vast stores of pleasure. But if Celia is perverse enough to wish to hoard her 'Trumpery', she will be left with insubstantial mock-comforts such as a blameless reputation. The final line forms a stern condemnation of this wrong-headed choice, 'Sense' standing for 'sensual satisfaction' as opposed to 'a Fantastick Name' – a mere figment of the imagination.[7]

Rather more ominous hints regarding the ultimate fate of the lady, should she remain unmoved, are voiced in *Verses put into a Lady's Prayer-book*. John Harold Wilson pointed out that this poem is surely indebted to two by Malherbe,[8] the second of which ends in the promise, 'Faites-moy grace, et vous l'aurez.' Exhortations to ladies to the effect that they might spend their time more profitably than in religious occupations are not unusual in England either; Sedley's *To a Devout Young Gentlewoman* is one example. Rochester's poem is more elaborate than Malherbe's, and certain turns of phrase in it show that he handled religious phraseology[9] with the off-hand ease of someone brought up on it. Interestingly enough, however, he speaks of 'the Gods' (and, in one instance, 'Heav'n') rather than 'God' (to match Malherbe's 'Dieu'). Perhaps the reason was as simple as a wish to avoid unnecessary recriminations due to blasphemy.

Another deviation from Malherbe is the progress of love in the final lines. The idea that pity often paves the way for love is a traditional one. Whether threats are the proper means to induce pity is, of course,

---

[7] The use of 'fantastic' as a pejorative term meaning 'purely imaginary' is widespread in the seventeenth century.

[8] Originally in *Notes and Queries* 187 (12 August 1944), 79; Walker reproduces the poems (p. 237).

[9] An interesting exploration of Christian terms as employed in this lyric is found in Larry Carver's 'Rascal before the Lord: Rochester's Religious Rhetoric', originally published in *Essays in Literature* 9 (Fall 1982); Vieth has reprinted it in a collection of essays on Rochester edited by himself, *John Wilmot, Earl of Rochester: Critical Essays* (New York and London, 1988). The relevant discussion is found on pp. 95–8 in Vieth's collection.

debatable; but the poem is essentially a light-hearted one, and the speaker's 'Despair' probably should not be taken too literally.

The last two lines have a Metaphysical flavour. Jeremy Treglown has suggested that the metaphor may serve ironic purposes here, evoking Crashaw's *Steps to the Temple* and Adam's words on ascending to God 'by steps'.[10] The yoking-together of earthly and heavenly joys can also be felt to recall Donne's *Extasie* (rather to the detriment of Rochester's lines).

The addressee of *Verses put into a Lady's Prayer-book* may well find the notion of purchasing salvation by means of fornication (or adultery) too much to take. A more mundane punishment for unyieldingness is depicted in the song beginning '*Phillis*, be gentler I advice':

> *Phillis*, be gentler I advice,
>   Make up for time mispent,
> When *Beauty*, on its *Death-Bed* lyes,
>   'Tis high time to repent.
>
> Such is the *Malice* of your *Fate*,
>   That makes you old so soon,
> Your pleasure ever comes too late,
>   How early e're begun.
>
> Think what a wretched thing is she,
>   Whose *Stars*, contrive in spight,
> The Morning of her love shou'd be,
>   Her fading *Beauties Night*.
>
> Then if to make your ruin more,
>   You'll peevishly be coy,
> *Dye* with the scandal of a *Whore*,
>   And never know the joy.

The inexorability of the *carpe diem* argumentation and the total absence of feeling ensure that this lyric could never be accused of possessing ingratiating qualities. Like Ovid (*Ars Amatoria* III.59–80), and like many generations before and after them, Restoration men and women accepted that the first signs of age brought a woman's power and

---

[10] 'The Satirical Inversion of Some English Sources in Rochester's Poetry', *The Review of English Studies* 24 (1973), 45–6. There are other roughly contemporary instances of such gradual ascending; thus, for instance, Godfrey Goodman said that 'if there were any [ioy in the creature], thy minde might be transported and carried, by the ladder or bridge of the creatures, to the loue of thy creator', in *The Fall of Man; or The Corruption of Nature, proved by the light of our naturall Reason* (London, 1616), p. 153.

influence to an end (see pp. 125–6 below). The *carpe diem* lyrics thus had a very real basis in fact. What makes the argumentation in this song questionable from a purely factual point of view is its confident reliance on Phillis' late amorousness. The speaker seems to expect that she will, duly compelled by fate, fall in love at the time when her beauty deserts her, and he rudely implies that this moment is imminent. Did he have any reason to anticipate such a state of affairs?

To judge from the frequency with which amorous older women occur in seventeenth-century literature, the combination of female senescence and unseemly desires seems to have been a stock notion. As Elisabeth Mignon has shown,[11] superannuated coquettes were figures of fun in a number of Restoration comedies. And, of course, no representation of a flirtatious older woman could be crueller than Dorset's last poem on the Countess of Dorchester. At a time when a woman was considered past her best at twenty-five and old at thirty, her 'rambling days' (Mignon's charming term) were so quickly over that late awakenings probably did come upon a fair number of previously-virtuous ladies.

Phillis must indeed be wretched if she discovers love at the point in time when her pursuers begin to back off. But there is that which is even worse, and that is not making use of any final opportunities. Nobody is going to believe that an ageing beauty will not snatch at whatever pleasure is yet to be had, and a woman's long-lasting efforts to preserve her reputation may end in her losing it without any compensation whatever.

The contention that one might as well be a sinner in deed as in name is not, of course, original either. Sedley has two pretty stanzas on the subject:

> Fair *Aminta*, art thou mad,
>   To let the World in me
> Envy Joys I never had,
>   And censure them in thee?
>
> Fill'd with Grief, for what is past,
>   Let us at length be wise,
> And to Love's true Enjoyments hast,
>   Since we have paid the Price.[12]

---

[11] See her study *Crabbed Age and Youth: The Old Men and Women in the Restoration Comedy of Manners* (Durham, N.C., 1947).

[12] *The Poetical and Dramatic Works of Sir Charles Sedley*, ed. Vivian de Sola Pinto (London, 1928), vol. I, p. 23.

Obviously, no ethical considerations operate at all.

The forces at work behind such wilful murders of reputations are glumly commented on in the second part of *Youth's Behaviour, or Decency in Conversation Amongst Women* (published in 1664):

Moreover, there is I know not what unhappiness in some persons, that doth expose them to the Tongues of the Detractors; and this more often happens to the Vertuous than to others, because their Denials do beget them Enemies, and thereby they often put themselves in Danger (as *Susanna*) to be accused of a Crime they never could commit. (p. 57)

With the exception of the compliments of *The Advice* – not a little marred by the comparison of the lady's beauty to dead soil 'mannured' by love –, Rochester's persuasion-to-enjoy poems are completely shorn of the conventional praise with which generations of poets attempted to flatter their ladies' pride as a preliminary to softening their hearts. More than that, some of the threats uttered in these poems are downright insulting. Whether Rochester, who knew women well enough to create memorable female protagonists (above all, of course, the matchless Artemiza), really composed them 'for [his] *Pintles* sake' is open to doubt. It is hard to imagine any woman – at any time in history – who would be in that humour won. It is no less difficult to accept the idea that a man who knew anything about women would set out to break their resistance without offering a sop to their vanity, choosing to offend it instead. Perhaps these poems should be seen as deliberate distortions of a genre with which a cynical intellect like Rochester's had had every opportunity to become thoroughly bored. Perhaps, too, his hatred of pride and vanity was so ingrained in him that he could not bring himself to pander to them even for the sake of an erotic conquest. Or perhaps conquests of that kind did not, after all, interest him very much.

The inclusion of the little lyric 'Leave this gawdy guilded Stage' in the persuasion-to-enjoy category is attended by reservations. Most importantly, it does not, properly speaking, constitute a plea for sexual surrender. It may well be addressed to a *de facto* mistress; commentators usually connect it with Mrs Barry. The poem is one of the relatively few that exist in Rochester's holograph. It is very likely to have direct biographical relevance; in his Introduction to Rochester's *Letters*, Jeremy Treglown suggests that it may have been written in 1676–7, when Barry's theatrical career kept her very busy indeed.

One amusing, and slightly touching, aspect of the poem is that it constitutes a man's plea to a woman not to devote too much time and

energy to her job. Her work is not intrinsically valuable or dignified; it
certainly does not deserve to have her expend herself in her professional
duties, to the detriment of her and her partner's love life. This is one of
those reversals of classic sex-role patterns that have passed unnoticed by
previous critics (cf. p. 82 below on *The Fall*). What 'the office' is and
has been to countless women, 'the Stage' is to the male petitioner in
this lyric.

That unconventional dimension should not obscure the fact that
'Leave this gawdy guilded Stage' is steeped in tradition. Treglown has
pointed out[13] that exhortations to quit the iniquitous world of the
theatre are nothing new, quoting Jonson's *Ode to Himselfe* which begins,
'Come leave the loathed Stage'. As usual, youth and beauty are
prerequisites in lovemaking. The concluding alexandrine couplet may
seem slightly cryptic:

> Twixt strifes of Love and war the difference Lies in this
> When neither overcomes Loves triumph greater is.

If 'neither' is taken to mean 'neither combatant in the relevant strife',
the lines form a neat paradox: in war, someone is expected to win; in
love's battles, neither party defeats the other, and mutual pleasure is the
essential triumph. This contention forms a refreshing contrast to the conquests and vanquishing (however pleasurable for the vanquished) that
abound in Restoration love poetry. Even so, it is of course in no way
original. Ovid's *Ars Amatoria*, for example, pointed out that the greatest
fulfilment in love calls for both partners to be equally 'overcome'
(ii.727–8, 'tum plene voluptas / Cum pariter victi femina virque
iacent').

If this poem was written by Rochester to Elizabeth Barry, it is likely
to be a comparatively late one. Despite all the dangers of theorising on
chronology, it is difficult not to wonder whether the mutuality present
in this slight piece, as well as in *The Mistress*, represents a growth in
personal maturity compared to such an early effort as *The Advice*,
written by a man in his early twenties. Mutuality is not a concept that
can be easily applied to the other great lyrics of discontent, *The Fall* and
'Absent from thee'. Still, they too bespeak an awareness of the woman
addressee as a person, and as a person of vital importance to the speaker.
Such an awareness is hard to find in the coldly rational pieces.

In the persuasion-to-enjoy poems, the male speaker is, by and large,

---

[13] 'Satirical Inversion', 43.

in control of the situation; if the addressee fails to relent, it will be all the worse for her. It is in the poems of adoration that the lady assumes the upper hand. The worshipper in *The Discovery*, for instance, professes not to harbour any hopes. Three others embody a favourable dimension of some sort. The divine glories of the radiant heroines in *The submission* and 'T'was a dispute 'twixt heav'n and Earth' are overwhelming to the point of being debilitating; but it is not expressly stated that the admirer will never enjoy them at close range. In the *Song* beginning 'While on those lovely looks I gaze', a note of something like complacency insinuates itself towards the end.

The Discovery is an early and not very accomplished poem, featuring Petrarchist clichés[14] and recalling the *amants malheureux* of the French ethos of love associated with d'Urfé and, later, with Mlle de Scudéry; 'Toujours aimer, toujours souffrir, toujours mourir' was the lot of these hapless creatures.[15] Even Ovid was no stranger to amorous servitude and admitted as much (see, for instance, *Amores* II.xvii.1–2). In seventeenth-century English poetry, where all these non–native influences prevailed, the sighs of unrequited love emitted by despondent males assume the force of a gale. It was only natural for the young Rochester to experiment in the same vein.

Perfect love in the noblest French tradition demanded that the unhappy lover should never reveal the cause of his woes (cf. below on the *Pastoral Dialogue between Alexis and Strephon*). As if languishing were not enough, his torment must remain a secret. The sole favour demanded of the lady in Rochester's *Discovery* is that she should allow the world to see her conquest, and it is implied – with less than perfect gallantry – that this ought to please her vanity. (The title of the poem, of course, refers to the revealing, the 'discovery', of his passion.)

The two poems beginning 'Could I but make my wishes insolent' and 'Insulting *Beauty*, you mispend' are slightly less chivalrous. In the first, the speaker's admiration of the loved one's beauty and worth does not prevent him from implicitly challenging her taste in suffering a worthless moron to woo her – an early manifestation of that hatred of fools that is so typical of Rochester.

For all his extreme woe, which he compares to the pain of a burning martyr, the unhappy lover is not beyond criticising his idol for having encouraged him, and his concluding lines revert to her lack of discrimination:

[14] See Farley-Hills, *Rochester's Poetry*, p. 45.
[15] A famous quotation from *Suréna*. See Pelous, *Amour précieux*, p. 46.

Tis some releife in my extreame distress
My rivall is Below your power to Bless.

The lady in 'Could I but make my wishes insolent' was at least courted
by another man, however inadequate his motives; but the addressee in
'Insulting *Beauty*, you mispend' has no suitors other than her adoring
slave. To be sure, he imputes the indifference of other men to the
dullness of mankind, or to the possibility that her conquering eyes have
been 'partial', singling him out – but the implications are hardly
flattering for the lady. As was the case in 'Could I but make my wishes
insolent', this lyric concludes on a note of petulance; she will be sorry
when her coldness has killed him. The suggestion that no man will love
her after the languishing speaker's death is hardly conducive to
seduction.

The idea that a woman could kill with disdain also occurs in the
intriguing exchange of poems by Rochester and his wife, the *Song*
beginning 'Give me leave to raile at you' and *The Answer* ('Nothing
adds to your fond fire'). As this exchange does not readily fit into any
of the categories I have drawn up, it might as well be discussed in this
context of pleading, threats of death, and disdain.

Rochester's *Song* begins with the impetuous demand that his lady
allow him to abuse her verbally without retaliating by being ungracious
to him:

> Give me leave to raile at you,
> I aske nothing but my due;
> To call you false, and then to say,
> You shall not keepe my Heart a Day.
> But (Alas!) against my will,
> I must be your Captive still.
> Ah! be kinder then, for I,
> Cannot change, and wou'd not dye.
>
> Kindnesse has resistlesse Charmes,
> All besides but weakly move,
> Fiercest Anger it disarmes,
> And Clips the Wings of flying Love.
> Beauty does the Heart invade,
> Kindnesse only can perswade;
> It guilds the Lovers Servile Chaine
> And makes the Slave grow pleas'd and vaine.

The stanzas are remarkable, not for their poetic merit but because they
argue (rightly or wrongly) that the husband's aggressiveness, accusations

and boasts of inconstancy are only a pose. If the lady will ignore them and remain generous to him, she will allay his outbursts, keep him faithful to her and enjoy his good-tempered service.

Lady Rochester, no doubt made wise by experience, did not accept this plea at face value. Still, she rewarded it by revealing her self-protective devices with great frankness:

> Nothing adds to your fond fire,
> More than Scorne, and cold disdaine,
> I to cherish your desire,
> Kindnesse us'd, but 'twas in vaine.
> You insulted on your Slave,
> Humble Love you soone refus'd
> Hope not then a Pow'r to have
> Which Ingloriously you us'd.
>
> Thinke not Thirsis I will e're
> By my Love, my Empire loose,
> You grow Constant through despair,
> Love return'd, you wou'd abuse.
> Tho' you still possesse my heart,
> Scorne, and Rigour, I must feigne,
> Ah! forgive that only Art,
> Love, has left your Love to gaine.
>
> You that cou'd my Heart subdue;
> To new Conquests, ne're pretend,
> Let your Example make me true
> And of a Conquer'd Foe, a Friend.
> Then if e're I shou'd complaine,
> Of your Empire, or my Chain,
> Summon all your Pow'rfull Charmes,
> And fell the Rebell in your Armes.

The finishing touch, coming after a display of psychological insight, devotion and wry humour ('Let your Example make me true'), is rather a noble expression of generosity. The Rochesters' correspondence – even stripped of conventional phrases which need not have signified a great deal – confirms the emotional bond between the spouses.

It is easy to sentimentalise this exchange of mediocre *Gelegenheitsverse* heavily overlaid with conventional power language, dissemblance and military metaphors. There is no reason to trust Rochester when he claims that harshness from his wife would kill him, as even her unkindness could not make him stop loving her. Even so, it is a

curiously touching set of verses, if only because of the clear-sightedness
and affection shown by the lady. Her longing for a 'Friend' to take the
place of the 'Conquer'd Foe' recalls the emphasis Milton placed on the
cheerful, companionate union of loving spouses.[16] It is very much a
wish and not a fact, not unlike the hoped-for bliss beyond all quarrels
and jealousies in the last stanza of *The Mistress*.[17]

Even in the poems where a Rochesterian speaker ostensibly conforms
to the accepted behaviour of a chivalrous admirer, a tone of discord can
often be heard. He may resort to such base means as blackmail, and his
servitude is rarely as abject and unconditional as the pastoral tradition
demands. One of the very few lyrics where the celebration of a beautiful
girl is not undercut by intimations of unchivalrousness is *The submission*.
It starts off with a classic acknowledgement of *innamoramento*, where
Love is invited to rule at his discretion. 'To this moment a Rebell I
throw down my Arms', the first line, suggests that the new worshipper
was no easy conquest for Cupid. (Similarly, the Sedley lyric entitled *The
Submission* argues that victory over a previous scoffer is a special kind of
triumph.)

Not only is the lady presented with unmitigated admiration; she is
equipped with traits beyond the inevitable conquering eyes and charms:

> When Innocence, Beauty, and witt doe Conspire,
> To betray, and engage, and enflame my Desire,
> Why should I decline what I cannott avoyd
> And let pleaseing hope by base fear be destroy'd.
>
> ...
>
> There can be no danger in sweetness and youth
> Where Love is secur'd by Good nature and Truth
> On her beauty I'le gaze, and of pleasure Complain,
> While every kind look adds a link to my Chain.

This is, for once, a true celebration of a girl who is not only lovely to
look at, but also delightful to know. She is young, pretty and intelligent;
she has the good taste to allow 'kind looks' to gladden the speaker's

---

[16] See Hagstrum, *Sex and Sensibility*, ch. 2. Milton was not an innovator in this respect;
descriptions and celebrations of conjugal happiness based on mutual devotion, respect and
loyalty abound in the sixteenth and seventeenth centuries. See, for instance, Alan Macfarlane,
Marriage and Love in England: Modes of Reproduction 1300–1840 (Oxford, 1986), ch. 3.

[17] If any real woman is implicated in the creation of that poem it is, ironically enough, Elizabeth
Barry, not Elizabeth, Countess of Rochester. If Burnet's account of Rochester's last illness is to
be trusted, the Rochesters did find that harmony a short time before he died (see p. 83 in the
Critical Heritage reproduction of Burnet's text).

heart; and she is sweetly innocent into the bargain. Olinda recalls those heroines in Restoration comedy who are bright, attractive and witty while remaining tantalisingly virtuous.[18] A virtue which holds such dangers may well cause the would-be lover to devote considerable energy to persuading himself that all will be well. She seems to be fond of him; surely the sweet young thing will not deceive him, her love being 'secur'd by Good nature and Truth'.

The words 'Truth' and 'secur'd' are of peculiar importance in Rochester's poems on love. Artemiza's noble eulogy on love affirms that it is the 'most gen'rous passion of the mynde':

> The softest refuge Innocence can fynde,
> The safe directour of unguided youth,
> Fraught with kind wishes, and secur'd by Trueth[.]

At the safe bosom of the faithful lady in 'Absent from thee', 'Love and Peace and Truth does flow'. The jealousy suffered by Corinna's lover in the *Ramble* is made especially painful in that her actions betray those moments when he had let go of all reservation, 'Wrapt in security and rest' (see pp. 100ff. below). There are two kinds of felicity in Rochester's love poetry: sexual union at the physical level, and mental and emotional security at the level of the mind. Wherever his poems afford us a glimpse of the two together, we come as close to a representation of true love as he can give. Sadly, and characteristically, it is never celebrated as an enduring achievement – not even in *The submission*.

What prevents the mutual inclination of the speaker and the lovely girl (supposing he is right in assuring himself of her liking for him) from proceeding to a truly satisfying conclusion is that she seems too dear for his possessing. In the end, the speaker is overwhelmed by the perfection of the creature whose praises he sings, and he recoils, dazzled, from his idol. Her 'weak Temple' would put up little resistance, but the adoring slave is powerless to conquer this citadel. Delight may be 'Loves end', but the 'Rapture' in which the speaker 'dissolves' is not that of shared erotic fulfilment. The most the speaker can cope with is imagining sexual intercourse with the girl he extols; reality would clearly be beyond him.

The submission seems somewhat uncharacteristic of Rochester. The courtly *soumission absolue* and the unstinting praise of the creature who is not only beautiful but innocent, truthful and witty as well are difficult

---

[18] Cf. Cowley's portrayal of the infinite allure of innocence in 'The Innocent Ill', pp. 145–6 in A. R. Waller's edition of Cowley's *Poems* (Cambridge, 1905).

to reconcile with, say, the arrogance of '*Phillis*, be gentler I advice' or the suavity of *Love and Life*. Still, the delectable Olinda is not the only Rochester female to be beyond cajoling, bullying and abuse. Corinna in *The Imperfect Enjoyment* is too gorgeously seductive for her own good; and Cynthia's rival in 'T'was a dispute 'twixt heav'n and Earth' is another prodigy. None of these ladies has a single deficiency, and yet they figure in love poems where ardour is allied to non-fulfilment. There is something emasculating about their very perfections.

The last-mentioned lyric hence also suggests that a woman may be too radiantly beautiful, imperilling her would-be lover's ability to stand the course of their relationship. It embodies a pleasing paradox: the addressed lady represents Earth in a beauty contest against Heaven's candidate, Cynthia/Artemis. She outshines the goddess, herself assuming the role of deity to her admirer, who compares her cautious veiling of her divinity to a similar practice on the part of Apollo, brother of Artemis.

Like *The submission*, this poem represents an attitude which students of Rochester's 'sexual politics' have failed to notice: intercourse – at more levels than one – with an eminently desirable lady, on an equal footing, is not possible. An erotic dimension is certainly present in the concluding stanzas of both poems, but the dissolving and possessing are not set in a framework of mutual, uninhibited enjoyment. The superiority of the lady is too shattering.

The *Song* beginning 'While on those lovely looks I gaze' seems initially to fit into this pattern of a male worshipper crushed by the woman's glory, but the second half of the poem brings a radical change of tone and perspective:

> But, if this murder you'd forego,
>   Your Slave from Death removing,
> Let me your Art of Charming know,
>   Or learn you mine of Loving.
>
> But whether Life or Death betide,
>   In Love 'tis equal measure;
> The Victor lives with empty Pride,
>   The Vanquish'd dyes with Pleasure.

In the first two stanzas,[19] the speaker is a narrator describing a lovely lady pursued by a too-aspiring male. Suddenly, in stanza three, the 'I' of the poem is himself the wretched suitor, and the lady is directly

---

[19] Walker prints the poem as four stanzas, Vieth (and others) as two.

addressed as 'you'. The shift is accompanied by a hint that the would-be lover's adoration may end in a rather more expedient death than the solitary demise of the heartbroken.[20]

The fourth stanza brings in another paradox. Whether the lady comes to love the speaker or remains immovable, the outcome is similar: either she is 'Victor' and lives on 'with empty Pride' while he meets his 'pleasing happy Ruin' in dying for love; or he triumphs, bestowing an enjoyable erotic 'death' on her, but in that case 'empty Pride' will attend his survival.[21] Consequently, this short lyric (of sixteen lines) explores several kinds of dissatisfaction, from the despair of the unsuccessful wooer to the ultimate discontent of the triumphant lover.

The last poem in the non-fulfilment category may be one of Rochester's earliest works. In Walker's edition, the *Pastoral Dialogue between ALEXIS and STREPHON* heads the 'Love Poems' section (following 'Juvenilia'); Vieth includes it among the 'Prentice Work'. However, the copy-text employed by both editors (published in 1682–3) states that the poem was written by Rochester 'At the BATH, 1674'.[22]

The first seven stanzas of the *Pastoral Dialogue* – exactly half the poem – contain no hint of opposing opinions. Both Alexis and Strephon complain of the torment inflicted on them by the entrancing Corinna, who – like several other Restoration ladies – combines a 'sweet Form divinely Fair' and a 'Cruel Mind'. They are chivalrous enough not to blame the lady for the latter; it was instilled by 'the Gods', just as her beauty was created by 'some Cruel Powers above'.

At first, in fact, it is Strephon rather than Alexis who seems to chafe at the bonds of amorous servitude, questioning Fate and arguing – like the speaker in *The Discovery*, and against the rule of *soumission absolue* – that love should not have to be hidden. In so doing, he briefly opposes the discretion which *l'éthique tendre* of France enjoined. There were English precedents for such a stance, though; see, for instance, Cowley's 'The Discovery':

> By Heaven I'll tell her boldly that 'tis She;
> Why should she asham'd or angry be,
> To be belov'd by Me?

[20] Cf. the poem 'The Thraldome' in Cowley's *The Mistress* (pp. 67–8 in Waller's Cowley edition), where twenty-eight lines of abject slavery end in the ambiguous plea that the tyrant Love employ the speaker not in building pyramids or quarrying in stony hearts, but in 'dig[ging] the *Mine*'.   [21] See Farley-Hills, *Rochester's Poetry*, pp. 46–7.

[22] On the dating of this poem, see p. 172 in Vieth's edition and Farley-Hills, *Rochester's Poetry*, p. 52. Walker acknowledges that Farley-Hills may be right; see p. 230 in his edition.

We are thus unprepared for the sudden change on Alexis' part from orthodox worship to a the-devil-take-her attitude. In contemporary France, however, a corresponding duality could often be seen as *l'esprit galant* gradually began to challenge *l'éthique tendre*.[23] During a period of transition, suitors adopted the manners of both and displayed either attitude according to their own convenience. Pelous quotes (p. 198) a stanza by Charleval in which the poet admits that he 'mixes the impatience of the satyr with the respect of the shepherd'.

Strephon, however, remains unconditionally faithful to his love. Like his namesake in Sedley's *A Pastoral Dialogue between THIRSIS and STREPHON*, he is a model of constancy. Except for his momentary lapse in lines 33–5, when he questions the need to conceal love, he is the *parfait amant tendre* throughout.

By contrast, Alexis comes to display distinctly ungentlemanly sentiments in stanza 11. Not only is he ready to transfer his affections to a more receptive object; he readily admits to a vindictive streak:

> ALEX. Rather what Pleasure shou'd I meet
> In my Tryumphant scorn,
> To see my Tyrant at my Feet;
> Whil'st taught by her, unmov'd I sit
> A Tyrant in my Turn.

This gloating over a humiliated woman does not sound much like the light-hearted champions of *la galanterie*. Even so, Alexis' willingness to offer his 'humble heart' to a less reluctant mistress was entirely in accordance with current fashions in France.

In England, though, many would have approved of Strephon's insistence that love and life are inseparable, with love a 'Divine Flame' which cannot be extinguished at will. Pastoral dialogues were popular throughout the seventeenth century; Marvell wrote several, and Lovelace, Waller, Etherege, Sedley and Dryden rendered the exchanges of various lovers with names such as Damon, Thyrsis, Clorinda and Phillis. Rochester himself was, of course, often referred to as 'Strephon' by his admirers (his wife called him Thyrsis in the exchange discussed above). One of them was Aphra Behn, a self-avowed worshipper of love. The pastoral dialogue was thus by no means a stale genre in the years of the Restoration. It usually dealt with the doubts and distress of love – forsaken mistresses and despairing swains were much in evidence –, but the potential vindictiveness evinced by Rochester's

---

[23] See Pelous, *Amour précieux*, pp. 195ff.

Alexis is a fairly drastic sentiment in a seventeenth-century English pastoral.

The quality which made Corinna seem unconquerable to the sighing shepherds was one that seventeenth-century love poets abhorred like no other. 'Honour' keeps holding out against the ardent pleas of wooers and is roundly cursed in consequence. Cowley's poem 'Honour' in *The Mistress* may serve as an example of a multitude of lyrics on the subject; 'the happy *work*' of obtaining a declaration of love concluded, the anticipation of total conquest is thwarted by 'bold *Honour*', '*Empty* cause of *solid* harms!' In another complaint on 'Womens Superstition', Cowley lamented that women still worship the old gods; '*Honour*'s their *Ashtaroth*, and *Pride* their *Baal*'.

Rochester thus took up another convention when he rendered the clash of Love and Honour in the lyric called *Womans Honor*. Like so many of his contemporaries, he represented the combatants as conflicting deities. As Shadwell's witty rake Rains asserts, 'those old Enemies Love and Honour will never agree' (*Epsom Wells*, v.i).

The speaker in Cowley's 'Honour' slyly reassures himself that he will get the better of Honour if he attacks at night, as the offensive quality only shows itself when the world looks on. Rochester's protagonist has a puissant deity on his side, but Love despairs of being able to lure the enemy out of his shelter. The mere sight of 'the mightier *God*' would drive Honour away; but as long as the latter stays barricaded in the woman's heart, Love is powerless to effect a change.

In seventeenth-century poetry, the word 'kind' often functioned as a synonym for 'sexually compliant'. Phillis' unkindness gives her rebuffed admirer much pain, but – as was the case with her namesake in '*Phillis*, be gentler I advice' – it entails even greater affliction for herself:

> Let me still languish and complain,
> Be most unhumanly deny'd,
> I have some pleasure in my pain,
> She can have none with all her *Pride*.
>
> I fall a Sacrifice to *Love*,
> She lives a Wretch for *Honours* sake,
> Whose Tyrant does most cruel prove,
> The diff'rence is not hard to make.

Most of Rochester's attacks on pride are directed against mankind in general, or at the mighty men of this world; *Womans Honor* lashes out at the same vice in women. Rochester will have enjoyed Sir William

Davenant's song *Against Womens pride*, printed in the Folio edition of the latter's *Works* in 1673:

> If neither Sun nor Moon can justifie
> Their pride, how ill it Women then befits
> That are on Earth but *Ignes fatui*,
> That lead poor-men to wander from their Wits?

The last stanza in *Womans Honor* has a misogynist ring to it, too. Women's conception of honour is paltry as well as misguided, whereas men have a sense of honour that benefits and exalts mankind. [24]

ANTICIPATION AND ASSEVERATION: FULFILMENT EXPECTED

When Love and Honour engage in *To Corinna. A SONG* ('What Cruel pains *Corinna* takes'), the conflict is rendered in very different terms. Both combatants have seconds, Nature and Virtue respectively, and the end of the combat is a foregone conclusion: Love and Nature will win the day. Virtue is weak and inept, Honour an empty convention. Corinna's attempts to assume their armour are consequently 'harmless' and 'helpless'. The victory of Love and Nature is the more certain as they have in effect already taken possession of the lady; her heart is soft, her eyes are kind, and her compliance virtually guaranteed. The 'scorn' she pretends to – probably expressed in words, since her eyes are 'so very kind' – is a meaningless gesture intended to safeguard whatever reputation for chastity she might possess. It is an act of dissemblance; but the suitor is not deceived and was never meant to be. Ladies who pretend to virtue though they have it not are stock characters in Restoration comedy. The 'dear, dear honour' of Wycherley's Lady Fidget is a classic example; all the Court Wits joined in making fun of them.[25]

In Rochester's lyric, the male is confident of success. He may pretend, in his turn, to be the lady's 'Vassal';[26] but she will actually submit to

---

[24] A woman poet of Aphra Behn's calibre would make no such distinctions; in her *The Golden Age*, she condemns honour, the 'Foe to Pleasure, Nature's worst Disease', in an all-out attack. This poem was probably written in the late 1670s. Maureen Duffy places it in 1679; see her *The Passionate Shepherdess: Aphra Behn 1640–1689* (London, 1977), p. 176.

[25] See, for instance, the conclusion of Gatty's song in Act v of Etherege's *She Would if She Could* (p. 213 in Verity's 1888 edition of Etherege's *Works*). The 'Affected Rules of Honour' recall line 6 in Etherege's *Song* 'Tell me no more you love' (p. 24 in James Thorpe's edition of *The Poems of Sir George Etherege* (Princeton, 1963)), 'Dull laws of Honor...'

[26] On vassalage and *The Fall*, see my article 'Rochester and *The Fall*: The Roots of Discontent', *English Studies* 69.5 (October 1988), 408.

being 'undone' by him, and he is in control of the situation. A brief exchange between Dryden's Melantha and Rhodophil (*Marriage A-la-Mode*, III.ii.67–8)[27] crystallises the Restoration mood when it came to feigned resistance, a topic reviewed below (pp. 52ff.):

> MEL. I hope you will not force me?
> RHO. But I will, if you desire it.

In the small *Song* 'Att Last you'l force mee to confess', the man is also to some extent in control of the situation. Here, though, it is he who prefers to dissemble by means of verbal 'scorne'. His reason suggests that he needs some sort of protection from the lady:

> Att Last you'l force mee to confess
> You need noe arts to vanquish
> Such charmes from Nature you posses
> 'Twere dullness, nott to Languish;
> Yett spare A Heart you may surprize
> And give my Tongue the glory
> To scorne, while my unfaithfull eyes
>   Betray a kinder story.

'Nature' is once more on the side of the angels, having created a girl who has no need to rely on 'arts' (cf. pp. 50 and 65). Her suitor acknowledges her power, but he is afraid she will make too complete a conquest of him. In Restoration love lyrics, 'surprise' often means 'conquer', 'take over (suddenly)'; that is obviously the sense of the word here. By means of verbal attacks, the wooer hopes to keep his 'heart', his innermost being, safe from the lady's influence, while his eyes cannot but admit that he languishes for her.

Contemporary poems imply that tongues and eyes are not in fact very good at performing dissimilar commissions. Again, one of Cowley's *Mistress* poems may be quoted in evidence:

> Thy *Tongue* comes in, as if it meant
>   Against thine *Eyes* t'assist my *Heart*;
> But different far was his intent:
>   For straight the *Traitor* took their part.
> And by this new foe I'm bereft
> Of all that *Little* which was left.

---

[27] P. 274 in vol. XI of the University of California edition of *The Works of John Dryden* (eds. J. Loftis, D. S. Rodes and V. A. Dearing; 1978).

The act I must confess was wise;
    As a dishonest act could be:
Well knew the *Tongue* (alas) your *Eyes*
    Would be too strong for *That*, and *Me*.
And part o'th' *Triumph* chose to *get*,
    Rather than *be a part* of it.[28]

It would be wrong to maintain that the speaker in Rochester's 'Att Last you'l force mee to confess' is doubtful of his ultimate success. If he were, he would hardly dare to submit such a petition to the lady, and his 'confession' was clearly extorted by her, which means that she cannot be indifferent to him. But this lyric has none of the smugness of 'What Cruel pains *Corinna* takes'. As in so many of Rochester's love poems, a hint of uneasiness can be discerned. The suggestion that the speaker fears that he will love too well betrays a level of sensibility which was not there in, for instance, '*Phillis*, be gentler I advice'.

The last of the poems in the 'fulfilment expected' group is very different from the other two. The *SONG of a young LADY To Her Ancient Lover* has elicited a very wide range of reactions from critics throughout the ages. Most academic commentators have admitted to finding the situation 'rather repulsive'.[29] Reba Wilcoxon represents the other extreme, arguing that the *Song* is a 'poignant' poem about a woman who 'is a warm and involved human being – a projection of Rochester's deepest needs in that she is a wholly sexual and deeply affectionate partner'.[30]

To a seventeenth-century reader of the young lady's song, the situation outlined in it would not have been 'repulsive' so much as utterly bizarre. It is hard to think of a historical period that has insisted as vehemently as the Restoration did on love being the exclusive business of young people – 'young' corresponding to the teens and early twenties, fifteen being a highly suitable age for the female. The speaker of Rochester's poem would not have had the effrontery to pose as 'young' if she had been beyond her teens.[31] When Rochester referred to Charles II at the age of forty-three as being in 'his declining yeares',

---

[28] 'Counsel', stanzas 5 and 6; p. 95 in Waller's edition. In Rochester's lyric, the eyes are 'unfaithfull' – disloyal – to the tongue; in Cowley's verses the tongue is the '*Traitor*'. Cf. Rochester's *Song* beginning 'As *Chloris* full of harmless thought', lines 19–20.

[29] Farley-Hills, *Rochester's Poetry*, p. 60. See also John R. Clark, 'Satiric Singing: An Example from Rochester', originally in *The English Record* 24 (Fall 1973), 16–20. Vieth reprinted it in his *Critical Essays* collection (pp. 165–72).

[30] 'Rochester's Sexual Politics', 146–7. See also Hammond's commentary in his edition of Rochester's poetry, where the *Song* is described as 'a human and strangely moving poem' (p. 75). [31] See Elisabeth Mignon, *Crabbed Age and Youth*, pp. 21ff.

he expressed an uncontroversial view. Restoration literature pokes merciless fun at middle-aged and older men with sexual ambitions and designs.[32] No wonder such men were uncomfortably aware of being at a disadvantage when paying attention to young ladies. When the future Duke of Newcastle courted Margaret Lucas, thirty years his junior, he besought her to bear in mind that 'Old and dry wood makes the best fier',[33] thus anticipating Dorset's well-known lyric *The Fire of Love* (written when the poet himself was around forty-seven).

Rochester's *Song* operates on two temporal planes. The young lady's lover is certainly referred to as 'Ancient', but he is not yet 'Old, / Aking, shaking, Crazy Cold'. As she is not at this point compelled to resort to 'Art' – characteristically inferior to the bounties of Nature in Rochester's poetry – to satisfy him, his potency is apparently still unimpaired. The third stanza reassures him that she will be able to deal with the impotence of old age when it does manifest itself. The element of *anticipated* crisis and remedy is not unimportant in the poem as a whole.

The young lady is highly affectionate; but nothing is said about her own needs and wishes. She serves, in Vieth's words, as a kind of 'generalized fertility principle'[34] bestowing new life on her 'oddly passive' partner. The words 'principle' and 'passive' seem to me to hold one clue to the poem. Wilcoxon supplies another – unwittingly, perhaps – when she writes that this woman is 'a projection of Rochester's deepest needs'.

Perhaps the reason why the *Song of a Young Lady* has made many people uncomfortable is that it is not a poem about real people, or a real relationship, at all. Rather, it is about an anxiety and the kind of reassurance that a person who suffers from such an anxiety would dream of. Few men at any time or age escape worries about sexual failure; Rochester certainly had them. Not one of his first-person lyrics describes mutual sexual gratification with a willing and committed partner as an actual and wholly satisfying event. Such gratification is either an-

---

[32] Cf. Mignon's extensive discussion of Dryden's *The Assignation* in *Crabbed Age and Youth*, especially pp. 68–71. See also Sedley's *Advice to the Old Beaux*.

[33] Quoted in Hilda L. Smith, *Reason's Disciples: Seventeenth-Century English Feminists* (Urbana, Ill., 1982), p. 88. Cf. Claude Dulong's account of Corneille's wooing of the 'Marquise'; *L'Amour au XVIIème siècle*, pp. 154–9.

[34] Vieth, '"Pleased with the Contradiction and the Sin"', 48. Vieth's observations – for instance on the successive lengthening of the stanzas – are often striking, but some of his statements seem fanciful (the poem constitutes Rochester's 'enthusiastic celebration of this uncommon relationship'; the third stanza sees the situation 'metamorphosed into a joyous pagan fertility pageant').

ticipated ('What Cruel pains *Corinna* takes'), bungled (*The Imperfect Enjoyment*), subsequently betrayed (*A Ramble in Saint James's Parke*), or somehow disappointing (*The Fall*). Rochester was only in his mid-twenties when he wrote to Savile that they had both proved themselves 'Errant fumblers' with women, and there is no reason to doubt that he means exactly what he says – he is no better at dealing with women than his fat bachelor friend.

The evidence of the poems themselves, supported by the letter to Savile, is unambiguous: these lyrics were written by a man who was plagued by sexual as well as emotional disharmony. The vision of the young lady, immensely reassuring, unshakeably devoted, entirely unconcerned for herself and infinitely resourceful, is the answer to all these troubles. In her capable hands, the male can forget all responsibility for his own and his partner's happiness. No wonder she is not real. Nor is the 'ancient person', that curiously depersonalised figure,[35] whose age – his sole distinctive attribute – makes him a suitable vehicle for sexual anxiety.

The poems on 'fulfilment expected' hence comprise two lyrics where the enjoyment of a lovely lady seems a realisable ambition and one where the realisation of erotic ambition is wholly entrusted to a lady. Only in the *Song* beginning 'What Cruel pains *Corinna* takes' is the male, as it were, on top of things. In this small group of poems, too, the vulnerability of masculinity makes itself felt.

MASTURBATION AND PENETRATION: FULFILMENT ACHIEVED

If the Young Lady comes across as a phantom of delight rather than as a realistically conceived woman speaker, the essential action in the *Song* 'Fair *Cloris* in a Piggsty lay' definitely takes place in the realm of dreams. Sleepers are not sinners, and erotic dreams dispensing with ethics and responsibilities have been material for poetry from antiquity onwards.[36] They were certainly popular with Renaissance and Res-toration poets.[37] So, of course, was the pastoral (cf. p. 45 above).

---

[35] *Ibid.*, 48–9.
[36] See, for example, H. M. Richmond, *The School of Love: The Evolution of the Stuart Love Lyric* (Princeton, 1964), pp. 50–7.
[37] Farley-Hills (*Rochester's Poetry*, pp. 65–9) adduces previous and contemporary instances, supplying useful comments on the implications of 'Floras Cave'. It might be added, though, that Marvell had employed a cave image for similar purposes in his pastoral on Clorinda and Damon. So did Jean Dehénault in his verses on 'Une grotte étroitte et profonde'; see pp. 69–70

Rochester's 'Fair *Cloris*' is thus connected with two well-established poetic genres, but it constitutes a break with the conventions of both.

First of all, Rochester's mock-pastoral is about the erotic dream of a woman, attended by masturbation. This may not be unique; but I have not come across another Restoration instance. Second, it parodies pastoral paraphernalia in a manner both brutal and delicious.[38] Making Cloris a swineherdess supplies a suitable stage-prop (the grunting herd, which her dream translates into a groaning lover) as well as marvellously comic details (such as the 'bosom Pigg'). With the exception of the equally hilarious *Signior Dildo*, this song is arguably the only poem in the Rochester canon where obscenity is wholly amusing. The frivolous tone never wavers, and it is emphasised by the humorously bland concluding line, 'She's Innocent and pleas'd'.

The fact that it is a third-person narrative (like *Signior Dildo*) has much to do with its light-heartedness. Rochester never wrote a first-person poem in which sexual passion is a subject of merriment. For similar reasons, the narrative element is important in the *Song* beginning 'As *Chloris* full of harmless thought'. That poem has the distinction of being the sole running account of straightforward heterosexual arousal and consummation in Rochester's poetry.

Before we turn to this other member of the fulfilment-achieved category, though, one topic that concerns both these songs ought to be addressed: that of sexual violation viewed against a Restoration background. Cloris in the pigsty dreams of being raped by a deceitful swain; Chloris beneath the willows represents the idea that women say no but mean yes. A modern reader, living at a time when the latter notion is soundly and unceasingly discounted in all sorts of fora every day of the week, may find it difficult to relish the comic dimensions of the two songs.

To seventeenth-century readers, however, the assertion that 'Virgins Eyes their hearts betray, / And give their Tongues the lie' was accepted wisdom. Scores of poets urged their male addressees to push ahead regardless of feminine objections. Dorset's *The Advice* and *Advice to Lovers* make the point with some ferocity.[39]

in Frédéric Lachèvre's edition of *Les Oeuvres de Jean Dehénault, Le Libertinage au XVIIe siècle*, vol. IX (Paris, 1922). The conventions burlesqued by Rochester in his *Song* are neatly illustrated in Dryden's 'Song of the Zambra Dance' from *The Conquest of Granada*.

[38] As Griffin says, 'Rarely if ever was a pastoral artifice so deftly yet so crudely parodied' (*Satires Against Man*, p. 103).

[39] See Brice Harris' edition of *The Poems of Charles Sackville Sixth Earl of Dorset* (New York and London, 1979), pp. 83–5.

Across the Channel, too, various experts insisted that women really wanted masterful men. La Rochefoucauld's devastating maxim is one example:

La plupart des femmes se rendent plutôt par faiblesse que par passion; de là vient que, pour ordinaire, les hommes entreprenants réussissent mieux que les autres, quoiqu'ils ne soient pas plus aimables.[40]

Even women subscribed to this notion. Thus, for example, Ninon l'Enclos – whose wide experience and tough common sense lent some support to her claim to represent all women – announced:

Je vous dis de la part des femmes: il est des instants où elles aiment mieux être un peu brusquées que trop ménagées; les hommes manquent plus de coeurs par leur maladresse que la vertu n'en sauve.[41]

No attempt to inhibit anachronistic reactions can altogether stifle a present-day reader's disgust at Pepys' dispassionate, if bilingual, account of how he raped Mrs Bagwell in her and her husband's home, a graphic illustration of Restoration attitudes to resisting women.[42]

Jacqueline Pearson summarises views on rape in the seventeenth century in the following harsh terms:

The period reveals a good deal of male – and, occasionally, female – cynicism about the very possibility of rape: 'a Woman's never to be Ravisht against her will', for women really desire to raped, and 'No Woman ever fell out with a Man about that business'. No woman need suffer rape: she can always choose to die instead, so that if she survives she must be guilty of 'so vile, so base a Crime'. Satirical writings emphasise the culpability of the victim or deny the very possibility of rape: women are so libidinous rape is impossible. Lucretia committed suicide only for fear of discovery but otherwise would have 'killed herself – before she had deny'd', and Susanna resisted the elders only because they were old.[43]

After this review of sexual violence in a seventeenth-century context, it is important to point out that no violation actually takes place in either of Rochester's two songs. Sleeping Cloris is excited by her dream of being raped; but psychologists agree that dreams and fantasies about rape – effectively removing all responsibility for sexual behaviour from a woman – are not unusual and certainly do not imply any wish for the

---

[40] No. 301 in the 1665 edition. Quoted by Pelous, *Amour précieux*, p. 200.
[41] Quoted by Dulong, *L'Amour au XVIIème siècle*, p. 192.
[42] See Richard Ollard, *Pepys: A Biography* (London, 1974), p. 100.
[43] *The Prostituted Muse: Images of Women & Women Dramatists 1642–1737* (London and New York, 1988), p. 96 (footnotes omitted).

real thing. Chloris beneath the willows is simply seduced by an
accomplished swain who is able to benefit from the lucky minute, the
'Shepherd's Hour'.[44] She yields because she is sexually aroused for the
first time, experiencing a force stronger than the bribes of princes:

> A sudden passion seiz'd her heart
>   In spight of her disdain,
> She found a pulse in e'ry part
>   And love in e'ry Vein:
> Ah Youth quoth she, what charms are these
>   That conquer and surprise;
> Ah let me! for unless you please
>   I have no power to rise.
>
> She faintly spoke and trembling lay
>   For fear he should comply ...

It is difficult to understand how Farley-Hills can make a 'violent rape'
of this encounter (*Rochester's Poetry*, p. 41). Exactly the same combination of circumstances occurs in Aphra Behn's poem *On a Juniper-
Tree, cut down to make Busks* (quoted from Montague Summers' 1915
edition of Behn's *Works*, vol. VI, p. 149):

> Beneath my shade the other day,
> Young *Philocles* and *Cloris* lay,
> ...
> I saw 'em kindle to desire,
> Whilst with soft sighs they blew the fire;
> Saw the approaches of their joy,
> He growing more fierce, and she less Coy,
> Saw how they mingled melting Rays,
> Exchanging Love a thousand ways.
> Kind was the force on every side,
> Her new desire she could not hide:
> Nor wou'd the Shepherd be deny'd.
> Impatient he waits no consent
> But what she gave by Languishment,
> The blessed Minute he pursu'd;
> And now transported in his Arms,
> Yeilds to the Conqueror all her Charmes,

---

[44] On this convention, see Treglown, 'He knew my style, he swore', in his *Spirit of Wit*, pp. 86–9.
Cf. the following lines from Etherege's *Song* 'See how fair Corinna lies': 'In the tender minute
prove her'; 'While the happy minute is, / Court her, you may get a kiss, / Maybe favors that
are greater' (p. 31 in James Thorpe's edition of Etherege's poems).

His panting Breast, to hers now join'd,
They feast on Raptures unconfin'd;
Vast and Luxuriant, such as prove
The Immortality of Love.   (lines 24–58)

Clearly, Behn agreed with Ninon l'Enclos that there were times when women preferred men to be assertive rather than gentle.

The two songs on a shepherdess named C(h)loris form the only instances in Rochester's poetry where sexual climaxes are described in sensual terms (unlike lines 121–2 in the *Ramble*) as being entirely enjoyable and having no bitter aftertaste (unlike lines 15–16 in *The Imperfect Enjoyment*). There are other references to orgasms in his poems; but those references are never as unreservedly favourable, even celebratory, as these passages.

It is significant that the 'fulfilment achieved' category only contains two specimens, and that they are both narratives that in no way involve the narrator himself. Another distinctive feature in these poems is that sexual gratification is unaccompanied by emotional involvement: the swineherdess has a dream lover; the other Chloris is a victim/ beneficiary of circumstances, 'the happy minute' and a chance encounter. It is no accident that these two representations of simple erotic pleasure are purely physical, divorced from the finer feelings that are so often associated with pain and anxiety.

RENUNCIATION AND AMBULATION: BEYOND FULFILMENT

The preceding section of this chapter drew attention to some features that set the two poems on Cloris the dreamer and Chloris the seduced virgin apart from the rest of Rochester's love poetry. Perhaps the most complete contrast to them is offered by a poem which argues that sexual climaxes are just not worth having.

The Platonick Lady, unaccountably neglected by most Rochester critics, is in fact a very interesting lyric. The female speaker's insistence that she hates 'the Thing is call'd Injoyment' may make a reader familiar with Rochester's poetry dismiss it as deliberately freakish, a mere exercise ridiculing a foolish notion. Actually, though, the Platonick Lady's stance has some underlying affinity with attitudes implied in other poems with a first-person male speaker. This contention will be discussed later; first, the poem needs to be placed in its literary and social/historical context.

As several scholars have pointed out, line 7 ('I hate the Thing is call'd

Injoyment') echoes Petronius' familiar statement, 'Foeda est in coitu et brevis voluptas' (paraphrased by Ben Jonson as 'Doing a filthy pleasure is, and short'). Restoration readers were thoroughly familiar with the idea that the consummation of erotic passion would be followed by disappointment and was hence best postponed, or never implemented at all. Sir John Suckling played a crucial part in the creation of what became an anti-fruition convention.[45] Edmund Waller's *In Answer of Sir John Suckling's Verses* quotes and comments on Suckling's views in a constellation of pros and cons (labelled that way in the poem). The poem supplies an informative and exhaustive two-page summary of the arguments involved; some excerpts may serve to illustrate their nature:

> CON. Fruition adds no new wealth but destroys,
> And while it pleaseth much, yet still it cloys.
> …
> PRO. Blessings may be repeated while they cloy;
> But shall we starve, 'cause surfeitings destroy?
> …
> CON. Women enjoy'd, whate'er before they've been,
> Are like romances read, or scenes once seen:
> …
> PRO. Plays and romances read and seen, do fall
> In our opinions; yet not seen at all,
> Whom would they please?
> …
> CON. They who know all the wealth they have are poor;
> He's only rich that cannot tell his store.
> PRO. Not he that knows the wealth he has is poor,
> But he that dares not touch nor use his store.[46]

Cowley also wrote a poem 'Against Fruition' in which he sides with Suckling. The concluding couplet contains a simile borrowed by Rochester in lines 11–12 of *The Platonick Lady*:

> *Love*, like a greedy *Hawk*, if we give way,
> Does over-gorge himself, with his own *Prey*;
> Of very *Hopes* a surfeit he'll sustain,
> Unless by *Fears* he cast them up again:
> His spirit and sweetness dangers keep alone;
> If once he lose his *sting*, he grows a *Drone*.

---

[45] A thorough and illuminating discussion of this convention is supplied by Richard E. Quaintance Jr in ch. 3 of his fine dissertation.

[46] Pp. 72–4 in Thomas Park's 1806 edition of Waller's *Poetical Works*.

In another *Mistress* lyric, however, Cowley attacks the platonic ethic; 'Platonick Love', like Donne's *Extasie*, views love as encompassing both souls and bodies.

In France, the doctrine of platonic love enjoyed its greatest vogue in the mid-seventeenth century. Madeleine de Scudéry was one of its priestesses. Her multi-volume *roman Le Grand Cyrus* appeared by instalments in the years around 1650. A dialogue between 'Sapho' (commonly equated with Mlle de Scudéry herself) and her woman friend Cydnon defines platonic love in the following terms:

> Je veux qu'on espère d'être aimé... mais je ne veux pas qu'on espère rien davantage, car enfin c'est ... la plus grande folie du monde de s'engager à aimer quelqu'un si ce n'est dans la pensée de l'aimer jusques à la mort ... J'entends ... qu'on m'aime ardemment, qu'on n'aime que moi et qu'on m'aime avec respect. Je veux même que cette amour soit une amour tendre et sensible, qui se fasse de grands plaisirs de fort petites choses ... [47]

This conception of love was soon challenged by *la galanterie*, and by 1670 it was widely felt to be outmoded on both sides of the Channel. Shadwell's Bevil, on being told by Lucia that 'Methinks 'twere enough to arrive at Platonick Love at first', impatiently replies, 'The pretence to that is more out of fashion in this active Age, than Ruffs and Trunkbreeches are.'[48]

Unlike Mlle de Scudéry's Sapho, the speakers in the English antifruition poems openly acknowledged and accepted the existence of sensual desire. Their basic argument was that amorous passion palls after the sexual climax. That this was by no means an unfashionable notion is shown by the exchange between Palamede and Doralice in Act v of *Marriage A-la-Mode*:

> PAL. Yet if we had but once enjoy'd one another; but then once onely, is worse then not at all: it leaves a man with such a lingring after it.
> DOR. For ought I know 'tis better that we have not; we might upon trial have lik'd each other less, as many a man and woman, that have lov'd as desperately as we, and yet when they came to possession, have sigh'd, and cri'd to themselves, Is this all?[49]

The first four lines of Rochester's *The Platonick Lady* form an orthodox presentation of *l'amour platonique*, speaking of lifelong devotion, modesty and male compliance with the woman's wishes:

---

[47] Quoted in Georges Mongrédien's anthology *Les Précieux et les Précieuses* (Paris, 1963), p. 128.
[48] *Epsom Wells*, v.i (p. 176 in Summers' edition).
[49] Pp. 305 and 306 in the University of California Press edition.

>   I could Love thee 'till I dye,
>   Wouldst Thou Love mee Modestly;
>   And ne're presse, whilst I live,[50]
>   For more than willingly I would give.

The following couplet, however, has an erotic dimension which would
make Mlle de Scudéry *rougir*; and the last two stanzas of the poem are
characterised by a sensuality that is comparatively rare in Rochester's
verse. Coition disgusts the Platonick Lady, though; in the second stanza,
she maintains that

>   It cutts off all that's Life and fier,
>   From that which may be term'd Desire.
>   Just (like the Be) whose sting is gon,
>   Converts the owner to a Droane.

What the lady advocates, then, is sex play without penetration. It is not
a very refined attitude by any standards, and in conjunction with the
conventional opening lines it forms a mockery of the traditional
platonic viewpoint. Her refusal to grant 'the feate' – sexual intercourse
and orgasm – is not dictated by considerations of honour, virtue and so
on; she simply does not think it is of any value, since it kills 'Life and
fier'. Hence, she is closer to the anti-fruition apologists than to such
promoters of platonic love as the French *précieuses* and 'Orinda'.[51] At
one level, the woman who claims to be well versed in the art of love, but
who nevertheless begins her plea with references to stock platonic
notions, may be said to constitute a parody of these ladies and their
literary effusions.

But in a more profound sense, *The Platonick Lady* forms part of a
pattern that comprises the great majority of Rochester's love poems. It
is a pattern of dissatisfaction with, pulling away from, and failing
adequately to perform sexual intercourse. In its fusion of erotic ardour
and non-consummation, *The Platonick Lady* has affinities with the non-
fulfilment poems (see above); and in its evasion of joint commitment to
an actual, mutually satisfying sexual relationship it recalls the 'irrespon-
sibilities' of the Ancient Person and the sleeping Cloris. Fastidiousness
and revulsion attend several of Rochester's poems on erotic love; and

---

[50] The last word is printed as 'love' in Walker's edition. As D. J. Womersley has pointed out
(review of Walker in *Notes and Queries* 33.2, June 1986), this is clearly a misprint. Walker has
corrected it in the paperback edition.
[51] On Katharine Philips as an advocate of platonic love, see Philip Souers, *The Matchless Orinda*
(Cambridge, Mass., 1931), pp. 258ff.

resentment at being cursed with sexual appetite surfaces in poems such as the lampoon on the whore Sue Willis. Consequently, it could be argued that the Platonick Lady's asseveration,

> I hate the Thing is call'd Injoyment,
> Besydes it is a dull imployment

is not without a certain uncomfortable personal relevance.

If an uncomfortable feeling arises in the present-day reader of *A DIALOGUE BETWEEN Strephon and Daphne*, he or she need not blame it on anachronistic disapproval of seventeenth-century attitudes. The poem is an exhibition of multi-level deceit and dissembling. Much of the dialogue is conventional enough. Strephon cynically rejects his mistress' attempts to persuade him to stay with her. As was the case with Alexis' envisaged triumph over Corinna, Strephon's callousness, even cruelty, offends against the idiom of the traditional pastoral. Not only does he announce his decision to leave Daphne; he breaks the golden rule for straying partners by taking care not to leave her a shred of self-respect. He starts off by insulting her ('fond Fool, give o're'), then tells her that his past love for her was no more than childish covetousness:

> Love, like other little Boys,
> Cries for Hearts, as they for Toys:
> Which, when gain'd, in Childish Play,
> Wantonly are thrown away.

When she concludes from this that love is 'Flattering or insulting ever, / Generous and grateful never' – fair comment, one would have thought –, Strephon upbraids her for being unfair:

> Nimph, unjustly you inveigh;
> Love, like us, must Fate obey.
> Since 'tis Nature's Law to Change,
> Constancy alone is strange.

Even in the late seventeenth century, this was a cliché. Strephon then, in dubious taste, compares Nature's changes – thunder followed by calming rain – to arousal followed by 'Show'rs that fall, / Quench the fire, and quiet all.'

Pathetically, Daphne recalls the pleasure those showers gave her, acknowledging that 'They kill'd Love, I knew it well, / I dy'd all the while they fell.' She goes on to ask the name of her triumphant rival, hoping, for Strephon's sake, that the lady is beautiful. Instead of a proper answer, her ungrateful swain supplies a glowing description of his new flame:

> *Daphne* never was so fair:
> *Strephon*, scarcely, so sincere.
> Gentle, Innocent, and Free,
> Ever pleas'd with only me.
> Many Charms my Heart enthral,
> But there's one above 'em all:
> With aversion she does flye
> Tedious, trading, Constancy.

In this strophe, Strephon's tactlessness reaches a peak. Not only does he point out that the new girl shares his views where Daphne does not; he also praises her attractions by comparing his cast-off mistress unfavourably to her. To cap it all, he professes a more genuine infatuation for her than he had for Daphne (though the cynic can still be heard in the word 'scarcely'). Not surprisingly, his interlocutor is crushed by his cruelty. He has one stab left to administer, though: when she asks him to say he would have liked to stay with her, he does not even offer her this scrap of comfort. His final insult is to advise her to follow his example.

It is at this point – one eight-line strophe from the end – that the reversal occurs. Daphne, who has so far had the reader's unreserved sympathy, reveals yet another plane of deceit:

> Silly *Swain*, I'll have you know,
> 'Twas my practice long ago:
> Whilst you Vainly thought me true,
> I was false in scorn of you.
> By my Tears, my Heart's disguise,
> I thy Love and thee despise.
> Woman-kind more Joy discovers
> Making Fools, than keeping Lovers.

Two factors contribute to the uneasiness that this volte-face[52] leaves in the reader. The first is a 'certain doubt as to whether Daphne's final assertion that she has been lying is not in itself a face-saving and despairing lie' (Anne Righter, 'John Wilmot', 63). After all the piled-up agony, it is hard to accept that the tears, pleas and laments were merely feats of dissemblance – dissemblance, too, of a kind that makes

[52] Anne Righter's apt term; see 'John Wilmot', 62.

Strephon's past feigning a kindergarten effort. This reservation raises some obstacles in the way of enjoying what Reba Wilcoxon calls Strephon's 'comeuppance'.[53] It is not possible to be absolutely sure that he really gets one – and anyone who takes Daphne at her word has to acknowledge that any sympathy he/she may have felt for her was misplaced. That entails admitting that the reader has been deceived as well.

The second factor also involves reader response and reader entrapment. Granting that Daphne is telling the truth, what does that make of her – and of Strephon? Despite his programmatic declarations in respect of inconstancy, it is clear that they are merely an excuse; he has simply found someone new and is keen to extricate himself from the old relationship. Strephon reveals his imperfect dedication to the principle of inconstancy when naively announcing his gratification that the new girl is 'Ever pleas'd with only me'. The ensuing assertion, according to which her greatest charm is that she loathes constancy, is ridiculously contradictory. Daphne, on the other hand, is the proper practitioner of inconstancy. If she is telling the truth, her motive for betraying Strephon in the past was not mere inclination (what Strephon pompously called Fate and Nature). She did it because she enjoyed making a fool of him, not because she followed the dictates of fancy. In so doing, she violated the libertine ethos according to which the maximising of sensual pleasure is the worthiest of pursuits.

At the end of the poem, then, the reader has to choose: is Daphne's last speech just a piece of desperate bravado, or is she in fact a much more repulsive creature than the lout Strephon? I suspect that the reader's discomfiture was deliberately engineered by Rochester, who must have spent considerable time over this carefully constructed poem (of seventy-two lines, thirty-six for each interlocutor). Irrespective of what his intentions may have been, the poem shatters the framework of the pastoral convention.[54]

Daphne has a male counterpart in the speaker of the poem *Against Constancy*. A candidate for the title of Rochester's most unpleasant lyric, this poem advocates sexual promiscuity on grounds that have nothing whatever to do with sensual pleasure. The irrelevance of sexual desire and gratification *per se* makes the use of the term 'libertine' misleading

[53] 'Rochester's Sexual Politics', 143.
[54] See Peter Porter's essay 'The Professional Amateur' in Treglown, ed., *Spirit of Wit*, pp. 66 and 68, and Treglown, 'Scepticism and Parody in the Restoration', *The Modern Language Review* 75.1 (January 1980), 22–3.

in connexion with this poem.[55] Inconstancy is extolled not because it is enjoyable, but because it confers socially desirable sexual-athlete status on the practitioner.

According to the speaker of this lyric, there are five reasons for hiding behind the sham of constancy, all of them contemptible: impotence (associated, as so often, with old age); fear of losing a partner as a result of infidelity; venereal disease; low sex drive; and fear of failure with other than tried-and-true partners.

In respect of *Against Constancy*, the importance of distinguishing between Rochester and the protagonist of a poem is especially apparent. The last two stanzas offer strong evidence in favour of a rigorous separation between poet and speaker. The forbiddingly obsessive tone of the last stanza[56] comes after four lines of swaggering:

> But we, whose hearts do justly swell,
>   with no vain-glorious pride,
> Who know how we in love excell,
>   long to be often try'd.

The poet whose works constantly express disgust with pride and vanity, as well as a painful awareness of erotic insufficiency, would never describe himself in those terms. This speaker is not merely a fiction; he is the bearer of particularly un-Rochesterian qualities.

Against Constancy seems to me to be a deliberate parody acting on two levels: a satirical glance at the tell-me-no-more convention, as previous critics have affirmed; and an attack on men to whom sexual intercourse merely serves to advance social aspirations. Such abusers of erotic pastimes are castigated in other Rochester poems, too, notably the *Ramble* (see pp. 97ff. below).

Another dimension is suggested by Dustin Griffin, who – after a brief outline of the argumentation in the poem – concludes, 'Inconstancy... becomes a proof... that the lover is neither dull nor defective. Impotence is the unspoken fear.'[57] The point underlines the overwhelming importance, personally as well as socially, of sexual prowess. A characteristic of many ages and societies, it was very much a Restoration

---

[55] Cf. John Wilders, 'Rochester and the Metaphysicals', in Treglown, ed., *Spirit of Wit*, p. 52 ('[the poet] assumes the simplified role of the libertine'). However, Wilders' comment on the poet's striking 'a deliberately challenging posture' is surely justified. Jeremy Treglown, who points out that the poem seems indebted to the 'Tell me no more' tradition, says that it 'argues in favour... of sexual enjoyment' as well as of promiscuity ('Satirical Inversion', 43); this statement seems unwarranted to me. On the 'Tell me no more' poems, see also Richmond, *The School of Love*, pp. 109ff.   [56] See Wilders, 'Rochester and the Metaphysicals', p. 53.

[57] *Satires Against Man*, p. 116.

concern. In Wycherley's *The Country Wife*, of course, pretended impotence serves as a cover for sexual promiscuity. Another memorable feature of the play, however, is the public ignominy of the allegedly impotent Horner. It is hard to think of another time or society in modern history where it would be perfectly permissible for a man to jeer at another's impotence to his face, and in front of the taunter's own womenfolk.

Hence, even the bragging, aggressive *Against Constancy* possesses an undertone of sexual *malaise*. It has a dash of *Existenzangst*, too: the speaker does not foresee any gradual decline, with concomitant impotence, for himself. Unlike the rake in *The Disabled Debauchee*, he does not expect to see old age:

> Then bring my Bath, and strew my bed,
>   as each kind night returns,
> Ile change a Mistress till i'me dead,
>   and fate change me for worms.

The collocation of 'worms' and 'try'd' – the last words of the last two stanzas – cannot but recall Marvell's *To his Coy Mistress*. The former serves as an emblem of death in both poems, the forces of decay becoming active as the human body lies passive in the grave. The latter word had specifically sexual connotations in the late seventeenth century, and they are clearly present in both poems, too. But the implications inherent in Rochester's final stanza are grimmer than those of Marvell's lines. The coy mistress had a chance to cheat the worms of their feast on her long-preserved virginity; the speaker in *Against Constancy* knows that his compulsive promiscuity can only end in death.

A complete contrast to *Against Constancy* – one that shows up the brittleness of its argumentation, and the jarring emptiness of its use of words such as 'heart' and 'love' – is supplied by one of Sedley's best-known lyrics:

> Not *Celia*, that I juster am
>   Or better than the rest,
> For I would change each Hour like them,
>   Were not my Heart at rest.
>
> But I am ty'd to very thee,
>   By every Thought I have,
> Thy Face I only care to see,
>   Thy Heart I only crave.
>
> All that i[n] Woman is ador'd,

> In thy dear Self I find,
> For the whole Sex can but afford,
>   The Handsome and the Kind.
>
> Why then should I seek farther Store,
>   And still make Love a-new;
> When Change itself can give no more,
>   'Tis easie to be true.

Without disavowing the libertine values, this speaker claims to see them all fulfilled in his relationship with his beloved. He refuses to take any credit for it; her 'dear Self' is the sole author of their joint felicity. Nothing in the entire Rochester canon corresponds to this tender security in the love of a perfect woman.

If there is any addressee to whom the 'Tell me no more' and the domestic exhortations in *Against Constancy* are directed, it may be a superior servant. It is hard to imagine a mistress or spouse at the receiving end;[58] and late-seventeenth-century drama contains a number of trusted valets and similar persons who do not scruple to comment on their masters' behaviour to their faces. At any rate, the argumentation is independent of the recipient's identity. In *Upon his leaving his Mistriss*, however, the interlocutor is the ostensible subject. This poem is the only Rochester lyric that attempts to let a deserted partner down lightly. The opening disclaimer is actually chivalrous, and the reason for the speaker's departure is couched in terms intended to deprecate him and exalt her. However, the remainder of the poem makes a kind of Messalina of the mistress, and not even a Restoration context can make sexual promiscuity on a national scale seem admirable. The speaker pretends to regard Celia's capacity as the laudable attribute of a superior creature, and he keeps up this pretence to the end:

> See the kind Seed-receiving Earth,
> To ev'ry Grain affords a *Birth*;
> On her no Show'rs unwelcome fall,
> Her willing *Womb*, retains 'em all,
> And shall my *Celia* be confin'd?
> No, live up to thy mighty *Mind*,
> And be the Mistriss of *Mankind*.

That Rochester did not find feminine sexual voraciousness appealing in itself is suggested by the following lines from the *Allusion to Horace*:

---

[58] Angeline Goreau regards this lyric as an instance of 'Rochester ... warn[ing] his mistress'; see her *Reconstructing Aphra: A Social Biography of Aphra Behn* (Oxford, 1980), p. 171.

I've noe Ambition on that idle score,
But say with Betty Morice, heretofore
When a Court-Lady, call'd her Buckleys Whore,
I please one Man of Witt, am proud on't too,
Let all the Coxcombs, dance to bed to you.

The departing lover never states his real reason for 'leaving' his mistress. If he were serious about wishing her to be 'the Mistriss of *Mankind*', he could have continued to partake of the 'joy' she was fashioned for, along with all his fellow men. The implication seems to be that he does not wish to live with her 'inclination'.

If he was repelled by her appetites – 'Sense', as David Brooks has pointed out, stands for an 'impulse toward sensual pleasure' –,[59] he did not deviate from contemporary attitudes. Many late-seventeenth-century men were convinced that women were sexually insatiable and more lustful than men, and Restoration writers often express male inability to believe in a woman's virtue.[60]

A point which has intrigued critics is that the lady is told to act in accordance with her 'mighty *Mind*' in welcoming all men as her lovers, and various interpretations of this seemingly incongruous expression have been offered.[61] In fact, the mind concerned is not the only 'mental and spiritual' quality in this poem. Those women who are content with one man are described as 'meaner Spirits' whose 'aims' and 'thoughts' counsel them to concentrate their efforts ('*Arts*') on pleasing a sole member of the male sex. Their exclusive behaviour is hence the result of deliberation and policy, not natural inclination (or virtue, for that matter). Celia, as the speaker asserts, is in a different class; therefore, it is not perhaps so surprising that her 'mind' should run on a very different mode of life. It is significant that the speaker invites her to obey not Nature or inclination, but the precepts suggested to her by her cognitive faculties. In a peculiarly Rochesterian manner, physical pursuits are envisaged as the outcome of mental instigation. Implicitly, too, the female intellect is – once again – maligned.

The expression 'mighty *Mind*' could be a wicked allusion on Rochester's part to a highly dissimilar poem. *Upon his leaving his Mistriss* was probably written in the mid-1670s; Vieth places it in 1674–5. In

---

[59] P. 106 in Brooks' edition of *Lyrics and Satires of John Wilmot Earl of Rochester* (Sydney, 1980).
[60] See Robert H. Michel, 'English Attitudes towards Women, 1640–1700', *Canadian Journal of History* 13.1 (April 1978), 43–4. Cf. also p. 53 above.
[61] See, for instance, Farley-Hills, *Rochester's Poetry*, p. 63, and Vieth, '"Pleased with the Contradiction and the Sin"', 42.

December 1673, Margaret, Duchess of Newcastle, had died, and
Shadwell (whose benefactress she had been) penned an *Elegy* praising
her virtue and constancy, as well as her mental and spiritual ability:

> She was not as most of her frail Sex are;
>   Who 'ave Fruitful *Wombs* but Baren *Brains*,
>   She left the best Remains:
>   Though we no Issue of her Body find
>   Yet she hath left behind
>   The Nobler Issue of her mighty *Mind*.[62]

Rochester – who had no reason to revere the memory of the 'incomparable Princess', freely libelled by others – may have enjoyed
imputing that quality to a woman who was in every sense her opposite.

The elaborate excuses made by the departing speaker may not only be
a device to cover up the shame of a cuckold;[63] they may also serve as lip-
service to inconstancy, a woman's this time. In any case, this lyric leaves
the strong impression of a male withdrawing from female sexuality.
Thus, even the beyond-fulfilment poems with their seemingly self-
reliant speakers fail to conceal the fundamental anxieties and am-
bivalence that are so characteristic of Rochester's lyrics. The poems in
the post-fulfilment category make no attempt to deny them.

PERTURBATION, IMPUTATION AND REFUTATION: POST-FULFILMENT I

The poems assigned to the post-fulfilment category are divided into
two sub-groups: those whose chief concern is fear of losing what one
possesses (I), and those where dissatisfaction with what one possesses is
an underlying and disturbing reality (II).

The simplest representative of the first group is one of the very few
Rochester poems whose argumentation is perfectly coherent and
straightforward. The *Song* 'My dear Mistris has a heart' celebrates a girl
as lovely and compliant as Sedley's Celia. Instead of acknowledging that
her perfections will keep him true to her, however, the lover fears that
they, and her 'wildness', will make her leave him in due course.

'Wildness' was an alluring trait in the fashionable Restoration set of
values. A wild person was wayward, self-willed and opposed to moral
standards of behaviour; the word implies defiance of dullness (*OED*

---

[62] Vol. v, p. 236, in Summers' edition of Shadwell's *Works*.
[63] See Wintle, 'Libertinism', p. 160.

II.7a). Wildness clearly belongs among the attributes of wit. It was attractive in men and women alike, but a quality that required careful handling:

CARO. What, you hanker after an acquaintance with *Rains* and *Bevil*? thou art
    a mad wench, but they are so very wild.
LUC. An they be naturally wilder than I, or you either for all your simpering,
    I'll be condemn'd to Fools and ill company for ever.[64]

For all the delightful naughtiness that a wild mistress possesses, her lack of unfashionable qualities such as fidelity and reliability will inflict the pangs of jealousy on one who truly loves her. The speaker in 'My dear Mistris has a heart' enumerates the very qualities that made a girl praiseworthy in the eyes of a Restoration libertine: 'kindness', beauty, intelligence (suggested by the hyperbole 'Angels listen when she speaks') and contempt of conventional virtue. Unlike the despicable sophist in *Love and Life*, however, he is a man whose enjoyment of present bliss is undermined by anticipations of the lady's defection. His tribulations form an illustration of Hobbes' contention according to which it is not enough to have secured happiness or success; we must be able to rest assured that the future will bring more of the same. In chapter 7 of *The Elements of Law*, Hobbes states that 'there can be no contentment but in proceeding' and that 'FELICITY ... consisteth not in having prospered, but in prospering.' More than once, Rochester's lyrics touch on the ruinous effects that fears for the future have on a person's ability to relish whatever good he owns at the moment.

Similar fears beset the nymph in the *Song* beginning 'Injurious Charmer of my vanquisht Heart':

> Injurious Charmer of my vanquisht Heart,
> Canst thou feel Love, and yet no pity know?
> Since of my self from thee I cannot part,
> Invent some gentle Way to let me go.
>   For what with Joy thou didst obtain,
>   And I with more did give;
>   In time will make thee false and vain,
>   And me unfit to live.

Apparently, the nymph's sole reason for concern is her idea that a girl's sexual surrender is inevitably followed by the man's contempt for, and unfaithfulness to, herself. When this state of affairs ensues, she, the ruined maiden, will be 'unfit to live'.

---

[64] *Epsom Wells*, I.i, p. 113 in Summers' edition.

The shepherd counters that this notion is but a figment of her imagination and rejects her attempt to define him as a faithless braggart. He is in a position of strength, being as confident of her love for him as of his own for her:

> Frail Angel, that wou'dst leave a Heart forlorn,
> With vain pretence falshood therein might lye;
> Seek not to cast wild shadows o're your scorn,
> You cannot sooner change than I can dye.

Dialogues of this kind, ending in mutual reassurance, are no novelty (see, for instance, Lovelace's *Dialogue. Lucasta, Alexis,* 'Tell me *Alexis* what this parting is'), nor is the contention that life without love is worthless (as Etherege's *Upon Love in Imitation of Cowley* shows). Rochester's 'Injurious Charmer' song is sung off-stage in his *Valentinian,* as part of the hero's scheme to seduce Lucina.[65] It should be effective for the purpose, as it opposes the idea that a woman who yields to a man is bound to lose his love in due course while ending in anticipation of consummated desire.

Whether the famous lyric *Love and Life* would convince a lady who (like the speaker's Phillis) considered herself the victim of 'Inconstancy, / False Hearts, and broken Vows' is less certain. With a Rochester lyric, imagining the situation that gave rise to the speaker's utterance is often a fruitful approach. In *Love and Life,* he is on the defensive. Phillis has apparently accused him of past misconduct and voiced apprehensions about the future.[66] In so doing, she has joined a formidable throng of seventeenth-century ladies; but the answer she receives is not like any other.

Replies to such expressions of concern on the part of insecure partners have usually fallen into one (or more) of three main categories. One is made up of protestations that vows made while in the throes of desire cannot be binding. Another typical reply – as we have already seen in the *Dialogue* between Strephon and Daphne – is that inconstancy is a law of nature and not something that human beings can prevent. The third mode of apologia-cum-reassurance is that the present moment is too precious to be disturbed by fruitless fretting about a future which nobody can know anything about in any case.

Many critics have testified to the excellence of Rochester's *Love and Life* and sought to define what sets it apart from other representatives of the apology-for-inconstancy genre. Some have emphasised the fright-

---

[65] See p. 240 in Walker's edition, and Vieth's textual note on p. 218 in his.
[66] Cf. Treglown, 'He knew my style', p. 90.

ening aspects inherent in a view of time that sees it, and human life, as moments plucked out of emptiness.[67] Others have stressed the logical acumen shown by the speaker.[68] Dustin Griffin, a sure-footed and sharp-eyed close reader, mentions the speaker's 'sense that external and irrational forces ... control his actions'.[69]

Jeremy Treglown, followed by several other critics, has pointed out that Rochester borrows the presentation of time from Hobbes (*Leviathan* I.iii);[70] but Hobbes' discourse on prudence, experience and expectation does not have a great deal to do with the situation outlined in *Love and Life*. The three stanzas are less concerned with epistemology than with averting recrimination:

> All my past life is mine noe more
>   The flying Houres are gon
> Like transitory Dreames giv'n ore
> Whose Images are kept in Store
>   By Memory alone.
>
> Whatever is to come is not
>   How can it then be mine,
> The present Moment's all my Lott
> And that as fast as it is got
>   Phillis is wholy thine.
>
> Then talke not of Inconstancy,
>   False Hearts, and broken Vows,
> If I, by Miracle can be,
> This live-long Minute true to thee,
>   Tis all that Heav'n allows.

The past no longer has anything to do with the speaker, who aligns the events of the 'flying Houres' with dreams. Everyone knows that nobody can help their dreams; he cannot therefore be held accountable for that set of images stored by memory.

Still, the past did contain moments that were 'mine' (since they are now 'mine noe more') and thus existed. The future, by contrast, has no being at all. Of course, the speaker cannot be expected to exercise any degree of control over something that he not only does not possess, but that does not exist in the first place.

---

[67] Cf. for instance Righter, 'John Wilmot', 60, and Everett, 'The Sense of Nothing', pp. 10–11. Reba Wilcoxon takes a more down-to-earth view, seeing the poem as 'a witty exercise in logic and epistemology'; see her 'Rochester's Philosophical Premises', 199.

[68] In addition to Wilcoxon, see Vieth, '"Pleased with the Contradiction and the Sin"', 51.

[69] *Satires Against Man*, p. 112.   [70] See Treglown, 'Satirical Inversion', 44.

The assertion that Phillis owns the speaker's present – all he can give to her – and his fidelity for a brief moment is also less than reassuring. The last lines of the poem deny his responsibility even for that. It is 'Heav'n' that 'allows' it 'by Miracle' – his wishes and feelings have nothing to do with it. Clearly, this is not a case of an Epicurean insisting on making the most of the present.[71]

Love and Life spells a total, and exceedingly unheroic,[72] denial of responsibility and commitment. Perhaps the most remarkable thing about this much-praised poem is that its melodious elegance manages to impart a note of suave persuasiveness to an argumentation that could hardly be more offensive to human beings for whom love is the most generous passion of the mind.

Phillis in *Love and Life* must face the fact that her lover disavows all personal obligations to her and proclaims himself unable to adopt any active measure to ensure her happiness. She, as a person, means nothing to the man, a circumstance easily realised if one compares the last stanza of *Love and Life* to Sedley's 'Not *Celia*, that I juster am'. In the latter lyric, the lover's fidelity is the natural corollary of his devotion ('I am ty'd to very thee'). Conversely, the speaker of Rochester's poem is faithful for a minute thanks to divine intervention – and even that moment of truth is conditional ('If I ... '). The lover claims not to possess a future; the relationship certainly does not have one.

SELF-FLAGELLATION, JOINT TRIBULATION AND DEPRECIATION: POST-FULFILMENT II

Rochester's three finest lyrics turn on the realisation that the physical union of lover and mistress, a central concern in all his poems on love, does not yield true satisfaction. The 'feat' coveted in so many love lyrics of the seventeenth century does not produce security and contentment. The reasons for this failure vary; but an innate inability to relax in trusting serenity features in all three poems in this category – 'Absent from thee', *The Mistress* and *The Fall*.

Lovers who tell their ladies that other distractions can only be temporary, and are decidedly inferior in any case, are as commonplace in literature as in life. Matthew Prior summed up an entire poetic genre

---

[71] Farley-Hills relates the poem to the *carpe diem* theme (*Rochester's Poetry*, p. 81); but K. E. Robinson does not see a 'celebration of a sensualist present' in it ('Rochester's Dilemma', *The Durham University Journal* 71.2 (n.s. 40.2; June 1979), 228).

[72] According to Farley-Hills (*Rochester's Poetry*, p. 85), the 'love of the two lovers' becomes 'an heroic defiance of an indifferent universe'.

when he reassured Cloe that the other women he admits to having amused himself with 'were all but my visits, but thou art my home'. Rochester's *Song* beginning 'Absent from thee' diverges sharply from this complacent tradition in that the speaker knows that his separation from his lady will cause nothing but suffering and will only end when he is saturated with pain. In addition, he knows that even then the heavenly restorative, his lady's love, will be powerless to hold him for any length of time. If he lives, he will in all likelihood stray again and could be lost in the process. The only reliable means of preventing this is his death.

Regarded from this angle, the argumentation of the poem seems downright grim. I suspect that the popularity of 'Absent from thee' is in some measure due to its despair having communicated itself even to readers who have not given much thought to that argumentation.

John Wilders has said that this poem is 'distinguished by its extraordinary honesty',[73] and the glib double-talk found in several other love lyrics by Rochester is certainly missing here. Even so, the speaker cannot be entirely absolved from a manipulative purpose, nor from shirking responsibility. As in the case of *Love and Life*, the situation which gave rise to the speaker's utterance forms a useful point of departure:

> Absent from thee I languish still,
>   Then ask me not, when I return?
> The straying Fool 'twill plainly kill,
>   To wish all Day, all Night to Mourn.

The speaker has clearly announced his intention to leave his lady, and she has asked him when he will be back. The question bothers him, and he evades an answer. So far, the first stanza poses no problems; but these lines are nevertheless puzzling. What are the implications of 'Then' in the second line? Who is envisaged as wishing and mourning, and in what kind of situation?

What the speaker seems to be saying is that the lady should not ask him to state a day on which he will return to her *because* he is always unhappy when he is away from her. This is not such a *non sequitur* as it might seem. If he had set a date, he would have imposed a dimension of concreteness on their separation. A *terminus ad quem* would provide a focal point for 'wishing', transforming absence from a painful condition to an unendurable one.

[73] 'Rochester and the Metaphysicals', p. 56.

There are other reasons for the man's reluctance to name the day of his return. First of all, he does not know it himself. He goes away in quest of pain and will only come back when exhausted with suffering:

> *Dear*; from thine Arms then let me flie,
>   That my Fantastick mind may prove,
> The Torments it deserves to try,
>   That tears my fixt Heart from my Love.
>
> When wearied with a world of Woe,
>   To thy safe Bosom I retire
> Where Love and Peace and Truth does flow,
>   May I contented there expire.

The speaker cannot, at the moment of departure, tell when he will have attained that weariness. An additional reason for not wishing to speculate on the duration of his absence may simply be that the departing 'Fool' finds it terrible to think of all he will have to suffer before he has reached that point.

The suggestion made above that the speaker to some extent evades responsibility is substantiated in the fourth stanza:

> Lest once more wandring from that Heav'n
>   I fall on some base heart unblest;
> Faithless to thee, False, unforgiv'n,
>   And lose my Everlasting rest.

This man, whose mind and emotions are clearly in a turmoil, is very different from the slick equivocator in *Love and Life*. Still, they do have one point in common: whatever happens to them, especially in amorous contexts, is the result of forces they cannot control. The frightening possibility of losing the lasting peace which the 'Absent' speaker can never possess in life is envisaged as the result of an accident. The idea that it might be in his power to steer clear of an unworthy partner, or to extricate himself from an unsatisfactory relationship, never occurs to him.

Without the fourth stanza, 'Absent from thee' would be a far simpler and less troubling poem. Not only does it supply a tragic reason for the wish to die contented in the lady's embrace, demolishing the comparative serenity of lines 11–12; it also states, in plain terms, that the 'straying' involves infidelity. Up to line 14, the torments which the man is destined to undergo could have been thought to be of a more general nature. But the last three lines of the poem, although they ostensibly deal with the possible consequences of renewed 'wandring', imply what the lady has to expect from the impending absence.

The cruelty of those implications, and the total lack of any idea of responsibility for his actions and eventual fate, rather detract from any sympathy one may have felt for the speaker. Still, he is certainly an honest if not an honourable man. Hence, there is no need to mistrust the statement in stanza two that it is his *mind* that prompts his straying. David Vieth is one of the few critics who have noted this striking feature of Rochester's song, claiming that it is 'surprising' to find 'that the speaker's attachment to his mistress is emotional ("fixed *heart*") whereas his motivation for straying is intellectual ("fantastic *mind*")'.[74] It is indeed unusual to find the speaker of a love lyric (at any point in time) explaining an urge to stray in cerebral terms; but in a Rochesterian context it is by no means unexpected. Sexual activity as the result of cerebration rather than erotic arousal is a recurring feature in Rochester's 'love poems'.

Nor do we need to suspect insincerity when the man who is about to leave proclaims that the experiences which lie ahead – probably sexual, at least in part – will bring pain rather than pleasure. After all, sexuality in Rochester's poetry is associated with a massive assemblage of pains and very little joy.

'Absent from thee', then, is a poem about the compulsion to seek out what will hurt. That compulsion demands the absence of the speaker from his beloved. These two concepts, pain and absence, are relevant not only to 'Absent from thee' but also to another lyric which deals with the pursuit of pain. In *The Mistress*, it is presence that entails suffering, not absence.[75] Still, the sufferer's inability to keep himself away from what torments him is an essential feature in this poem, too.

The theme of absence is endemic to love poetry. In fact, separation between lover and beloved may almost be said to be a basic condition in the writing of plangent verses on love; if the object were present, it would either be described or pleaded with (or, of course, enjoyed). In the most celebrated examples, absence imposes acute suffering on the one who loves, but does not serve to abate his/her passion; it can also be gallantly denied, in claims that the lover's devotion transcends the

---

[74] '"Pleased with the Contradiction and the Sin"', 43.

[75] On pain and absence in 'Absent from thee' and *The Mistress*, see my article 'Rochester and Jealousy: Consistent Inconsistencies', *The Durham University Journal* 80.2 (n.s. 49.2; June 1988), 220–1.

separation and creates a presence in absence. The great Renaissance
sonneteers were experts in dealing with absence along such lines, and
seventeenth-century love poetry continued the tradition. As A. M.
Gibbs points out in his commentary on Sir William Davenant's poem
To Mr. W. M. Against Absence, absence is 'a common *topos* in
seventeenth-century poetry'.[76]

It is the more interesting to realise that Rochester's treatment of
absence in 'Absent from thee' and in *The Mistress* has markedly original
features. In the first-mentioned lyric, the speaker deliberately seeks the
pain of absence. More than that, he begs to be excused from adding to
it by having to think about absence as a fixed period of time. He desires
to be exempted from lethal wishing and mourning; the implication
seems to be that he would rather not think of his true love any more
than he can help. If I am not reading too much into the first stanza at this
point, here is another unchivalrous dimension (in addition to the
admission of possible infidelity in stanza four). I cannot think of any
other literary presentation of absence that fuses these aspects.

The treatment of absence in *The Mistress* contains some rather
traditional components; but the entire 'absence complex' in this poem
also, as far as I am aware, lacks a counterpart. The first characteristic of
absence is conventional enough: time passes slowly when the speaker is
apart from his love, unlike the time spent with her. But lines 6–8 of *The
Mistress* develop the well-worn conceit of the lady's eyes feeding the
lover's ardour in an unexpected direction:

> But, oh how slowly Minutes rowl,
>   When absent from her Eyes
> That feed my Love, which is my Soul,
>   It languishes and dyes.
>
> For then no more a Soul but shade,
>   It mournfully does move;
> And haunts my Breast, by absence made
>   The living Tomb of Love.

Since the lover's soul and his love are one and the same, and since the
lady's eyes are what sustains the latter, absence literally brings about the

---

[76] Sir William Davenant, *The Shorter Poems, and Songs from the Plays and Masques*, ed. A. M. Gibbs
(Oxford, 1972), p. 410. See also the discussion of classical and Renaissance poetry on absence
in Richmond, *The School of Love*, pp. 146–54. A sad, and charming, lyric on absence is Waller's
The Self-Banished, where voluntary exile is embraced for reasons entirely different from those
of Rochester's 'Absent from thee' speaker.

death of the soul. In the insubstantial form of a classical underworld 'shade', it pays sad visits to the seat of its old life, the lover's breast, now only physically alive.[77]

The mere collocation of absence, love, death and the soul is not in itself unique. One contemporary instance is supplied by Richard Flecknoe's rambling Character 12, 'Of Absence', 'To the Lady – Written at *Bruxelles* in French':

Absence is the *Abscinthe* or bitterness of *Love*, that weans us from the delightful presence of those we love; 'tis the *night* and *winter* of *Amity*: when our *Sun* being set, or retir'd into another *Hemisphere*, we are sad, and restlesly long for its return; and if *Death* be nothing else, but onely a separation of *Soul* and *Body*, *Absence* certainly wou'd be worse and more grievous then *Death* it self; since it separates the *Soul* even from the *Soul*, but that *fortior quam mors dilectio*; As Love ha's power over *Death*, so *Time* and *Place* ha's no power over *Love*. 'Tis the *touch-stone* and *trial* of our *Loves*; and when in *presence* of those we love, we are all eyes to look on them; and in *absence*, all thought to think on them; 'tis a sign our *Love* is perfect and true indeed ... [78]

The striking difference between this discourse and the description of absence in *The Mistress* is that in the latter, love does not survive separation and the soul does not survive the death of love. Absence is not a time for keeping love alive by thoughts of the beloved. It does not make the heart grow fonder; it starves the heart to death. The reassurance that 'our *Love* is perfect and true indeed' has to be sought in the presence of the beloved – where it is granted by the pains of jealousy.

The review of absence in the two lyrics has hence brought us back to the other concept that is relevant to both: pain. In 'Absent from thee', the pain which the voluntary exile would have to undergo was twofold: separation from his true love; and tormenting experiences in a world of woe. *The Mistress*, on the other hand, represents absence as a painless because lifeless state. The pain comes from doubting the loved one's constancy; it simultaneously proves the sufferer's own.[79]

In both poems, then, pain is actively sought and envisaged as the preliminary to uninterrupted bliss. For that bliss to become a fact in

---

[77] As in my 'Rochester and Jealousy' article (219, n.32), I want to draw attention to David Brooks' emendation of line 16, 'Short Ages, lieving Graves'. Brooks introduced it in his edition of Rochester's poems (p. 138), explaining his reasons in a short article called 'A Conjectural Emendation for Rochester's "The Mistress"', *Bibliographical Society of Australia and New Zealand Bulletin* 5.2 (1981), 75–8. Brooks' argumentation has been questioned, but it seems natural and convincing to me.

[78] *Aenigmatical Characters, Being Rather a New Work, then a New Impression of the old* (London, 1665), pp. 18–19. [79] See 'Rochester and Jealousy', 221–2.

'Absent from thee', the erstwhile sufferer has to die. The desired outcome in *The Mistress* is less drastic; but the hope expressed in the two concluding lines of that poem is hardly solid enough to balance all that has gone before. The appellation 'happy ending' is clearly inapplicable to both lyrics.

With regard to the point of view of the lady in the case, 'Absent from thee' is a good deal further from the possibility of a happy ending than *The Mistress*. The best that the deserted woman can hope for is that the absence of the man she loves so sincerely will be terminated by his return, promptly followed by the termination of his life in her arms – a bleak prospect for her as well as for him. Her embrace is referred to as a 'Heav'n'; her function seems, logically enough, to consist in affording absolution. *The Mistress*, by contrast, depicts a situation characterised by mutuality. The hoped-for resolution to the lovers' tribulations will be the outcome of their joint triumph over the pangs of fear and jealousy.

This is one of the most radical differences between these two poems, which have such important points in common. Even for a reader not primarily interested in Rochester's personal history, biographical speculations are hard to resist when looking for explanations of that divergence. 'Absent from thee' is traditionally associated with Lady Rochester and *The Mistress* with Elizabeth Barry. There is a fair quantity of evidence in favour of that view. Rochester's letters supply most of it. For instance, his tempestuous relationship with Mrs Barry lends pertinence to lines like 'You think we disagree'; Lady Rochester's impatience during her husband's prolonged and repeated absences is also on record. In an early letter to his wife, the new-wedded lord avers that 'there is Left for mee...noe Heaven but in y^r Love'. If the tentative dating of that letter (1667, Treglown) and the poem (1674–5, Vieth) is correct, and if the biographical relevance commonly held to prevail with regard to 'Absent from thee' is accepted, Rochester felt much the same after seven years of marriage. Whether such protestations made the loneliness of the Countess easier to bear is another matter.

In connexion with the pursuit of pain which plays such a vital part in 'Absent from thee' and in *The Mistress*, a passage from *A Very Heroicall Epistle in Answer to Ephelia* might be called to mind. The speaker of this poem, usually believed to be a satirical representation of Rochester's enemy Mulgrave (see p. 344 below), proclaims ''tis my Maxim, to avoyd all paine'. Griffin has pointed to the relevance of Epicurean doctrine in this context; Farley-Hills, while omitting any mention of Epicurus, parenthetically suggests that the Bajazet passage be 'compare[d] ... to the idea expressed in *The Mistress* that "pain can ne'er deceive"'.[80] The avoidance of pain is crucial to Epicureans. Anyone wishing to make a reasonably coherent Epicurean of Rochester would hence have to contend with the satirist's irony in the *Very Heroicall Epistle*, as well as with the two great love lyrics where pain is regarded as a necessity.

In fact, the ante-penultimate stanza of *The Mistress* (which Peter Porter called 'one of the finest declensions in [Rochester's] entire corpus'[81]) forms as vigorous an attack on Epicurean values as can be imagined in a secular context:

> Fantastick Fancies fondly move;
> And in frail Joys believe:
> Taking false Pleasure for true Love;
> But Pain can ne're deceive.

Samuel Butler had voiced a similar view in his *Satire upon the Weakness and Misery of Man*, a poem in which, according to one of his editors, the otherwise 'arch and droll' satirist is 'serious and severe':[82]

> Our pains are real things, and all
> Our pleasures but fantastical.

It would be difficult to argue that the *Mistress* stanza is merely an exponent of the poet's irony. It is vital to the argumentation of the poem, and if it is not taken seriously, then neither can *The Mistress* be.

But should *The Mistress*, and 'Absent from thee', be taken seriously? What reasons can be adduced for contending that these lyrics are the outcome of an essentially sincere impulse? This is a question which no student of Rochester can escape. Much recent Rochester criticism has focused on the 'values' expressed in the poet's work. Obviously, it is impossible to offer judgements on an artist's values if one is not sure when he or she might be pulling the audience's collective leg. Rochester, after all, was a highly talented satirist, and a master of persiflage; how does one assess such a writer's relative degree of seriousness in his lyrics?

I do not think that a reliable scale can be constructed, but some elucidation might be gained from shifting the emphasis from arguments to concerns. When a certain complex of emotions and ideas is dealt with repeatedly and at length in works of high quality, it is not unreasonable

---

[80] *Satires Against Man*, p. 63, and *Rochester's Poetry*, p. 125, respectively.
[81] 'The Professional Amateur', p. 67.
[82] Reginald Brimley Johnson in vol. II of *The Poetical Works of Samuel Butler* (London, 1893), p. 182. (The quoted Butler lines are 81–2 of the *Misery of Man*.)

to suppose that this mattered a great deal to the artist. In a Rochesterian context, it seems to me that discontent with what one recognises as a valuable possession is such a concern. The love lyrics generally suggest that sexual compliance is something worth striving for; but in those poems where it has evidently been granted, it never yields complete satisfaction.[83] In the poet's entire *œuvre*, hypocrisy and stupidity are constantly held up to scorn. Significantly, both 'Absent from thee' and *The Mistress* bespeak a fear of, and disgust with, falsehood.

In neither lyric is the speaker satisfied with the true love he believes is his. The 'straying Fool' acknowledges that he can never find *permanent* contentment even in his true love's arms. The lover in *The Mistress* distrusts the reliability, even the reality, of the couple's commitment; jealousy is the 'only Proof' that they 'love, and do not dream'.[84] Such features suggest that these two lyrics deal with concerns that were vital to the poet and are hence to be taken seriously.

Rochester's first-person speakers are – as was pointed out above – forever impelled by cerebral whims, pressures and persuasions. 'Fantastick mind' could, in fact, serve as a collective designation of much of their argumentation. Emotions are certainly present, too; admiration, pique, jealousy, fear of loss and fear of commitment all have important parts to play. In 'Absent from thee', though, the restless intellect is the potent detacher of a fixed heart; in that poem, at least, mind is stronger than feeling.

Where does that leave physical desires, especially the lust which so many have regarded as characteristic of Rochester's poetry? Very far down on the 'concern' scale. Even a poem such as 'Leave this gawdy guilded Stage' has more to say about standards in lovemaking than about the urgency of desire and the glory of satisfaction.

In 'Absent from thee' and *The Mistress*, lust does not matter at all. Nothing stands in the way of the men enjoying their women's bodies, but that fact has nothing to do with either the pain the speakers suffer or the hopeful resolution they envisage. Vieth's contention that 'the one thing absolutely clear about ["Absent from thee"] seems to be the desirability of the speaker's "dear" or "love"'[85] is misleading: the lady is commended for her worth, not for her beauty or desirability. The

---

[83] Except in the third-person narrative of Chloris under the willow tree. See p. 55 above.

[84] Faith in the touchstone value of jealousy is, incidentally, a widespread Restoration notion; Aphra Behn's poem *To Lysander* affirms that 'Jealousy alone can prove, / The surest witness of my Flame', and in *Marriage A-la-Mode* Rhodophil tells Doralice, 'Faith I am jealous, and that makes me suspect that I love you better then I thought' (v.i; p. 307 in the University of California Press edition).   [85] '"Pleased with the Contradiction and the Sin"', 42.

lover of *The Mistress* is driven to madness by his lady's wounding eyes, but mere sensual gratification will not cure him; he has surely had that already.[86] It is her enduring love, the fixed treasure of her heart, that he is yearning for, as she yearns for his.

Hearts in Rochester's love poetry can mean many things. In the three lyrics belonging to this category, though, the heart is 'the seat of love or affection' (*OED* 10a); the exception being line 14 in 'Absent from thee', where 'base heart' stands for a worthless partner. The inability of the speaker's heart to remain securely attached to the lady he professes to love is a major cause of the suffering contained in 'Absent from thee' and *The Mistress*. To the lady in the former, the admission that her beloved's heart will not stay with her when he goes is another of the cruel blows she has to sustain on his departure.

In the seventeenth century, the inability of a lover's heart to find a permanent home could be the subject of ironic poetic discourse (as in Cowley's rueful 'The Heart fled again'). With regard to 'Absent from thee' and *The Mistress*, though, I cannot detect any tongue-in-cheek dimension in the lines on imperfectly fixed hearts. Nor do I see any reason to regard the lover's tribute of his heart in *The Fall* as the handing over of an inferior commodity.

In *The Fall*, too, pain is a focal issue; but it is different from the torments of the straying fool in 'Absent from thee' and the fears and jealousies suffered by the couple in *The Mistress*. Those afflictions, acute as they were, held the hope of ultimate bliss after being endured. Torment in *The Fall* is permanent, because it is an aspect of the human condition. The third stanza of this lyric drives home the contrast between the perfect happiness enjoyed by Adam and Eve and the flawed pleasures of mankind after the Fall.[87] In *The Fall*, then, pain is not sought, because it is always present and impossible to transcend – infernal rather than purgatorial.

When Rochester's speaker equates the lot of post-lapsarian man with Hell, he voices a bold but not unprecedented sentiment. In seventeenth-century religious debate, especially among Ranters and Cambridge Platonists, Hell was sometimes interpreted as a state rather than a place.[88] More particularly, the reality of an 'inner Hell' in this life was

---

[86] Cf. Righter, 'John Wilmot', 65, and my 'Rochester and Jealousy', 221.

[87] For an investigation of seventeenth-century ideas on love before and after the Fall in relation to Rochester's poem, see my 'Rochester and *The Fall*', esp. 401–3.

[88] On the occurrence and development of such views, see D. P. Walker's highly readable study *The Decline of Hell: Seventeenth-Century Discussions of Eternal Torment* (London, 1964); C. A. Patrides, 'Renaissance and Modern Views on Hell', *Harvard Theological Review* 57 (1964),

experienced as an awareness of the loss of Heaven's perfect harmony and the presence of a conscience racked with guilt and regret.

Of course, those contemporaries of Rochester's who did not believe in the eternal torment of the soul after death were a minority. Most Restoration clerics, for instance, would definitely agree with the predecessor who issued the glum warning:

They that go thither [i.e., to Hell] shall find it no metaphore.[89]

Still, disbelief in the traditional Christian Hell was at least not unheard of, and Rochester expressed it twice, the second time in his translation of Seneca's *Troades* chorus (see p. 146 below).

In *The Fall*, Rochester reduces the vast corpus of Christian debate and dogma on Heaven and Hell, knowledge and the Fall to one metaphor: erotic pleasure. The bliss of Paradise consisted in the complete and natural harmony of the bodies and wills of the lovers. Knowledge lost man this unthinking joy; the Fall introduced such curses of cogitation as hope and fear, anticipation and disappointment. This idea was by no means original; Butler, for instance, wrote that

as knowledge cast Adam out of Paradise, so it do's all those who apply themselves to it, for the more they understand, they do but more plainly perceive, their own wants, and Nakednes, as he did, which before in the State of Ignorance, were hidden from him, untill the eies of his understanding were opened, only to let him see his losses, and the Miseries which he had betrayd himself unto. For the world appeare's a much finer thing to those that understand it not then to those who do, and Fooles injoy their Pleasures with greater Appetite and Gust then those who are more sensible of their vanity, and unwholsomnes.[90]

Nor is the doleful recapitulation of the unsatisfactoriness of life's delights in Rochester's third stanza a novelty. Malherbe had voiced similar regrets in much the same terms:

> Il n'est rien ici-bas d'éternelle durée:
> Une chose qui plaît n'est jamais assurée:
> L'épine suit la rose, et ceux qui sont contents
> Ne le sont pas longtemps.
>
> ('Victoire de la constance: Stances', lines 13–16)

217–36; and Keith Thomas, *Religion and the Decline of Magic* (London; I have used the second impression of 1971, where the relevant passages are found on pp. 170–1 and 573).
[89] Bishop Thomas Bilson in *The Effect of Certain Sermons* (London, 1599), p. 52. Quoted by Patrides, 'Renaissance and Modern Views', 223.
[90] P. 15 in Hugh de Quehen's edition of *Samuel Butler: Prose Observations* (Oxford, 1979), from 'Learning and Knowledge'.

Que rien n'est ici-bas heureux parfaitement,
Et qu'on ne peut au monde avoir contentement,
Qu'un funeste malheur aussitôt n'empoisonne.
('Quoi donc c'est un arrêt qui n'épargne personne', lines 2–4)

As Jean Hagstrum maintains, evocations of the Miltonic Bower of Bliss
served to emphasise the unsatisfactoriness of latter-day love in many
eighteenth-century works.[91] *The Fall* might be adduced as a seventeenth-century instance. If Dorset and Dryden knew and appreciated
Paradise Lost,[92] it is likely that Rochester possessed some degree of
familiarity with it, too. Milton's description of the amorous felicity
enjoyed by the lovers in Eden is in no way incompatible with the second
stanza in *The Fall*:[93]

Naked beneath cool Shades they lay,
    Enjoyment waited on desire;
Each member did their wills obey:
    Nor could a wish set pleasure higher.

In terms of the history of ideas, then, the content of lines 1–12 of
Rochester's poem does not amount to anything more than a collocation
of current, if not orthodox, opinions and contentions. What makes *The
Fall* unique and (in my view) moving is the way in which these opinions
and contentions are used in it. In the fourth stanza, they are compressed
and subjugated by the exigencies of an actual relationship:

Then, Cloris, while I duty pay,
    The nobler Tribute of a heart;
Be not you so severe, to say
    You Love me for a frailer part.

The speaker, who has acted as if the quality of sensual pleasure were his
sole concern, sees that his own inadequacies in this respect may lose him
a mistress who means something to him beyond such pleasure. Affection
and apprehensiveness on a very personal plane introduce a new
dimension of pain. I believe that the words 'nobler' and 'frailer' should
be taken at their face value here. The lover fears that he might not be
able to satisfy his mistress. His amorous defects may not be his fault; he

---

[91] *Sex and Sensibility*, pp. 14–15.
[92] See Vivian de Sola Pinto, *Sir Charles Sedley 1639–1701: A Study in the Life and Literature of the
Restoration* (London, 1927), p. 94.
[93] Lines 7–8 might embody an echo of a song in Etherege's *The Comical Revenge, or, Love in a Tub*
(II.iii): 'Our reason we'd banish, our senses should sway, / And every pleasure our wills should
obey.'

has blamed them on the Fall of Man and the subsequent condition of mankind. But if Cloris chooses to value sensual pleasure more than true love, the vassal may not be allowed to retain the favours of his sovereign.

Taking 'nobler' and 'frailer' to mean just that does not amount to a denial of the irony in this situation. A man who has acted as if erotic enjoyment were all-important realises that if this is what his mistress feels, his sufferings are twofold: first, the awareness of a discrepancy between perfect pleasure and the dull delights that are his lot; and second, the fear that his partner in these less-than-ideal joys will remove herself, and them, from him. In the end, emotional commitment turns out to be more important than that sensual pleasure which so many Rochester poems have seemed to advocate.

As was the case in 'Leave this gawdy guilded Stage', a traditional sex-role pattern is reversed: the man is afraid that the woman only wants him for whatever sexual services he is able to provide. Consequently, there is an element of wry humour in the final stanza; but it adds to, rather than detracts from, its pathos.

In *The Fall*, then, the degree of fixity on the part of the lady's heart is the problematic factor. In 'Absent from thee', it was the man's; in *The Mistress*, neither heart was securely in the partner's keeping; here, at last, is a man's plea for mercy in the form of emotional generosity. Even in this group of three lyrics, numbering sixty-eight lines altogether, Rochester's range and variety once again assert themselves.

Several critics have commented on the lack of palpable sensuousness in *The Fall*. 'There is very little erotica in Rochester's poetry', says David Farley-Hills in his discussion of this lyric.[94] *The Fall* 'depicts the ... lovemaking [of Adam and Eve] in abstract and wholly unerotic terms', maintains Carole Fabricant;[95] and Barbara Everett points out that 'the absence of the sensuous' in the second stanza is particularly striking.[96]

All this is surely true; and statements like these pave the way towards comprehending the fundamental paradox of Rochester the love lyrist: the sexual union of man and woman is an essential factor in almost all the poems, regardless of the circumstances, and yet this vital issue is curiously insubstantial in itself. Contentment and satisfaction in sensual pleasure are conspicuously absent. The poems reviewed in this chapter have displayed a very considerable variety; but, with one exception (the

[94] *Rochester's Poetry*, p. 48.   [95] 'Rochester's World', 339.
[96] 'The Sense of Nothing', p. 18.

'lucky-minute' *Song*), they never celebrate the consummation of a heterosexual relationship. Nobody who reads these lyrics can miss grasping that erotic pleasure is important, but no reasons for its importance are ever indicated. At the centre of Rochester's poems on love, there is an empty space.

3

'The Imperfect Enjoyment' and 'A Ramble in Saint James's Parke'

This chapter in the Men and Women section focuses on two poems where love, or rather the betrayal of love, is a major concern. Walker has placed the longer of the two among the 'Satires and Lampoons'. Nevertheless, *A Ramble in Saint James's Parke* is, like *The Imperfect Enjoyment*, a poem about a lover's disappointment. In both, too, anger directed against the faithless agent dominates the second half.

The word 'half' is no approximation. Exactly thirty-six of the seventy-two lines that make up *The Imperfect Enjoyment* are devoted to the shortcomings of the offender, and out of the 166 lines of the *Ramble*, 84 constitute reproaches and curses whose target is the vile Corinna. Narrative and expostulation are thus evenly balanced in both poems.

When David M. Vieth's edition of Rochester's poems first made *The Imperfect Enjoyment* and *A Ramble in Saint James's Parke* available to a large public, readers and critics alike reacted strongly to their obscenity.[1] Today – twenty-five years later – this topic seems rather stale. A far more pressing issue is the question of the interplay of mind, body and feeling in *The Imperfect Enjoyment* and the *Ramble*. In the course of an analysis of the two poems, the following chapter addresses that question.

The two halves of *The Imperfect Enjoyment* – the narrative and the expostulation[2] – are not the only neatly proportioned subdivisions in this poem. Eighteen lines on joint erotic arousal and one-sided orgasm

---

[1] In the early 1970s, Reba Wilcoxon called the former 'blatantly shocking in sexual language and imagery'; see her 'Pornography, Obscenity, and Rochester's "The Imperfect Enjoyment"', *Studies in English Literature 1500–1900* 15 (Summer 1975), 375.

[2] John O'Neill, who has also noted that the poem is divided into two sections, calls the first 'narrative' and the second 'a commentary on the events in the narrative'; see 'Rochester's "Imperfect Enjoyment": "The True Veine of Satyre" in Sexual Poetry', *Tennessee Studies in Literature* 25 (1980), 60. (The latter description seems inaccurate to me.)

84

are followed by another eighteen describing the consequences of the latter. Nine lines on the previous record of the speaker's penis as related to its present state ensue, and the poems ends with a twenty-seven-line burst of invective directed at 'Thou treacherous, base, deserter of my flame'. The discussion of *The Imperfect Enjoyment* will, by and large, adhere to this outline; but before any detailed comments can be offered, the literary background of this poem should be reviewed.

Restoration scholars have long been aware of the existence of a group of English imperfect-enjoyment poems in the late seventeenth century. It was Richard E. Quaintance Jr, however, who mapped out the history and development of this minor 'genre' in sixteenth- and seventeenth-century France and England,[3] showing that its foundations were laid in classical Rome.

Ovid's *Amores* III.7 and Petronius' *Satyricon* 128–40 are concerned with the failures of men to have sexual intercourse with willing and accomplished female partners. Rochester was no doubt familiar with both, and debts to Ovid's poem can be observed in *The Imperfect Enjoyment*. Rémy Belleau's *Impuissance* (beginning 'Quel desastre nouveau')[4] and Mathurin Régnier's fourth elegy, called *Impuissance. Imitation d'Ovide* ('Quoy? ne l'avois-je assez en mes voeux desiree')[5] deal with the same situation. Again, there is reason to believe that they were known to Rochester. He may also have come across two other French poems, Payot de Morangle's *L'Occasion perdue. A Cloris. Stances* and Benech (?) de Cantenac's *L'Occasion perdue recouverte*.[6] The latter was translated by Aphra Behn as *The Disappointment*, a poem first printed in the 1680 edition of *Poems on Several Occasions* attributed to Rochester. Another translation of Cantenac's poem appeared in *Wit and Drollery* (London, 1682).

By contrast, Rochester's *The Imperfect Enjoyment* tells the story of a premature ejaculation,[7] followed by the inability to produce a renewed erection without delay (see below). *Ejaculatio praecox* also occurs in Charles Beys' *La Iovissance Imparfaite*, on which Etherege based his

---

[3] Quaintance's article in the *Philological Quarterly* of 1963 (vol. 42; 'French Sources of the Restoration "Imperfect Enjoyment" Poem', 190–9) only gives, as Dustin Griffin has said, 'the bare bones of his dissertation research'. The whole body of it can be consulted in Quaintance's 'Passion and Reason', pp. 158–213.   [4] Published in *Le Cabinet satyrique* in 1618.

[5] Published in Régnier's *Satyres* in 1613. In the Librairie Marcel Didier edition of Régnier's *Oeuvres complètes* (ed. Gabriel Raibaud, Paris, 1958), the poem is found on pp. 228–35.

[6] Published in 1654 and 1660 respectively; see p. 161 in Quaintance's dissertation.

[7] Cf. Wilcoxon, 'Pornography', 382; Griffin, *Satires Against Man*, p. 93; and O'Neill, 'Rochester's "Imperfect Enjoyment"'. See also William Ober, *Boswell's Clap and Other Essays: Medical Analyses of Literary Men's Afflictions* (Carbondale, 1979), pp. 247–52.

poem *The Imperfect Enjoyment*. While Beys' and Etherege's speakers regret the outcome of the sexual encounter, neither is prepared to be blamed for it. Nor is the apportioning of blame a vital issue, as the partner also achieves an orgasm, albeit 'separement' (Beys, stanza 16).

Another poem on Quaintance's list has been attributed to Rochester, an attribution rejected by scholars from John Harold Wilson onward.[8] Beginning with the line 'Fruition was the question in debate', it recounts a course of events similar to the one found in Beys/Etherege. John H. O'Neill[9] has added a further member to the group, an undistinguished eighteen-line lyric beginning 'Bless me you stars! for sure some sad Portent'.

Keith Walker adduces an additional instance, relating it to lines 62–3 of Rochester's *The Imperfect Enjoyment*. It is a poem from Richard Head's racy narrative *The English Rogue*; Walker quotes the last four lines (p. 242 in his edition). Ken Robinson mentions another 'comparable piece', the lyric beginning 'Base mettell hanger by your Master's Thigh!'.[10]

O'Neill, following Quaintance, has briefly demonstrated the intricacy of the putative links between all these poems. The song from *The English Rogue* testifies to the 'mishmash of borrowings'[11] that characterises this genre. Its first two lines are very similar to the beginning of the 'Bless me you stars!' *Song*, and the last two coincide with the conclusion of *One Writeing Against his Prick*. The situation delineated in it, like that in the majority of imperfect-enjoyment poems, involves sudden, inexplicable impotence affecting a usually highly potent man. It is peculiarly distressing in that it strikes just as he is about to capture a particularly coveted prize. In this respect, too, Head's rogue (the appellation is an understatement) resembles most of his brothers in misfortune.

Thanks to the labours of several scholars, it is possible to view Rochester's *The Imperfect Enjoyment* against the background of a genre. However, none of the compilers has given any attention to the existence of antithetical works, where premature ejaculation is followed by renewed erection and a satisfactory conclusion. One such poem is

---

[8] 'Two Poems Ascribed to Rochester', *Modern Language Notes* 54 (1939), 458–60.

[9] 'An Unpublished "Imperfect Enjoyment" Poem', *Papers on Language and Literature* 13.2 (Spring 1977), 197–202.

[10] 'The Art of Violence in Rochester's Satire', in Claude Rawson and Jenny Mecziems, eds., *English Satire and the Satiric Tradition* (Oxford, 1984), p. 97. This poem, under the heading *One Writeing Against his Prick*, was printed by Harold Love in his selection for the *Penguin Book of Restoration Verse* (Harmondsworth, 1968), on p. 184 (not 84, as Robinson says on p. 97, n.14 in his article).   [11] O'Neill on the 'Fruition' poem.

attributed (wrongly)[12] to Rochester in *The Works of the Right Honourable The Earls of Rochester, and Roscommon*.[13] Called, appropriately, *The Perfect Enjoyment*, it begins along much the same lines as the opening of Rochester's *The Imperfect Enjoyment*, but the mistress' 'busy Hand' manages to restore the lover's erection after ejaculation. Nathaniel Lee's popular play *Theodosius* (produced in 1680) contains a *Song* depicting a similar process, the shepherd Damon '[rallying] again by the force of [Phillis'] Charms'.[14]

In most of the imperfect-enjoyment poems, the unhappiness of the situation is emphasised right from the start; for instance, the first line of Belleau's poem speaks of 'desastre' and 'malheur'. The first twelve lines of Rochester's *The Imperfect Enjoyment*, however, contain no hint of impending calamity. They form a lusciously erotic description of mounting mutual excitement. Some details belong to imperfect-enjoyment stock-in-trade, such as the girl's tongue when kissing[15] and her nakedness.[16] The former is adroitly employed, though; engaged in other pursuits than speaking, it still conveys a wordless command. The lightning imagery, mentioned by Quaintance as being peculiar to Rochester,[17] also occurs in *The Perfect Enjoyment*:

> My fierce Assault, made with a Lover's Hast,
> Like Lightning piercing, and as quickly past,
> Thus does fond Nature with her Children play,
> Just shews us Joy, then snatches it away.

These lines stress the transitoriness of thunderbolts, but the opening lines of *The Imperfect Enjoyment* do not evoke such unfavourable associations.

In fact, this poem which ends in so much bitterness begins with a passage that is unique in Rochester's poetry in that it presents an ecstatic male speaker anticipating the imminent gratification of his desire, ardently embraced and desired by a gorgeous girl. Not even the 'As Chloris full of harmless thought' *Song* can be said to parallel these lines. That lyric is a narrative of happy-minute seduction (see p. 54 above),

[12] Vieth ascribes it to Mulgrave; see pp. 481–3 in *Attribution*.

[13] Pp. 80–3 in the third edition, printed for E. Curll, London 1709. This edition includes 'Some Memoirs of the Earl of Rochester's Life' by St Evremond.

[14] This song is easily accessible in Love's Penguin volume, pp. 157–8. The *Covent Garden Drollery* of 1672 (reprinted by G. Thorn-Drury in 1928) contains two songs where similar feats are performed.   [15] Cf., for instance, Ovid's *Amores*, III.7.9.

[16] Cf., for instance, line 10 in Régnier's poem.

[17] P. 211 in Quaintance's dissertation. It should be noted that the reference to Jove's lightning, albeit differently applied, also occurs in the relevant *Satyricon* passage; it might have stuck in Rochester's mind.

accomplished after initial resistance (of much the same kind as that offered by Beys' and Etherege's ladies). In *The Imperfect Enjoyment*, the blissful intercourse of an 'equally inspir'd' couple is promised and very nearly realised – but the promise remains unfulfilled.

In referring to the anticipated union as one of his 'Soul' and her 'Heart', the speaker in Rochester's *Imperfect Enjoyment* conforms to Renaissance and Baroque usage. With regard to 'heart', this kind of metonymy is common in Rochester's poetry. Régnier's *Impuissance* supplies a similar instance in line 16, 'Et sa langue mon cœur par ma bouche embrasa' (cf. also line 20, 'Et son ame exaloit maint souspir amoureux'). To sixteenth- and seventeenth-century people, the boundaries between soul, mind, heart and body were vague and shifting. Quaintance, commenting on a typical passage from Beys' poem, quotes Montaigne's words on 'the narrow seam between the soul and body, through which the experience of the one is communicated to the other' (p. 198 in Quaintance's dissertation).

Quaintance helpfully draws attention to the relevance of Montaigne's essay on the power of the imagination (1.21). Montaigne had argued that 'une forte imagination produit l'evenement'. He illustrated this contention with examples drawn from bodily illness, devoting a sizeable part of the essay to the problem of impotence. According to Montaigne, the untimely recollection of a story of sexual failure, affecting someone else, had the power to induce impotence. After the first failure, apprehension formed a powerful threat to new attempts. The cure recommended by Montaigne shows how little present-day sex therapists could have taught him; he advocated frank advance acknowledgement of the problem, thus removing the expectation of success and the obligation to perform.

One of the few objections that can be raised against Quaintance's analysis – with regard to Montaigne as well as to Rochester – is that it places too great emphasis on cognitive aspects. The 'imagination' discussed by Montaigne is certainly a wide concept, but its harmful effects on potency are not the results of too much 'conceptualizing' etc. (see p. 172 in Quaintance's dissertation). On the contrary, rational endeavour is powerless against the wilful, unpredictable operations of human fancies.

As Griffin points out with reference to Rochester, thinking is 'a natural part of love-making'.[18] The decision to 'throw / The *All-*

---

[18] *Satires Against Man*, p. 96.

dissolving Thunderbolt' is expressly said to be the outcome of a message conveyed by the speaker's 'thoughts'. The subsequent failure to re-establish erection is not due to the meddling intellect; it has other causes:

> Smiling, she chides in a kind murm'ring *Noise*,
> And from her *Body* wipes the clammy joys;
> When with a Thousand Kisses, wand'ring o're
> My panting *Bosome*, — is there then no more?
> She cries. All this to Love, and *Rapture's* due,
> Must we not pay a debt to pleasure too?
> But I the most forlorn, lost *Man* alive,
> To shew my wisht Obedience vainly strive,
> I sigh alas! and Kiss, but cannot Swive.
> Eager desires, confound my first intent,
> Succeeding shame, does more success prevent,
> And *Rage*, at last, confirms me impotent.
> Ev'n her fair Hand, which might bid heat return
> To frozen *Age*, and make cold *Hermits* burn,
> Apply'd to my dead *Cinder*, warms no more,
> Than Fire to *Ashes*, cou'd past Flames restore.
> Trembling, confus'd, despairing, limber, dry,
> A wishing, weak, unmoving lump I ly.

It is clear from Corinna's reaction (her smile, the gentleness of her remonstrances, and her acknowledgement of '*Love*' and '*Rapture*') that she is aware of the reason for her lover's inability to hold back — her overpowering 'charms'. I take her words about the 'debt to pleasure' to mean that while the force of the physical urge, kindled by intense attraction, may be beyond control, there is more to lovemaking than that. '*Pleasure*' is less ungovernable than '*Rapture*',[19] and pleasure she still expects to have. It is an expectation whose legitimacy the speaker does not question for a moment.

In his anxiousness to obey her, the speaker loses sight of his 'first intent'. It is not clear what the expression refers to, but an experienced lover would know that recuperation takes some little time. In the words of Lucretius, translated by Dryden:[20]

> Then, when the gather'd bag has burst its way,
> And ebbing tydes the slacken'd nervs betray,
> A pause ensues; and Nature nods a while,

---

[19] The latter word was used metonymically in line 15. Its erotic connotations were, of course, reinforced by Carew's famous poem.

[20] *De Rerum Natura*, IV.1115ff. An excerpt from Dryden's translation is reproduced in Love's Penguin volume, where the quoted passage is found on p. 198.

> Till with recruited rage new Spirits boil;
> And then the same vain violence returns,
> With flames renew'd th'erected furnace burns.

As was to be expected, mere effort of will does not produce the desired effect, and this realisation is embodied in the elegant line which exploits the different meanings of 'succeed'. Rochester's triplet is tightly knit – the vain attempt is followed by shame, and all hope being lost, helpless fury 'confirms me impotent'.

If the speaker had taken thought, he would probably have realised that his eagerness to save the situation would be counter-productive. But at this point, he is neither impelled by physical appetite nor prompted by 'thought' – his sole motivating force is his wish to satisfy Corinna. That wish validates the term 'Love' that recurs in lines 49 and 60.

In none of the other texts belonging to the imperfect-enjoyment category is genuine concern for the unsatisfied partner a feature of any importance. The men whose potency failed them may curse themselves or the overwhelming – and hence enfeebling – attractions of the woman concerned. Only in Rochester's poem is the man's failure due to his desire to please his lady. While other temporarily incapacitated men bewail the loss of a golden opportunity, Rochester's protagonist regrets the disappointment suffered by a partner he truly cares for – a disappointment which is, moreover, indirectly caused by his feelings for her.[21]

The genuine pathos of lines 35–6 ('Trembling, confus'd … I ly') rapidly fades before the hyperboles of the following nine lines on the disserviceable penis:

> This *Dart* of love, whose piercing point oft try'd,
> With *Virgin blood*, *Ten thousand Maids* has dy'd;
> Which *Nature* still directed with such *Art*,
> That it through ev'ry *Cunt*, reacht ev'ry *Heart*.
> Stiffly resolv'd, twoud carelessly invade,
> *Woman* or *Man*, nor ought its fury staid,
> Where e're it pierc'd, a *Cunt* it found or made.
> Now languid lies, in this unhappy hour,
> Shrunk up, and Sapless, like a wither'd *Flow'r*.

At this point, Rochester may be directly indebted to Ovid:

> At nuper bis flava Chlide, ter candida Pitho,
> Ter Libas officio continuata meo.

---

[21] On the emotional aspect in the poem, cf. Wilcoxon, 'Pornography', 388–9.

Exigere a nobis angusta nocte Corinnam,
Me memini numeros sustinuisse novem.[22]

Ovid's account of his successes, rendered in such a situation, is somewhat comic in its petulance. Even so, his boasts – including nine performances within the space of one short night – are rather more realistic than the claim to have disposed of ten thousand maidenheads. If the latter is a deliberate, and grotesque, exaggeration, what about the avowed indifference to partners? I have suggested (p. 21 above) that the reading '*Boy*' replace '*Man*' in line 42, but that alteration does not do much to reduce the indiscriminateness of the reviled object. The point of the depersonalisation of sexual 'partners' is surely that mere lust impels itself. Lines 37–45 thus form a counterpart to the preceding nine lines, where the failure of the penis is imputed to misguided efforts to please the lady. Accordingly, the two passages, of equal length, establish the antithesis of reciprocation and solipsistic indifference.

Even today, many people would find lines 37–45 of *The Imperfect Enjoyment* obscene. This is to a great extent a matter of taste and hence best left out of the discussion here. Still, a comparison with a poem by Claude de Chouvigny, baron de Blot l'Eglise, may provide a complementary perspective. Blot expresses a similar indifference in the following terms:

L'un ayme le c ... d'une fille,
L'autre le c ... d'un beau garçon,
L'autre n'ayme garçon ny fille
Et ne chérit que son flacon.
Pour moy, je bois, je ris, je chante,
Et je f ... ce qui se présente.[23]

Rochester's lines seem to me to possess far greater merit in that they express a condition in a juxtaposition of opposites which, in turn, forms part of a wider context. Peter Porter once, in a well-found phrase, referred to 'the almost lacy precision of Rochester's writing' in connexion with the poem on Sue Willis.[24] Contemplation of the contrast between Blot's lines and Rochester's may enhance one's respect for Rochester's artistry, not only as a craftsman, but also as an explorer of the human predicament.

---

[22] Lines 23–6 of *Amores* III.7, quoted from the 1670 Hackiana edition of *P. Ovidii Nasonis Opera Omnia: In tres Tomos divisa, cum integris Nicolai Heinsii* (Lyons), vol. I, p. 478.

[23] P. 11 in *Les Chansons libertines de Claude de Chouvigny, baron de Blot (1605–1655)*, ed. Frédéric Lachèvre (Paris, 1919; vol. VI of Lachèvre's *Le Libertinage au XVIIe siècle*).

[24] 'The Professional Amateur', p. 63.

According to John O'Neill, critics have regarded *The Imperfect
Enjoyment* either 'as a psychological and confessional poem, an account
of its author's experience', or 'as a philosophical poem, a statement of
the tragic limits of earthly happiness'.[25] Dissatisfied with both readings,
O'Neill proposes that *The Imperfect Enjoyment* should be viewed as a
satire on pride – the pride of the flesh. He also outlines a parodic element
in the poem and argues that line 45 forms a deliberate allusion to
Spenser's *Faerie Queene*, I.viii.41, line 369 ('and all his flesh shronk up
like withered flowres'). O'Neill's view of *The Imperfect Enjoyment* rests
on one other factor: the speaker's reference to his penis (in line 10) as
'The *All-dissolving Thunderbolt*'. Here, O'Neill maintains, 'a dangerous
excess, a form of pride' sets in.

In my view, this conception of *The Imperfect Enjoyment* rests on too
slender a basis. Neither the alleged Spenserian reminiscence of the Red
Crosse knight beset by pride nor the thunderbolt line lends enough
support to it. When Rochester's poems attack pride – and all the satires
do so, vehemently and at length – subtlety is not a salient feature. The
kind of pride they denigrate is human presumptuousness, vain ideas of
personal superiority and puffed-up ambition, not anything that could be
called 'the pride of the flesh'. Besides, the hubris that O'Neill discerns
in line 10 is diminished by the circumstance adumbrated in lines 7–9 and
echoed in line 60 – the command issued by the lady. Nevertheless,
O'Neill's probing into the 'irrationality' of the concluding apostrophe
is thought-provoking, and he offers several pertinent observations on
the poem.[26]

The final section of *The Imperfect Enjoyment* has elicited very different
reactions. Reba Wilcoxon feels that its tone is a mixture of comic and
tragic.[27] Other critics have taken up their stands at various points along
the scale from funny to serious. David Farley-Hills, for instance, regards
the entire poem as 'an extremely funny burlesque';[28] conversely, Carole
Fabricant stresses 'the bitterness of its tone'.[29] Several scholars have
spoken of the 'disgust' that characterises the final part.[30] Many years
ago, J. H. Wilson wrote that Etherege's and Rochester's poems are

---

[25] 'Rochester's "Imperfect Enjoyment"', 58. O'Neill mentions Griffin as a representative of the
first group and Carole Fabricant as belonging to the second (59).

[26] Such as 'After all, *ejaculatio praecox* and temporary impotence must be fairly unremarkable
events in the life of a rake. What is remarkable is the fact that this rake cannot accept them as
such' (62).   [27] 'Pornography', 380.   [28] *Rochester's Poetry*, p. 112.

[29] 'Rochester's World of Imperfect Enjoyment', 347.

[30] See, for example, Griffin, *Satires Against Man*, pp. 91 and 98–9, and K. E. Robinson, 'The Art
of Violence', pp. 97–8.

'actually … frank studies of impotence written from the depths of spiritual revulsion'.[31]

To most readers, all these – partly conflicting – evaluations probably make some sort of sense. That is in itself suggestive of complexity. Another noteworthy factor is the technical brilliance evinced in these twenty-seven lines. The barrage of auditory effects in the following two couplets is remarkable, both in its intensity and in the way it produces an impact without seeming too elaborate:

> Like a Rude roaring *Hector*, in the *Streets*,
> That Scuffles, Cuffs, and Ruffles all he meets;
> But if his *King*, or *Country*, claim his Aid,
> The *Rakehell Villain*, shrinks, and hides his head[.]

Lines like these – packed with alliteration and chimes, and with the element of *double entendre* well in hand – bear the stamp of the skilful craftsman. This phenomenon is curiously contrasted with the violence of the vocabulary and the ludicrous excesses of lines such as:

> And may *Ten thousand* abler *Pricks* agree,
> To do the wrong'd *Corinna*, right for thee.[32]

Another indication that the conclusion of *The Imperfect Enjoyment* is the product of painstaking desk-work is found in the treatment of the *miles gloriosus* motif.[33] Comparing an uncompliant penis to a soldier deserting his commander is a commonplace; Ovid, for instance, accused the deserter of leaving its master 'inermis' (*Amores* III.vii.71). Rochester, however, develops the notion in a way that brings out the dimension of fear. The traitor is not merely false – its falsehood is emphasised first and last, in lines 47 and 70 – but a coward to boot. This aspect is expressly formulated in the couplet that forms the core of the execrations unleashed by the speaker, lines 60–1:

> But when great *Love*, the onset does command,
> Base Recreant, to thy *Prince*, thou darst not stand.

'Recreant' (both senses recorded by the *OED* seem to apply here, including B1, 'one who yields in combat; a cowardly or faint-hearted person') and 'darst' suggest base trepidation. Among the members of the imperfect-enjoyment genre, it is Belleau's *Impuissance* that comes closest to Rochester's poem in this respect;[34] 'Mon V. faict le poltron', it is 'couard et craintif', 'Brave sur le rempart et couard à la breche'.

---

[31] *Court Wits*, p. 101.

[32] On the face of it, one ought to be enough. Cf. line 38 ('With *Virgin blood, Ten thousand Maids* has dy'd').   [33] Aptly designated by Quaintance; see p. 210 in 'Passion and Reason'.

[34] Quaintance was the first to note this similarity; see p. 210 in his dissertation.

Fear is a powerful feeling, and *The Imperfect Enjoyment* is fundamentally concerned with the incompatibility of physical function and
emotion. The lines on those whores to whom the offender stood up
without fail (50–1, 59 and 63–5) are not, in my view, predominantly
remarkable for the disgust or revulsion they express. Rather, they
suggest complete indifference. An interesting feature in the image of the
'*Fucking Post*' (lines 63–4) is the essential passivity of the male organ. It
simply serves as an impersonal instrument. Appropriately, those who
make use of it are themselves driven by mere physical appetite. '*Brutal
Valor*' in line 58 is a term with literal significance: the penis only
functions at the level of animal copulation, a point reinforced by the
'*Hogs*' simile.

In other words, the second half of *The Imperfect Enjoyment* codifies the
impossibility of giving sexual satisfaction where emotion comes into
play, at least in the speaker's case. This appears to be the reason why he
does not envisage a renewed attempt. Several other disappointed and
disappointing lovers in imperfect-enjoyment works were able to redeem
their initial disgrace; Rochester's speaker does not even admit the
possibility of a second chance.

It seems to me that the most striking way in which Rochester's poem
deviates from the others in this genre has been neglected by critics. His
Imperfect Enjoyment is the only poem in which the inability to restore
erection immediately after premature ejaculation results in furious
imprecations. When, for instance, Ovid's and Belleau's speakers inveigh
against their *partes pessimae*, the latter have failed utterly. No comparable
poem suggests that an event like the one described in Rochester's poem
is reprehensible. The premature ejaculation itself was not presented as
blameworthy. Nevertheless, dreadful suffering – and Rochester knew
how distressing urinary disorders could be – is wished on the traitor in
a triplet which makes Belleau's envisaged punishments, though
distasteful (such as intercourse with a two-toothed hag who can
remember Joan of Arc), seem rather trivial. Why, then, does Rochester's
speaker attack the 'deserter of his flame' more vehemently than any
other imperfect-enjoyment protagonist – for a crime which very few,
at any time, would regard as such?

If the inability to make love twice running without an intervening,
however brief, period of recuperation were to be equated with
impotence, most men would suffer from that complaint for the greater
part of their lives. Despite the existence of 'perfect-enjoyment' verses,
there is little reason to believe that the Restoration thought any

differently on this point. Still, most of the critics who have discussed Rochester's poem have used the word 'impotence', and the poet did so himself ('And *Rage*, at last, confirms me impotent').

Impotence is clearly an issue not only in *The Imperfect Enjoyment*, but in other Rochester poems as well.[35] In *The Disabled Debauchee* and the *Song of a Young Lady to her Ancient Lover*, it is envisaged as an attendant upon old age. Old men's potency was expected to be poor; it was no fault of theirs. *The Fall* suggests that a man's wish to please a woman he is genuinely committed to may be hampered by defects that are not his, but those of fallen humanity. At no time does Rochester describe the simple failure to have an erection in the first place.

That situation, from which other poets – following Ovid – did not recoil, would not, I think, have been possible for Rochester to address. Instead, he created another where the anger and shame of impotence could be explored without exposing his speaker to the ignominy of present, realised, impotence proper. This way, a sensitive subject is probed under the cover of another protective device (like old age and the condition of man after the Fall). The bravado displayed in the tales of past exploits would serve a similar purpose.

To be sure, such a reading can be criticised as being too reductively biographical, and others are certainly possible. If it is accepted, however, it says something about Rochester that goes beyond asserting that he worried about sexual failure. Recognising his ability to employ distancing techniques, and to apply a variety of conventions – down to burlesque hyperbole – to his private fears, amounts to recognising a serious artist.

While *The Imperfect Enjoyment* and *A Ramble in Saint James's Parke* are often discussed in conjunction, critics are apt to find the latter darker in tone. Both open on an optimistic note, tell of subsequent betrayal and end in vengeful diatribe. Elements of burlesque occur in both, too. But the *Ramble* is, as several scholars have indicated, a more unsettling poem. Expostulations directed against one's own recalcitrant penis are, of course, more likely to make a comic impact than the grim determination to wreck the life of another human being. However, there are other reasons for the general impression that the *Ramble* is less funny than *The Imperfect Enjoyment*.

To begin with, though, something might be said about the

---

[35] Fredelle Bruser was among the first Rochester critics to draw attention to this fact; see 'Disproportion', 387–8.

similarities. Curiously enough, few critical analyses have given much space to the emotion/rationality/sensuality complex that seems to me to lie at the heart of both poems. The *Imperfect Enjoyment* speaker fails to satisfy his mistress because his eager desire to please her frustrates his 'first intent', which I have taken to refer to the rational realisation that a renewed attempt should not be undertaken right away. Rationality and sensuality can co-operate successfully, but feelings impair the smooth functioning of the body. The peculiar passivity and indiscriminateness displayed by the stolid '*Fucking Post*' in *The Imperfect Enjoyment* has a counterpart in the equally undiscriminating 'devouring Cunt' of the rambler's Corinna. Both organs represent sexual activity completely devoid of emotion. In neither case is that activity held to be reprehensible in itself; pain and fury are produced by the realisation that it does not allow for, or coexist with, the most generous passion of the mind. It should also be noted that both poems *look back on* such activity – it forms part of a comparative retrospect, not an actual situation.

Most critical discussions of the *Ramble* speak of 'compulsive promiscuity', 'mechanical sex', 'nymphomania', 'blind fury of fornication', 'mindless pleasure' and so on. According to David Farley-Hills, the 'point' of the *Ramble* is that 'we are all victims of this sexual madness'.[36] An inspection of the motives of the five *dramatis personae* in the *Ramble* yields a rather different picture.

The speaker of the poem sets out for the park in honour of a principle, leaving his boon companions to their slanderous gossip:

> ... I who still take care to see
> Drunkenness Reliev'd by Leachery
> Went out into Saint James's Park
> To coole my head and fire my heart.

Alternating between convivial drinking and lovemaking was in accordance with the Restoration libertine's standards of behaviour (see p. 11 above). Similar turns of phrase occur in *The English Rogue*, during the 'hero's' visit to a brothel:

Having well warmed our selves with Wine, knowing that our bloods began to heat; *Well*, said [the madam], *I guess at the intent of your coming hither ... Come, I see by your countenances, that ye were born sons of mirth and pleasure ... If you want Subjects to exercise your parts on, we'll have more wine, and when ye are inflamed, ye shall have the benefit of a Cooler.*[37]

---

[36] *Rochester's Poetry*, p. 109.

[37] Pp. 76–7 in the 1666 edition of *The English Rogue described, in the Life of Meriton Latroon, a Witty Extravagant.*

The *Ramble* protagonist does not seem to have made an 'Assignation' with Corinna; their meeting is apparently accidental. Given the customary conditions and clientele of the Park, he could be sure of having his 'Drunkenness Reliev'd by Leachery' in some way without making previous arrangements. Unlike his predecessor, the 'auncient Pict', he lived at a time when no visitor to St James' Park had any need to fear having to resort to solitary masturbation. Still, what awaited him there was undoubtedly a 'Jylting'; to that extent, a kind of fellowship is established between the two men.

Before Corinna's reasons for turning him down on sight can be considered, the forces impelling her three suitors should be scrutinised. 'Sexual madness', a 'blind compulsion to fornicate' and so on do not seem to have a great deal to do with them. Their chief motive power is of a very different kind: social ambition.[38]

Rochester devoted some thirty lines to his description of the three fops – a fair quantity for a not very prolific poet. The first, on whom the lion's share is bestowed, is the prototype of the would-be hanger-on at the Court of Charles II. He has connexions there, from whom he picks up information which will give him something to imitate in his endeavour to be like the best people. This ambition rules his life. His senses, his reason, and his actions are all completely subjugated by it. The other two young blades are also desirous of impressing people, though the ambitions of the second are not expressly said to extend further than his landlady. All three are cheats – 'Knights of the Elboe and the Slurr' – and thus in the business of fraud and treachery at a particularly low (in every sense of the word) level.

These vain, affected pretenders to social standing are surely not 'making up to' Corinna merely for the sake of her physical attractions. It is her status as the mistress of a man who keeps the company they aspire to that really whets their appetite. The rambler is clearly a man of some distinction, to judge from the circles he frequents (the first two lines of the poem seem to form a précis of Court tittle-tattle, of which Rochester was reportedly inordinately fond). By obtaining Corinna's favours, the would-be wits will kill several birds with one stone: they will have enjoyed a lady who belongs to the best people – a feather in their caps –; and by interviewing her in the process, they will have learned all sorts of intimate details about her distinguished lover. That will give them something else to imitate, as well as providing them with

---

[38] This aspect of the *Ramble* is analysed in my article 'Rochester and Jealousy', 216–18; the following discussion incorporates a paragraph from that analysis.

the pleasant feeling of having a hold over the rambler, whose pillow-
talk Corinna passes on to them.

If the speaker of the *Ramble* adheres to a libertine principle and the
three sparks are out to raise their social status, what are Corinna's
motives? Is she a nymphomaniac, a victim as well as a perpetrator of
compulsive fornication, as some Rochester critics have maintained?
Why does she take up with the three fools, rather than joining her
admiring lover?

In fact, the speaker makes it very clear that lust is *not* her reason for
this humiliating choice. Corinna is 'Joyfull and pleas'd', not because she
anticipates sexual satisfaction but because she is flattered. Neither her
intellect nor her sensual appetite influences her conduct ('neither Head
nor Taile perswade'). Flattery has always been the seducer's most
efficacious weapon, a fact on which a contemporary of Rochester's
sombrely reflected:

No Woman's virtue in the World (if young) can be so strong a Fort to her, but
it may be rendered to the perpetual showers of flatterie, and complement,
which play upon it.[39]

Much of the rambler's fury is due to his idol's having yielded to the
effusions of such despicable males. Another Restoration writer portrayed their kind in the following terms:

A *Town-Gallant* is a Bundle of *Vanity*, composed of *Ignorance*, and *Pride*, *Folly*,
and *Debauchery*; a silly *Huffing* thing, three parts *Fop*, and the rest *Hector*.[40]

The behaviour of this type of man betrays strenuous efforts to copy the
Court-Wit circle. The determination to draw an inviolable line of
demarcation between the true wits of that circle and their uncouth
imitators is an interesting feature of Rochester's verse (see, for instance,
Timon and *The Imperfect Enjoyment*). And these are the men Corinna
prefers to the *Ramble* speaker, these odious social climbers who woo and
win her with platitudes of inexpressible inanity! In taking up with them,
she certainly does not have 'pleasure for excuse'. What motivates her is
one of the three defects which are always seen as inexcusable in
Rochester's *œuvre*: vanity, or pride (cf. lines 36 and 83). The three
young blades represent the other two, folly and hypocrisy (or stupidity
and insincerity).

It has been suggested[41] that the foolishness of the three sparks is a

[39] Richard Graham, *Angliae Speculum Morale; the Moral State of England* (London, 1670), p. 74.
[40] *The Character of a Town-Gallant, exposing the Extravagant Fopperies of some vain Self-conceited
    Pretenders to Gentility and good Breeding* (London, 1675), p. 2.
[41] See, for example, Farley-Hills, *Rochester's Poetry*, p. 71.

point in their favour where Corinna is concerned. Morophilia, the love of fools, is a phenomenon with a long history,[42] and it is harboured by some women in Rochester's poems. The fine lady in *Artemiza to Chloe* is a staunch defender of morons in love, not because they are particularly potent (the traditional belief) but because such men are easily deceived and dominated. Chloris in *To A Lady, in A Letter* is said to be indifferent to the stupidity of her admirers, as long as 'their Codds [are] full'. The most striking example of morophilia in a downright sexual context is found in lines 33–4 of *Signior Dildo*:

> Our dainty fine Dutchesse's have got a Trick
> To Doat on a Fool, for the Sake of his Prick ...

The *Ramble* is not, properly speaking, illustrative of morophilia. The folly of the three young blades is not so much a cause of Corinna's offensive preference as an aggravating circumstance:

> But to turn damn'd abandon'd Jade
> When neither Head nor Taile perswade
> To be a Whore in understanding
> A passive pott for Fools to spend in.
> The Devill play'd booty sure with Thee
> To bring a blott on Infamy.

The concluding couplet is another of Rochester's dizzying hyperboles. Corinna, in betraying her intelligence as well as her sensual appetite, has sunk even below the 'Infamy' imputed to her fifteen lines earlier. Sullying perfidy is a feat that calls for infernal assistance. The fall of Corinna, from a divine apparition (lines 35–40) to the devil's confederate, has been completed.

In the *Ramble*, as so often in Rochester's poems on love, the protagonists are hence motivated by mental rather than physical urges. But of course Corinna's flattered pride and the social aspirations of the fops do not prevent them from being sexually aroused:

> So a prowd Bitch does lead about
> Of humble Currs the Amorous Rout
> Who most obsequiously doe hunt
> The savory scent of salt swoln Cunt.

Three levels of sexual activity can, I think, be discerned in the *Ramble*. The lowest is represented by these four people, who abuse sex for

---

[42] The subject is extensively covered in Quaintance's 'Passion and Reason', ch. 2. See also Griffin, *Satires Against Man*, pp. 87–8.

ulterior and contemptible motives. 'Meer lust' ranks well above it. To be sure, it is also accompanied by emotional indifference and a total lack of discrimination; but it does have 'pleasure for excuse', and that excuse possesses some degree of validity in itself. The speaker accounted for Corinna's envisaged indulgence in it with socially inferior men as 'quench[ing] a fire [he] rais'd'. St James' Park is the 'abode' of such activity, and the rambler himself went there in deliberate pursuit of it.[43] It is thus in no way blameworthy, however 'promiscuous'.

The third and highest level of erotic activity is illustrated in the following passage:

> You that cou'd make my heart away
> For noise and Colour and betray
> The secretts of my tender houres
> To such knight errant Paramours
> When leaneing on your faithless breast
> Wrapt in security and rest
> Soft kindness all my powers did move
> And Reason lay dissolv'd in Love.

At an earlier point in the poem (line 108), the rambler invited pity in referring to himself as 'humble fond beleiveing mee'. Here, emotionally charged words such as 'heart', 'tender', 'security', 'rest' and 'Soft kindness' (even allowing for the secondary meanings of the first and last of them) pave the way for the remarkable admission in line 132. The speaker in the *Ramble* uses the very expressions that have signalled genuine devotion throughout Rochester's love poetry. More than that, 'security' and 'rest' spell peace and contentment, so infinitely desirable and so heartbreakingly elusive. With the lovely girl who jilts him for the flattery of three miserable cheats, he knew such moments, moments when the boundaries between lust, rationality and emotion vanished, 'And Reason lay dissolv'd in Love'.

The issue of craftsmanship and conscious artistry that was touched on in respect of *The Imperfect Enjoyment* should be reviewed in relation to the *Ramble*, too. This in some ways highly accomplished poem employs parody with great skill.[44] A number of conventional ideas and prejudices

---

[43] On the meaning of the word 'ramble' in the late seventeenth century, see John D. Patterson, 'The Restoration Ramble', *Notes and Queries* 28.3 (n.s.; June 1981), 209–10.

[44] See Griffin, *Satires Against Man*, pp. 28–30. Wilcoxon stresses the use of mock-religious language in the poem; see 'The Rhetoric of Sex in Rochester's Burlesque', *Papers on Language and Literature* 12 (Summer 1976), 280–1. Biblical associations of various kinds are proposed by Thomas K. Pasch in an article which presents a very different view of the *Ramble* from the one suggested in this chapter. See 'Concentricity, Christian Myth, and the Self-Incriminating Narrator in Rochester's *A Ramble in St. James's Park*', *Essays in Literature* 6 (Spring 1979), 21–8.

are brought up in the *Ramble* and made to serve varying purposes. Contrary to the traditional Neoplatonic notion that a beautiful body must house a fair soul, the rambler joins a large company of disgruntled men[45] when exhorting:

> But mark what Creatures women are
> How infinitly vile when fair:

That Catholic priests, Jesuits included, practised sodomy was a conviction widely held in seventeenth-century England[46] (see lines 145–6 of the *Ramble*). At that time, too, medical men were constantly subject to imputations of atheism (line 149).[47]

One might ask why the speaker expects Corinna's future marriage to give him the best opportunity for revenge. Surely it would be more to the point to blacken her reputation at an earlier date, so as to prevent her from marrying at all? The only reason I can see for postponing his malicious slander is that such a campaign, launched without delay, might be taken for the hurt pride of a jealous lover and thus be turned against himself. Besides, Corinna betrayed the speaker's trust; now he anticipates destroying her future husband's trust in her.[48] Such an event would, considering a husband's power over his wife, ruin the very foundations of her existence.

Quite a few of the rhymes in the *Ramble* are impure, and some lines do not rise above mere doggerel. Nevertheless, some passages contain cleverly sustained metaphorical elaborations, such as the ingestion metaphor in lines 113–22 (with the chiming combination 'dram of sperm'); and the Jesuit couplet (lines 145–6) has a slippery elegance. In the tetrameter couplet, caesuras can be expected to be rarer than in the iambic one, and there are not many in the *Ramble*. The enjambments in lines 125–7 increase the pace of the accusations, and the slowing down that results from the end-stopping in lines 129–32 lends added weight to the crucial line 'And Reason lay dissolv'd in Love'.

[45] See, for instance, Ovid's *Amores* II.17; William Ram(e)sey's *The Gentleman's Companion* supplies a seventeenth-century example (p. 93).

[46] See, for example, Thompson, *Unfit for Modest Ears*, pp. 125 and 153. Oldham's *Satyrs upon the Jesuits* mention buggery among their vices; see, for instance, III.93–4 and IV.294 (pp. 29 and 53 respectively in Harold F. Brooks' Oldham edition).

[47] Sir Thomas Browne quotes 'the scandall of my profession' as one reason why he might be thought not to have any religion at all (section 1 of *Religio Medici*).

[48] Ken Robinson suggests that a 'mirroring-punishment' is adumbrated in lines 159–60; 'Just as Rochester experiences sexual resentment because he has been supplanted ... so ... she would suffer sexual anguish as her lover was ripped from her' ('The Art of Violence', p. 100). The wilful destruction of Corinna's husband's confidence in her might be regarded as another kind of 'mirroring-punishment'. A third instance is supplied below.

Just as there are three levels of sexual activity in the *Ramble*, the poem reflects on three aspects of humanity: the mental, the sensual and the emotional. Corinna betrays all three. For good measure, she offends against social standards too. While the rambler's fury may well be augmented by the immediacy of the situation – it was perhaps easier to 'bear' her past infidelities because he did not witness them, waiting for her to 'come home' –, it is neither illogical nor irrational.

Logic and rationality may seem curious terms to apply to the conclusion of the *Ramble*, even by negative implication. They can, however, be seen to operate in a particularly interesting passage:

> May stinking vapours Choak your womb
> Such as the Men you doat upon
> May your depraved Appetite
> That cou'd in whiffling Fools delight
> Begett such Frenzies in your Mind
> You may goe madd for the North wind
> And fixing all your hopes upont
> To have him bluster in your Cunt
> Turn up your longing Arse to the Air
> And perrish in a wild dispair.

Here, the noisome insubstantiality of Corinna's choice, the three fops, forms the centre of an extended metaphorical complex manifested in the words 'vapours', 'whiffling', 'North wind', 'bluster' and 'Air'. The idea that boreal inclemency would be a suitable focus for Corinna's desire, however demented it might appear at first sight, actually makes sense. Her intercourse with the young flatterers is, in a sense, incorporeal, the outcome of vanity and ambition attended by 'Tune', 'Nonsense', 'noise' and 'Colour' (lines 75 and 126). There is no matter in it, no 'body', only unsavoury air. Characteristically, Corinna's imagined passion fuses sensual, mental and emotional aspects; her yearning for the north wind will be conceived in her 'Mind', entrenched in her 'hopes', and shown in her turning up '[her] longing Arse to the Air'. The woman who rejected true substance would hence be condemned, if the spell worked, to a hopeless hankering for its opposite. The mirroring-punishment drawn up in these ten lines could hardly have been more apposite.

In the *Ramble* as in *The Imperfect Enjoyment*, love has been betrayed, and it is this treachery that informs the concluding objurgations. The exaggerations may well strike readers as amusing, and the debts to the genre of burlesque are obvious. One marvellously funny detail is the invocation 'Some power more patient now Relate / The sence of this surpriseing Fate' – lines 87–8 – just before the torrent of abuse beginning, 'Gods! that a thing admir'd by mee / Shou'd fall to so much Infamy.' The hudibrastic metre is certainly no coincidence. On the face of it, there is no reason to quarrel with Farley-Hills' categorisation when he includes the *Ramble* in 'Rochester's Burlesque Poetry'.[49]

Even so, both the *Ramble* and *The Imperfect Enjoyment* seem to me to hold an unmistakable note of distress. In this they resemble those post-fulfilment love lyrics which turn so uncomfortably on pain and absence. In the midst of the grotesqueries and grimaces, a small throbbing presence keeps insisting that 'pain can ne're deceive', and that it is about the only thing that cannot.

[49] See pp. 105–6 in *Rochester's Poetry*.

4

'A Letter from Artemiza in the Towne to Chloe in the Countrey'

NORM AND STRUCTURE IN *ARTEMIZA TO CHLOE*

A Letter from Artemiza in the Towne to Chloe in the Countrey – the longest poem in the Rochester canon drawn up by Vieth and sanctioned by subsequent scholars – is consistently praised by modern Rochester critics,[1] but there is a lack of incisive critical analysis of it. This is partly the result of uncertainty about the basis and direction of its satire, an uncertainty which is, in its turn, largely due to critics finding Artemiza's own stance and credibility difficult to define.

Hardly any analysis of the poem omits a consideration of the extent to which Artemiza herself can be said to constitute a 'norm'. Most of them express reluctance to regard her in this way.[2] If the author did not care to supply a 'norm', the reader will have to construct his/her own *point d'appui* for the satire to be effective as such. The most obvious solution is to make Artemiza herself a satirical creation. Both Vieth and Weinbrot, accordingly, claim to see her undergoing an unfortunate development as the poem progresses. To Vieth, she begins 'as a spokesman [*sic*] for romantic love [but] degenerates…into a gossip-monger' (p. 18 in the *Moriae Encomium* essay); Weinbrot, in terms of

---

[1] A survey of opinions on *Artemiza to Chloe* is supplied in an article by David Sheehan, 'The Ironist in Rochester's "A Letter from Artemisia in the Town to Chloe in the Country"', *Tennessee Studies in Literature* 25 (1980), 72ff.; the article is reprinted in Vieth's *Critical Essays*, where the relevant presentation is found on pp. 299–300.

[2] See Griffin, *Satires Against Man*, pp. 133ff.; Howard D. Weinbrot, 'The Swelling Volume: The Apocalyptic Satire of Rochester's *Letter From Artemisia In The Town To Chloe In The Country*', *Studies in the Literary Imagination* 5 (1972), 25; Vieth, 'Toward an Anti-Aristotelian Poetic: Rochester's *Satyr against Mankind* and *Artemisia to Chloe*, with Notes on Swift's *Tale of a Tub* and *Gulliver's Travels*', *Language and Style* 5 (Spring 1972), 135; and Vieth's 'The *Moriae Encomium* as a Model for Satire in Restoration Court Literature', in Vieth and Griffin, eds., *Rochester and Court Poetry*, p. 15.

much greater indignation, claims to find her accepting the fine lady's judgements and even 'encouraging such hellish values to take root' ('The Swelling Volume', 34). Griffin thinks that she is 'satirized by herself and by the reader' (*Satires Against Man*, p. 133).

Does Artemiza deserve all this censure, or even part of it? Did Rochester set her up as a target of satire rather than as – or as well as – a satiric spokeswoman? This issue must be confronted before going on to review others that are raised by the poem, notably the conflict between wit and folly, 'sexual politics', and the position of women poets and scholars in Restoration society.

The first thing to bear in mind when scrutinising Artemiza's discourse is that it is made up of a familiar letter to a friend or relative of the same sex. Such communications were, and are, rambling and informal by their very nature. Two well-known women letter-writers of the seventeenth century expressed their dislike of excessively polished epistolary efforts in the following terms:

I wonder at nothing more than at the ambition of printing letters: since, if the design be to produce wit and learning, there is too little scope for the one; and the other may be reduced to a less compass than a sheet of gilt paper, unless truth were more communicative. Business, love, accidents, secret displeasure, family intrigues, generally make up the body of letters; and can signify very little to any besides the persons they are addressed to.

Letters mee thinks should bee free and Easy as ones discourse, not studdyed, as an Oration, nor made up of hard words like a Charme.[3]

The ease with which the opening salutation glides into the first line of the poem suggests that the correspondents are closely acquainted. Henry Care's *Female Secretary* (1671) allowed a woman letter-writer to 'almost joyn ... together' title and first line when writing to 'those with whom you are more familiar', supplying the example:

Coz,
    I understand by your Letter, & c.[4]

If anyone has a right to be annoyed with Artemiza, it is surely poor Chloe who is languishing for gossipy news and is not afforded a single titbit. The Corinna story deals with a woman in whom she has no reason to be interested and a nameless man. It will hardly make up for

---

[3] Mary Evelyn and Dorothy Osborne, quoted in Sister Mary Humiliata, 'Standards of Taste Advocated for Feminine Letter Writing', *The Huntington Library Quarterly* 13 (1949–50), 265 and 266.   [4] Quoted by Sister Mary Humiliata, 'Standards of Taste', 269.

the total absence of details about 'who, and who's togeather' – an informal expression which retains its colloquial directness even today – among the people she knows. Towards the end, Artemiza seems to feel that her voluminous letter is indeed lacking in the sort of substance Chloe desired. Exhausted as she is, she therefore holds out promises for better things in her next missive. Countless letter-writers throughout the ages have resorted to similar 'this isn't what you wanted to hear, I know, but I'll make up for it next time' formulae.

At least Chloe cannot accuse Artemiza of keeping her in false hopes. The moment Artemiza has disposed of her scruples in the matter of writing verse, she expresses her regret at not being able to write the kind of thing her correspondent longs to hear. That sentiment is immediately followed by the famous lines on love and its debasement:

> But how, my dearest Chloe, shall I sett
> My pen to write, what I would faine forgett,
> Or name that lost thing (Love) without a teare
> Synce soe debauch'd by ill-bred Customes here?
> Love, the most gen'rous passion of the mynde,
> The softest refuge Innocence can fynde,
> The safe directour of unguided youth,
> Fraught with kind wishes, and secur'd by Trueth,
> That Cordiall dropp Heav'n in our Cup has throwne,
> To make the nauseous draught of life goe downe,
> On which one onely blessing God might rayse
> In lands of Atheists Subsidyes of prayse
> (For none did e're soe dull, and stupid prove,
> But felt a God, and blest his pow'r in Love)
> This onely Joy, for which poore Wee were made,
> Is growne like play, to be an Arrant Trade;
> The Rookes creepe in, and it has gott of late
> As many little Cheates, and Trickes, as that.

This, as Weinbrot suggests, is Artemiza's 'norm' ('The Swelling Volume', 35). If she is in some way to be regarded as a butt of the poem's satire, then either her ideal must have ludicrous dimensions, or she must be seen to be false to it herself.

To begin with the former condition, there is nothing in Artemiza's description of love that looks out of place in the context of Rochester's *œuvre*. The key words 'safe', 'secur'd' and 'Trueth' are characteristically associated with the kind of love that transcends mere lust. They occur in *The submission* (lines 13–14), 'Absent from thee' (lines

9–12) and the *Ramble* (lines 129–32),[5] in passages where true love is envisioned but remains unachieved – a fact which only serves to align them with the *Artemiza to Chloe* lines, where unfulfilment introduces, concludes and underlies the portrayal of love.

There is nothing fatuous or facile about that portrayal. Artemiza decidedly opposes marriage (see lines 28–9) and never conjures up a vision of lasting and pervasive bliss. True love is a 'Cordiall dropp' that does not prevent the draught of life from being nauseous; it merely serves to make life bearable – just. Artemiza stresses that love was designed by the Creator as the sole joy of human life, and now she has to acknowledge that even that no longer exists. It is hardly a sentimental attitude.[6]

A chief characteristic of Artemiza's 'lost thing (Love)' is genuine devotion to another person and an interest in his/her happiness ('gen'rous passion', 'softest refuge' etc.). 'Gen'rous' probably means 'noble' as well as 'liberal', and it is noteworthy that the passion is said to be 'of the mynde' – a feeling which engages the whole person, not a mere physical attraction divorced from thought, inclination and conscious commitment. Such powerful affections may be unfashionable in Restoration society; but several of Rochester's most memorable speakers admit to caring about partners. In his verse, the uneasy coexistence of mind and body is not made any smoother by the stirrings of emotion. Like the stanza on perfect paradisal love in *The Fall*, and lines 130–2 in the *Ramble*, Artemiza's lines create a vision of a state where hearts and minds lie down with bodies and true harmony is achieved.

In other words, Artemiza's presentation of the 'Passion Love' does not differ markedly from comparable passages in the remainder of Rochester's poetry – certainly not to such an extent that it seems to invite satire (but see p. 109 below on the woman speaker as a safeguarding device). Are there any other reasons for believing that the spokeswoman should be regarded with scorn?

---

[5] In respect of the *Submission* quotation, cf. Griffin, *Satires Against Man*, p. 140. Wilcoxon, in 'Rochester's Sexual Politics' (145), has noted the relevance to *Artemiza to Chloe* of the last two passages.

[6] I cannot find that Artemiza is 'innocent but wilfully sentimental', as Everett calls her (at the outset of the poem); see 'The Sense of Nothing', p. 30. John E. Sitter also imputes sentimentality to Artemiza, whose 'fond fictions' allegedly 'render her more vulnerable than reliable'; see 'Rochester's Reader and the Problem of Satiric Audience', *Papers in Language and Literature* 12.3 (Summer 1976), 297. (While this view seems odd to me – a person as thoroughly disillusioned as Artemiza is hardly 'vulnerable' –, Sitter makes a number of valuable points in his article, which was reprinted in Vieth's *Critical Essays*).

If there are, I have not found them. On the contrary, there is further evidence that her point of view is, as Richard E. Quaintance Jr. called it, 'established ... in a manner impregnable to ironic subversion'.[7] First of all, there is her name. As several critics have noted, 'artemisia' is (in the words of the *OED*) 'a genus of plants ... distinguished by a peculiarly bitter or aromatic taste, including the Common Wormwood'. It would seem to be the name of a satirical observer rather than a stooge. The associations evoked by its bearers in ancient history reinforce the impression of independence and strength.[8]

Artemiza's lines on true love are more programmatic than those passages in other Rochester poems with which they have affinities. This distinction, however, is hardly enough to imply overt satiric intent. When it comes to her views on what forces should direct human behaviour, there is a degree of resemblance, both with regard to substance and attitude, to the stance of the speaker in the *Satyr against Reason and Mankind*. Like this man, she consistently advocates 'Natures rule'. True, what he regrets is that the healthy instincts given by Nature to men and animals alike (see pp. 223–4) are perverted by men's pride – including the pride of reason – and fear; Artemiza, on the other hand, deplores women's surrender to dictates of fashion largely created by themselves. Despite this difference with regard to the targets of their respective attacks, the *Satyr* speaker and Artemiza both castigate the offences of their respective sex against Nature, contending that those offences are foolish human fabrications which bring nothing but unhappiness on their misguided creators.

As the *Satyr* speaker acknowledges the existence of '*right Reason*', the function of which is to enhance the satisfaction of man's appetites, so Artemiza recognises that the worthiest freedom involves some restraint – compliance with 'Natures rule, or Loves advice', which even monarchs must obey. Spurning such gentle masters, however, women embrace a 'meaner Liberty', subjugating themselves under the fickle and ignoble sway of Fashion. As a result, they wilfully corrupt their innate ability to discriminate ('tast' and 'Choyce'), refusing to allow such generous feelings as admiration and approval. Forsaking pleasure, they set themselves no higher aim than the vain and selfish assurance that

---

[7] 'Passion and Reason', p. 34.
[8] See, for instance, pp. 29–30 in Everett's 'The Sense of Nothing' and p. 33 in Rothstein's *Restoration and Early Eighteenth-Century Poetry*. Admittedly, though, a woman bearing that name could be an object of Augustan satire. In Pope's imitations of Dorset, one 'Artemesia' (a woman who actually recalls Rochester's fine lady in several respects) is scorned as being 'All Flutter, Pride, and Talk'.

they behave, and are seen to behave, in accordance with the momentary prescriptions of the 'publicke Voyce'.

Throughout lines 40–69, Artemiza emphasises the *passion* – that is, the powerful feeling – of love. She does not come across as a prude; her slighting words on marriage and her praise of the joy and pleasure of love do not suggest that she is an advocate of chastity. What she does state in those thirty-odd lines that constitute her 'platform' is what innumerable women have held before and after her: that 'love's the finest thing around', and that sexual intercourse ('the Action Love') without tenderness and affection has little to offer in the way of genuine pleasure. Those women who have forgotten that in their desire to comply with current trends have prostituted themselves – '[turned] Gipsyes' – for a worthless commodity.[9]

It is very much a woman's point of view. I have argued that there is nothing ridiculous about it against the background of the Rochester canon, and that some components in Artemiza's eulogy and lament on love are reminiscent of important contexts in Rochester's poems where the speaker's identity is not obviously distinguished from his own. Still, I would hazard a guess that one reason why Rochester gave such lines on love to a woman speaker was that he could not, as a fashionable man of wit, risk being identified with an attitude that might be thought to be outmoded, larmoyant and – literally – effeminate.

It took a man like Richard Head, who had no Court Wit reputation to lose, to venture to publish such sentiments without the cover of a persona:

It is pity, that *Love*, which is the holiest Passion of the Soul, should meet with so many impious Persons which corrupt it, and, contrary to its own inclinations, make it deserve their designs, by turning natural Love into self-Love, making the Spring head of good, the Original of all our Evil.[10]

So could a poet much respected by Rochester, but without fashionable ambitions. Edmund Waller's *Divine Poems* voice his mental kinship with Artemiza in this respect; man is, he says, 'with love, of all created things the best, / Without it, more pernicious than the rest' (*Canto* IV). When Dryden discourses along similar lines, his spokesman is the noble Almanzor in the second part of *The Conquest of Granada*, who announces (I.i.145–6) that 'Love's a Heroique Passion which can find / No room in any base degenerate mind.'

---

[9] Keith Walker rightly points out that 'gipsy' here means 'a cunning, deceitful, fickle' woman; the *OED* supplies the synonyms 'baggage' and 'hussy'.

[10] From *Proteus Redivivus: or the Art of Wheedling, or INSINUATION* (1675), p. 101.

Artemiza has defined her own position, and the remainder of the poem displays a succession of debased sexual relationships to bear her out. Even Corinna's victim was first taken in not by the charms of her person, but by her sprightly demeanour and 'fine' London talk which dazzled the 'o'regrown Schooleboy'. Like the three young blades in the *Ramble*, he was originally in the business of pretence, too. In other words, Artemiza makes her point clearly and goes on to prove it with energy and panache.

There is another reason why Artemiza does not come across as a personage to be held in derision or contempt, and that is her self-irony. The introductory passage shows us a good-humoured speaker who is able to frame, and quietly enjoy, a joke at her own expense – arguably the most disarming accomplishment of all. Her tone is never strident or self-righteous, even when her criticisms are at their most stringent; but the beginning and conclusion of the poem are especially appealing in their gentle self-mockery.

It is noteworthy that the feminine inconsistency she observes in herself, with rueful amusement, does not involve her innermost personal beliefs. True, her realisation that writing poetry is hazardous in itself, especially for a woman, does not prevent her from doing so. On the contrary, the lurking danger and 'shame' of the undertaking actually whet her appetite for it. But this delight in unbecoming conduct is surely no more than a mischievous desire to go against conventional wisdom, and her 'conviction' does not run very deep. She 'convinc'd' herself, to begin with; and her rationale in so doing was one she later shows she in fact particularly dislikes: deference to public opinion.[11] Besides, she is only writing for Chloe's benefit, and at her request. Even the 1670s found nothing much to object to in women's writing so long as they were not foolish enough to publish.[12]

Consequently, I think Artemiza's standards are solid and explicit enough to serve as a 'norm' of sorts (the use of that term in this context is not entirely appropriate; see p. 140 below). Whether they also represent beliefs held by Rochester the man is impossible to state with any confidence (cf. pp. 237ff. below on the status of the *Satyr* speaker). It seems sufficient to me that this poem, which deals so extensively with

---

[11] According to Vieth, in 'The *Moriae Encomium* as a Model' (p. 18), Artemiza here 'displays the kind of perverseness that we have already seen qualifying the positions of the fine lady and the men of wit' and is later 'intimidated ... by the female automatons who follow fashion in love'. I fail to understand these accusations.

[12] See Jean Elisabeth Gagen, *The New Woman: Her Emergence in English Drama 1600–1730* (New York, 1954), p. 67. See also pp. 130f. below.

male and female fools, never — in my view — supplies any tenable reason for regarding the speaker herself as belonging to the latter category.

Nor do I find Vieth's and Weinbrot's condemnations of Artemiza comprehensible. As far as I can see, she is not in any sense a gossip-monger, as Chloe will have found out to her chagrin. The greater part of her letter is given to presenting examples of the 'ill-bred Customs' she deplored in lines 36–9 and 50–3. There is no suggestion that she takes a different view of them at the end of the fine lady's lengthy discourse. Artemiza, who had to admit that the loquacious lady, flawed as she was, possessed plenty of laudable qualities, finally dismisses her in lines 256–7 with much fainter praise ('some graynes of Sense') than she granted her in previous passages. The idea that Artemiza somehow comes to subscribe to the lady's opinions appears totally unfounded to me.

It is curious that a scholar of Weinbrot's stature should come close to wilful misrepresentation of a Rochester speaker. Vieth, while being less censorious about Artemiza, is at least ungracious in his assessment of her; so is John Harold Wilson. This hostile attitude cannot but make one wonder whether her sex might have something to do with it. It is difficult to avert a suspicion that Artemiza's peculiarly feminine, whimsical humour has failed to communicate itself to these men, all three of them eminent Restoration scholars, and that this accounts for their harshness towards her. Three hundred years after Rochester created her, Artemiza seems in this limited sense to fulfil her own prophecy and stand scorned though she succeeds.[13]

Much critical ingenuity has been devoted to the structure of *Artemiza to Chloe*, and comments on the 'Chinese-boxes' set-up,[14] where one

[13] It must be admitted, however, that the occasional woman critic has also found Artemiza puzzling. To Carole Fabricant, she assumes 'disparate stances' and is 'a figure of ambivalent sentiments'; 'The Writer as Hero and Whore: Rochester's *Letter from Artemisia to Chloe*', *Essays in Literature* 3 (Fall 1976), 152 and 153. See also Doody, *The Daring Muse*, pp. 71–2. But Anne Righter (Barton) appreciates Artemiza's integrity and essential femininity: 'Artemesia herself ... is a kind of seventeenth-century Elizabeth Bennet. Witty and self-aware, both amused and exasperated, she is the sister of Jane Austen's heroines' ('John Wilmot', 55). Another woman critic with a fondness for Artemiza, 'who beguiles us into giving her a hearing', is Reba Wilcoxon; see 'Rochester's Sexual Politics', 143–6. Felicity A. Nussbaum also observes that Artemiza's 'contradictions resemble a knowing irony more than a blundering inability to cope with the lewd town'; this is one of a number of perceptive remarks on the poem in her *The Brink of All We Hate: English Satires on Women, 1660–1750* (Lexington, Ky., 1984), p. 74.

[14] This simile is adapted by Farley-Hills in his book *The Benevolence of Laughter: Comic Poetry of the Commonwealth and Restoration* (London, 1974), p. 178. A somewhat over-ambitious structural model for *Artemiza to Chloe* is proposed by Vieth in 'Toward an Anti-Aristotelian Poetic', 140.

woman describes to another what a third woman has said about a fourth, invariably accompany discussions of Artemiza's status. But if one accepts her position as the argumentative basis of *Artemiza to Chloe*, no elaborate structural devices seem necessary. Artemiza puts forward her view of the state of love in contemporary London life to Chloe. She then proceeds to illustrate it by presenting the personage of the fine lady, who in turn illustrates *her* argument – the greater merit of fools in love – by telling the story of Corinna. That story also reflects on Artemiza's views (see p. 115). To all four women, the subject of love is a major concern; in this, their femininity unites them.

This common interest is of course very differently conceived in the four of them. Chloe, according to Artemiza who should know, is simply keen to have some news about the state of current relationships. Artemiza is saddened by the degeneration of the only good thing in life to the point where it has become a shabby commerce. The fine lady is primarily concerned with the establishing of female hegemony in the sex struggle. To Corinna, the subject is not a matter of contemplation or argumentation, but of survival.

The downfall of love, says Artemiza, has largely been brought about by women; and the fine lady is one of the perpetrators of this crime.[15] She is a heartless creature, dedicated to the pursuit of fashionable status, whose brusque dismissal of her dutiful husband[16] is unpleasantly offset by her gross flirtation with the monkey. Several Rochester critics have noted the *double entendre* in her exclamation 'Oh I could live, and dye with thee'.[17] But the compliments she lavishes on the animal (which Artemiza's detached eyes see for the 'dirty chatt'ring Monster' he is) betray that his main attraction lies in his exotic fashionableness.

Affections are unknown to this grossly affected person; but her own actions and effusions do not exhaust her illustrative function. By having her, and not Artemiza, tell the story of Corinna and her dupe, Rochester

---

[15] The comparison with gaming ('play' in line 51), and crooked gaming at that, shows how deeply the former 'onely blessing' has sunk. Rochester repeatedly refers to gambling in emphasising a censorious attitude. So did several of his contemporaries, notably Etherege and Dryden.

[16] 'Obsequiously' in line 81 will have its old meaning (*OED* 1) of 'compliant with the will or wishes of another, esp. a superior; prompt to serve, please, or follow directions'. Her rudeness could actually be said to be unfashionable; as Dryden's *Marriage A-la-Mode* makes clear, spouses were expected to be very fond in public and indifferent in private. Gwendolen's insistence, in *The Importance of Being Earnest*, that her future husband be affectionate 'especially when there are other people present' thus had the force of tradition behind it.

[17] Line 145 constitutes one of the most obvious verbal echoes from *Marriage A-la-Mode* in *Artemiza to Chloe*; in II.i.17, Melantha sighs, 'Oh Count *Rhodophil*! Ah *mon cher*! I could live and die with him.'

heightens the dramatic efficiency of the lurid narrative. It is a tale of seduction, prostitution, gratuitous cruelty, starvation, corruption, theft and murder – and the unconcerned narrator blithely concludes that 'Fooles' of the kind that Corinna cheated, robbed and killed were made by 'Nature' for the express purpose of 'patch[ing] up Vices, Men of Witt weare out'! Considered against Artemiza's own view of Nature, as the source of healthy inclinations and as co-creator (God and Nature seem interchangeable in lines 147, 150, 154 and 159), the lady's final assumptions are 'impertinent' indeed.

This word, which Artemiza repeatedly applies to the loquacious 'visiter',[18] means 'grotesque' or 'absurd', as editors inform us. 'Impertinent' talkers of both sexes would seem to have been as great scourges during the Restoration as in later ages.[19] But for all the fine lady's shocking insensitivity and ridiculous behaviour, she is not stupid. Anne Righter may exaggerate slightly when arguing that she is 'a fully realized character of some integrity' ('John Wilmot', 55), but it is certainly true that she is no 'mere caricature'. Perhaps the most chilling aspect of her tale of Corinna is that she makes it sound not only true, but rather commonplace. Her narrative style makes the wreck of a country family, after six centuries of placid rural life, as a result of the machinations of a greedy London whore seem no more remarkable than a run-of-the-mill sub-plot in a Restoration comedy. Indeed, she even invests it with a providential dimension.

The reason for her failure to perceive the ethical implications of her story is that her moral sense has been wiped out by her exclusive commitment to the standpoint that fools were created for the material convenience of women. Her contempt of folly extends not only to 'kind-keeping Fooles' such as Corinna's victim; she has no mercy on his wife and child(ren) either, precisely because they come of the same 'Booby-breede' as he. The ruin of his legitimate offspring is commented on in the complacent couplet:

> And as the Race of such an Owle deserves,
> His owne dull lawful progeny he starves.

[18] Dryden's Melantha in *Marriage A-la-Mode* is at one point described as 'the most eternal Visiter of the Town' (I.i.190). Hannah Woolley's *The Gentlewoman's Companion*; *Or, a Guide to the Female Sex* (London, 1675), shows us just how appallingly the fine lady behaves: 'When you enter into a Room by way of a Visit, avoid the indiscretion and vanity of a bold entrance without Ceremony, but do it quietly and civilly. And when you come near the person you would salute, make your Complement, and render your Devoir modestly, and with some gravity, shunning all bawling noise or obstreperousness' (p. 49).

[19] See, for instance, Samuel Butler's *Character* of an 'Impertinent', p. 282 in Charles W. Daves' edition of *Samuel Butler 1612–1680 Characters* (Cleveland and London, 1970).

This woman, to whom Artemiza in all fairness ascribes 'a discerning Witt', thus despises stupidity wherever it occurs while warning women to steer clear of intelligent men. The rational basis of this seeming paradox is provided by the fine lady's complete absorption in materialistic considerations and her dedication to fashion.

Another paradoxical element in *Artemiza to Chloe* is found in the function of the Corinna story. As was pointed out above, it serves to illustrate two opposing viewpoints – the fine lady's and Artemiza's.

To start with the former's point of view, the vicissitudes of Corinna's life bear out her contention that women should not have anything to do with clever men, but that if they have, fools serve to remedy the unfortunate consequences. Corinna has 'run / Through all the severall Wayes of being undone', but in fact she has only been 'ruined' twice: first, when she was 'Couzen'd … by Love' – that is, seduced by someone she liked and trusted –, and second, when she gave up her profitable career as a prostitute to 'doate upon a Man of Witt'. The disastrousness of that commitment does not only consist in its brevity; the fickleness of witty men was a stock notion in the Restoration. What led to everyone's scorning her was his 'ill-natur'd Jest', that is, the cruel public taunts with which he disengaged himself from her. If he had simply tired of her and palmed her off on somebody else, things would only have been back to where they were before she met him. Her great misfortune is that he makes a fool of her in public and thus effectively cuts her off from subsequent employment by any man who cares about his reputation. The implications of the word 'Jest' are brought out in *The Man of Mode* by Dorimant's answer to Young Bellair's 'I cou'd find it in my heart to resolve not to marry at all':

Fie, fie, that would spoil a good jeast, and disappoint the well-natur'd Town of an occasion of laughing at you. (Etherege, *The Man of Mode*, I.i.459–61)[20]

The connexion between an 'ill-natur'd Jest' and the condition – abhorred by fashionable Restoration Londoners like no other – of being a laughing-stock is hinted at in two lines from Rochester himself; they occur in the prologue to Settle's *The Empress of Morocco*:

> You Men would think it an ilnatur'd Jest,
> Should we laugh at you when you did your best.
>
> (lines 7–8)

---

[20] P. 34 in John Conaghan's 1973 edition (Edinburgh). Incidentally, Dorimant's ridding himself of Loveit is no gentlemanly performance either.

It should be noted that the fine lady, whose polemical purposes require her to be Corinna's supporter throughout, does not ascribe her falling in love with a man of wit to a lack of judgement on the young whore's part. It would not do to have Corinna appear stupid; hence the blame is put where it can do no harm to the narrator's principles, on 'Fate, or [Corinna's] ill Angell'.

What makes Corinna's misfortunes a potentially sensitive issue to Artemiza is that they were the result of her twice yielding to the 'Passion Love'. As long as she ran her affairs on a business footing, she did very well out of them. This may be one of the reasons why Artemiza has to acknowledge that there are 'some graynes of Sense' in the fine lady's torrents of talk.

Of course, Artemiza could defend her own commitment to feelings in love by pointing out that Corinna's affections were bestowed on two men who did not reciprocate in kind. Her original seducer hardly qualified as a harbourer of emotions that could be described as 'The softest refuge Innocence can fynde, / The safe directour of unguided youth', nor did her subsequent abuser feel any 'gen'rous passion' towards her. The fact that Corinna loved the wrong men could be said to reflect more unfavourably on her than on love itself. Still, Artemiza's grudging acknowledgement that there is something in what the lady says, and the sheer scope that Corinna's adventures are given in the letter, suggest that she cannot dismiss the other woman's description of the havoc caused by amorous love out of hand. This may be held to weaken her stance; but it could also be regarded as evidence of Artemiza's fair-mindedness, in which case it supports rather than undermines her trustworthiness. Whichever view one takes of this, the skill with which Rochester brings out the conflicting values of the two women speakers by providing the Corinna test case is surely remarkable.

Even if Corinna's changing fates might make Artemiza concede that the 'Passion Love' is not without its perils, she could counter that Corinna's sufferings are to a great extent due to that power of the 'publicke Voyce' which Artemiza detests. Before the 'Man of Witt' exposed her to public ridicule, she had been a pampered society pet, and her brief love affair with an intelligent man would not in itself diminish those attractions which the fine lady so eloquently expresses in lines 193–6. It was public opinion, brutally turned against her by her inconstant lover, that reduced her to a 'Memento Mori' practically overnight.

That lesson is not lost on Corinna, who after a wretched winter of discontent stakes her last half crown on retrieving her fortunes. She does so by seducing a country bumpkin, whose fresh arrival in town guarantees that he knows nothing of her disgrace. The effect of London on such youths as he is graphically described in the one line 'Turnes Sparke, learnes to be lewd, and is undone'. It was a standard fate of rural 'young Masters'; a contemporary guide to polite society describes it in the following terms:

A third sort is a Company of raw mopish youths, who come to town burthen'd with the wary precepts of their Parents, who having a little breath'd the freedom of the Town make a loose into all manner of vanity and debaucheries.[21]

Restoration comedy supplies plenty of examples of the same phenomenon. The cheating of rural oafs (of all ages and both sexes) by slick London performers was a stage convention for decades.

Corinna is smart enough to present this poor fool with the dual attraction of a dashing London creature who pretends to admire his bucolic virtues. The fine lady's account of this shameless and desperate deception is marvellously contrived:

> This o'regrowne Schooleboy lost-Corinna wins,
> And att first dash, to make an Asse, begins:
> Pretends, to like a Man, who has not knowne
> The Vanityes, nor Vices of the Towne,
> Fresh in his youth, and faithfull in his Love,
> Eager of Joyes, which he does seldome prove,
> Healthfull, and strong, he does noe paynes endure,
> But what the Fayre One, he adores, can cure.
> Gratefull for favours does the Sexe esteeme,
> And libells none, for being kind to him.
> Then of the Lewdnesse of the tymes complaines,
> Rayles att the Witts, and Atheists, and mainteynes,
> 'Tis better, then good Sense, then pow'r, or Wealth,
> To have a love untainted, youth, and health.
> The unbred puppy, who had never seene
> A Creature looke soe gay, or talke soe fine,
> Beleaves, then falls in Love, and then in Debt...[22]

---

[21] *The Art of Complaisance, or the Means to oblige in Conversation* (London, 1673), pp. 72–3.

[22] Like David Brooks (p. 125 in his edition of Rochester's lyrics and satires), I take the verbs 'complaines', 'Rayles' and 'mainteynes' to refer to Corinna, like 'Pretends' in line 228. They seem to form part of the 'fine talk' mentioned in line 241. The word 'then' in line 236 also supports this reading. Lines 234–5 clearly refer to the young fool. Vieth's punctuation, with a series of semi-colons, creates some confusion regarding the subjects in this passage.

No wonder the lady approves of Corinna's deft touch; the latter certainly turns her bitter experiences to good use. She does not grant her favours often enough for their allure to pall, having learnt the hard way that generosity is bad policy. The irony of this 'diseas'd, decay'd' and half-starved prostitute praising her swain's 'faithfull Love' (he grossly deceives his country wife) and 'health', pretending not to care about 'pow'r, or Wealth', and complaining of the 'Lewdnesse of the tymes' would have delighted a Restoration playhouse audience. Here, as in *Tunbridge Wells*, Rochester shows his dramatic skill in a miniature 'scene' as memorable as any composed by 'refin'd Etheridge' or 'Slow Witcherley'.

It is hard to imagine that such an audience would condone homicide, however, and yet the fine lady implicitly sets the seal of her approval on Corinna's final manoeuvre. When the poor young man's infatuation is at its height, the narrator seems to agree that ' 'Tis tyme, to poyson him '. Corinna has no intention of being abandoned again and takes care that it will not happen. Like the women poisoners Juvenal abhorred, she murders in cold blood ('*illam ego non tulerim, quae cõputat, & scelus ingens / Sana facit*', Satire 6, lines 651–2; quoted from the de Luyne edition, with a French translation by M. de Marolles, of *D. Junii Juvenalis et Auli Persii Flacci Satyrae* (Paris, 1671), p. 83).

It is Corinna, not Artemiza, who accounts for the element of successive vitiation in *Artemiza to Chloe*. Her amorous career begins with an error of judgement and ends in murder for gain. While the amoral fine lady appreciates the outcome of the story, I can find no evidence that it is in any way palatable to Artemiza. Her concluding assurance that her next letter, joined with the present one, will fill a volume of tales 'As true, as Heaven, more infamous, then Hell' may be hyperbolic; but the tale of Corinna has its share both of truth and of infamy, and I see no reason to believe that Artemiza is indifferent to the fact.

Dustin Griffin, who like David Farley-Hills has many important things to say about *Artemiza to Chloe*, argues that 'while Artemisia is concerned with the practice of love, the fine lady, more remote from experience, asks about the theory of love' (*Satires Against Man*, p. 144). It seems to me that both Artemiza and her counterpart are concerned with theory as well as with practice, but that both basically argue in favour of a principle and are 'theorists' to that extent. The 'practical' element is provided by the Corinna story. I have tried to show how this piece of merciless reality reflects on the attitudes and beliefs of both women speakers in the poem. Jeremy Treglown has remarked that most of Rochester's satires have an 'air of hectic improvisation'; *Artemiza to Chloe*, however, again in Treglown's words, possesses 'distancing devices of voice within voice and story within story'.[23] An attempt to imagine the Corinna tale told by Artemiza herself on the basis of her own observations indicates the degree to which the poem's success is indebted to this 'voice within voice' structure.

WIT, FOLLY AND SEXUAL POLITICS IN *ARTEMIZA TO CHLOE*

In her praise of natural impulses, and her regret at seeing them ousted by man-made scourges, Artemiza resembles the speaker in the *Satyr* (see p. 108 above). It says something about the subtlety with which the conflict of values is handled in *Artemiza to Chloe* that Artemiza's counterpart, the fine lady, also deplores pursuits attacked in the *Satyr against Reason and Mankind*. Her reasons, of course, differ a great deal from those of Artemiza and the *Satyr* speaker. *Their* concern is with the quality of pleasure and – to a limited extent – with personal integrity; *her* guiding principle is the cementing of female superiority and control.

It is against that background that her animosity against wit, knowledge and reason – qualities also maligned in the *Satyr* – should be contemplated. The *Satyr* speaker regrets their interference with the operations of the senses, which entails the corruption of sensual pleasure as well as of clear judgement (see pp. 193ff. below). His chief accusation against them is that they make men deceive themselves; the fine lady disapproves of them because they prevent women from deceiving men. She does not dispute that cognitive effort brings reliable insights, but she insists that everybody would be much better off without them. To her, reason is a 'glaring light', not an *ignis fatuus*; but it is far more pleasant for everyone to dwell in semi-darkness.

Much of the Artemiza/fine-lady opposition actually turns on their different conceptions of wit and folly. Both women regard both qualities as means by which human beings work their weal or woe. For neither of them, however, do wit and folly constitute absolute standards – they are always subjugated by a ruling principle.

To Artemiza – and here, again, she comes close to the *Satyr* speaker – wit is a corruptible human capability which ultimately has little to do with happiness or moral worth. She gently mocks the 'Men of Witt'

---

[23] '"He knew my style"', p. 84.

who risk their reputations in the notoriously perilous waters of public writing, as dangerous in their way as 'doubts boundless Sea'. The degree to which wit has become a social norm is implied in line 64. Here, Artemiza complains that female fashion worshippers will not admire or approve – spontaneous, outward-going feelings – because ''tis below witt'. But the most interesting use of the word in Artemiza's own discourse is found in lines 151 and 164, where she grants that her *bête noire* was born with a fair measure of intelligence and has used it in order to amass considerable knowledge. The fine lady is, in her view, a fascinating mixture of wit and folly. Both ingredients would seem to have been congenital, which makes Artemiza wonder what Nature, which she herself places above human efforts and ambitions, might have 'meant / When this mixt thinge into the World shee sent'. However, the fine lady has used her wit and 'Sense' to compound her folly. Nature, says Artemiza, is not responsible for the worst excesses of human foolishness; they are the result of misapplied intelligence.[24] Like the satirical observers in the *Satyr* and *Upon Nothing*, she distrusts and despises formal learning, another characteristic that aligns her with other Rochester speakers and makes it hard to conceive of her as an object of satiric scorn.

Like Artemiza, the fine lady uses 'wit' and 'sense' to mean 'intelligence, perspicacity and common sense'. The chief usefulness of her kind of wit is that nobody can deceive you if you have it. Fools, in her book, are too obtuse to see through the tricks played on them; and by aspiring to the high social status of men of wit without being clever enough to play that risky game, they lay themselves open to exploitation, too. Indirectly, then, she and Artemiza would agree that the ambition to keep one's end up in polite society is ruinous to those deficient in wit. But while Artemiza shows no animosity against people who are simply stupid (she grants that even they glory in true love), the fine lady sees their worldly misfortunes as no more than their due. Her amorality is in evidence throughout, whereas Artemiza's strictures on folly are reserved for those who actively corrupt themselves, either by sacrificing Nature for Fashion or by warping their minds with learning.

The fine lady proves her 'discerning Witt' by an unanswerable accusation directed at male fools: their vanity and conceit contribute

---

[24] As Pinto states (*Enthusiast in Wit*, p. 124), this point is made by Dryden as well, in his Epilogue to *The Man of Mode*. In fact, it is also expressed by Etherege himself in Medley's comment on Sir Fopling Flutter: 'He is like many others, beholding to his Education for making him so eminent a Coxcomb; many a Fool had been lost to the World, had their indulgent Parents wisely bestow'd neither Learning nor good breeding on 'em' (i.i.363–6 in Conaghan's edition).

very much to their undoing. It is not only sheer stupidity that makes them unable to see through smart women's wiles; they have such a good opinion of themselves that they are only too ready to believe the most outrageous flatteries. The lady's sneer has a cutting edge:

> But the kinde easy Foole apt, to admire
> Himselfe, trusts us, his Follyes all conspire,
> To flatter his, and favour Our desire.
> Vaine of his proper Meritt he with ease
> Beleaves, wee love him best, who best can please.
> On him Our grosse dull common Flatt'ries passe,
> Ever most Joyfull, when most made an Asse.
> Heavy, to apprehend, though all Mankinde
> Perceave Us false, the Fopp concern'd is blinde,
> Who doating on himselfe,
> Thinkes ev'ry one, that sees him, of his mynde.

The recurrence of the word 'admire' in line 124 is a masterstroke on the poet's part. On two previous occasions it concluded end-stopped lines (64 and 107) and denoted a feeling for others; the enjambment in lines 124–5 makes its application in this context of self-love especially effective.

But even if we, and Artemiza, are prepared to concede that the lady has a valid point here, that admission is quickly undercut by the realisation that the same accusation could be turned against herself. As Artemiza says, she knows 'Ev'ry ones fault, and meritt, but her owne'. Her vanity is of enormous proportions. For hours on end, this loud-mouthed and garrulous woman completely dominates the gathering. On her arrival, she pours out questions but never waits for an answer, being more concerned with upholding her own opinion than with taking in the opinions of others.[25] Her clumsy attempts at self-exculpation in the matter of her appearance bear testimony to the want of 'discretion' (see p. 128 below) Artemiza finds in her.

For someone as devoted to fashion as the fine lady, it might seem illogical to attack the great trend-setters in society, the men of wit. But it should be remembered that this grotesque female pseudo-wit does not challenge the social status of these men: it is 'in Love' that they should be avoided. Love, to her, is nothing more than a battle for power[26] in

---

[25] In this respect, too, she resembles Dryden's Melantha in *Marriage A-la-Mode*; see p. 129 below. David Sheehan is surely right in insisting that Artemiza's attack on her is unambiguous (pp. 304–6 in Vieth's *Critical Essays*).   [26] Cf. Wilcoxon, 'Rochester's Sexual Politics', 146.

which – in the words of a present-day American politician – 'you're either doing it to them or they're doing it to you'.

One of the parallels between the fine lady and Artemiza – parallels that also serve to point up the contrasts between them – is the low opinion they have of their own sex. Artemiza, of course, argues that her 'silly Sexe' was chiefly responsible for the lovelessness that characterises polite society. The fine lady makes no bones about admitting that women are the repositories of 'frailtyes, Arts' and so on, though to her those terms have no real meaning.

Artemiza is, if we are ready to take her word for it, truly grieved by this state of affairs; she claims that it vexes her woman's heart. The fine lady does not care what defects a woman might have, so long as she is not stupid but uses her female weapons to advantage in the Restoration sex war, a subject that calls for separate discussion.

Artemiza has frequently been referred to as the fine lady's 'counterpart' in this discussion of *Artemiza to Chloe*. If the scope for comparison is widened to include the entire Rochester canon, however, it could be argued that the latter's opposite number is found in the *Song* beginning 'Love a *Woman*! y'are an *Ass*' (see pp. 23ff. above). The cynical male speaker of this poem goes even further than the fine lady; not content with asserting the supremacy of his sex over the other, he declares himself ready to dispense with women altogether. If you do not care about having offspring ('To get supplies for Age, and Graves', something only the lower classes need to depend on), a woman is of no use at all. Sexual satisfaction is better supplied by a nimble page-boy than by '*Forty Wenches*', a point Juvenal had also made in his sixth Satire (lines 33–4). In any case, the best things in life exist independently of women.

This Rochester speaker's point of view was not unique in seventeenth-century England. In the 1680s, the misogynist satirist Robert Gould expressed relief at divesting oneself of a tiresome wife in similar terms. Once free of her, the long-suffering husband was able to

> Enjoy your *Book*, your *Bottle*, and your *Friend*
> Three of as choice companions Heav'n can send.[27]

The *Fragment of a Satire on Men* ('What vaine unnecessary things are men') experiments with a similar attitude on the part of women.

[27] Quoted in Eugene Hulse Sloane, *Robert Gould Seventeenth-Century Satirist* (Philadelphia, 1940), p. 95.

Rochester's *œuvre* thus covers both extremes in the battle of the sexes
and plenty of ground between them. An inquiry into the reasons for –
and significance of – this divergence must take the Restoration background, historical as well as literary, into account.

From a purely quantitative point of view, most of the Rochester
passages where 'love' and 'heart' occur combine professions of
admiration with intimations of sexual ambitions, the latter tending to
overshadow the former. In some cases, not even a shade of the amorous
passion outlined by Artemiza is evoked by 'love'. No instance of the
word is more sharply distinct from that emotion than lines 13–16 in
'Love a *Woman*! y'are an *Ass*', where it is stripped of any emotional and
heterosexual significance. A mere physical craving, it is easily satisfied
by a boy who commands certain skills. Also, it is merely an occasional
interruption of the chief employment, 'Drinking, to engender *Wit*'.

In giving predominantly sexual overtones to 'love', Rochester
conformed to Restoration practice. Not only the Court Wits regarded
love mainly as a physical matter.[28] In the latter part of the seventeenth
century, the upper classes generally despised ardent devotion and
regarded love as a matter of sensual appetite which should preferably be
gratified with a minimum of fuss and inconvenience.[29] And yet those
who professed such views were inordinately preoccupied with this
ostensibly uncomplicated business; obviously, 'love in the Enlightenment was not as simple as it seemed'.[30] The range of connotations
adhering to 'love' and 'heart' in Rochester's poetry constitutes evidence
of its complexity.

Artemiza to Chloe bears witness to the obsession with love/gallantry
described by Morton Hunt. As we have seen, all four women involved
in the poem have an interest and/or a stake in what Etherege's Lady
Cockwood called 'the great business of this town'.[31] On her arrival,
immediately after her apologetic remarks on the ravages that country
life has worked on her appearance, the fine lady inquires, 'How is Love
govern'd? Love, that rules the State … ?'

These questions at once sum up the importance of sexual intrigue in
Restoration London and the way such matters were regarded – as
manifestations of power ('govern'd', 'rules'). It is not surprising that
Kate Millett's term 'sexual politics' has been applied to Rochester's

---

[28] On the love poetry of these men, see J. H. Wilson, *Court Wits*, pp. 85–108.
[29] See Morton M. Hunt, *The Natural History of Love* (New York, 1959), p. 256.
[30] *Ibid.*, p. 256.
[31] *She Would if She Could*, v.i; p. 233 in Verity's 1888 edition of the *Works* of Etherege.

poems. From the youthful pastoral efforts to the lampoons of the late 1670s, his love poetry is forever concerned with power-structured relationships, men and women controlling, influencing and dominating one another.

In asserting that love 'rules the State', the fine lady is echoing a view expressed in Rochester's satire on Charles II:

> Nor are his high Desires above his Strength,
> His Sceptter and his Prick are of a Length,
> And she may sway the one, who plays with th'other...

This may not in fact have been true, but people believed it at the time and took considerable pains to curry favour with the Royal mistresses. If they did not wield much political power, the King's easy-going temperament certainly made them useful advocates for anyone seeking advancement.

In Rochester's poetry, intimations of worldly power in connexion with sexual relationships are thus a feature based on amorous activities in Court circles. It is interesting to note the high frequency of 'power language' in the love poems. Mistresses, actual and would-be, have conquering eyes or are 'Love's citadels'; their admirers are slaves in chains or vassals; and the ladies themselves form the battle-ground of the two great combatants, Love and Honour. There is much talk of vanquishing, submission and tyranny. Is there any evidence that Rochester 'rejects enslavement of either of the sexes', as Reba Wilcoxon claims,[32] and that – consciously or not – he regarded sexual equality as an ideal?

While the poems supply examples of men chafing at the bonds their lust imposes on them, they also contain ecstatic passages on the glories of amorous slavery. I have found nothing to suggest that Rochester was in any way interested in, let alone committed to, the notion of sexual equality. The instances where reciprocal affection, allied to sensual pleasure, is implied have less to do with the rejection of male or female dominance than with the indivisible harmony that is a feature of perfect love (as portrayed in the opening stanzas of *The Fall*). Those who enjoy such raptures certainly represent an 'ideal' where '"power *over* others" ...no longer exists' (Wilcoxon summarising Millett, 'Rochester's Sexual Politics', 137). The sad and significant fact is that nobody is ever seen to do so. Adam and Eve did, according to the speaker of *The Fall*;

---

[32] 'Rochester's Sexual Politics', 137.

so did lovers of past, less depraved times, if we are to believe Artemiza. But Rochester's poems never celebrate the actual achievement of true concord in love, and it is difficult to see the above-mentioned 'ideal' as a 'persistent theme' (Wilcoxon's terms).

It would have been remarkable if Rochester had – deliberately or not – been a supporter of sexual equality. Even Restoration feminists would not usually demand the implementation of schemes to promote full equality with men.[33] (One champion of women's rights who did just that was a man, and a Frenchman: regarded against the background of seventeenth-century attitudes towards women, Poulain de la Barre's *De l'égalité des deux sexes, discours physique et moral où l'on voit l'importance de se défaire des préjugéz*, published in Paris in 1673, is one of the most radical feminist tracts ever printed.[34]) The main concern of such pioneers as Bathsua Makin and Hannah Woolley was to improve the education of women.[35] The view that women were indeed 'the idlest/silliest/dullest part of *Gods Creation*'[36] was in no way extreme; Makin, Woolley and somewhat later Mary Astell saw that poor educational opportunities and a lack of stimulating occupation were to blame. Joachim Heinrich laconically summarised the position of aristocratic women in the latter half of the seventeenth century in the following words: 'Die Frau galt besonders in den adligen Kreisen als ein Spielzeug für die Männer, als ein Werkzeug für die Befriedigung der sinnlichen Leidenschaften' (*Die Frauenfrage*, p. 55). She was given very little chance to develop beyond those functions. Nor were conditions much improved when, several

---

[33]   See, for instance, Robert H. Michel, 'English Attitudes towards Women', 36.

[34]   It appeared in an English translation in 1677, *The Woman as Good as the Man: Or, the Equality of Both Sexes*. On Poulain's audacity and wide-ranging social thought, see Michael A. Seidel, 'Poulain de la Barre's *The Woman as Good as the Man*', *Journal of the History of Ideas* 35.3 (July–September 1974), 499–508. It should be added that one Englishman did claim full equality for women in the 1670s – William Ram(e)sey in *The Gentleman's Companion* (1672).

[35]   The many excellent recent studies of women in the seventeenth century – such as Antonia Fraser's *The Weaker Vessel* (New York, 1984), Sara Heller Mendelson's *The Mental World of Stuart Women: Three Studies* (Brighton, 1987) and Smith's *Reason's Disciples* – should not obscure the fact that fine scholarly studies were written earlier in this century, too. One of them is Gagen's *The New Woman*; another is Doris Mary Stenton's *The English Woman in History* (London and New York, 1957). Myra Reynolds' *The Learned Lady in England, 1650–1760* (New York, 1920) is a pioneering work of enduring value. For bibliographical purposes, Joachim Heinrich's admirable *Die Frauenfrage bei Steele und Addison: Eine Untersuchung zur englischen Literatur- und Kulturgeschichte im 17./18. Jahrhundert* (Leipzig, 1930; the volume is no. 168 in the Palaestra series) remains indispensable. Historians and demographers such as Lawrence Stone, Keith Thomas, Alan Macfarlane and Peter Laslett have made magnificent contributions to this field of study.

[36]   Of these three options regarding line 4 in 'Love a *Woman*! y'are an *Ass*', Walker favours the first and Vieth the second. Many Restoration gentlemen would wholeheartedly agree with them all.

decades after Rochester's death, the young Lady Mary Wortley Montagu wrote to the ageing Bishop Burnet complaining that lack of schooling and total concentration on their appearance made upper-class women 'the most useless and most worthless part of the creation'. As if this were not enough, 'a learned woman' would be despised as 'a talking, impertinent, vain, and conceited creature' (see Heinrich, *Die Frauenfrage*, p. 82). One wonders whether the recipient of this lament remembered certain features in Rochester's poems.

One of the best-known works that reflect the condition of nobly born women in the late seventeenth century is *The Lady's New Year's Gift: or, Advice to a Daughter* by George Savile, Marquess of Halifax (1688 and many subsequent editions). It constitutes a set of rules for decent female conduct, especially in marriage, which proceeds from the 'Inequality in the Sexes' as an established fact. The book was published eight years after Rochester's death, but – as Sarah Wintle points out – it was written by the elder brother of Rochester's best friend,[37] and its precepts are thus presumably of some relevance to values held in the poet's circle. Halifax was no bigot; on the contrary, his temperate character earned him a nickname that has survived through the centuries, 'the Trimmer'.[38] Even so, his instructions to a marriageable daughter (for whom he felt great affection) are hard to stomach for a modern reader. She must at all times serve and obey her husband; even his infidelities must be borne with 'Discretion and Silence', cardinal virtues according to Halifax (see below). 'Vanity, Affectation, and Impertinence' are faults to which women are prone; his daughter must do her best to eschew them.

By way of consolation, Halifax reminds the girl that she, as a woman, is able to exert greater power through her eyes than men can do through their laws. The idea that women rule by means of their beauty and charm was a traditional one (cf. lines 143ff. in Juvenal's sixth satire). Even some feminists subscribed to it and accepted that middle age put an end to women's opportunities in this line. Rochester's Timon speaks of '*Age, Beauties* incurable Disease', and the *carpe diem* lyrics of the Court Wits are liberally sprinkled with dark hints that this disorder may soon be in evidence.

As Harold F. Brooks has shown, the 'battle of sex' and 'the conflict of true wit and good breeding against the pretence of them or the want

---

[37] See 'Libertinism', pp. 138–40.
[38] On the life and times of Halifax, see H. C. Foxcroft, *A Character of the Trimmer: Being a Short Life of the First Marquis of Halifax* (Cambridge, 1946).

of them'[39] dwell at the core of Restoration comedy. Both are present in *Artemiza to Chloe* and in several other Rochester poems as well. More than that, they are actually interwoven. Not only does the fine lady claim that fools are better keepers and husbands than men of wit; even Artemiza adopts the language of power when speaking of the folly of women in relinquishing the sovereign liberty that is their birthright – 'Our silly Sexe, ... borne, like Monarchs, free.'

Rochester often overturns conventions; there are plenty of examples in this book. However, I can find no support for Wilcoxon's idea that he deliberately rejected the dominance of either sex in amorous matters. This would involve a very marked defiance of customary Restoration views on the relations between the sexes, and when Rochester is being defiant one does not usually have to look very hard for signs of it. On the other hand, Sarah Wintle's suggestion that Rochester's libertinism led him to consider the point of view of female as well as male libertines is well supported by her argumentation. Wintle maintains that such considerations caused Rochester to 'confront problems that lurked underneath everyday prejudice' ('Libertinism', p. 134) and that the result is an element of imbalance and uncertainty. This line of reasoning allows her to make several important observations (see especially p. 148). Wintle's view does not require Rochester to step out of the sex-battle paradigm altogether; it merely involves a certain amount of probing within it.

One 'problematic implication' (Wintle's term) is articulated in the fragment beginning 'What vaine unnecessary things are men' – the idea that it is perfectly possible to manage without the other sex. Even sexual satisfaction can be had without recourse to men; but, as the woman speaker wryly admits, that works both ways:

> Besides the Beastly men wee dayly see
> Can Please themselves alone as well as wee[.]

Whatever the substitute, dildo, page boy or thumb, Rochester's poetry hence more than once suggests that heterosexual intercourse is an expendable business.

It is no accident that both Vieth and Walker place this fragment next

---

[39] 'Principal Conflicts in the Restoration Comedy of Manners: The Battle of Sex, and Truewits v. Witwouds and Lackwits', *The Durham University Journal* 80.2 (n.s. 49.2; June 1988), 210–12. See also Wilkinson's dissertation, especially the second part, which offers plenty of informative discussions and illustrative examples regarding these conflicts.

to *Artemiza to Chloe* in their editions of Rochester's poems.[40] Lines 3–20 emphasise the depth of humiliation to which women have fallen in 'This ill bred age':

> Whence comes that meane submissivness wee finde
> This ill bred age has wrought on womankinde
> Fall'n from the rights their sex and beautyes gave
> To make men wish despaire and humbly crave
> Now 'twill suffice if they vouchsafe to have,
> To the pell Mell, Playhous and the drawing roome
> Their Woemen Fayres, these Woemen Coursers come
> To chaffer, chuse and ride theire bargaines home,
> Att the appearance of an unknown face
> Up steps the Arrogant pretending ass
> Pulling by th'elbow his companion Huff
> Cryes Looke, de God that wench is well enough
> Faire and well shap't, good lipps and teeth 'twill doe
> Shee shall bee Tawdry for a month or two
> Att my expence, bee rude and take upon her
> Shew her contempt of quallity and honour
> And with the generall fate of errant Woman
> Bee very proude awhile, then very Common...

The comparison to horse-market trading is a demeaning one for women and men alike. This woman speaker does not overtly blame the former for their 'meane submissivness', but she does imply that at least part of their degradation is of their own doing.

This implicit accusation is contained in the speech of the 'Arrogant pretending ass'. The young woman of his choice will respond to her elevation by putting on airs, becoming an arrogant pretender in her turn. The last four lines quoted above constitute one of the many passages in Rochester's poetry where vainglorious pretence is followed by ruin or, in other words, pride comes before a fall. If 'womankinde' had been invulnerable to this Rochesterian arch-vice, its members might still have exercised 'the rights their sex and beautyes gave'.

A characteristic which would have prevented such deplorable behaviour as showing 'contempt of quallity and honour' is the one that was so highly praised by all writers of seventeenth-century conduct manuals, discretion. Halifax, as we saw, placed it beside 'Silence' as one of the chief qualities of a good woman, and the praise of 'discreet' ladies

---

[40] In *Enthusiast in Wit*, Pinto pointed out that it 'is in a very similar vein to Artemisa's letter. Here again a woman is supposed to be the speaker and here again bitter contempt of men is the main theme' (p. 127).

was a standard feature in those books and pamphlets that purported to raise the status of women. In *The Man of Mode*, the unaffected modesty and good sense of Emilia are reluctantly acknowledged by Medley and Dorimant, the latter allowing that she is 'a discreet Maid', adding, 'I believe nothing can corrupt her but a Husband.'[41]

No wonder men who were out to make easy conquests were greatly annoyed when they found this characteristic in a would-be mistress. In the *Mistress* poem called 'Discretion', Cowley exclaimed:

> *Discreet?* what means this word *Discreet?*
> A Curse on all *Discretion!*
> This *barbarous term* you will not meet
> In all *Loves-Lexicon.*

Dorset, in a poem as dominated by sexual politics as any Rochester lyric, expressed a lover's disgust with this impediment to his ambitions in the following stanza:

> My love is full of noble pride
> And never will submit
> To let that fop, discretion, ride
> In triumph over it.[42]

Clearly, discretion meant something more to the seventeenth century than it does today. Nowadays, it stands for little more than prudence in discourse. The definition in the *OED* (III.6) suggests a wider applicability – 'ability to discern or distinguish what is right, befitting, or advisable, esp. as regards one's own conduct or action'.[43]

It is this much-vaunted ability to exercise good judgement and suit one's words and actions to the occasion that is lacking in the fine lady, according to Artemiza. The implications of that defect are far more serious than a present-day reader of lines 167–8 may assume. In stating that the lady has everything except discretion, Artemiza confirms that her natural wit and acquired learning are, in practice, of no value to her or anyone else. In fact, they have combined to make a fool of her.

The fine lady is also conspicuously deficient in that other great virtue

---

[41] 1.i.414–20. Discretion was a quality valued in men, too. In 1669, the English ambassador in France, Ralph Montague, wrote to Arlington recommending that Rochester be allowed to return to England (this was after the Killigrew ear-boxing rumpus). The ambassador said that 'If hereafter he continues to live as discreetly as he has done ever since he was here, he has other good qualities enough ... to make him acceptable wherever he comes' (see Pinto, *Enthusiast in Wit*, p. 72).

[42] *The Advice* ('Phyllis, for shame let us improve'), p. 77 in Harris' edition of Dorset's poetry.

[43] Keith Walker quotes illuminating passages on 'discretion' from Hobbes' *Leviathan* in his comment on line 168 in *Artemiza to Chloe* (p. 280 in Walker's edition).

which women should cultivate, according to Halifax, namely silence. Even the poets of antiquity complained of garrulous women; the indefatigable nag was a stock figure in mediaeval literature; Jonson's *Epicoene, or The Silent Woman* (acted on the Restoration stage) made comedy out of a man's horror of loquacious females; and seventeenth-century writers on good manners never tired of exhorting women to curb their unfortunate tendency to gabble.[44] Richard Flecknoe's *Character* of 'a Talkative Lady' gave her listener 'a dayes *Head-ache* just as soon as [he got] into her company', and Richard Allestree's *The Ladies Calling* (1673) regretted the growing use of profanities by women. The verbosity of the fine lady was thus a familiar phenomenon in polite Restoration society. Whether she herself was meant to recall one particular Restoration woman, whose contemporaries testified to her garrulity and verbal coarseness, will be considered in the following section.

WOMAN SCHOLAR AND WOMAN POET

Previous Rochester critics have noted the striking similarities between the fine lady's discourse and that of the ridiculously affected Melantha in Dryden's *Marriage A-la-Mode*, which was of course dedicated to Rochester. Melantha is extremely fond of French expressions; she actually uses the word 'embarrass' and praises it as being 'a delicious *French* word' (cf. line 98 in *Artemiza to Chloe*). 'Let me die' is one of her favourite phrases in English. Like the fine lady, Melantha does not wait for answers to her questions; her future husband, overwhelmed by her ceaseless prattling, glumly concludes that he will have to 'kiss all night, in [his] own defence, and hold her down ... and give her the rising blow every time she begins to speak'.[45]

Beyond these resemblances, however, Melantha and the fine lady have little in common. The former is a city lady determined to climb in society; the latter is the wife of a country squire (Rochester cannot resist aiming a kick at his detested 'Knights'). The most important differences between the two women, however, are found in the fine lady's polemical purpose and the fact that she has

> turn'd o're
> As many Bookes, as Men, lov'd much, reade more ...

[44] On silence being urged on women, see Jerome Nadelhaft, 'The Englishwoman's Sexual Civil War: Feminist Attitudes towards Men, Women, and Marriage 1650–1740', *Journal of the History of Ideas* 43.4 (October–December 1982), 565–6.

[45] II.i.88–90 in the 1978 University of California Press edition (vol. XI of *The Works of John Dryden*), p. 245.

In other words, she is one of a rare species in Restoration England – a learned lady.

As was to be expected at a time when women's education was so poor that many well-born ladies were barely literate, a woman scholar was a prodigy, and not one that commanded much respect or admiration. Myra Reynolds and J. E. Gagen have shown how the learned lady came to be a stock comic figure in late-seventeenth-century drama, partly due to the influence of Molière's *Les Femmes savantes*, first acted in 1672. Most people in the Restoration years, women as well as men, would have replied in the negative to the question contained in the subtitle of the great Dutchwoman Anna Maria van Schurman's *The Learned Maid, or Whether a Maid may be a Scholar?* (translated into English in 1659). Even those who agreed that she might would probably add a proviso to the effect that the maidenly scholar should at least have the discretion not to inflict her work on the public.

But one Englishwoman did publish no less than a dozen folio volumes, some of them with titles such as *Philosophicall Fancies*, *Observations upon Experimental Philosophy* and *Orations of Divers Sorts*. Those who had something to gain from flattering her – the universities of Oxford and Cambridge, for instance, and men like Joseph Glanvill – showered fulsome compliments on her. To others, she was 'Mad Madge' or (posthumously) that 'Shame of her Sex, Welbeck's illustrious Whore'. Only the fact that she was a nobleman's wife protected Margaret Cavendish, Duchess of Newcastle, from being mocked to her face.

Rochester's fine lady undoubtedly owes some features to Dryden's Melantha, but others may have been supplied by this the most famous – or infamous – learned lady of the Restoration period. Rochester's character is not by any means a portrait of the Duchess of Newcastle. For one thing, her elderly husband was certainly not a 'Knight', and she was genuinely devoted to him; she is not known to have 'turn'd o're' any gallants; and she is not on record as having extolled the merits of fools in love. What does bring her to mind when one contemplates the fine-lady character in *Artemiza to Chloe* is her resemblance to the latter with regard to dress and demeanour, as well as in the matter of erudition.

When Margaret Cavendish came to London in the spring of 1667, London society was exceedingly curious about her. Pepys (11 and 26 April 1667) had to go to some trouble to see her 'antique dress' and to find that she was 'naked-necked, without any thing about it'. The

Duchess was famous for wearing very low-cut dresses, even for that age of all-but-bared bosoms; but Mary Evelyn, who disliked her, admitted that she – at forty-four – had the figure for it. What the diarist's young wife found especially deplorable about the great lady was her posturing – 'her gracious bows, seasonable nods, courteous stretching out of her hands, twinkling of her eyes, and various gestures of approbation' – as well as her conversation, which was 'airy, empty, whimsical and rambling ... terminating commonly in nonsense, oaths, and obscenity'.[46] In truth, the Duchess' dress and manners did tend to strike observers as decidedly eccentric. Sir Charles Lyttelton, who met her in 1665, recorded that she did not curtsy like other women but 'made legs and bows to the ground with her hand and head',[47] masculine fashion. Not unnaturally, Restoration society enjoyed mocking her unusual appearance and manners.

It seems to me that the fine lady's 'Countrey nakednesse', 'fifty Antique postures', 'fourty smiles, as many Antique bows' and so on may well have made contemporary readers connect Rochester's learned lady with 'Mad Madge of Newcastle'. By all accounts, the Duchess was never at ease in society and frequently sought to cover her shyness by exaggerated loquaciousness. Although she never expressed such outrageous notions as Rochester's fine lady, she was known to be a champion of her sex and vigorously opposed to women's enslavement in marriage to tyrannous husbands. To that extent, she could be said to have some points in common with the fine lady where sexual politics is concerned, too.

The fact that the lady calls herself 'Rude, and untaught, like any Indian Queene' (line 99) if anything strengthens the Newcastle connexion. The Duchess openly and repeatedly deplored her deficient formal education, writing lengthy apologies which served as prefaces to her works. They were no empty disclaimers. 'She was simply uneducated', says her gallant biographer, Douglas Grant (*Margaret the First*, p. 111); her spelling was wild and her grammar shaky, and her discourses in prose and poetry owed nothing to those formal structures with which men's education made them familiar. To hostile listeners,

---

[46] Evelyn's *Diary*, ed. Austin Dobson (London, 1906), II.271.

[47] See Douglas Grant, *Margaret the First: A Biography of Margaret Cavendish Duchess of Newcastle 1623–1673* (London, 1957), p. 184. Rochester knew Lyttelton in rather a special way; see Pinto, *Enthusiast in Wit*, pp. 66 and 69. He was acquainted with other people who knew the Newcastles, too; one of them was Shadwell, whose tributes to the couple were ironically termed his 'northern dedications' in *MacFlecknoe*. (In fact, *Epsom Wells* was dedicated to the Duke.)

she may well have recalled Juvenal's pseudo-masculine, pseudo-learned woman, whose torrential speech ('like a philosopher') created a horrible din (Satire 6, lines 440–3) before which 'grammarians' and other learned men took cover.

The allusion to Dryden's (and perhaps, to some extent, Sir Robert Howard's) heroic drama *The Indian Queen* brings in another dominant female character who was both 'untaught' and 'naked', words that occur in the Epilogue to that play.[48] Restoration readers who knew the play will have relished the fine lady's damning herself out of her own mouth in aligning herself with the bloodthirsty, usurping Zempoalla. When the play was acted in 1663–4, this lady's dress was the talk of the town,[49] just as Margaret Cavendish's was to be a few years later.

The Duchess of Newcastle held views that would not recommend her to present-day feminists. Like so many other writers on sexual politics in the Restoration, she maintained that women rule thanks to their beauty, though she was careful to point out that this 'governing' had to be done with tact, 'so as men perceive not how they are Led, Guided, and Rul'd by the Feminine Sex'.[50] A similar realisation is voiced by the woman speaker of Rochester's country wife's lament, 'What vaine unnecessary things are men'. She acknowledges that an overbearing wife would only drive her husband into the arms of a more complaisant whore, who would receive the 'cloathes' that should have been the spouse's; her conclusion is couched in a beautiful specimen of 'power language': 'Thus Tyrannyes to Commonwealths Convert'. Or, in other words, a tyrannous wife must needs resign her power and enter into a community of interests with the mistress, securing whatever advantages can be had out of the man.

Like most feminists, Margaret Cavendish came in for a good deal of resentment and ridicule from members of her own sex. One censurer, often quoted in studies of 'Margaret the First', was Dorothy Osborne. On hearing that the then Marchioness of Newcastle had published poetry, she wrote to her future husband William Temple: 'Sure the poore woman is a litle distracted, she could never bee soe rediculous else as to venture at writeing book's and in verse too.'[51]

---

[48] P. 231 in the 1962 edition of the play by John Harrington Smith and Dougald Macmillan, vol. VIII in *The Works of John Dryden* from the University of California Press.

[49] See the Commentary in Smith and Macmillan's edition, p. 282.

[50] For pertinent quotations, see Mendelson, *The Mental World*, pp. 22–3, and Stenton, *The English Woman*, p. 158.

[51] *The Letters of Dorothy Osborne to William Temple*, ed. G. C. Moore Smith (Oxford, 1928), p. 37.

This reaction to an enterprise undertaken with great enthusiasm by Margaret Cavendish, an ardent devotee of poetry, lends special pertinence to Artemiza's self-admonitory strictures in lines 17–19:

> Bedlam has many Mansions: have a Care.
> Your Muse diverts you, makes the Reader sad;
> You Fancy, you'r inspir'd, he thinkes, you mad.

Men might lose their reputations if they ventured to expose their writings to the public. Women would – regardless of any inherent value in their works – be held to have lost their sanity merely by publishing. Where such a climate of opinion prevailed, it was clear that a woman poet could not win. Is Artemiza's account of the perils of pen(wo)manship historically accurate?

To begin with, her initial comparison of unsuccessful male writers to shipwrecked merchants (the words 'returnes' and 'stocke' imply a commercial outlook) is undoubtedly pertinent. Poetry *was* 'dang'rous', and the highest stake – a reputation for wit – could be lost virtually overnight. An unenthusiastic playhouse audience could make or break a play and its author in a few days. The prologues and epilogues of Restoration plays are forever urging audiences to have mercy on authors and actors alike, resorting to more or less fantastic arguments in the process. The very fervour of these pleas – often contributed by influential personages willing to deflect censure from the author – indicates the magnitude of the interests at stake. Sir Carr Scroope's Prologue to *The Man of Mode* affirms:

> Like Dancers on the Ropes poor Poets fare,
> Most perish young, the rest in danger are;
> This (one wou'd think) shou'd make our Authors wary,
> But Gamester like the Giddy Fools miscarry.

Scroope referred to playwrights as 'Poets', and the word 'poem' could stand for a literary work irrespective of genre (*OED* 1b). For instance, Dryden called *Marriage A-la-Mode* 'that Poem, of which you were pleas'd to appear an early Patron' in his dedication of that play to Rochester. The 'stormy pathlesse World' in lines 9–13 of *Artemiza to Chloe* is likely to be the realm of *belles-lettres* in general, but writing in numbers – 'Verse' – is a particularly hazardous occupation, especially for a woman.

And yet one woman managed to write, publish and even earn a living by writing 'poems' of various kinds. The achievement of Aphra Behn, often called the first professional woman writer in Britain, becomes all the more remarkable when one considers the times in which she lived. Even those who admired her work found the writer's sex impossible to take in their stride. Behn herself characterised her literary ability as 'my masculine part the poet in me'.[52] Etherege had voiced a similar attitude towards the Duchess of Newcastle when crediting her with fusing 'Your sex's glory and our sex's pride'.[53] The only 'petticoat author' who managed to command universal respect, Katherine Philips – the 'matchless Orinda' –, was praised by Cowley in similar terms.[54] Clearly, a woman writer was as unnatural, and as rare, a phenomenon as a woman scholar.

Unnatural women like Margaret Cavendish and Aphra Behn were vilified as being disgraces to their sex. The former was dubbed 'Welbeck's illustrious Whore' at about the time when *Artemiza to Chloe* was written; some years later, similar abuse was poured on Behn, especially by the misogynist Gould. Artemiza had said that 'Whore is scarce a more reproachfull name, / Then Poetesse' (lines 26–7); Gould, who knew Rochester's poetry, held that

> *punk* and *Poetess* agree so Pat,
> You cannot well be *This* and not be *That*.[55]

If the fine lady has certain traits in common with the Duchess of Newcastle, Artemiza herself resembles Aphra Behn in more ways than one. Her humour and intelligence, her aversion to marriage,[56] and her conviction that love is the most important thing in life can all be paralleled in the 'incomparable Aphra' – and then, of course, she proves herself an accomplished poet. While it is tempting to regard these similarities in personality and outlook as deliberate parallels, chronological considerations enjoin caution. Such Behn poems as *The Golden Age*, which strongly resemble some of Rochester's libertine verse, were almost certainly written in the late 1670s. Aphra herself proclaimed that

---

[52] See Duffy, *The Passionate Shepherdess*, p. 248.

[53] 'To Her Excellency the Marchioness of Newcastle, after the Reading of her Incomparable Poems'; p. 394 in Verity's edition of Etherege's *Works*.

[54] See his *Ode* 'on *Orinda's* Poems'. The main reasons why Orinda did not rouse antipathy were her personal modesty and her favoured subject matter, pastoral friendships. 'Orinda's inward virtue' (Cowley) was generally acknowledged, and she took care not to give offence. See Souers, *The Matchless Orinda*, esp. ch. 8, and Smith, *Reason's Disciples*, pp. 153–6.

[55] Quoted in Mendelson, *The Mental World*, p. 162. See also Reynolds, *The Learned Lady*, pp. 372ff., and Nussbaum, *The Brink*, p. 73.

[56] Mendelson reviews Behn's 'anti-matrimonial sentiment', which was clearly perceptible in her play *The Forc'd Marriage*, first acted in 1670 (*The Mental World*, p. 121).

Rochester 'did [her] Faults Correct';[57] it is a suggestive expression, but the exact nature of their acquaintance at the time when *Artemiza to Chloe* was written is hard to ascertain. The idea that she might have had something to do with the creation of Artemiza can be no more than a pleasing speculation.

Whatever sympathy Rochester may have felt for the talented Aphra Behn, struggling to make a living by her pen, it must be acknowledged that a late 'occasional' poem of his expresses typical Restoration disapproval of women writers. In *The Earl of* ROCHESTER's *Answer, to a Paper of* Verses, *sent him by L. B.* Felton, *and* taken out of the Translation of Ovid's Epistles, 1680, a male speaker upbraids a woman who has attacked him in verse:

> Were it not better far your Arms t'employ,
> Grasping a Lover in pursuit of Joy,
> Than handling Sword, and Pen, Weapons unfit:
> Your Sex gains Conquest, by their Charms and Wit.

Walker's notes suggest that these lines were occasioned by a 'letter of reproach' sent to Rochester by Lady Betty Felton, who may have had reason to feel ill-treated. They might be no more than a weary gesture dismissing a bothersome woman's complaints. Placed by Walker in the 'Epigrams, impromptus, jeux d'esprit' section, the poem is a rather flat, sometimes even awkward, piece. But as there seems to be no doubt about the authorship, there is no escaping the conclusion that one of the very last pieces of poetry Rochester wrote contains a dully conventional view of writing women.

ARTEMIZA TO CHLOE AS A REFLECTION OF ITS TIME

To what extent is *Artemiza to Chloe* reliable as a source of information about late-Restoration manners and morals? Was the 'Passion Love' really in such a bad way in the 1670s, and were the sentiments of the fine lady still fashionable when she returned to London with her fool of a husband? The poem implies that women who resided in the country felt sadly cut off from the place, and the activities, on which their interests centred; is there any historical basis for such an attitude? And, at the

[57] In her lines *To Mrs W. On her Excellent Verses (Writ in Praise of Some I had made on the Earl of Rochester) Written in a Fit of Sickness*, easily accessible in Farley-Hills' *Critical Heritage* volume, pp. 105–6.

strictly factual level, was it legally possible to bequeath an estate to an illegitimate child?

To begin with the last and most specific question, the fine lady's statement that the gulled oaf left one of his 'solid comforts', his estate, to Corinna's bastard does seem odd in view of the prevalence of property settlement in centuries of English history. In the seventeenth century, primogeniture was certainly the norm;[58] *Tunbridge Wells* provides a graphic description of its outcome from the point of view of younger sons. It is unlikely that the estate of a 'great Family' (even allowing for a degree of irony in the expression) would be unbound by settlement regulations. The young fool was married and had legitimate offspring; he had 'rob[bed] his wife' (presumably depleting her jointure[59]), which suggests that customary provisions had been made with regard to her property.

The estate need not have been entailed, though. Quite a few seventeenth-century landowners were able to bequeath their estates according to their wishes and did so.[60] (The 'young Masters Worship' may have had a daughter or daughters; we do not know the sex of his 'dull lawfull progeny'.) But could bastards inherit? According to one historical source (1650), a bastard could 'never be heir unto any man', but a somewhat later writer says 'the Parents of a Bastard may by Deed executed in their Lifetime, or by last Will, give or devise their Lands to their Bastards.'[61] This is apparently what happens in the case of Corinna. Rochester, who was himself a landowner, the son of a mother who had struggled for years to see her own offspring provided with rightfully inherited estates, the husband of an heiress with estates of her own, and the father of children of both sexes,[62] would be likely to know what was legally possible in that line.

As for the town/country contrast implied in *Artemiza to Chloe*, it reflects a classical, as well as classic, theme. Horace's poems depicted the

---

[58] See, for instance, Lawrence Stone, 'Social Mobility in England, 1500–1700', *Past and Present* 33 (April 1966), 37.

[59] The jointure was a sum set aside for a bride to be used for her own upkeep in the event of her husband's death. Cf. the glum discourse on the drunkard who ruins his family and squanders his estates in Scrivener's *Treatise Against Drunkennesse*: He 'wooes his distressed wife a second time for to release her Joynture … In the mean time the Timber falls … and that Ax is laid to the Entail, to cut that off too' (pp. 97–9).

[60] See Christopher Clay's fascinating article 'Marriage, Inheritance, and the Rise of Large Estates in England, 1660–1815', *The Economic History Review*, second series, 21.3 (December 1968), 503–18, esp. 504 and 510–11.

[61] See Alan Macfarlane, 'Illegitimacy and Illegitimates in English History', in P. Laslett, K. Oosterveen and R. M. Smith, eds., *Bastardy and Its Comparative History* (London, 1980), p. 73.

[62] His own bastard daughter by Elizabeth Barry was not born until 1677.

difference between worldly urban pursuits and rural virtues, and Juvenal's satires castigated Roman depravity; both were read, and imitated, in the seventeenth century. Verse letters exchanged between dwellers in town and country formed something of a special genre. One example of such a correspondence in the Restoration years is found in the mildly bawdy *Letter from Mr. Shadwell to Mr. Wicherley* and the recipient's *Answer* in the same vein.[63]

Male writers on town versus country would often uphold the merits of the latter.[64] One notices that the fine lady's husband was not at all happy about the trip to London; it took some skilful manipulation on her part to engineer it. From a woman's point of view, however, the bustle of the city has always formed a powerful attraction. Doomed to the tedium of rural existence, many generations of Englishwomen have longed for 'seasons' and 'visits' in London. Chloe – and the fine lady when she is at home – hence represent a plight lamented for centuries.

Further seventeenth-century evidence to the effect that women regarded country life as an affliction is supplied by *Marriage A-la-Mode*. In Act III, scene i, the perspicacious and level-headed Court lady Artemis – the resemblance of her name to that of Rochester's heroine may not be fortuitous – says that 'when I am out of Town but a fortnight, I am so humble, that I would receive a Letter from my Tailor or Mercer for a favour'. Shortly before this tongue-in-cheek admission, she has been discussing the hardships of country life with Melantha and the fashionable wife Doralice:

DOR. In the Countrey! nay, that's to fall beneath the Town; for they live there upon our offals here: their entertainment of wit, is onely the remembrance of what they had when they were last in Town; they live this year upon the last years knowledge, as their Cattel do all night, by chewing the Cud of what they eat in the afternoon.

---

[63] See Summers, ed., *The Works of Thomas Shadwell*, vol. v, pp. 227–32. Incidentally, this exchange substantiates the dichotomy of country ale versus the stronger stuff of the city that is hinted at by the fine lady in *Artemiza to Chloe* (lines 87–90 and 213). It also contains a parting salutation which resembles Artemiza's closely enough to bring out the brilliance of the latter in a comparison: 'I wou'd turn o're the Leafe, but know / My Muse has tyr'd her self and you. / And so Adieu' (Wycherley).

[64] Characteristically, Abraham Cowley, who advocated the temperate pleasures of a life close to Nature, was a diligent imitator of Horace. Cf. for instance his 'Paraphrase upon the 10th *Epistle* of the first Book of *Horace*', pp. 416–18 in Waller's 1906 edition of Cowley's *Essays, Plays and Sundry Verses*. A delicately sympathetic account of the boredom awaiting women in the country is given by Pope in his epistle *To Miss Blount on her leaving the Town after the Coronation*. Rachel Trickett has suggested that it may draw on the rather grim picture of rural life painted by Harriet in *The Man of Mode*; see her *The Honest Muse*, pp. 166–7. Incidentally, Trickett applies the adjective 'Horatian' to Rochester (p. 143; but cf. also p. 97).

MEL. And they tell, for news, such unlikely stories; a letter from one of us is such a present to 'em, that the poor souls wait for the Carriers-day with such devotion, that they cannot sleep the night before.[65]

Naturally, capital life has always set the fashions for the country at large, but the development of London in the late seventeenth century provides a particularly interesting backdrop to the conversation of these ladies. At this time, London became the biggest city in Europe, passing even Paris. Considering that the population of France was four times that of England, this meant that a much larger number of English men and women were in touch with, or affected by, life in the capital than their French counterparts. During the seventeenth century, the city grew with extraordinary rapidity, despite temporary depletions due to plague outbursts and the like. The demands of the capital for food and fuel affected economic structures and social habits, and the innate human desire to 'ape one's betters' began to assume the expression of ladies demanding merchandise of the kind that was currently used in London.[66]

Considering that the fine lady had been away from the capital for a while, one may well wonder whether her up-the-fools tenet was still fashionable on her return. Since she does not wait for an answer to her question 'who are the Men most worne of late', the poem's readers are never told.

We must turn to other contemporary sources for evidence in this and other respects concerning the vicissitudes of 'love', and a good deal of it is provided by two plays which were popular in 1674 – Shadwell's *Epsom Wells* and Dryden's *Marriage A-la-Mode*. The fact that Rochester knew them well is shown by allusions to both in his poems; Dryden even implies that Rochester collaborated in the writing of his play ('it receiv'd amendment from your noble hands, e're it was fit to be presented').

The charming heroines of *Epsom Wells*, Carolina and Lucia, are conscious of their audacity in even thinking of becoming familiar with the witty rakes Rains and Bevil. Carolina, acknowledging their attraction, says that 'we are already so much pester'd with gay Fools, that have no more sense than our Shock-dogs, that I long for an acquaintance with witty men as well as thou dost. But how can we

---

[65] P. 261 in the University of California Press edition.
[66] This paragraph relies heavily on an article by E. A. Wrigley, 'A Simple Model of London's Importance in Changing English Society and Economy 1650–1750', *Past and Present* 37 (July 1967), 44–70; see esp. 44–5, 50–1, 62 and 67.

bring it about without scandal?'[67] Bevil and Rains, realising – much to their consternation – that the two young ladies have aroused something that could be called affection in both of them, are impressed with that commendable inclination:

BEV. I love these Women the more, for declaring against Fools, contrary to most of their Sex.
RAINS. I hate a woman that's in love with a fulsom Coxcomb, she's a foul feeder ...[68]

If we are to believe Shadwell's young couples, fools were felt to be safe, unlike the men of wit who were scandalous by definition. Carolina and Lucia may have the courage – and 'wildness' – to defy the customary practice of their sex and take up with wits, but in so doing they clearly go against the prevailing fashion. On the evidence of *Epsom Wells*, then, the fine lady would seem to adhere to conventional wisdom among women.

One aspect of 'love' in the Restoration that is illustrated both in Artemiza's lines on the 'Passion Love' and in the fine lady's callous cogitations is the absence of tenderness and real affection in relationships. *Marriage A-la-Mode* provides chilling instances (as well as one pair of true lovers, Leonidas and Palmyra). Rhodophil claims to have been ashamed of being so unfashionable as to have loved his wife for 'a whole half year, double the natural term of any Mistress'. When 'the World began to laugh' at him, he turned against her and she against him, the result being that 'when we are alone, we walk like Lions in a room'. His friend Palamede realises that 'you dislike her for no other reason, but because she's your wife', and Rhodophil cynically answers, 'And is not that enough?' (I.i.142–54). The clothes metaphor employed by Rochester's fine lady is also paralleled in *Marriage A-la-Mode*. Doralice, Rhodophil's wife, is resolved not to have a married man for a lover, 'for a man to come to me that smells o' th' Wife! I wou'd as soon wear her old Gown after her, as her Husband' (V.i.231–3).

Acknowledgements to the effect that romantic love was unfashionable in the post-Restoration years abound in contemporary literature and other records; to quote just one example, Lucia in *Epsom Wells* says 'Love is so foolish and scandalous a thing, none now make use of any

---

[67] I.i, p. 113 in Summers' edition of *Epsom Wells*. See also pp. 134 and 154, where the scandalousness of witty men is reiterated.
[68] IV.i, p. 155 in Summers' edition. On morophilia in Rochester's poetry, see pp. 99 above and 291f. below.

thing but ready money' (III.i).[69] Obviously, Artemiza has no reason to entertain any great hopes for a restoration of true love. As described by her, love is not so much a 'norm' as an impossible ideal. A norm is a criterion to which matters and manners can be seen to measure up, or fail to do so; Artemiza sees nothing around her that could even tentatively be held up against her conception of 'That Cordiall dropp'.

This chapter has drawn attention to some properties of the poem that seemed to call for closer investigation than they had so far received, above all the delicate shifts and contrasts in point of view. But skill in perfecting the voice-within-voice structure is not the quality most worthy of note in *Artemiza to Chloe*. Its most remarkable feature is the character of Artemiza herself. She transmits a picture of late-seventeenth-century 'love' that could hardly be more depressing; she expresses her own genuine regrets at this state of affairs; contemporary sources vouch for the basic accuracy of her description – and yet a whiff of irrepressible, sharp-witted good humour comes off the pages. At a time when misogyny was rife and several authors translated Juvenal's sixth satire with gusto,[70] Artemiza criticised the behaviour of her own sex and the mores of her day with pointed accuracy allied to low-pitched irony. Her letter may be a 'satire against women',[71] but it allows for no smugness on the part of the other sex. More than that, it imparts Horatian grace to Juvenalian subject matter, and the result – as well as the speaker herself – is irresistible.

---

[69] Cf. also *Marriage A-la-Mode* II.i.306–9 and Fraser, *The Weaker Vessel*, p. 272 (on the fate of the Verney sisters).   [70] See Nussbaum, *The Brink*, pp. 77ff.
[71] Wilson, *Court Wits*, p. 131.

PRIDE AND PHILOSOPHY

——◆◆◆◆◆——

5

'*Upon Nothing*'

Throughout Rochester's poetry, traditional conceptions and conventions are taken up, briefly explored and burlesqued or distorted – sometimes subtly and as it were in passing, occasionally violently and thoroughly. *Upon Nothing* is an instructive instance of the latter. In this much-admired poem, according to Dr Johnson 'the strongest effort of his Muse', Rochester's constant animus against pride, folly, and vanity, especially as displayed by clergymen, schoolmen and statesmen, is given particularly incisive and sustained expression.

As previous critics have emphasised,[1] the poem has a social as well as a metaphysical dimension. A tripartite structure was drawn up by David Farley-Hills (*Rochester's Poetry*, p. 176), and as an introductory comment on *Upon Nothing*, his outline is helpful; but the more time one spends trying to unravel Rochester's paradoxes and rationalise his argumentation, the more one comes to realise how unsatisfactory any external structure is when applied to his poem. At times, the only thing that seems to stand up in it is the addressee.

Many people have pointed out that Rochester draws on the Christian conception that God created the universe out of nothing. Also, Dustin Griffin showed that Rochester joined a well-established literary tradition when writing an encomium on Nothing, and that he was surely fully aware of the fact.[2] Indeed, an appreciation of the lengths to which he

---

[1] See, for instance, Griffin, *Satires Against Man*, pp. 266–80, and Farley-Hills, *Rochester's Poetry*, pp. 173–8. In Barbara Everett's 'The Sense of Nothing', this poem plays an important part throughout.

[2] Like several other Rochester critics, Griffin refers to H. K. Miller's pioneering essay, 'The Paradoxical Encomium: With Special Reference to Its Vogue in England, 1600–1800', *Modern Philology* 53 (1956), 145–78. Another important source is Rosalie L. Colie's *Paradoxia Epidemica: The Renaissance Tradition of Paradox* (Princeton, 1966). See also Gillian Manning's 'Rochester and *Much A-Do about Nothing*', *Notes and Queries* n.s. 33 (December 1986), 479–80, where a

went in his onslaught on divines and politicians calls for some awareness
of that tradition.

By and large, previous praisers of Nothing had either amused
themselves and their readers by defining its glories in negative terms (for
instance, the 'Song of Nothing' declares that 'A fool that says Nothing,
may pass for a wit'[3]) or explored the creation-ex-nihilo dogma.
Rochester is indebted to both approaches, and to representatives of
them, but his *Upon Nothing* does not belong to either and possesses a
high degree of originality. The first seven stanzas are best quoted
together:

> Nothing thou Elder Brother even to Shade
> Thou hadst a being ere the world was made
> And (well fixt) art alone of ending not afraid.
>
> Ere Time and Place were, Time and Place were not
> When Primitive Nothing, somthing straight begott
> Then all proceeded from the great united what –
>
> Somthing, the Generall Attribute of all
> Severed from thee its sole Originall
> Into thy boundless selfe must undistinguisht fall.
>
> Yet Somthing did thy mighty power command
> And from thy fruitfull Emptinesses hand
> Snatcht, Men, Beasts, birds, fire, water, Ayre, and land.
>
> Matter, the Wickedst offspring of thy Race
> By forme assisted flew from thy Embrace
> And Rebell-Light obscured thy Reverend dusky face.
>
> With forme and Matter, Time and Place did joyne
> Body thy foe with these did Leagues combine
> To spoyle thy Peaceful Realme and Ruine all thy Line.
>
> But Turncote-time assists the foe in vayne
> And brib'd by thee destroyes their short liv'd Reign
> And to thy hungry wombe drives back thy slaves again.

Discussions of *Upon Nothing* have tended to emphasise the conflation of
theories regarding the Creation that Rochester seems to have brought
about. Thus Griffin argues that the poem

popular poem, also called the 'Song of Nothing', is shown to have existed before Rochester's;
as Manning suggests, it may well have constituted an influence on him.

[3] The poem was contained in *Merry Drollery Compleat*, first collected in 1661 (I have used the
1875 reprint).

tells ... as many as three different stories of creation: (1) Nothing begot something [sic], and from their incestuous union all else followed (st. 2); (2) Something was severed or sundered from Nothing, as Eve was sundered from Adam's side, and subsequently severed or 'snatched' from Nothing's hand 'men, beasts', etc. (sts. 3–4); (3) with terms now shifted from concrete to abstract, from 'Something' to 'Matter', Matter is born of Nothing but frustrates Nothing's desire for incestuous union, fleeing from its embrace, joining in rebellion against Nothing with Form, Light, Time, and Place (sts. 5–6). (Satires Against Man, p. 270)

This 'multiple account', Griffin believes, is probably due to a deliberate introduction of discrepancies rather than a failure on the author's part to control the poem.

The first stanzas of Upon Nothing do pose some intriguing questions, but a conflict of three dissimilar accounts of the Creation is not perhaps their prime feature. Nothing certainly begot Something, but there is no need to envisage any incestuous unions. Something, which is part of all created things – 'the Generall Attribute of all' – seems to have called 'Men, Beasts' and so on into existence by actively invading unresisting Nothing's realm. This creative ability on the part of Something is not a result of its being severed from Nothing; on the contrary, Something is dissolved in Nothing when severed from it – perhaps the most vexatious paradox of Rochester's impious stanzas. Fusion is brought about by separation; consequently, created things and beings only exist in conjunction with Nothing.

As for Matter, it certainly belongs to Nothing's line, even if it is not necessarily 'born of' this ancestor. Also, the desire of Nothing to embrace 'the offspring of its Race' need not be more incestuous than the wish to hold on to one's progeny usually is. The exact parentage of Form, Light, Time, Place and Body is uncertain. Form assists Matter, thus giving rise to tangible phenomena; Light is a 'Rebell', too, opposing the darkness of Nothing; Time and Place came into being at the time when Nothing begot Something, perhaps issuing together with Something from 'the great united what'. It is logical for Body to be the foe of Nothing, as bodies are the result of Form and Matter coming together after Matter's escape from Nothing.

Griffin is surely right when maintaining that Rochester's poem deliberately mocks the views of the Creation reflected in Cowley's Hymn to Light[4] and in the Davideis, where he has noted several striking

[4] The suggestion was first put forward by Pinto in 'John Wilmot', p. 367. Griffin's discussion is found on pp. 270–2 in Satires Against Man.

parallels. Cowley's Light kindles life, beauty and joy, dispersing fear, grief and vice. By contrast, the sole reference to light in *Upon Nothing* presents this agent as an unlawful opponent of the permanent order. Its unsuccessful insurrection is ironically described as having, temporarily, 'obscured' the 'dusky face' of Nothing. The verb means 'to make less visible, intelligible, or beautiful' as well as 'to darken'; but to anybody who had any Latin – as Rochester did – the latter meaning would obtrude and lend a paradoxical zest to the line.

Another debt to Cowley, indicated by Griffin (followed by Walker), is to the older poet's *Life and Fame*, where Life is addressed as '*Nothings younger Brother*'. Where Cowley thus has 'Life', Rochester writes 'Shade' – a sardonic inversion indeed, although the remainder of Cowley's poem certainly emphasises the brevity and transitoriness of life. Other seventeenth-century writers besides Cowley had preceded Rochester in establishing family relationships among abstract concepts; Samuel Butler, for instance, argued that 'Error as wel as Devotion is the Natural Child of Ignorance, and the elder Brother'.[5]

Time in *Upon Nothing* is a special case. While in league with Form, Matter, Place and Body, it forms a powerful opposition to Nothing – powerful enough to threaten what the speaker ironically terms its 'Peaceful Realme'. But Time is persuaded to withdraw its support from the rebels, thus condemning all created things to annihilation in their source, the 'hungry wombe' of Nothing.

The reason why all this argumentation seems absurd is not that it is made up of components belonging to different stories of the Creation, but that it is fundamentally impossible to argue about Nothing as if it were a positive entity. Applying the rhetorical device used in those praises of Nothing that are based on the 'Nothing is better than … ' matrix, we can conclude that nothing existed before the world was made and that nothing lasts forever. We might inquire about the origins of the world, and find our question answered by the query itself, bereft of its question mark: What is the creative principle from which the earth and all that lives on it proceeded. As for the sexual 'confusion' discussed by Griffin and others – Nothing is a 'Brother' and 'begets' Something; later on it has a hungry womb and a capacious bosom –, that confusion can be resolved by the realisation that nothing can be a brother and have a womb at the same time.

In fact, the first seven stanzas of *Upon Nothing* supply a striking

---

[5] See 'Religion' in de Quehen's edition of *Samuel Butler: Prose Observations*, p. 34.

illustration of Hobbes' comments on absurdity, 'to which no living creature is subject, but man onely. And of men, those are of all most subject to it, that professe Philosophy' (*Leviathan* I.v, 'Of REASON, and SCIENCE'). Hobbes continues:

For it is most true that *Cicero* sayth of them somewhere; that there can be nothing so absurd, but may be found in the books of Philosophers. And the reason is manifest. For there is not one of them that begins his ratiocination from the Definitions, or Explications of the names they are to use ...

The soundness of the 'names', the definitions and concepts on which reasoning rests, is the touchstone of scientific labour, according to Hobbes. When he discourses on the dangers of vain philosophy in part 4 of *Leviathan*, 'Of the Kingdome of Darknesse', he stresses the importance of proper definitions of a number of phenomena, 'Body, Time, Place, Matter, Forme' heading the list. These are of course the very concepts with which Rochester's speaker builds his exposition of absurd reasoning, with the addition of 'Light', the quality which directly opposes the darkness disseminated by that '*Confederacy of Deceivers, that to obtain dominion over men in this present world, endeavour by dark, and erroneous Doctrines to extinguish in them the Light, both by Nature, and of the Gospell*' (the introductory passage of ch. xliv and of *Leviathan* part 4).

   Upon Nothing hence demonstrates that even these terms, for which suitable definitions could, according to Hobbes, be had, will form part of an argumentation that leads nowhere when the whole reasoning proceeds from 'names that signifie nothing', to quote Hobbes again (I.v). The affinity between chapters I.v and IV.xliv of *Leviathan* on the one hand and Rochester's poem on the other – much more material could be adduced – seems too great for coincidence. However, Hobbes did not deny the possibility of arriving at true insights on the basis of sound ratiocination, or 'Reasoning aright', whereas *Upon Nothing* unequivocally negatives the idea. In addition, the 'Kingdome of Darknesse' may contain 'Phantasms of the braine' that prevent human beings from perceiving the light of the Scriptures, but it is not itself a product of the imagination. The operations of Christ's enemies are a distressing reality to Hobbes, who argues that misinterpretation of the Scriptures keeps men in darkness. Conversely, Rochester's speaker addresses a dusky ruler who not only does not exist, but whose very non-existence is the reason why created things are impermanent.

   The fact that *Upon Nothing* firmly denies the possibility of immortality has made it natural for commentators to connect it with Rochester's brilliant translation of a passage from Seneca's *Troades*:

> After Death, nothing is, and nothing Death,
> The utmost Limit of a gaspe of Breath;
> Let the Ambitious Zealot, lay aside
> His hopes of Heav'n, (whose faith is but his Pride)
> Let Slavish Soules lay by their feare;
> Nor be concern'd which way, nor where,
> After this Life they shall be hurl'd;
> Dead, wee become the Lumber of the World,
> And to that Masse of matter shall be swept,
> Where things destroy'd, with things unborne, are kept.
> Devouring tyme, swallows us whole
> Impartiall Death, confounds, Body, and Soule.
> For Hell, and the foule Fiend that Rules
> Gods everlasting fiery Jayles
> (Devis'd by Rogues, dreaded by Fooles)
> With his grim griezly Dogg, that keepes the Doore,
> Are senselesse Storyes, idle Tales
> Dreames, Whimseys, and noe more.

The memorable metaphor 'the Lumber of the World' constitutes a departure from Seneca, as does the representation of Death's fictitious kingdom as 'fiery Jayles / (Devis'd by Rogues, dreaded by Fooles)'. Rochester's parenthesis forms a swift but venomous thrust directed at the divines who fashioned the glories of Heaven and horrors of Hell, equally insubstantial, to serve their own worldly ends. The implications of this accusation are perhaps the gravest charge Rochester ever made against Christian dogma and those who uphold it.

Still, he will have read a pagan philosopher who warned his disciples not to allow menacing priests to distract them with fear of eternal punishment in Hell: in the first book of Lucretius' *De Rerum Natura*, the eulogy on Epicurus is followed by disgust at the abuses of popular religion and a caution against its practitioners (see especially lines 101–11).

Analyses of *Upon Nothing* are apt to become too ponderous and bogged down in abstractions, losing sight of the irreverent flippancy that is one of the poem's salient characteristics. Kristoffer F. Paulson criticised this exaggerated solemnity in his note on 'the great united what', which he regards as a deliberate bawdy pun on 'twat'.[6] The

---

[6] 'Pun Intended: Rochester's *Upon Nothing*', *English Language Notes* 9 (December 1971), 118–21.

suggestion has been favourably received, and it works well in the context. Vieth has remarked (*Rochester Studies*, p. 64, item 161) that the figure denoting 'nothing' is 'o', 'an immemorial symbol of the female genitalia'; and previous discussions of *Upon Nothing* have reminded us that 'nothing' had sexual connotations in the Renaissance and that Rochester will have known this and made use of it.

Even so, the realisation that the complicated introductory stanzas may trick us into ridiculously serious analyses of obstreperous philosophical concepts should not lead us to dismiss the poem as lacking a serious dimension. The humour of the paradoxes and the insolence of the concluding reflexions on various nations, and on kings and whores, do not prevent *Upon Nothing* from being a stinging attack on three particularly influential segments of the population in Rochester's day – the divines, the learned men of the Universities, and the people who governed the realm.

From the point of view of a Christian theologian, the account of the Creation in *Upon Nothing* is blasphemous in more ways than one. Rochester's speaker burlesques an orthodox Christian notion, that of God's creation of the world *ex nihilo*; he implicitly aligns God with Nothing (the eternal aspect, among others), with the 'great united what' (the source of all created things), and with Something (the creative effort that brought forth the four elements), augmenting the audacity of the proceeding by means of the bawdy connotations of the first two concepts; he denies the notion of immortality; he maintains that theology and ethics do not possess any substance whatsoever; and he accuses those whose task it is to save men's souls, bringing them the comfort of religion, of being worse than useless in their obtuse hypocrisy. Rochester the man may not have been an atheist – he is said to have denied it emphatically more than once[7] –, but it is difficult to see how *Upon Nothing* could be saved from the imputation of atheism. 'Agnosticism' (Farley-Hills) is too mild a term in the face of its wholesale broadsides directed against several of the fundamental tenets of Christianity.

One illustration of Rochester's irreverence is provided by a look at Crashaw's English translation of a Latin epigram, in *Steps to the Temple*:

> O Mighty *Nothing*! unto thee,
> *Nothing*, wee owe all things that bee.
> God spake once when hee all things made,

---

[7] To Burnet and Giffard; see Burnet's account, p. 53 and note in Farley-Hills' *Critical Heritage* volume. Cf. pp. 361ff. below.

He sav'd all when he *Nothing* said.
The world was made of *Nothing* then;
'Tis made by *Nothyng* now againe.[8]

Crashaw's poem refers to the passage in Matthew 27:12 where Jesus, accused by the chief priests and elders, answered nothing. In Crashaw's lines, two aspects of Nothing are woven into a sacred paradox fusing the creation of the world with its redemption.[9] It is difficult to tell whether Rochester knew this poem; Crashaw was a friend of Cowley's and much admired by him, and Rochester was certainly familiar with Cowley, who could have acted as a mediator. Be that as it may, Crashaw's and Rochester's poems both extol Nothing and exploit the paradoxical uses of the concept, but Crashaw's wit is made to serve Christian faith while Rochester's is turned against it.[10]

In the lines *To the Post Boy* Rochester states that his other transgressions, considerable as they are in kind as well as in quantity, are but 'poor things' in view of the fact that he has also 'blasphemed my god and libelld Kings' (on these self-accusations, see p. 360 below). In David Vieth's edition, the editor suggests that the blasphemy might be taken to occur in *A Satyr against Reason and Mankind*, 'which evoked several verse replies from clergymen' (p. 131 n.14); but the mockery of the *Satyr* is far less blasphemous than the onslaught on Christian theology in *Upon Nothing*. In the *Satyr*, the folly, hypocrisy and vanity of men form the prime target, one of the worst offences being the presumptuousness of believing oneself to be the 'Image of the Infinite'. *Upon Nothing* explicitly denies that infiniteness, in addition to performing the sacrilegious alignments mentioned above. Both poems attack clergymen, but *Upon Nothing* is more radical, removing every bit of ground from below their feet. While the *Satyr* criticises certain notions and doctrines, the former poem asserts that there is no foundation for any doctrine at all.

That, of course, goes for doctrines other than those which primarily belong to the domain of theology, and *Upon Nothing* is patently unkind to the terms and conceptions of traditional academic scholarship. In an interesting discussion of this poem,[11] Reba Wilcoxon says that 'the

---

[8] *The Poems English Latin and Greek of Richard Crashaw*, ed. L. C. Martin (Oxford, 1927), p. 91.
[9] See George Walton Williams, *Image and Symbol in the Sacred Poetry of Richard Crashaw* (Columbia, 1963), pp. 25–6.
[10] Cf. Isaiah's words on the dumbness of the coming Saviour in verse 7 of that fifty-third chapter from which the dying Rochester apparently derived great comfort (see p. 363 below).
[11] In 'Rochester's Philosophical Premises', 187. Howard Erskine-Hill helpfully points out that the polemic thrust in *Upon Nothing* is directed against 'the purveyors of religious or philosophical

irony turned upon abstractions in general' is 'more central than the challenge to Christian orthodoxy'. It seems to me that both these aspects are rooted in the same attitude, and that it is difficult to establish a line of demarcation between 'abstractions in general' and 'Christian orthodoxy'. The late seventeenth century was a time when philosophers, schoolmen, clergymen and the men of the 'new science' moved freely all over the field of learning, both literally and figuratively, unconcernedly overstepping the boundaries which later ages have liked to set up for their respective disciplines. One instructive example of this interdisciplinary commerce is found in the fact that Richard Bentley, about a dozen years after Rochester's death, was appointed to deliver the so-called Boyle lectures on the 'folly and unreasonableness of atheism'. The famous scientist had caused these lectures to be preached 'for proving the Christian religion against notorious infidels', and the great scholar and librarian Bentley – at one time tutor in the household of Rochester's adversary Edward Stillingfleet – referred to the work of Isaac Newton in his attempts to confute atheism, a proceeding at which Newton expressed his gratification.[12] Stillingfleet, the King's Chaplain who became Bishop of Worcester, may have remembered his old enemy when contemplating Bentley's words on the possibility, and probability, of creation out of nothing (pp. 140–4 in Dyce's edition) – especially in the face of Bentley's conclusion that the 'universal maxim, that *nothing can proceed from nothing*', 'only expresses thus much, that matter did not produce itself, or, that all substances did not emerge out of an universal nothing. Now, who ever talked at that rate?' At least, Stillingfleet could have made the concluding question a somewhat less rhetorical one.

Another instance of the connexion between contemporary science and theological doctrines with special reference to nothing is supplied by the eminent botanist Nehemjah Grew, whose *Cosmography* discoursed on the impossibility of nothing as a point of departure for the creation of the world. Dr Johnson's *Dictionary* excerpts the following argument (see under *nothing*):

It is most certain, that there never could be *nothing*. For, if there could have been an instant, wherein there was *nothing*, then either *nothing* made something, or

---

metaphysics', making no distinction between them; see 'Rochester: Augustan or Explorer?' in G. R. Hibbard, ed., *Renaissance and Modern Essays Presented to Vivian de Sola Pinto in Celebration of his 70th Birthday* (London, 1966), p. 56.

[12] See *The Works of Richard Bentley, D. D.*, ed. Revd Alexander Dyce, vol. III (London, 1838; a facsimile was printed by Ams Press, New York, in 1966), pp. 201ff.

something made itself; and so was, and acted, before it was. But if there never could be *nothing*; then there is, a being of necessity, without any beginning.

Christian metaphysics is not the sole target of *Upon Nothing*'s irreverent nihilism. The quotation from Grew makes use of concepts reviewed some seventeen centuries earlier by that inveterate enemy of religious superstition and fervour, Lucretius. The first doctrine expounded in *De Rerum Natura* is that 'nothing comes from nothing' (1.150ff.). Some of Rochester's mock-scientific terms ('Generall Attribute', 'Originall', etc.) suggest that *Upon Nothing*, by glancing at Lucretius, was intended to include pagan as well as Christian philosophy in its extirpation of *all* theoretic reasoning on the Creation.

The tenth stanza of *Upon Nothing* (lines 28–30) seems aimed at all who practise any one of the disciplines nowadays denoted by the concepts philosophy and science; it is preceded here by the eighth and ninth stanzas, subsequently discussed in conjunction with it:

> Though Misteries are barr'd from Laick Eyes
> And the Divine alone with warrant pries
> Into thy Bosome, where thy truth in private lyes
>
> Yet this of thee the wise may truly say
> Thou from the virtuous Nothing doest delay
> And to be part of thee the wicked wisely pray.
>
> Great Negative how vainly would the wise
> Enquire, define, distinguish, teach, devise,
> Didst Thou not stand to poynt their blind Phylosophies.

The five verbs of line 29 constitute a summary of the acquisition and transfer of academic learning in any field. Rochester's speaker sardonically states that the pursuit of such learning would be utterly pointless unless it had a mighty guarantor – and that guarantor is the very opposite of the substance and fact sought by scholars.

The semantic properties of the word 'poynt' have been variously explained; but Paul Hammond is surely right when he argues that the *OED* II.5b definition is the most satisfactory one.[13] Not recorded until 1704, some thirty years after the composition of *Upon Nothing*, it reads: 'To give point to (words, actions, etc.); to give force, poignancy, or sting to; to lend prominence, distinction, or poignancy to'. Affirming that nothing lends force and poignancy to those ideas and conceptions that are completely dependent on nothing amounts to denying the

---

[13] See p. 113 in his edition of Rochester's poems.

value of scientific/philosophic knowledge twice over in the most relentless manner.

A distinction between theologians and other philosophers (in a wide sense) is implied in the two preceding stanzas. Only 'the Divine' – here in the sense of 'theologian' rather than 'minister' – is authorised to perceive 'Misteries', 'barr'd from Laick Eyes', and to approach the bosom of Nothing, 'where thy truth in private lyes'.[14]

While the Anglican clergy comes under fire in lines 43–5 ('Reverend Shapes', 'Lawn-sleeves'), the reference to 'Misteries' and the emphasis on attempts to penetrate secrets seem to imply that Puritan divines bear the brunt of the satire in lines 22–4. A typical target would be Richard Sibbes, attacked by Rochester in the *Satyr*.[15] In his 'The Fountain Opened; or, The Mystery of Godliness Revealed', Sibbes insisted that godliness is a great mystery, that 'In Christ, all is mysteries' and that the gospel, also a mystery,

should teach us ... *not to set upon the knowledge of it with any wits or parts of our own* ... It is a mystery, and it must be unveiled by God Himself, by his Spirit. If we set upon this mystery only with wits and parts of our own, then what our wits cannot pierce into, we will judge it not to be true, as if our wits were the measure of divine truth.

Sibbes' argumentation here is, by and large, reducible to the kind of attitude ridiculed in the relevant stanza: Religion is full of mysteries which the common man should not try to unravel by his own efforts; the divine only can speak of them with any authority, but even he has to have them revealed to him. One is reminded of Hudibras' Ralpho, who 'could deep mysteries unriddle / As easily as thread a needle' thanks to 'new-light', the 'dark lanthorn of the Spirit' which – as Griffin has pointed out[16] – was one of the instances that contributed to making the *ignis-fatuus* motif a topos by the time Rochester took it up in his *Satyr*.

The word 'Yet' at the beginning of the next stanza (line 25) implies a difference between the divine, licensed to pry, and the secular 'wise' who, while lacking that authority, may still make some statements about the nature of Nothing. As in other Rochester poems (such as *The*

---

[14] Here Vieth's reading, '*the* truth' (italics added), found in several manuscripts, seems preferable as imparting an immediate generality to the concept of truth which is in keeping with the argumentation in the following stanza. There is no actual contradiction, of course.

[15] On Rochester and Sibbes, see pp. 163ff. While mysteries play an important part in the views of Anglican churchmen, too (Burnet, for instance, discussed them at length with Rochester; see p. 172 below), Puritan divines were especially apt to dwell on them and their significance to the Christian believer.　　　[16] *Satires Against Man*, pp. 212–13.

Disabled Debauchee and *Artemiza to Chloe*), the connotations of 'wise'
and 'wisely' are decidedly profane. The wicked wisely pray to be
turned into nothing, so as to escape eternal punishment for their sins.[17]
Truth – otherwise so elusive in the poem – is expressly granted to the
contention of the wise that nothing keeps nothing away from the
virtuous, which amounts to saying that virtue goes unrewarded. These
lines form a joint denial of an afterlife whose terms are conditioned by
our conduct during this earthly existence (cf. above on Rochester's
translation of the passage from Seneca). The fools who dress up Nothing
in a bishop's lawn sleeves, noblemen's furs and scholars' gowns (see
below) 'look wise' along with their void dummy, adopting the solemn
appearance of the sapient and noble (lines 43–5). 'The wise' in lines 25
and 28 thus reads like an ironic bow to those men of learning whose
efforts and operations Rochester's speaker thinks nothing of. It is given
special emphasis by the recurrence of 'wise', 'wisely', 'wise' in lines 25,
27 and 28, moved down the line one step at a time, and by the rhymes
in stanzas eight and ten. When the word returns as an adjective in line
45, it is again emphasised as the last word of the stanza.

Having dealt with the men of sacred and secular philosophy, the
satirist of *Upon Nothing* turns to the men of the state, blasting their
ambitions, their abilities and their functions in the next four stanzas:

> Is or is not, the two great Ends of ffate
> And true or false the Subject of debate
> That perfect or destroy the vast designes of State –
>
> When they have wrackt the Politicians Brest
> Within thy Bosome most Securely rest
> And when reduc't to thee are least unsafe and best.
>
> But (Nothing) why does Somthing still permitt
> That Sacred Monarchs should at Councell sitt
> With persons highly thought, at best for nothing fitt,
>
> Whilst weighty Somthing modestly abstaynes
> ffrom Princes Coffers and from Statesmens braines
> And nothing there like Stately nothing reignes?

'Is or is not' and 'true or false' are the two components with which the
great schemes of statecraft – such as the alliance of Charles II and Louis
XIV, often referred to as the 'Grand Design' – stand or fall. The irony
of this postulate is further strengthened by the coldly scornful

---

[17] This is Griffin's reading of line 27 (*Satires Against Man*), p. 275.

appositions. 'Is or is not' sums up the basic condition of any phenomenon; as David Brooks says,[18] they are 'two predicates which may apply to anything', and these sentences describe the '"two great ends of Fate" for anything'. Ascribing 'Ends' – intentions – to fate, which carries such strong overtones of unalterable and inscrutable causality, and suggesting that these ends are decisive when it comes to creating grand political plans, effectively reduces the relevance of men's efforts. Referring to true or false as 'the Subject of debate' may seem facilely cynical to a later age, but to an intelligent Restoration man who saw the country's government at first hand, as a courtier and as a member of the House of Lords, it probably summarised the essence of contemporary politics.

For the political situation in Restoration England makes almost any other era in the country's history seem laudable in comparison. J. R. Jones paints the scene in the darkest colours:

Deceit and double-dealing on the part of kings, ministers and politicians, cynicism on the part of the people, produced an appalling debasement of politics. Nothing was taken on trust or at its stated face-value. Self-interest, hypocrisy and corruption were taken for granted. Politicians, like revellers in a carnival, were assumed to be wearing masks in order to conceal their true features, and to aid them in the seduction of their victims. Indeed, Charles's most effective political attribute was his skill in the art of dissimulation ... Few ministers or politicians were given credit for any measure of integrity. Altruism and a sense of duty and responsibility were apparently obsolete virtues.[19]

The two lines that introduce the onslaught on contemporary statesmen thus indicate that Restoration politics was a game where appearance and reality were crucial, as well as dubious, entities. The next stanza goes on to maintain that they, and thereby the art of government, are best when reduced to nothing. Joining the Christian/Puritan mysteries in the safe bosom of Nothing – aptly contrasted with the 'wrackt Brest' of the statesman –, appearance ('true or false') and reality ('Is or is not') find their proper home in annihilation.

The word 'politician' has a somewhat pejorative ring to it today, but its connotations were not altogether pleasant in the sixteenth and seventeenth centuries either (as the Marlovian voyage on 'two

---

[18] P. 135 in his edition of the *Lyrics and Satires of John Wilmot Earl of Rochester*. See also Hammond's comment on the relevance of the Aristotelian tag *on kai mē on*, p. 113 in his Rochester edition.

[19] *Country and Court: England 1658–1714* (London, 1978), vol. v in *The New History of England*, pp. 2–3. This informative and readable work is of great value to a student of seventeenth-century literature, and I am indebted to it on several points.

politicians' rotten bladders' and Shakespeare's 'scurvy politician'
suggest). In Rochester's time, it could refer to anybody who resorted to
dubious and subtle methods to further his own ends; but in the context
of *Upon Nothing* it clearly denotes a person involved in government.

The breast of a Restoration politician had every reason to be 'wrackt'
by doubts regarding appearance and reality. The penalties for errors of
judgement could be severe, as the respective fates of Clarendon and
Clifford prove. These two men, despite their many weaknesses, gave
Charles II loyal service according to their lights. The former's downfall
in 1667, followed by distasteful and vindictive impeachment proceedings, will have made an impression on the new courtier Rochester,
whose courtesy M. A. had been bestowed on him six years earlier by
means of a kiss from the then-powerful Lord Chancellor.[20] Rochester
may not have had any personal sympathy for Clarendon, who was not
a popular figure among the Court Wits;[21] but the lack of such feelings
will not have prevented him from regarding Clarendon's fate as an
example of the dangers inherent in even the most distinguished political
career. Clifford was known personally and well to Rochester, too, ever
since the days of the Second Dutch War when they were shipmates in
the perilous and abortive Bergen action.[22]

Rochester has acrimonious things things to say about politics, and
those who practise it, elsewhere. In the six-line *Lampoon upon the English
Grandees* (called *Impromptu on the English Court* by Vieth and *Epigram on
the English Court* by Hammond), probably written later than *Upon
Nothing*, he castigates Charles' lack of application in matters of statecraft
when suggesting that the King was the opposite of 'a great polititian'.
In the prose Bill where Rochester praises his ware and attainments as
'Alexander Bendo', he goes out of his way to be rude to politicians.
Having maintained that his own craft is 'much more Safe' (the crucial
word again) than the art of 'Government', which 'no ways belongs to
my Trade, or Vocation', he slyly concludes that the practice of a
mountebank is 'equally honest, and therefore more profitable' than that
of the politician. Taking the comparison a step further, he writes:

[20] Clarendon was Rochester's mother's brother-in-law; see Basil Greenslade's intriguing account
   of personal and political relationships, 'Affairs of State', in Treglown, ed., *Spirit of Wit*,
   especially pp. 96–100.
[21] According to J. H. Wilson, Rochester was one of Clarendon's 'bitter enemies'; see *A Rake and
   His Times: George Villiers 2nd Duke of Buckingham* (London, 1954), p. 82.
[22] The latter piece of information is supplied by Burnet. It was at Clifford's house that John
   Evelyn met Rochester in 1670, afterwards describing him as 'a very prophane wit' in his *Diary*
   (24 November).

The Politician (by his example no doubt) finding how the People are taken wth Specious Miraculous Impossibilities, Plays the same Game, Protests, declares, promises I know not what things wch he's sure can ne'er be bro^t about; the People believe, are deluded, and pleased. The expectation of a future good, which shall never befall them, draws their Eyes off a present Evil; thus are they kept & established in Subjection, Peace, & Obedience, He in Greatness, wealth and Power: so you see the Politician is, & must be a Mountebank in State Affairs, and the Mountebank no doubt, (if he thrives) is an errant Pollitician in Physick.

This attack on politicians is less overtly abusive, and much shorter, than Butler's *Character* of 'A Modern Politician'.[23] Still, its brief, cool exposition on the treachery and greed of this race of men is just as damaging as Butler's tirade, which – among many other things – accuses them of 'forgeting to discern between Good and Evil' and of being unable to perceive a 'Distinction of Virtue and Vice'. The resemblance between Butler's fulminations and Rochester's cutting imputations – in *Upon Nothing* as well as in the Bendo Bill – is great with regard to the actual content of their charges. It is in the expression that the two writers differ, Rochester proving the validity of Butler's own warnings against long-windedness.

Concepts like 'secure' and 'safe' are vital components in Rochester's verse (see pp. 100 and 106 above). The references to security and (un)safety in the relevant *Upon Nothing* stanza differ from other instances in that they occur in a political rather than a personal context. Hobbes' central doctrine regarding the conferring of sovereignty by common consent is founded on the need for security – a concept which recurs throughout his discussions 'Of Common-Wealth', as does 'safety'. Rochester, whose debt to Hobbes was considerable (cf. pp. 174ff. and 237ff. below), shows his independence even of this philosopher when he allows his speaker to conclude that there is no such thing as security in public life.

Hobbes stipulated that sovereign power could be wielded by a monarch or by an assembly. That power was the result of the people's decision, not a divine prerogative. The expression 'Sacred Monarchs' in the next stanza is thus also un-Hobbesian, but it occurs in a context which is decidedly unflattering to crowned sovereigns in general.[24] The

---

[23] Pp. 29–45 in Daves' edition of Butler's *Characters*. The Bendo passage is quoted from Pinto's 1961 edition of *The Famous Pathologist, or The Noble Mountebank* (Nottingham University Miscellany, no. 1), p. 34.

[24] In the titles of Rochester's juvenile tributes to Charles and Henrietta Maria, the Royal personages are addressed, in the approved fashion of the time, as 'Sacred Majesties'.

two monarchs Rochester knew personally, Charles II and Louis XIV, are decried in other poems of his, notably the *Satire on Charles II*. *Upon Nothing*, which proclaims that statecraft as such is essentially a nullity, does not explicitly attribute the same quality to monarchs themselves; it is the uselessness of councillors that forms the main butt of the satire. Even so, some of the venom rubs off on the rulers who surround themselves with nitwits, and the subsequent references to 'Princes Coffers' and 'Kings promises' imply that the practical capacities of kings are as non-existent as their loyalties (see below).

It is a mark of Rochester's structural skill and awareness that he does not forget the nature of the interrelationship of Nothing and Something when he takes it up again in stanzas 13 and 14 (lines 37–42). Nothing may be the more venerable (non)entity; but it is only by gracious permission of Something, the 'Generall Attribute of All' (that is, also of sacred monarchs, statesmen's brains and princes' coffers), that it takes over heads and treasuries. Something is always the active principle, ultimately bound to lose itself in the sublime passivity of Nothing.

The allusions to proceedings in the council and to the emptiness of princely coffers are no mere generalities. Before its reconstruction in 1679, the Privy Council had played a rather less essential part under Charles II than it ought to have done. It tended to burden itself with trivia.[25] Its size – there were fifty Privy Councillors in the mid-1670s – will have had something to do with its inefficiency, as will Charles' growing predilection for relying on private advice. Still, the lack of competence and dedication on the part of councillors in general can be discerned behind the Council's gradually slipping grasp of vital governmental business, and a sharp observer such as Rochester will have known where to direct his insults to make them sting. The contempt of the Council that transpires from this stanza will not have displeased Charles; the somewhat veiled authority for the inadequacy of councillors – 'highly thought' – may well be an indirect reference to the King.

The next stanza proclaims that the most striking quality of 'Statesmens braines' is their non-existence, thus levelling the political satire at persons higher up than mere councillors. If, as seems likely, *Upon Nothing* was written in 1673 or 1674 (see below), Rochester may

---

[25] See p. 52 in J. R. Jones' *Country and Court*. The satire called *The King's Vows*, assigned to 1670 by George deF. Lord, contains an expression of the King's determination to 'have a Privy Council to sit always still' (p. 161 in Lord's *Poems on Affairs of State* volume). Edward Raymond Turner's *The Privy Council of England in the Seventeenth and Eighteenth Centuries: 1603–1784*, vol. 1 (Baltimore, 1927), provides much interesting information on Charles II and his Council, including the decline in the latter's importance; see especially pp. 381 and 402–7.

have had Buckingham, Shaftesbury and Arlington in mind. For various reasons, the status of the former Cabal ministers was rather shaky at this time.

The date given for *Upon Nothing* by Walker, 'before 1673', was based on his assumption that the above-mentioned 'Song of Nothing', printed in 1673, echoed Rochester's poem. Gillian Manning's research (see n.2) has invalidated this view by showing that the 'Song' in question had been in existence long before that. One detail in *Upon Nothing* that might be read as a temporal indication is the expression 'Princes Coffers' in line 41. Walker, relying on a note by Harold Love, mentions Charles' bankruptcy in 1672 as a reason for it (p. 262 in his edition). It is certainly possible that the 'Stop of the Exchequer', which entailed the King's failure to honour his debts, prompted that contemptuous reference to the poverty of princes. Charles' impecuniousness was a dominant feature of his reign and the reason for many of his unpalatable manoeuvres. At no time, however, was his lack of means so acute as in 1672 and 1673, nor its consequences so shockingly obvious. In the light of the dramatic events of 1672 and 1673, the latter year seems a likely year of composition. The 'Stop' scandal remained fresh in people's minds for some years, however, so this suggestion is highly tentative. One example of the vividness with which the King's financial difficulties remained imprinted on the minds of critical subjects is the lampoon *The History of Insipids*. Written in or around 1675,[26] it attacks the 'Stop' in acrimonious terms. The poem also repeats the allegation, frequently made against the King, that Charles shamefully neglected loyal Stuart followers:

> Old Cavaliers, the Crown's best guard,
>   He leaves to starve for want of bread.
> Never was any prince endu'd
> With so much grace and gratitude[27]

– a bitter reproach directed at the man who is surely also the target of lines 49–50 in *Upon Nothing*, the last three stanzas of which partly summarise and partly extend the argumentation in the previous seven:

> Nothing who dwell'st with fooles in grave disguise
> ffor whom they Reverend Shapes and formes devise

[26] On the authorship of this poem, sometimes ascribed to Rochester, see Frank H. Ellis, 'John Freke and *The History of Insipids*', *Philological Quarterly* 44 (October 1965), 472–83. David Vieth calls Ellis' ascription to Freke 'conclusive'; see Vieth's *Rochester Studies*, p. 103 (items 280–1). Present-day scholars tend to wish to keep an open mind; see, for instance, p. xvii in Walker's Introduction. See also p. 303n. below.

[27] P. 245 in Lord's *Poems on Affairs of State*.

Lawn-sleeves and ffurs and Gowns, when they like thee looke wise:

ffrench Truth, Dutch Prowess, Brittish policy
Hibernian Learning, Scotch Civility
Spaniards Dispatch, Danes witt, are Mainly seen in thee;

The Great mans Gratitude to his best freind
Kings promises, Whors vowes towards thee they bend
fflow Swiftly into thee, and in thee ever end.

The first of the concluding stanzas looks back to the preceding attacks
on divines, statesmen and learned men. Nothing, still passive, is not
merely the unalterable receptacle that houses the end of their ambitions;
the classic disguise metaphor expresses the vanity of their pursuits in
another way: Nothing supports the robes and insignia that are the
outward characteristics of their exalted functions. The 'fooles' who
devise those sober garments for Nothing themselves look like nothing
at all; the 'Lawn-sleeves and ffurs and Gowns' in which they dress their
fellow nullity are clearly the emblems of their respective trades and
stations. Lawn sleeves, as Vieth and others tell us, are part of a bishop's
regalia. Walker suggests that 'ffurs and Gowns' should be taken to refer
to scholars and judges respectively. Unlike Butler, though, Rochester
has little to say against the legal profession, and the 'Gowns' look like
an allusion to the men of the universities. 'Ffurs' were part of some
kinds of academic dress in the seventeenth century, too, but here they
could well form an attribute of statesmen. All Charles' more important
ministers were peers of the realm and consequently wearers of the fur-
trimmed robes of the mighty.

Up to the last two stanzas, *Upon Nothing* has formed a massive attack
on those categories of men who count for something but are good for
nothing. At the conclusion of the poem, however, the satirist widens his
scope as he indulges in national prejudice of a kind that is still with us.
The choice of nations to be insulted need not have been very deliberate.
France, the Netherlands and Spain were the three countries with the
greatest involvement in British foreign policy in Rochester's day;
Denmark was a country with plenty of contacts with England; and the
examples of Scotland and Ireland are instances of uncharitableness
beginning at home. Taken altogether, the selection is one that would
appeal to a large number of Englishmen, and that might be a sufficient
cause for it.

While the respective allegations are neither unusual nor profound, a
few of them merit some consideration. Keith Walker has found 'the

ironic reference to "Dutch Prowess" ... very puzzling ',[28] adding, in his notes: 'In what sense the Dutch lacked this quality has not been satisfactorily explained.' Elaborate explanations hardly seem necessary, though. Rochester had fought the Dutch in operations where their lack of valour was less apparent than poor British strategy (especially in the Bergen affair) and where he had seen many shipmates die. Accusing the enemy of cowardice is standard practice for fighting men of all races and times. It might be added that Rochester's letters betray a special animosity against the Dutch,[29] though none of the passages where he reviles them has anything to say about their courage. Still, Dutch foot-soldiers were not renowned for their valour;[30] Boileau mocked their cowardice in his fourth epistle (1672). According to a French writer on various European nations in the late seventeenth century, the Dutch did not much care about 'what other Nations call point of honour, the Motto of many being this, *No Honor but Profit*'.[31]

The unkind reference to 'Brittish policy' may be viewed as yet another kick aimed at those statesmen – including the monarch – whose conduct of the country's affairs was particularly unedifying at this time ('policy' here means, as Walker says, 'political sagacity ... ; statecraft; diplomacy' according to *OED* 1.3). Considering the respect and affection which Rochester himself clearly felt for his Scots tutor Sir Andrew Balfour – obviously a kind and courteous man –, the slur on Scotsmen's manners may seem surprisingly ungracious. Still, Rochester had known other Scotsmen since, notably the unappealing Lauderdale. In any case, the libels in these lines may not represent the poet's personal views so much as current prejudice, the indulgence of which would be relished in his circle.

The same circle will have seen the face of Charles II behind the 'Great man' and the 'Kings promises' in the last stanza. As we have seen, the King was often blamed for failing to reward those who had stood by

---

[28] P. x; see also p. 262, where some possible explanations are put forward, among them Harold Love's suggestion that 'the reference may be to the ill success of the Dutch land defence against the French'. 'Dutch courage' might be relevant; see Waller's *Instructions to a Painter*, lines 227–44 (p. 30 in Lord's *Poems on Affairs of State*).

[29] See pp. 160 and 167 in Treglown's edition of Rochester's *Letters*. There was much popular hatred against the Dutch at this time. Dryden took part in fanning it; see James Anderson Winn, *John Dryden and His World* (New Haven and London, 1987), p. 239. Marvell's poem *The Character of Holland* does not flatter the Dutch either.

[30] Johan Huizinga has said that the Dutch preferred taxing their strength and valour at sea to displaying 'kriegerischen Geist' as soldiers; see *Holländische Kultur des siebzehnten Jahrhunderts* (Jena, 1933), p. 17.

[31] Jean Tailhard, *A Treatise concerning the Education of Youth: The Second Part*, p. 167. This English translation was printed in London in 1678.

him in the days before he, in G. R. Cragg's telling phrase, 'won by default the throne which he had been unable to regain by force'.[32] Rochester himself had no reason for complaint; Charles always took an interest in Henry Wilmot's son and was in fact astonishingly tolerant towards him. He is even reported[33] to have made light of the young peer's best-known epigram:

> God bless our good and gracious King
>   Whose promise none relyes on
> Who never said A foolish thing
>   Nor ever did A wise one.

Whatever good intentions the King may have had, the insubstantiality of 'Kings promises' was another matter for daily object lessons at the Restoration Court, not least in the last years of the so-called Cabal,[34] 1672 and 1673. Characteristically, Bishop Burnet begins the third book of his *History*, from 1673 to 1685, with the brief statement: 'The proceedings of the former year had opened all men's eyes.' With its cautious plurals ('Sacred Monarchs', 'Kings promises'), *Upon Nothing* is less direct in its accusations against Charles than the *Satire on Charles II*, but there is no mistaking the target. In *Upon Nothing* alone, the poet's words to the Post Boy, 'I have blasphemed my god and libelld Kings', are substantiated in full.

A further indignity suffered by the promises of kings is to be coupled with 'Whors vowes', another verbal commodity in plentiful supply at a Court where chastity and fidelity were rare virtues. In contemporary parlance, adulteresses and fornicatresses were called whores as well as downright prostitutes, and the first two categories were so abundant in the elevated society of the time that Rochester, in a late letter to Henry Savile, wrote that 'hypocrisy [is] the only vice in decay amongst us. Few men here dissemble their being rascals and no woman disowns being a whore.'[35] Obviously, no great faith could be placed in vows articulated by these ladies.

All created things come to nothing in the end, affirms the speaker of *Upon Nothing*, but the 'Great mans Gratitude to his best freind, / Kings promises, Whors vowes' disintegrate even more quickly than the rest. The shift from epistemological to social criticism towards the end of the

---

[32] In the Preface to his *Puritanism in the Period of the Great Persecution: 1660–1688* (Cambridge, 1957; I have used the 1971 reprint).   [33] See Pinto, *Enthusiast in Wit*, p. 74.

[34] The ministry composed of Clifford, Arlington, Buckingham, Ashley and Lauderdale, whose initials made up the singularly apt designation.

[35] 21 November 1679. See Treglown's edition of the *Letters*, p. 232.

poem has been felt to constitute a structural weakness, but it must not be forgotten that the edge of the satire is always directed at the kinds of pretence that go with influential positions in society. *Upon Nothing* is not so much a 'satire against man' (Griffin's collective term for Rochester's poetry) as a satire against the delusions, conceitedness, stupidity and faithlessness that characterise the operations of people of consequence in public life, whether they be theologians or noble ministers.

Modern critics have found it difficult to share the enthusiasm of the eighteenth century for *Upon Nothing*. Vieth, Farley-Hills and Griffin[36] all profess but limited admiration for Dr Johnson's favourite. In my view, however, the poem is a masterpiece: the argumentation possesses the elegant concentration and stringency that are Rochester's in his best moments; the satire is incisive rather than abusive, but enlivened by the impudent irreverence that is such a powerful attraction in his verse; the versification is brilliant, the alexandrine rounding off the couplet (except in line 42, 'And nothing there like Stately nothing reignes' – an accident, or a deliberate reduction to emphasise 'nothing'?) to form an unusual and striking metre; and the continual subversions of notions current in Rochester's time exhibit the peculiar dynamics of that time with rare force and lucidity. But *Upon Nothing* is more than that. It is an extremely intelligent rebuttal of any and all claims of the human intellect to be able to guide mankind in any sort of direction at all, let alone a sound and consistent one. Nor does it suggest that any other aspect of human life might be able to redeem this deficiency. Rochester's poem constitutes the apex – or, rather, the nadir – of nihilism in English poetry.

---

[36] For instance, Griffin says that 'the two halves of the poem are imperfectly joined' (*Satires Against Man*, p. 278). There are exceptions to these censorious views, though; Anne Righter, for one, does not hesitate to call it a 'great poem' ('John Wilmot', 66).

6

'A Satyr against Reason and Mankind': the context

At one level, Rochester's *Satyr* constitutes a digest of religious and philosophical notions in the seventeenth century as well as of people and events in Restoration society. The compactness of that digest is an achievement in itself. The 225 lines of the poem comprise an astounding variety of ideas and arguments; it is remarkable that the inconsistencies that have been noted in it are not more numerous and fundamental.

The sheer wealth of material that must be reviewed and considered when elucidating the *Satyr* in its context precludes a discussion of the kind given to *Upon Nothing*, where references and implications were woven into a stage-by-stage analysis of the poem as a whole. Dustin Griffin found it necessary to examine the issues in two long chapters, called 'The Background to Rochester's "Satyr"' and 'A Reading of the "Satyr Against Mankind"' respectively. A similar subdivision is adopted here. Textual matters form a suitable point of departure for this initial chapter. They are followed, in turn, by considerations of the content and significance of the adversarius' speech against the background of developments in seventeenth-century theology; the poem's debts to Hobbes and Montaigne; and, finally, the occurrence of pertinent lines of thought in the satires of Boileau. The ensuing chapter offers a passage-by-passage discussion of the poem, ending in an assessment of its peculiar qualities and distinctive character.

TEXTUAL ISSUES

The first question that confronts a student of the *Satyr* is the matter of its length. Most Rochester scholars have agreed that lines 174–225, sometimes called 'The Apology' or the 'Addition', may well have been written somewhat later than the main body of the poem. A number of the extant manuscripts lack this epilogue; so does the first printed version, the 1679 folio leaflet.[1] Despite this chronological hiatus, the epilogue is usually treated as an integral part of the *Satyr*, and for excellent reasons. There is no reason to doubt Rochester's authorship, which makes it a legitimate member of the canon. In addition, it supplies the complementary 'favourable' perspective of classical satire.[2] The twenty-four lines given to the rudely interrupted interlocutor are too few, too designedly pregnable and too ferociously massacred to serve as a foil to the satirist's indignation.

Vieth's change of copy-texts entails the exclusion from his edition of four lines included by Hammond and Walker, who followed the 1680 printed text throughout. They occur in the epilogue description of a good churchman, a description which gives more space to the vices that such a man should refrain from than it does to the virtues he should be seen to practise:

> Who from his Pulpit, vents more peevish Lyes,
> More bitter railings, scandals, Calumnies,
> Than at a Gossipping, are thrown about,
> When the good *Wives*, get drunk, and then fall out.

While these lines (198–201 in Walker's edition) do not constitute one of the most pungent satirical passages in the poem, the actual charge is not unimportant. Fanning dissension from the pulpit was a weapon which Restoration clergymen could and did resort to when the political situation seemed to call for it. It invested them with considerable power in their confrontations with civil authorities. In view of their historical implications, then, the lines may be said to be better in than out.[3]

The puzzle posed by the alternative readings in line 74 is a trickier one. Vieth (like Hayward and Pinto before him) makes the speaker cry out that the gist of the 'mighty Man's' protests had already been expressed in 'Patrick's *Pilgrim*, Sibbes' soliloquies'. Walker, on the other hand (like Hammond and Brooks), adopts the reading '*Patricks Pilgrim, Stillingfleets* replyes', which occurs in about a third of the texts collated by him. The difference is not so trivial as it might appear. The

---

[1] See Vieth, *Attribution*, pp. 370–5.

[2] The balance of 'negative' attacks and 'positive' precepts to virtue in classical satire has been related to English poetry by, among others, Mary Claire Randolph in 'The Structural Design of the Formal Verse Satire', *Philological Quarterly* 12 (1942), 368–84, and Howard D. Weinbrot, 'The Pattern of Formal Verse Satire in the Restoration and Eighteenth Century', *PMLA* 80.4, part 1 (September 1965), 394–401.

[3] Vieth has rejected them as a scribal interpolation. In 'A Question of Copy-Text: Rochester's "A Satyr against Reason and Mankind"', *Notes and Queries* 19.5 (vol. 217 of the continuous series; May 1972), 177–8, Kristoffer F. Paulson defended the authenticity of these lines.

case for Stillingfleet was put by Kristoffer F. Paulson in 1971.[4] His
argument, accepted not only by the most recent editors but also by
several critics, was that an attack on the Puritan divine Richard Sibbes
(who had died in 1635) amounted to wasting powder on dead hawks.
Conversely, Stillingfleet was not only very much alive but also a
coming man of appreciable influence. He was thus a more suitable
quarry, especially as Charles II had some reason to regard him with
disfavour.

Paulson points out that Stillingfleet's sermon preached before the
King on 24 February 1675 seems to attack lines 1–173 of Rochester's
Satyr. Paulson's assumption that Stillingfleet's indignant defence of 'the
excellencies of humane nature' prompted Rochester's epilogue appears
plausible to me. So does his contention that lines 193–7 allude to
Stillingfleet's presumptuousness in daring to subject the mores of the
Court, not excepting Charles' own habits, to public criticism (though
this was not by any means an infrequent occurrence; see p. 230 below).
However, I doubt that 'Sibbes' soliloquies' should give way to
'Stillingfleet's replies' in line 74.

Paulson expresses the idea that 'Stillingfleet's replies' was actually the
original reading and that 'Sibbes' ... ' was a censored one, brought in at
a later date. He bases this argument on the fact that Stillingfleet, who
was engaged in several religious controversies, wrote a large number of
'replies' in the course of his disputes. It is true that some of Stillingfleet's
rejoinders to men who debated with him in print were called 'replies'.
Still, only one of them seems to have existed before 1675, a piece of
polemical writing directed against Catholicism.[5] While the capacity of
speculative human reason is involved in the argumentation, that 'reply'
was primarily concerned with the Scriptures as a criterion of religious
certainty. A few 'answers' on various controversial topics hardly make
up for this lack of pertinent 'replies'; most of Stillingfleet's 'answers'
were written after 1675, too.

The idea that an attack on Stillingfleet could in any way have harmed
the interests of the man who lampooned the King, the heir to the
throne, and various influential men and women at Court without
suffering any dire consequences is not an immediately convincing one
either. If the names of Patrick and Ingelo did not require the perfunctory

---

[4] 'The Reverend Edward Stillingfleet and the Epilogue to Rochester's *A Satyr against Reason and
Mankind*', *Philological Quarterly* 50 (1971), 657–63.

[5] 'A Reply to Mr. Serjeant's Third Appendix' (London, 1665), in *The Works of Dr. Edward
Stillingfleet* (London, 1707–10), vol. IV, pp. 626–58. See Robert Todd Carroll, *The Common-
Sense Philosophy of Religion of Bishop Edward Stillingfleet* (The Hague, 1975), pp. 44 and 60–2.

initial-dash 'disguise', it is difficult to see why Stillingfleet's name should be so controversial as to call for total, if temporary, obliteration.

A more likely supposition is that Rochester originally wrote 'Sibbes' soliloquies' and that this was later changed – by him, or by someone else who knew of Stillingfleet's 'reply' to the *Satyr* in his sermon – to '*Stillingfleets* replyes'. If this was the case, the question is which reading should be preferred.

As late as 1984, David Vieth categorically denied the pertinence of Paulson's arguments (*Rochester Studies*, p. 77). He also dismissed the idea that the epilogue to the *Satyr* could have been in any way inspired by Stillingfleet's sermon. The same censorious attitude prevails in Vieth's comment on David Trotter's essay 'Wanton Expressions'.[6] Griffin was 'not fully [convinced]' by Paulson's argument (p. 195n. in *Satires Against Man*).

Since there can be no absolute certainty either way, and since Stillingfleet does seem to come under fire in the epilogue (see below), a relevant query is whether the loss of Sibbes is a loss to the poem. Was he as negligible a target as Paulson, Trotter and Walker suggest?

In fact, the expositions, treatises and sermons of Richard Sibbes contain a large amount of material that can be related to Rochester's *Satyr*. Sibbes' discourse on sanctified versus carnal reason,[7] while in no way original,[8] comes close to the kind of 'reason' extolled by the adversarius in the *Satyr*. His treatment of the symbolic properties of light, and of the superiority of sight over the other senses, is interesting when held up against the *ignis-fatuus* passage in the *Satyr*; the latter implicitly contradicts everything Sibbes has to say about '*pure*' light, which '*admits of no contagion*', and about '*the most glorious and noble*', as well as '*sure*', sense of sight.[9] Sibbes' teachings on the fear of God ('*It must be general* at all times, in all actions')[10] form another doctrine which

---

[6] The essay forms part of Treglown's collection, *Spirit of Wit* (pp. 111–32). Vieth's reaction is found on p. 137 in his *Rochester Studies* (item 372).

[7] See, for example, 'The Fountain Opened; or, The Mystery of Godliness Revealed' in Sibbes' *Works*, ed. Alexander Grosart (7 vols., 1862–4), vol. I, p. 467, and 'Bowels Opened: or, Expository Sermons on Canticles IV.16, v.6' in vol. II of the *Works*. See also 'The Soul's Conflict with Itself', vol. I, p. 245, where reason is described as 'a beam of God'; the relevance of this locus was indicated by Griffin, *Satires Against Man*, p. 195.

[8] Similar lines of thought can be found in other seventeenth-century writers, for instance Pascal and Glanvill. See Louis I. Bredvold, *The Intellectual Milieu of John Dryden: Studies in Some Aspects of Seventeenth-Century Thought* (Ann Arbor, 1934; I have used the 1956 reprint, where the reference to Pascal is on p. 39); and Basil Willey, *The Seventeenth-Century Background: Studies in the Thought of the Age in Relation to Poetry and Religion* (London, 1934), p. 172.

[9] See, for instance, 'The Christian Work', vol. V, pp. 28–30, and 'The Excellency of the Gospel above the Law', vol. I, pp. 250–1.   [10] See 'The Christian Work', vol. V, p. 12.

would have seemed repugnant to one who regarded omnipresent fear (although differently conceived) as one of the two chief scourges of mankind.

Perusing Sibbes' writings is not an inspiring task, and it is not surprising that Pinto and Griffin seem to be the only Rochester scholars who have undertaken it. Somewhat unexpectedly, Griffin finds the term 'soliloquies' difficult to account for. He quotes another passage from 'The Soul's Conflict' (vol. I, p. 191) where the word occurs ('Here, therefore, is a special use of these soliloquies'), whereupon he records his puzzlement at Rochester's 'singling out' Sibbes' 'soliloquies'.[11] But the word 'soliloquies' need not be taken as literally as that. The speaker of the *Satyr* is saying that 'all this we know / From ... Sibbes' soliloquies', and it is a very apt descriptive term for the kind of discourse that prevails in much of what Sibbes wrote. Questions and protracted answers, as well as expositions with the odd objection thrown in (and disposed of at great length), are typical features of his devotional works. Indeed, 'soliloquies' could almost be used as a generic term for them.[12]

Pinto stresses the anti-sensual dimension in Sibbes' writings and argues that the harshness of his calls to virtue would have roused Rochester's antagonism.[13] This is surely a relevant point, and so is Pinto's assumption that Sibbes' works may have been favourites of Rochester's mother. Griffin agrees, saying that Rochester as a child might have 'been force-fed Sibbes by his pious Puritan mother, and carried with him a distasteful memory'. This is all the more likely considering that Richard Sibbes was a great favourite with titled Puritan families in the youth of the then Anne St John; she may even have known him personally.[14] Such undigested morsels of religious instruction could easily account for Rochester's reference to a dead-and-gone Puritan.

Whether Rochester had Sibbesian passages at the back of his mind when selecting divines fit for abuse in the *Satyr* we cannot know. The relevances suggested here may be purely fortuitous. Sibbes was not an original thinker; also, many of his notions can be paralleled in later works by Anglican as well as Puritan divines. This review of possible

---

[11] P. 194 in *Satires Against Man*. This passage does not, contrary to Griffin's claim, contain the only occurrence of 'soliloquies' in Sibbes' writings; see, for instance, vol. I, pp. 286ff.

[12] Pinto seems to have felt much the same way about the word; see his comment on it in his edition of Rochester's poems, p. 218.   [13] *Enthusiast in Wit*, pp. 25–6.

[14] Sibbes' editor Grosart mentions several families in Oxfordshire and surrounding counties where the divine was a lionised guest; see the Introduction to *Works*, vol. I, p. cxviii.

links is merely intended to answer the question posed at the outset of the discussion. I think the loss of Sibbes from the *Satyr* does constitute an unfortunate omission, and I would be glad to see Pinto's and Vieth's reading of line 74 reinstated in future reprints of Rochester's poem.

THE *SATYR* AND SEVENTEENTH-CENTURY RELIGIOUS TRENDS

One point made by Griffin in his remarks on Sibbes is that 'Rochester may have wanted to extend his attack to include a Puritan divine (to match the Anglican Patrick)' (*Satires Against Man*, p. 195). Of course, Ingelo was an Anglican too; if Sibbes is allowed to disappear, all the recognisable clergymen butts in the *Satyr* are Anglicans. Griffin's conditional assumption touches on an interesting aspect of the presentation of religious values, stances and the like in the poem. Which school of religious thought does the adversarius represent? Can he in fact be said to represent any one direction in Restoration religious life? Raman Selden, referring to his 'Geneva bands', unhesitatingly labelled him 'a Puritan divine';[15] but, as Vieth pointed out in his notes to the poem, such bands were worn by many Restoration clergymen.

The importance of this question extends beyond providing a gloss on the 'mighty Man' and his background. He constitutes the only explicit counterclaim to the poem's attacks on reason and mankind and is hence a vital focus for its satire. If his convictions were not familiar to the poem's readers, the efficiency of that satire would suffer. Consequently, the nature and provenance of those convictions are crucial.

Stripped of their rhetorical embellishments and broken down to stark statements, the 'Band, and Beard's' claims are fivefold: (1) God gave man, and man only, an immortal soul. (2) He created man in His own image. (3) He gave man reason, thus raising him above animals. (4) Reason enables man to transcend his physical capabilities and to understand the wonders of the Creation. (5) Thanks to reason, man can arrive at reliable ethical rules, the adherence to which will determine his condition after death. All these issues are essential components in the religious and philosophical developments and controversies of the seventeenth century. A brief consideration of each of them in turn should help a present-day reader to gain a firmer grasp of the religious-philosophical background of the *Satyr*.

---

[15] In *English Verse Satire 1590–1765* (London, 1978), p. 94.

While many contemporary clergymen would have frowned at hearing man described as 'blest' and 'glorious' (see below), the idea that the Almighty had given men immortal souls was indisputable to Puritans and Anglicans alike. Theologians from both quarters had attacked Hobbes' contention that there is nothing in Scripture to prove that men's souls survive the deaths of their bodies, as well as his view that only the faithful will be given eternal life at the Resurrection.[16] Hobbes was not alone in holding this opinion. For instance, Sir Thomas Browne recorded that he had once believed, like 'the Arabians', 'That the Souls of men perished with their Bodies, but should be raised again at the last day.' The mere mention of such a conception drew censure from his critics.[17] A more unexpected believer in 'mortalism' was Milton's Adam (*Paradise Lost*, x.792).[18] In the 1660s and 1670s, the so-called Latitudinarians[19] made considerable efforts to uphold the notion of immortality, a fact that suggests that it was widely questioned.

General arguments for the immortality of the human soul had of course been put forward in print before the Restoration. For example, Walter Charleton's *The Immortality of the Human Soul, Demonstrated by the Light of Nature* appeared in 1657. This work of Christian apologetics in dialogue form, written by a physician and scientist (who was to become a friend of Dryden's), favours the view that reason should be allowed to assist faith in comprehending 'sacred Truths'. Charleton is an interesting personage in a Rochester context. The writer of a popularised account of *Epicurus' Morals*, he was also a notable expounder of the philosophy of Pierre Gassendi, who had argued that Epicurean doctrines could be made to form part of Christian natural philosophy. Some of the ideas disseminated by Charleton may well have met with a measure of interest from Rochester.[20]

---

[16] See *Leviathan*, chs. 38 and 44.

[17] See *Religio Medici*, I.7, written in 1635 and first printed in 1642. The objections made by Sir Kenelm Digby and Alexander Ross are analysed in James N. Wise's book *Sir Thomas Browne's Religio Medici and Two Seventeenth-Century Critics* (University of Missouri Press, 1972); see pp. 63–9 and 131–40.   [18] See Willey, *The Seventeenth-Century Background*, p. 241.

[19] The term, originally a disparaging one, has come to stick to the (comparatively) liberal Anglican clergymen of the late seventeenth century, such as Gilbert Burnet, Edward Stillingfleet, Simon Patrick, Joseph Glanvill, and John Tillotson. See G. R. Cragg, *From Puritanism to the Age of Reason* (Cambridge, 1950), ch. 4, especially pp. 66–7. Christopher Hill has argued that the characteristic moderation of the Latitudinarians must have provoked Rochester; his lively discussion is found in the essay on Rochester in *The Collected Essays of Christopher Hill*, vol. I, *Writing and Revolution in 17th Century England* (Brighton, 1985), pp. 302–3. David Trotter has reasoned along similar lines in 'Wanton Expressions'.

[20] On Charleton and Dryden, see Phillip Harth, *Contexts of Dryden's Thought* (Chicago and London, 1968), especially pp. 21–5 and 103–4. Charleton's interest in Gassendi's philosophy is briefly discussed in John Redwood's *Reason, Ridicule and Religion: The Age of Enlightenment in*

In 1659, the Cambridge Platonist Henry More,[21] theologian and religious poet, published an anti-Hobbesian discourse with a title resembling Charleton's, *On the Immortality of the Soul*. This work made Joseph Glanvill commit a treatise of his on the same subject to his desk drawer,[22] but what he did publish about the 'great question' of the soul's nature is significant. Glanvill concluded that the relationship between body and soul is beyond rational explanation,[23] and Robert Boyle held a similar view.[24] The doctrine of the immortality of the soul had many defenders; another of them was the Nonconformist Richard Baxter, whose *Reasons of the Christian Religion* (1667) contained arguments explicitly directed at contemporaries with Epicurean inclinations.[25] Charles Blount's *Anima Mundi*, printed in Amsterdam in 1679 in evasion of the Licensing Act, argued that the immortality of the soul was a subject on which no agreement had ever prevailed; it was certainly a vexed question in his own lifetime.[26]

In emphasising the '*everlasting* Soul' of man, the adversarius has hence taken the opportunity to reiterate a statement frequently made in the theological debate of the Restoration period. His allusion to Genesis 1:26–7 drives home another point where controversy was rife, but the teaching of orthodox Christians in every camp unequivocal. The Biblical account of the Creation was frankly disbelieved even by people who would not label themselves atheists. One of them was Rochester himself, who told Burnet that 'the first three Chapters of *Genesis* he

England (London, 1976), p. 110. Griffin mentions Charleton's *Epicurus' Morals* and draws attention to some parallels between it and arguments in Rochester's *Satyr*, but rightly points out that the Epicurean ideas he quotes are commonplaces; see pp. 15, 170n., and 183n. in *Satires Against Man*. Glanvill admired Gassendi, but others regarded the Frenchman's atomism and Epicurean ideas with suspicion as promoting atheism; see Bredvold, *The Intellectual Milieu*, pp. 52n. and 65.

21 The Cambridge Platonists were, like the Latitudinarians with whom they had very strong affinities, committed to rational theology and the progress of natural science. On the relationship between Cambridge Platonists and Latitudinarians, see Cragg, *From Puritanism to the Age of Reason*, and Barbara J. Shapiro, *Probability and Certainty in Seventeenth-Century England* (Princeton, 1983), pp. 106ff.

22 See Jackson I. Cope, *Joseph Glanvill: Anglican Apologist* (St Louis, 1956), pp. 5–6.

23 See *The Vanity of Dogmatizing*, ch. 3.iii, originally published in 1661.

24 See Shapiro, *Probability and Certainty*, p. 88. For the general differences between Glanvill's and Boyle's theories of certainty, see Henry G. Van Leeuwen, *The Problem of Certainty in English Thought 1630–1690* (The Hague, 1970), pp. 90.

25 See Bredvold, *The Intellectual Milieu*, pp. 64–5. The seventeenth-century French literary Epicureans were convinced of the mortality of the human soul; see J. S. Spink, *French Free-Thought from Gassendi to Voltaire* (London, 1960), ch. 8, especially pp. 166–8.

26 See Harth, *Contexts of Dryden's Thought*, p. 75. Harth also supplies a useful reminder of censorship and its consequences at this time, pointing out that Blount's work had been handed about in manuscript long before it was published (pp. 81–3 and n.).

thought could not be true, unless they were Parables' (p. 66 in the *Critical Heritage* reproduction). This was a more polite way of expressing what Claude de Chouvigny, Baron of Blot l'Eglise, had rendered in the following terms two or three decades earlier:

> Messieurs, encore un mot
> Avant que je me taise:
> Je ne suis pas sy sot
> De croire à la Genèse.[27]

But even if Christians of all confessions were agreed that man had been created in God's image, the adversarius' elevated view of mankind in general (*'Blest glorious* Man!', *'this fair frame'*) was not universally shared. Laments for the depravity of man in his fallen estate, some of them clearly influenced by St Augustine, occur time and again in seventeenth-century devotional and philosophical works.[28] It should be remembered, too, that even among Restoration theologians who promoted the progress of rationalist thought in religion and science, the limitations of human reason were clearly articulated. In this respect, the eulogies of the 'mighty Man' cannot be said to be typical of leading Restoration divines as we know them from their writings (cf. below).

Genesis 1:26 and 28 declares that man should have dominion over animals. The idea that human reason was the main source of man's privileged position is another notion upheld by seventeenth-century churchmen while being undercut by sceptical philosophers and men and women of letters. The wretchedness of man compared to the life of animals, which is at least free from malice and viciousness, was a topic especially frequently addressed in seventeenth-century France (see pp. 187 and 200f. below). Comparisons between men and animals, with special reference to their rational faculties, were not unusual in England either and had in fact become a somewhat stale subject towards the end of the century.[29]

When the adversarius stresses the superiority of man over beasts, and connects it with the faculty of reason, he is voicing an idea which both Puritans and Anglicans would subscribe to. Sibbes, for example, had

---

[27] *Les Chansons Libertines de Claude de Chouvigny, baron de Blot l'Eglise*, p. xxvii.

[28] One instance among many is supplied by Glanvill's *Vanity of Dogmatizing*, pp. 10–13 in Bernhard Fabian's 1970 Olm facsimile (Heidelberg and New York); here Glanvill employs metaphors not unlike Rochester's own (in the *ignis fatuus* passage, and to some extent in lines 66–71).

[29] See, for instance, Sir William Temple's essay *Of Popular Discontents*, contained in *The Works of Sir William Temple, Bart.* (London, 1757), vol. III, p. 34.

said that 'the judgment of man enlightened by reason is above any creature',[30] and the exaltation of reason is a standard feature in the works of Anglican divines.

Up to now, the 'Band, and Beard' has voiced notions that could be heard from any pulpit in seventeenth-century England, both before and after the Restoration. By and large, even Catholic divines would – despite their comparative emphasis on faith rather than reason – agree with his basic convictions.[31] When it comes to the actual functions and capabilities of human reason, though, the claims made by the interlocutor become controversial.

No Puritan theologian would endorse the view that man's reason endows him with the authority and ability to expound the mysteries of the universe, including Heaven and Hell. Puritan eschatology is the province of divine revelation, not of human intellect. Supernatural knowledge must infuse the understanding of man. However the concept 'reason' is defined,[32] it is the faculty of a base creature whose saving virtue, if any, is humility.

Catholic controversialists would feel equally offended by the adversarius' claims for human reason. To them, the authority of the Church was at all times superior to the individual insights attained by the exercise of the notoriously fallible human intellect. Much Protestant/Catholic polemics in the late seventeenth century focused on the problem of faith and certainty. Against the Roman Catholic claim of infallibility, Anglican churchmen like Stillingfleet and Tillotson argued that moral certainty was the only basis for religious belief; that this basis was a sufficient one; and that moral certainty could be reached with the aid of reason.[33]

It would seem, then, that Rochester's 'Band, and Beard' ultimately represents post-Restoration Anglicanism with its consistent emphasis on reason. But if this is what Rochester had in mind, the satirist's distortions are gross. No leading Anglican churchman would make such drastic

---

[30] 'The Excellency of the Gospel above the Law', *Works*, vol. IV, p. 234.

[31] See pp. 20–1 and 73–6 in Bredvold's *The Intellectual Milieu*.

[32] All studies of seventeenth-century religion have had to contend with the difficulties inherent in defining 'reason' and 'revelation'. Most of them have arrived at the conclusion that narrow definitions defeat their purpose and that 'reason' should, in a late-seventeenth-century context, be interpreted in a wide sense as denoting the capacities of the human intellect. For a reminder of the connexion between reason and religious worship in the thought of a Cambridge Platonist, see James Deotis Roberts, Sr, *From Puritanism to Platonism in Seventeenth Century England* (The Hague, 1968), pp. 66ff. on Whichcote.

[33] Many studies have dedicated much space to discussions of Protestant–Catholic disputes. For a brief summary, see Shapiro, *Probability and Certainty*, pp. 101–4.

claims for a faculty whose limits were drawn up time and again in the
course of theological debates. Latitudinarians like Stillingfleet, Patrick
and Burnet, to mention three men known to Rochester, granted that
much matter of religious belief was *above* reason, but – and this was the
essential point – not *against* it.[34]

Burnet's conversations with Rochester on religious matters contain
passages which form excellent illustrations of the Latitudinarian's
attitude to reason. The two men's conflicting views on mysteries and
rationality in the religious life afford sidelights on the *Satyr* issues; pages
72–4 in Farley-Hills' *Critical Heritage* reproduction are especially
relevant. In this conversation, Rochester – who had written the *Satyr* a
couple of years earlier – appears as a rationalist. The mysteries of the
Christian religion, he argues, are incomprehensible and hence un-
believable, merely making way 'for all the Jugglings of Priests'. Burnet
counters that human beings cannot understand everything that goes on
in Nature – reproduction, for instance –, but that this does not prevent
such processes from taking place. Rochester's objections to 'Mysteries'
and 'things against [his] Reason' suggest that he was not familiar with
those devotional works where the supra-rational was carefully balanced
against the rational and found to be, at least, not irrational. This is hardly
surprising. Still, whether he wanted to or not, he will have heard a good
many sermons, at Court and in the country, which will have reflected
the manner in which contemporary clergymen relied on and invoked
reason. It was obviously not congenial to him. Having heard reason
praised from the pulpit, and being unaware of the limitations imposed
on it in religious treatises whose argumentation had to be much more
cautiously worded than the occasional sermon, he may have placed
what he regarded as current clergyman jargon in the adversarius'
mouth.

That gentleman's high-flown rhetoric and inflated claims for the
capacities of reason need not of course be misrepresentations due to the
poet's lack of detailed knowledge about developments in contemporary
theology. They may simply be deliberate exaggerations, set up to form
satisfactorily large targets for rebuttal. If they are, it must still be granted
that the substance of the 'Band, and Beard's' contentions are middle-of-

---

[34] For an illuminating précis of Robert Boyle's view of the capacities of reason, see Richard S.
Westfall, *Science and Religion in Seventeenth-Century England* (New Haven, 1958), pp. 168–9.
Boyle, an exponent of the new science who was also a devout Christian, held that 'The proper
function of human reason is not to teach us supernatural things but to lead us to a supernatural
teacher – that is, to God – and to defend the things that He teaches from the charge of being
contradictory or impossible.'

the-road views which any clergyman at the time could have uttered, whether he was an ex-Covenanter or a bred-in-the-bone Anglican. Some of them could have been voiced by a Roman Catholic priest, too. This generality increases the efficiency of the *Satyr*'s attack on the clergy; so does the fact that the notions so confidently expressed by the adversarius were under attack from outside Christian orthodoxy.

The final ethical dimension of his speech fits into this picture. The claim that reason alone is the agent that procures the information we need to '*give the World true grounds of hope and fear*' may be an exaggeration, but the concern with living well so as to secure the desired kind of afterlife was a vital issue.

It should be borne in mind that the adversarius never speaks about leading a virtuous life, nor does he refer explicitly to life after death. All he says is that reason helps us '*find out what's acted*' in Heaven and Hell, and that it tells us what goes on in those parts of the Universe of which we can have no direct perceptions. Armed with that knowledge, we will know what to anticipate. To the typical Anglican clergyman of Rochester's day, man's chance of earthly happiness and eventual salvation lay to a great extent in his making the right use of those principles and faculties with which he had been naturally endowed. Latitudinarians and Cambridge Platonists repeatedly emphasised the importance of morality; in fact, their sermons were more apt to concentrate on moral obligations than on theological matters. An illustrative example is supplied by Glanvill, who held that the end of morality was 'to restore the empire of our *minds* over the *will*, and *affections*', morality consisting in 'subduing *self-will* and ruling our *passions*, and moderating our *appetites*'.[35]

This seems to be the sort of attitude that the *Satyr* speaker attacks in lines 98–111. The kind of reason imputed to the interlocutor in those lines – 'Your *Reason*' – is not in fact articulated by him in his short speech. He says nothing about killing desires, destroying appetites or deferring to the clock rather than to one's hunger pangs. But the speaker is not conscious of a discrepancy between the adversarius' claims and his own reply. He has plainly heard it all before and consequently answers what he is sure the other man would have gone on to say, as well as what he actually had a chance to say.

To uphold the necessity of leading a virtuous life before the Court of Charles II cannot have been an easy or congenial task. Still, Court

---

[35] 'Anti-fanatical Religion and Free Philosophy', quoted in Cope, *Joseph Glanvill*, p. 57.

chaplains and other notable London preachers never wearied of it, perhaps partly for that very reason. Rochester must have heard them *ad nauseam*. Some of that nausea can, I think, be felt behind the speaker's impatience and rudeness.

Describing the attempts made by rational theologians to refute atheism, Barbara Shapiro has presented the following summary of the content of such writings:

The first step in the attack on enthusiasts and atheists was to establish the basic principles of religion by means of the unaided reason. Although the lists of basic principles varied slightly, they usually included the existence of God and his attributes, the immortality of the soul, the existence of rewards and punishments after death, and the need to worship the deity and live a moral life. A large number of works dealt with one or more of these topics, and together they make up a not inconsiderable portion of the major theological writings of the era.[36]

This account of Anglican attitudes in the second half of the seventeenth century agrees fairly well with the claims put forward by the 'Band, and Beard'. Whether or not Rochester read any of the essays and treatises written by the influential churchmen of his time, he knew their tenets and arguments well enough to make sure that his adversarius was a figure whom his readers would have no difficulty in recognising.

HOBBES AND MONTAIGNE – DEBTS AND DEPARTURES

When the *Satyr* was written, Christians of all denominations had spent more than two decades attacking Thomas Hobbes. The label 'atheist' was overtly fixed to Hobbes at about the time when Rochester joined the Court of Charles II.[37] As Samuel I. Mintz has pointed out, the term 'atheism' did not, in the seventeenth century, merely refer to the denial of God's existence; 'it also meant any arguments which tended in that direction, even if only by implication'.[38] Hobbes' philosophy was widely felt to 'tend in that direction', and many orthodox Christians were appalled by its implications as they viewed them. To a twentieth-

---

[36] *Probability and Certainty*, p. 83.

[37] In 1666, a Bill against atheism, clearly aimed at Hobbes, was brought into the Commons. It was never passed, but Hobbes was forbidden to publish in England. Like so many other controversial English authors, he resorted to publishing in Holland instead. See D. D. Raphael, *Hobbes: Morals and Politics* (London, 1977), p. 14.

[38] *The Hunting of Leviathan: Seventeenth-Century Reactions to the Materialism and Moral Philosophy of Thomas Hobbes* (Cambridge, 1962), p. 39.

century reader, Hobbes' alleged atheism is at best an elusive quality, and many modern scholars have denied or modified the charge.[39]

Inevitably, Hobbes' own name came to be a byword of atheism. Mintz's account (*The Hunting of Leviathan*, pp. 50–1) of the recantation made by one Daniel Scargill, Fellow of Corpus Christi College, Cambridge, in 1668 provides a neat illustration of guilt by association. Scargill rues having professed 'that I gloried to be an *Hobbist* and an *Atheist*' and laments his past indulgence in 'great licentiousness, swearing rashly, drinking intemperately' as well as in other vices which have a familiar ring to the Rochester student. One of the best-known contemporary accounts of the poet, the entry in Anthony Wood's *Athenae Oxonienses*,[40] contains a regretful parenthesis on the influence of the Court on the young Earl, '([it] not only debauched him but made him a perfect Hobbist)'. Obviously, Hobbism is even worse than mere loose living.

Leaving the question of Rochester's atheism aside,[41] the nature and extent of Hobbes' influence on the poetry is clearly an important issue. It has been discussed and reviewed by several critics, for instance Thomas H. Fujimura, who argued that such an influence probably operated with regard to the *Satyr*.[42] It seems to me that Fujimura and others have made a good case for the poem's indebtedness to Hobbes, although the nature of that indebtedness calls for further investigation.

While several expressions and contentions in the *Satyr* resemble Hobbesian statements, others contradict essential elements in Hobbes' philosophy. It would have been convenient to begin with the similarities, go on to the differences, and present a joint appraisal of Hobbes' significance in the *Satyr* context by way of conclusion, but this is unsatisfactory in practice. Nearly every Hobbesian context evoked by Rochester's *Satyr* entails contrast as well as affinity when brought into conjunction with the poem. In fact, this is a recurrent phenomenon

[39] See the summary offered by Raphael, *Hobbes*, pp. 85–7, as well as F. C. Hood's *The Divine Politics of Thomas Hobbes* (Oxford, 1964).

[40] 1692; it is easily accessible in the *Critical Heritage* volume, pp. 170–3.

[41] See pp. 360ff. below.

[42] 'Rochester's "Satyr against Mankind": An Analysis', *Studies in Philology* 55.4 (October 1958), 576–90; it was reprinted by Vieth in his *Critical Essays*. See also Pinto, *Enthusiast in Wit*, pp. 26–9; Griffin, *Satires Against Man*, pp. 168–73; and Robinson's 'Rochester and Hobbes and the Irony of *A Satyr against Reason and Mankind*', *The Yearbook of English Studies* 3 (1973), 108–19. Ford Russell has contributed important observations on Rochester and Hobbes, partly correcting Fujimura, in his 'Satiric Perspective in Rochester's *A Satyr against Reason and Mankind*', *Papers on Language and Literature* 22.3 (Summer 1986); see especially 246–7 on fear and power.

where influences on Rochester are concerned: virtually every similarity connotes a discrepancy.

One of the most striking verbal resemblances between the *Satyr* and Hobbes' *Leviathan* occurs in line 78, where human life is said to be 'short' and 'void of all rest'. It recalls the passage – surely the most-quoted of all – in chapter 13 of *Leviathan*, where Hobbes summarises the 'state of nature', 'where every man is Enemy to every man'. It is a condition dominated by 'continuall feare, and danger of violent death', where the life of man is 'solitary, poore, nasty, brutish, and short'.

But to conclude from this that Rochester and Hobbes have similar views on the condition of man would be a mistake. Hobbes' famous words refer to a state where no sovereign rules, no binding laws exist and every man has to fend for himself. He would have been the first to deny that Restoration England was such a society.[43] The *Satyr* speaker, on the other hand, expresses a view which applies to human beings generally, including educated men in a civilised nation.

Lines 33ff. ('His wisdom did his happiness destroy', etc.) suggest that every human being is born with the option of enjoying the world, but fails to realise it as he falls victim to pride, wisdom and wit. By contrast, Hobbes argues that man's original condition, the state of nature, is as far removed from enjoyment as it is possible to be. Only by attaining security through joint submission to the laws of a commonwealth can men know that peace which is their most urgent desire.

The condemnation of 'humane Nature' in lines 124ff. does not have much to do with Hobbes either. The expression 'Savage *Man*' may seem to imply a reference to Hobbes' state of nature, but the description of man's baseness has no counterpart in Hobbes' characterisation of that state. Hobbes never says that man is depraved or vicious in his natural state, however repellent those actions may seem which he undertakes to avert what he regards as dangers to him. On the contrary, 'Force, and Fraud, are in warre the two Cardinall vertues.'

Fortunately, man may come out of this 'ill condition', and one of the instruments he will then have to rely on is his reason. Hate, lust, ambition and covetousness, and the crimes they are apt to produce, are, says Hobbes, 'so annexed to the nature, both of man, and all other living creatures, as that their effects cannot be hindred, but by extraordinary use of Reason, or a constant severity in punishing them' (ch. 27). This is a very different view from the one held by the *Satyr* speaker. Hobbes

---

[43] In fact, he has to resort to 'savage people in many places of *America*' for an example, and admits that there was probably never a time when this state prevailed all over the world (ch. 13).

declares that all created beings are afflicted with these 'infirmities' (animals are hence no better than men); these qualities are part of our very nature, forming a marked contrast to the 'instinct' praised by the satirist; and they must be restrained.

Unlike the *Satyr* protagonist, Hobbes advocated education and felt, with Bacon, that 'knowledge is power'.[44] However forbidding his view of man, 'natural' and 'civilised', may appear,[45] it is less disheartening than the one communicated by Rochester's poem. Man may, according to Hobbes, achieve the peace and security he longs for – if he is reasonable enough to comprehend that this calls for him to surrender the right to follow his own natural impulses, so that he can enjoy the protection of a commonwealth and its laws. This kind of argumentation is far from the satirist's insistence on the soundness of man's natural instincts against the perversions of rational thought.

One *Satyr* feature that has been associated with Hobbes is the emphasis on sense perception.[46] The satirist suggests (lines 8–9) that the five senses are more reliable as purveyors of information about the world around us than that man-made quality, the 'Sixth sense' (see p. 193 below). He also says that 'sense' is a better guide than reason (line 13) and that it provides the soundest advisory principle for action (lines 100ff.). By contrast, the adversarius stresses the happy ability of reason to transcend '*material sense*'. In the latter cases, 'sense' does not refer solely to the sense organs; and the last two instances where 'sense' occurs in the *Satyr* (lines 197 and 216) imply 'common sense', as opposed to '*Nonsense*' (line 89), rather than 'transmitter(s) of sense perceptions'.

Hobbes' philosophy rests on his view of the functions of the senses. In F. S. McNeilly's words:

... in Hobbes's philosophy thinking is nothing more than a succession of images (or conceptions) which originate in sense experience. According to Hobbes, the world, and our experience of it, is all to be explained in terms of the actions and interactions of physical objects – motions of bodies. We see objects as coloured, feel them as hot and cold, and so forth. The colour and the heat,

---

[44] See Raphael, *Hobbes*, p. 11.

[45] The popular idea according to which Hobbes argued that men are wicked, wolflike creatures who prey on one another has been attacked by several scholars. One example is Paul J. Johnson, 'Hobbes and the Wolf-Man', in J. G. van der Bend, ed., *Thomas Hobbes: His View of Man* (Amsterdam, 1982), pp. 31–44.

[46] See, for instance, Fujimura, 'Rochester's "Satyr"', 579 and 583, and Robinson, 'Rochester and Hobbes', 110–12. These two critics argue that Rochester 'follows Hobbes' (Robinson, 'Rochester and Hobbes', 109). A similar opinion is put forward by Raymond K. Whitley in 'Rochester: A Cosmological Pessimist', *English Studies in Canada* 4 (Summer 1978), 188–9.

however, are not properties inhering in the objects, but are how the objects appear to us: they are *appearances* in us, caused by the action of the objects on our sense organs...We ourselves are material objects, with physical sense organs which react to the stimulus of objects external to us. We have knowledge of these objects only through the images which they cause in us; and these images, strictly speaking, are merely our awareness, not of the objects causing them, but of the physical state of our own organism – produced by the action of the objects upon it.[47]

In affirming the supreme importance of the sense organs, Hobbes is not making the sort of claims for them that the speaker in the *Satyr* does. Hobbes is concerned with describing processes of understanding, not with evaluating the respective merits of intellectual and sensual capacities. When, in chapter 6 of *Leviathan*, he discourses on good and evil, he states that these terms 'are ever used with relation to the person that useth them: There being nothing simply and absolutely so'. What we want, we call good; what we dislike we call evil. 'Appetite' and 'aversion' are the terms chosen by Hobbes to designate those 'motions' which determine whether something is good or bad to us. The only absolute rules in this respect are those applied by the representative of the power whose decrees we have agreed to abide by.

Again, a resemblance has turned out to involve a contrast. By and large, previous Rochester critics have tended to draw attention to similarities rather than discrepancies, but one instance where Rochester departs from Hobbes has been noted (originally by Fujimura): the treatment of fear in the *Satyr*. To Hobbes, fear is the quality that impels men to seek security and to avoid breaking the laws (ch. 27). True, crimes may be committed through fear; but judged by its effects, it could be said to be a constructive passion.

In my opinion, the difference between Hobbes' view of fear in chapter 27 and the presentation of fear in the *Satyr* lies not so much in its effects on people's actions; it is more a matter of how those actions are regarded in relation to an ideal. In Hobbes' state of nature men make ceaseless war against one another for fear of domination and oppression. The *Satyr* depicts mankind as engaged in an endless arms race, every twist of the upward spiral being caused by renewed fear. Fear compels people to abide by the laws of the state, according to Hobbes; outwardly praiseworthy behaviour is the result of fear, says Rochester's speaker. No great difference – but while Hobbes has no quarrel with the

[47] *The Anatomy of Leviathan* (London and New York, 1968), pp. 31ff.

actions caused by fear, the *Satyr* deplores them. All the glorious feats of those who have been driven by 'base fear' are actually sheer hypocrisy; if people lived according to their instincts, as the *Satyr* speaker has advocated before, a mass of public virtue would vanish – an outcome which Hobbes would hardly regard as favourable.

Fujimura argued that Hobbes, unlike the *Satyr*, saw desire for power, not fear, as man's main motive ('Rochester's "Satyr"', 585–6), but this is a questionable view on two grounds. First, Hobbes shows that the desire for power is closely related to the fear of coming under oppression (chs. 13 and 14); there is thus no real contradiction between the two passions, but more of a confluence. Second, the *Satyr* also associates fear with 'That lust of *Pow'r*, to which [man's] such a *Slave*'.

There are other *Satyr* passages which bring Hobbes to mind without signalling such marked discrepancies as the contexts reviewed above. One is the insistence (in lines 161–73) on the necessity of doing unto others as they do unto one another, and unto you, even if it means being dishonest. Hobbes says (in ch. 15) that 'he that should be modest, and tractable, and performe all he promises, in such time, and place, where no man els should do so, should but make himselfe a prey to others, and procure his own certain ruine'. (This somewhat cynical opinion is not, of course, peculiar to Hobbes and Rochester.) The occurrence of such typically Hobbesian terms as 'appetites' and 'voluntary' bespeaks familiarity with Hobbes, and the presentation of the two paragons has Hobbesian features (see p. 236 below). Further possible Hobbes parallels are mentioned in the ensuing chapter (pp. 221 and 227). It seems clear to me that Rochester was well acquainted with Hobbes' philosophy, but that he adapted its terminology and ideas to his own very personal uses. The fact that Hobbes' person (well known to the Court Wits) and work were so hysterically maligned by those divines and schoolmen whom Rochester detested so heartily will only have increased his appeal to the young courtier.

Excerpting odd pieces of *Leviathan*, juxtaposing them with *Satyr* arguments and proclaiming a set of similarities is not a very demanding task. Subjecting Montaigne's *Essais* to a similar exercise is easier still. The very nature of that unique project ensures that it submits tractably to quotation-for-a-purpose operations. Montaigne's self-explorations were not aimed at producing a consistent set of beliefs or a hierarchy of ideas. The cast of his mind made the unprejudiced testing of heterogeneous notions natural as well as desirable to him. In fact, it is one of the miracles of the *Essais* that their analyses of evidence and opinion can allow for so much diversity and width without wearying the reader or making him/her lose the author's distinctive voice. According to a German proverb, it is the tone that makes the music; the captivating charm of the *Essais* stems from the man's personal tone rather than from the themes he discusses or the arguments he considers.[48]

S. F. Crocker's early study of Rochester's *Satyr* led him to conclude that of the possible sources he had consulted, Montaigne's *Apologie de Raimond Sebond* was the one that most resembled the poem.[49] Crocker broke the *Satyr* down into fourteen leading ideas and related each of them to passages from Montaigne's *Apologie*, as well as to excerpts from Boileau and a few of the French *libertinage* poets.

Some of the passages which Crocker relates to the *Satyr* are true parallels. This is the case with Montaigne's denunciation of the presumptuousness and vanity of men who aspire to a kind of knowledge that is beyond their understanding. The bitter attacks on man's unwarranted pride and on the idea that he is superior to the rest of Creation definitely come into this category, too.

Other alleged links are more tenuous, and some hardly deserve the name at all. Two instances of the latter concern qualities reviewed above in connexion with Hobbes: sense perception and fear.

Crocker claims that Montaigne 'expressly stipulates that man should follow the dictates of the senses'. He quotes two passages as evidence, passages where the philosopher states that 'les sens sont le commencement & la fin de l'humaine cognoissance' and that man's notion of holding an advantage over other created beings is small reason for self-glorification. However, the conviction that we can only know what the senses have transmitted to us – a classical Epicurean idea – is not the same as the notion that they are our best guides for action. Far from claiming that we should rely on our senses to guide us aright, Montaigne writes:

Cette mesme pipperie, que les sens apportent à nostre entendement, ils la reçoiuent à leur tour. Nostre ame par fois s'en reuenche de mesme, ils mentent, & se trompent à l'enuy … Il semble que l'ame retire au dedans, & amuse les puissances des sens. Par ainsin & le dedans et le dehors de l'homme est plein de

---

[48] This is not to say that Michel Eyquem the man and his private circumstances are always at the centre of the *Essais*. See, for instance, the discussion of the different *mois* of the *Essais* in ch. 4 of Pierre Moreau's *Montaigne: L'Homme et l'œuvre* (Paris, 1953; pp. 42ff.).

[49] 'Rochester's *Satire against Mankind*: A Study of Certain Aspects of the Background', *West Virginia University Bulletin* 3, Philological Papers vol. 2 (May 1937), 57–73.

foiblesse & de mensonge ... Si les sens sont noz premiers iuges, ce ne sont pas les nostres qu'il faut seuls appeller au conseil ...[50]

As for fear, the lines quoted by Crocker have little to do with it and nothing at all with the presentation of fear in the *Satyr*. Crocker's passage is taken from the well-known pages where, at the beginning of the *Apologie*, Montaigne vents his disgust at the abuses of religion. It would be difficult to find any paragraph in the *Essais* that would seem directly relevant to the *Satyr* in this sense. The short essay that Montaigne wrote on fear (I.xviii) will not do as a quarry for such material. It does mention the possibility of achieving military victory as a result of a frenzied wish to escape from battle. This, however, has nothing in common with the *Satyr* argument that men's best passions are inspired by fear and that 'all Men, wou'd be *Cowards* if they durst'.

Not even on the subject of men and animals does Montaigne's *Apologie* actually offer a parallel to Rochester's *Satyr*. Crocker's claim that 'The idea of the superiority of animal to man is frequently stated by Montaigne' ('Rochester's *Satire against Mankind*', 67) is not borne out by the *Essais*. It is true that animals possess certain laudable qualities in greater measure than men – loyal friendship is one example –, but Montaigne does not argue that beasts are generally 'better far' than people. There are differences in degree, but not in kind:

... nous ne sommes ny au dessus ny au dessous du reste : tout ce qui est soubs le Ciel, dit le Sage, court vne loy & fortune pareille ... Nous deuons conclure de pareils effects, pareilles facultez, & de plus riches effects des facultez plus riches : & côfesser par côsequent, que ce mesme discours, cette mesme voye, que nous tenôs à oeuurer, aussi la tiennêt des animaux. (1598 edition, pp. 453–4)

Still, both Rochester and Montaigne refer to animals in their attempts to demonstrate the vanity of man's pretensions to supremacy in the Creation, and their turns of phrase are often similar. The *Apologie* contains several examples, and so do other *Essais* where Montaigne regrets that man, a 'miserable animal', will ruin his chance of pure enjoyment and augment his misery by 'art and study' instead of simply relishing the powers with which he is endowed in his natural condition (cf., for instance, I.xxx, *Des Cannibales*). These lines of thought come very close to some of the argumentation in the *Satyr*.

---

[50] Quoted from *Les Essais de Michel Seigneur de Montaigne* (Paris, 1598), pp. 608–10. Donald M. Frame has stressed that according to Montaigne, 'all [man's] instruments of knowledge, notably the senses, are demonstrably deficient and deceptive'; see *Montaigne's Essais: A Study* (Englewood Cliffs, 1969), pp. 28–9.

Montaigne's frequently quoted words about the differences between men and animals, 'il y a plus de distance de tel à tel homme qu'il n'y a de tel homme à telle beste' (in the opening passage of *Essais* I.xlii), form a 'striking parallel' to the conclusion of the *Satyr*, as Crocker maintained ('Rochester's *Satire against Mankind*', 71). Montaigne's point of departure is Plutarch's contention that there is a greater difference between man and man than there is between beast and beast. Actually, as John F. Moore pointed out, Plutarch's *Gryllus* offers an even closer parallel to Montaigne's adaptation; it reads: 'I do not believe that there is such difference between man and beast in reason and understanding and memory, as between man and man.'[51] Contemplation of the distance between an ideal man like Epaminondas and people of Montaigne's own acquaintance led him to this estimation. Rochester's speaker also sets up the conception of an ideal man, or rather two ideal men, against those he sees around him. Despite the existence of the Plutarch locus, with which Rochester may well have been familiar, the similarity in expression and application seems great enough to permit the conclusion that the *Satyr* is directly indebted to the *Essais* on this point.

If it is correct to see a deliberate allusion to the *Essais* in the last line of the *Satyr*, it should be borne in mind that this reference is not to the *Apologie* but to *De l'inequalité qui est entre nous*, in the first book (the *Apologie* is in the second). Are there grounds for assuming that Rochester knew the *Essais* as a whole?

I think there is circumstantial evidence to suggest this. Some of these indications are found in parallels between ideas expressed by Montaigne and Rochester respectively; others have more to do with divergences than with resemblances. An example of the former is Montaigne's view of human life as a flux in which people and conditions are constantly changing. To a poet whose denials and refutations of fixity of any kind are as frequent and vehement as Rochester's, this contention will have seemed like confirmation on a vital issue.[52] Himself moving from one position to another, in his public and private life as well as in his writings, Rochester is not likely to have overlooked the statement towards the end of *Essais* II.i according to which there is 'autant de difference de nous à nous mesmes, que de nous à autruy'.

It might seem odd to propose that differences between his own attitudes and Montaigne's may have served to attract such a wilful and

---

[51] 'The Originality of Rochester's *Satyr against Mankind*', *PMLA* 58.2 (June 1943), 393–4n.
[52] See Treglown, *Letters*, p. 17.

irritable intellect as Rochester's. Still, it seems to me that Montaigne's mixture of modesty and authority, allied with his freedom from cant and self-righteousness, must have held a powerful appeal for the young Englishman who moved on partly similar territory a hundred years later. Like Montaigne, Rochester belonged to the exalted circles of his nation and saw the management of his country's turbulent affairs at first hand. Again like his predecessor in France, he found plenty to abhor in those who wielded power, receiving a succession of object lessons in vanity, treachery and greed. The poise attained by Montaigne was foreign to Rochester's feverish restlessness, but he will have recognised that it was not based on self-deception, ignorance of the affairs of men, or religious or moral bigotry. Serenity is too strong a word to use of Montaigne's view of human life and his own place in it, but the stretches of enlightened tranquillity found in the Frenchman's writings must have seemed refreshing to Rochester's unquiet mind. While Montaigne's wholehearted commitment to the Catholic faith and to retired rural existence was uncongenial to Rochester, he had some experience of both. According to Burnet, his wife was 'for some years misled into the Communion of the Church of *Rome*', partly at her husband's instigation, and the periods spent on their country estates gave him plenty of opportunities for leading a contemplative life. The fact that he did not cling to it does not mean that he saw nothing good in it.[53]

Another reason for believing that Rochester read Montaigne is the sheer entertainment value of the *Essais*. Whether he read them in Florio's 1603 translation or in one of the many French editions that kept appearing every few years up to 1669, he cannot have failed to relish their vigorous, lucid style, their 'spoken flavour', the immediacy of their imagery, and their humour, ranging from gentle irony to the richly comic.

Finally, in the 1670s the *Essais* possessed the glamour of the scandalous, not unlike the writings of Hobbes. Still popular among the *beaux esprits* of France, they had come under heavy attack from theologians.[54] In 1676, after several years of lobbying, they were put on the *Index librorum prohibitorum*. Montaigne was accused of not caring about the soul's salvation (Pascal) or about knowing God (Bishop Bossuet); and

---

[53] Cf. *ibid.*, pp. 15 and 19–20.
[54] See ch. 27 in Alan M. Boase's *The Fortunes of Montaigne: A History of the Essays in France, 1580–1669* (first published in 1935; I have used the 1970 reprint issued by Octagon Books, New York).

warnings were issued against the dangerous pleasure of reading the
Essais and being seduced by them and their underlying call to
concupiscence (Malebranche). In England, Montaigne – naturally
enough – did not arouse enmity of this kind. The essays of Abraham
Cowley owed a great deal to his example. Before that, he had inspired
Bacon and was thus a respected name among Royal Society men.
Dryden was able to quote him on occasion, and so no doubt were other
Restoration poets. To Rochester, however, who spent time in France in
the late 1660s and early 1670s, Montaigne would have had the additional
appeal of priestly disapproval.

THE QUESTION OF BOILEAU

The first scholarly reaction of any length to Crocker's article was John
F. Moore's defence of the originality of the *Satyr*. Moore's article, which
mentions some resemblances and divergences between Rochester's
poem and Boileau's eighth satire, is geared to demonstrating Rochester's
relative independence of previously suggested 'sources'. By way of a
preamble, he voices a general reservation against making too much of
parallels between Montaigne's *Essais* and the work of any later writer.
This reservation is based on the nature of the *Essais* in that they
constitute a 'collection of ideas culled from earlier writers'.[55] According
to Moore, Rochester may well have gleaned the content of statements
made by Montaigne from the Frenchman's predecessors. The possibility
that he also derived Montaignean ideas from Montaigne's successors can
be seen in some of the resemblances to Cowley, Sir Thomas Browne
and others suggested in this book.

The reason why critics have given attention to a possible influence of
Boileau's on Rochester is simple: he had been known to express his
admiration for the French poet, and his contemporaries were aware of
it and ready to perceive parallels between the two poets' work. Samuel
Johnson, relying on Burnet, makes the straightforward statement that
'his favourite author in French was Boileau, and in English Cowley',
and scholars of different generations have referred to these preferences as
to an established fact.

Rochester's grounds for appreciating Cowley are obvious. His
partiality for Boileau may, at first sight, seem harder to explain. To most
modern readers, the name of Boileau, author of *L'Art poétique*, has a

---

[55] Moore, 'The Originality', 393. In this, of course, Montaigne was typical of his time. The
exhibition of original ideas was not a priority with seventeenth-century writers either.

decidedly fusty smell which makes him seem an unlikely influence on a restive Court Wit.[56] In fact, the traditional conception of L'Art poétique as a tedious treatise on correct writing does not stand up to an open-minded perusal of it. One thing that enlivens Boileau's discourse is his unkind treatment of several of his contemporaries. He always thought of himself as a satirist, schooled by the great ancient master of the art, Horace;[57] and it was Boileau the satirist – only eleven years older than himself – whom Rochester admired. Some of Boileau's satires first appeared in a pirated edition in 1666 (the 'monstrueuse' edition); it was soon followed by bona fide ones. When Rochester encountered Boileau, the latter was hence a fairly recently discovered, and frequently criticised, writer of satirical poetry, 'un genre sans grand éclat'.[58] Again, Rochester's predilection for controversial writers is in evidence.

Like Rochester, Boileau had the audacity to direct sharp attacks at the powerful people of his day, finding several victims among the nobility and the clergy as well as in the academic world. The 'monstrous edition' even contained a few naughty lines behind which his fellow countrymen would immediately have seen the great Colbert.[59] His ungracious treatment of a number of colleagues in the literary satires, and his engagement in the conflict between 'ancients' and 'moderns', soon involved him in disputes which recall Rochester's quarrels with Mulgrave and Scroope.

It is Boileau's eighth satire, 'A Monsieur M[orel], Docteur de Sorbonne', that has been said to have inspired Rochester's Satyr. The relationship between the two has been variously described from Augustan times to our own. Thomas Rymer commented on it, vigorously and chauvinistically preferring Rochester,[60] and Voltaire as well as Horace Walpole mentioned the connexion. In a well-known statement towards the end of his pages on Rochester in Lives of the English Poets, Dr Johnson implied that Rochester's debt to Boileau was a considerable one, remarking succinctly: 'Of the Satire against Man Rochester can only claim what remains when all Boileau's part is taken away.' That Rochester 'imitated' Boileau was a contention put forward by several subsequent commentators, and it was only in the twentieth

[56] For influences in Rochester's Allusion to Horace, see pp. 332–3 below.
[57] See, for example, Joseph Pineau, L'Univers satirique de Boileau: L'ardeur, la grâce et la loi (Geneva, 1990).
[58] See René Bray's introduction to the poet in Boileau: L'Homme et l'œuvre (Paris, 1942), p. 15.
[59] Ibid., p. 21. The lines are often quoted; see for instance the notes to C.-H. Boudhors' 1934 edition of the Satires, part of the Oeuvres complètes, p. 191.
[60] In the Preface to the Reader in Tonson's 1691 edition of Rochester's poems.

century that the nature and extent of this influence were again sharply questioned. A. F. B. Clark set the tone for modern critics when referring to Johnson's statement and continuing: 'With all respect to Johnson, "Boileau's part" does not seem to me to be a very great one.'[61]

While drawing attention to several pertinent passages in Boileau's eighth satire, both Crocker and Moore emphasised the differences between that poem and the *Satyr*. Not until 1969 was the case for Boileau brought up again, in Paul C. Davies' article 'Rochester and Boileau: A Reconsideration'.[62] Davies' brief discussion does not add much substance to a joint consideration of the two poems. Its chief merit lies in the valuable presentation of relevant passages from Boileau's other satires, notably the fourth. Joseph Warton had said (in 1782) that Rochester's *Satyr* was 'from the fourth of Boileau';[63] Davies does not refer to this statement but helps to show that it need not have been a mere *lapsus calami*.

Despite all this inconclusive theorising about the influence of Boileau's eighth satire on Rochester's most famous poem, the two texts have rarely been subjected to sustained comparative scrutiny. Most critics have pointed out that Boileau's use of an adversarius could have influenced Rochester and that his satire, like Rochester's, compared mankind unfavourably to animals. Verbal similarities, above all the image of man who 'Voltige incessamment de pensée en pensée' (line 36), have been noted. There is a shortage of concrete discussions, though.

That Rochester should have been unaffected by an entertaining satirical discussion, written by a man whose work he admired and was familiar with in the early 1670s, on the shortcomings of mankind in relation to animals seems unlikely to me. Boileau's satire was first published in 1668. Some six years later, Rochester devoted a long satirical poem to the defects of mankind as compared to animals, including an interlocutor whose arguments are torn to shreds by the satirist. However differently Boileau used his *docteur*, and although the adversarius device occurs in classical satire as well, the idea that Boileau's example prompted the appearance of the 'Band, and Beard' appears perfectly credible.

There are further points that connect the two satires. Neither Boileau

---

[61] *Boileau and the French Classical Critics in England (1660–1830)* (Paris, 1925), p. 114.

[62] *Comparative Literature* 21 (Fall 1969), 348–55.

[63] In his *Essay on the Genius and Writings of Pope, Volume the Second*, p. 110; see Farley-Hills' *Critical Heritage*, p. 207.

nor Rochester denies that man is equipped with reason; this is precisely what makes him so unfortunate. When Boileau's *docteur* calls man's reason his torch and faithful pilot (line 235), the satirist retorts that it is of precious little service to him. When the light of that torch falls on a rock, he heads straight for it instead of staying away from it, which would have been a far more sensible course (cf. the '*Mountains* of Whimseys' in the *Satyr*). Both poets assert that learned institutions house fools and that the efforts of scientists exploring the universe have brought small benefits. The *Satyr*'s insistence on the necessity of being a knave among knaves has points in common with the cynical parental advice in Boileau's satire (cf., for instance, line 193).

Like Rochester, Boileau is rude to the governing bodies and to high dignitaries. The machinery of the law, with all its puffed-up officers, is something animals do not need. Beasts know 'Ni haut, ni bas Conseil, ni Chambre des Enquestes' (line 148) and are all the better for it. Their natural instincts make it possible for them to live according to 'laws' which prevent them from making senseless war on one another: 'L'Homme seul, l'Homme seul en sa fureur extrême, / Met un brutal honneur à s'égorger soi-même.'

Man is superstitious and frightened of the figments of his own imagination, says Boileau. Up to 1683, when pressure from 'personnes de piété' resulted in their removal, two lines in the eighth satire read: 'De Fantosmes en l'air combatre leurs desirs, / Et de vains argumens chicaner leurs plaisirs.'[64] Disapproved of as being too 'libertines', they resemble the 'Whimseys, heap'd in his own *Brain*' of the *Satyr*. That poem's outline of right reason (lines 99–109) seems relevant to the French satire in this respect, too.

All these points of resemblance are just that – there is similarity, but no identicalness and no obvious reference. A comparative reading of the two poems reveals a good deal of dissimilarity as well.

To begin with, Boileau's satire gives little space to those two passions that are presented as the prime curses of mankind in Rochester's poem, pride and fear. Of course, pride in intellectual attainments is indirectly given a dressing-down in the attacks on academic stupidity ('un Docteur n'est qu'un sot'). Still, Boileau does not argue that pride is a major reason for the miserable condition of mankind. It is significant that his poem starts by affirming that man is the most *stupid* animal, whereas Rochester's begins by referring to man as a *vain* animal.

[64] See p. 360 in Boudhors' edition of Boileau's *Satires*.

Other examples show that the faults which Boileau's satire imputes to man are not the same as the ones castigated in the *Satyr*. For instance, the French poem deplores man's lack of wisdom, 'Sagesse', 'Une égalité d'ame', of which he has less than other creatures, being forever restless, inconsistent and unreliable. This is not one of the human features impugned in the *Satyr*. Boileau gives much more space than Rochester does to the folly of avarice and ambition. Also, the Frenchman's preoccupation with lucre has no counterpart in the English poem. Boileau's animus against the legal and medical professions is not paralleled in the *Satyr* either.

Conversely, the *Satyr* contains much important matter that is hardly, if at all, present in the poem Rochester was supposed to have imitated. The exposition on wit is one example; the emphasis on action and 'right reason' ruled by sense is another. The wanton wickedness of man, who viciously destroys his neighbour 'to do himself no good', is an even grimmer defect than the contemptible vices deplored by Boileau. Another vital difference is that there is nothing in Boileau's satire to parallel the 'Apology' or 'Addition' in the *Satyr*.

While it seems quite possible to me that Boileau's poem was 'the inspiration of' Rochester's, as Davies suggests ('Rochester and Boileau', 355), I doubt that 'he had it in mind as he was writing'. The former phrase implies that Boileau supplied the impulse to write a satire decrying man and his reason at the expense of animals and their sound instincts, which seems plausible. But Davies' second claim would mean that Rochester kept referring to the French poem while composing his own. The variety and extent of the divergences between the two satires, as well as the character of those divergences, make such a procedure less than likely; it is certainly difficult to make the term 'imitation' – however widely defined – fit the relationship between the poems.

One detail which can be taken to support that contention is the occurrence of a particular animal in both satires. Boileau's concludes with a lengthy discussion of the merits of an ass compared to the defects of man. At the end of the comparison, which rouses the indignation of the *docteur* who resents 'cet exemple odieux', the satirist imagines what the ass would say were he able to comment on the important people he sees in a Paris street. If the animal had the voice he possessed in Aesop's day, he would surely exclaim: 'Ma foi, non plus que nous; l'Homme n'est qu'une beste!' This is the last line of Boileau's poem. I find it hard to believe that the man who wrote 'Our *Sphere* of Action, is lifes happiness, / And he who thinks Beyond, thinks like an *Ass*' had that poem on his desk, or at the back of his head, while he was writing his own. In the *Satyr*, the expression 'thinks like an *Ass*' is obviously a term of censure such as Boileau's adversarius might have used. It is a small point, of course; but it appears to me to lend some weight to the view of Boileau's influence that has been put forward in this chapter.

7

'A Satyr against Reason and Mankind' : the argumentation

Rochester's most famous long poem directs its satirical thrusts at much the same targets as *Upon Nothing*: the pride, vanity, folly and treachery of men, especially those who would govern and influence others. The *Satyr*, however, is more inclusive and more complex. Like *Upon Nothing*, it attacks cognitive effort and intellectual occupations, but it does grant cerebral activity one permissible domain: that of directing the actions of humans in such a way as to help them derive the greatest possible gratification from the operations of their senses. In Rochester's love poems, mental urges drive men to seek contentment in sensual pleasure, only to find it sadly flawed. Unlike these frustrated protagonists, the *Satyr* speaker is not concerned with having experiences but with arguing a case, and the qualities of the senses are only part of it.

A modern reader who approaches Rochester's *Satyr against Reason and Mankind* with a collection of present-day opinions about it at his/her elbow cannot but wonder at the diversity of those opinions. How is it possible that such a superficially straightforward poem can have been so variously interpreted? On the face of it, it seems to make some eminently paraphrasable statements about the human condition. If those statements do not proceed in neat sequential stages, at least they are hardly overtly contradictory. But even on this point, two leading authorities object. David M. Vieth holds that the argumentation in the poem splits into two halves, the 'libertine' and the 'Hobbesian' subdivisions, which cannot be logically reconciled.[1] David Farley-Hills repeatedly maintains that an analysis of the *Satyr*'s arguments leads to complete impasse.[2] Different views of the poem's formal status have produced diverging ideas on what, and who, is actually satirised in it.

---

[1] See 'Toward an Anti-Aristotelian Poetic', 124–9.
[2] See, for instance, *Rochester's Poetry*, p. 184.

Repeated perusals of the considerable quantities of knowledgeable reasoning that have gone towards elucidating the poem's attack on precisely that activity are apt to induce weariness in the student. He or she may be left feeling that the unsound mental landscape of lines 14–19 lurks alongside his/her own pursuit of clarification. The idea of the satirist proving his point at his reader's expense across three centuries is a somewhat uncomfortable one.

Much of the controversy aroused by the *Satyr* is caused by disagreement regarding structural aspects. One example is the question of whether the poem's speaker is Rochester himself or a *persona* who is satirised in his turn.[3] Another is the result of uncertainty over epistemological versus ethical aspects. The vast amount of seventeenth-century thought and discussion on issues reflected in the *Satyr* may lead critics in different directions, too.

In a consideration of possible overall 'interpretations' or 'readings' of the *Satyr*, two questions are predominant: how is the human condition portrayed in the poem? and what choices are open to those who share it?

The introductory lines, 1–7, immediately establish that even the existence of a dog or a monkey would have been preferable to the human predicament. Such an existence is not an option, though; these lines make it clear that wishing one had been an(other) animal instead is pointless. The advantage held by beasts in comparison with men plays a vital part in the *Satyr*, but the initial manifestation of this idea is negative – man is inexorably fettered to his lot. These lines tell us comparatively little about the reasons for the superiority of beasts; they are mostly deferred to the latter half of the poem (lines 114–40). All we are given to understand at this point is that men and animals belong to the same kind – man is expressly included among the animals –, but that man's pride in his rationality makes him an inferior species.

Dustin Griffin has suggested that the whole poem turns on the paradox that it is better to be an animal than a man, which is defensively argued in a manner resembling the scholastic *quaestio* procedure.[4] I think

---

[3] See p. 238 below. James E. Gill's 'Mind against Itself: Theme and Structure in Rochester's *Satyr against Reason and Mankind*', *Texas Studies in Literature and Language* 23 (Winter 1981), 355–76, reviews some pertinent material in this respect.

[4] Griffin's helpful remarks on the term 'paradox' which could, in Rochester's day, mean 'a statement or tenet contrary to received opinion or belief' (pp. 200–3 in *Satires Against Man*) are followed by an exposition on this structural principle. Before him, Charles A. Knight had maintained that the preference of beasts to men 'dominates most of the poem and is its formal organizing device'; see 'The Paradox of Reason: Argument in Rochester's "Satyr against Mankind"', *The Modern Language Review* 65 (1970), 255. Other critics have held that classical

this structural model, ingenious as it is, fails to accommodate much that is not directly relevant to the man/beast comparison. Another objection to it is that the superiority of animals over men is presented in such a way that its essential function is to emphasise the baseness of human beings. 'Being an animal' is not a realisable preference. What the satirist is really concerned with is humiliating man.[5]

His choice of animal examples lends special weight to the degradation of mankind. The beasts which the speaker regards as being above human status are not independent wild creatures, which could have been invested with some sort of natural nobility. Nor are they docile providers of nourishment whose practical and pastoral functions might have given them a smatch of honour. Instead, he speaks of three animal categories whose main characteristic in relation to seventeenth-century man was that they served his diversions. Dogs were used in various sports and were entirely at the mercy of their human masters; so were monkeys, providers of drawing-room amusement. Bears, trained or baited,[6] were employed in human entertainment of a kind that seems particularly callous and cruel today. (Of course, bear-baiting involved dogs, too.) Despite the demeaning treatment these three species undergo at human hands, and whatever unpleasant qualities they might have in themselves (Rochester's letters and other poems do not betray any great fondness for dogs and monkeys), their masters are more contemptible than they.

The conclusion of *Tunbridge Wells*, often related to the *Satyr*, makes a similar point. The disgusted observer voices his personal sense of shame at making use of that 'wiser Creature', his horse, whose superiority lies in his 'doeing only things fit for his Nature'. Natural inclination versus non-natural reasoning forms the nucleus of lines 8–13 in the *Satyr*:

rhetoric played a part in the organisation of the *Satyr*; see, for instance, Ronald W. Johnson, 'Rhetoric and Drama', 367. A. D. Cousins argues that Rochester in writing his *Satyr* adapted the five- or six-part structure of the deliberate oration; see 'The Context, Design, and Argument of Rochester's *A Satyr against Reason and Mankind*', *Studies in English Literature 1500–1900* 24.3 (Summer 1984), 434.

[5] This concern is emphasised in Isabelle White's '"So Great a Disproportion": Paradox and Structure in Rochester's *A Satyr against Reason and Mankind*', originally published in the *Kentucky Philological Association Bulletin* (1976), 15–23. It has been reprinted, most recently in Vieth's *Critical Essays*, where the relevant passage occurs on p. 285.

[6] Cf. Pepys on the Bear Garden of London, 27 May 1667. A bear-warden and his beast play an important role in the first part of *Hudibras*. Bear-baiting was disapproved of by the Puritans, like other cruel animal sports, but became fashionable again after the Restoration; see Keith Thomas, *Man and the Natural World: A History of the Modern Sensibility* (New York, 1983), p. 158.

> The senses are too gross, and he'll contrive
> A Sixth, to contradict the other Five;
> And before certain instinct, will preferr
> *Reason*, which Fifty times for one does err.
> *Reason*, an *Ignis fatuus*, in the *Mind*,
> Which leaving light of *Nature*, sense behind ...

This short passage combines some of those terms that provide the argumentative raw materials of the poem: 'senses/sense, instinct, Nature' as opposed to 'Reason'. It also explains that this is where men and animals differ. Man is not content to be guided by the senses. In his unwarranted pride, he must needs improve on them by his own efforts. His creation, the 'Sixth' sense, actually goes against those five which he shares with animals – a classical error according to Epicurean philosophers.[7] Now as well as in the seventeenth century, the concept 'sixth sense' denotes some faculty of perception which is only conjectured to exist. In the *Satyr* context, the application of this term to man's contrivance merely emphasises its spuriousness.

Recoiling from the senses because they seem intellectually coarse and impure is not a sign of admirable refinement but of conceit. Only men commit this folly. Those who spend their whole lives indulging in it – by implication philosophers and learned men in general – are especially ludicrous because they take pride in that which works their ruin. The classical notion of the dangers of intellectual hubris was often voiced by other seventeenth-century authors, too. Samuel Butler was one of them; his *Character* of 'An Hermetic Philosopher' ridicules certain thinkers who

very much contemn any Knowledge, that is either derived from Sense or reducible to it; and account Demonstration too gross and low an Aim for the sublime Speculations of the Intellect.[8]

If the speaker's insistence on the dignity and importance of the senses was uncontroversial in itself, his claim for instinct as opposed to reason was unorthodox in Rochester's time. In the seventeenth century, as in our own, the word 'instinct' was usually connected with animal rather than human behaviour. (True, Pascal juxtaposed 'cœur' and 'instinct'; but he was referring to a 'first knowledge' which served as a basis for rational thought processes.[9]) Calling this faculty in man 'certain' while

---

[7] Cf., for instance, the claims made for the five senses in Lucretius' *De Rerum Natura*, IV.499–512.
[8] P. 153 in Daves' edition of Butler's *Characters*.
[9] *Pensées*, 282. A clarifying discussion of these concepts is offered by Edward John Kearns, *Ideas in Seventeenth-Century France: The most important thinkers and the climate of ideas in which they*

giving reason fifty-to-one odds entailed taking up an extreme position – extreme enough to qualify for the description 'paradox' (in the sense of going against accepted opinion).

To refer to sense as 'light of *Nature*' constituted another breach against current beliefs and designations. Irrespective of the extent to which contemporary theologians and philosophers accepted the validity of sense data, they will have taken exception to this use of the light metaphor. For Puritans ('new light'), Cambridge Platonists ('candle of the Lord'),[10] Cartesians ('lumière naturelle') and Anglicans[11], light in an epistemological context stood for a God-given guide whose ultimate purpose was to lead man to salvation. However differently their respective 'light' was conceived, it certainly transcended mere sense perception and sensual capacities. Lines 12–13 in Rochester's *Satyr* hence entail the subversion of a term with particularly exalted connotations in his day.

Those connotations were, of course, in keeping with the traditional association of light with truth – especially divine truth – and darkness with doubt and misery. Seventeenth-century literature offers many examples; Cowley alone contributes a considerable number. Night is the time of sorrow and confusion; daylight sets mankind on its proper course again.

When reason is called an '*Ignis fatuus*, in the *Mind*', that crucial concept – the cornerstone of seventeenth- and eighteenth-century history of ideas – suffers one of the worst insults ever inflicted on it. The 'light' of an *ignis fatuus* is not only notoriously faint and deceptive; it is also literally the product of decay. (Newton later defined it – in the *Opticks*, quoted by Dr Johnson in his *Dictionary* – as 'vapours arising from putrified waters'.) The *ignis-fatuus* metaphor was growing into a topos in Rochester's time, as Griffin reminds us.[12] However, the suggestion that the faculty of reason is inherently contaminated as well as misleading will still have been able to strike his contemporaries as both unexpected and repugnant. The beginning of the journey through the arduous landscape of the mind – in 'errors Fenny – *Boggs*' – could be taken as an indication that Rochester knew how *ignes fatui* arise and deliberately alluded to it. The metaphorical suggestion of the in-

---

worked (Manchester, 1979), p. 100. Lord Herbert of Cherbury also spoke of an innate 'natural instinct' which should direct the 'discursive reason'; see Cope, *Joseph Glanvill*, p. 71.

[10] Griffin mentions the possible relevance of this concept (pp. 186–7 in *Satires Against Man*).

[11] Two examples among many are Sir Matthew Hale's *Light of Nature and Natural Reason* and Stillingfleet's *Origines Sacrae* II.v on 'natural light'.   [12] P. 213 in *Satires Against Man*.

salubrious birth of reason is itself a condemnation of its nature, well matching the subsequent delineation of its effects.

In the summer of 1674, the year when Rochester is believed to have written the Satyr (see, for instance, p. 282 in Walker's edition), Martin Clifford published A Treatise of Humane Reason. While in no way a masterpiece, this work acquires interesting dimensions when read along-side Rochester's Satyr. Clifford's avowed 'end' is 'Happiness', which aligns him with the satirist in line 96 of Rochester's poem. His argumentation, however, relies on his own reason, a feature which would have aroused the Satyr speaker's indignation.

According to Clifford, those who would disapprove of his using his reason as a guide would

seek to terrifie us with the example of many excellent Wits, who, they say, by following this Ignis fatuus (for so they call the only North-Star which God has given us for the right steering of our course) have fallen into wild and ridiculous Opinions ... (Treatise, A 4, 'Licensed on July 24, 1674, by "Ro. L'estrange"')

This is such a striking parallel to lines 12–30 of Rochester's Satyr that one cannot help wondering if the resemblance is coincidental. Rochester and Clifford are likely to have been personally acquainted and aware of each other's writings.[13] The quoted lines could constitute an allusion to the Satyr's denigration of reason; after all, they do offer an instance of ignis fatuus being used as a metaphor for reason (later in his treatise, on pp. 62–3, Clifford applies the same metaphor to false revelation). There are of course a plethora of ignes fatui in Restoration literature; but apart from the Satyr, this is the only instance I know of where reason is explicitly said (nota bene by Clifford's opponents) to be a will-o'-the-wisp. Theoretically, it could be argued that Rochester borrowed the reason/ignis fatuus metaphor from Clifford; but in view of the wording of the latter's passage and his inferior status in relation to Rochester, it does not seem likely. If this locus in Clifford's Treatise does glance at Rochester, the Satyr must have been in existence before the summer of 1674. Vieth's Attribution suggests that it was written 'between the middle of 1674 and the end of 1675' (p. 293); the Clifford parallel offers an opportunity to modify that provisional dating, if only by a matter of months.

---

[13] See p. 315n. below. A 'Character' of Clifford appended to Albertus Warren's An Apology for the Discourse of Humane Reason Written by Ma. Clifford, Esq., Being a Reply to Plain Dealing (1680) suggests that the two men had several interests in common. Plain Dealing, incidentally, is the title of an attack by Marvell on Clifford's treatise; it was only one of a number of unfavourable 'replies' to Clifford's cogitations.

A further parallel to Rochester's use of the will-o'-the-wisp image is
found in another passage from Butler's 'Hermetic Philosopher'. This
Character

controuls his fellow Labourers in the Fire with as much Empire and Authority,
as if he were sole Overseer of the *great Work*, to which he lights his Reader like
an *ignis fatuus*, which uses to mislead Men into Sloughs and Ditches; for when
he has mired him in the *Chaos*, and told him, that the *Philosophers Stone* is
Water, or a Powder, he leaves him in the Dark. (Daves' edition, p. 141)

It is not surprising that Rochester's lines appear to have lingered in the
memories of the poet's contemporaries and successors. The dimness of
Reason in the opening lines of Dryden's *Religio Laici* has been noted as
a similar instance;[14] another possible echo of Rochester's *ignis fatuus*
occurs in *The Hind and the Panther*, lines 1.73–4. As far as English
literature is concerned, it was the mid- and late-seventeenth-century
poets that turned the metaphor into a stock symbol of human error.

One of the basic questions with which a *Satyr* reader is faced is what
kind of reason the poem attacks. Like 'light', 'sense' and other central
terms, 'reason' is a word with manifold connotations. The speaker
advocates 'right reason', which is not just a matter of compulsive
obedience to the dictates of the senses – it does call for some degree of
deliberation, too (lines 99–111). In a limited way, the poem itself is
dependent on the validity of deductions, as critics have noted.[15]

The passages that explicitly deal with reason, lines 11–30 and 55–113,
must be considered together in any attempt to explain the respective
character of 'wrong' and 'right reason' in the *Satyr*. The reason whose
ill consequences are portrayed in lines 11–30 is characteristically
divorced from action:

> *Reason*, which Fifty times for one does err.
> *Reason*, an *Ignis fatuus*, in the *Mind*,
> Which leaving light of *Nature*, sense behind;
> Pathless and dang'rous wandring ways it takes,
> Through errors Fenny – *Boggs*, and Thorny *Brakes*;
> Whilst the misguided follower, climbs with pain,
> *Mountains* of Whimseys, heap'd in his own *Brain*:
> Stumbling from thought to thought, falls headlong down,
> Into doubts boundless Sea, where like to drown,

---

[14] See Irène Simon, '"Pride of Reason" in the Restoration and Earlier Eighteenth Century',
Revue des langues vivantes 25.5 (1959), 380.
[15] Cf. Knight, 'The Paradox of Reason', 258–9.

Books bear him up awhile, and make him try,
To swim with Bladders of *Philosophy*;
In hopes still t'oretake th'escaping light,
The *Vapour* dances in his dazling sight,
Till spent, it leaves him to eternal Night.
Then Old Age, and experience, hand in hand,
Lead him to death, and make him understand,
After a search so painful, and so long,
That all his Life he has been in the wrong;
Hudled in dirt, the reas'ning *Engine* lyes,
Who was so proud, so witty, and so wise.

This reason removes itself from the faculty of sense, acting on man's thoughts and in his brain and only there. Consequently, it is not the power that 'is ordinarily employed in adopting thought or action to some end' (*OED* III.10); it is, in more than one sense, an end in itself. The abortive 'progress' of the human reasoner illustrates step-by-step ratiocination unconcerned with sense data. Hence, the satirist's onslaught focuses on the mental activity of the physically passive, those who 'Retire to think, cause they have naught to do'.

That is how the adversarius comprehends it, too. The reason praised by him is a cerebral capacity whose express purpose is to sever man and physical sensation – '*We take a flight beyond material sense*'. Like the satirist, he uses a metaphorical journey to illustrate his argumentation – subversions, perhaps, of the pilgrim's-progress pattern in devotional literature. (The speaker instantly parodies the 'flight' in lines 84–7.)

On this point, the satirist has no difficulty in picking up the cue from the 'formal Band, and Beard'. The reason commended by the latter was, as the *Satyr* speaker correctly affirms, a 'supernatural gift', and he does not care for non-natural things. Another kind of 'supernatural gift' is found in *Hudibras* I.i.472ff., where Samuel Butler describes the divine revelation which enabled Squire Ralpho to explain 'deep Mysteries'. In his presentation of the tailor's '*Knowledge*', Butler emphasises the word 'gift' and explores its humorous possibilities (Ralpho, for example, 'ne're consider'd it, as loath / To look a gift-horse in the mouth'). Referring to divine inspiration as a gift was sectarian jargon (originally derived from 1 Corinthians 12:4,[16]), and Butler, of course, made good use of any opportunity he had to burlesque contemporary religious cant. For any *Satyr* reader who had also read *Hudibras* (in Rochester's lifetime, that would apply to a majority), Butler's play on 'gift' would

---

[16] See John Wilders' Commentary, p. 331 in his edition, *Samuel Butler Hudibras* (Oxford, 1967).

immediately lend a slightly ironic dimension to the word as it occurs in Rochester's poem. Ralpho's new light and the *Satyr*'s reason are very different capacities, but both are described as *ignes fatui* and both are presented, tongue in cheek, as divine implements bestowed on man for the better procurement of his salvation.

Among seventeenth-century Anglicans, reason was held to lead man up to those mysteries of faith that are above reason, helping him to accept them. Both Cowley and Butler referred to it as a human compass.[17] To find uncompromising literary condemnations of the rational faculty in man, we have to cross the Channel. In seventeenth-century France, derogatory references to human reason abound. When Boileau, in his fourth satire, says that 'Souvent de tous nos maux la Raison est le pire' (line 114), he is joining two or three generations of literary *libertins* in France. Since the early decades of the century, Théophile de Viau and his followers had advocated a hedonism which saw compliance with Nature, manifested in the senses, as the guiding principle. The *libertins* were often students of Epicurus, and of his disciples Lucretius and Gassendi. One of their leading exponents, Jacques Vallée Des Barreaux (1599–1673), knew Théophile as a young man and lived long enough to be celebrated as the grand old man of *le libertinage* in the *salons* of the 1660s. It has been suggested that Rochester may have known him personally.[18] Whether he did or not, I think Rochester is very likely to have read at least some of the French poet's literary output. The *libertins* published little; their verses were copied and handed round among kindred spirits, like those written by Rochester himself.

Previous Rochester critics have pointed to resemblances between *libertinage* representatives such as Mathurin Régnier and Jacques Des Barreaux and Rochester.[19] More work needs to be done in this field, though. For one thing, there are other parallels – some of them striking – which have not yet been pointed out and commented on. However, similarities are merely one aspect of literary relationships. Another, and an important and hitherto neglected one with regard to Rochester and the *libertins*, consists in defining those discrepancies which suggest

---

[17] Griffin quotes the relevant passages from Cowley's poem *Reason* on pp. 185–6, and from Butler's prose discourse on 'Reason' on p. 211n. of *Satires Against Man*.

[18] The likelihood of such a meeting is mentioned in Emile D. Forgues' article on Rochester ('John Wilmot, Count of Rochester') in *Revue des deux mondes* 10 (August 1857), 826.

[19] Both Griffin and Farley-Hills have drawn attention to several pertinent passages in the works of these two French poets, the former quoting three sonnets by Des Barreaux on pp. 177–80 in *Satires Against Man*.

independence and transcendence on the part of the 'influenced' writer. The attacks on reason in the *Satyr* and in *libertinage* poems respectively supply an illustrative example in this respect.

The following sonnet by Des Barreaux, printed under the heading 'La raison fait le malheur de l'homme', contains several ideas whose relevance to the *Satyr* is apparent:

> Ce n'est qu'un vent furtif que le bien de nos jours,
> Qu'une fumée en l'air, un songe peu durable;
> Nostre vie est un rien, à un point comparable,
> Si nous considérons ce qui dure toujours.
>
> L'Homme se rend encor luy mesme misérable,
> Ce peu de temps duquel il abrège ses jours
> Par mille passions, par mille vains discours,
> Tant la sotte raison le rend irraisonnable.
>
> Plus heureuses cent fois sont les bestes sauvages,
> Cent fois sont plus heureux les oyseaux aux bocages
> Qui vivent pour le moins leur âge doucement.
>
> Ha! que naistre comme eux ne nous fait la Nature,
> Sans discours ny raison, vivant à l'avanture,
> Nostre mal ne nous vient que de l'entendement.[20]

Like Rochester's speaker, Des Barreaux argues that man is the author of his own woes in that he does not, or cannot, escape the evil workings of his reason and his wish for knowledge. His reason inflicts passions and 'mille discours' on him. The result of this is that he becomes, in the terms of Des Barreaux's neat paradox, 'irraisonnable'. Animals are far happier than men, but the kind of life they lead is out of man's reach.

Other sonnets by Des Barreaux supplement this lament on man's misfortune in being equipped with reason, exhorting man – victim of regret, sorrow and fear, and a creature who spends his time in various unexalted pursuits – not to think himself superior to the rest of the animals. However, these complaints about reason are not made on the same grounds as those expressed in lines 11–30 of the *Satyr*. The discrepancy between man's pride in his rationality and the actual manifestations of reason is certainly there; but those manifestations do not parallel the ones found in the beginning of Rochester's poem. What Des Barreaux regrets is the corollary of reason, the unhappy habit of

---

[20] Lachèvre, ed., *Disciples et successeurs de Théophile de Viau: La Vie et les Poésies inédits de Des Barreaux (1599–1673) – Saint-Pavin (1595–1670)*, vol. II of *Le Libertinage au XVIIe siècle* (Paris, 1911), p. 245.

looking before and after. In addition, he sardonically notes the inability
of reason to ennoble man, to raise him above such mean pursuits as nose-
picking and urinating.

Des Barreaux had an adept pupil in Mme Deshoulières. Her *Les
Moutons: Idylle* brings reason, pride and a man/animal contrast together
in a way that is relevant to Rochester's argumentation as well as to that
of Des Barreaux:[21]

> L'ambition, l'honneur, l'interest, l'imposture,
>   Qui font tant de maux parmi nous,
>   Ne se rencontrent point chez vous.
> Cependant nous avons la raison pour partage,
>   Et vous en ignorez l'usage.
> Innocens animaux n'en soyez point jalous,
>   Ce n'est pas un grand avantage.
> Cette fière raison dont on fait tant de bruit,
>   Contre les passions n'est pas un seur remède.
> Un peu de vin la trouble, un enfant la séduit;
>   Et déchirer un cœur qui l'appelle a son aide,
>   Est tout l'effet qu'elle produit.
>   Toujours impuissante et sévère,
>   Elle s'oppose a tout, et ne surmonte rien.
>   ...
> Paissez Moutons, paissez sans règle et sans science:
>   Malgré la trompeuse apparence
> Vous estes plus heureux et plus sages que nous.

Here, it is the insufficiency of reason that is regretted. It is useless as a
guard against the passions and only serves to impede enjoyment.
Towards the conclusion of Boileau's fourth satire, 'la Raison' also
appears as an ineffectual spoilsport:

> C'est Elle qui farouche, au milieu des plaisirs,
> D'un remords importun vient brider nos desirs.
> La Fâcheuse a pour nous des rigeurs sans pareilles;
> C'est un Pêdant qu'on a sans cesse à ses oreilles,
> Qui toûjours nous gourmande, et loin de nous toucher,
> Souvent, comme Joli, perd son temps à prescher.[22]

To that extent, Boileau's charges against reason are much the same as
those voiced in the poems of Des Barreaux and Mme Deshoulières.

---

[21] On the relevance of *Les Moutons* to *The Fall*, see my 'Rochester and *The Fall*', 403. The
Deshoulières text is quoted from Frédéric Lachèvre's edition of her *Poésies libertines,
philosophiques et chrétiennes* in vol. XI of *Le Libertinage au XVIIe siècle* (Paris, 1924), pp. 67–8.

[22] Lines 115–20. (Claude Joly was vicar of St Nicolas des Champs; see p. 237 in Boudhors'
edition.)

However, he goes on to criticise the people who wish to give reason divine status on earth – dreamers who claim that it has power to lead men to salvation.

There can be no doubt that Rochester was familiar with this French tradition of decrying reason. It is noteworthy, though, that his own treatment of it stresses its epistemological aspects so much more than its practical-ethical ones. Most of the lines given to the presentation of reason in the *Satyr* depict its cognitive inadequacy. Though this dimension is not entirely lacking in the French poems against reason, it is far less in evidence than in the *Satyr*. Even the famous Des Barreaux sonnet which recommends that 'Estudions-nous plus à jouir qu'à connoistre, / Et nous servons des sens plus que de la raison' ('Mortels, qui vous croyez ...') does not dispute that reasoning brings insights. The sad thing is that the more the spirit raises itself by gaining knowledge, the better able it is to perceive the source of its distress. 'Je renonce au bon sens, je hay l'intelligence' exclaims the sonneteer, all in accordance with the motto of the poem, 'Qui multiplicat intellectum multiplicat afflictionem.'

It is in the *Satyr* lines on 'right reason' (100–9) that we find an echo of the exasperation articulated by French poets at the sensual frustrations caused by meddlesome 'raison'. The adversarius said nothing about killing desires; the transition from epistemology to ethics – or, rather, to principles of practical conduct in daily life – is one made entirely by the satirist himself. It does, however, reflect the insistence on moral behaviour which was such a vital concern among Anglican clergymen. Any representative of that category would be offended at the suggestion that the best reason can do is to find ways of augmenting our sensual gratifications.

Indeed, applying the concept of right reason, with its religious overtones,[23] to the kind of 'reasoning' that is adumbrated in lines 100–9 almost looks like a deliberate affront directed against contemporary theologians. The scope within which 'right reason' is allowed to function here is a narrow and exclusively physical one. 'Distinguishing by sense' – that is, allowing the senses to provide the guidelines for reasoning – is not in itself such an obnoxious expression in an age where empirical philosophy was gaining ground, however controversial its manifestations might be. Imparting moral authority to the senses (line 101) is of course another, and far worse, matter. But the crowning insult

---

[23] See ch. 9 in Robert Hoopes' *Right Reason in the English Renaissance* (Cambridge, Mass., 1962). Cf. also Ronald W. Johnson, 'Rhetoric and Drama', 370.

to orthodox Christian reason and its advocates lies in the choice of examples of reasonable behaviour. According to lines 102–9, the only acceptable rational activity consists in finding ways to enhance one's physical pleasures and to satisfy one's appetites, unhampered by any intervening considerations. As if this implicit denial of all spiritual and cognitive values were not bad enough, the speaker suggests that anybody whose reason tells them to go against their physical inclinations is perverse and despicable. Using the expression 'reforming Will' about the deliberate nurturing of desires so as to increase their expected satisfaction is another subversion of concepts current in the clerical sphere.

This is not the sum of the indignities inflicted on speculative human reason in the *Satyr*. Even the components in the landscape of the mind outlined in lines 15–19 add to them. The references to the bogs and brakes of error are obviously uncomplimentary even to the mind of a present-day reader. In Rochester's time, however, mountains and oceans were also regarded with marked dislike.[24] The former were characteristically referred to as 'savage' and 'deformed' (as in Marvell's *Upon the Hill and Grove at Bill-borow*); the latter were uniformly seen as frighteningly vast as well as hazardous and tiresome to traverse. Naturally, both were regarded as sterile, too. These unpleasant overtones add to the effectiveness of the metaphors. '*Mountains of Whimseys*' and 'doubts boundless Sea' thus do not merely give vast dimensions to man's mental aberrations; they invest them with a measure of fruitlessness, distaste and impassability as well.

The deluded reasoner in the *Satyr* suffers more hardships than the man in Boileau's eighth satire, who 'Voltige incessamment de pensée en pensée'. During his painful attempt to proceed from one thought to another, he loses whatever foothold he had in his own freakish notions and is suddenly engulfed in doubt which offers him nothing solid to hold on to. Books can only sustain him for a limited time, and the swimming-bladders of philosophy are powerless to carry him to firm ground. He can only flounder around in doubt until he has exhausted the air whose insubstantiality alone keeps them, and him, afloat. Learning, too, is merely scum on the surface of doubt. When the deceptive light fizzles out, so, at long last, does the reasoner's life. At its

---

[24] See Myra Reynolds, *The Treatment of Nature in English Poetry: Between Pope and Wordsworth* (Chicago, 1909), where a number of seventeenth-century instances are quoted (pp. 7–15). Marvell's attitude to mountains, and its representativeness, are investigated in Marjorie Hope Nicolson's *Mountain Gloom and Mountain Glory: The Development of the Aesthetics of the Infinite* (Ithaca, 1959); see especially pp. 34–5 and 68–9.

close, experience shows him the extent of its errors. Understanding having replaced doubt, he is no longer struggling in the water; but the substance that now clings to him, clogging and halting his functions, is the most humiliating of all.

The sea of doubt is boundless but not bottomless, and it is on its miry sea-floor that reasoning man finally rests (see below). Dying, he recognised the width of his self-deception. Once absorbed by 'eternal Night', he is just a useless implement – 'engine' used metaphorically of a human being means 'agent' or 'tool'.[25] The instrument bogged down in darkness and filth was wielded by speculative reason and has reaped its just deserts, disgrace and destruction.

The word 'dirt' has several senses that can be applied to this passage. The most immediately pertinent one appears to be the second meaning listed in the *OED*: 'unclean matter, such as soils any object by adhering to it; filth; *esp.* the wet mud or mire of the ground, consisting of earth and waste matter mingled with water'. It seems likely to me that the dirt in which the reasoning engine lies huddled is that which covers the floor of the sea where his wretched light went out and death overtook him. There are other readings, though.[26] Thus, for example, phrases like 'fall to dirt' and 'lay all in the dirt' used to mean 'come to nothing'. Consequently, the line could also be read as an expression of the utter nothingness to which the agent of reason is ultimately reduced.

The potential polemical significance of 'engine' adds to the dishonour of the reasoner. Ever since the publication of Descartes' *Discours de la méthode*, more than forty years before that of the *Satyr*, the French philosopher's theory of 'l'animal-machine' had been debated among the intellectuals of France. Descartes had argued that the bodies of men and animals are mere machines, albeit superbly made, and that man alone has been invested with a soul and a mind. Animals are automata. This, of course, goes right against the theriophilic strain in French philosophy and literature from the Renaissance onwards, and many men and women of letters contested the doctrine.[27] Gassendi countered that animals possess intelligence as well as men, and that the only

---

[25] The *OED* quotes an example from Marvell (*The Rehearsal Transpros'd*, 1.92, 1672), 'that Politick Engine who ... was employed ... as a Missionary amongst the Nonconformists' (see under *engine*, 10).

[26] Cf. for instance Griffin, in *Satires Against Man*, p. 218: '"Huddled in dirt" may mean wretched, debased, and humiliated, grovelling in the dust, or, more likely, dead in a fresh grave.'

[27] See, for instance, Leonora Cohen Rosenfield, *From Beast-Machine to Man-Machine: The Theme of Animal Soul in French Letters from Descartes to La Mettrie* (New York, 1940), pp. 158–67, and A. Lytton Sells, *Animal Poetry in French and English Literature & the Greek Tradition*

difference is one of degree. The *précieuses* of Paris were incredulous; Mme de Sévigné thought Descartes must have been joking, and even the philosopher's niece, Catherine Descartes, did not defend him. Madeleine de Scudéry wrote a little epitaph for a lap-dog whose 'esprit' was said to '[demonter] / Le systeme de la machine'.[28] Among other explicit objections to Descartes in the late seventeenth century, La Fontaine's *Discours à Madame de la Sablière* praises the resourcefulness of animals. Clearly, the *beaux esprits* of the mid- and late 1600s were collectively up in arms against the Cartesian idea.

I find it difficult to believe that Rochester never heard of all this opposition to a theory which must have seemed repugnant to him.[29] He may well have been tempted to adduce his own oblique protest against it. If he did, he would not have been the first Englishman to ridicule Descartes' theory: Samuel Butler was there before him. Rochester could easily have heard about Descartes' animal-automaton without reading so much as a line from the *Discours*; Butler, who spent years among the books of his rich employers, surely knew more than that. These lines from *Hudibras* I.ii (53–60) read like a wicked passing stab at Descartes:

> But let that pass: they now begun
> To spur their living Engines on.
> For as whipp'd Tops and bandy'd Balls,
> The learned hold, are Animals:
> So Horses they affirm to be
> Mere Engines, made by Geometry,
> And were invented first from Engins,
> As *Indian Britans* were from *Penguins*.[30]

Not even Descartes' admirers in France or England[31] were very happy about the beast-machine idea. One further reason for suspecting that

(Bloomington, 1955; the volume is no. 35 in the Indiana University Publications, Humanities Series), pp. 114–22. Keith Thomas' *Man and the Natural World* contains an excellent summary of the Cartesian argument and its implications; see pp. 33–5. The following presentation of literary and philosophical reactions to Descartes' theory is greatly indebted to Rosenfield and Sells. [28] Quoted on p. 117 in Sells' *Animal Poetry*.

[29] Griffin is less confident in this respect; in a footnote he suggests that the reader might 'compare' Rochester's 'engine' to 'the anti-theriophilist Descartes' description' of men and animals (*Satires Against Man*, p. 218n.), but says nothing about the implications of such a comparison.

[30] Pp. 30–1 in John Wilders' edition. Wilders cautiously says that it is 'possibly an allusion' to Descartes' *Discours* (p. 342), but another author, Wallace Shugg, is sure it was indeed a deliberate reference; see his 'The Cartesian Beast-Machine in English Literature (1663–1750)', *Journal of the History of Ideas* 29.2 (April–June 1968), 280–1.

[31] Sells (p. 116 in *Animal Poetry*) and Keith Thomas (*Man and the Natural World*, p. 35) point out that Henry More disagreed violently with it. The admiration of the Cambridge Platonists for Descartes is well known (see, for instance, Kearns, *Ideas in Seventeenth-Century France*, p. 78).

Rochester knew of and scorned it might possibly be discerned in the satirist's view of the relative desirability of simian existence. Descartes had used a monkey as an example of the mindlessness of beasts. According to him, it would be possible to construct a machine representing a living monkey, which would act and look so like a real one that it could not be distinguished from the actual animal.[32] The satirist's preference could be taken to imply a rejection of this claim.

The hapless '*Engine*' was decoyed and deluded by reason, but the causes of his falling victim to it were innate in himself. Line 30 enumerates them. His pride, wisdom and wit, essentially human qualities not found in other animals, rendered him vulnerable to the evils of reason. The following lines, down to the '*Band, and Beard's*' interruption, depict their nefarious operations. The greater space is given to the least universal defect, wit; but the exposition is headed by the foulest of human passions in the satirist's view: pride.

> *Pride* drew him in, as *Cheats*, their *Bubbles* catch,
> And makes him venture, to be made a *Wretch*.
> His wisdom did his happiness destroy,
> Aiming to know that *World* he shou'd enjoy;
> And *Wit*, was his vain frivolous pretence,
> Of pleasing others, at his own expence.
> For *Witts* are treated just like common *Whores*,
> First they're enjoy'd, and then kickt out of *Doores*:
> The pleasure past, a threatning doubt remains,
> That frights th'enjoyer, with succeeding pains:
> *Women* and *Men* of *Wit*, are dang'rous Tools,
> And ever fatal to admiring *Fools*.
> Pleasure allures, and when the *Fopps* escape,
> 'Tis not that they're belov'd, but fortunate,
> And therefore what they fear, at heart they hate.

C. F. Main's insistence that '*the Satyr* lashes one principal vice: pride' has been contested,[33] and rightly. The attempt to subsume all the concerns of the poem under this one heading is not successful; too much refuses to go in under it. Thus, for example, the other great defect in human nature, fear, serves as a companion piece to pride and produces another type of evidence of man's depravity (see below). But Main's

---

[32] See Kearns, *Ideas in Seventeenth-Century France*, p. 59.

[33] See Main's 'The Right Vein of Rochester's *Satyr*', in *Essays in Literary History Presented to J. M. French*, ed. R. Kirk and C. F. Main (New Brunswick, 1960, and New York, 1965), pp. 93–112. Vieth attacked it with customary grimness in his *Rochester Studies*, p. 75 (item 194), as well as in his article 'Toward an Anti-Aristotelian Poetic'.

emphasis on pride is partly warranted, not by structural consistency but by sheer repetition and vehemence. References to pride occur nine times in the poem (lines 7, 30, 31, 114, 175, 189, 193, 203 and 208), and there are several instances of its neighbouring vice, vanity. The fact that beasts are not contaminated by it is driven home twice, in lines 6–7 and 114–16. While it is the curse of mankind generally, it is especially rampant in the mighty. On three occasions, pride is specifically imputed to the clergy, and the portrait of the virtuous clergyman characteristically begins with the adjectives 'meek' and 'humble'. Not even the equally elusive honest statesman lacks it. In his case, though, pride is envisaged as turned to a 'good' use: he is just enough to realise that he is prone to avarice, and his pride refuses to let him sink so low as to indulge in it! From this very Rochesterian paradox, it transpires that even the greatest vice may assume the functions of a virtue, becoming the source of a good passion (cf. line 143).

In associating pride with high social status, the satirist is of course merely adhering to the proverbial dimensions of the term.[34] But in lines 31–2, pride is not simply seen to go before destruction in a worldly sense ('my pride fell with my fortunes'). By making man believe himself capable of attaining intellectual glory, it paves the way for the loss of any joy in human life.

For the poem does not deny that such joy is a possibility. Despite its gloom and savagery, it twice speaks of happiness (lines 33 and 96) – once, it is true, as a lost treasure, but once also as an extant and achievable, if limited, quality. What keeps it from men is their cursed propensity for cognitive endeavour. 'Wisdom' joins pride as the second great snare luring man away from his proper occupations.

Pride hence made the pursuit of reason seem feasible, but it is wisdom that makes it desirable. From the days of Paradise onwards, man has neglected the enjoyment immediately at hand for the dubious prospect of knowing intangible things. The words 'wise/wisdom' and 'philosopher/philosophy' are about as prevalent in the *Satyr* as those belonging to the pride/vanity constellation. According to the satirist, thinking is worse than useless if it does not lead to favourable action,[35] and wisdom consists in knowing how to act in order to secure what you desire (lines 117–22). Few literary works have allowed these concepts such narrow space as the *Satyr*. When it comes to delineating the virtues and potentials of human thought, its antipole is Wordsworth's *Ode*.

[34] Cf. Butler's *Character* of 'A Modern Politician', p. 35 in Daves' edition.
[35] This view holds good in respect of the good-men prototypes, too; see p. 236 below.

Where the concepts pride and knowledge are concerned, occasional parallels can be found in the works of Butler and Cowley. In the former's remarks on 'Learning and Knowledge', for instance, he maintains:

The end of all knowledge, is to understand what is Fit to be don; For to know what ha's been, and what is, and what may be, dos but tend to that. (de Quehen's edition, pp. 11–12)

Cowley's The Tree of Knowledge suggests that pride in intellectual ability is grotesque in view of the wretchedness of man's endeavours in this respect; he

> Yet searches Probabilities,
> And Rhetorick, and Fallacies,
> And seeks by useless pride
> With slight and withering Leaves that Nakedness to hide.[36]

Later in the Satyr, the speaker has something to say about those who believe themselves able to fathom extraterrestrial phenomena. At this point, he is content with lashing the folly of wasting one's time and energy in trying to learn about the world, instead of putting those resources to use in enjoying it.

An interesting question in this context is what 'Wit' stands for in lines 35ff. The indefinableness of this concept was a familiar bugbear even to those generations who used it so widely that the flavour of their times still clings to it. Cowley's Ode: Of Wit explores the device of negative definition (''tis not ... '), to conclude with a piece of blatant flattery, triumphantly avoiding the issue. With a term whose meaning oscillates between human intelligence and facile verbal cleverness, traversing sense, judgement and fancy, the issue is one that begs to be avoided.

The delineation of wit in the Satyr suggests a much narrower and less admirable capacity than the qualities implied by 'wit' in other Rochester poems, where the word tends to denote 'discernment', 'taste' and so on (see, for instance, line 16 in Tunbridge Wells and line 60 in the Epilogue to Love in the Dark). The wit frowned on by the satirist appears as a kind of buffoonery, a negative social talent fed by malevolence allied to perspicacity.

A contemporary courtesy-book writer, Obadiah Walker, distinguished between wit, memory and judgement. Wit, in his view, was less stable than judgement, a far worthier quality. He defined wit as 'the

---

[36] On The Tree of Knowledge as related to The Fall, see 'Rochester and The Fall', 401.

mother of facetiousness, conceits, jests, raillery, satyricalness, which is almost *synonymum* to wit'.[37] Obadiah Walker also stressed its potential as a mischief-maker in society. The *Satyr* speaker seems to take a similar view.

The entertainment supplied by wits is obviously a finite resource, like that provided by whores. Sooner or later, the wit has exhausted his usefulness and is discarded. The nature of that usefulness is defined by lines 43–5: it consists in causing merriment by means of slandering other people in an amusing manner. Once this diversion has palled, the fool can only hope that he himself will, by some lucky chance, escape being made fun of at the next house visited by the traducer.[38]

One may well wonder why Rochester, whose wicked sallies and impertinences were notorious at Charles' Court, should ostensibly criticise such pastimes in the *Satyr*. Also, it might seem odd that 'wit' in this somewhat debased and highly limited sense should be mentioned along with pride and wisdom as being one of the characteristics of man as an instrument of reason.

Did Rochester, using the speaker as his mouthpiece, deliberately attack a type of conduct for which he was himself infamous, or is the speaker the object of the satire – perhaps in that he disapproves of a pastime that does afford 'pleasure' (line 43), if only to fools? The latter alternative would have to be chosen by anyone who believed Rochester incapable of self-criticism. Regardless of the different views held by various Rochester critics in respect of his adoption of *personae*, it would be difficult to find anyone who would maintain that he was. The poem *To the Post Boy* is the most patent evidence of the poet's rebellious frankness turned against himself (see pp. 357ff.). There are other instances in his poems and letters which also prove that his contempt for hypocrisy did not allow him to disavow his own reprehensible conduct.

Indeed, nobody was in a better position to deplore the acquisition of short-lived popularity by defaming others than the second Earl of Rochester. He had first-hand experience of being 'kickt out of *Doores*' as a result of such pursuits, and he more than once voiced his disgust at the attempts made by fools to exploit the company of the man of wit (cf., for instance, *Timon*).

The reasons why the speaker – whether or not he expresses Roches-

---

[37] *Of Education. Especially of Young Gentlemen*, in two parts (Oxford, 1673). The discussion of wit is found on pp. 122–5.

[38] Vieth's placing of the comma in line 45, 'And therefore what they fear at heart, they hate', yields the better sense.

ter's own views – decries the practice of wit as described here are
threefold: it gives no real satisfaction to the consumer; it is directly
harmful to the performer; and both are driven to it by pretence. The
fool's brief enjoyment of slurs on others is essentially conditioned by his
wish to feel superior to them, and the wit is impelled by vanity.
Needless to say, no beast would waste a second on such spurious
pleasures. As Butler said of wit (p. 56 in de Quehen's edition of his *Prose
Observations*), 'It is the worst Trade in the world to live upon.'

Pride is thus involved in the presentation of wit, but what does it have
to do with wisdom? Not very much on the face of it, but there is one
fundamental similarity: the wit draws on his mental qualities (thus
neglecting his senses, the sole providers of genuine enjoyment) in a show
of superficial cleverness which only leads to his own ruin. Hence his
efforts, like the reasoner's journey, illustrate the fruitlessness and pain
inherent in any exercise of the human intellect.

It is this latter aspect that disturbs the adversarius, easily envisaged as
a man with plenty of experience when it comes to wit – he is patently
a natural target for the venom of a gifted lampooner. No wonder he is
eager to voice his agreement with the satirist on this score. Their
disapproval has different causes, though, and the 'Band, and Beard' is
not so obtuse as not to realise it. His dislike of wit – '*this gibeing jingling
knack*' – is due to its being an unkind and paltry pastime which debases
the glorious mental faculties of man; the satirist is plainly uninterested
in its meanness. This is why the 'mighty Man' believes that his own
poetical talents would lend themselves more profitably to the abuse of
wit, talents maliciously exhibited in the slack triplet,

> *Perhaps my* Muse, *were fitter for this part,*
> *For I profess, I can be very smart*
> *On* Wit, *which I abhor with all my heart*:

The adversarius' whole case amounts to a defence of those very qualities
and pursuits that the satirist has disparaged. Throughout his short
speech, the intellectual capacity of man is extolled as the greatest of
human attributes, conferred by the Almighty Himself.[39]

The satirist professes to find this view downright blasphemous:

> This supernatural gift, that makes a *Myte* –,
> Think he's the Image of the Infinite:
> Comparing his short life, void of all rest,
> To the *Eternal*, and the ever blest.

[39] See pp. 167–74 above on the ideological content of lines 58–71.

The presumptuousness of man, the infinity and incomprehensibility of God, and the wretchedness of the human intellect return time and again in the works of late sixteenth- and seventeenth-century sceptics.[40] To mention just one example which Rochester may have read and will have heard of, Father Pierre Charron held that human beings are too feeble and God too infinite for man to possess any knowledge of the nature and existence of the Almighty.[41] The so-called Pyrrhonists (drawing on the teachings of the Greek sceptic Pyrrho of Elis) proclaimed that there is no point in seeking to obtain reliable knowledge at all; Montaigne's *Apologie* develops this basic contention.[42] In the matter of divine wisdom, God's infiniteness was a classic sceptical tenet, reiterated in the disputes between sceptics and rationalists. Rochester's contemporaries will have regarded the expression 'the Infinite' in the light of those disputes. To them, the arguments and counter-arguments of adversarius and satirist will have come across as a literary reflection of a major philosophical issue.

Two years after Rochester's death, Dryden took up the theme in *Religio Laici*. The Preface to that poem makes it clear that he sides with the speaker in Rochester's *Satyr* where this particular question is concerned:

And indeed, 'tis very improbable, that we, who by the strength of our faculties cannot enter into the knowledg of any *Beeing*, not so much as of our *own*, should be able to find out by them that Supream Nature, which we cannot otherwise define than by saying it is Infinite; as if Infinite were definable, or Infinity a Subject for our narrow understanding. They who wou'd prove Religion by Reason, do but weaken the cause which they endeavour to support: 'tis to take away the Pillars from our Faith, and to prop it only with a twig ...[43]

[40] The term 'scepticism' is another of those concepts whose diverse applications have clouded arguments and provoked misunderstandings to such a degree that one approaches them with apprehension and handles them with diffidence. For the purposes of this discussion, scepticism means 'lack of confidence in man's ability to obtain and assert absolute knowledge by exercising his own mental powers'. Those who are familiar with developments in the history of ideas during the seventeenth century will not need reminding that scepticism in this sense was not by any means irreconcilable with Christianity, nor with the pursuit of scientific learning.

[41] See, for instance, the summary of Charron's arguments (in *Les Trois Veritez* and *Sagesse*) provided by Richard A. Popkin, *The History of Skepticism from Erasmus to Descartes* (New York, 1961), pp. 58–63.

[42] Louis Bredvold claimed that 'it moves toward a complete Pyrrhonism' (*The Intellectual Milieu*, p. 33). See also Dale Underwood, *Etherege and the Seventeenth-Century Comedy of Manners*, Yale Studies in English, vol. 135 (New Haven and London, 1957), p. 23.

[43] Quoted from John Sargeaunt's edition of *The Poems of John Dryden* (Oxford, 1925), p. 95. In the words of the poem itself: 'How can the *less* the *Greater* comprehend? / Or *finite Reason*

Dryden takes issue with specific schools of thought in the realm of religion. The *Satyr* is less precise in its attacks on man deluded by reason. According to K. E. Robinson, the 'vain *Animal*' is the scholast, and the target of the satirist, even in the opening lines, is the misguided views of schoolmen ('Rochester and Hobbes', 111). Is it possible to categorise the victims/perpetrators of reason, and if so, can we conclude that they all belong to the old Aristotelian school of learning?

When the introductory lines speak of 'that vain *Animal*', they seem to refer to mankind at large. After all, the speaker is talking about a species to which he unhappily belongs, not about the tiny academic community. The follower of reason resorts to the works of philosophers in his distress, but there is no suggestion that he is himself a member of their profession. Nor do the lines on wit adumbrate a gowned personage. The 'mighty Man's' claims for human reason are not expressly limited to people who have enjoyed the benefits of a higher education. The first references to academic learning occur in the satirist's reply to him. It is the adversarius' brand of reason

> That frames deep *Mysteries*, then finds 'em out;
> Filling with Frantick Crowds of thinking *Fools*,
> Those Reverend *Bedlams*, *Colledges*, and *Schools*;

Some ten lines further down, the academics are in for another kick; they are those

> *Cloysterd Coxcombs*, who
> Retire to think, cause they have naught to do.

Coxcombs in this context are, to quote Johnson's definition, 'superficial pretender[s] to knowledge or accomplishments'. Obviously, the cloisters of religious houses and academic colleges are their natural habitat.

From these scathing but scanty references to formal education, I do not think it is possible to conclude that the satirist's attacks are aimed at traditional scholasticism (still prevalent in the academic life of the Restoration[44]). Rather, they seem directed against the pursuit of learning *per se*. This assumption is supported by the names Patrick and Ingelo, divines associated with Latitudinarianism, and by the oblique reference to Glanvill in lines 86–7 (see pp. 213ff. below). All these men

---

reach *Infinity*? / For what cou'd *Fathom* GOD were *more* than *He*.' Of course, *Religio Laici* propounds quite different arguments from those of the *Satyr* in other respects; these three lines (39–41) were preceded by a dismissal of sensual pleasure as the *summum bonum* (lines 33–5).

[44] See Cragg, *From Puritanism to the Age of Reason*, p. 6.

were heartily opposed to rigid scholasticism and welcomed the new philosophy[45] – and all are exposed to the satirist's abuse.

Dustin Griffin has drawn attention to two aspects of Ingelo's religious-allegorical romance *Bentivolio and Urania* which would have been offensive to Rochester (*Satires Against Man*, pp. 190–2):[46] Ingelo's exalted view of man; and his attacks on Epicurus and his followers. The former component is certainly relevant to the claims made for man in the adversarius' speech; the latter is more closely connected with the killing-desires attitude imputed to him. It might be noted that the satirist speaks of the 'Pathetique Pen' of Ingelo, thus apostrophising the romancer's ability to move his readers; but the passages quoted by Griffin are from the prefaces to the various volumes, not from the story itself. From what I have read of it, pertinent passages in the actual romance are rare.

Ingelo's book thus only corresponds to the 'mighty Man's' speech in a very limited way, and the pertinence of Patrick's *Parable of the Pilgrim* is more dubious still. Exaltation of man really is not a feature in it;[47] the only passages which seem relevant to the *Satyr* are those where sensual pursuits are castigated. The phrases quoted by Griffin on meditation and prayer, activities which may enable man to 'receive communications from above, and to be made partakers of a Divine Nature', have very little to do with the proud flight of reason sketched by the adversarius. If Rochester ever read the *Parable of the Pilgrim*, he is more likely to have reacted to its discourses on sensual pleasure and on the restlessness of irreligious men.

Both these books were popular in the Restoration, whatever difficulties a modern reader might have with them, and Rochester had

---

[45] *Ibid.*, p. 65; see also Cope, *Joseph Glanvill*, pp. 115–18. Quotations from Patrick's writings and informative comments are supplied by John Hoyles in *The Waning of the Renaissance 1640–1740: Studies in the Thought and Poetry of Henry More, John Norris and Isaac Watts* (The Hague, 1971), pp. 12–13, 16, 29–30 and 49.

[46] Pinto records (in his edition of Rochester's poems, p. 217) Sir Walter Raleigh's comment on this book in *The English Novel* (1894), according to which *Bentivolio and Urania* '[marks] the lowest depth to which English romance-writing sank'. While being unqualified to validate or contest that statement, I can testify to the virtual unreadableness of this work. Though not otherwise given to daytime naps, I repeatedly fell asleep over the Bodleian copy and have not as yet managed to read it through. While Griffin's diligence in respect of this book commands admiration, his avoidance of the word 'read' ('I have consulted a copy in the Yale University Library', p. 190n. in *Satires Against Man*) allows for a suspicion that the same might apply to him.

[47] Griffin holds that such exaltation 'is implicit in the very idea of the earthly pilgrimage to heaven' (p. 193 in *Satires Against Man*), but the humility of man is a classic feature in this genre. Patrick's pilgrim is not a lordly creature who proceeds assured of success, any more than Bunyan's; in fact, his lack of purposefulness and strength is distinctly tiresome.

at least heard of them. Whether he ever sat down to read them is hard to guess. The lack of a distinct agreement between what the 'Band, and Beard' actually says and what Patrick and Ingelo wrote makes such active study seem doubtful. In fact, it was rather easier to find parallels in Sibbes (see pp. 163–7 above). 'The Pathetique Pen of *Ingello*' and '*Patricks Pilgrim*' may simply have been selected as well-known specimens of Anglican belief, to match the adversarius' predominantly Anglican/Latitudinarian views (see pp. 171ff. above).

Ingelo held degrees from Edinburgh, Cambridge and Oxford, whereas Patrick was a Cambridge man. But it was the '*Colledges*'[48] of Oxford – Exeter and Lincoln, to be precise – that were responsible for the education of the man who indirectly comes under fire in lines 86–7. This couplet occurs within a sustained onslaught on reason as the originator of futile cognitive efforts. It is an onslaught whose ferocity might detract from the impact of the simile in these lines:

> So charming Oyntments, make an Old *Witch* flie,
> And bear a Crippled Carcass through the Skie.

Still, that simile possesses a boldness easily lost on a modern reader, and its relevance to the endeavours of rational thinkers is greater than it might seem.

The focal point of these issues is a name: Joseph Glanvill. As Walker and other Rochester editors following John Hayward have recorded, but not deemed worthy of commenting on, the *Satyr* lines resemble a passage from Glanvill's *Sad(d)ucismus Triumphatus*:

> *There are* Actions *in most of those* Relations *ascribed to* Witches, *which are* ridiculous *and* impossible *in the nature of* things; *such are* (1) *their flying out of* windows, *after they have anointed themselves, to remote places.*[49]

Summoning reason and philosophy to his aid, Glanvill later conjectures that the phenomenon is explicable: body and soul can be separated without death (as is affirmed by 'great Philosophers'); and

> the *Witches anointing* her self before she takes her flight, may perhaps serve to keep the Body *tenantable*, and in fit *disposition* to receive the *Spirit* at its return. (p. 14)

---

[48] In Butler's 'Heroical Epistle of Hudibras to Sidrophel', lines 81–2, the knight mentions the conjurer's having 'gain'd, o'th' *Colledge*, / A Quarter-share (at most) of Knowledge'. According to Wilders, this is a reference to the Royal Society, which met at Gresham College (p. 406n. in his *Hudibras* edition). The satirist's '*Colledges*', in the plural, throws a wider net, but that most important body in the learned community could hardly escape being included in the attack.

[49] Section 3.2, p. 9 in Bernhard Fabian's Olm facsimile edition of 1978 (Hildesheim and New York).

What comes across to us as the superstitious nonsense of a distant age was accepted religious wisdom in Rochester's day. Calling it into question amounted to atheist heresy.[50] Hobbes, who had denied the power of witches (in chs. 2 and 12 of *Leviathan*), met with the indignant outcry of the educational establishment. Even such admirable scientists as Boyle believed in witches. Their reason was simple: evil spirits and witches are evidence of the existence of a spiritual world. In times where divine miracles are rare, we may look to the realm of darkness for proof that there is a reality beyond material things. For Glanvill, supernatural evidence of this debased nature confirmed the immortality of the soul. Indeed, disbelief in witches amounted to disbelief in immortality and all the intangible truths of religion; 'no spirits, no God'.

Glanvill was, in fact, fighting a losing battle. In the years just before the Restoration, there had been a decline in the condemnation of witches. The trend was reversed in the 1660s, and Glanvill's book on witchcraft was first published in 1666, with two reprints in 1667.[51] Fresh outbreaks of alleged sorcery occurred in southern England, and Glanvill's treatise appeared just as the panic was at its height. But there had been scoffers all along – mainly, as Glanvill saw, among 'the looser *Gentry*, and the small Pretenders to Philosophy and Wit'.[52] That segment of the population was one where Rochester felt more at home than among the Anglican clergy. The social category so contemptuously described by Glanvill – and, of course, Hobbes and his successors – carried the day as far as witchcraft was concerned. Glanvill and Rochester both died in 1680. Despite the popularity of *Saducismus Triumphatus*, the 'climate of opinion' (to quote Glanvill's own famous expression) had no place for it a few decades later.

There is of course no proof that Glanvill is the intended target of lines

[50] Many scholars have analysed the role of witchcraft in seventeenth-century religious life. To a reader unfamiliar with the subject, Basil Willey's discussion of *Sad(d)ucismus Triumphatus* still offers an introduction that could hardly be improved on (pp. 194–204 in *The Seventeenth-Century Background*). See also Cope, *Joseph Glanvill*, pp. 61–3 and 91–103; Thomas, *Religion and the Decline of Magic*, pp. 681–98 (in the second impression of 1971); and Shapiro, *Probability and Certainty*, pp. 194ff. On Hobbes' views regarding witchcraft and the attacks he had to sustain as a result of them, see Mintz, *The Hunting of Leviathan*, pp. 102–9.

[51] See Cope, *Joseph Glanvill*, p. 93.

[52] See Willey, *The Seventeenth-Century Background*, p. 196, and Thomas, *Religion and the Decline of Magic*, p. 693 (in the 1971 edition). Jackson Cope (*Joseph Glanvill*, p. 102n.) and Barbara Shapiro (*Probability and Certainty*, p. 208) record Richard Baxter's comment, in a letter to Glanvill (1670), that scoffers were to the fore 'at Court and ye Innes of Court' – another indication that Rochester's own social environment disbelieved in witchcraft. One unconvinced reader of Glanvill's discussions was Samuel Butler, whose 'Criticismes upon Bookes and Authors' (p. 137 in de Quehen's edition of Butler's prose) shows up the inconsistency of Glanvill's polemical stance.

86–7. The couplet could simply be read as a reference to popular belief, with no personal polemics intended. But the inclusion of the witch simile in this particular context is suggestive. In lines 80–93 the satirist denounces academic attainments and the places where they may be obtained. The witch lines are set in an overall attack on reason as a component in the acquisition of learning. The appreciation that greeted Glanvill's writings on witchcraft was largely due to his attempt to apply scientific arguments in them. His work was thus regarded as the forward-looking labour of a man who was not only a noted clergyman but also an exponent of the new science, and who explicitly invoked 'the Rules of *Reason*, and *Philosophy*' in his undertaking.[53] Another reason for surmising an implicit allusion to Glanvill is that this learned divine was personally known to Charles' Court; he became Chaplain in Ordinary to the King in 1672. If lines 86–7 are taken as the covert insult of a nobleman courtier directed against a Court chaplain, it would only be one instance among many of Charles' courtiers goading the clergy, much to the King's amusement.[54]

In comparing reason to the ointment which enabled a witch to fly, the satirist gives the last twist to his parodic explorations of the flight metaphor. In lines 88–91, reason is again the subject:

> 'Tis this exalted Pow'r, whose bus'ness lies,
> In *Nonsense*, and impossibilities.
> This made a Whimsical *Philosopher*,
> Before the spacious *World*, his *Tub* prefer ...

'*Nonsense*' is a highly apt designation for the province of that faculty which the satirist has so consistently set up against sense (in a seventeenth-century context, the word carried much the same connotations as it does today), and 'impossibilities' sums up those futile intellectual endeavours that the satirist ridiculed before. However, the claim that it was reason that made Diogenes of Sinope stay in his tub is less immediately comprehensible viewed against the background of previous lines.

Vieth's commentary in his Rochester edition is sparse but usually highly informative. In respect of the philosopher in a tub, however, it is less than illuminating:

---

[53] See, for instance, pp. 13 and 14 in the Olm facsimile of *Saducismus Triumphatus*.
[54] Cf. J. H. Overton, *Life in the English Church (1660–1714)* (London, 1885), p. 8: 'Besides the indirect injury [the King] did by his libertinism both in deed and in opinion, he was directly [the Church's] enemy; he notoriously disliked the clergy and set his courtiers against them.' On the contempt of the Wits for clergymen, see also J. H. Wilson, *Court Wits*, p. 77.

Diogenes the Cynic, well known for dwelling in a tub, taught that virtue consists in the avoidance of all physical pleasure and that pain and hunger are positively helpful in the pursuit of goodness. (p. 97)

In fact, as Dale Underwood has shown,[55] Diogenes the Cynic had several points in common with the Restoration libertines. His asceticism was the result not of a wish to mortify the flesh in pursuit of goodness, but of his desire to attain the greatest possible freedom from human needs. With regard to bodily appetites, Diogenes and the speaker in the *Satyr* are actually in agreement: they should be gratified with a minimum of fuss and delay. In his conversations with Burnet, Rochester voiced much the same views.

It is possible that Rochester did not know of these similarities, or that he disregarded them. The gravamen of the charge against Diogenes in the *Satyr* is that he chose to forgo worldly pleasures because of some idea he had. In that limited sense, the traditional image of the philosopher in his tub was of course perfectly adequate.[56]

The couplet on Diogenes, supplemented by the two lines on 'Cloysterd Coxcombs', marks a turning point in the satirist's reply to the 'Band, and Beard'. Up to now, he was busy demonstrating the absurdity, and the presumptuousness, of his opponent's claims for reason. Those claims were basically of an epistemological nature, although they had ethical implications ('*give the World true grounds of hope and fear*'). The following section of the satirist's speech, from line 94 to line 111, shifts the emphasis to what he feels that reason *can* do. That shift entails a remove from the thin air of speculation to the earthy domains of practical action:

> But thoughts, are giv'n, for Actions government,
> Where Action ceases, thoughts impertinent:
> Our *Sphere* of Action, is lifes happiness,
> And he who thinks Beyond, thinks like an *Ass*.
> Thus, whilst against false reas'ning I inveigh,
> I own right *Reason*, which I wou'd obey:
> That *Reason* that distinguishes by sense,
> And gives us *Rules*, of good, and ill from thence:

[55] *Etherege*, pp. 18–20. See also Arthur O. Lovejoy and George Boas, *Primitivism and Related Ideas in Antiquity* (Baltimore, 1935), vol. 1 of *A Documentary History of Primitivism and Related Ideas*, pp. 120–9.

[56] In his strictures on the failures of philosophers to live according to their own precepts, Sir Thomas Browne (*Religio Medici*, i.55) said that '*Diogenes* ... was the most vainglorious man of his time, and more ambitious in refusing all Honours, than *Alexander* in rejecting none.'

That bounds desires, with a reforming Will,
To keep 'em more in vigour, not to kill.
Your *Reason* hinders, mine helps t'enjoy,
Renewing Appetites, yours wou'd destroy.
My Reason is my *Friend*, yours is a *Cheat*,
Hunger call's out, my Reason bids me eat;
Perversly yours, your Appetite does mock,
This asks for Food, that answers what's a Clock?
This plain distinction Sir your doubt secures,
'Tis not true Reason I despise but yours.

Changing from critic to preceptor, the speaker proceeds to outline the nature and functions of 'right/true *Reason*'. The narrowness of its realm has already been commented on (see p. 201 above). The insistence on action is in keeping with the emphasis which the entire poem gives to it (see pp. 227 and 236 below). Both these aspects form the starkest possible contrast to the 'boundless Universe' and the incorporeal qualities of reason that were prevalent in lines 66–89. In fact, the contrast seems too marked for coincidence.

The actions governed by thoughts prompted by right reason guided by the senses have but one purpose: that of securing the greatest possible satisfaction for bodily appetites. There is nothing to suggest that this process might be affected by other people pursuing the same aim for themselves. The issue of man's behaviour to others of his species is reviewed later on, in lines 129–73. The passage is thus a libertine's credo, representative of a long tradition in France and to some extent in England,[57] but a particularly reductive one. For instance, it says nothing about nature and the appropriateness and joy of living according to her laws, a point repeatedly made by Théophile de Viau and his successors. This unmitigated advocacy of total sensuality hardly deserves to be graced by the term Epicurean. The very plainness of the satirist's language and his example (hunger and food)[58] underscores its lack of any ingratiating qualities.

By contrast, Rochester's predecessors and contemporaries generally put the libertine's case with persuasive deftness, eschewing extremist positions. The following stanza from *Les Philosophies* by the (as yet unconverted) abbé de Choisy makes a point not unlike the one contained in lines 102–3 of the *Satyr*, but the tone is radically different:

---

[57] See Underwood, *Etherege*, pp. 11–17.
[58] Griffin notes the difference in style between the preceding passage and the lines on 'right reason' (*Satires Against Man*, pp. 222–3).

> Rendez-vous donc à mon système,
> Mais usez-en tout à loisir;
> Eloignez-vous de tout extrême;
> N'épuisez ni soif, ni désir;
> Le plaisir est le bien suprême,
> Mais l'excès n'est point un plaisir.[59]

The combination of pleasure and moderation is praised by Cowley in his essay *On Liberty*, in a passage which goes on to chide the 'Lustful and Luxurious' for being mere 'servants of the Belly':

Why, I'le tell you who is that true Freeman, and that true Gentleman; Not he who blindly follows all his pleasures (the very name of Follower is servile) but he who rationally guides them, and is not hindred by outward impediments in the conduct and enjoyment of them.[60]

Like the contrast between the functions of reason in lines 66–89 and 94–111, the brashness of the lines on 'right reason' seems calculated, and for the same reason, namely polemical effectiveness. The speaker's stance is so extreme that it must incite disagreement even in the most docile reader, not to mention his immediate target, the Restoration divines and philosophers represented by the adversarius.

The following passage invites objections, too:

> Thus I think Reason righted, but for *Man*,
> I'le nere recant defend him if you can.
> For all his Pride, and his Philosophy,
> 'Tis evident, *Beasts* are in their degree,
> As wise at least, and better far than he.
> Those *Creatures*, are the wisest who attain,
> By surest means, the ends at which they aim.
> If therefore *Jowler*, finds, and Kills his *Hares*,
> Better than *Meres*, supplyes Committee Chairs;
> Though one's a *States-man*, th'other but a *Hound*,
> *Jowler*, in Justice, wou'd be wiser found.

Sir Thomas Meres belonged to the Country Party in the Commons and was thus a member, and an influential one, of the opposition. That Charles bore him no grudge in 1672–3 can be seen from the King's wish that Meres should be made Speaker at that time.[61] He, and the Court

---

[59] Quoted in Spink, *French Free-Thought*, p. 158.

[60] P. 384 in A. R. Waller's edition of the *Essays, Plays and Sundry Verses of Abraham Cowley* (Cambridge, 1906).

[61] See D. T. Witcombe, *Charles II and the Cavalier House of Commons 1663–1674* (Manchester and New York, 1966), p. 128n. A thorough account of Meres and his work (he is said to have been named to 686 committees during the Cavalier Parliament!) is found in Basil Duke Henning's *The History of Parliament: The House of Commons 1660–1690*, vol. III (London, 1983), pp. 48–59.

generally, will not have been pleased with Meres' 1673 criticism of particularly sore points (such as the Chancellor's writs and the King's embarking on the Third Dutch War without consulting Parliament).[62] Still, whatever relish a reader who belonged to the Court circle may have felt at seeing Meres estimated to be less wise than a capable hound, even he will have been provoked by the comparison – at least to the point where he would object, 'but surely the intrinsic worthiness of the ends and aims must be considered, too, not merely the degree of success in achieving them'.

This is precisely the reaction the satirist has induced by what appeared to be gross exaggerations and distortions. Having engineered its build-up, he is ready for it when it comes. Lines 123–58 ('You see how far *Mans* wisedom here extends' up to 'For all Men, wou'd be *Cowards* if they durst') constitute a blow-by-blow slashing of man's claim to dignity and moral worth. As in the lines on wit (35–44), man is now viewed in a social context;[63] the interpersonal perspective takes over and prevails to the end of the poem. These thirty-six lines are divided into two distinct passages of equal length by the anadiplosis in lines 140–1 ('for fear; / For fear'). Both are concerned with man's behaviour to others of his species. The first passage exhibits man's reprehensible actions towards his fellows and their background in mere wantonness; the second argues that even apparently laudable conduct is motivated by a selfish passion, fear for one's own safety. The former involves a thorough-going comparison with (other) animals. This perspective is relinquished in the latter, the satirist apparently feeling that there is no need for an animal contrast to human hypocrisy. It is worth noting that the *Satyr* favours beasts not because they are virtuous, but because they lack human vices. The superiority of beasts is thus consistently couched in negative terms. Not until the 'Apology' or 'Addition' does the speaker provide anything that could be called a delineation of virtue (see pp. 225ff. below).

The issue of wisdom/reason/philosophy being settled to man's disadvantage, with the piteously small loophole in the lines on right reason, the satirist turns to the moral nature of man as manifested in actions, the only criterion he will allow. He finds that while beasts destroy one another due to their instinct for survival ('hunger' and 'Love'), men work the ruin of others under the influence of sheer caprice. Animals do not hide their aggressiveness ('Teeth, and Claws');

---

[62] See Witcombe, *Charles II*, pp. 130–1.   [63] Cf. Gill, 'Mind against Itself', 560–1.

men conceal their hostility under the disguise of its opposite, benevolence. In calling man 'Savage' and 'Unhumane', the satirist operates on two levels: while superficially suggesting that man is beastly, these words remind us that he is in fact beastlier than the beasts.[64] The distress of men's victims brings no tangible benefit to the perpetrators. Watching the sufferings of others must hence be a sufficiently enjoyable diversion for men to go to some trouble to bring them about. It is hard to imagine a harsher condemnation of humanity.

Its counterpart was written a dozen or so years later, in *The Hind and the Panther*:

> Beasts are the Subjects of Tyrannick sway,
> Where still the stronger on the weaker Prey.
> Man only of a softer mold is made;
> Not for his Fellows ruine, but their Aid.
> Created kind, beneficent and free,
> The noble Image of the Deity.
> ...
> But when arriv'd at last to humane Race,
> The Godhead took a deep consid'ring space:
> And, to distinguish Man from all the rest,
> Unlock'd the sacred Treasures of his Breast:
> And Mercy mixt with reason did impart,
> One to his Head, the other to his Heart:
> Reason to Rule, but Mercy to forgive:
> The first is Law, the last Prerogative.
>
> (1.245–50, 255–62)

In this history of the human race, the speaker can dispense with practical illustration. Another poet, however, drew on experiential material when applying himself to the man/beast issue in a religious poem. Waller's *Divine Poems* speak encouragingly of divine love and the comforts of the Scriptures, but observation of men and animals leads him to comparisons resembling those of Rochester's satirist:

> For greedy wolves unguarded sheep devour
> But while their hunger lasts, and then give o'er:[65]

---

[64] Cf. Scrivener's *Treatise Against Drunkennesse*, p. 78: 'And if that be true which *Chrysostome* saith ... that for a Man to be compared to a Beast, is to be worse than a Beast, because he was ordained to be much better ... what may we think of those Men to whom Beasts are compared, but not equallizing them in Beastlinesse? In all cases we say Comparisons are odious; but in this case, abominable, and confounding.'

[65] This natural regulation of appetite and supply among animals was commented on by many seventeenth-century writers, among them Godfrey Goodman in his *Fall of Man*; see pp. 78–9. (Goodman also argued that man is a far more miserable creature than the beasts; see, for instance, pp. 27–8.) Jeremy Treglown has demonstrated that Sir William Davenant's works

> Man's boundless avarice his want exceeds,
> And on his neighbours round about him feeds.
> His pride and vain ambition are so vast,
> That, deluge-like, they lay whole nations waste.[66]

Those resemblances are surely coincidental, however, and it would be hard to find two more dissimilar attitudes to fear than those put forward by Waller (in *Of the Fear of God*) and the speaker in Rochester's *Satyr*. The former – not unlike Sibbes – argues that fear of God is a means to escape damnation. A nobler attitude was articulated in Browne's *Religio Medici* (1.52); here, in a heart-lifting paragraph, Browne wrote: 'I feare God, yet am not afraid of him; his mercies make me ashamed of my sins, before his judgements afraid thereof... I can hardly think there was ever any scared into Heaven...'

The all-pervading fear that prompts human action in Rochester's *Satyr* is of an aggressively worldly kind. The 'security' it compels man to strive for is a comfortable position in this life, not in a subsequent existence. Its materialistic nature may make it seem natural to associate it with fear as discussed by Hobbes (see pp. 178f. above).[67] The references to 'Arm(e)s' and 'lust of *Pow'r*' (lines 140–5) could be seen to connect this *Satyr* passage with Hobbes' remarks on natural man's 'continuall feare, and danger of violent death' (ch. 13). The definitions in chapter 6 of *Leviathan* are pertinent, too:

> *Aversion*, with opinion of *Hurt* from the object, FEARE. The same, with hope of avoyding that Hurt by resistence, COURAGE.

It should be remembered, though, that Hobbes' emphasis with regard to fear in a purely materialistic context is on external causes. For instance, men in the state of nature have every reason to fear death; it is an 'object' that calls forth aversion and fear, not an innate compelling passion; and man in a commonwealth must fear breaking its laws, for such crimes will not go unpunished.[68]

The satirist's presentation of fear focuses on its role as dictating actions that would seem virtuous and benevolent, but are in truth hypocritical manifestations of misguided self-interest. The persuasiveness of lines

---

contain passages very similar to Rochester's, in this respect and in others; see 'Rochester and Davenant', *Notes and Queries* 23.12 (vol. 221 of the continuous series; December 1976), 557–8.

[66] *Of Divine Love*, canto IV, lines 7–12. (Cf. also the conclusion of *Of the Fear of God*, canto I.) Quoted from Park's edition of Waller's *Poetical Works*, p. 135.

[67] For Hobbes' comments on the fear of God, see, for instance, *Leviathan*, ch. 31.

[68] On fear and benevolence in Hobbes' ethics, see Bernard Gert, 'Hobbes and Psychological Egoism', in B. H. Baumrin, ed., *Hobbes's* Leviathan: *Interpretation and Criticism* (Belmont, Calif., 1969), pp. 107–26.

140–1 may detract from this perspective. The preceding passage (lines 123–40) compared the *worst* things men can do to the gravest charges that can be brought against animals, concluding that man is by far the greatest offender. Here, in lines 143–58, the speaker demonstrates that even the *best* actions of human beings are base in origin.

Rochester's *Satyr* was not the only literary expression of disgust with human deceptiveness and villainy. Butler's *Satire upon the Weakness and Misery of Man* avows:

> Our holiest actions have been
> Th'effects of wickedness and sin...
>
> ...
>
> The best of all our actions tend
> To the preposterousest end.
>
> (lines 25–6 and 41–2)

And Cowley's long essay *Of Liberty*, a work which Rochester can be shown to have been familiar with,[69] discourses on human ambition in terms that strongly resemble lines 144–52 of the *Satyr*:

> Let us first consider the Ambitious, and those both in their progress to Greatness, and after the attaining of it. There is nothing truer than what *Salust* saies, *Dominationis in alios servitiam suam Mercedem dant,* They are content to pay so great a price as their own Servitude to purchase the domination over others.
>
> ...
>
> ... That it is the nature of Ambition ... to make men Lyers and Cheaters ... to cut all fri[e]ndships and enmities to the measure of their own Interest, and to make a good Countenance without the help of good will. And can there be Freedom with this perpetual constraint? What is it but a kind of Rack that forces men to say what they have no mind to?
>
> ...
>
> I do but slightly touch upon all these particulars of the slavery of Greatness: I shake but a few of their outward Chains; their Anger, Hatred, Jealousie, Fear, Envy, Grief, and all the *Etcaetera* of their Passions, which are the secret, but constant Tyrants and Torturers of their life ... (Waller's edition of Cowley's *Essays*, pp. 378, 380 and 384)

Cowley's suggested remedy, however, is not recourse to natural instinct and sensual gratification enhanced by deliberation, but a competency-lives-longer life of the traditional happy-man variety.[70]

---

[69] An important late letter to his wife contains four lines from a Martial translation appended by Cowley to this essay. Rochester was apparently quoting them from memory. See Treglown's edition of the *Letters*, p. 242. (This letter was written several years after the *Satyr*, but Rochester's familiarity with Cowley's essay may have been of long standing.)

[70] See Maren-Sofie Røstvig, *The Happy Man: Studies in the Metamorphoses of a Classical Ideal 1600–1700* (Oslo and Oxford, 1954), vol. I, pp. 76–7 and 93–5.

In the *Satyr*, it is fear that impels man to strive for those outward glories, honour and fame; but fear is also the source of man's 'lust of *Pow'r*' which, in its turn, lurks behind every show of personal friendliness. In the first half of lines 123–58, amiable gestures masked underlying malice; in the second, friendliness disguises worldly ambition. Lack of sincerity is common to both displays of cordiality. Another element that occurs in both halves of the description of human behaviour is the word 'betray'. Man betrays man; but every man is himself betrayed by the fear that is at the core of his being. The other great evil passion that bedevils mankind is pride. Pride blinds him to his limitations, making him waste his life in the vain pursuit of knowledge and wisdom. Fear drives him to exalt himself above others, repressing his healthier inclinations and falsifying his motives to himself and to the external world he is so anxious to control. Taken together, these two fundamental human passions make man destroy himself while destroying others. Beasts are indeed fortunate to be exempt from both.

Since human nature is corrupted by pride and fear, all that a man can do is try to make the best of those traits which Nature gave to men and (other) animals alike: instinct, senses, appetites, the satisfaction of the latter being increased by the judicious application of reason. Against the background of the total depravation of humanity that is depicted with such masterful strokes in lines 123–58, the passage on 'right *Reason*' gains a new dimension. What appeared to be an *outré* stance comes, by subsequent qualification, to seem like a sane option. Incapable of genuine benevolence, man can do nothing for other men, and while in the grip of pride and fear he does himself no good either – a point repeatedly stressed by the satirist (see lines 16, 28, 32–4, 36, 88–9, 132 and 151–2). All that remains is to trust natural instinct, not human passions – Nature, not human nature.

This is the point where many Rochester critics have lost their bearings. Overlooking the distinction between those characteristics that man *shares with the other animals* and those that are *specifically human*, they have found a contradiction between the advocacy of nature, sense and instinct and the viciousness of man acting according to his base urges. Griffin says that the poem '[changes] its valuation of human appetites' which are, in lines 130–8, implicitly condemned as 'lawless and wanton'.[71] Farley-Hills contends that the argument, at this point in the poem, 'has come to the paradoxical position that *neither* man's

---

[71] *Satires Against Man*, p. 237.

reason *nor* his instincts are satisfactory guides to conduct' and 'is at a complete impasse', leading the reader 'into a state of intellectual impotence'.[72] To Vieth, the *Satyr* consists of two mutually contradictory halves; in the first, human beings can, theoretically, achieve the 'norm of pleasure' represented by animals, but in the second 'man, victimized by his depraved nature, cannot rise to [their] moral level'.[73]

Unlike these scholars, I cannot find an inherent contradiction, still less an irreconcilable division, in the *Satyr*. Nor do I think it necessary to try to establish a 'unity' by way of the self-dramatisation of the speaker, as James E. Gill has attempted to do.[74] The fact that the speaker who attacks reason himself proceeds by ratiocination is paradoxical, but not logically impossible to the point where some elaborate explanatory structure must be erected to make it acceptable. He is careful not to rely on mere postulates and abstractions. Tangible examples are steadily adduced to support his argumentation, all in accordance with his views on sense perception and action. He certainly puts his reason to use beyond that realm of bodily appetite to which he wished to see reason restricted, but that irony can surely be savoured without the need for far-reaching theoretical deliberations on cohesion, open-endedness and so on. After all, his ratiocination purports to direct others to that narrow province.

The satirist's subsequent advocacy of knavery has also been quoted as a sign of inconsistency and argumentative weakness. It is hardly illogical, though:

> And honesty's against all common sense,
> *Men* must be *Knaves*, 'tis in their own defence.
> *Mankind's* dishonest, if you think it fair,
> Amongst known *Cheats*, to play upon the square,
> You'le be undone –
> Nor can weak truth, your reputation save,
> The *Knaves*, will all agree to call you *Knave*.
> Wrong'd shall he live, insulted o're, opprest,
> Who dares be less a *Villain*, than the rest.
> Thus Sir you see what humane Nature craves,

---

[72] *Rochester's Poetry*, p. 184.   [73] 'Toward an Anti-Aristotelian Poetic', 127.
[74] Gill's analysis ('Mind against Itself') contains useful suggestions, but the contortions of his *persona* seem unnecessarily complicated. A subsequent article of his, called 'The Fragmented Self in Three of Rochester's Poems' (*Modern Language Quarterly* 49.1 (March 1988), 19–37), has done nothing to convince me that 'a growing awareness of the triumphs and despairs of postmodern thought' makes Rochester's poetry 'more compelling than [it was] ten years ago' (37).

> Most Men are *Cowards*, all Men shou'd be *Knaves*:
> The diff'rence lyes (as far as I can see)
> Not in the thing it self, but the degree;
> And all the subject matter of debate,
> Is only who's a *Knave*, of the first *Rate*?

The speaker is convinced that all any man can do is to look after his own interests. As '*Mankind's* dishonest', self-preservation leaves him no other option but to be a knave among knaves, and preferably better at it than most. The statement that 'honesty's against all common sense' does not conflict with the claims made elsewhere for 'sense'. In any case, the meaning of the expression 'common sense' here might be the third in the *OED*, 'The general sense, feeling, or judgement of mankind, or of a community'. Mankind, then, is inherently dishonest, and the community at large – not unnaturally – puts a very low price on honesty. Even those whose inclinations are not towards knavery (there are differences in degree, the satirist admits) thus have no choice, as long as they want to live among men.

On this point, Rochester's satirist could call on Hobbes, Butler and even Cowley to support him:

For he that should be modest, and tractable, and performe all he promises, in such time, and place, where no man els should do so, should but make himselfe a prey to others, and procure his own certain ruine, contrary to the ground of all Lawes of Nature, which tend to Natures preservation. (Hobbes, *Leviathan*, ch. 15)

Most Men owe their *Misfortunes* rather to their Want of *Dishonesty*, than Witt. (Butler, 'Sundry Thoughts', ed. de Quehen, p. 1) The Reason why Fooles, and Knaves thrive better in the world then wiser and honester men, is because they are nearer to the Generall Temper of mankind, which is nothing but a Mixture of Cheat and Folly ... ('Learning and Knowledge', *ibid.*, p. 11)

If twenty thousand naked *Americans* were not able to resist the assaults of but twenty well-armed *Spaniards*, I see little possibility for one Honest man to defend himself against twenty thousand Knaves ... He will find no less odds than this against him, if he have much to do in humane affairs. (Cowley, *The dangers of an Honest man in much Company*, *Essays*, p. 443)

The five ensuing lines follow the ending of the original *Satyr*, if we grant the assumption that the 'Apology' was a subsequent addition:

> All this with indignation have I hurl'd,
> At the pretending part of the proud World,
> Who swolne with selfish vanity, devise,

> False freedomes, holy Cheats, and formal Lyes
> Over their fellow *Slaves* to tyrannize.

The expression 'pretending part' could be read as a partial vindication of mankind, but it is more of an identification of the addressee. The 'World' is 'proud' – no part of mankind is free from the taint of pride – but the satirist's rage is specifically directed at those who would deliberately place themselves above others. 'Pretending', 'swolne', 'vanity' are words that recall the three target groups of *Upon Nothing*, statesmen, influential divines and learned men. So, by implication, does the line 'False freedomes, holy Cheats, and formal Lyes'. 'Freedomes' denoting 'privileges' are one of those commodities at the statesman's disposal which he may dispense in order to secure or reward loyal support. 'Holy Cheats' can be read as a reference to those spurious threats and promises with which the clergy subjugate their flocks. 'Formal Lyes', finally, points in the direction of academic learning; 'formal' here seems to mean 'in accordance with established rules, methodical' (applicable to both the ancient and the modern philosophy). If this reading of line 177 is accepted, it can be seen to summarise the deceitful measures with which politicians, clergymen and academics oppress their fellows. These powerful men resort to fraud not 'in their own defence', to avoid being victimised by knaves, but to victimise others no worse than themselves. It is from these social ranks that the two good-men prototypes in the 'Apology' are recruited. The statesman comes first:

> But if in *Court*, so just a Man there be,
> (In *Court*, a just Man, yet unknown to me)
> Who does his needful flattery direct,
> Not to oppress, and ruine, but protect;
> Since flattery, which way so ever laid,
> Is still a Tax on that unhappy Trade.
> If so upright a *States-Man*, you can find,
> Whose passions bend to his unbyass'd Mind;
> Who does his Arts, and *Pollicies* apply,
> To raise his *Country*, not his *Family*;
> Nor while his Pride own'd Avarice withstands,
> Receives close Bribes, from *Friends* corrupted hands.

The designation 'just Man' is reminiscent of Hobbes, who discourses on the justness of men and actions (*Leviathan*, ch. 15) and on justification by works and faith respectively (ch. 43). The definition of 'a just man' in the former context comes close to the imaginary upright statesman:

A Just man ... is he that taketh all the care he can, that his Actions may be all Just: and an Unjust man, is he that neglecteth it. And such men are more often in our Language stiled by the names of Righteous, and Unrighteous; then Just, and Unjust; though the meaning be the same.

Interestingly enough, the model statesman is not required to abstain from practising the fundamentally insincere art of flattery. The satirist, like so many Restoration observers,[75] recognises that it is an inescapable feature in elevated political activity. Nor, as we remember, was the righteous politician exempt from pride. But this and other 'passions' are subservient to an incorruptible mind, and that mind supplies the guidelines for his actions. This is precisely what the *Satyr* speaker prescribed in line 94, 'thoughts, are giv'n, for Actions government' — a general statement of a much less controversial nature than the ensuing definition of the proper use of reason. True to the speaker's thorough-going commitment to action, he is primarily interested in what the good statesman achieves in practical terms. The possessor of that illusory quality, an 'unbyass'd Mind', is able to perform as unrealistic deeds: his actions are geared to helping his fellow men, in a limited sense (line 182) as well as on a national scale (line 188). In so doing, he abstains from securing advantages for himself and his family — not because he is too virtuous even to contemplate it, but because his 'unbyass'd Mind' shows him that such conduct is unworthy.

When the satirist affirms that a 'just Man' does not, as far as he is aware, exist at the contemporary Court, he is voicing a virtually incontestable opinion (cf. pp. 153ff. above on *Upon Nothing*). Even high politicians who at least possessed appreciable amounts of moral courage and loyalty to their Royal master hardly qualified for the term 'just' as applied by the *Satyr* speaker. Such basically faithful servants as the previously mentioned Clarendon and Clifford, for example, were not blind to personal advantage and had sadly inflexible minds.[76] For all their admirable qualities, there was nothing saintly about them (except perhaps in comparison with men like Buckingham), and selfless benevolence towards their fellow men was not a salient characteristic in either.

[75] Cf. Butler's *Character* 'A Modern Politician', p. 34 in Daves' edition of the *Characters*, and the *Savile Correspondence: Letters to and from Henry Savile, Esq. ... including letters from his brother George Marquess of Halifax* (London, 1858), p. 37.

[76] See, for instance, David Ogg, *England in the Reign of Charles II* (Oxford, 1934; I have used the paperback edition of 1963), vol. I, p. 150, and Cyril Hughes Hartmann, *Clifford of the Cabal: A Life of Thomas, First Lord Clifford of Chudleigh, Lord High Treasurer of England (1630–1673)* (London, 1937), pp. 307–11.

The virtues of the good statesman are to a great extent defined in negative terms. This is even truer of the second paragon, the humble clergyman. More than twice as long as the statesman passage, and charged with far greater vehemence, this exposition on vice and virtue in ecclesiastical life reflects that loathing of clerical insincerity which repeatedly surfaces in Rochester's writings (and conversations with Burnet):

> Is there a *Church-Man* who on *God* relyes?
> Whose Life, his Faith, and Doctrine Justifies?
> Not one blown up, with vain Prelatique Pride,
> Who for reproof of Sins, does *Man* deride:
> Whose envious heart makes preaching a pretence
> With his obstrep'rous sawcy Eloquence,
> To chide at *Kings*, and raile at Men of sense.
> Who from his Pulpit, vents more peevish Lyes,
> More bitter railings, scandals, Calumnies,
> Than at a Gossipping, are thrown about,
> When the good *Wives*, get drunk, and then fall out.
> None of that sensual *Tribe*, whose Tallents lye,
> In *Avarice, Pride, Sloth*, and *Gluttony*.
> Who hunt good Livings, but abhor good Lives,
> Whose Lust exalted, to that height arrives,
> They act Adultery with their own *Wives*.
> And e're a score of Years compleated be,
> Can from the lofty *Pulpit* proudly see,
> Half a large *Parish*, their own *Progeny*.
>   Nor doating *Bishop* who wou'd be ador'd,
> For domineering at the *Councel Board*;
> A greater *Fop*, in business at Fourscore,
> Fonder of serious *Toyes*, affected more,
> Than the gay glitt'ring *Fool*, at Twenty proves,
> With all his noise, his tawdrey Cloths, and Loves.
>   But a meek humble Man, of honest sense,
> Who Preaching peace, does practice continence;
> Whose pious life's a proof he does believe,
> Misterious truths, which no *Man* can conceive.

The virulence of this attack on the clergy as a whole and, if my assumptions are correct, on at least two individual members of it (see below), is brought home to us with peculiar clarity when we realise that the speaker imputes all the seven cardinal sins to churchmen. Pride, avarice, sloth and gluttony are stated together in line 203; the detestable preacher is said to have an 'envious heart' (line 195); and lines 205–9 make it very clear that lechery is a frequent clerical occupation. Wrath, however, is only present by implication, in lines 197–9 on the irate pulpit orator.

This may not be the only instance in English literature of the deadly sins *in corpore* being attached to those who practise Christianity,[77] but it would be difficult to find a corresponding example, even at this time when Church discipline was at a low ebb and the clergy complained bitterly of popular contempt.[78]

One who frequently spoke out against the denigration of religion and its servants was Edward Stillingfleet. In a sermon preached before Charles and the Court in the spring of 1667, the then incumbent of St Andrew's, Holborn, Prebendary of Islington in St Paul's Cathedral, and Chaplain in Ordinary to the King – still only thirty-two years old – passionately accused his audience of disrespect to religion:

> Methinks, among persons of civility and honour, above all others, religion might at least be treated with the reverence and respect due to the concernments of it; that it be not made the sport of entertainments, nor the common subject of plays and comedies. For is there nothing to trifle with but God and his service? Is wit grown so schismatical and sacrilegious that it can please itself with nothing but holy ground? Are prophaneness and wit grown such inseparable companions, that none shall be allowed to pretend to the one but such as dare be highly guilty of the other?[79]

The text of this sermon was 'Fools make a mock of sin'. Rochester, then twenty years old and a newlywed Gentleman of the Bedchamber, may have heard, or heard of, it. In any case, his *Satyr* imputes both folly and sin to the body of men of whom Stillingfleet was such a prominent member.

A better-known sermon of Stillingfleet's, and one that directly concerns Rochester, was the one preached on 24 February 1675, on the text 'Lest any of you be hardened through the deceitfulness of sin'. (It was subsequently 'printed by his Majesty's special command',[80] which

---

[77] For example, Morton W. Bloomfield mentions an amusing and well-written fifteenth-century satire, *Why I Can't Be a Nun*, on pp. 205–6 of his *The Seven Deadly Sins: An Introduction to the History of a Religious Concept, with Special Reference to Mediaeval English Literature* (Michigan, 1952).

[78] See ch. 8 in Overton, *Life in the English Church* (especially pp. 301–9 and 325–30).

[79] In *Twelve Sermons by Bishop Stillingfleet* (London, 1696); quoted by Overton, *Life in the English Church*, p. 242.

[80] See William Holden Hutton, *The English Church: From the Accession of Charles I to the Death of Anne (1625–1714)* (London, 1903), p. 215. On Rochester and Stillingfleet, see Kristoffer Paulson's 'The Reverend Edward Stillingfleet'.

says as much about the King's quizzical humour as about the merits of the discourse.) This sermon is not only an attack on Court immorality; it also incorporates 'Stillingfleet's reply' to Rochester's *Satyr*:

> ... because it is impossible to defend their extravagant courses by *Reason*, the only way left for them is to make *Satyrical Invectives* against *Reason*; as though it were the most uncertain, foolish and (I had almost said) unreasonable thing in the World: and yet they pretend to shew it in arguing against it: but it is a pity such had not their wish, *to have been Beasts rather than Men*, (if any men can make such a *wish* that have it not already) that they might have been less capable of doing mischief among mankind ...

If the conclusion of the poem was written after these fulminations were uttered, the poet's contention that clergymen are sinners in every sense – including the very worst – of the word may well have something to do with Stillingfleet's diatribe. It would probably give Rochester considerable gratification to level such charges against the clergy, placing them cheek-by-jowl with five lines that seem to refer particularly to the preacher who had repeatedly associated the Court and its ways with 'sin'.[81]

Stillingfleet was not of course the only preacher who would 'chide at *Kings*, and raile at Men of sense'. Men like Robert Frampton and Thomas Ken criticised the behaviour of Charles II without losing his favour; Richard Ollard quotes the King's remark that he would 'go and hear little Ken tell me of my faults'.[82] I have found no evidence of open hostility on the King's part towards Stillingfleet, whom he made Dean of St Paul's in 1678; but the fact remains that Stillingfleet did not receive a bishopric until William was King. Perhaps his persistent controversies with Catholics told against him with a monarch who had Romanist sympathies.[83]

Be that as it may, there is some reason to assume that the 'obstrep'rous sawcy Eloquence' of the vain preacher in lines 193–7 is at least in part a dig at the celebrated orator Stillingfleet. He was, after all, unusually audacious in his denunciation of the King and Court; Overton, commenting on the 1667 sermon, says that 'one hardly knows whether

---

[81] Commenting on Stillingfleet's association of sedition with 'Sin' in a 1673 sermon before Charles, Carroll dryly points out that Stillingfleet chose 'a metaphor which he knew Charles and his Court could relate to'; *The Common-Sense Philosophy*, p. 23.

[82] *The Image of the King: Charles I and Charles II* (London, 1979), pp. 110–11.

[83] On Charles' religion, see, for example, Ollard, *The Image of the King*, pp. 103–14. The bizarre story of his proposed 'conversion' to Rome as part of a deal with Louis XIV – the 'Grand Design' – is fascinatingly told and documented in Hartmann, *The King My Brother* (London, 1954).

to admire most the eloquence or the moral courage of the preacher' (*Life in the English Church*, p. 242). If the 'Apology' part of the *Satyr* followed the 1675 sermon, Rochester had every reason to hit back at the man who preached it, and he seems to have done just that.

Personal resentment may account for the lines on 'peevish Lyes' and so on being so closely associated with the lines on Stillingfleet (assuming they do refer to him). If they were written shortly after Stillingfleet's sermon, the disgusted Rochester may indeed have felt that 'scandals', 'Calumnies' and the like (in the sense of 'opprobrious censure' and 'false charges') were adequate representations of that clergyman's utterance. But this particular quarrel with a churchman may have receded into the background at this point, widening the applicability of these lines as compared to 196–7. (Also, it should be borne in mind that they might, as Vieth contends, be a scribal interpolation; see p. 163 above.)

Whatever their origins, the lines on pulpit ire reflect Restoration distaste for seditious preaching. The role played by zealous churchmen in the immediate past was only too fresh in people's minds, and the new taste for 'plain' instead of 'witty' preaching[84] was allied to the prevailing fear of enthusiasm. Many people concurred in Samuel Butler's views, in the *Character* called 'The Seditious Man' (p. 192 in Daves' edition):

If he be a Preacher, he has the Advantage of all others of his Tribe; for he has a Way to vent Sedition by Wholesale; and as the foulest Purposes have most need of the fairest Pretences; so when Sedition is masked under the Veil of Piety, Religion, Conscience, and holy Duty, it propagates wonderfully among the Rabble, and he vents more in an Hour from the Pulpit, than others by News and Politics can do in a Week.

The clergy may not have enjoyed much social prestige at this time, but in their congregations their influence – political as well as religious – was considerable. As parish priests, they were in a position to impose their views on the illiterate and uninformed common man; as chaplains – often an unenviable position – they could try their persuasive powers on members of wealthy households; and as high dignitaries in the Church, especially bishops, they could bring great pressure to bear on Court and Parliament. The failure of Charles' proposed Declarations of

---

[84] See, for instance, Cope, *Joseph Glanvill*, pp. 159ff. on Glanvill's part in this development, and W. Fraser Mitchell, *English Pulpit Oratory from Andrewes to Tillotson: A Study of Its Literary Aspects* (London and New York, 1932).

Indulgence is a case in point.[85] The first of these attempts was defeated in 1662 and the second some ten years later. On both occasions, the victor's name was Gilbert Sheldon.

As Sheldon's biographer Victor D. Sutch remarks, with engaging forthrightness, 'it is difficult to know what to think of Sheldon'.[86] To commentators with a Puritan bias, his name is the symbol of post-Restoration persecution. Anglicans acclaim his devotion to the Church and credit him with having done more than anybody else to secure its survival in the turbulent years of Charles' reign. Friends of scholarship and architecture recall Sheldon's generous patronage of learning and the decisive part he played in Christopher Wren's career.[87] Admirers of tolerance, magnanimity and personal piety find little to attract them in Sheldon's biography.

The attitude of Charles II to the man who became Archbishop of Canterbury in 1663 shifted in the course of the late 1660s and early 1670s. Sheldon's efficient blocking of the first Declaration of Indulgence did not destroy his influence with the King. However, his subsequent implacable opposition to anything that smacked even faintly of toleration roused Charles' displeasure. It has been recorded that the Archbishop refused the Sovereign the Sacrament because of his immoral life.[88] If this actually happened, the enormity of such a refusal is sufficient cause for real enmity on the King's part.

At any rate, Charles' growing dislike of the Archbishop is a fact. Other facts forge strong links between Sheldon and the 'doating *Bishop*' in line 210 of the *Satyr*. Sheldon was born in 1598 and thus nearly 'Fourscore' in 1675; his attendance at and influence on the Privy Council could well be described as 'domineering', especially by an unsympathetic observer; he was deeply involved in all sorts of political schemes and measures, including many not even remotely connected

[85] See J. R. Jones, *Country and Court*, pp. 150–1 and 177–8.

[86] *Gilbert Sheldon: Architect of Anglican Survival, 1640–1675* (The Hague, 1973), p. vii. (The book is vol. 12 in the Series Minor of the International Archives of the History of Ideas.) See also Overton, *Life in the English Church*, pp. 19–20 ('The discrepancies between the various estimates of him are almost ludicrous'). In Nathaniel Salmon's *The Lives of the English Bishops from the Restauration to the Revolution* (London, 1733), Sheldon is passionately defended against such (according to Salmon) 'wretched Table-talk' as Gilbert Burnet's claim that he 'seem'd not to have a deep sense of Religion, if any at all: And spoke of it most commonly as of an Engine of Government ... By this means the King came to look on him as a wise and honest Clergyman' (pp. 11–12).

[87] See, for instance, Sutch, *Gilbert Sheldon*, pp. 151–2.

[88] Ollard (*The Image of the King*, p. 110) and W. H. Hutton (*The English Church*, p. 197) refer to it as an accepted fact; Sutch is more cautious but does not appear to disbelieve the story (*Gilbert Sheldon*, p. 103).

with the Church;[89] he made diligent use of 'all the politician's traditional array of ploys' (Sutch, *Gilbert Sheldon*, p. 136), proving his fondness for 'serious *Toyes*'; and for all his candour and impatience with hypocrisy, he was a man who stood upon his dignity. Even Sheldon's friends would have found the words 'meek' and 'humble' singularly inapplicable to him.

The lines on the ageing ('doating' referring, of course, to impairment of the intellect due to advancing age) bishop seem to me to form a lampoon on the prelate who repeatedly shattered Charles' attempts to promote religious toleration.[90] This was one of the few great issues to which the King was truly committed. His defeat in 1673 was humiliating as well as decisive. (It was, incidentally, preceded by an all-out Anglican pulpit campaign against Catholicism which could well have struck a loyal Stuart courtier as downright seditious.) It would be hard to envisage a more complete contrast to the 'meek humble Man', 'Preaching peace', than the indomitable Gilbert Sheldon, of whom Overton wrote 'that he was more of a statesman than a divine, [and] that spiritual mindedness was, to say the least, not a conspicuous trait in his character'.[91]

As it happens, lines 210–15 of the *Satyr* do not make up the only suggestion of anti-Sheldon sentiment in Rochester's poetry. The impromptu *Rhime to Lisbone* contains a wish that 'the Bishop' who officiated at Catherine's wedding to Charles be transported to a hotter climate. This 'Bishop' was none other than Gilbert Sheldon, Bishop of London in 1662.[92]

While Sheldon's private morals may have been far from impeccable, neither he nor Stillingfleet – the former a bachelor, the latter a twice-married man with a large brood of legitimate children[93] – has much to do with the portrait of lascivious clergymen in lines 205–9. The lechers

---

[89] Sutch speaks of his 'acknowledged business acumen' leading to Sheldon's serving on innumerable committees for secular matters (such as poor relief, river navigation and limiting the number of hackney coaches in London; see pp. 131–2 in *Gilbert Sheldon*).

[90] Pinto's belief that the *Satyr* refers to Thomas Barlow, Bishop of Lincoln, born in 1607, is rather strange (p. 219 in his edition of Rochester's poetry).

[91] *Life in the English Church*, p. 20.

[92] See Vieth's edition of Rochester's poems, p. 20, and p. 303 in Walker's. The same charitable wish was extended to Clarendon, popularly believed to have played a decisive part in arranging the marriage. Still, there is of course no evidence of a real animus against these two gentlemen in this *tour de force*.

[93] Sheldon was, according to Pepys, 'as very a wencher as can be' (29 July 1667), and *The History of Insipids* alludes to him as a '[bishop] that [loves] a wench' (line 36; see p. 245 in Lord's *Poems on Affairs of State*). On Stillingfleet, see James Nankivell, 'Edward Stillingfleet, Bishop of Worcester, 1689–99', *Transactions of the Worcestershire Archaeological Society* 22 (1945–6), 17–18.

who can see 'Half a large *Parish*, their own *Progeny*' come across as
vicars contentedly settled in 'good Livings', not as celebrated divines in
the front line of religious debate. The satirist never places the 'large
Parish[es]' in a definite geographical location, but there is a distinct
country flavour about the lines. Rochester was a man who spent long
periods of his life in the country, on his and his wife's estates. He will
have been as familiar with the rural clergy as he was with London
preachers.

The idea that clergymen had strong sensual tastes and physical
abilities to match is not peculiar to Restoration England. The parson
who pretends to minister to the minds of his parishioners' wives while
actually seducing them is a stock figure in Continental country lore.
When the rambler in St James' Park talked about a 'well hung Parson'
he was not aiming a gratuitous insult (or compliment) at the clergy, but
simply alluding to attributes that parsons were popularly believed to
possess.

Were the Restoration clergy guilty of scandalous conduct of this
kind? The *Satyr* speaker's allegations are, as I have tried to show, rather
more specific than they have hitherto been given credit for being. It is
unlike him to devote five lines to a scurrilous accusation which is totally
unfounded.

David Ogg draws a vigorous two-page portrait of the Restoration
parson, concluding that while there were notorious exceptions, he was
generally a fairly decent man who 'maintained at least a glimmer of
spirituality in a country-side almost completely insulated from the
outside world' (*England in the Reign of Charles II*, vol. I, p. 135). The
exceptions were painfully evident, though, and a sore point with
established churchmen. Glanvill's battle with Marvell over Samuel
Parker (see pp. 250ff. below) shows what a sensitive issue the morals of
clergymen were. In his pamphlet *An Apology and Advice for Some of the
Clergy, Who Suffer Under False, and Scandalous Reports Written on the
Occasion of the Second Part of the Rehearsal Transprosed*, Glanvill states that
'now the usual Scandals that such Enemies endeavour to fasten on the
Clergy are, those of *Drinking*, and *Women*'.[94] Samuel Butler's unclassi-
fied notes show that he knew such allegations well and did not disbelieve
them, as the savage irony of these lines bear witness:

---

[94] See Cope, *Joseph Glanvill*, pp. 34–5. The pamphlet, probably written in 1673, was anonymous,
but Cope does not doubt Glanvill's authorship. Cf. also Trotter, 'Wanton Expressions', pp.
128–9.

Incontinence is a less Scandalous Sin in Clergy-men then Drinking, because it is manag'd with greater Privacy, then the other Iniquity, which is apt to expose them to greater Freedom, and tempt them naturally, to venture too far without their Necessary Guard of Hypocrisy, without which they are in perpetuall Danger of being Discoverd, that is to say, undon. The Flesh has a greater Advantage against the Spirit, in zealots then any other Sort of men ... (de Quehen's edition, p. 213)

Sedley's ten-line epigram 'To Flavia' speaks of a 'deep Divine' whose usefulness to the lady concerned was exclusively physical. Sutch's *Gilbert Sheldon* supplies an entire catalogue of disgraceful clergymen, several of whom were notoriously debauched (pp. 152–3).

Clearly, Ogg's good-enough clergymen suffered from the existence of thoroughly reprehensible colleagues. Nor were their sins limited to drunkenness and profligacy. In line 204, the satirist jeers at those who 'hunt good Livings, but abhor good Lives'. Here he is voicing his disgust with the grasping ways of clergymen, and again he has a fellow critic in Butler, whose 'Modern Politician' speaks of those 'Hypocrites' 'who, though they do not *live by their Faith*, ... do that which is nearest to it, get their living by it'.[95] Even Burnet did not deny that Rochester's bitterness against the hypocritical obsequiousness of clergymen anxious for preferment was, at least in part, founded on fact. The appalling poverty of many Restoration ecclesiastics makes their desperation understandable,[96] but so is the courtier's distaste at witnessing the servile manoeuvres of those who should be beyond the reproaches they levelled against others.

The four lines on the 'meek humble Man' offset the more than twenty in which the odious practices of contemporary churchmen are reviled. His envisaged virtues summarise their vices: pride, insincerity, aggressiveness and sensual immoderation. Lines 218–19, looking back to 191–2, address the classical issue of faith as compared to knowledge based on tangible evidence. The good churchman is required to forgo both sense and reason,[97] believing without proof and being seen to do so by the evidence of his actions.

When the satirist calls the two worthy men '*God-like*', he is not

---

[95] See also Butler's 'A Fanatic', p. 127 in Daves' edition.

[96] Actually, John Eachard related the destitution of clergymen to their dissolution, suggesting that sensual pursuits formed the sole comfort of the 'smally beneficed'; see *The Grounds & Occasions of the Contempt of the Clergy and Religion Enquired into* (London, 1670), p. 109.

[97] His 'honest sense' is a faculty close to 'uncorrupted soundness of mind' (*OED* 1.11 under 'sense'). Isabelle White stresses his irrationality; see '"So Great a Disproportion"', p. 287 in Vieth's *Critical Essays*.

applying a conventional hyperbole to them. These two prototypes of goodness, so far invisible to the speaker's jaded eye, are truly godlike in that they possess superhuman qualities which can only have been instilled by a higher power. Their ability to transcend human nature in practical action is one of which the satirist has seen no living proof. All other human beings are the victims of their own humanity and of the humanity of their fellows, betrayed by their own folly and the wanton cruelty of their kind.

The honest statesman and the pious clergyman are obviously different from each other. The former acts on the national scene, and the substance of his actions is practical benefit justly allotted. The latter's sphere of action is defined by his faith which makes him serve as a shining example of unworldly goodness. For all their dissimilarity, however, they have vital points in common: fear and pride cannot corrupt them; they are not motivated by self-interest; and they are committed to the well-being of others. These qualities do not only raise them above humans; the last two also establish their superiority above beasts.

The satirist concludes that the existence of these men would mean that '*Man* differs more from *Man*, than *Man* from *Beast*'. In so doing, he seems to conceive of two human categories, the virtuous and the rest of mankind, beasts forming a category in between.[98] Each of the '*Man*' classes is thus closer to '*Beast*' than to the other human category.

Even the presence on earth of such paragons – and its hypothetical character is driven home again and again – would not alter the gloomy view held by the *Satyr* speaker of the vast majority of humans. Consequently, the idea that the conclusion to the poem offers something akin to a 'conditional recantation'[99] is misguided. It is significant that the existence of good men would impel the speaker to express a modification of his unorthodox view '*to them*' (italics added). No general admission of error is contemplated. Nor is the highly limited concession outlined in line 221 the sole, or even the most important, outcome in such a case. It is merely the preliminary to a vow of allegiance and surrender to any rules drawn up by these worthies.

This is an aspect which *Satyr* critics have, somewhat surprisingly, tended to pass over. Why should this bold spirit, the satirist, consider

[98] Griffin's organisation of his 'three-tiered hierarchy' looks like a rather tortuous superfluity (pp. 242–3 in *Satires Against Man*).

[99] Several critics have followed Pinto (*Enthusiast in Wit*, p. 157) in applying designations of this kind to the 'Apology'. Pinto, however, does point out that 'even if Rochester is convinced of the existence of truly good men, he will still retain his former opinion of the rest' (p. 158).

relinquishing those principles for practical action which he put forward with such determination merely on the say-so of a few virtuous men? And how can he even entertain the notion that the vast majority of impious and dishonest self-seekers, the *'Rabble World'*, would join him?

The idea of an entire population voluntarily subordinating itself to the rule of a sovereign power is a central Hobbesian conception. In my view, few *Satyr* passages come as close to the ideas of Hobbes as lines 222–3. As previous lines of argumentation in the poem have suggested, the speaker's view of mankind in general cannot be characterised as 'Hobbesian'. Here, though, the *Satyr* speaker seems to move close to Hobbes' ideas on the establishing of a commonwealth. He clearly has not accepted the civilisation he is actually living in as an improvement on the 'state of nature'. But these men, he seems to say, would be my sovereigns. They would be heartily minded to the common weal, each in his own way, supplementing the other; they would rule justly and in a spirit of peace. Show them to me, and to the world at large, and we will submit to their sway.

The idea that mere men, however virtuous, could be 'adored' would seem repellent to the men of the Church. From the point of view of a Restoration theologian, it would be far seemlier for a former scoffer newly convinced of the existence of true nobility and moral worth in mankind to recant to God and submit to the guidance of the clergy, who claim to be His representatives on earth. Naturally, such a notion never crosses the satirist's mind. True to his conviction that the Infinite is unknowable, and the senses the sole purveyors of reliable knowledge, he would attach his subservience to those whom he *saw* to be worthy.

This man, whom critics have so often charged with inconsistency, actually seems to possess a remarkably well-regulated mind. Not even the view of the good churchman as someone who would restrain his indulgence in sensual pleasure is a contradiction. It is, after all, what his faith tells him to do, and he – unlike his vicious colleagues – obeys. This is not to say that the satirist shares that faith; on the contrary, he makes it abundantly clear that he does not. What the *Satyr* speaker would be prepared to accept is the evidence of his own senses that there are men who, for no worldly gain whatsoever, elevate themselves above the passions of mankind. It should not be forgotten that their ability in this respect has nothing to do with rationality, howsoever defined. The adversarius' *'shining* Reason' is very far removed from their respective virtues.

If the satirist thus puts his case with far greater skill and less

contradiction than most Rochester critics have been ready to grant, does
this mean that we could drop designations like 'the satirist' and 'the
Satyr speaker' and boldly speak of 'Rochester' instead? It is clear from
this long discussion that I do not believe the satirist is himself satirised.
He is nowhere made a fool of, and minor flaws in his argumentation do
not jeopardise his case. That case has several components which come
close to personal statements made by Rochester on various occasions.
The thrusts directed at people whom Rochester may have had reason to
dislike – whether on private grounds or in loyalty to Charles II –
bespeak a patent biographical relevance.

For my own part, I have answered this question already in that I have
avoided ascribing sentiments voiced in the *Satyr* to Rochester. My
reason for being cautious on this score has nothing to do with more or
less subtle *persona* theories and their ramifications. It is far simpler, and
it has already been expressed in previous chapters: I do not think we
know enough about what Rochester really felt and thought at any one
time to be able to impute wide-ranging, long-lasting and clearly
definable views to him. His constant restlessness, physical and mental,
his merciless perspicacity and his distrust of anything that posed as
established wisdom make any set of clear-cut convictions sit uneasily
upon him. Even the satirist's argumentation, which contains much that
agrees with the picture of Rochester we gain from some biographical
source material, seems reductive and rigid when viewed in conjunction
with other parts of that material. To mention just one example, the
satirist derides the very notion of friendship between men; Rochester at
some point between 1673 and 1675 addresses a letter to his close friend
Henry Savile, claiming that 'if there bee a reall good upon Earth 'tis in
the Name of freind, without wch all others are meerly fantasticall'.[100]

The speaker in the *Satyr* seems to me to represent opinions and
convictions for which Rochester the man felt some sympathy and
which Rochester the poet endeavoured to express as efficiently as
possible. This entailed the assumption of stances he did not necessarily
share, as well as the expression of contentions whose uncompromising
nature need not have had a basis in Rochester's own mind. Such
distinctions do not, of course, apply to Rochester alone. Writers of
satires throughout the ages have sharpened their arguments by stripping

---

[100] *Letters*, pp. 92–4. Characteristically, the fine words on friendship are offset by melancholy
observations as to its rareness, especially among poor men. It might be mentioned that Griffin
sees male friendship as an 'avenue to security' for Rochester (*Satires Against Man*, p. 19),
emphasising Savile's importance to him.

them of personal reservations. Enhancing polemical efficacy and directing aggression to where it hurts most form part of the satiric artist's trade. What the man himself may have felt is a different matter, and I cannot see that there is any urgent need to try to bring these two dimensions together where the *Satyr* is concerned.

In fact, an attempt to fuse them would detract from those qualities that seem to me to form the essence, and the uniqueness, of the *Satyr against Reason and Mankind*. This poem places the reader right in the storm centre of the late seventeenth century. In little more than two hundred lines, it brings a painfully chaotic period to life, a time when scholasticism was slowly forced to yield to the new science, when Parliament asserted its power over the Sovereign without having to resort to decapitation, and when Anglicanism secured its supremacy in the religious life of the nation. These processes (or at least the first two) have come to seem as marks of progress to later generations, and yet they involved people and events whose lack of morally inspiring qualities was glaring. An unusually sharp-witted courtier not yet thirty years old put his artistic talents to use in castigating them, and the result is a poem that crystallises its time with incomparable vividness.

COURT AND SOCIAL

———————◆◆◆◆———————

8

' *Tunbridge Wells* '

The structure of *Tunbridge Wells*, a poem more dutifully than enthusiastically praised by Rochester critics, may well seem haphazard,[1] but it is not a fortuitous series of satirical observations. Variegated as the scenes in this Restoration comedy of less than 200 lines are, they consistently display Rochester's characteristic loathing of folly, hypocrisy and false pride. The beginning and ending are not without a certain symmetry. The third line of *Tunbridge Wells*, as well as the third line from the end, refers to the speaker mounting his horse. What lies between the two rides is a set of experiences that makes him take a very different view of that everyday action. In addition, observing the ways and follies of the world in the course of some kind of itinerancy is not unprecedented in classical satire (cf., for instance, Horace's fifth satire in the first book).

The pace of the poem is heightened by the verbs of movement which describe the speaker's involuntary encounters with pretentious fools and hypocrites. Having 'trotted' to the Wells, he 'turns his head' and beholds the fat knight, with drastic results. He then 'silently slinks' down to the lower walk, where he chances on the 'Buckram Puppet'; 'runs' to the upper end and is cursed with meeting a group of clergymen; takes pains to 'evade' listening to the 'Irish Crew'; 'conveys himself' to a position 'Amidst the Croud'; 'runs away' only to end up in the vicinity of the two barren wives; and 'gets a nearer view' of some impoverished cadets pretending to be dashing officers. Finally, he takes himself off again, once more on horseback.

Not only are the vices of the spa visitors by and large reducible to the three especially abhorred by Rochester; these people keep condemning themselves out of their own mouths, too. From first to last, the speaker

---

[1] Cf. Treglown's remarks concerning the organisation of *Tunbridge Wells* on p. 83 in '"He knew my style"'.

is a disgusted listener as well as a nauseated observer. The 'Wells' form
the meeting-place of 'Fooles, Buffoones, and Praters'; the knight bawls
and censures; the second fool speaks 'all Proverbs, Sentences, and
Adage'; the churchmen tell of their disorders; the Irishmen talk, but
being made to listen to them is a prospect the speaker will not even
contemplate; the wooing couple and the two wives are quoted at
length; and the would-be heroes in uniform sing a bawdy song. The
listener summarises:

> Our selves, with noyse of Reason wee doe please
> In vaine: Humanity is our worst Disease.

These lines reject both those capacities which are traditionally held to
place man above animals: the rationalism he lays claim to, and the gift
of speech. The realisation that these human characteristics are worse
than useless provides a neat transition to the concluding lines on the
superiority of the horse. Within the compass of a single morning, the
creature who was regarded as a mere means of transportation has thus
come to be viewed as a nobler being than his rider.

Although *Tunbridge Wells* depicts a 'true Medley' of people from all
walks of life, the speaker's main interest is directed towards people with
social ambitions (as was that of the *Ramble* protagonist). A certain
animus against the gentry is discernible in the lines on the 'Bawling
Fopp' and the credulous owner of a 'good Estate' who hopes for an
heir. The young 'Gallant' and the impecunious younger sons also seem
to belong to social strata below, but not very far below, that aristocracy
to which Rochester belonged. This feature could be felt to reflect the
characteristic pecking-order disgust with the person just below yourself,
as well as the contempt for the booby-squire character which is so
prevalent in Restoration comedy.

Three early manuscripts gave names to the 'Bawling Fopp' and the
'Buckram Puppet' (see p. 267 in Walker's edition). The former was
identified as 'Sir Nicholas Crisp' and the latter as 'Sir Francis Dorrell'.
Whether the attacks were deliberately levelled at these men we cannot
know, but Rochester often had personal targets in view, and it is at least
a possibility. In the case of the 'meere Sir Nich'las Cully', the identical
first name and surname initial lend some support to the supposition.
These two men were both about Rochester's own age; like himself, too,
they were connected with the Inns of Court. Crisp's title was hereditary
('Nature, contriv'd the Fool shou'd be a Knight'). A Middle Temple
man, he was a baronet when, on 20 April 1674, he obtained a licence to

marry one Judith Adrian. If he is indeed the butt of lines 8–22, his visit to Tunbridge Wells might have represented a well-advised attempt to augment his physical fitness in connexion with his marriage. Sir Frances Dorrell or Dayrell, on the other hand, was knighted at Lincoln's Inn on 29 February 1671/2. He died in 1675, aged twenty-nine[2] – another *terminus ad quem*, if lines 41–50 do in fact refer to him, for the writing of *Tunbridge Wells*, in addition to its 1675 publication in *Proteus Redivivus*. (Quite apart from any *de mortuis* considerations, Rochester would not have bothered to flog a dead horse.)

Sneering at the gentry would come naturally to a peer who enjoyed privileges that accentuated the boundary between his class and the squirearchy.[3] However, a Restoration writer did not have to belong to the nobility to make fun of foolish knights and country gentlemen, as Etherege, Wycherley and Shadwell demonstrate.

The latter playwright is a man whose influence on *Tunbridge Wells* is especially patent. Shadwell's comedy *Epsom Wells* marks his development from Jonsonian 'humours satire' towards the fashionable, witty comedy of manners;[4] and *Epsom Wells* has much in common with Rochester's poem. In fact, previous comments on Rochester's debts to Shadwell have passed over several striking resemblances.[5]

If Dryden's notorious accusation against Shadwell was true, and Sedley collaborated in the writing of Shadwell's play, Rochester would have had a special reason to take an interest in *Epsom Wells*. (Line 16 in *Timon* could be read as an indication that Rochester shared Dryden's view in this respect.) But there are further grounds for believing him to have been familiar with the play. In the first place, *Epsom Wells* was a great success. The production that opened at Dorset Garden in December 1672 was followed by two command performances at Court.[6] To Rochester, the King's approval would be a commendation, quite apart from congenial elements such as witty, charming and

---

[2] This biographical information was supplied by William Arthur Shaw, *The Knights of England*: *A Complete Record* (2 vols., London, 1906) and by the *Alumni Oxonienses* (Crisp) and *Cantabrigienses* (Dorrell/Dayrell).

[3] See Ogg, *England in the Reign of Charles II*, vol. I, pp. 136–8.

[4] See Don R. Kunz, *The Drama of Thomas Shadwell* (Salzburg, 1972), pp. 114ff.

[5] See, for instance, Selden's essay 'Rochester and Shadwell' in Treglown, ed., *Spirit of Wit*.

[6] See Kunz, *The Drama of Thomas Shadwell*, p. 114, and the 'Theatrical History' presentation attached to *Epsom Wells* in Montague Summers' edition of *The Complete Works of Thomas Shadwell*, vol. II, p. 99.

courageous young rakes, thorough-going cuckolding at all levels and copious imbibing of wine.[7]

The choice of a fashionable spa for a satire on contemporary society was a natural one. Drinking mineral well-water was an increasingly popular restorative for a variety of disorders, and Bath, Epsom and Tunbridge were frequented for other than health reasons, too. Contemporary accounts of high life in spas supply vivid pictures of the 'goings-on' in these watering-holes of the upper classes and those who would tack themselves on to, or alternatively sponge off, them. In the early 1660s, the new French ambassador named Tunbridge Wells 'Les Eaux de Scandale'.[8] He had ample opportunities to study the place, for the Court resided there on more than one occasion. Pepys mentions Queen Catherine's stays at Tunbridge in 1663 and 1666. Tradition has it that it was there, in 1668, that Charles took up with two of his better-known mistresses, the actresses 'Moll' Davis and Nell Gwyn.[9] A sojourn at a spa thus offered opportunities for the sort of experiences that are delicately referred to as 'holiday romances' in the columns of modern agony aunts.

Shadwell's play shows that Epsom harboured profligate visitors, too, although Tunbridge enjoyed an even greater reputation for fast living. Like Rochester's poem, *Epsom Wells* begins with a morning scene. Bisket, 'a Comfit-maker, a quiet, humble, civil Cuckold', praises the fine taste of the waters 'after being fudled last Night'. (As Vieth points out in his editorial comments on *Tunbridge Wells*, the waters were held to be especially efficacious when taken just after sunrise.) Kick, like Cuff a 'cheating, sharking, cowardly Bully', has also turned up at the wells after a night of heavy drinking, resolved to 'wash away [his] Claret'.

Rochester's speaker has prudently lined his own 'Squeamish Stomach' in like manner before arriving on the scene. The two initial lines of *Tunbridge Wells*, with their stale classical allusions[10] whose mocking tone is reinforced by the bawdy implications of 'head' and

[7] Contemporaries apparently associated it with licentious behaviour; see, for instance, the *Young Gallant's Academy* of 1674, p. 57.

[8] See Hartmann, *La Belle Stuart* (London, 1924), pp. 33 and 43.

[9] See Maurice Ashley, *Charles II: The Man and the Statesman* (London, 1971), p. 153. The diaries of Pepys and Evelyn contain several references to Tunbridge Wells. The faith placed in its waters by many Englishmen, from aristocrats to country vicars, is illustrated in, among other works, Gladys Scott Thomson, *Life in a Noble Household 1641–1700* (London, 1937; reprinted 1950), pp. 221–4, and Alan Macfarlane, ed., *The Diary of Ralph Josselin 1616–1683* (London, 1976), p. 586.

[10] For two contemporary instances, see *Hudibras* II.ii.29–32 and Cowley's Horace paraphrase, *The Country Mouse*, lines 52–5 (p. 415 in Waller's edition of Cowley's *Essays*).

'Lapp',[11] are further deflated by the swift introduction of fools, cuckolds, whores and the like. The explosive vomiting in line 10 completes this initial plunge into low-style satire.

The fit of nausea confirms the diagnosis in the narrator's case: he suffers from a gastric disorder.[12] In Walker's edition, and in most of the extant texts of the poem, line 7 reads 'To undertake the Dose, *it* was prescrib'd' (italics added; 'it' here clearly refers to the previously-mentioned stomach); Vieth has 'that was prescribed', which is of course much less precise. The stomach in question may seem unduly sensitive even for a diseased organ, since the mere sight of the 'thing unweildy' induces emesis; but the appellation 'Sir Nich'las Cully' brands the newcomer as a truly revolting creature.

As Rochester editors briefly record, Sir Nicholas Cully is a character in Etherege's comedy *The Comical Revenge; or, Love in a Tub*. What no commentary points out is that this man is as offensive a personage as 'refin'd Etheridge' ever created: knighted by 'OLIVER', he pretends loyalty to the King; he is gullible, drunk, cowardly and of very humble origins; and his manners are so boorish and uncouth that they disgust even a modern reader innocent of seventeenth-century rules of polite conduct.

Rochester's knight is rich, as he issues from that emblem of wealth, a coach and six (cf. p. 252 below on Samuel Parker), and will be in a position to 'purchase some inspireing pretty Toy'. He is also fat, since a cart would have been a better means of conveyance considering his bulk. He is a dolt, being 'as wise as Calf' (*OED* 1c under *calf*), and he possesses all the strength and valour of a blustering hector ('as bigg as Bully'; *OED* 1 under *big* and II.3 under *bully*). In addition to these unattractive characteristics, he does not have the sense to keep his mouth shut. 'Censure' here (line 16) probably does not mean 'to find fault with' but 'to pass judgement, to form or give an opinion' (*OED* I.3 under *censure*). Such nice occupations should of course be left to those who have 'Witt', judgement and taste. His 'Traine' – identified, as

---

[11] See Farley-Hills, *Rochester's Poetry*, pp. 191–2. Cf. the recurrence of these ambiguous parts of the anatomy in the *Dialogue* beginning, 'When to the King I bid good Morrow', line 9.

[12] Farley-Hills attributes 'the spleen' to the narrator, but the only evidence for that diagnosis, besides his general misanthropy, is his calling it 'that wise Disease'. Admittedly, though, vomiting on beholding a revolting creature need not be indicative of illness. The observer of a quack-doctor would, according to a Restoration 'character' writer, be similarly affected. In this description of a mountebank – published in 1676, and possibly in some way connected with the Bendo escapade –, the author avers that the quack's '*Looks* are enough to give one a *Stool* or a *Vomit*' (*The Character of a Quack-Doctor, or the Abusive Practices of Impudent Illiterate Pretenders to Physick Exposed*, London, 1676, p. 1).

Walker says, as 'his sisters' in two extant manuscripts – consists of persons as obese and abominable as himself:

> Nature, has done the Bus'nesse of Lampoone,
> And in their lookes, their Characters has showne.

Nature has been doubly unkind in contriving that 'the Fool shou'd be a Knight' and doing 'the Bus'nesse of Lampoone' – malicious operations for one so repeatedly commended in Rochester's poetry. The use of 'Characters' in line 28 is surely a pun involving several meanings: 'character' in the sense of mental or moral constitution, alphabetic sign (Nature has 'written' a lampoon) and description of a person's qualities (*OED* 4b, 11 and 14). 'Character' also means 'the face or features as betokening moral qualities' (*OED* 10), which ties the varied senses of the word together when applied in this context.

In Walker's edition, these lines are followed by a six-line bracketed passage. It praises the virtues of dildoes, in view of the impossibility of summoning enough sexual appetite to have intercourse with such repellent creatures. Vieth did not include the six lines in his edition, and Walker admits that 'they seem to be an intrusion' (p. 266). Their abrupt crudity in a poem not otherwise obscene (by Restoration standards) supports that impression.

The second 'Fopp' is also offensive to eyes and ears alike. A stiff, conceited dunce (one appealing *OED* definition under 'buckram', 3b, is 'stuck up'), he keeps delivering himself of irrelevant, sententious clichés. The elegant chiasmus in line 44 lends a touch of class(icism) to the essential insubstantiality of this platitude-spouting fool, a classical type 'full of high sentence, but a bit obtuse'.

His 'Spanish guise' indicates another quality in low esteem among the Court Wits. As David Brooks points out in his commentary (p. 118 in his Rochester edition), 'Spaniards had the reputation of always seeming grave.' Describing the effects on Sir Henry Bennet (later Lord Arlington) of that gentleman's stay in Madrid, Ronald Hutton says that he 'acquired ... a taste for rich clothes and ponderous dignity'.[13] The 'Master of the Ceremonies' at a spa was responsible for the en-

---

[13] *The Restoration: A Political and Religious History of England and Wales 1658–1667* (Oxford, 1985), p. 192. One character in the 1678 comedy *Tunbridge-Wells: Or a Days Courtship* – believed to be by Thomas Rawlins, but the authorship is not certain – poses, '*in Spanish habit*', as one 'Don Roderigo de los Blustrados hectoromanos Bullirockos' (p. 41 in the edition published in London in 1678).

tertainment of visitors;[14] this pompous nitwit will not have been a success at the job.

A striking topical allusion occurs in lines 47–8, where a trivial everyday act is contrasted with clandestine machinations at the highest political level. The 'Buckram Puppet'

> Can with as much solemnity, buy Eggs,
> As a Caball, can talke of their Intrigues.

It was in the spring of 1673, when Charles was forced to surrender his Declaration of Indulgence and accept the Test Act, that the ministry known as the Cabal fell apart. Clifford resigned his office as Lord Treasurer, thus indirectly proclaiming himself a Catholic. Other members of the Cabal soon came under tough Parliamentary pressure and lost much public and Royal favour. A new chief minister, Sir Thomas Osborne – Earl of Danby from 1674 –, took over the Treasury, and the men of the Cabal were left to make more or less successful attempts to regain prestige and influence. The Cabal was never popular, and a note of contempt can be heard in Rochester's couplet. True, it had assisted Charles in operations geared to asserting his Royal prerogative – and Rochester, for all his impudence, was a loyal courtier according to his lights –; but once its breakdown was inevitable, the King withdrew his support from the Cabal ministers.

The allusion to the collapsed Cabal supplies another *terminus a quo* for *Tunbridge Wells*, in addition to the initial staging of Shadwell's *Epsom Wells* (December 1672) and the publication of the second part of Marvell's *The Rehearsal Transpros'd* in the winter of 1673–4.[15] Summer was the fashionable time for going to Tunbridge Wells, as Pepys (22 July 1663), Evelyn (15 August 1661) and other contemporary sources confirm.[16] A sunrise at five suggests a later point in time than

---

[14] See Lewis Melville, *Society at Royal Tunbridge Wells in the eighteenth century – and after* (London, 1912).

[15] Walker, noting that the Parker passage does not appear in the *Proteus Redivivus* text, says that it may be a later addition (p. 266). Beyond this omission in Head, I cannot find anything to support this suggestion. That omission may be due to cautiousness on Head's part. After all, the 'Bayes' lines form the only passage in *Tunbridge Wells* where a well-known and easily identifiable public personage comes under attack. His text contains other changes, too; the 'Irish Crew' libel is made to refer to prostitutes, even more uncontroversial targets than Irishmen (and Head was Irish by birth). See also Hammond's review of Walker's edition (in *The Review of English Studies* 37, May 1986, 264–5), where the textual difficulties connected with *Tunbridge Wells* are discussed.

[16] See, for instance, Lodwick Rowzee, *The Queens Wells. That Is, A Treatise of the nature and vertues of* Tunbridge *Water* (London, 1671; this is a reprint of the original edition of 1632), pp. 50–1.

March/April, too. Vieth's provisional dating – the early months of 1674 – should hence, I think, be modified to June/August, 1674 (cf. p. 262 below).

Both the witless knight and the solemn utterer of misplaced trivia were presumptuous as well as stupid, and the 'new scene of Foppery' in lines 53–81 trounces that Rochesterian arch-vice, pride. The assembled clergymen bore one another with their complaints, some laying claim to a particularly respectable one, 'the Spleene' (see below),

> But none had Modesty enough to 'plaine,
> Their want of Learning, Honesty, and Braine,
> The generall Diseases of that Traine:
> These call themselves Ambassadors of Heav'n,
> And sawcily pretend Commissions giv'n;
> But shou'd an Indian King, whose small Command
> Seldome extends beyond Ten Miles of Land;
> Send forth such wretched Tooles in an Ambassage
> He'd find but small Effects of such a Message.

The collocation of the Almighty and an 'Indian King' in this passage (lines 59–67) is a daring one, but it is hardly blasphemous. On the contrary, blasphemy is committed by those who claim to be sent by God. Their lack of serviceable abilities – including powers of persuasion – is such that even the smallest worldly potentate would find them useless as purveyors of his wishes ('Message' here meaning 'a body of persons conveying a communication'; *OED* 3). These lines draw up a contrast between the greatness of God – never articulated, but never challenged either – and the vanity shown by despicable humans believing themselves to reflect that greatness. The severity of this passage resembles the anger displayed in lines 76–9 of the *Satyr*, a parallel case in this respect. It is noteworthy that the poetry of Rochester, who by his own admission 'blasphemed [his] god', more than once expresses sharp disapproval of human pretensions based on a belief that man can in some way represent the Deity. A confirmed atheist would be more likely to ridicule such pretensions than censure them with patent indignation.

The clerics in question – 'Curates, Priests, Canonicall Elves' – represent different strata in the ecclesiastical hierarchy. 'Canonicall' is obviously a term of disparagement in Rochester's poem,[17] as it is in the libertine Song – published in Playford's *Choice Songs and Ayres* in 1673 – from *Epsom Wells*, II.i:

---

[17] 'Elves' is an abusive word here, too, as Hammond and Walker have shown.

Such is the poor Fool who loves upon duty,
Because a Canonical Coxcomb has made him,
And ne'er tastes the sweets of love and of beauty,
But drudges because a dull Priest has betray'd him ...

The distempers from which these churchmen suffer do not, however, suggest any implicit abuse on the satirist's part. The pleasantly alliterative 'Scurvy, Stone, Strangury' were common disorders in the late seventeenth century. The term 'scurvy' was occasionally used as a designation for the blood disease purpura, as well as for the disease that most of us immediately associate with ships; but Rochester applied it to the latter illness in Alexander Bendo's Bill, where it is referred to as 'that Labes Britannica or grand English disease' and held up as a cause of 'Stones in the Kidneys and Bladder'.[18]

'Stone' and 'Strangury' refer to disorders of the urinary system, the former of course denoting kidney and bladder stones and the latter difficulty in urinating. Neither was felt to be a embarrassing condition; OED quotations confirm their social acceptability as well as their distressing characteristics. The latter are evoked by the Imperfect Enjoyment speaker's imprecations directed against his disobliging penis, 'May Strangury, and Stone, thy Days attend'. Clearly, the constellation 'Scurvy, Stone, Strangury' was a natural one to Rochester.

Bendo's Bill also mentions 'Spleen', but only in passing and as part of the human – female, in this case – anatomy. In line 57 of Tunbridge Wells, the 'Spleene' means 'melancholia; what is now called "depression"'.[19] Not a disorder readily admitted to today, it was a fashionable one in Restoration England, implying that the sufferer possessed refined sensibilities and mental capacity.

It should be borne in mind that seventeenth-century men and women did not regard illness as an external invader which could and should be attacked by the mechanical application of equally external standard remedies.[20] This is as good a place as any to mention the advances and conflicts in Restoration medicine. The latter involved traditional Galenists on the one hand and experimental chemists on the other. In

[18] See pp. 34–5 in Pinto's edition of The Famous Pathologist. Gladys Scott Thomson's book on the Russell family testifies to the commonness of the disease; practically the entire household – including servants – received anti-scorbutic treatment at some point (pp. 312–14).

[19] David Brooks' Rochester edition, p. 118. See Ogg, England in the Reign of Charles II, vol. II, p. 718.

[20] Cf. Marjorie Hope Nicolson, The Breaking of the Circle: Studies in the Effect of the 'New Science' upon Seventeenth-Century Poetry (Evanston, Ill., 1950; I have used the revised edition of 1960), p. 218.

Richard Foster Jones' words, 'the controversy between ancients and moderns finds full expression in the relentless war which the chemical doctors were waging against the Galenists and their "method"'.[21]

This combat was one that the educated public was well aware of. Many noblemen followed the King's example and made chemical experiments, among them Rochester himself and the man to whom Dryden affixed the imperishable string of attributes, 'Chymist, Fidler, States-man, and Buffoon'.[22] Shadwell's Bevil in *Epsom Wells* – one of the rake-heroes – lightheartedly alludes to the opposition between Ancients and Moderns in medicine when asserting that he and his boon companions 'like subtle Chymists extract and refine our pleasure, while [those insipid-temperate Fools] like Fulsom Galenists take it in gross' (1.i). Alexander Bendo's Bill indicates that Rochester was aware of the state of medicine. Quacks, of course, thrived on the war between its scientific representatives, and the Bill cleverly avoids commitment in either direction.[23] In addition, it succeeds in combining socio-political satire and self-irony with professed benevolence and an impressive display of medicinal lore. The result is that even deliberate absurdities do not rob it of a certain degree of authority.

To return to Rochester's poem, the illnesses of the 'sufferers' in *Tunbridge Wells* agree with the catalogue of complaints for which the waters were held to be beneficial in his day. Dr Rowzee praised the effects of the *Queens Wells* (the queen in question being Henrietta Maria) on stomach and urinary disorders, scurvy, venereal disease, and green-sickness, as well as on 'spleen' and spiritual *malaise* such as 'hypochondrial melancholy'.[24]

The leader of the clerical fools' parade, Archdeacon Samuel Parker, is likewise the arch-dunce and the most offensive among the gentlemen of the cloth. Against him, specific accusations are levelled, as well as the more general aspersions in lines 53–67.

Rochester editors usually provide a short background sketch of the

[21] *Ancients and Moderns: A Study of the Rise of the Scientific Movement in Seventeenth-Century England* (St Louis, 1961), p. 206.

[22] In the mid-1660s, the 'Modern' Edward Bolnest dedicated his *Medicina Instaurata* to Buckingham, who was credited with having two laboratories of his own, one at home and one at Court. See R. F. Jones, *Ancients and Moderns*, p. 211.

[23] The quack in the 1676 *Character* referred to above (p. 245, n.12) would profess loyalty to the Moderns, but without knowing anything about them; 'he rails at *Galen* and *Hippocrates* ... without knowing whether they were *Men* or *Women*; but admires *Van Helmont* blindfold, and fancies him & *Paracelsus* to be two jolly *Dutch Burgomasters* ... ' (p. 2).

[24] See pp. 41–8 in Rowzee's publication on '*Tunbridge* Water'. His list is faithfully reproduced by Thomas Benge Burr in *The History of Tunbridge Wells* (London, 1766), pp. 75–84. Rowzee was insistent that 'the best time of the day to take the water was betimes in the morning'.

Parker-Marvell quarrel to which the poem alludes in lines 69–76. We are told that Parker, Archdeacon of Canterbury from 1670, had aroused Marvell's displeasure which was vented in *The Rehearsal Transpros'd*, and that the expressions 'Importance Comfortable' and 'Lazy dull distemper' in *Tunbridge Wells* are derived from two expressions that were used by Parker during the dispute and ridiculed by Marvell in the two parts of *The Rehearsal Transpros'd*. Parker's attempts, in his *Ecclesiastical Politie* (1670), to advocate the supremacy of the Sovereign in religious matters as well as in worldly concerns are stated as being the main reason for Marvell's disapproval, and we are reminded that the name 'Bayes' was borrowed from the Duke of Buckingham's parody of the heroic play, *The Rehearsal*. All this is quite true, and highly relevant to Rochester's lines. Still, the question of why Rochester should have taken such an interest in the quarrel, even to the extent of devoting several lines to the worsted combatant, is not answered by the brief factual remarks that an editor's space allows. Even the fuller re-capitulation in Vieth's *Attribution* (pp. 276–8) does not resolve it.

In view of Charles' absolutist leanings, one might have assumed that the King would approve of Parker's insistence that the civil power should exercise authority in religious matters, too. Religion, however, was one area where Charles had no wish to assert the authority of the Crown. Charles II was personally and genuinely committed to the principle of religious toleration (see pp. 232–3 above).[25] In fact, the King himself intervened on Marvell's behalf when the licenser wanted to suppress a second edition of *The Rehearsal Transpros'd*, part 1.[26] Contemporary sources state that Charles read Marvell's work several times and enjoyed it greatly.[27] His appreciation was apparently quite unaffected by the fact that Marvell's own background was solidly Nonconformist, to say nothing of Marvell's attacks on the Court party in Parliament and the stinging satires he directed against the King himself and the Duke of York.

Royal approval would be one reason for Rochester's reading and praising *The Rehearsal Transpros'd*, but it is not the only one. Like his

---

[25] Ronald Hutton's recent biography *Charles the Second: King of England, Scotland and Ireland* (Oxford, 1989) casts doubt on this commitment on the King's part, but Hutton allows for other views than his own fairly censorious ones in this and other respects, and I remain convinced of Charles' serious intent in the matter of religious toleration.

[26] *Dictionary of National Biography*, vol. XII, p. 1213 (under Marvell). See Pierre Legouis, *Andrew Marvell: Poet, Puritan, Patriot* (Oxford, 1968), pp. 194ff.

[27] See, for instance, Warren L. Chernaik, *The Poet's Time: Politics and Religion in the Work of Andrew Marvell* (Cambridge, 1983), p. 122.

Sovereign, Rochester will have appreciated its entertainment value. Marvell's comic touch and appeal to the good sense of good-humoured, witty people are irresistible.

Finally, Rochester's complimentary reference to *The Rehearsal Transpros'd* will have had yet another reason: a loathing of Samuel Parker the man. Even those who did not detest him the way Burnet did (see below) had to admit that Parker had a very good opinion of himself, and that unworldly Christianity was not a conspicuous feature in his character. The fact that Parker did very well for himself under the monarch he had wanted no part of before the Restoration does not make him an unusual man in any way; but his talents in that respect do seem to have been unusually pronounced. To the question 'what was the best body of divinity', he is reported to have replied that 'that which would help a man to keep a coach and six horses was certainly the best' (*DNB*, vol. xv, p. 273). This may be a misrepresentation, like so many famous sayings; but there seems to be no doubt that Parker had a taste for the good things of this world. In addition, he does not appear to have been a man much given to self-scrutiny. In Burnet's *History of My Own Time*, Samuel Parker is said to have been 'so lifted up with pride that he was become insufferable to all that came near him'.[28]

Marvell's attacks on Parker in *The Rehearsal Transpros'd* mercilessly expose those three qualities that constantly provoke Rochester's most mordant satire: vanity, stupidity and insincerity. When the *Tunbridge Wells* speaker maintains that 'Marvell has enough, expos'd his Folly', he is in fact delivering an accurate description of Marvell's method in *The Rehearsal Transpros'd*. Throughout their over 700 pages, the two parts of the book turn quotations from Parker's own writings against him, making the divine damn himself out of his own works. Even to a modern reader, Marvell's fiendishly clever, if sometimes grossly unfair and outrageous, manipulations of 'Mr. Bayes'' own words provide amusement of a high order.

The two phrases singled out by the speaker in *Tunbridge Wells* form excellent examples of Marvell's technique and surely stuck in Rochester's memory for that reason. In his Preface to Bishop Bramhall's 'Vindication of himself and the Episcopal Church from the Presbyterian Charge of Popery' – the piece which provoked the first part of *The Rehearsal Transpros'd* – , Parker had mentioned '*matters of a closer and more comfortable importance to himself and his own Affairs*'. This pompous

---

[28] iii.211; quoted by *Dictionary of National Biography*, vol. xv (under Parker), pp. 272–3.

phrase refers to Parker's marriage, but whether or not Marvell was aware of that, he '[concludes] that it must be one of... three things; either his Salvation, or a Benefice, or a Female'.[29] After disposing of the first two, Marvell decides, all mock-innocence, that Parker must mean a mistress.

Likewise, in the second part of *The Rehearsal Transpros'd*, Marvell quotes Parker's explanation for his delay in replying in print to the first part. The Archdeacon blamed this deferral on his having been prevented by 'a dull and lazy distemper'. Marvell promptly holds Parker's vanity – in believing that anyone could take the slightest interest in his health – up to scorn, suggesting that Parker, having 'enter'd his *closer Importance* upon Record' in 'his late Preface', expects the reading public to take an interest in 'his close Stool', too.[30] No wonder such venomous innuendoes led to 'all the laughers [being] on Marvell's side',[31] Rochester included.

Marvell had made uncomplimentary references to Parker's ungainly figure, and the word 'Cobb' in line 68 of *Tunbridge Wells* '[contains] the notion "rounded", "roundish mass", or "lump"' (*OED* ii), as well as meaning 'leading man', the explanation offered by Rochester editors. Many people went to the spas to lose weight, especially to Epsom, whose waters were laxative, and to Bath, which was given a number of opportunities to restore the figures of Court ladies. Parker could clearly do with some weight reduction, although his main object in taking the waters, according to the satirical observer, is the final cure of his infamous 'distemper'. Marvell had slyly suggested that it might be a venereal disorder, masking as 'scurvy', but then professed to doubt whether such an infirmity would accost 'a Personage of his Figure and Character' (ii.9) – another unkind stab at Parker's appearance. The *Tunbridge Wells* speaker clearly accepts Marvell's libellous theory.

The following six lines of *Tunbridge Wells*, 82–7, form one of the disparaging references to the Irish in Rochester's poetry and is by far the harshest.[32] For a man who held the Irish title of Viscount of Athlone (the survival of his grandfather's exploits in Ireland), penning these lines was

---

[29] *The Rehearsal Transpros'd*, a facsimile edition printed by Gregg International Publishers in 1971 (Farnborough), p. 8 (part 1).

[30] See *The Rehearsal Transpros'd*, ii, pp. 2–3. Then as now, it was considered bad manners to bore people with one's health worries; according to the *Rules of Civility* (translated from the French in 1671), ''tis unpleasing ... to hear a man always complaining of his distempers in company; and implies either stupidity or hypocrisie' (p. 41).

[31] *Dictionary of National Biography*, vol. xii, p. 1213.

[32] Cf. *Upon Nothing*, line 47, and the lampoon on 'Irish whore', 'To longe the Wise Commons have been in debate'. See p. 158 above and pp. 303ff. below. On the plight of the Irish in

less than generous, even if they need not be read as expressions of his personal view:

> Next after these, a fulsome Irish Crew,
> Of silly Macs were offer'd to my view;
> The things did talke, but th'hearing what they said,
> I did my self the kindnesse to evade:
> Nature, hath plac'd these Wretches beneath Scorne,
> They can't be call'd soe vile, as they are borne.

The status of native Irishmen in Restoration England was never an enviable one, and occasional bouts of extra-strong anti-Papist sentiment did nothing to improve it.[33] Some leading politicians – Ashley, for instance – loathed anything and anyone Irish, and even the efforts of the Lord-Lieutenant of Ireland, the otherwise fairly influential Duke of Ormonde, were powerless to redress the balance. Insulting the Irish was thus an uncontroversial pastime. The speaker in *Tunbridge Wells* cannot be bothered to assign any specific faults or vices to them. Being born in Ireland evidently disqualifies one even from the privilege of being criticised. Rochester's readers will have sympathised with the speaker's dislike of Anglo-Irish speech, which educated Englishmen clearly found both repellent and ridiculous.[34]

Having removed himself from such obnoxious company, the satirical observer and eavesdropper finds himself in the 'true Medley' of lines 90–7, the elements so mixed in it that not even a 'Conventickle, Play, or Fair' could match it for variety. Fairs, of course, always drew all sorts of visitors, and Restoration playhouses had very heterogeneous audiences indeed. 'Conventickles' are explained by Walker, quoting Johnson, as 'An assembly for worship. Generally used in an ill sense, including heresy or schism' (p. 268 in Walker's edition). In a Restoration context, though, the connotations of the word were rather more specific.

Conventicles were Protestant Dissenter services, and a few years before the Test Act Charles II had been forced to accept the new Conventicle Act of 1670, which forbade such religious meetings.

Rochester's day, see Edward MacLysaght, *Irish Life in the Seventeenth Century* (Dublin 1939; I have used the 1979 paperback edition).
[33] Cf., for instance, Ogg, *England in the Reign of Charles II*, vol. II, p. 394.
[34] See, for instance, the presentation of the late-seventeenth-century book called *Bog-Witticisms* in *A New History of Ireland III. Early Modern Ireland*, ed. T. W. Moody, F. X. Martin and F. J. Byrne (Oxford, 1976; I have used the corrected edition of 1978), pp. 551–2 (Alan Bliss, 'The English Language in Early Modern Ireland').

Measures had been taken against conventicles before, and a similar Act had been passed, after initial baulking, in 1664.[35] In the mid-1660s, and again in the early 1670s, militia and other disciplinary forces were set to detect such gatherings. Third offenders could be transported to the colonies for seven years.[36] A relentless campaigner for the rigorous enforcement of the Conventicle Act was Archbishop Sheldon.[37] The King viewed the proceedings with the distaste he always felt in cases of religious persecution. However, it was necessary for Charles to accept what Marvell called 'the terrible Bill against Conventicles', as it constituted – again in Marvell's words – 'the Price of Money'.[38]

By suggesting that people from very different social backgrounds could be seen at a conventicle, Rochester's speaker directs an ironic jab at upper-class Dissenters for the mixed company they keep. However, he is also alluding, with ostensible insouciance, to an activity which was not supposed to take place at all and which a well-connected person should in any case know nothing about. Such nonchalance must have annoyed staunch Anglicans – Sheldon and his protégé Parker, for example – considerably.

In the midst of this motley company, the speaker introduces a young couple whose conversation has often been praised as wonderfully vivid. The 'Gallant' and 'Damsell' – the latter pretending to ill-health by 'Leaning on Cane' while relying on her 'Hood' to disguise her – are obviously meeting by appointment, probably made the night before. It is a truly shocking arrangement by ordinary standards, but this is a Restoration spa, and practically anything goes. As Shadwell's Lucia said resignedly in Act IV of *Epsom Wells*, 'the freedom of *Epsom* allows almost nothing to be scandalous'.

The very lack of propriety in the rendezvous is comically set off by the would-be courtly style of address initially employed by the couple.

---

[35] A thorough discussion of the conventicle concept, and of conventicles in practice, at this time is found in Patrick Collinson's article 'The English Conventicle', *Studies in Church History* 23 (*Voluntary Religion*, Oxford, 1986), 223–59. It might be added that the suggestion that someone frequented conventicles seems to have been a fairly common expression of contempt. Otway's *The Soldier's Fortune*, for instance, mentions 'every parish bawd that goes to conventicle twice a week', and *An Exclamation from Tunbridge and Epsom Against The Newfound Wells at Islington* (1684) ironically claims that 'a Citizen could as soon perswade his *Spouse* to forswear *Conventicles*, as prevail with her not to visit us once a year'.

[36] See R. Hutton, *The Restoration*, pp. 199–201 and 207–12.

[37] See J. R. Jones, *Country and Court*, p. 176.

[38] In a private letter to his nephew, quoted by John Dixon Hunt in *Andrew Marvell: His Life and Writings* (London, 1978), p. 166. (Dixon Hunt's book is also informative on *The Rehearsal Transpros'd*, as is Annabel M. Patterson's *Marvell and the Civic Crown* (Princeton, 1978), especially pp. 173–8 and 189–210.)

The moronic compliments of the young gallant reflect the conventions that prevailed in polite conversation between the sexes, as well as traditional conceits of courtly love.[39] The latter is exemplified by the exceedingly fatigued metaphor of the lady's eyes outshining the sun, which wearied Shakespeare a good many decades earlier. The reference to meteorological clemency as a result of the coveted person's presence also reads like a parody of the stilted language felt by some to be appropriate for a suitor.[40] The young woman's reply is just as obedient to formal requirements and just as bathetic.

Even at this early point, the caricature is a triumph. When the wooer resumes the initiative, the young lady having – very properly – put the ball back in his court, its character alters. The 'Gallant' has plainly exhausted his meagre store of opening gambits and plunges into the first subject he can think of that has anything to do with the damsel's affairs. The fact that it is nothing more elevated than her extraordinarily bad luck at cribbage (a game also referred to in *Epsom Wells*, 1.i) heightens the irony. The extreme indelicacy of line 120 – 'Gad-Damme Madam, I'm the Son of a Whore' – allows this deliberate perversion of fashionable dialogue to end with the kind of language Sir Nicholas Cully might have used. Contemporary moralists frowned on the ever-prevalent use of bad language in ordinary conversation. Some amusing and illustrative strictures are provided by a Restoration *Character*:

He admires the Eloquence of, *Son of a Whore*, when tis pronounced with a good Grace, and therefore applyes it to *every* thing; So that if his *Pipe* be faulty … Tis a *Son of a Whore Pipe* … For *New-minted Phrases* he has much enricht our Language: Twas he brought, *I beg your Diversion*, into fashion, and [he] may have a Patent for the sole use (as first Inventer) of that Noble Complement, *Let me be Damn'd, and my Body made a Gridiron to Broil my Soul on to Eternity, If I do not Madam, love you confoundedly*.[41]

In respect of language, it might be added that some of the effectiveness of the *Tunbridge Wells* passage, even with readers unfamiliar with conventions in seventeenth-century polite conversation, is surely due to the perennial body language that is so graphically described in it.

---

[39] A very helpful introduction to the significance of conduct books in Restoration comedy is supplied by Wilkinson's *The Comedy of Habit*. See also Ogg, *England in the Reign of Charles II*, vol. I, p. 117.

[40] Not everybody would agree that such addresses were suitable in the circumstances; see, for example, *The Refin'd Courtier, or a Correction of several Indecencies crept into Civil Conversation* (1663; ascribed to Nathaniel Waker, it is an adaptation of Della Casa's *Galateo*).

[41] *The Character of a Town-Gallant*, p. 5.

The young woman's answer in lines 111–13 is not indicative of intelligence. Nor, of course, is her quick surrender to a 'suitor' whose address is so glaringly deficient in wit and judgement. She shows a congruent want of sense in allowing that surrender to be sealed by the bestowal of baubles from a pedlar's stall.[42] The outcome of the 'prattle' – one of many stresses on offensive talk in *Tunbridge Wells* – is that the would-be wit infects his lady with the itch ('Scotch Fiddle'). She clearly catches it in bed with him, sexual intercourse and/or infested bedclothes being classic transmitters of this distressing condition.

The swift telescoping of events, from the awkward pseudo-fashionable conversation to the unsavoury complaint, is another pace-augmenting dimension in *Tunbridge Wells*. The whole gallant–damsel episode provides a sharply etched presentation of a Restoration 'love' story in a mere twenty-eight lines – an achievement that any contemporary playwright might envy.

It only takes one line, into which contempt and flight are compressed, for the speaker to move his focus and settle it on another set of spa visitors. The two ladies whose conversation is recorded in lines 133–48 have come to the Wells for the same reason as Queen Catherine – to procure heirs for their husbands. Despite the epithet 'Ladyshipp', neither necessarily belongs to a titled family. It was a courteous appellation at the time; Mrs Woodly in *Epsom Wells* is repeatedly addressed in this manner.

Epsom Wells, as several Rochester critics have stated, also mentions the alleged effects of the well waters on infertility.[43] At one point in the play, Cuff and Kick allude to the practice of barren wives to conceive as a result of adulterous liaisons at the Wells. That this was by no means unheard of is confirmed by the *Exclamation* of 1684 (see n.35). The anonymous writers praised the expediency of a wife's temporarily ridding herself of her 'peivish Yoak-fellow', whose visits would only have to be endured at weekends ('on which you are sure to be very Sick'). At Tunbridge or Epsom, their advocates claimed,

disappointed *Wives*, met with seasonable Refreshments; the *Barren* by vertue of our *Metalsome* Waters, and the application of an *able Doctor* behind a Bush,

---

[42] She obviously did not heed the gloomy warnings in such manuals as the second part of *Youth's Behaviour, or Decency in Conversation Amongst Women* (London, 1664), p. 33: 'It is too often seen that young Gentlewomen by Gifts are courted to interchange, and to return the Courtesie; Rings indeed and Ribbands are but Trifles, but believe me, they are not Trifles that are aimed at in such Exchanges.'

[43] See, for instance, Selden, 'Rochester and Shadwell', p. 185, and p. 269 in Walker's Rochester edition.

found Nature relieved, grew Fruitfull and blest their *rejoycing Husbands* with many an hopefull *Heir*.

The speaker of *Tunbridge Wells* is able to catch his breath again while walking close to the ladies and eavesdropping on their conversation. Their silent companion, the teenage daughter, is a main topic and probably has to submit to hearing her condition discussed in terms that later ages might find, and surely have found, distasteful.

In fact, a Restoration reader – male or female – will not have found her complaint or the proposed remedy at all unusual or even offensive. The pale, dyspnoeic girl, with her headaches and amenorrhoea, is a textbook case of a disorder which affected girls and young women for centuries, the so-called 'green-sickness' or 'chlorosis'.[44] 'Green-sick' girls occur in literature well before the seventeenth century, but Rochester's description is unrivalled in its lucid brevity. (As 'Dr Bendo', he claimed to be able to cure the disorder; see pp. 35–6 in Pinto's edition of the Bill.)

At this time, the greatest physician of the late seventeenth century, Thomas Sydenham, advocated the use of steel tonics in chlorosis.[45] The presence of the chlorotic girl at a spa whose waters contain iron was thus in accordance with contemporary medical wisdom; but so was the cure proposed by the childless lady. Ever since Tudor times, physicians had themselves maintained that copulation was the best remedy. In Molière's play *L'Amour médecin* (first performed in 1665), sottish doctors hint that Lucinde is a sufferer (this is of course not the case; she is malingering and already has a lover). That lovemaking was indeed the best doctor in such cases was argued in *Aristotle's Master-piece*, a widely read manual on procreation which was translated into English in the 1680s and remained popular for decades (it had little, if anything, to do with Aristotle).[46] In 1665, Richard Flecknoe's *Aenigmatical Characters* suggested that the

---

[44] A present-day specialist, Irvine Loudon, has put forward the suggestion that 'chlorosis' actually refers to two pathological conditions which he terms 'chloro-anorexia' and 'chloro-anaemia' respectively; see 'The Diseases called Chlorosis', *Psychological Medicine* 14 (1984), 27–36. The *Tunbridge Wells* patient clearly suffers from the first-mentioned complaint, which primarily affected upper-class girls aged fourteen to twenty-one and invariably involved amenorrhoea.

[45] See Fielding H. Garrison, *An Introduction to the History of Medicine* (Philadelphia and London, 1917), p. 262.

[46] See Robert Michel, 'English Attitudes', 56, and Roy Porter, '"The Secrets of Generation Display'd": *Aristotle's Master-piece* in Eighteenth-Century England', in Robert P. Maccubbin, ed., *Unauthorized Sexual Behaviour during the Enlightenment*, special issue of *Eighteenth-Century Life* 9 (n.s.; May 1985), 7–8.

pallor and weakness of a 'Green-sickness Girle' might well be remedied by 'a good *Husband-man*', 'which they say she wants extreamly'.

The words 'those' or 'them' as euphemisms for the menses were the usual familiar expressions, short for 'the flowers', 'the terms' or 'the courses'. The subject was not taboo in conversation, certainly not among women, who did not even have to know one another very well before feeling free to discuss it.[47] Male diarists referred to it, and Charles II wrote a highly explicit letter to his sister on his wife's gynaecological condition.[48] The presentation of the women's talk would thus seem to be a reasonably faithful reproduction of an ordinary conversation on a subject of a fairly intimate but not downright indelicate nature.

The passage that concludes this 'scene' is coarser both in tone and in implication. The assertion that trusting husbands go to considerable trouble and expense in order to be rewarded by a set of horns and a bastard heir has a grim ring to it. The consequences of a wife's adultery have always been viewed in connexion with wealth and property.[49] The idea that estates inherited from one generation to the next would pass into the hands of 'heirs' wholly unrelated to previous owners entails a special kind of social upheaval, to say nothing of personal grief and disappointment.

Still, bastards inheriting is a timeless phenomenon, and there is no lack of examples from different epochs affecting the most exalted circles in England. Compared to the sanctions imposed on adultery in other countries, the English always had a fairly lax attitude to extra-marital sexual intercourse.[50] The Restoration was a time when paternity was a particularly vexed and shaky issue. In Court circles, adultery was rife; titles and riches were bestowed on the King's illegitimate offspring, and bastards were born into several aristocratic families. The fact that Anne Hyde was pregnant when the Duke of York married her seemed mildly shocking to some, but the suspicion that the child might not have been fathered by him – bruited about by James himself soon after the marriage – was far worse. Here was the heir presumptive to the throne,

---

[47] See Patricia Crawford, 'Attitudes to Menstruation in Seventeenth-Century England', *Past and Present* 91 (May 1981), 49.

[48] See, for instance, Lady Antonia Fraser's biography *King Charles II* (first published in 1979; I have used the 1988 Futura edition, where the relevant passage is quoted on p. 260).

[49] Cf., for example, Guido Ruggiero's *The Boundaries of Eros: Sex Crime and Sexuality in Renaissance Venice* (Oxford, 1985), esp. pp. 55–9. See also Macfarlane, *Marriage and Love*, pp. 242–3, and Michel, 'English Attitudes', 51.

[50] Cf. Macfarlane, *Marriage and Love*, pp. 239–42.

himself suggesting that his own firstborn (the baby boy did not survive) was in no way related to the Royal Family!

For all their apparent flippancy, Rochester's lines hence touch on a troubled issue. The intimation that the envisaged cuckolding in lines 155–8 was made possible by the wiles of a midwife rests on a less sensitive basis.

The social status of midwives was poor in the fifteenth, sixteenth and seventeenth centuries. Their prestige did begin to improve in the mid-seventeenth century, but it was still far from great in the Restoration years. The gradual increase was connected with the licensing practice that began in the seventeenth century. Up to 1642, bishops had the authority to license midwives (the Church was very much concerned in the matter, as the midwife had to be able to baptise a dying infant in the absence of a clergyman). It then passed to the physicians at Surgeon's Hall.[51]

Despite this seeming confirmation of professional skill, actual medical competence played a very small part in the licensing procedure. What the licence certified was, by and large, that the midwife was a person of good character. The fact that this was felt to be a matter of paramount importance is in itself proof of the suspicion with which these women were regarded. Even people who did not fear that midwives resorted to black magic were well aware that they had particular knowledge of the secrets of reproduction, and that awareness was not always a comfortable one. When Rochester's speaker calls the local midwife who suggested the Wells 'truest Friend to Letchery', he voices the uneasy feeling, shared by many, that midwives were able to manipulate human sexuality in treacherous ways. A seventeenth-century oath taken by midwives suggests what kinds of malpractices they were suspected of committing, or at least conniving at. The second item is directly related to the accusation put forward in *Tunbridge Wells*:

Item, Yee shall neither cause nor suffer any woman to name, or put any other Father to the Childe, but onely him which is the very true Father thereof indeed.[52]

The final 'scene' in *Tunbridge Wells* portrays two wretched 'Cadets', a word which – as Walker states – can mean 'younger sons' as well as

[51] See Thomas Rogers Forbes, *The Midwife and the Witch* (New Haven and London, 1966), pp. 112 and 152.

[52] *Ibid.*, p. 146. This oath was anonymously published in 1649. In the comedy *Tunbridge-Wells* (by Rawlins?), one Mrs Parret is, in the words of the *dramatis personae* presentation, 'Parcel Midwife, parcel Bawd'.

'army volunteers aiming for a commission'. Everything about these men is shabby, a reflection of their poverty. The 'Thirty Pounds a yeare' suggest that they receive something in the nature of a trooper's pay, which was 2s.6d. a day with full pay and 2s. a day 'subsistence money'.[53] Subsistence money was often all a soldier received for a long time. Despite the valiant efforts of the Paymaster-General from 1661 to 1679, Stephen Fox,[54] colonels – who were responsible for seeing that the men under their command were paid – were constantly kept short of the necessary funds to pay them in full. The difference between subsistence and full pay (the so-called 'off reckonings') was frequently in arrears for months, in some cases even years.

Even so, younger sons could do worse than embark on a military career in Britain's first standing army (not counting the Cromwellian army). True, it was never a popular body; taxpayers loathed it, feeling that it had much to do with the King's perpetual shortage of cash, and the people generally viewed it with suspicion as a possible instrument of tyranny. At Court, making fun of soldiers was a frequent amusement. Still, it usually was not difficult to recruit officers for the six standing regiments. An English officer was unlikely to have to serve in the colonies, the worst thing that could happen to a soldier. Anyone who could buy a commission did not lead a bad life, especially if he had some private means and was not obliged to live on his pay alone.

A modern reader may well wonder how it was possible for the cadets to pose as officers if they were in fact troopers, but at this time there were no great differences in respect of dress between commissioned and non-commissioned soldiers. The red lining of these men's coats, the two pistols, and their sashes – 'Scarfe about the Arse'[55] – imply that they belong to the Royal Horse Guards, who wore blue coats faced with red. Like all troopers in regiments of Horse, they carried a pair of pistols; unlike non-commissioned rank in most Foot regiments, they wore sashes like their officers.[56] Consequently, their uniforms would not give

[53] See Correlli Barnett, Britain and Her Army 1509–1970: A Military, Political and Social Survey (London, 1970), p. 138.
[54] See John Childs, The Army of Charles II (London, 1976). The following paragraphs rely heavily on Childs' and Barnett's books.
[55] Cf. lines 28–30 in Sir Carr Scroope's In Defence of Satyr, p. 365 in Lord's Poems on Affairs of State; the poem is also reprinted by Walker (pp. 136–7).
[56] In addition to Barnett's and Childs' studies, Clifford Walton's History of the British Standing Army, A. D. 1660 to 1700 (London, 1894) has been extremely helpful. Further information was supplied by Captain Edmund Packe's An Historical Record of the Royal Regiment of Horse Guards, or Oxford Blues (London, 1834), and by W. Y. Carman, British Military Uniforms from Contemporary Pictures: Henry VII to the Present Day (London, 1957; a contemporary account of a review describes the 'Oxford Blues' as being 'Coated and Cloaked Blew, lined Red', p. 29).

their deceit away – except by being extremely dirty, non-commissioned soldiers having to make do with the same coat and breeches for years. Their 'Hair ty'd back' looks like an attempt to imitate the hairstyle, or rather wig-style, popular among officers after 1670 (see Walton, *History*, p. 368).

The Horse Guards was not one of the most prestigious regiments. Typical troopers were, according to Childs, 'younger sons of the poorer gentry who hoped that experience in the Horse Guards would fit them for commission in later years' (*The Army of Charles II*, p. 24). This description agrees fairly well with the kind of impression made by the two would-be officers. The satirical observer scorns their pathetic efforts, limiting their 'Command' to dogs and servants of the lowest kind and ridiculing the notion that officers would have to be content with 'a [cast-off] Spavined Horse' and 'Rusty Pistolls'.

If the dating suggested above (pp. 247–8) is correct, the Third Dutch War (ended in February, 1673/4) was over when *Tunbridge Wells* was written. If so, the two men had just missed a good opportunity of gaining a commission in the field; raising the money to buy one seems out of the question. They may even have been among those troopers who were perforce disbanded after the war (ten per troop, on 6 April 1674; see p. 28 in Packe's *An Historical Record*). In any case, their presence at the Wells would appear to have been dictated by the direst need, more particularly the need of a dowry. That would explain their 'appearing' at an expensive watering-place filled with the daughters of wealthy families.

Their pretences were not unprecedented, it seems; Flecknoe's 1665 *Characters* mentions 'one who falsely styles himself Collonel' (p. 45). He is really a coward who was anxious to avoid fighting. Like many another braggart in uniform, 'He drunk formerly when he shou'd be fighting, and now talks onely of fighting in his drink.'

The fact that Rochester's unprepossessing pair is 'singing a Bawdy-Song' at this hour, and in such a place, suggests that they, too, are far from sober. The notorious intemperance of Charles' standing army was one component in its lack of discipline. 'Its behaviour before the public was nothing less than disgusting', according to Childs, who reports especially disgraceful brawls in 1673.[57]

The sashes mentioned in line 171 of *Tunbridge Wells* made Paul Hammond ascribe commissioned rank to the two brawlers; John Harold Wilson also referred to them as having 'commissions in the army' (*Court Wits*, p. 133).

[57] *The Army of Charles II*, pp. 214–15. In spite of this, and the ridicule heaped on the army by non-military courtiers, some peers had their own units. The Duke of Buckingham was one

An additional reason for the satirical narrator's scorn may be that although Rochester himself did at one time have a cavalry commission, his military career – over when he was but twenty – was a naval one. He had, after all, seen action against the Dutch and conducted himself with conspicuous bravery, according to his commander.[58] Perhaps the naval veteran's dislike of the other branch of the service has something to do with the contempt expressed in these lines.

A typically Rochesterian paradox follows in lines 174–7: the pretences of the soldiers are compared to the appreciation given to an animal because he is dressed in human garb and made, man-like, to ride on another animal – whereas the 'Trump'rie' actually degrades the beast. Another caustic observer of contemporary manners, describing the 'ridiculous ... sight' of a young man going through various motions to win a mistress, had concluded: 'An ape, methinks, never looks so like himself, as when he has on my young Masters suit' (The Refin'd Courtier, p. 46). To this writer, human dress accentuated the traditionally unfavourable characteristics of the ape – affectation, silliness and wantonness, among others. Rochester's speaker utters an even more venomous denunciation of human beings: while those who call the ape 'the Young Gentleman' think they are elevating the beast, they are in fact demeaning him in that they pay their tribute of respect to that which is not in the animal's nature.

This significance of the ape lines emerges when they are viewed in conjunction with the conclusion of Tunbridge Wells:

> Blesse me thought I, what thing is Man that thus
> In all his shapes, he is rediculous?
> Our selves, with noyse of Reason wee doe please
> In vaine: Humanity is our worst Disease.
> Thrice happy Beasts are, who because they be
> Of Reason voyd are so of Foppery;
> Faith I was soe asham'd that with remorse,
> I us'd the Insolence to mount my Horse;
> For he doeing only things fit for his Nature,
> Did seeme to me by much the wiser Creature.

The first couplet in this passage embodies the chief concern of Tunbridge Wells. At the same time, it articulates a vital distinction between this

example; another is Rochester's enemy Mulgrave, whose 'Earl of Mulgrave's Foot' was formed in 1673 and disbanded in 1674. On Mulgrave's military career, see p. 351 below. Childs quotes disparaging remarks made on the army by Rochester's closest friend Henry Savile (pp. 214–15).   [58] See, for instance, Treglown, Letters, p. 16.

poem and the roughly contemporary, and much gloomier, *Satyr.*
Tunbridge Wells depicts a succession of men and women – representatives of 'Man ... in all his shapes' – whose behaviour and appearance
'[excite] contemptuous merriment', to quote Johnson's definition of
'ridiculous'. The *Satyr*, also directed against 'Reason' and 'Humanity',
is less concerned with the outward face of mankind than with human
motives and actions. No wonder the latter satire is both bleaker and
more profound.

A thorough-going manifestation of 'rediculous' humanity in *Tunbridge Wells* is the 'noyse' made by humans pretending to utter rational
discourse (see pp. 241–2 above). A secondary meaning of 'noise' is
'much and/or loud talk' (*OED* 6 and b), and all the castigated fools
bluster, babble and bawl. This mark of our humanity, with which we
flatter ourselves, is in fact a symptom of an affliction worse than any of
those which the Wells are expected to alleviate: the incurable and
terminal condition of being human.

The conclusion that the humble horse is a 'wiser Creature' than his
rider is hence inevitable. As was the case in the *Satyr*, the superiority of
animals is associated with beasts without any inherent nobility. Three
horses occur towards the end of *Tunbridge Wells*, the poor wretch that
belonged to the soldier, the equally wretched creature that had to carry
a monkey in a show to entertain humans, and the speaker's own mount.
Even the fact that they serve humans does not prevent them from being
better than those who make use of them, because it is in their nature to
yield service. The man who is conscious of shame in commanding that
service articulates an insight partially developed in the *Satyr*: it is better
to obey natural impulses than to betray one's nature by posturing and
cheating,[59] especially as the profits gained by pride and insincerity are so
despicable in themselves.

Harold Love maintained that *Tunbridge Wells* is more concerned with
abuse than with actual portrayal.[60] (Others have echoed that view.[61]) I
find such a distinction difficult to draw; so much of the abuse is
descriptive, and the descriptions are themselves abusive. A study of the
historical context of *Tunbridge Wells* helps a present-day reader develop

---

[59] It is not to be wondered at that Richard Head thought *Tunbridge Wells* an apt illustration for
his book on *The Art of Wheedling, or INSINUATION* (the supplementary title of *Proteus
Redivivus*).
[60] See his essay 'Rochester and the Traditions of Satire' in Love, ed., *Restoration Literature: Critical
Approaches* (London, 1972), pp. 149ff.
[61] See, for instance, Bruce King, *Seventeenth-Century English Literature*, Macmillan History of
Literature (London, 1982), p. 198.

a greater awareness of the ironical dimensions that Rochester's contemporaries recognised and enjoyed. Such an awareness should augment our own pleasure in this poem which – while obviously more superficial than the *Satyr* – energetically dissects foolish pretentiousness in Restoration society.

9

' *Timon* '

Rochester scholars have often dealt with *Timon* and *Tunbridge Wells* in succession. These two predominantly social satires came into being at roughly the same time, and there is, as David M. Vieth has said, a 'special relationship' between them.[1] Endorsing the arguments put forward by Harold F. Brooks in 1938,[2] Vieth concluded that both poems were written in the spring of 1674.

But if one accepts the idea that Rochester was highly aware of events and developments in France, the summer of 1674 seems more likely. There are two grounds for believing him to have been well informed in this respect: his personal and long-standing acquaintance with the French Court and with several English envoys to France, who were in a position to convey news and gossip to him – and his passion for the latter commodity. Burnet's account of the tricks to which Rochester resorted in order to supply his readers with up-to-date calumnies may not be literally true; but he certainly appears to have attained a high degree of accuracy. It is hard to imagine that his level of ambition was lower where French business was concerned.

AFFAIRS OF FRANCE

Timon twice refers to the military achievements – the 'success' – of Louis XIV and the French army. The most spectacular martial victory of 1674 from Louis' point of view was the conquest of Franche-Comté. The entire campaign lasted from February to July, but the decisive breakthrough was accomplished by mid-May (the capitulation of

[1] See *Attribution*, pp. 271–95.
[2] See Brooks' 'The Date of Rochester's "Timon"', *Notes and Queries* 174 (28 May 1938), 384–5.

Besançon) and early June (the fall of Dôle, then the capital of the province). Louis, who arrived in Franche-Comté in the early days of May, took all the credit for the outcome of the campaign. It was only to be expected from a monarch convinced of his greatness as a military commander; he had done the same in 1672, after the *Blitzkrieg* against the Dutch.

Franche-Comté in 1674 has often been depicted as something of a sitting duck, but according to the Marquis of Pomponne, the province was well supplied with arms and munition; it also harboured a population that would have been willing and able to use them. The apparent ease with which Louis' conquest was achieved was partly due to the misuse of enemy resources. Characteristically, Pomponne repeatedly refers to 'la bonne fortune du roy' as a vital reason for his success.[3]

To the rest of civilised Europe, Louis XIV may well have appeared to possess divine assistance in the early summer of 1674. The host's wife in *Timon* expresses a similar view in line 58 (see below). After the setbacks of 1673, the sun seemed safely settled on 'his most Christian Majesty' once again.

The reference to 'the *French Kings* success' in *Timon* hence suggests late May 1674 as a *terminus a quo* for the poem. But what about the lines on Souches and Turenne, on which Brooks based his dating of the satire?

> Will *Souches* this year any *Champoone* drink?
> Will *Turene* fight him? without doubt says *Huffe*,
> When they Two meet, their meeting will be rough.

Brooks' study of the *London Gazette* for the spring of 1674 led him to conclude that 'all likelihood of an encounter between Turenne and Souches was over' in mid-June. On the contrary, the two generals could have faced each other as late as July.

While Louis was covering himself with glory in Franche-Comté, Turenne was reduced to covering Louis' operations, commanding a comparatively small body of men in Alsace. His task was to prevent allies against France from breaking through into the beleaguered province. It was a 'chétive occupation pour un général de son mérite',[4]

---

[3] *Mémoires du Marquis de Pomponne*, ed. J. Mavidal (Paris, 1860), pp. 142–53. Pomponne was Secretary of State for Foreign Affairs until dismissed by Louis after the peace of Nijmegen (1678).

[4] Camille-Georges Picavet, *Les dernières années de Turenne: 1660–1675* (Paris, 1918), p. 401. This paragraph relies heavily on Picavet's book, especially pp. 397–424. Additional information,

and when victory in Franche-Comté was assured, Turenne proposed a more active role for himself. In the principality of Juliers/Jülich, on the left bank of the Rhine, the Imperial general Souches stood with 30,000 men. Turenne wanted to advance towards him by way of Trèves/Trier, but Louis and Louvois – the powerful Secretary of State for War – refused to allow him to move away from Alsace. Not content to remain inactive, Turenne crossed the Rhine, fought the Austrian commander Caprara and the Duke of Lorraine at Sintzheim on 16 June, received some reinforcements, and invaded the Palatinate. The latter step alarmed Louis, who was afraid Turenne had advanced too far. The marshal was fairly close to the forces of the Imperial general Bournonville, and there was a possibility that Souches might join his colleague. In July, Louis promised Turenne reinforcements if Souches made such a move. Consequently, there were two occasions in June and July where Turenne and Souches might have met on the battlefield.

Turenne's letters during the summer of 1674 repeatedly mention threats against Champagne. No such invasion took place, partly thanks to his strategic skill throughout the Alsace campaign. According to a contemporary source, the country folk of Champagne hailed him as their liberator during the first week of 1675, obviously relieved that no Imperial troops had been given the opportunity to drink 'any *Champoone*' during the preceding year. Turenne returned to the Court in triumph in January, 1675, but Souches had been dismissed from his command a couple of months before.[5]

In a manner characteristic of – if by no means exclusive to – the seventeenth century, Timon's host and his fellow-diner Huffe discuss military operations solely with reference to the commanders, reflecting the attitude of those men themselves. As Heinrich Peter (*Der Krieg des Großen Kurfürsten*, p. 213) stated, the great generals tended to regard war as a chess game where the personal honour of the players overshadowed the real issues.

In view of all these circumstances, June or July 1674 seems to me to be the most likely month of composition with regard to *Timon*. Another French affair remains to be considered in the light of that date, though: the lines on the French King's divided affections.

particularly on Souches' moves (or rather the lack of them), was provided by Heinrich Peter's *Der Krieg des Großen Kurfürsten gegen Frankreich 1672–1675* (Halle, 1870), especially pp. 213–47.
[5] According to the *Allgemeine Deutsche Biographie*, vol. XXXIV, p. 700 (Berlin, 1971; this is a reprint of the first edition of 1892), 'Souches hatte überhaupt wenig Freunde, viele Gegner.' In view of the scope and severity of the charges levelled at him, it is not surprising.

Timon's hostess is only interested in one aspect of the new master of Europe, his *amours*:

> We chancd to speak of the *French Kings* success;
> My *Lady* wonder'd much how *Heav'n* cou'd bless,
> A *Man*, that lov'd Two *Women* at one time;
> But more how he to them excus'd his Crime.

All Rochester editors unhesitatingly identify the 'Two *Women*' as Louise de La Vallière and Madame de Montespan. The latter is undoubtedly one of them, but the relevance of the former is dubious.

In 1674, Louis XIV's liaison with Madame's shy, blonde lady-in-waiting had been over for a long time. It is true that she remained *maîtresse en titre* for a couple of years afterwards, but in effect she was reduced to serving as a cover for the mistress who supplanted her in 1667, Madame de Montespan. Louis' relationship with that lady was a highly problematic one, as she had a husband by whom she had two children. Worse than that, the Marquis de Montespan was, legally, the 'father' of her children by the King and thus in a position to assert his authority over them. Consequently, the children's governess from 1669 to 1673, the widowed Mme Scarron, had to live with them in strict seclusion. In 1673, however, she appeared at Court, richly apparelled and with her own establishment. In late 1674, she acquired the property, and the name, of Maintenon.

Whether the future Mme de Maintenon was the King's mistress in 1673 is doubtful, but in the course of 1674, the relationship clearly reached that stage. Mme de Sévigné was dropping hints as early as 1672, but they merely prove that the King was seriously interested.[6]

Nobody who knew anything about the Court of Louis XIV would have regarded Louise de La Vallière and Mme de Montespan as two of a kind in 1674. Rochester was certainly aware of the former's fall from grace. In a letter dated '1671–4' by Jeremy Treglown, he tells his wife of a doll he has bought for their daughter, 'the very person of the Duchess la Vallière, late mistress to the King of France, dried up and pined away to a very small proportion by fasting' (*Letters*, p. 85). This account of the reduction to doll size of Louise de La Vallière implies that Rochester also knew of the self-castigation she undertook. She is, for instance, reported to have worn a hair-shirt under her finery long before she entered the severe Carmelite convent where she spent over thirty years atoning for her six years of sinful splendour.[7]

---

[6] See Marcel Langlois, *Madame de Maintenon* (Paris, 1932), p. 26.
[7] See J. Lair, *Louise de La Vallière et la Jeunesse de Louis XIV* (Paris, 1882; second edition), p. 300.

That event took place in mid-April, 1674. The whole Court was watching as that most pathetic of royal mistresses, calm and smiling, turned her back on Versailles. It was a day to remember – and a few days later the Court was on its way to the mud and glory of Franche-Comté.

The 'Two *Women*' that Louis XIV loved are thus more likely to have been Mme de Montespan – with whom he maintained sexual relations throughout the 1670s – and the new favourite, Mme Scarron, soon to be Mme de Maintenon.

Everybody who was somebody in Whitehall must have known about La Vallière's departure, and about the '*French Kings* success' in Franche-Comté, by late May 1674. But what about Turenne's designs, the French fears for Champagne, and Louis' uncertainty regarding the movements of the Imperial troops? Would Rochester have been informed about such matters?

Several people connected with the Court of Charles II took a personal interest in Turenne. Buckingham had served under him;[8] so had James, Duke of York,[9] in those distant days when he was widely regarded as a more promising prince than his elder brother. Throughout 1673, Buckingham was desperate to lead an English army against the enemies of France; Dryden ridiculed his eagerness in an obsequious letter to Rochester, dated April–May 1673 by Treglown.[10] Monmouth and Churchill – both well known to Rochester – were operating near, and with, Turenne in the summer of 1674. One must also remember that incredible feats of intelligence were performed throughout Europe at this time when no news travelled faster than a courier riding post and a sailing vessel. To mention just one example, an entry dated 17 April 1674 in the Bulstrode papers accurately summarises Swiss anxiety as a result of the Franche-Comté campaign, predicting that the French 'will master that county before it's releived by any of their neighbours'.[11]

[8] See Wilson, *Court Wits*, p. 206, and *A Rake and His Times*, ch. 1.
[9] See, for instance, p. 22, n.11 in Lord's *Poems on Affairs of State*. James and Turenne were personal friends; see Suzanne d'Huart, ed., *Lettres de Turenne* (Paris, 1971), p. 505. Turenne apparently relied greatly on the British soldiers under his command in 1672–4; see C. T. Atkinson, 'Charles II's Regiments in France', *Journal of the Society for Army Historical Research* 24 (1946), 53, 61 and 129–31.
[10] See pp. 88–9 in Rochester's *Letters*. One rather wonders what the Earl of Rochester thought of the commoner Dryden's invitation to '[laugh] at the great Duke of B–'. Cf. Winn, *John Dryden*, p. 251.
[11] *The Bulstrode Papers*, vol. 1 (*1667–75*), privately printed in 1897 (*The Collection of Autograph Letters and Historical Documents formed by Albert Morrison*, second series (1882–1893)), p. 266. Incidentally, the devastation of the unhappy Palatinate at the hands of Turenne's soldiers was a popular topic of conversation at Charles' Court in 1674; see, for instance, Otto von Schwerin

Clearly, public servants in England were able to draw on excellent sources regarding Continental developments.

Like Timon's host and hostess, Europeans in all nations were mesmerised by all things French. These were the years when Louis XIV established the hegemony of France. Her army, reorganised by Louvois, became the strongest in Europe; Colbert even managed to create a respectable fleet despite the King's total lack of interest; French literature, especially the drama, conquered larger territories than the French army; and Louis built one of the most stupendous royal castles in the known world. No wonder the *dramatis personae* of *Timon* took a keen interest in what went on in the country of which England was in a limited, but very real, sense a poor relation.

Two further aspects of *Timon* with a French connexion remain to be considered: the host's repudiation of French fare; and the ludicrous scene where the four bullies come to blows over the issue of French military valour. Both features are especially interesting in that they reflect prevalent English attitudes to France and her dominating role, in matters of taste as well as in a political sense.

Timon hopes that the meal he is about to receive will in some measure compensate for his having to put up with the company. He begins to suspect the worst, however, when his host announces that the food and drink are unaffected by French *raffinement*:

> I thought the *Dinner* wou'd make some amends,
> When my good *Host* cryes out – y'are all my *Friends*,
> Our own plain *Fare*, and the best *Terse* the *Bull*
> Affords, I'll give you and your *Bellies* full:
> As for *French Kickshaws*, *Cellery*, and *Champoon*,
> *Ragous* and *Fricasses*, introth we'ave none.

The meal does no credit to domestic traditions. The beef – the English staple food *par excellence* – is tough and the vegetables overgrown, and Timon seems to find the other solids inedible as well. None of the herbs and spices employed in French late-seventeenth-century cooking are allowed to season the traditional sauces.[12] Timon seems to be compelled

d.J., *Briefe aus England über die Zeit von 1674 bis 1678*, ed. Leopold von Orlich (Berlin, 1873), pp. 9 and 11.

[12] See William Younger's (gold) mine of information, *Gods, Men, and Wine* (London, 1966), p. 375. Cf. *Hudibras*, II.i.595–8 ('*season ... as French* cooks use, / Their *Haut-gusts, Bouilles*, or *Ragusts*'). Interestingly enough, St Evremond – possessor of one of the finest palates in England, and well known to Rochester – disliked 'Ragous, or Kick-shaws', too; see Younger, *Gods, Men, and Wine*, p. 376.

to satisfy his hunger with the wine, slaking his thirst with sips of small
beer – a mixture which would by itself account for his subsequent
haggard appearance.

His host's prejudice against French fare is characteristic of his class, the
country squire of the old-Cavalier strain. As Griffin pointed out,[13] the
character Clodpate in Shadwell's *Epsom Wells* also reviled '*French
Fricasies and Ragousts*', and so did many other stout-hearted Englishmen. Fielding's classic song *The Roast Beef of Old England* continued the
tradition, lamenting the enfeebling effects of French *ragoûts*.

The taste of Timon's host is obviously perverted by national
prejudice, and it is presented in that light. His rejection of Sillery wine
and champagne in favour of red wine from a tavern[14] reinforces that
impression. Champagne came into fashion at the time of the Restoration,[15] and St Evremond estimated it above any other wine. Sillery
was also a discerning nobleman's tipple; Younger describes how the
cellar at Woburn received it from the 1660s onwards.[16]

The mere fact that the host brings up these characteristic French
delicacies indicates how familiar French preferences were in certain
English circles. The fight over the question of whether cowardice lurks
behind the fine martial show of the French indicates that some
Englishmen went so far as to identify themselves with that nation and
her honour:

> Damn me (says *Dingboy*) the *French*, *Cowards* are,
> They pay, but the *English*, *Scots*, and *Swiss* make *War*.
> In gawdy *Troops*, at a review they shine,
> But dare not with the *Germans*, *Battel* joyn;
> What now appears like courage, is not so,
> 'Tis a short pride, which from success does grow;
> On their first blow, they'll shrink into those fears,
> They shew'd at *Cressy*, *Agincourt*, *Poytiers*;

[13] *Satires Against Man*, pp. 37–8.

[14] Claret was a favourite among the upper classes of the seventeenth and eighteenth centuries; see
Younger, *Gods, Men, and Wine*, p. 361. 'Terse' from the Bull – surely, as Love has suggested,
a local inn (see p. 275 in Walker's Rochester edition) – would not have been of the finest sort,
and Timon may have felt as aghast at the proclaimed provenance of the wine as did Lady Peter
Wimsey on learning that her husband had accepted an invitation to drink public-house sherry
at the Vicarage (Dorothy L. Sayers, *Busman's Honeymoon*, ch. 14).

[15] See Younger, *Gods, Men, and Wine*, pp. 346 and 348, as well as J. C. Drummond and Anne
Wilbraham, *The Englishman's Food: A History of Five Centuries of English Diet* (London, 1939),
p. 402.

[16] *Gods, Men, and Wine*, pp. 347–8. Incidentally, the Marquis of Sillery was counted among the
small and select company of *grands seigneurs* who are alluded to as 'l'ordre de Costeaux' in
Boileau's third satire (line 107; see pp. 216–17 in Boudhors' commentary).

Their loss was infamous, *Honor* so stain'd,
Is by a *Nation* not to be regain'd.
What they were then I know not, now th'are brave,
He that denies it – lyes and is a *Slave*
(Says *Huffe* and frown'd) says *Dingboy*, that do I,
And at that word, at t'others *Head* let fly
A greasie *Plate*, when suddenly they all,
Together by the Eares in Parties fall.

Not only is the situation itself absurd; Dingboy's arguments are foolish in the extreme – though not without a limited pertinence in respect of foreign recruitment (see below). The Hundred Years War was rather too long ago to be of any great relevance, as Huffe remarks in his brief reply; but of course references to ancient campaigns have a way of cropping up during any debate on the martial honour of a nation. In the 1670s, vacillation was a characteristic of Leopold I and some German princes; the French certainly did not suffer from any lack of pugnacious resolution. The fact that the successes of 1672 had not led to a resounding victory over Holland was less due to lack of perseverance on their part than to the resourcefulness and diplomatic skills of the young William of Orange. Despite a certain caution on both sides in the Franco-German conflict in 1674, the courage of the French forces was by no means inferior to that of the Imperial ones. Turenne, as was stated above, was only too eager to 'with the *Germans*, *Battel* joyn'.

The matter of foreign mercenaries and French subsidies is a slightly more sensitive one from the French point of view. It is true that Louis XIV paid Charles II to wage war against the Dutch. French money helped equip English naval forces which were felt by many Englishmen to have been made to bear the brunt of supposedly Anglo-French engagements with the Dutch at sea. A number of British regiments – English, Scots and Irish – supplemented the French army in 1672–4,[17] even after the separate peace between England and Holland had been concluded in February 1674.[18] As anybody whose juvenile literary fare included G. A. Henty will remember, Scots soldiers served in the French armies throughout the seventeenth century.[19] From 1671 onwards, though, the most stable recruitment of foreign soldiers

---

[17] See Atkinson, 'Charles II's Regiments', 53–65 and 129–36.
[18] See K. H. D. Haley, *William of Orange and the English Opposition, 1672–4* (Oxford, 1953), pp. 185, 189 and 192–3. Naturally, the Dutch disapproved.
[19] Rather more scholarly, but still entertaining, confirmation is provided by Stephen Wood's *The Scottish Soldier* (Edinburgh, 1986), p. 13. See also Atkinson, 'Charles II's Regiments', 57.

involved Swiss troops.[20] As many people in and outside the cantons realised, supporting France was not really in the Swiss interest. Still, successful French diplomacy, Swiss fear of displeasing the new super-power, and the judicious application of bribes secured this excellent supply of fighting men. To that extent, French money may be said to have bought soldiers from abroad. Even so, foreign troops never made up more than a rough quarter of the French army, and in any case enrolment outside the national territory was a feature in all the more considerable Continental armies at this time.

French affairs are clearly a vital concern in Rochester's *Timon*, and it is strange that hardly any scholarly attention has been given to this element. Instead, Rochester critics have concentrated on the poem's debts to the *repas-ridicule* tradition represented by Horace, Régnier and Boileau; the significance of the narrator's name; the values represented by Timon and his *persona* function; and the occasional touches of obscenity in the poem. With the exception of the last-mentioned element (the coarse bits represent typical Court-satire usage), these are important features, and they will be dealt with in the following pages. One topic will, by and large, be deferred to the chapter on Rochester's *Allusion to Horace*, though: the references to contemporary authors and their works (see pp. 322–3 and 330 below).

MODELS AND CHARACTERS

The similarities and differences between *Timon* and Boileau's third satire have been discussed at some length by Griffin, Farley-Hills and Love.[21] They have drawn attention to such similarities between Boileau's and Rochester's satires as an interviewer who demands an explanation of the wan visage of the narrator; the description of a displeasing meal, in which that narrator has been lured to participate expecting to be in good company; the development of a fight complete with plate-throwing; and a discussion of the merits of contemporary writers. Rochester's poem differs from Boileau's in being shorter, giving much less space to the actual food, providing a hostess (and some obscenities), and having the guests come to blows over the martial virtues of the

---

[20] See André Corvisier, *L'Armée française de la fin du XVIIe siècle au ministère de Choiseul: Le soldat*, vol. I (Paris, 1964), pp. 259 and 263.

[21] See pp. 36–41 and 174 in Griffin's *Satires Against Man*, pp. 155–60 and 186–90 in Farley-Hills' *Rochester's Poetry*, and pp. 158–63 in Love's 'Rochester and the Traditions of Satire'.

French instead of over literary disagreements. As Love points out, Rochester inserts quotations in the literary debate (there are some in Boileau's satire, but they are short and fairly insignificant in comparison). It is very cleverly done, too. The four men of more than dubious taste and judgement appear especially ridiculous when owlishly (mis)quoting purple passages from solemn plays whose grandeur makes a delicious contrast with their befuddled state.

Among the other points that demonstrate Rochester's indebtedness to Boileau, as well as his skill in adaptation, are odd lines such as 'Pensant qu'au moins le vin dûst reparer le reste' (line 70 in Boileau's satire; cf. line 69 in Rochester's). Further instances are Boileau's

> Et leur premiere ardeur passant en un moment,
> On a parlé de paix et d'accommodement.
>
> (lines 227–8)

In *Timon*, this conclusion to the row becomes:

> Their rage once over, they begin to treat,
> And Six fresh *Bottles*, must the peace compleat.

'Treat' here means 'To deal or carry on negotiations ... with a view to settling terms' (*OED* 1.a.*intr.*); Rochester hence retains Boileau's humorous metaphorical comparison between the end of the 'lutte barbare' and a peace treaty between warring nations.

The fact that Rochester's bullies fight over military honour and not over literature has been noted several times. Actually, though, Boileau mentions warfare as well. Having said that every diner expressed his views on various affairs of state,[22] Boileau's 'P' continues:

> Puis delà s'embarquant dans la nouvelle guerre,
> [Chacun] A vaincu la Hollande, ou battu l'Angleterre.
>
> (lines 165–6)

The smug Frenchmen are sure that they could have vanquished either combatant in the Second Dutch War. Their superiority makes a delightful contrast to Huffe's and Dingboy's heated rhetoric in lines 163–7 of *Timon*.

Rochester's debts to Régnier's eleventh satire, often connected with Boileau's poem, are less patent. As Farley-Hills maintains, the tone of

---

[22] 'Reglé les interests ... et reformé l'Estat' (lines 63–4); cf. Rochester's 'Some regulate the *Stage*, and some the *State*' (line 112).

Régnier's narrative is closer to *Timon* than to Boileau, whose fastidious speaker employs a more polished idiom.[23] The reluctance of the speaker to take part in the meal, and his failure to eat a great deal, are common to Boileau, Régnier and Rochester. Régnier's rambling tale (448 lines to Boileau's 236 and Rochester's 177) also contains a discussion on the merits of certain poets (lines 227ff.), and the fare includes sauces and fricassée (lines 262–3; they are unfortunately spilt over the speaker's feet). Striking parallels between Régnier's and Rochester's *repas-ridicule* satires are hard to find, though.

Nor is it easy to demonstrate any direct indebtedness on Rochester's part to a classical exponent of that genre, Horace's *Satire* II.8. As in *Timon*, the host in Horace's poem is officious and anxious for his guests to enjoy – and be impressed by – the meal he offers them; but there is nothing wrong with the actual cooking. When the diners refuse to eat, it is not because the food is inferior, but because they are disgusted by the vulgarity of their host and his ostentatious extravagance. There can be little doubt that Rochester knew Horace's satire, but as in the case of Régnier, direct influence is hard to prove. The relationship between Boileau's work and *Timon* is the only one that might deserve to be called 'imitation', and even here 'adaptation' is a better term. It might be pointed out, by the way, that *repas affreux* were represented in English poetry before *Timon*. One fine example, complete with a host's glowing but unfulfilled promises, is found in Herrick's *The Invitation* ('To sup with thee thou didst me home invite').

Much of the scholarly discussion regarding the extent to which *Timon* has been affected by Horace, Régnier and Boileau has focused on the speaker's character and functions, and this is where previous analyses have tended to diverge. Not only is Rochester's Timon viewed in different ways by various commentators; the same applies to his predecessors. An example – and the most interesting one from the point of view of *Timon* – is found in Griffin's and Farley-Hills' highly dissimilar views on Boileau's 'P'. To the former, he is 'an urbane Horatian man of good taste';[24] the latter, by contrast, sees him as a 'fussy, bad-tempered sybarite', arguing that 'we are meant to laugh at him as much as at the boors he describes'.[25]

It is true that Boileau himself claimed that his 'P' character was ridiculous because he described a bad meal as if it were a major

---

[23] Incidentally, the ridiculous pedant in Régnier's poem estimates 'un langage poly' above all other things (line 230).   [24] *Satires Against Man*, p. 36.
[25] *Rochester's Poetry*, p. 187.

calamity,[26] and the fastidiousness of the narrator does have an amusing dimension. Still, the wry conclusion of Boileau's satire has a certain self-ironic appeal. Besides, one need not be a spoilt gourmet to shudder at the truly nightmarish account of the repast he is served.

What of Timon, then? Are 'we' supposed to find him ridiculous, too? What values does he stand for? Does he represent Rochester's own point of view? Is he a 'scourging satirist' in the Elizabethan tradition, as Farley-Hills repeatedly insists? And what of his name – is he an utter misanthrope, like Shakespeare's Timon of Athens?

A close look at this speaker fails to confirm both the 'anger' which Farley-Hills keeps imputing to him and the 'uncertainty' in his attitudes that bothers Griffin. Like the speaker in *Tunbridge Wells*, he describes people and manners that disgust him, but he is rather less upset by them than his counterpart in *Tunbridge Wells*.[27] His expostulations are comparatively mild; he condescends to take some part in the conversation; he stays out of the tussle (as does his host); and he only leaves when he has seen peace restored. On the whole, he behaves like an *honnête homme*. His language may be drastic and occasionally obscene, but this is a result of Rochester's 'translating out of what we may loosely call a neoclassical mode of satiric discourse into the reigning native mood, lampoon'.[28]

Should Timon be identified with Rochester? David Vieth, having pointed out that many Augustan poems employ the *persona* device, finds such an identification admissible. The relevant passage from Vieth's *Attribution* states the case clearly:

Far from being satirized ... Timon represents the norm of values by which judgment is passed upon other characters in the poem – the host, his wife, and the four hectors. Timon's function is something like that of the 'gentlemen of wit and sense' in the comedies of Shadwell, who embody the standards violated by the humor characters. Thus Timon may be a projection of the values, and conceivably the identity, of the author of the poem.

The identification of Timon with Rochester is at least plausible. Timon's personality resembles Rochester's, and his name as well as his attitudes suggest the misanthropy which was associated with the Earl. (p. 286)

The final sentence calls for some discussion on two points, though. First, does Timon possess anything that might be called a 'personality', and second, is 'misanthropy' a proper designation for his 'attitudes'?[29]

---

[26] See p. 212 (the commentary) in Boudhors' edition of Boileau's satires.
[27] See Love, 'Rochester and the Traditions of Satire', p. 161.   [28] *Ibid.*, p. 160.
[29] Farley-Hills also attributes a 'personality' to Timon; see *Rochester's Poetry*, p. 189.

What *Timon* tells us about the speaker of the poem is that he is young; writes occasional poetry and sometimes reflects on that of others; is familiar with the ways of whores and gamblers; and is an intimate acquaintance of the Court Wits Sedley, Buckhurst and Savile (particular friends of Rochester's). He has certain standards when it comes to eating and drinking, and he shares the general Restoration view that women past their prime are useless for amorous purposes. These characteristics are typical of the inner circle of Court Wits and hardly amount to a personality. As for his attitudes, there is nothing positive about them. He hardly eats anything, despises the drink and the other guests, makes no contribution to the literary discussion, and keeps out of the scuffle. Although he refers to the company as 'we' in lines 57, 89 and 111, everything that goes on is essentially beneath his active involvement. Even his parting resolution – to avoid certain drinking practices and the society of bullies – is limited and negative. He undoubtedly has norms and standards, but they are only discerned by way of what is offensive to them.

The essential negativity of the *Timon* speaker becomes apparent when he is compared to the narrator in *Tunbridge Wells*. In the concluding lines of that poem speaks a real misanthropist. His contention that 'Humanity is our worst Disease', and his attempts to eschew close contact with various revolting representatives of the human race, make him a more suitable bearer of the name 'Timon' than the reluctant dinner guest.

The second question raised by Vieth's last sentence is what significance one should attribute to the speaker's name. Farley-Hills, who finds the tone of the poem 'scornful', 'jaundiced' and 'angry', is convinced that Shakespeare's *Timon of Athens* is highly relevant to Rochester's *Timon*, and that Rochester in fact named his speaker after Shakespeare's character.[30] The 'parallels' he quotes are dubious, though, and Rochester's Timon acts and speaks in a manner which has very little in common with the raging bitterness of Shakespeare's protagonist.

Another Timon who has been suggested as a reason for Rochester's choice of name is the sceptic philosopher and poet Timon of Phlius.[31] A review of other more or less likely Timons is provided by Griffin in a footnote;[32] but both Griffin and Hammond have expressed well-

---

[30] See pp. 186, 188, 135 and 136 in *Rochester's Poetry*. It should be remembered that the Timon Restoration audiences knew was Shadwell's adaptation of Shakespeare's play, first acted in 1678.
[31] See, for instance, Vieth's headnote in his edition of Rochester's poems, p. 65.
[32] P. 40, n.33 in *Satires Against Man*.

considered warnings against attaching too great, and too specific, significance to the name. Incidentally, Shakespeare's Timon was not the only representative of the misanthrope known to Renaissance and Baroque readers; there was Shakespeare's source, North's Plutarch, and Lucian's dialogue *Timon the Misanthrope* (the latter was translated by Erasmus, and it is referred to in his *Praise of Folly*[33]). As Keith Walker says, with gentle finality, 'The significance of "Timon" is obscure, and perhaps not very important.'[34]

In fact, the poem was simply called 'Satyr' in most seventeenth-century manuscripts and editions. One contemporary text carries the title 'Satyr upon a Diner', which shifts the emphasis from Timon to his host.

This gentleman, whose insistence on his company is the root cause of Timon's woes, is introduced in line 5 as 'a dull dining *Sot*'. The verb is surely used in the sense of 'To furnish or provide [a person] with a dinner; to entertain at dinner' (*OED* 3 under *dine*).[35] The portrait of the host in *Timon* is interesting – not because of its subtlety, but because it comprises several features belonging to a clearly defined segment of Restoration society, and because it supplies a positive counterpart to the negativity of the man called Timon.[36]

The host is a man with social ambitions (like the fools in the *Ramble*, for instance), but he is more than that. He claims to be one of the Cavalier country gentlemen who lost money and estates during the Commonwealth:

> And now the *Wine* began to work, mine *Host*
> Had been a *Collonel* we must hear him boast
> Not of *Towns* won, but an *Estate* he lost
> For the *Kings* Service, which indeed he spent
> Whoring, and Drinking, but with good intent.
> He talkt much of a Plot, and *Money* lent
> In *Cromwells* time.

There were many people who had suffered such losses and were bitter about not receiving compensation for them after the Restoration. Their plight was sometimes a pitiable, if irremediable, one, but Timon is unmoved by the host's lugubrious reminiscences and ascribes his losses to less exalted occupations than the loyal support of the exiled

---

[33] See p. 39 in Clarence H. Miller's translation of *The Praise of Folly* (New Haven and London, 1979).   [34] P. 274 in his Rochester edition.

[35] Walker believes that the word 'Diner' in the Harvard MS title should be 'Dinner'.

[36] The words 'positive' and 'negative' are used in their traditional senses and have nothing to do with moral evaluation.

Sovereign. The unrefined origins of the 'dull dining *Sot*' are reflected in the meal, served with 'all that *Country Bumpkins*, call good Cheer'. His taste for beef, for instance, is very much that of a country squire, frowned on by fashionable society.[37]

The host's lack of refinement shows in his deficient literary judgement, too. Not only does he praise a poor piece of verse in the mistaken belief that his unwilling companion wrote it; he also does not seem to be much of a reader at the best of times. When literary matters are discussed, he is out of his depth. His wife's repeated attempts to conduct the conversation along such lines are rudely interrupted by his indelicate toast, which can only add to her grievances. Having listened wordlessly to the four hectors crying up their respective favourites, he finally adds his ha'p'orth in the form of the second couplet from Dryden's *The Indian Emperour*. One suspects that he has learnt it by heart (unlike Huffe and Halfwit, he does not misquote) just for such an occasion, his bad taste showing in the choice of this rather shaky simile.[38] Having delivered this contribution to the lofty discussion, he shows his true character in exclaiming:

> But pox of all these *Scriblers*, what do'e think.
> Will *Souches* this year any *Champoone* drink?
> Will *Turene* fight him?[39]

The ex-colonel thus heavy-handedly brings the discussion back to his home ground, with results he could hardly foresee.

The 'Diner's' lack of cultural polish shows in other ways, too. Like a true 'Bumpkin, or Country-Squire', he 'salutes a Man' by 'lay[ing] violent Hands upon him'.[40] Praising the four bullies as 'Men, *Tam Marte quam Mercurio*', he makes use of a very tired cliché. In fact, some twenty lines of *Timon* reproduce his tactless, inelegant and blustering talk, and about 50 of the poem's 177 lines are directly concerned with him. The portrait of the host hence takes up about the same space in the poem as literary matters do. It runs to almost twice the number of lines given to his lady, whom critics have found much more absorbing.

---

[37] For an amusing illustration from the *Sociable Letters* of Margaret, Duchess of Newcastle, see Grant, *Margaret the First*, p. 168.

[38] It is a 'vulnerable' one, as Dryden's modern editor John Loftis points out (p. 325 in vol. IX of the University of California Press edition of *The Works of John Dryden*), and Rochester obviously relished tearing it to shreds.

[39] In Vieth's edition, lines 151–4 are all given to Huff(e), but Brooks gives the first three to the host and has Huff(e) answer 'Without doubt' and so on, which makes far better sense.

[40] See Butler's *Character* with that title (p. 75 in Daves' edition). The physical accosting of unfortunate men by importunate fools is of course a classical topos; several critics have pointed to the instance in Horace's ninth satire of the first book.

Two passages are devoted to the delineation of this personage, who has no counterpart in the *repas-ridicule* satires of Horace, Régnier and Boileau:

> In comes my *Lady* strait, she had been *Fair*,
> Fit to give love, and to prevent despair.
> But *Age*, *Beauties* incurable Disease,
> Had left her more desire, than pow'r to please.
> As *Cocks*, will strike, although their *Spurrs* be gone,
> She with her old bleer *Eyes* to smite begun:
> Though nothing else, she (in despight of time)
> Preserv'd the affectation of her prime;
> How ever you begun, she brought in love,
> And hardly from that Subject wou'd remove.
> We chancd to speak of the *French Kings* success;
> My *Lady* wonder'd much how *Heav'n* cou'd bless,
> A *Man*, that lov'd Two *Women* at one time;
> But more how he to them excus'd his Crime.
> She askt *Huffe*, if *Loves* flame he never felt?
> He answer'd bluntly – do you think I'm gelt?
> She at his plainness smil'd, then turn'd to me,
> *Love* in young *Minds*, preceeds ev'n *Poetry*.
> You to that passion can no *Stranger* be,
> But *Wits*, are giv'n to inconstancy.
> ...
> My *Lady* she
> Complain'd our love was course, our *Poetry*,
> Unfit for modest Eares: small *Whores*, and *Play'rs*
> Were of our Hair-brain'd *Youth*, the only cares;
> Who were too wild for any virtuous *League*,
> Too rotten to consummate the Intrigue.
> *Falkland*, she prais'd, and *Sucklings*, easie Pen,
> And seem'd to taste their former parts again.

The hostess has been regarded as a 'resilient old lecher',[41] a character who 'demonstrates how social behavior can become a mode of sexual sublimation',[42] and 'a fool prattling obsessively of what she can no longer enjoy'. It has been suggested that her frustrated sexual appetite turns her into a 'portrait ... in Rochester's gallery of impotents'.[43] These comments seem somewhat exaggerated to me. There is no doubt of her coquettish behaviour, nor of Timon's stern disapproval of flirtatiousness

---

[41] Farley-Hills, *Rochester's Poetry*, p. 189.   [42] Carole Fabricant, 'Rochester's World', 343.
[43] The last two quotations are from Griffin's *Satires Against Man*, p. 39.

in someone who has lost her power, but not the desire, to please. Her avid interest in love is not, however, necessarily the expression of superannuated and unsatisfied lust. Not only is it one common to representatives of her sex at, and in, any age; it is also one that was particularly prevalent in polite seventeenth-century society. In the *salons* of the *précieuses*, the nature of love was the topic *par préférence*. In England, too, wherever women spoke or wrote, love was at the centre of their discourse, as in lines 32–63 and 101 of *Artemiza to Chloe*. There is nothing overtly hypocritical about the hostess' lament for the demise of chivalrous love in lines 101–8. She calls the simultaneous *amours* of Louis XIV a 'Crime', and who is to say that she does not mean it? Timon censures her 'affectation', the flirtatious behaviour which she acquired and employed in her prime and has not since unlearned. He illustrates it in her stilted manner of speaking, which is effectively offset by Huffe's rude question and her husband's toast.

Perhaps the most interesting aspect of modern critical reactions to the lady is the way in which Timon's contempt for her has rubbed off on present-day readers. To him, she is a nuisance and a bore, an object which has lost its usefulness and whose failure to act accordingly is especially irritating. His attitude is typical of his time in every way; but one may well wonder why modern critics should, implicitly, look down on her as something of a sexual aberration when the poem gives no solid support to such a reading. To a post-Restoration reader, one would have thought that the faded beauty – whose conversation, significantly, twice refers to youth – might be viewed as a slightly pathetic creature rather than as a freak.

Still, the lady is of course a stylised figure, just like her husband. Unfashionable as their tastes are, the couple illustrate the dedication to the subjects of love and war that dominated Restoration gatherings, in the country as well as at Court:

The two great subjects which make up the Conversation of the Court, are Love and War. If the thoughts of the more brave and active Spirits, are taken up with Sieges, ingagements, and the acquisition of glory, those of the vain effeminate and impertinent, are no less busied in the Conduct of an Amarous Intreague.[44]

Late-seventeenth-century conduct books also touched on the classical theme of keeping the peace at meal-times[45] often enough to make one suspect that scenes such as the one described in *Timon*, lines 168–73, were far from unusual. Nor is there anything out of the ordinary about the

---

[44] *The Art of Complaisance*, p. 63.   [45] One famous example is Horace's *Ode* I.xxvii.

four bullies. They form a pretty gallery of Restoration fops – uncouth Huffe, whose rough nature is excited by rumbling rhetoric; Dingboy, whose discourse is packed with fashionable oaths; and Kickum and Halfwit, who claim to admire noble feelings rendered in heroic verse. The host's and Timon's decision to let them fight till they tired of it, without interference, was informed by a conviction that no great harm would be done. Not only were their swords 'safe' (presumably deposited somewhere else in the house); hectors were by definition ineffectual fighters:

He is all for light skirmishes and pickeering, but cares not to engage his whole body, but where he is sure to come off. He is an exact judge of honour, and can hit the very mathematic line between valour and cowardise... When he is engag'd in a quarrel, he talks and looks as big as he can, as dogs, when they fall out, set up the bristles of their backs, to seem taller than they are. It is safer for a man to venture his life than his conversation upon him.[46]

To judge from Timon's silence, this describes his views exactly.

The company at the old Cavalier's table is thus made up of stock characters. Timon's 'alas' in line 5 indicates that their society, in combination with a miserable meal, was such an appalling experience that he would have preferred to run up gambling debts to particularly obnoxious creditors. All his six fellow-diners (including the lady) bore him intensely, and perhaps it is partly this account of desperate boredom that makes *Timon* less absorbing than the other more ambitious satires. Unfortunately, Timon is something of a bore himself. As Jeremy Treglown has observed,

... the satire is itself, arguably, in poor taste: a vivid, contemptuous account of a dinner party at which Timon is, however unwillingly, a guest, reviling the appearance, behaviour and conversation of his hosts and fellow guests behind their backs and criticizing the quality of the meal.[47]

Timon certainly has its enjoyable passages, such as the deprecating and often quoted couplet 'A *Song* to *Phillis*, I perhaps might make, / But never Rhym'd, but for my *Pintles* sake' and the twisted quotations from the heroic plays, complete with Timon's sardonic comments.[48] The narrative, with its persistent tense shifts, is lively enough. But it lacks the

---

[46] Butler's *Character* of 'An Hector'; pp. 278–9 in Daves' edition.

[47] '"He knew my style"', p. 77.

[48] In fact, *Timon* could be said to be more satisfying as a literary satire than as a social one; cf. pp. 322–3, 330 and 334 below.

nervous energy of *Tunbridge Wells*, the savage authority of the *Satyr*, the incisive, good-humoured wit of *Artemiza to Chloe* and the gimlet impudence of *Upon Nothing*. Its 'snobbery of manners' has its points, but the mockery of social folly lacks the sting of Rochester's great attacks on pride and hypocrisy. True, both these characteristics are implicit in the silly pretentiousness of the diners, but that is altogether a slighter thing than the vanity lashed in, for instance, the *Satyr* and *Upon Nothing*. Generally speaking, *Timon* has more to offer the historian than the poetry lover – or the true misanthropist.

10
Court satires and lampoons

The scope of the social satire in *Tunbridge Wells* and *Timon* is much wider than in *Signior Dildo*, the satire on Charles II ('I'th'Isle of Britaine'), *Mistress Knights Advice to the Dutchess of Cleveland in Distress for A Prick*, the *Dialogue* of the warring mistresses ('When to the King I bid good Morrow'), the four-line squib on Cary Frazier, and *On Mistress Willis*. Although erotic activities feature in fashionable life at the spa, they only form one dimension among several in the varied texture of *Tunbridge Wells*. By contrast, the six satires and lampoons mentioned above focus on the genitalia of the men and (especially) women at the Court of Charles II. *Signior Dildo* and the satire on the King are the longest and most interesting poems of the six, and the greater part of the ensuing chapter is devoted to them. The subject matter of the *Lampoone* beginning 'To longe the Wise Commons have been in debate' relates that poem to this group; and the plea for 'cleanly sinning' in the *Song* whose first line is 'By all *Loves* soft, yet mighty Pow'rs' might be appended to it, too. Hence, these two poems will be reviewed under the 'Court Satires and Lampoons' heading, although that designation is not entirely adequate in the case of the *Lampoone* and of little relevance to the *Song*.

SIGNIOR DILDO

Considering that Rochester is a poet whose name remains indissolubly associated with 'wickedness', he wrote comparatively little in the way of indecent poetry and (leaving *Sodom* out of account) none that can very well be termed pornographic.[1] His

---

[1] In the sense defined by Roger Thompson (*Unfit for Modest Ears*, p. ix), 'intended to arouse lust, create sexual fantasies or feed auto-erotic desires'. Cf. Griffin, *Satires Against Man*, p. 89n.

obscenities[2] are no worse than those of his court-satirist colleagues, as various modern anthologies have demonstrated.[3] More than that, the share of his total output that might be referred to as 'bawdy'[4] is very small. To a certain extent, of course, all these properties are lodged in the eye of the beholder. It may be a personal defect in respect of humour that makes me regard *Signior Dildo* as Rochester's only bawdy poem of any length. In fact, the conclusion of 'Fair *Cloris* in a Piggsty lay' is the only other instance in Rochester's *œuvre* which seems to me to be downright 'amusing about sex' (to quote Thompson's definition of 'bawdy'). Elsewhere, indecency is always, at some level, linked with pain, revulsion and/or disappointment. *A Ramble in Saint James's Parke* supplies a particularly striking illustration of this darker side to Rochester's 'wicked' verse.

What is it, then, that makes *Signior Dildo* funny where the *Ramble* is not? To some degree, of course, the difference is a matter of tone. The thumping anapests and the swift movement of the poem, 'from Whore to Whore', accentuate its epigrammatic impudence. Above all, though, the total absence of personal involvement is the decisive factor. The speaker is not concerned in the 'action' at all; indeed, the poem itself is a negation of personal involvement. In one sense, the theme of *Signior Dildo* is – as some critics have suggested[5] – the sexual independence of woman on man. Lust may be satisfied in a manner which is literally impersonal. The artificial phallus provides one solution to the unsettling disharmonies found in the men-and-women poems. At least, it disposes of the pain that always attends human intercourse.

This is not to say that Rochester advocated the severance of sexual relations between men and women. In the first place, the 'solution' does nothing for the male sex, as the conclusion of *Signior Dildo* makes abundantly clear. More important than that, it is – in the literal meaning of the word – an unnatural one. The dildo belongs among the paraphernalia of 'art', whose inferiority to 'nature' is repeatedly implied in Rochester's poetry. The Restoration libertines, like their

[2] Thompson (*ibid.*) defines the obscene as being 'intended to shock or disgust, or to render the subject of the writing shocking or disgusting'.

[3] Such as, for instance, the *Poems on Affairs of State* volumes; Harold Love's Penguin anthology of Restoration verse; the Gyldenstolpe manuscript edited by Bror Danielsson and David M. Vieth (*The Gyldenstolpe Manuscript Miscellany of Poems by John Wilmot, Earl of Rochester, and other Restoration Authors*, Stockholm, 1967); and John Harold Wilson's *Court Satires of the Restoration* (Columbus, 1976).

[4] Again, Thompson's preface to *Unfit for Modest Ears* supplies a plain and workable definition, 'intended to provoke amusement about sex'.

[5] See, for example, Wilcoxon, 'Sexual Politics', 142, and Wintle, 'Libertinism', p. 153.

predecessors in France, were adherents of the natural impulse, especially in sexual matters. Rochester's *Satyr* expresses that allegiance in no uncertain terms. *Signior Dildo* cannot be read as a celebration of female sexual independence, achieved by artificial means. On the contrary, it joins *Upon Nothing* in forming a beautifully accomplished paradoxical encomium.

Comments on *Signior Dildo* – I have never seen anything that could be called a detailed critique of the poem – usually speak of its women as if they formed a homogeneous group. The ladies are regarded as collectively representing female sexual appetite.[6] Actually, however, they respond differently to the potentialities of the dildo, and those differences are not without significance.

Jeremy Treglown has suggested that the poet's choice of women was less than deliberate:

There is every likelihood that 'Signior Dildo'... was composed rapidly in company: its basis – rhyming on all the gossip-worthy names he could think of or had suggested to him – is like that of a party game.[7]

It is an attractive idea, and there may well be some truth in it. *Signior Dildo* is certainly rather a haphazard work. Many variants of the poem exist,[8] and the fact that it easily admitted additions by other hands testifies to the looseness of its structure. Still, I do not think that the selection of women's names (only three of which are actually 'rhymed on', one of these ladies being represented by her husband's first name) was quite that fortuitous.

Before the women – and men – whose sexual predilections and pursuits are reviewed in the poem are subjected to scrutiny, something should be said of the ostensible subject, or rather object, of *Signior Dildo*. Artificial penises were imported from France and Italy during the Restoration years; Rochester himself and Savile are said to have had a hand in the trade.[9] The burning of a confiscated consignment is alluded to in line 64 of *Signior Dildo*, as well as in the poem *Dildoides* attributed to Samuel Butler.[10] From the poet's point of view, the arrival of an Italian royal bride in England was hence a natural occasion to choose as a starting-point. Representing the imported phallus as a member of her

---

[6] See, for instance, Wilcoxon, 'Mirror of Men's Fears: The Court Satires on Women', *Restoration: Studies in English Literary Culture, 1660–1700* 3.2 (Fall 1979), 48, and John H. O'Neill, 'Sexuality, Deviance, and Moral Character in the Personal Satire of the Restoration', *Eighteenth-Century Life* 2 (1975), 16–17.   [7] In '"He knew my style"', pp. 84–5.
[8] See pp. 186–8 in Walker's edition.
[9] See pp. 62–3 in Treglown's edition of Rochester's *Letters*.
[10] See Pinto, *Enthusiast in Wit*, p. 73, and Wilcoxon, 'Mirrors', 48.

train is a powerful comic device. Describing this emblem of depersonalised 'intercourse' as a person in his own right, equipped with a
number of laudable qualities, is a never-failing source of humorous
effects.

This non-personage possesses a string of attributes that were in short
supply at Court. The Signior is noble but modest, cheap, discreet,
vigorous, a potential preserver of marital fidelity, ready to serve all
shapes and sizes without fail and healthy ('sound, safe') into the bargain
– the latter being a virtue which should recommend him especially
warmly to a Court whose members were forever undergoing treatment
for venereal disease. The fact that the dildo has been carefully invested
with all these qualities is another of those comic elements in the poem's
make-up which suggest that it may not, after all, have been a spur-of-
the-moment effort.

A further indication of this kind is provided by the destination of
Signior Dildo. 'He' was allegedly an attendant upon the new Duchess
of York, and there is something of an anti-Yorkist bias in the poem. The
hint of hostility against the entourage of the heir presumptive may be
regarded in the light of the rift between Buckingham, on whose side
Rochester would be insofar as he was on anybody's, and the Duke.[11]
That conflict was at a crucial stage in 1673 and early 1674. The anti-
York element shows in the selection of aristocratic women. Anne
Hamilton, wife of Robert Carnegie, Earl of Southesk, was one of the
Duke's better-known mistresses; Count Gramont tells the disgraceful
story of how her husband came to know of her infidelity.[12] The
Countess of Falmouth and Ralph Montague's wife Elizabeth, the latter
a bride when the poem was written (between 26 November 1673 and 26
January 1673/4[13]), had both harboured hopes of marrying James when
his first wife died. Dorothy Howard's name is not blackened by any
source of Restoration gossip known to me;[14] but *Signior Dildo* certainly
infers that she has been 'ranging' – gone a-roving, that is – with the
Duke. The Duchess of Modena is, of course, his new mother-in-law.
Among the women who are expressly said to have availed themselves

[11] Cf. Winn, *John Dryden*, pp. 245 and 248.
[12] Pp. 176–8 in Allan Fea's 1906 edition of the *Memoirs of Count Gramont* by Anthony, Count
Hamilton (London). Cf. also Fea's *Some Beauties of the Seventeenth Century* (London, 1906), pp.
263–8. Rochester apparently remained on friendly terms with her; see pp. 187–8 in Treglown's
edition of Rochester's *Letters*.
[13] See p. 271 in Walker's edition. The dating was established by Vieth (p. 192 in his edition of
Rochester's poems).
[14] As J. H. Wilson points out, John Evelyn (11 July 1675) described her as 'a most virtuous and
excellent creature' (see p. 19 in *Court Satires*).

of the Signior's services – six altogether –, four belong to the York sphere, including his bride and her mother. At a time when anti-Papist sentiment ran high in an England seething with disapproval of the Duke of York's new Catholic marriage, that fact is suggestive (see below).

Some of the other ladies were probably included simply because they had a reputation for loose living – among them the notorious Cleveland (Barbara Palmer, *née* Villiers, Countess of Castlemaine) and wanton Betty Felton.[15] The expression 'dainty fine Dutchesse's' in line 33 presumably refers to the two Duchesses whose dainty finery was a result of their long-standing associations with the King, in other words, Cleveland and Portsmouth.[16] Tom Killigrew was of course the man whose ears Rochester boxed in the King's presence, one of his worst social offences.[17] Libelling Killigrew's wife as a woman of uncouth manners might have seemed permissible, especially as it gave Rochester another chance to insult the Dutch.[18] The popularity of that nation was at a very low ebb in England at this time. The fact that the lady was the stepmother of one of his cronies would not have weighed heavily with him.

A far graver offence against the ethics of friendship occurs in the seventh stanza:

> The Countesse of Falmouth, of whom People tell
> Her Footmen wear Shirts of a Guinea an Ell:
> Might Save the Expence, if she did but know
> How Lusty a Swinger is Signior Dildo.

Suggestions that the fine ladies of Restoration society sometimes looked for erotic amusement with their social inferiors, servants included, are plentiful in Restoration literature. Rochester has himself contributed several instances. In one of them, *Mistress Knights Advice*, Cleveland is told to bribe her prospective simple lovers with ale. The Falmouth stanza in *Signior Dildo* implies that Mary Bagot, widow of the Earl of

---

[15] On the latter, see Wilson, *Court Satires*, pp. 47–8, 72, 75 and 238. Philippa Temple, mentioned in line 49, was the victim of more than one scurrilous satire; see, for instance, pp. 72 and 110 in Harris' edition of Dorset's poems. Cleveland's predilection for plebeian lovers is satirised in Marvell's *Last Instructions to a Painter*, lines 79ff. (p. 104 in Lord's *Poems on Affairs of State* volume).

[16] I do not think it likely that Frances, widowed Duchess of Richmond, is also implied here, as Wilson proposes (*Court Satires*, p. 18. Walker accepts the suggestion; see p. 272 in his edition). The former Frances Stuart, so ardently desired by Charles II in the 1660s, had her detractors – Dorset's satire *Colon* libels her, calling her 'salt' (lustful) –; but her conduct and the way she came by her title set her too far apart from the other two for a joint reference to seem probable.

[17] See, for instance, Pinto, *Enthusiast in Wit*, p. 71.

[18] On Rochester's aversion against the Dutch, see also p. 159 above.

Falmouth – whose name has, incidentally, been linked with those of the incorrigible Henry Jermyn[19] and of the King himself[20] – was reduced to persuading her servants to go to bed with her by means of buying expensive clothes for them.

It may not be the most insulting innuendo in *Signior Dildo*; but in view of the fact that it was directed against a woman who was being wooed by one of Rochester's best friends, it is an ungentlemanly one. Buckhurst, the future Earl of Dorset, was infatuated with Lady Falmouth at the time when *Signior Dildo* was written and married her shortly afterwards.[21] Clearly, respect for the sentiments of a friend did not trouble the composer.

There is further evidence of this not particularly appealing trait in the poet Rochester. As J. H. Wilson has suggested, the twelfth stanza (lines 45–8) probably refers to the Countess of Shrewsbury:[22]

> The countess of the Cockpit (who knows not her Name)
> She's famous in Story, for a Killing Dame:
> When all her old Lovers forsake her I Trow
> She'l then be contented with Signior Dildo.

The restraint suggested by the arch parenthesis is a thin veil indeed. All the world knew that Anna Maria Brudenell/Talbot, widowed Countess of Shrewsbury, had been living openly in the Cockpit[23] with the man who had fatally wounded her husband in a duel. In January 1674, the Duke of Buckingham faced his ordeal in Parliament as a result of the scandalous affair. Buckingham was often in trouble, but this situation was one of the worst he encountered. One would have thought that his young friend Rochester – who did support him in a subsequent scrape[24]

---

[19] See Fea, *Some Beauties*, p. 114. This Henry Jermyn was the nephew of the Earl of St Albans with the same name (see below). His inadequacies as a lover, as well as those of the future Duke of Marlborough, are the subject of the last line of *Mistress Knights Advice*.

[20] See Arthur Irwin Dasent, *The Private Life of Charles the Second* (London, 1927), pp. 238–9.

[21] The genuine warmth of his feelings for her can be sensed in letters written at this point. See Brice Harris, *Charles Sackville Sixth Earl of Dorset: Patron and Poet of the Restoration*, Illinois Studies in Language and Literature, vol. 26.3–4 (Urbana, 1940), pp. 58–61.

[22] *Court Satires*, p. 19.

[23] A designation for an appendage to Whitehall. The Duke of Buckingham moved into quarters there when he took over the post of Master of the Horse on Albemarle's death; see ch. 10 in Wilson's *A Rake and His Times*.

[24] See J. H. Wilson, *Nell Gwyn: Royal Mistress* (New York, 1952), p. 201. This biography has not been superseded by Roy MacGregor-Hastie's *Nell Gwyn* (London, 1987), whose accuracy can be sampled in the following quotation: 'Nell's old friend and colleague Elizabeth Barry was brought to bed of a daughter by Rochester ... As the Countess of Rochester had died recently, she toyed with the idea of persuading the Earl to marry Elizabeth, but nothing came of it' (p. 138). As the Countess survived her husband, that was not perhaps surprising.

– would have had better things to do during these days than adding even the faintest breath to the fanning of flames which threatened irreversible damage to a boon companion. However, *Signior Dildo* may well have antedated the climax of Buckingham's tribulations by a couple of weeks.[25]

Buckingham, often referred to as a close friend of Rochester's, constitutes a fascinating sidekick to Charles II. The two men were brought up together; spent many years abroad and acquired foreign tastes and languages; married plain, barren and devotedly loyal wives for political reasons; shocked even their permissive age with the way they conducted their illicit liaisons; played the parts of rescuing heroes in two different London fires; and were both committed to religious toleration – one of the few consistent (and, in the eyes of posterity, consistently admirable) political ambitions either man ever had. It is somewhat surprising that Rochester's poetry, with all its more or less covert allusions to the King, contains so few references to Buckingham.[26]

In one sense, however, neither Buckingham nor the King fares so badly in *Signior Dildo* as he might have done: ladies associated with them are said not to be in need of artificial phalli. The Countess of Shrewsbury will only have to fall back on Signior Dildo when 'all her old Lovers forsake her'. The morophilia imputed to Cleveland and Portsmouth is not, of course, flattering to Charles, although his association with the former was over at this point. However, the only woman who expressly rejects the service of the dildo is one of the King's mistresses, the singer and actress Mary Knight:

> He civilly came to the Cockpitt one night,
> And profer'd his Service to fair Madam Knight,
> Quoth she, I intrigue with Captain Cazzo
> Your Nose in myne Arse good Seignior Dildo.

Knight has the good taste to prefer a 'living prick', like Cary Frazier (see below), and there can be no doubt as to whose 'Cazzo' she is intriguing with. For a woman constantly referred to in terms such as 'a minor member of the royal seraglio',[27] she looms large in Rochester's Court

---

[25] In early January 1674, Rochester was himself banished from the Court as a result of inadvertently handing the King a lampoon on himself. Vieth suggests that Rochester may have intended to give Charles a copy of *Signior Dildo*. See p. xxvii in the Introduction to Vieth's edition of Rochester's poems.

[26] The only poem that actually mentions him is the *Allusion to Horace*, line 122, where Buckingham is one of the men whose literary judgement Rochester professes to admire.

[27] Wilson's description; see p. 19 of his *Court Satires*.

lampoons. Besides showing commendable judgement in *Signior Dildo*,
she demonstrates erotic expertise in *Mistress Knights Advice* and the
Dialogue.

Cleveland is a different matter. The *Signior Dildo* passage is not the
worst contemporary libel on Rochester's beautiful and reckless cousin;
but in view of her allegedly distended vagina (a commonplace in
writings of this kind), she is clearly not the discerning man's choice. Nor
was her current lover renowned for nice discrimination in amorous
matters. Unlike Buckingham and Charles, he is not spared the indignity
of being thought expendable thanks to the newly arrived Italian:

> Our dainty fine Dutchesse's have got a Trick
> To Doat on a Fool, for the Sake of his Prick,
> The Fopps were undone, did their Graces but know
> The Discretion and vigor of Signior Dildo.
>
> That Pattern of Virtue, her Grace of Cleaveland,
> Has Swallow'd more Pricks, then the Ocean has Sand,
> But by Rubbing and Scrubbing, so large it do's grow,
> It is fit for just nothing but Signior Dildo.

There can be little doubt that Rochester had a particular 'Fool' in mind
here. John Churchill being otherwise engaged in late 1672 and 1673,
Cleveland had taken another lover – another John, the Earl of
Mulgrave.[28] Combining an attack on the perpetual target Cleveland
with an indirect stab at his own arch-enemy must have given Rochester
considerable pleasure.

There are other traces of animosity in *Signior Dildo*, invalidating
David Farley-Hills' opinion that the poem possesses 'little satirical
content'.[29] Old Henry Jermyn, Earl of St Albans, is presumably
bringing the dildo to a lady he is no longer able to gratify by natural
means:

> St Albans with Wrinkles and Smiles in his Face
> Whose kindnesse to Strangers, becomes his high Place,
> In his Coach and Six Horses is gone to Pergo,[30]
> To take the fresh Air with Signior Dildo.

[28] See Wilson, *Nell Gwyn*, pp. 135, 140 and 149. In April, 1674, he was replaced by Rochester's
best friend, Savile, who may (as Rochester editors have pointed out) be the 'Harris' who
figures in line 30 on the wife of Ralph Montague. Montague, incidentally, was another man
well known to Rochester, who had reason to be grateful to him (see p. 128n.).
[29] *Rochester's Poetry*, p. 112.
[30] On the doubtful meaning of 'Pergo', see Walker's edition, p. 273, and Wilson, *Court Satires*,
p. 19. Mrs E. Duncan Jones has suggested to Walker that Rochester may be referring to Pyrgo
(sometimes spelt Pergo) near Brentwood in Essex. The Restoration used the word 'Pego' as a

St Albans was widely regarded as a worthless, ancient lecher. An ardent Francophile, he was employed as ambassador extraordinary to France in the 1660s. What political influence he had was bound up with the favour with which Queen Henrietta Maria regarded him; it was in fact rumoured that he had married her, or at least had an affair with her.[31] The line 'Whose kindnesse to Strangers, becomes his high Place' suggests, with decorous subtlety, that Rochester knew of this allegation.

Another, characteristically Restoration-flavoured, satirical thrust is aimed at the citizens of London in the sixteenth stanza:

> Were this Signior but known to the Citizen Fopps
> He'd keep their fine Wives from the Foremen of Shops,
> But the Rascalls deserve their Horns shou'd Still grow,
> For Burning the Pope, and his Nephew Dildo.

Derogatory references to the merchants and officials of the City of London and their families abound in Restoration Court literature, including the current courtesy books.[32] The very term 'citizen' is one of abuse when employed by these writers. The Bendo escapade will have afforded its perpetrator particular satisfaction in that his gullible victims were mostly drawn from this segment of the London population. The destruction of dildoes referred to in line 64 was an event which touched Rochester himself, and pope-burning was a popular City pastime, especially in late 1673.[33]

The narrator of *Signior Dildo* claims to be outraged by both sorts of conflagration, but the fusion of the burnt offerings and the family relationship proclaimed between them have an anti-Catholic tinge. Most of the ladies whose relative interest in, or fitness for, the signior makes up most of the poem's substance were Catholics (including the Duchesses of Cleveland and Portsmouth and the Countess of Shrewsbury). The York household was, of course, the focus of English Catholicism. It would hardly be correct, though, to call *Signior Dildo* an anti-Papist satire. It reflects the formidable hostility against Catholics that was felt everywhere in England at the time, but it scarcely does more than that. Buckingham, a Protestant with a pro-Dissenter bias,

---

synonym for 'penis' (see Thompson, *Unfit for Modest Ears*, pp. 122–3), and Sir Francis Fane's *Iter Occidentale* speaks of women who travel to take the warm waters as being 'on Pilgrimage to St Pego'. There might be some connexion there, but it seems doubtful.

[31] See *Dictionary of National Biography*, vol. XXIX, p. 343, and *Poems on Affairs of State*, vol. I, pp. 100–1. According to Gramont, St Albans was Queen Henrietta Maria's lover and treated her shabbily; see p. 105 in Fea's edition of the *Memoirs*.

[32] See, for instance, the second part of *Youth's Behaviour, or Decency in Conversation Amongst Women*, p. 79, and *The Young Gallant's Academy*, p. 56.

[33] See John Miller, *Popery and Politics in England 1660–1688* (Cambridge, 1973), p. 131.

lived with a Catholic; so did Rochester himself, and partly as a result of his own preference, if Burnet's account of Lady Rochester's religion is correct. Neither in Rochester's poems nor in his letters have I come across anything that could be called anti-Catholic sentiment. The libellous comments on the Duke of York seem less concerned with his faith than with his personal qualities.

The last four stanzas of *Signior Dildo* are pure burlesque. The satirical edge felt in many of the others recedes, personal attacks disappear, and the poem concludes with a splendidly mock-heroic Battle of the Phalli:

> Count Cazzo who carryes his Nose very high,
> In Passion he Swore, his Rivall shou'd Dye,
> Then Shutt up himself, to let the world know,
> Flesh and Blood cou'd not bear it from Signior Dildo.
>
> A Rabble of Pricks, who were welcome before,
> Now finding the Porter deny'd 'em the Door,
> Maliciously waited his coming below,
> And inhumanely fell on Signior Dildo.
>
> Nigh weary'd out, the poor Stranger did fly
> And along the Pallmall, they follow'd full Cry,
> The Women concern'd from every Window,
> Cry'd, Oh! for Heavn's sake save Signior Dildo.
>
> The good Lady Sandys, burst into a Laughter
> To see how the Ballocks came wobbling after,
> And had not their weight retarded the Fo
> Indeed 't had gone hard with Signior Dildo.

The paradoxical-encomium convention remains in evidence till the end, too – a happy one for the 'hero', and a disappointing one for the encumbered competitors[34] he displaced. If 'Lady Sandys' in line 89 is, as Rochester's editors have suggested, Nell Gwyn's friend Lady Lucy Hamilton Sandys,[35] the spectacle of the Catholic import's escape does not induce dejection in the entourage of the self-styled Protestant whore. The onomatopoeia of line 90 is another of Rochester's memorable auditory effects. The colloquialism 'Flesh and Blood cou'd

---

[34] See Farley-Hills, *Rochester's Poetry*, p. 112. In the case of *Signior Dildo*, Farley-Hills' repeated emphasis on the comic element in Rochester's verse – in this book as well as in *The Benevolence of Laughter* – seems entirely warranted. One rather wishes, though, that he had refrained from adding the pompous parenthesis according to which *Signior Dildo* is '(shocking only to the very impure)'.

[35] See, for instance, p. 59 in Vieth's edition. Nell Gwyn had lodgings in Pall Mall, as did Mary Knight.

not bear it' (line 80), which still comes across as such today,[36] has a literal dimension which heightens the humour of 'Count Cazzo's' sulky withdrawal. The use of an Italian appellation for this vain blusterer, literally reduced to impotent wrath, imparts a common note to the opposing parties in lines 77–80.

Another burlesque element in the concluding stanzas is that they suggest the two ways in which an offended Restoration courtier could seek redress, both abortive in this case: a challenge; and an ambush perpetrated by hired thugs. Rochester had some experience of both. The nature of that experience is a matter for the biographer;[37] here it is sufficient to say that he turns it to good account, providing his poem with another 'social' feature which would amuse his readers.

Signior Dildo, then, is probably less of an improvisation than it seems at first reading. Despite its narrow compass – sexual intrigue at Court –, it succeeds in being something more than a mere succession of libels. It catches some of the powerful political and religious under-currents at Whitehall, reflecting the crisis brought on by the Duke of York's second marriage. Nevertheless, it manages to do so without compromising the merry insolence of Rochester's sole bawdy poem of any length.

THE SATIRE ON CHARLES II

The belief that it was the lampoon beginning 'I'th'Isle of Britaine' that led to Rochester's banishment from the Court in January 1674 has long been held by Rochester scholars.[38] Even a cursory look at it makes one sympathise spontaneously with the offended King; it is obviously a scurrilous piece of work by any standards. However, Charles II tolerated much impudent, violent and *lèse-majesté*-ish behaviour from the Court Wits. Why should this lampoon have provoked him to the point of not wanting to look upon the writer's face for some considerable time? The nature of the accusations made in the satire on Charles II must be investigated before that question can be answered.

Few critics have given much space to this poem, and even fewer have stopped to ask themselves why it roused Charles' anger, rather than his

---

[36] Cf. *The Man of Mode*, Act I, line 140 (or 141): 'DORIMANT. Flesh and blood cannot hear this and not long to know her.'

[37] Cf., for example, Pinto's *Enthusiast in Wit*, pp. 93–6, and the 'Black Will' passage in the *Letters* (p. 120), which has been cited as evidence of his readiness to resort to the kind of commissioned violence that Dryden suffered at a later date, in the Rose Alley incident. On this much-discussed topic, see Winn, *John Dryden*, pp. 593–4.

[38] See, for example, Vieth's and Walker's editions of the poems (pp. 60 and 270 respectively).

fleeting displeasure. The most original discussion of it that I have seen draws attention to one vital aspect, the political dimension;[39] but it possesses other significant features, too.

One interesting quality is the essential contradictions in the poem. It starts as a panegyric on Charles II and his realm, albeit with an indecorous reason for the latter's fame, and the third line voices the traditional loyal subject's desire, 'oh long may hee reigne and thrive'. The fourth line ('The easiest King and best bred man alive') anticipates, practically word for word, those evaluations – written in the 1680s – of Charles' character that contemporaries have handed down to us.[40] The comparison between the peace-loving English monarch, a man whose distaste for physical violence and bloodshed was evident from his accession, and Louis XIV, who repeatedly plunged his country into protracted wars, is also entirely in Charles' favour.[41] The following four lines relate his unaggressive personality to his amorousness and credits him with unusual attainments in that line. The couplet

> Nor are his high Desires above his Strength,
> His Sceptter and his Prick are of a Length

has made the poem known as 'the sceptre lampoon'. There is little reason to assume that Charles would have been offended by it.

The first third of the poem is hence unreservedly laudatory. It is fairly unproblematic from a textual point of view, too. As editors affirm, the textual problems posed by this poem are great.[42] In some texts, the couplet which Vieth and Walker place at the end ('I hate all Monarchs' etc.) follows line 13. Also, the 'Restlesse he roalles about' couplet is sometimes found after line 21 in the poem as printed by Vieth and Walker.

The actual satire begins in line 12:

[39] This is O'Neill's footnote (n.24) in the 'Sexuality, Deviance' article (19). Ronald Paulson developed a similar line of thought a few years later, contributing interesting ideas on the 'Kingship' aspect. See 'Rochester: The Body Politic and the Body Private', in Louis L. Martz and Aubrey Williams, eds., *The Author in His Work: Essays on a Problem in Criticism* (New Haven and London, 1978), a Festschrift to Maynard Mack, pp. 106–7.

[40] Two typical accounts, by James Welwood and John Evelyn, are easily accessible in vol. VIII of *English Historical Documents 1660–1714*, ed. Andrew Browning (London, 1953), pp. 899–901. The word 'ease' is foregrounded in both, and they lay strong stress on the King's great innate gifts and his congenital good nature. Burnet, in a statement which exactly parallels Rochester's, called him 'the best bred man in the world'. See Ashley, *Charles II*, p. 145.

[41] Louis XIV could indeed be accused of 'Starving his People'; the effects of certain taxes were drastic, and the poverty of the French peasant appalled more than one British visitor to France. See John Lough, *France Observed in the Seventeenth Century by British Travellers* (Boston, Melbourne, Henley and London, 1984), ch. 2.

[42] Cf., for example, pp. 185 and 270–1 in Walker's edition.

And she may sway the one, who plays with th'other
And make him little wiser than his Brother.
Restlesse he roalles about from Whore to Whore
A merry Monarch, scandalous and poor.
Poor Prince thy Prick like thy Buffoons at Court
Will governe thee because it makes thee sportt.
'Tis sure the swaucyest that e're did swive
The proudest peremtoriest Prick alive.
Though Safety, Law, Religion, Life lay on't,
'Twould breake through all to make its way to Cunt.

The charges levelled at the King centre on his neglect of his royal duties. The poem plainly states that his love of pleasure enables mistresses and such 'Buffoons at Court' as the author himself to usurp the Sovereign's prerogative (the words 'sway' and 'governe' are significant).[43] A jibe at the Duke of York is thrown in for good measure. All this was commonplace stuff in contemporary satires. The *Poems on Affairs of State*, edited by George deF. Lord, show how the eulogies of the early 1660s gradually gave way to more and more abusive personal attacks on the Stuart brothers. Their mistresses, especially of course the King's, were reviled in what Lord calls 'appalling, but sometimes justified, invective', and Charles' personal defects 'were magnified until he was depicted as another Sardanapalus' (p. xliii). In that sense, lines 12–21 of the sceptre lampoon only form a trickle in a great tidal wave of abuse.

In the copy-text chosen by both Vieth and Walker, line 15 runs, 'Grown Impotent and scandalously poor'. The editors' alteration to the present reading had two consequences: the decline in Charles' sexual prowess is confined to the conclusion of the poem, where it is rendered in less explicit terms; and what might be seen as a covert reference to the Stop of the Exchequer disappears. Charles' constant dependence on Parliament for funds was, from the King's point of view, a burden and an obstacle that might well be called scandalous. It had consequences that merited that designation among the population at large, too, notably the subsidies from Louis XIV. At no time, however, was Charles' poverty so closely allied to scandal as in the months and years after the infamous Stop. The Third Dutch War had to be brought to some sort of conclusion as soon as possible, and public confidence in the spending policies of the King and his ministers was low. At this point in

---

[43] Cf. Welwood and Evelyn (pp. 899–901 in the *English Historical Documents* volume): 'he would submit his judgment in greatest matters to others of much inferior parts'; 'his too easy nature resigned him to be managed by crafty men'.

time, regardless of where their political sympathies lay, most people who took an interest in the country's affairs would probably regard 'scandalously poor' as a correct description of the Sovereign's situation.

Adopting the now-familiar epithet 'A merry Monarch' instead of 'Grown Impotent' completely alters the impact of line 15. Still, leaving the copy-text version unchanged would have resulted in a head-on clash between that line and lines 18–21. Those two couplets form a counterpart to the account of the '*Dart* of love' in *The Imperfect Enjoyment*, equally priapic and equally reckless. It should be observed that line 20 explicitly accuses the King of ignoring his highest duties when under the influence of his lust: his obligation to protect the freedom and well-being of his subjects, to uphold the laws of the realm and to defend the faith.

As always, Rochester's political satire is interwoven with personal attack:

> To Carwell the most Deare of all his deares
> The best Reliefe of his declining yeares
> Offt hee bewayles his fortunes and her fate
> To love so well and be belov'd so late.
> For though in her he setles well his Tarse
> Yett his dull graceless Ballocks hang an arse.
> This you'd beleive had I butt Tyme to tell you
> The Paynes itt Cost the poor laborious Nelly
> Whilst shee imployes, hands, fingers, mouth, and thighs
> E're shee can raise the Member she enjoys –

The ruler whose satyriasis made him lose sight of his royal duties has suddenly been replaced by an ageing roué who taxes the strength and ingenuity of his mistresses. John O'Neill partly resolved the contradiction by pointing out that physical impotence should be read as an image of political impotence, and the entire poem presents the King as politically impotent.[44] Still, the personal aspect cannot be left out of account entirely. In addition to having surrendered his political sovereignty, the wielder of the peremptory 'Member' has to resign the sexual sovereignty he acquired as a result of that surrender. As for the two principal mistresses of his 'declining yeares', the 'fate' of the French-born Duchess is to endure protracted intercourse of the 'qu'il vienne, qu'il vienne' type, and Nell Gwyn has to apply all her arts even to reach the point of departure.

[44] 'Sexuality, Deviance', 19 n.24. See also Ronald Paulson, 'Rochester', pp. 106–7.

It has been claimed that Rochester, in righteous indignation, accuses Charles of 'wast[ing] his time and his kingdom in trivialities',[45] and that the poet 'relish[es] the incongruity of a symbol of human dignity and magnificence devoting himself to such undignified pursuits'.[46] Such views imply an element of detached moral judgement that I cannot discern in this poem. It seems to me that Rochester started out by writing a good-humoured squib on his King, including all the usual charges against him but attenuating them by references to his love of peace and his lack of personal vainglory. Both these characteristics, especially the latter, are qualities greatly valued by the poet whose most cutting satire is forever directed against human vanity. Also, the attribution of one of his own foremost personal traits, restlessness, to Charles implies sympathy (conscious or not) rather than rejection. For a young man with Rochester's rebellious disposition, such an impudent description of his Royal master could easily be undertaken simply for fun, no real malice intended. If the lampoon had stopped at line 21, I cannot believe that its author would have been dismissed from the King's presence.

But in the passage on Charles' waning potency – a subject on which the King was understandably sensitive in any case[47] –, impudence gives way to contempt. For Charles, the sneering condescension of a much younger man who had him to thank for everything, including plenty of erotic opportunities, must have been intolerable. The actual situation in which he came to see the poem (if we are to trust the traditional story, conveyed by K. H. D. Haley[48]) cannot have helped. If you expect to enjoy some nasty verses on other people and find yourself reading a satire on your own person instead, the surprise will not augment your inclination to be merciful. Like many essentially kindly people, Charles II disliked having his good nature taken advantage of.

Four matters remain to be discussed briefly in connexion with 'I'th'Isle of Britaine': the way in which the poem reflects on the relative merits of Charles II and Louis XIV; the Portsmouth–Nell–Charles triangle; the degree to which the accusation contained in lines 12–13 of the poem was true; and the relationship between Rochester and the King in a more general sense.

---

[45] Wilson, *Court Wits*, p. 128.   [46] Farley-Hills, *Rochester's Poetry*, p. 123.
[47] Cf. O'Neill, 'Sexuality, Deviance', 18. Rochester's lampoon must be one of the first to address the subject; it certainly antedates *Portsmouth's Looking-Glass*. According to J. H. Wilson, Charles became sterile as a result of gonorrhoea in the mid-1670s and suffered a marked decline in sexual vigour and appetite as the decade wore on. See *Nell Gwyn*, p. 231.
[48] In *William of Orange*, pp. 60–1. (The reference is supplied by Vieth and others.)

The first two can be fairly quickly disposed of. Louis XIV comes off extremely badly at the hands of English satirists. Many of them – Marvell, for instance – were made deeply uneasy by Charles' pro-French manoeuvres. Louis is regarded as a bloodthirsty tyrant and a thoroughly bad influence on his kinsman in England. Rochester had no reason to harbour much respect or admiration for 'the french Foole'; Louis had snubbed him, and indirectly Charles II, when refusing to see him after the Killigrew ear-boxing incident.[49] The appellation 'Hector' was one which many people would have thought appropriate for Rochester himself, but he was always keen to distance himself from it (cf. p. 98 above). Applying it to Louis must have been gratifying. Nor can it be said to have been undeserved. The ruthlessness with which Louis XIV ruled his Court must have seemed forbidding to the young Englishman used to an easy-going and tolerant monarch.

Even so, the two Kings are jointly condemned in the final couplet. It is an unkind cut which lends some support to Ronald Paulson's contention that kingship is the real issue of this poem and that Charles is found wanting, just like his French 'brother'. Whether this somewhat blustering and deliberately provocative conclusion to the sceptre lampoon warrants the designation 'savage republican verse' is doubtful, though.[50]

The comparison between 'Carwell', Louise de Kéroualle, Duchess of Portsmouth, and Nell Gwyn is not one that Rochester's friend Nell would have relished. Their rivalry was a bitter one, and Nell never missed an opportunity to suggest that she, the base-born whore, was the King's true favourite.[51] Conversely, Rochester's lampoon states that she had to rely on the tricks of her trade to a greater extent than did her rival.[52]

Rochester's *Dialogue* ('When to the King I bid good Morrow') addresses the 'triple-combat' theme, involving Nell Gwyn, Portsmouth and Hortense Mancini, Duchess of Mazarin. Waller, the old gentleman poet, wrote a poem with that title which gallantly refuses to accord a

---

[49] See Pinto, *Enthusiast in Wit*, pp. 71–2. Cf. also Rochester's two-line impromptu, 'Lorrain he Stole'. On the comparison between Charles II and Louis XIV in this satire, see also Howard Erskine-Hill, *The Augustan Idea in English Literature* (London, 1983), p. 225.

[50] In his essay on Rochester in vol. 1 of his *Collected Essays*, Christopher Hill calls him 'the courtier and friend of Charles II who wrote savage republican verse' (p. 298). (No other instance suggests itself to me.)

[51] See Fraser, *King Charles II*, p. 289 (in the 1988 paperback edition); Wilson, *Nell Gwyn*, pp. 182 and 198; and Fea, *Some Beauties*, pp. 79–80.

[52] Nell's skill in that respect was commended by other writers; see p. 420 in the *Poems on Affairs of State*, vol. 1.

final victory to any one of the ladies. Rochester's *bagatelle* is not gallant in any sense. It is perhaps significant that Mazarin is not given any lines to herself, quite apart from the language difficulty. The combat was less vital to her; she had other fish to fry and did not pose a lasting threat to the Portsmouth/Gwyn duo. The King's stanza is only remarkable for the relaxed domesticity of the scene,[53] which contrasts with the unambiguous situations in the previous eight lines. The concluding stanza leaves no doubt as to where the ordinary Englishman's sympathies lay:

> People – Now Heav'ns preserve our Faiths Defendor,
> From Paris Plotts, and Roman Cunt,
> From Mazarine, that new Pretendor,
> And from that Politic Gramount.

Was this man-in-the-street fear that the King's judgement and actions might be adversely affected by his Catholic mistresses and their hangers-on justified?

A large number of contemporary writers, including satirists and diarists, were sure that this was the case. It is difficult to indicate precisely to what extent Rochester shared the conviction; the pertinent lines in the sceptre lampoon may simply express a current notion. All modern historians agree that Charles II's mistresses exercised very little, if any, influence on matters of statecraft.[54]

The petty day-to-day business of taking courses and getting places was a different matter. Anyone interested in worldly advancement during the reign of Charles II was well advised to be in the good books of the reigning mistress (cf. p. 123 above). Of course, there was a limit to the powers of promotion enjoyed by these ladies. According to Sir Francis Fane, Louise de Kéroualle asked the King to make Arlington Lord Treasurer the morning after their pseudo-wedding, only to hear her new royal lover's cool reply, 'Madam, you should have asked me that yesterday.'[55] In any case, Rochester's distress when, in 1675, he found himself out of favour with Portsmouth was genuine. His anxiety to set matters right with her can be studied in pages 106–9 of the *Letters*. The spectacle of the rude libeller pleading with his friend to save his hide

---

[53] Lady Antonia Fraser stresses this feature of the King's relationship with Portsmouth; see pp. 313–14 and 411 in her biography. Rochester would have been well-informed, perhaps from the horses' mouths, about the monarch's favourite pastimes; the cosy comforts which Charles extols in the *Dialogue* are not those of a man ruled by irrepressible sexual desire.

[54] It is significant that J. R. Jones' *Charles II: Royal Politician* (London, 1987) merely contains a handful of passing references to Portsmouth and her associates and only one to Cleveland.

[55] The anecdote is retold by Wilson in *Court Satires*, pp. 276–7.

is not an altogether pleasant one. Although he commends himself for never having 'pinn[ed] the dependence of [his] fortune upon her solicitations to the King', he is desperately worried lest she speak badly of him to Charles; 'I do not know how to assure myself the D. will spare me to the King.'

Was Rochester's eagerness to prevent Portsmouth from complaining of him to Charles simply dictated by material concern? The King had bestowed certain privileges and functions on him, associated with much-needed emoluments. Rochester, who took pains to avoid living off the fortune his wife had brought him,[56] would have been in acute financial trouble if those privileges had been withdrawn. Still, it is hardly likely that the King would have set such a scheme in motion. Charles was not vindictive; if he had been, Rochester would surely not have been made Ranger and Keeper of Woodstock in 1675.[57]

Rochester certainly seems to have been afraid that Portsmouth's denigration of his person might rouse real rancour in the man who had previously been so lenient towards him. Whether or not he feared material disadvantage, the King's displeasure was clearly a possibility he could not bear to contemplate. It would exclude Rochester from Court life which, tiring and irksome as it often was, had been his habitat for over ten years. It would also cut him off from the one older man who had shown himself consistently committed to his interests. This may not have been a matter of indifference to him.

It has frequently been suggested that Charles acted as a kind of father-figure to Rochester,[58] and it is a fair assumption. The King's behaviour to the son of Henry Wilmot was certainly that of a paternal benefactor. But what of the young man's response? Jane Lane has supplied a sketch of his feelings:

Rochester had not been at Whitehall very long before he conceived a hatred for the King which lasted to the end of his short life. His hatred for Charles was personal, though in his poems he pretended it had its roots in his own patriotism. Both men were superbly witty; but whereas Rochester's wit was always malicious, Charles's was nearly always good-humoured, and therefore much more telling. Charles Stuart, whatever his faults, was a big person; John Wilmot was essentially little.[59]

---

[56] One of the very few traditional gentlemanly virtues that can be attributed to Rochester, it has often been emphasised by his admirers.   [57] See Pinto, *Enthusiast in Wit*, p. 147.
[58] See, for instance, p. 27 in Treglown's Introduction to Rochester's *Letters*.
[59] *Puritan Rake and Squire* (London, 1950; the author's name – one with a Restoration connexion – is a pseudonym for Elaine Dakers), p. 79. While I disagree with this description, and question others in Lane's account, her chapter on Rochester is a thought-provoking one. Vieth dismisses

Nobody who does not believe Rochester to be the author of *The History of Insipids*,[60] or who does not take the slightly schoolboyish 'I hate all Monarchs' couplet literally, can credit this account. The charges made against Charles in the canonical poems are merely the conventional ones, and even they are sometimes touched with half-admiration and tolerance.[61] It should also be remembered that several malicious passages in Rochester's satires are directed against people and phenomena that were particularly obnoxious to the King. This bespeaks some degree of loyalty, and I think it is a point of some importance.

On the other hand, Rochester's writings about Charles contain little in the way of filial respect and affection. He came to the Court in his late teens, at a time when Charles' restoration was still a cause of joy in the nation, and at that point he may well have looked up to the King as a kindly but awe-inspiring elder kinsman. However, Rochester's intellect was too sharp, and his powers of observation too well developed, to allow him to retain any starry-eyed illusions for very long. He was, it would seem, an idealistic youth when he left Balfour's tutelage. Young Rochester may have suffered keenly as a result of the disappointment few of us escape in early adulthood, that of watching a revered authority topple off its pedestal. This would account for some particularly ungracious touches in his libels on the King. 'Personal hatred', though, is something else.

Even so, there is truth in Lane's comparison between the two men, harsh as it is to Rochester. Charles, with all his faults, possessed human virtues on a scale Rochester could never aspire to. Magnanimity was one of them, as nobody had better reason to know than 'Your *WILMOT's* son'.[62]

THE MINOR LAMPOONS

To such a man, the Irish Cattle Bill must have been distasteful, and the King was certainly unenthusiastic about it. Rochester's lampoon beginning 'To longe the Wise Commons have been in debate' alludes

it in one line as having no scholarly apparatus, which is perfectly true; but it contains much independent thinking about Rochester in his time, and I have found it stimulating to read.

[60] Frank Ellis' ascription to Freke has been challenged (see p. 157 above), but whoever wrote this bitter satire, I am convinced Rochester had nothing to do with it. As Lord affirms, 'In style, tone, and substance, *The History of Insipids* is unlike any other work of Rochester's', which amounts to saying that it does not sound a bit like him – and it does not. See p. 243 in Lord's *Poems on Affairs of State*.

[61] A point made by Farley-Hills; see *Rochester's Poetry*, p. 123.

[62] The conclusion of what purports to be a juvenile poem by Rochester, *To His Sacred Majesty* ('Vertues triumphant Shrine! who do'st engage', p. 3 in Walker's edition).

to this prohibition while associating it with the great Parliamentary concerns of early 1673. In characteristic Rochester fashion, the poem then goes on to apply the political perspective to the sexual mores of the Restoration Court.

In the early months of 1673, Parliament and King were locked in one of their most serious conflicts during Charles' reign. On 14 February, Charles realised that the Commons would not accept the Declaration of Indulgence which he had vowed to 'stick to' nine days before.[63] On 6 March, he knew that – unless Louis XIV supplied extra money, enabling Charles to dissolve Parliament – he would have to withdraw it in exchange for the funds he so urgently needed.[64] This defeat was one of the bitterest in Charles' life (see p. 233 above).

Such were the 'Trifles of State' which the 'Wise Commons' were debating, instead of taking measures to ensure the venereal health of Englishmen:

> To longe the Wise Commons have been in debate
> About Money, and Conscience (those Trifles of State)
> Whilst dangerous Greyvances daily increase,
> And the Subject can't riott in Safety, and peace.
> Unlesse (as agaynst Irish Cattle before)
> You now make an Act, to forbid Irish whore.

The irony of 'Trifles', 'Wise', 'dangerous Greyvances' and 'riott in Safety, and peace' is obvious. (It might be noted that 'safety' and 'peace' are two central qualities that should attend on perfect love and are never seen to do so; cf. pp. 42, 100 and 106.) It recalls the acrid line 32 in *Upon Nothing*, 'And true or false the Subject of debate'. The suggestion that the House of Commons should have more urgent business to attend to than the national finances, the royal prerogative and the fateful issue of religious discord is of course grotesque. It becomes even more so when considered against the interests that are claimed to be of paramount importance.

Another stab at the Commons is delivered in the sly parenthesis of line 5. Six years earlier, after a good deal of stalling and dragging of feet, Parliament had passed a bill prohibiting the importation of Irish cattle (it followed a partial ban). Despite Ormonde's warnings as to the consequences for Ireland, and despite the King's reluctance, the Irish Cattle Act was finally passed by both Houses. It was supported by

---

[63] The speech of Charles II in support of his Declaration of Indulgence (5 February 1672/3) is reprinted in *English Historical Documents*, vol. VIII, p. 77.

[64] For a brief account of these events, see J. R. Jones, *Charles II*, pp. 103–4.

landowners in parts of England and Wales, and Buckingham was a prime mover. As some people had foreseen, it brought little actual benefit even to those who pressed for it, and the King's Irish revenue suffered as well. In conjunction with severe winters and cattle disease, it produced distress in Ireland. The Irish, however, soon learnt to adapt to the ban and would not have fared too badly, had not the Third Dutch War hampered their commerce with other nations.[65] By the time Rochester wrote the *Lampoone*, the consequences of this injudicious Parliamentary decision were apparent.

The *Lampoone* is not only aimed against Parliament; the immediate culprits are the new Irish 'livestock' – the implicit comparison is an insult in itself – who 'Invade us with Impudence, beauty, and pox'. Some Irish ladies are explicitly mentioned: the Alice Clanbrassil who was satirised by Dorset (then Buckhurst) as 'The Antiquated Coquette' and the 'Cootes' and '[Mrs] Fox' whom Etherege remembered with a degree of nostalgia some fifteen years later.[66] The remainder of the poem is made up of a lament that these irresistible and wily invaders are not 'more modest, more sound, or lesse fayre'. The conclusion is devoted to the unfairness of it all, the line 'Is it just, that with death cruell Love should conspire' having acquired dreadful renewed pertinence in our own time.

This poem is interesting because of its political dimension. It demonstrates the peculiar nature of Rochester's political satire: topical innuendo, easily lost on a reader unfamiliar with Restoration history, fused with personal malice, often on a sexual basis.

The plea for sexual 'soundness' recalls poems where distaste for unclean women induces self-disgust or results in the advocacy of intimate hygiene. The venomous lyric *On Mistress Willis* makes a point resembling that of the *Lampoone*, but in even more forthright terms:

> Against the Charms our *Ballox* have
> How weak all human skill is
> Since they can make a Man a slave
> To such a Bitch as *Willis*.

---

[65] A thorough account of the Bill's stumbling passage through Parliament is supplied by Ronald Hutton, *The Restoration*, pp. 251–6. On the consequences for Ireland as they appeared to a well-informed man when the *Lampoone* was written, see Sir William Temple's 'Essay upon the Advancement of Trade in Ireland', dated Dublin, 22 July 1673 (printed in the *Miscellanea*, 1680; see especially pp. 107–8 and 120–1). See also John O'Donovan, *The Economic History of Live Stock in Ireland* (Cork, 1940), pp. 46–7 and 52–3.

[66] See pp. 33–5 in Harris' edition of Dorset's poems and pp. 181–2 in *Letters of Sir George Etherege*, ed. Frederick Bracher (Berkeley, 1974).

Again, the male sex is regarded as a helpless collective victim of their own appetites in collusion with beastly women. The ensuing description of the notorious prostitute, libelled by many, is one of double corruption; her mind and her body are equally vile. The unattractiveness of her personality was indicated by the satirist who, in 1689, said that Willis had progressed from Mrs Moseley's 'stable' to

> a playhouse, where a goatish peer
> Feeling her c – t liked it, but never her.[67]

Shadwell, praising the virtues of cheap and above all 'wholsom' country lasses in a verse letter to Wycherley, commiserated with his friend on the latter's being compelled to make do with some '*Chloris*, or ... *Phillis*, / (Who's as Expensive as *Su Willis*)'.[68]

The ability to cure venereal disease was hence one that the Restoration Court held in very high esteem. Chief among those who practised the art was the King's physician Sir Alexander Frazier. According to Pepys (19 September 1664), Frazier was an expert at dealing with other unwanted effects of sexual activity as well. He helped the ladies of the Court to 'slip their calfes when there is occasion', said the diarist caustically. This service, in conjunction with his curative skills, gave Frazier such high status at Court that he could, still in Pepys' words, 'do what he please[d] with the King'.

In view of this expertise, it was surely not unnatural for the medical man and his wife[69] to supply their daughter[70] with some kind of protective device:

> Her Father gave her Dildoes six;
> Her Mother made 'um up a score:
> But she loves nought but living pricks
> And swears by God sheel frig no more.[71]

In Ken Robinson's view, the young woman uses the 'living pricks' as human dildoes. She actually continues the occupation she has forsworn, at least in an ironical sense. This may be reading too much into four

---

[67] See Wilson, *Court Satires*, pp. 294–5. For an unusually detailed analysis of Rochester's poem, see Robinson, 'The Art of Violence', pp. 106–7.

[68] Vol. v of Shadwell's *Works*, p. 228.

[69] As Dresser to the Queen, Lady Frazier was well versed in Court habits, too.

[70] Useful information on Cary Frazier is provided in a biographical note in Wilson's *Court Satires*, pp. 239–41, as well as in his *Court Wits*, pp. 117 and 215; Fea, *Some Beauties*, pp. 286–9; Harris' edition of Dorset's poems, pp. 26–7, 127 and 133; and Vieth, *Attribution*, pp. 235–7.

[71] In an extensive discussion of these four lines, Ken Robinson holds that this act of generosity is a 'subversion of normal parental attitudes' (see 'The Art of Violence', pp. 107–9). On the contrary, it seems to me to denote understandable parental solicitude under the circumstances.

undistinguished lines of extempore verse, from which we gather little more than her enthusiastic preference ('loves', 'swears') for the natural object. That preference was shared by Mrs Knight in *Signior Dildo*, where it appeared in a favourable light. Referring to human beings exclusively by means of their genitals is, after all, standard Court-satire practice.

The squib on Cary Frazier may not have been an all-out attack on her. She does discard artificial stimuli once she has been introduced to the real thing, and Rochester may have appreciated her taste in sexual matters on other grounds, too. She was wooed by Sir Carr Scroope; but having sampled his capacities, she rejected him, aiming for royal favour instead. With this ambition frustrated, she married Charles, Viscount Mordaunt, in or around 1679. Vieth believes Rochester's lines to have been written in 1677, at a point when Scroope was mourning his defeat. If so, they constitute salt in his enemy's wounds.[72] On the other hand, the Scroope connexion could of course have worked in the opposite direction; Rochester may have felt that the mere existence of such an association would taint the woman in question. The possibility of her having had a brief affair with his other *bête noire*, Mulgrave, supports this alternative view.

Lawrence Stone has painted a forbidding picture of the filth and disease that inhibited sexual pleasure in seventeenth- and eighteenth-century England.[73] A man with experience of Continental standards in hygiene, as Rochester had, might well be disgusted by their absence in his own country. His *Song* 'By all *Loves* soft, yet mighty *Pow'rs*' is quoted by Stone as the 'first, and frankest' complaint occasioned by this state of affairs. Its recommendations could not be more lucid or specific:

> Fair nasty *Nymph*, be clean and kind,
> And all my joys restore;
> By using Paper still behind,
> And Spunges for before.

In rejecting intercourse during menstruation, Rochester was not being unusually fastidious. Most contemporary dispensers of advice on sexual matters took a similar view. The use of paper for the suggested purpose was common in England, too. In the 'nasty and stinking'[74] Court of

---

[72] According to contemporary lampoons, the liaison with Scroope resulted in Cary needing her father's professional services. See Wilson, *Court Satires*, pp. 239–40.

[73] See his chapter on 'Upper-Class Attitudes and Behaviour' in the fifth part of *The Family, Sex and Marriage In England* 1500–1800 (London, 1977).

[74] The result, according to Evelyn's classic description, of the King's spaniels performing their natural functions everywhere (including having and feeding puppies in the King's own bed).

Charles II, though, a young man who had spent some of his formative years on the Continent, under the guardianship of a highly cultured physician, would have had reason to feel squeamish on occasion.

The reward held out for 'cleanly sinning' is a long-standing relationship:

> If thou wou'dst have me true, be wise,
>   And take to cleanly sinning;
> None but fresh *Lovers Pricks* can rise,
>   At *Phillis* in foul linnen.

The last two lines, however, imply that the adoption of hygienic measures is a condition not only of fidelity, but also of performance. Even in these unexceptional lines, we thus catch a glimpse of the spectre whose presence is felt in so many of Rochester's poems on sexual topics: that of failing potency. 'Fresh *Lovers Pricks*' may be deficient in good taste; but like Signior Dildo, they are happily invulnerable to the hazards and disappointments that attend on men whose minds and bodies are not separate entities. As several of the love lyrics show, as well as poems such as *The Imperfect Enjoyment* and the *Ramble*, Rochester's poetry repeatedly dwells on the plight of the latter. The superior vigour of Signior Dildo, and the ailing regal organ in the sceptre lampoon, bear witness to the proximity of the spectre even in those Court satires where personal business is, superficially at least, laid aside.

Rochester's court-and-social poems are irreconcilable with the traditional image of the poet as the ultimate Restoration rake. Fashionable society activities, Court amours and drunken revels are viewed with cynical distaste, sometimes even with physical revulsion. The impatience and restlessness that could be felt in the love poems have their counterparts in the Court satires, too. Inferior minds express themselves in vile talk, and the realm of the senses is profoundly disappointing; bodies are diseased or unclean, food and drink abysmal. At no level does human intercourse, of whatever kind, afford satisfaction. If true worth and substance reside anywhere in human existence, it is not in that sphere.

CRAFT AND ART

———◆◆◆◆———

I I

'An Allusion to Horace'

From the very first, reactions to Rochester's *An Allusion to Horace* have varied greatly. This is only to be expected with a work which was born of, and itself fomented, controversy. But the *Allusion* is more than a record of Restoration skirmishes in the literary arena.[1] When he wrote it, the poet cannot have known that it would be his last ambitious poem of any length. In that sense, regarding it as his artistic testament is anachronistic. Nevertheless, this is the role which its position in Rochester's *oeuvre* and the nature of its chief concern impose on it.

The nature of that concern indicates the sphere to which Rochester's 'Fantastick mind' turned in his final productive phase, around the year 1676:[2] the question of what distinguishes good writing from bad, and how the former is to be achieved. Coming from the pen that produced three satirical views of the human predicament and five love lyrics which were all unsurpassed in their time,[3] an exploration of these issues deserves an attentive and unprejudiced hearing. In the *Allusion*, for once, Rochester appears to me to be speaking *in propria persona* without any disguises or reservations; hence, the sometimes awkward term 'Rochester's speaker' is dispensed with throughout this chapter.

Attitudes to the *Allusion* among late-twentieth-century critics reflect the variety of opinion referred to above. Three thoughtful and largely commendatory appraisals of the poem appeared in the 1970s and early

---

[1] Picking one's way through the literary quarrels of the 1670s is as laborious as trying to impose logical order on the Wars of the Roses. Shifting allegiances, sometimes within a year, constantly undercut attempts to map out a straight and consistent course of development.

[2] The *Allusion* was dated to the winter of 1675–6 by John Harold Wilson in 'Rochester, Dryden and the Rose-Street Affair', *Review of English Studies* 15 (July 1939), 298–301. Subsequent scholars have accepted this dating.

[3] Not, I think, an exaggerated claim for the *Satyr*, *Upon Nothing*, *Artemiza to Chloe*, *The Fall*, *The Mistress*, *Love and Life*, the *Song of a Young Lady* and the *Song* beginning 'Absent from thee'.

1980s,[4] but it came in for undisguised hostility as well.[5] Some scholars
have been troubled by the feeling that there is something atypical, if not
fundamentally unconvincing, about the *Allusion*.[6] A comment made by
James Anderson Winn is revealing in this respect:

> ... the 'I' of his poem cannot be completely identified with the actual rakish
> Earl, since the literary judgments cast in its sprightly verse are essentially those
> of Horace. (*John Dryden*, p. 293)

Such remarks imply a reluctance to accept that 'the rakish Earl' cared
enough about the art of poetry to think seriously about it, and that such
hard thinking on his part could involve Horatian conceptions and
convictions. To most people, the name of Horace immediately suggests
suave good taste and decorous irony. It is easily forgotten that Horace
the satirist could be both pungent and outspoken – and that his imitator
Rochester was able to temper malice and indignation with humour.
More important, instinctive resistance to a joint contemplation of
Horace and Rochester as satirists and craftsmen is apt to block one's
awareness of what Rochester is in fact saying in the *Allusion*.

Another aspect of the *Allusion* which has induced unhappiness, or
censoriousness, in its readers is the element of seeming disloyalty to
protégés and friends. At various points in time, Rochester had promoted
the interests of Crowne, Settle and Otway, as well as of Dryden himself;
here all these men are sharply criticised. Even the attention bestowed on
Rochester's close companions – Etherege, Wycherley, Buckhurst/
Dorset – is not unreservedly complimentary.

To some critics, then, 'the Satyr keeps revealing itself through the
Horatian toga'.[7] By contrast, Jos. A. Johnson has insisted that the
Allusion

> is not merely the personal or malicious lampoon it is often assumed to be. It is
> an original poem, definitely based upon and patterned after Horace, following
> Horace when appropriate and deviating when not. It is a poem with a concern
> more universal than the venting of one man's spleen; it is a poetic statement of

---

[4] Howard D. Weinbrot, 'The "Allusion to Horace": Rochester's Imitative Mode', *Studies in Philology* 69.3 (July 1972), 348–68; Jos. A. Johnson, Jr, '"An Allusion to Horace": The Poetics of John Wilmot, Earl of Rochester', *The Durham University Journal* 66.1 (n.s. 35.1; December 1973), 52–9; Pat Rogers, '*An Allusion to Horace*', in Treglown, ed., *Spirit of Wit*, pp. 166–76. It might be added that the introductory pages of Weinbrot's article give detailed consideration to the significance of the word 'allusion'.

[5] Farley-Hills condemned it as 'the least interesting' of the major satires (*Rochester's Poetry*, p. 197).   [6] Cf. Griffin, *Satires Against Man*, p. 257.

[7] Farley-Hills' arresting, if somewhat complicated, metaphor; p. 203 in *Rochester's Poetry*.

a consistent artistic principle; it is a poem which warrants further critical study
for its artistic judgments, for whatever it may reveal of the Restoration, and for
its own merits.[8]

The ensuing discussion of the *Allusion to Horace* proceeds from a similar
conviction.

HORACE AND DRYDEN

If the *Allusion* is the work of a serious artist about standards in writing,
rather than one among many records of Restoration literary bickering,
four major issues must be considered: Why should Horace be used as a
vehicle? What factors led to Dryden's being chosen as the main butt of
the satire? What ideals in respect of commendable authorship does the
Allusion uphold? And, finally, with what justice could the poet
Rochester appear as a spokesman for those ideals? The first two
questions are addressed in the following pages; the other two are
deferred to the next two sections of this chapter.

For Rochester, the idea of designing a polemical piece about literary
matters as a contemporary English adaptation of Horace's tenth satire of
the first book must have been close at hand. Later ages have credited the
Allusion with blazing a trail in this respect;[9] but Rochester himself is not
likely to have regarded it as a great innovation. *Upon his Drinking a Bowl*
and *Timon* had shown him, and others, what he could do in the way of
transposing classical and French works to his own time and place. The
translations from Ovid and Lucretius testify to his skill in paraphrasing
Latin texts.[10] Horace's tenth satire was quoted and ransacked for a
variety of purposes throughout the late seventeenth century, in France

---

[8] P. 58 in Johnson's '"An Allusion"'. For some reason, this discussion has not received much
attention. To be sure, its proportions are modest, and several of the views put forward in it
overlap those of Weinbrot and Griffin, which were published at roughly the same time. But
it makes a very important point about the *Allusion*, and I think it has been unfairly neglected.

[9] The *Allusion* has often been held up as the first example of an 'imitation' of the Classics along
the same lines as Pope's *Imitations of Horace*; see, for instance, Vieth's headnote (p. 120 in his
edition). In a seminal article on 'The "Imitation" in English Poetry, Especially in Formal
Satire, before the Age of Pope', *The Review of English Studies* 25 (1949), 124–40, Harold F.
Brooks filled in the English background with regard to such adaptations, placing Rochester's
poem in a more general context (133–4). A recent article by P. E. Hewison reconsiders the
'imitation' issue; see 'Rochester, the "Imitation", and "An Allusion to Horace"', *The
Seventeenth Century* 2 (1987), 73–94.

[10] A careful analysis of Rochester's Ovidian elegy ('O Love! how cold, and slow to take my
part!') is provided by Harold Love in his essay 'The Art of Adaptation: Some Restoration
Treatments of Ovid', in Antony Coleman and Antony Hammond, eds., *Poetry and Drama
1570–1700: Essays in Honour of Harold F. Brooks* (London and New York, 1981), pp. 141–4.

as well as in England.[11] Boileau translated scraps from it in his satires (see, for example, line 28 in the seventh satire); and of course Dryden repeatedly refers to it in his *Defence of the Epilogue* [*to the Second Part of* '*The Conquest of Granada*'] ; *or, An Essay on the Dramatic Poetry of the Last Age.*

Dryden's setting up Horace as an arbiter of good writing, quoting the tenth satire in the process, made that poem a particularly suitable weapon for an unveiling of Dryden's own defects.[12] But what about the reasons for attacking Dryden in the first place? Who was Dryden, what was he in 1675?

The first thing to realise about Dryden's standing as a poet in the mid-1670s is that he was the writer of panegyrics (*Astraea Redux*, for instance); *Annus Mirabilis*; various occasional verses, among them prologues and epilogues to plays, his own and those of others; and some comedies and heroic plays. The works which were to make him the first name in late-seventeenth-century English literature were as yet unwritten, and Rochester did not live to see them.

What Dryden had produced up to 1675, however, had won him the laureateship (fairly recently created), influential acquaintances, and widespread admiration, at Court and elsewhere. He was a man of some consequence (not least due to his Howard marriage) and undeniable talent. His social status was somewhere between the commoner hacks and the Court Wits, an uncomfortable position.[13] To Rochester, then, Dryden was not 'one of us' while still being important and gifted enough to be reckoned with.

Although the attack on Dryden in the *Allusion* is primarily directed against the poet and not against the man, hints of personal rancour are felt in lines 71–6 and 84–6. Having praised Sedley's mastery of the superficially innocent but inherently seductive love poem, Rochester voices his disgust with Dryden's clumsiness in erotic contexts:

---

[11] In respect of Horace's influence on French seventeenth-century satire, including the works of Régnier, Théophile de Viau and Boileau, see Jean Marmier, *Horace en France, au dix-septième siècle* (Paris, 1962).

[12] See Farley-Hills, *Rochester's Poetry*, p. 202, and Rogers, '*An Allusion*', p. 170.

[13] Winn's *John Dryden* demonstrates it in admirable detail; see, for example, pp. 225–7, 246–7 and 250–4. I am not convinced, though, that Rochester's post-1674 aggressiveness towards Dryden had anything much to do with the 'condescending attitude of an aristocrat who liked to believe that the making of poetry required noble birth' (p. 250). Rochester mentions several commoners among the men of letters whose judgement he bows to, including Shadwell and Samuel Butler, whose antecedents were humbler than those of other commoner writers admired by Rochester (Wycherley, for instance).

> Dryden, in vaine, try'd this nice way of Witt,
> For he, to be a tearing Blade thought fit,
> But when he wou'd be sharp, he still was blunt,
> To friske his frollique fancy, hed cry Cunt;
> Wou'd give the Ladyes, a dry Bawdy bob,
> And thus he got the name of Poet Squab:

The wording of the reproach suggests that it was directed against the maladroit, superannuated (at forty-odd) would-be Court Wit rather than against the poet. His monosyllabic exclamation comes across as a pathetic attempt to adopt the jargon of 'a tearing Blade'. The expression 'a dry Bawdy bob' surely does not refer to physical inadequacy but to miscarried attempts at *risqué* repartee.[14] While social *faux pas* are things easily overlooked in people one is genuinely fond of, they tend to become exceedingly irritating in those whom one instinctively dislikes. Lines 71–6 in the *Allusion* testify, tellingly, to Rochester's readiness to be annoyed by Dryden's awkwardness in polite society.

Lines 84–6 of the *Allusion* reveal another reason for Rochester's animus against Dryden:

> To his owne the while
> Allowing all the justnesse that his Pride,
> Soe Arrogantly, had to these denyd?

As always, pride rouses Rochester's wrath. Dryden's attitude to the masters of a past age is an offence of a kind that Horace's Lucilius is innocent of – Lucilius, whose strictures on Accius and Ennius were not accompanied by self-aggrandisement.[15] According to Rochester, Dryden pretends to greater distinction than his illustrious predecessors.[16] The penalty for such unforgiveable presumptuousness is delivered in lines 87–92 of the *Allusion*, which do not leave Dryden with a shred of comfort:

> And may not I, have leave Impartially
> To search, and Censure, Drydens workes, and try,

---

14 Vieth pointed out that 'a "dry-bob" is coition without emission' (p. 124 in his edition). Pat Rogers, acknowledging this gloss, suggested that the expression had wider implications (see pp. 172–3 in '*An Allusion*'). On Dryden's habit of intensifying sexual dimensions in his translations, see Hagstrum, *Sex and Sensibility*, pp. 52–3.

15 'Quum de se loquitur, non ut majore reprensis'; see lines 53–61 in Horace's tenth satire, book I. Horatian quotations are from the Hackiana edition of Q. *Horatius Flaccus*, with notes by J. Bond and C. Schrevelius (Lyons and Rotterdam, 1670), pp. 481–2.

16 Weinbrot's article skilfully demonstrates how Rochester's treatment of Dryden contrasts with Horace's attitude to Lucilius. This is one of the examples adduced by Weinbrot; see 'The "Allusion"', 361.

If those grosse faults, his Choyce Pen does Commit
Proceed from want of Judgment, or of Witt.
Or if his lumpish fancy does refuse,
Spirit, and grace to his loose slatterne Muse?

Dryden's writings on the nature of poetry have a great deal to do with Rochester's attack. Merely by setting himself up as an authority, he made himself vulnerable to criticism. But is Rochester fair when he accuses Dryden of believing himself superior to Shakespeare, Jonson, Beaumont and Fletcher?

Of Dramatic Poesy, An Essay, the *Epilogue to the Second Part of 'The Conquest of Granada'* and the *Defence of the Epilogue* are all studded with references to Jonson, Fletcher and Shakespeare.[17] A typical, if extensive, excerpt from the *Defence* might be quoted by way of illustration:

Shakespeare, who many times has written better than any poet, in any language, is yet so far from writing wit always, or expressing that wit according to the dignity of the subject, that he writes, in many places, below the dullest writer of ours, or any precedent age. Never did any author precipitate himself from such height of thought to so low expressions, as he often does. He is the very Janus of poets; he wears almost everywhere two faces; and you have scarce begun to admire the one, ere you despise the other. Neither is the luxuriance of Fletcher ... a less fault than the carelessness of Shakespeare. He does not well always; and when he does, he is a true Englishman; he knows not when to give over. If he wakes in one scene, he commonly slumbers in another; and, if he pleases you in the first three acts, he is frequently so tired with his labour, that he goes heavily in the fourth, and sinks under his burden in the fifth.

For Ben Johnson, the most judicious of poets, he always writ properly, and as the character required; and I will not contest farther with my friends who call that wit: it being very certain, that even folly itself, well represented, is wit in a larger signification; and that there is fancy, as well as judgment, in it, though not so much or noble: because all poetry being imitation, that of folly is a lower exercise of fancy, though perhaps as difficult as the other; for 'tis a kind of looking downward in the poet, and representing that part of mankind which is below him.

In these low characters of vice and folly, lay the excellency of that inimitable writer; who, when at any time he aimed at wit in the stricter sense, that is, sharpness of conceit, was forced either to borrow from the Ancients ... or, when he trusted himself alone, often fell into meanness of expression. Nay, he was not free from the lowest and most grovelling kind of wit ...

(Ker's edition, pp. 172–3)

[17] See, for instance, pp. 99, 160, 164–5, 167, 172 and 176–7 in W. P. Ker's edition of the *Essays of John Dryden*, vol. I (New York, reprinted 1961).

Although Dryden was doubtless sincere when proclaiming his 'love' and 'admiration' of Shakespeare and Jonson, he is a very Janus of critics when he discusses them. While he certainly does not claim to surpass them in genius, he does argue that the literary language of his own age is free from the 'faults' and 'incorrectness' he laments in theirs. This corresponds to what Rochester is saying in the *Allusion*, where he uses the word 'Stile' to denote the faculty in regard to which Dryden claims to be better than Shakespeare. ('Stile' seems to me a reasonably accurate term for those matters to which Dryden refers in speaking of the 'impropriety of language' evinced by Shakespeare and Fletcher.)

Rochester may to some degree have read Dryden's theoretical works the way the Devil reads the Bible; but he certainly seems to have read them. The *Allusion* is remarkable not only for the way in which Rochester uses Horace to 'get at' Dryden: he makes Dryden's own writings serve the same purpose.

When Rochester grants that Dryden's plays are 'Embroider'd' with 'Witt' and 'Learning', he refers to two characteristics valued by his victim.[18] The acknowledgement of Dryden's popularity is patently ironic, too. Unlike the austere arbiter who is content to please the few who know, the Laureate had stated that his 'chief endeavours [were] to delight the age' in which he lived.[19] More wicked than these compliments on having achieved less than exalted aims are Rochester's hints that Dryden did not adhere to his own precepts. The importance of 'refining' one's wit, of 'circumscribing' an over-fruitful fancy, and of choosing rhymes calculated to enhance the second line of a couplet was articulated by Dryden himself;[20] Rochester implicitly accuses him of failing all these worthy ideals.

There are other indications that the *Allusion* was deliberately charged with subtle anti-Dryden barbs. When Shadwell is praised for his 'bold Stroakes', 'Shewing great Mastery with little care', the choice of words is reminiscent of Dryden's *Prologue to Tyrannick Love*:

[18] See, for instance, p. 175, line 29 in Ker's edition (*The Defence of the Epilogue*). See also J. A. Johnson, '"An Allusion"', 55.

[19] See *A Defence of an Essay of Dramatic Poesy*, p. 116 in Ker's edition of Dryden's essays. It is interesting to compare the *Allusion* with Martin Clifford's abusive letters to Dryden, written in May–July, 1672; they are found in the *Clarendon State Papers*, vol. 87 in the Bodleian Library, and were printed in 1687 as *Notes upon Mr. Dryden's Poems in Four Letters*. Clifford's strictures resemble Rochester's in several respects; he accuses Dryden of theft, plagiarism, greed, indifference to the opinions of qualified judges, boring his readers and 'scattering ... Nonsense'. According to Clifford, Dryden's writings 'are like a Jack of all Trades Shop, they have variety, but nothing of value' (29 May 1672).

[20] In, for example, *An Essay of Dramatic Poesy* (pp. 95–6 and 105–6 in Ker's edition) and the *Defence of the Epilogue* (pp. 170–2).

Poets, like Lovers, should be bold and dare,
They spoil their business with an over-care.

Dryden will not have relished hearing these qualities attributed, by way of a compliment, to a rival. The fact that he was moving away from the idea that 'rashness is a better fault than fear' at this time[21] will not have helped at all. Rochester's line on Flatman's defects, 'And rides a Jaded Muse, whipt with loose Raines', may be read as an ironic reference to a similar equestrian feat in Dryden's *Prologue* (the writer of *Tyrannick Love*, says Dryden of himself, has 'loos'd the Reins, and bid his Muse run mad').

Another piece of critical prose in which Dryden was involved, this time as co-author, might be related to Rochester's *Allusion*. With Shadwell and Crowne, Dryden attacked Elkanah Settle in *Notes and Observations on the Empress of Morocco, Or, some few Errata's to be Printed instead of the Sculptures with the Second Edition of that Play*. The pamphlet, published in 1674, maintains that those who appreciated Settle's successful play were deficient in judgement. 'Fools' and 'Women' are mentioned as typically indiscriminate theatre-goers. Among 'Judicious Men' with Whitehall connexions, the play was disliked, claims Dryden in the Preface. Unable to deny the popular success of *The Empress of Morocco*, he ascribes it to stage tricks.[22]

In the *Allusion*, too, 'Fooles, and Women' represent poor judgement, whereas 'the shrew'd Judges in the Drawing-Roome' parallel Dryden's 'Judicious Men'. Again, Rochester has turned Dryden's own words against the kind of poor-quality writing which, he implies, Dryden himself represents.

In the mid-1670s, a reorientation in Dryden's artistic ideas took place.[23] He was relinquishing the idea that the poet's unconfined fancy should be allowed 'full scope and swing', and the pleasures of popularity were obviously becoming less alluring to him. The *Epilogue* to *Aureng-Zebe*, which was produced at the very time when Rochester is believed to have written the *Allusion*, argues, like that poem, that the appreciation of the discerning few is better than the applause of the mob:

---

21 Winn (*John Dryden*, p. 256) points out that Dryden saw – and criticised – his own youthful extravagance in Settle, who had expressed a view of inspiration akin to the one presented in the *Tyrannick Love* prologue.

22 The controversy was described by Frank C. Brown in *Elkanah Settle: His Life and Works* (Chicago, 1910). The whole subject can be studied in detail in Anne T. Doyle's recent *Elkanah Settle's The Empress of Morocco and the controversy surrounding it* (New York, 1987).

23 Winn discusses it with customary thoroughness in his chapter 'Another Taste of Wit', *John Dryden*, pp. 243–84.

Who would excel, when few can make a Test
Betwixt indiff'rent Writing and the best?
For Favours cheap and common, who wou'd strive,
Which, like abandoned Prostitutes, you give?
Yet scatter'd here and there, I some behold,
Who can discern the Tinsel from the Gold:
To these he writes ... [24]

When Settle replied to the censorious *Notes* written by Dryden,
Shadwell and Crowne, he dismissed the latter two as not being worthy
of his efforts. To Settle, they were not 'so fair marks as the First', that
is, Dryden. Rochester, too, clearly viewed Dryden as a target well
worth exercising his powers on. More than one Rochester scholar has
argued that the complimentary lines on Dryden in the *Allusion* are a
mere gesture without much significance:

> But to be just, twill to his praise be found,
> His Excellencies, more than faults abound.
> Nor dare I from his Sacred Temples teare,
> That Lawrell, which he best deserves to weare.

This passage translates lines 48–9 in Horace's tenth satire, 'neque ego illi
detrahere ausim / Haerentem capiti multa cum laude coronam'. In view
of the scathing all-round condemnation of Dryden articulated in the
Allusion, it does look slightly incongruous.

Still, there is evidence that Rochester thought highly of Dryden's
literary talents in the early 1670s. The latter's uneasy letter to the man he
still regarded as a benefactor when it was written, in 1673, was
obviously a reply to a communication of Rochester's. That communication was, in Dryden's words, 'the most handsom Compliment,
couched in the best language I have read' (Rochester's *Letters*, p. 86).
Rochester had clearly praised Dryden in emphatic terms. He would
have had nothing of importance to gain from showering flattery on the
older man, quite apart from the fact that he hated insincere adulation.
Hence, the appreciation he had apparently conveyed to Dryden must
have been genuine.

Less than three years later, this highly commended author provides
the focus of a satire on poor verse. More than that, in a letter to Savile
(placed in the spring of 1676 by Treglown) Rochester refers to Dryden
in terms that Dr Johnson was to apply to women preachers:

---

[24] P. 226 in Sargeaunt's edition of Dryden's poems.

You write me word that I'm out of favour with a certain poet whom I have ever admired for the disproportion of him and his attributes. He is a rarity which I cannot but be fond of, as one would be of a hog that could fiddle, or a singing owl. (*Letters*, pp. 119–20)

What caused this marked shift in Rochester's attitude to Dryden? The usual explanation is that Dryden had, as it were, joined the camp of Rochester's enemy Mulgrave around 1674, a move which is likely to have incensed his former patron.[25] In view of Rochester's disgust with Mulgrave, this circumstance seems relevant; but one may well wonder whether it is the whole truth. After all, the *Allusion* is an attack on Dryden's poetry rather than on his person, though personal antipathy is strongly felt in it. If Rochester thought Dryden wrote well up to 1673, would a mere transfer of allegiance account for the harsh criticism of Dryden's faults as a writer in the *Allusion*? Had anything been added to the Laureate's 'Volumes' between early 1673 and late 1675 that could account for this display of professional dissatisfaction on the part of another poet?

Two serious checks to Dryden's career roughly coincide with this time. The first was the failure of his play *The Assignation, or Love in a Nunnery*, dedicated to Sedley and published in 1673 (it had been acted in 1672). Dryden's literary rivals gloated over his disappointment, and it weakened his standing to some extent. Another blow was to follow: the ambitious transformation of *Paradise Lost* into a rhymed operatic play, *The State of Innocence and the Fall of Man*, was not staged. It was not printed until after Rochester's *Allusion* was written, but apparently hundreds of copies circulated before that. *The State of Innocence* seems to have been composed in some haste, and it does not belong to Dryden's most distinguished verse. I think it is quite possible that Rochester saw this work and disliked it. For one thing, the kind of piety that is articulated in *The State of Innocence* will hardly have recommended it to the author of that bitter lyric *The Fall*. The coyness with which prelapsarian sexual exploration is rendered is another aspect he is unlikely to have been impressed by.

Dryden's letter to Rochester also contained his newly written prologue and epilogue to a performance of Jonson's *The Silent Woman* in Oxford. Jeremy Treglown (*Letters*, p. 90n.) suggests that a reference in the prologue to 'haughty Dunces', who 'build their Poems the *Lucretian* way', were lines Dryden was 'nervous about'. He certainly

---

[25] See, for instance, p. 96 in Pinto's *Enthusiast in Wit*. It is generally agreed that lines 3–4 are an oblique reference to Mulgrave.

might have been, especially as his own letter calls Rochester 'that Rerum Natura of your own Lucretius'. No offence intended, surely – but the two very different contexts in which Lucretius is invoked form an instance of Dryden's lack of tact.

Another reason why Rochester may not have approved of Dryden's 'grosse flattery [of] the learned'[26] is that he himself held academic dignitaries in very low esteem (cf. pp. 158 and 211 above). Seeing them exalted in much the same terms that Dryden had employed in praising Rochester himself cannot have been altogether pleasant.

All these things may have contributed to Rochester's change of heart with regard to Dryden. The sly reference to *The Indian Emperour* in *Timon* could be taken as an indication that such a shift was taking place in 1674.[27] Dryden's reaction to Rochester's criticism, in the preface to *All for Love*, shows that he took his former patron's strictures hard. He had reason to do so: he knew that they were, at least in part, just; and he had spent the last few years gradually improving his writing along much the same lines as the ones Rochester advocates. It takes a saintlier character than Dryden's not to find justified criticism more painful than unfounded accusations.

Rochester had condemned him, drawing on Dryden's own idiom; in 1678, Dryden countered by weaving an unmistakable allusion to Rochester's *Satyr* into his reply:

We who write, if we want the talent, yet have the excuse that we do it for a poor subsistence; but what can be urged in their defence, who, not having the vocation of poverty to scribble, out of mere wantonness take pains to make themselves ridiculous?[28]

VIRTUES AND VICES

Two questions which directly involve Horace and Dryden were not addressed in the section primarily devoted to these two poets: first, to what extent does Rochester's outline of good versus bad writing rely on Horace? and second, what is basically wrong with Dryden's verse?

[26] Dryden's own words, and no exaggeration; p. 91 in the *Letters*.
[27] See p. 280 above. It must be borne in mind, though, that the *Timon* quotations are fairly harmless jests compared with the uncompromising censure of Dryden in the *Allusion*.
[28] Paul Hammond has drawn attention to this passage in Dryden's preface to *All for Love*. See 'Two Echoes of Rochester's *A Satire against Reason and Mankind* in Dryden', *Notes and Queries* n.s. 35.2 (vol. 223 of the continuous series; June 1988), 171. The quoted passage is found on p. 196 in Ker's edition of Dryden's *Essays*.

Both these issues are related to the question of what standards are advocated by the *Allusion* and hence best investigated from that point of view.

Four ideals are common to Horace's and Rochester's poems: restraint, concentration and economy of expression; stylistic variation, but without wearisome verbiage; pointed humour rather than virulent invective as a vehicle for satire; and indifference to popular acclaim, combined with a desire to satisfy a few men of impeccable taste. A minor virtue is grudgingly conceded by both poets: managing to please one's audience is an ability worthy of some, albeit limited, recognition.

What Horace and Rochester have against Lucilius and Dryden is that they place(d) quantity before quality. This is an accusation made against Lucilius in Horace's fourth satire of the first book as well as in the tenth. The prolific poet does not blot enough; rough, halting verse is the outcome. On one essential point, though, Rochester diverges from his Latin original: where Horace restricts his criticism to formal matters, Rochester is concerned with the lack of *substance* in Dryden's verse. Dryden's 'Sense', the 'substance, purport, or intention'[29] of what he says, is defective.

This vital difference between Horace and Rochester is often overlooked. Farley-Hills, for instance, repeatedly states that what Rochester objects to is Dryden's 'coarseness';[30] but that is primarily a Lucilian fault. What mars Dryden's works is 'looseness': his 'Volumes' are the products of a 'loose slatterne Muse'. His printed works are unconnected and rambling, and as an artist he is marked by inaccurate or careless thought or language.[31] Looseness signifies the antithesis of circumscribing (line 20). While Horace's Lucilius comes across as something of a rough diamond, his seventeenth-century counterpart Dryden is accused of not having a palpable core at all, let alone a hard one. His attainments are all superficial, more art with less matter. The wit and learning that made his plays popular are mere ornaments,[32] 'Embroider'd' on to a flimsy if voluminous fabric. The lack of solid substance in his works is indicated by the expression '[stuff] up' in line 9: the 'heavy Masse' is inert and meaningless. With such a radical indictment, little consolation is to be derived from the reassurance that one's 'Excellencies, more than faults abound' (line 78). If one's chief

---

[29] *OED* 23; 25 and 27 are relevant, too. Accusations of lack of 'sense' are very frequent in Restoration literary criticism.   [30] See *Rochester's Poetry*, pp. 200–3.

[31] See *OED* definitions 1j and 6a under *loose*. The dedicatory epistle of Dryden's *The Spanish Friar* is quoted as an instance of 1j; 'I ... am as much asham'd to put a loose indigested Play upon the Publick.'   [32] A point also made by Weinbrot; see 'The "Allusion"', 358.

defect is having nothing substantial to say, mere surface accomplishments are insufficient compensation. They are all Rochester leaves
Dryden with.

In the course of his deft analysis, Weinbrot shows how Rochester is
'truly anti-Drydenian' whereas Horace was 'truly pro-Lucilian' ('The
"Allusion"', 362).[33] I think it might be added that the *Allusion*
implicitly and ironically aligns Dryden not only with Lucilius, but also
with Horace himself. What Dryden attacks in his forebears Shakespeare,
Jonson and Fletcher is not a lack of 'gravitas' (Lucilius' charge against
Ennius; see line 54 in the Horatian original), but the unfavourable effects
of their age on their writings. Had they been contemporaries, they
would have been more 'correct';[34] they would have benefited from that
'*improvement of our Wit, Language, and Conversation*' which had,
according to Dryden, taken place since their time.[35] Horace's attitude to
Lucilius is similar: had he lived in Horace's own day, he would have
been more painstaking and his poetic style less harsh.[36] In other words,
Horace's view of Lucilius resembles Dryden's view of Shakespeare,
Jonson and Fletcher far more than it does Rochester's of Dryden.
Irrespective of whether this is the result of a deliberate design on
Rochester's part, regarding Dryden as a 'Horace' to Shakespeare and
Jonson's 'Lucilius' provides an additional satiric dimension. Its edge is
directed against that presumptuousness of Dryden's which disgusted
Rochester so intensely.

Still, Dryden is not the sole victim of the *Allusion*. Several other
Restoration writers are mentioned, some maligned and others praised.[37]
An investigation of the virtues and vices presented in the poem calls for
a certain amount of stock-taking on the contemporary literary scene.

To begin with a review of the minor victims, their faults are various:
John Crowne is boring; Elkanah Settle and Thomas Otway are inept in
their attempts to win popularity;[38] Thomas Flatman is a poor imitator

[33] See also Hewison, 'Rochester', 83.

[34] Dryden frequently uses this term in his criticism of his predecessors; cf. line 82 in the *Allusion*.
'Lewd' in line 83 does not, of course, mean 'lascivious' but 'ignorant, unskilful' (*OED* 4), and
Dryden repeatedly accused his predecessors of being defective in this sense.

[35] See the *Defence of the Epilogue*, p. 164 in Ker's edition.

[36] Cf. Horace's fourth satire in book I, line 8, as well as lines 67–71 in the tenth.

[37] An intriguing feature of the *Allusion*, noted by previous critics (see Griffin, *Satires Against Man*,
pp. 247–9, and Farley-Hills, *Rochester's Poetry*, pp. 202–3), is that so little of Rochester's praise
is unqualified; see the discussions of Etherege, Wycherley, Shadwell, Waller and Buckhurst/
Dorset below.

[38] The epithet 'puzzling' in line 19 seems to me to correspond to *OED* 2 under *puzzling*,
'laboriously trying to puzzle something out', although the first instance is from 1691, Roger
L'Estrange's sentence 'The servant ... is a Puzzling Fool.'

who lacks verve and terseness; Nathaniel Lee represents manly heroes as raving weaklings governed by unworthy passions, making them and himself ridiculous; Roger Boyle, Earl of Orrery, and John Caryll are mere 'scribling Authors', incompetent writers of indifferent plays.[39]

For all the variety of their shortcomings, none of which is paralleled by an instance in Horace's tenth satire, those defects have a common denominator. It is the same as the basic charge against Dryden, also independent of Horace: a lack of true substance. All is 'noise and Colour', like the fatuous compliments of the *Ramble* fops, the show of art without the power.

Some details may be mentioned in support of this view. 'Crownes tedious Scenes' is probably a reference to the masque *Calisto*, acted at Court in 1675 with an amateur cast, the Princesses Mary and Anne playing leading parts. The production was tremendously lavish and the libretto of 'prodigious length'.[40] John Evelyn referred to a performance of *Calisto* as being 'all ... pomp and serious impertinence'.[41] According to him, too, the fine ladies who appeared in it spent their time between entrances 'railing with the Gallants' in the 'tireing roome'. Such greenroom behaviour does not suggest that Crowne's text was held in high esteem by the actors or by members of the courtly audience.

Crowne is, of course, also mentioned in *Timon*, where a special characteristic of his is outlined in lines 135–40. Latter-day drama specialists have observed that Crowne's plays supply an occasional hint of that sentimentalism which was to become such a dominant feature in the English theatre of the eighteenth century.[42] Rochester must have been one of the first critical intelligences to have noted this novel trait. He does not appear to have thought highly of it, considering that he placed the observation in the mouth of the foolish hector Kickum.

---

[39] Line 96 refers to their plays. Orrery's *Mustapha* was revived in 1675, and according to a popular Rochester legend, he instructed Elizabeth Barry in the part of Isabella. See John Harold Wilson, *All the King's Ladies: Actresses of the Restoration* (Chicago, 1958), pp. 51–2. Caryll's *The English Princess* had probably been revived in the early 1670s; it was printed in a new edition in 1673. See William Van Lennep, ed., and Emmett L. Avery and Arthur H. Scouten, introd., *The London Stage 1660–1800*, part 1 (Carbondale, 1963–4), p. 199.

[40] The designation of Eleanore Boswell, *The Restoration Court Stage (1660–1702): With a Particular Account of the Production of* Calisto (Cambridge, Mass., 1932), p. 188. I have found no evidence to support the traditional notion that Rochester was behind Crowne's being commissioned to write the masque, so as to put Dryden's nose out of joint.

[41] Evelyn's comments can be studied *in extenso* in *The Life of Mrs. Godolphin* by John Evelyn of Wootton Esq., ed. Samuel Lord Bishop of Oxford (London, 1847), pp. 97–8.

[42] See, for example, Allardyce Nicoll, *A History of English Drama 1660–1900*, vol. I, *Restoration Drama 1660–1700* (Cambridge, 1923; I have used the fourth edition of 1955, where the relevant remarks are found on p. 270).

The *Allusion* maintains that Settle and Otway were unsuccessful in their attempts to entertain both 'the Rabble and the Court'. This is undoubtedly true of the latter, whose first play *Alcibiades* was not a major success.[43] In respect of Settle, though, the allegation seems odd. By any standards, *The Empress of Morocco* appears to have been very popular indeed, among the general public as well as at Court.[44] Dryden, of course, claimed that the seasoned judges of Whitehall looked down on it; but the play was twice acted at Court, which implies that it had admirers there. Perhaps the *éclat* of the *Empress* had waned somewhat in late 1675, at which time Settle's standing was not what it had been.[45] In any case, Rochester's *Allusion* places both Otway and Settle among those who attempt to amuse the multitude, an ambition which the poet regards with scorn.

The reference to Settle in *Timon* was not a flattering one either. There, truculent Huffe was enthusiastic about the turgid rhetoric of the *Empress*; Rochester burlesqued it when turning 'Their lofty Bulks the foaming Billows bear' into the absurdly alliterative '*Whose broad-built-bulks, the boyst'rous Billows, bear*'. In this masterly one-line parody, he showed what he thought of Settle's high-flown idiom.

Flatman has no 'Sense' either; he imitates Cowley and does it badly. 'Loose Raines' applies that significant term of censure, 'loose', to Flatman's Pindarics. As for Lee, the adjective 'Fustian' says it all: his style in *Sophonisba* is 'unnaturally pompous' and 'ridiculously tumid' (Dr Johnson). Both these men lack spirit and grace, and neither articulates anything of importance.

Nine men of letters are openly criticised in the *Allusion* – Dryden, Crowne, Settle, Otway, Flatman, Lee, Orrery, Caryll and Scroope.[46] The writers who receive praise from Rochester's pen are nine, too – Shadwell, Wycherley, Waller, Buckhurst, Sedley, Shepherd, Godolphin, Butler and Buckingham. One name hovers midway between these two categories, whose respective number equals that of the Muses: Etherege. Once the men whose work is regarded with favour have been reviewed, it will be time to return to him.

When Rochester states that Shadwell and Wycherley are the only really commendable writers of comedy, he excludes writers from both

[43] See Roswell Gray Ham, *Otway and Lee: Biography from a Baroque Age* (New Haven, 1931), pp. 42–5 and 86.   [44] See Nicoll, *Restoration Drama*, p. 117.

[45] See Brown, *Elkanah Settle*, pp. 15–18. One reason why Rochester may have regarded Settle with disfavour is that he seems to have suffered from a swollen head; Arthur Franklin White calls Settle 'vainglorious' in his study *John Crowne: His Life and Dramatic Works* (Cleveland, 1922), p. 34.   [46] The lines on Scroope are mentioned in the following chapter, p. 352.

categories: Dryden, Crowne, Orrery and Caryll[47] as well as Sedley.
(Buckingham's *Rehearsal* does not really belong to the genre.) He also
leaves out Etherege, author of three comedies, *The Man of Mode* among
them.

The two successful writers of comedies are especially interesting in
that they are each other's opposites. The two epithets 'hasty' and
'slow', neither a term of unreserved approbation, effectively brings out
the contrast between Shadwell and Wycherley. The former has enough
natural talent to be able to dispense with laborious editing and revising;
the latter, not a man for 'bold Stroakes', wins his victories on points.

The praise of Shadwell is, in a sense, inconsistent with other portions
of the *Allusion*.[48] The poem attacks Dryden for prolific and undistinguished writing; Shadwell, too, wrote much and quickly and did not
disguise the fact. He certainly did not subject every line to painstaking
scrutiny, an occupation strongly recommended elsewhere in the
Allusion. There is every reason to ask, as Raman Selden does, 'How
serious a flaw is the absence of "art" and "care"?' ('Rochester and
Shadwell', p. 179) The six lines devoted to Shadwell are unproblematic
in themselves:

> Shadwells unfinisht workes doe yet impart,
> Great proofes of force of Nature, none of Art.
> With just bold Stroakes, he dashes here and there,
> Shewing great Mastery with little care;
> And scornes to varnish his good touches o're,
> To make the Fooles, and Women, praise 'em more.

The trouble arises when they are laid beside the following passage (lines
98–101):

> To write what may securely stand the test
> Of being well read over Thrice at least
> Compare each Phrase, examin ev'ry Line,
> Weigh ev'ry word, and ev'ry thought refine...

Two things soften the contradiction somewhat. The first is that the
Allusion does distinguish between the kind of verse that is to be read

---

[47] Crowne's *The Country Wit* – whose première could have coincided with the writing of the
Allusion; see pp. 231 and 241 in *The London Stage* – and Caryll's *Sir Salamon Single* place them
in the category of comedy writers. On Orrery's comedies, see Kathleen M. Lynch, *Roger Boyle
First Earl of Orrery* (Knoxville, 1965), pp. 185–7.

[48] Raman Selden has drawn attention to this element of contradiction; see 'Rochester and
Shadwell', pp. 179–81. Cf. also Selden's *English Verse Satire*, p. 98.

over and over again and theatrical works. The word 'Rhimes' in line 1 surely refers to Dryden's poetry and his rhymed plays as well as to his rhymes in the narrower sense of the word. But Shadwell and Wycherley (and Etherege, for that matter) wrote comedies in prose. While this is a genre where 'Judgment' and 'paines' (line 51) pay dividends, too, it is nevertheless one where the repeated savouring, book in hand, of felicitous expressions is less important than sureness of touch in the presentation of men and manners.

This is what Shadwell does so well, according to Rochester. His plays demonstrate 'force of Nature' and 'great Mastery' in the creation of 'true Comedy'. In other words, they make salient points about the more entertaining facets of the human condition, and they make them with energy and dispatch. Shadwell's plays may hence be 'unfinisht', but 'loose' they are not.

Wycherley's gifts are of a totally different order. By the winter of 1675–6, three plays of his had been staged, with varying success. *The Plain Dealer* was not produced until roughly a year after the *Allusion* was written. Wycherley wrote his four plays in a period of five to six years, which does not sound particularly 'slow'; but he obviously devoted great care to their construction. His plots and characterisation are far more skilfully worked out than Shadwell's, with whom Allardyce Nicoll has compared him in an intriguing comment:

There is almost something of Shadwell in Wycherley's work. There is always the sense that the heart is struggling for entry into the world of the intellect.[49]

Maybe a similar feeling was what moved Rochester to name Wycherley as one who 'toucht upon true Comedy'. For all the skill of his intrigues and the polished wit of his dialogues, he has more to offer than mere cleverness. *The Country Wife*, for instance, moves precariously over sensitive ground; there is a good deal of cruelty and potential suffering beneath the sparkling brilliance of this play, maybe the greatest of all Restoration comedies. Rochester, who despised larmoyant pathos and ranting heroics,[50] was a connoisseur of the *comédie humaine*. It is possible,

---

[49] P. 238 in *Restoration Drama*. Cf. also J. A. Johnson, '"An Allusion"', 57, on Shadwell and Wycherley as related to the Jonsonian 'humours' comedy. On the subject of Wycherley's alleged slowness, cf. B. Eugene McCarthy, *William Wycherley: A Biography* (Athens, Ohio, 1979), pp. 99–100.

[50] His dislike of the latter is evident in, for instance, his sneers at Orrery's *Mustapha* with its impossibly noble princes. With regard to different approaches to *The Country Wife*, see Robert D. Hume's exploration of it in *The Development of English Drama in the Late Seventeenth Century* (Oxford, 1976), pp. 97–104. Hume has addressed the subject again with Judith Milhous in their

I think, that he saw a similar awareness in Shadwell and Wycherley, and that this recognition prompted him to regard them as superior to more superficial comedy writers.

Comedy is the first of the four literary genres practised by poets in whom Rochester finds laudable qualities. The second is panegyric verse, where Edmund Waller is the master:

> Waller, by Nature for the Bayes design'd,
> With force, and fire, and fancy unconfin'd,
> In Panigericks does Excell Mankind:
> He best can turne, enforce, and soften things,
> To praise great Conqu'rours, or to flatter Kings.

The first line of the five could be taken to suggest that Waller would have been a better choice as Poet Laureate than Dryden. The 'Bayes', however, do not only refer to this office; the Restoration poems belonging to the session-of-the-poets genre centred on Apollo's difficulties in deciding which aspiring poet to give his laurels to.[51]

Rochester's admiration of Waller has traditionally been thought to be reflected in Dorimant's quotations from that doyen of English verse in *The Man of Mode*. The *Allusion* emphasises Waller's natural gifts as a poet ('force, and fire, and fancy') while ascribing skill and tact ('turne, enforce, and soften') to him as well. One reason why he could never have been made Poet Laureate was the fact that he had composed several panegyrics on Cromwell. This is, of course, the underlying significance of line 58 in the *Allusion*, as all editors point out. True, Dryden had published a lamenting *Poem on the Death of His Late Highness, OLIVER Lord Protector* in 1659; but it could be overlooked, especially as it contained nothing overtly derogatory about the Stuart Charleses. Waller was universally respected in the Restoration years, and despite the turncoat innuendo, Rochester credits him both with native talent and with successful craftsmanship.

Having other men exalted far above him in the fields of comedy and panegyric verse will have annoyed Dryden, as a considerable share of his own literary output had been devoted to those genres. At this point, though, the man who would become the most illustrious late-seventeenth-century satirist had no reason to be jealous when another man was praised as the best writer of satires:

Producible Interpretation: Eight English Plays 1675–1707 (Carbondale and Edwardsville, 1985), where pp. 73–106 supply much food for thought on *The Country Wife*.

[51] For two examples, see pp. 327–37 and 352–6 in Lord's *Poems on Affairs of State* volume.

> For poynted Satyrs, I wou'd Buckhurst choose,
> The best good Man, with the worst Natur'd Muse:[52]

'The best good Man' may sound tautologous but is in all likelihood an allusion to that standing epithet, *vir bonus*.[53] It constitutes high praise, and Buckhurst – or Middlesex, as the future Earl of Dorset should properly be called in 1675–6 – apparently deserved it. No other Restoration Court Wit's name has escaped the censure of later and stricter ages, but Buckhurst's lovable personality has consistently won him friends throughout the centuries. The contradiction perceived by Rochester between the kind and generous man and the malicious satirist is no misrepresentation, though; Buckhurst's satires can be extremely abusive.[54]

One interesting discrepancy between Rochester and Horace might be noted at this point: Horace mentioned himself as a fairly successful satirist, better than Varro of the Atax if inferior to Lucilius. Rochester omits his own name, leaving all satirical honours with his friend. A wish to avoid an autobiographical bias[55] may, but need not, have been a reason; after all, the last 15 lines of the *Allusion* deal with Rochester's own standing as a man of letters. Perhaps he was simply reluctant to place himself in any one category. All the same, I think this reticence is typical of Rochester: for all his intolerance, he was not a conceited man. Even the concluding invocation of the judicious-men panel is headed by a conditional 'if'.

Despite Rochester's respectable output as a love lyrist, nobody could argue that the description of Sedley's success in the field could also be held to apply to him:

> For Songs, and Verses, Mannerly Obscene,
> That can stirr Nature up, by Springs unseene,
> And without forceing blushes, warme the Queene:
> Sidley, has that prevailing gentle Art,
> That can with a resistlesse Charme impart,
> The loosest wishes to the Chastest Heart,

---

[52] Uncertainty about punctuation has led some scholars to assume that the next few lines refer to Buckhurst, too. Vieth's edition set matters right on this score, though: it is clear that lines 61–3 refer to Sedley.

[53] For the classical source and a Restoration application of the expression, see George McFadden, *Dryden the Public Writer 1660–1685* (Princeton, 1978), p. 171.

[54] See, for instance, the lampoons on Edward Howard's *The British Princes*, pp. 7ff. in Harris' edition of Dorset's poems.

[55] Pat Rogers has said that Rochester 'evidently did not want to introduce too much by way of autobiography' ('*An Allusion*', p. 172).

Raise such a Conflict, kindle such a ffire
Betwixt declineing Virtue, and desire,
Till the poor Vanquisht Maid, dissolves away,
In Dreames all Night, in Sighs, and Teares, all Day.

The lines on Sedley form the longest passage devoted to any poet other than Dryden in the *Allusion*. It is also very elaborately designed. Like line 60 on Buckhurst, it turns on paradox; here, though, the paradox is carefully developed. The words 'Mannerly Obscene' ('decently indecent') introduce a succession of antitheses. At the same time, the language itself takes on an insidious sensuousness which has more in common with Sedley's seductive songs than with Rochester's usual energetic and unidirectional satiric style.

The rare reference to Queen Catherine serves to emphasise Sedley's skill in ripening the desires of virtuous ladies. If not even that emblem of chastity is insensible to the undermining effects of Sedley's songs and verses, the power of his 'Art' must be formidable. While his poems induce 'loose' wishes, they are anything but 'loose' – 'rambling', 'careless' – themselves. Softly awakening Nature in the subtlest of ways, they are the very opposite of the 'uselesse Words' of the blundering incompetents; there is matter in the sighs of line 70.

As usual, Rochester's précis of a colleague's work is well informed. Among Sedley's lyrics, there are no overt obscenities, but many of them speak of hidden fires and employ suggestive metaphors. The well-known strawberries-and-cream *Song* ('Smooth was the Water, calm the Air') is only one of many instances.[56]

The case of Etherege is an intriguing one.[57] The two lines Rochester gives to his friend 'gentle George' are sandwiched between an outline of what Shakespeare and Jonson have to teach their successors and an unveiled attack on another poet, Flatman, who resembles Etherege in that he does *not* imitate these two masters. It is not the happiest of positions, and a look at the Horatian original renders it more uncomfortable still; in relation to Horace's satire, Etherege is put in the place of 'pulc[h]er / Hermogenes' – translated as 'the fop Hermogenes'

---

[56] P. 36 in Pinto's edition of Sedley's *Works*, vol. I. Cf. also, for example, the *Songs* on pp. 16–17 ('Get you gone, you will undo me') and 20–1 ('*Phillis*, you have enough enjoy'd'), which contain such lines as 'My Dreams at Night were all of you, / Such as till then I never knew' and 'Love's Empire... Where even Tears and Sighs can show / Pleasures, the Cruel never know.'

[57] See Griffin, *Satires Against Man*, p. 255, and Rogers, '*An Allusion*', p. 171. Both these critics have addressed the matter of Etherege's function in the *Allusion*. Griffin is sure that Rochester is being entirely complimentary; Rogers is less certain.

in the Loeb edition.[58] Hermogenes not only does not have the sense to imitate his accomplished predecessors, says Horace; he has not even read them. The placing of Etherege in the *Allusion* is hence an unfavourable aspect in itself. The question of imitation and originality raises more complicated issues.

The seventeenth century certainly appreciated the kind of imitation which 'made it new'. The many compliments showered on Rochester himself for his skill in this respect speak for themselves.[59] While despising 'servile copying' (Thomas Rymer's phrase), however, Restoration critics did not regard the word 'original' as expressing unqualified praise. Calling a person a 'Sheere Originall' was tantamount to regarding him as a rather ridiculous and eccentric figure. It is significant that the fop Novel in Wycherley's *The Plain Dealer* damns himself out of his own mouth when announcing, 'I must confess I hate imitation, to do anything like other people. All that know me do me the honor to say I am an original, faith.'[60]

If the expression 'Sheere Originall' is, at the very least, attended by unflattering connotations, what of 'refin'd'? In a poem which lays such stress on the importance of a poet's 'refining' his thoughts, that word might, in any case, be regarded as a term of approbation. There is a difference between the contexts of lines 101 and 32, though. Refining thoughts is a matter of purifying them, clearing them 'from dross and recrement', as Dr Johnson says.[61] Applied to a human being, 'refine' had more to do with elegance and polish. In a Restoration context, it is still a compliment;[62] but even if it refers to Etherege's mode of writing rather than to his personal qualities, it does not possess enough force to nullify the detrimental elements mentioned above.

The lines on Etherege in *Timon* might be called to mind at this point:

Damn me (says *Dingboy*) in my mind *Gods-swounds*
Etheridge, writes *Airy Songs*, and soft *Lampoons*,

[58] The adjective 'pulcher', of course, basically means 'handsome'; the German classical scholar Ludwig Döderlein retained this meaning while giving the epithet a sneering tone, translating the expression as 'der Adonis Hermogenes' (p. 61 in his *Horazens Satiren: Lateinisch und deutsch mit Erläuterungen* (Leipzig, 1860)).

[59] Weinbrot recapitulates some of these statements in footnote 32 on p. 364 of his 'The "Allusion to Horace"'.

[60] Act II; p. 43 in the Regents Restoration Drama Series edition by Leo Hughes (London, 1967).

[61] Johnson's *Dictionary* quotes line 101 of Rochester's *Allusion* as an example, referring to the author as *Anon*.

[62] Rogers suggests that it might signify 'over-refined' here ('*An Allusion*', p. 171). It is certainly possible; Etherege had a reputation for being 'overdressed, in manners overrefined'; see Arthur R. Huseboe, *Sir George Etherege* (Boston, 1987), p. 36.

> The best of any *Man*; as for your *Nowns*,
> *Grammar*, and Rules of Art, he knows 'em not,
> Yet writ Two talking *Plays*, without one *Plot*.

First of all, poor Etherege suffers from guilt by association as a result of being mentioned along with Orrery, Settle, Crowne and Dryden and being praised by such a nincompoop as Dingboy. Secondly, his lack of studious application to '*Grammar*, and Rules of Art' is less than eulogistic, although Dingboy finds it a rare accomplishment in someone who was nevertheless able to write 'Two talking *Plays*, without one *Plot*' – the third stab at Etherege in *Timon*.

Knowledge of Rochester's friendship with Etherege has tended to reduce critical awareness of the injurious implications in *Timon* and the *Allusion*.[63] That friendship did not, apparently, suffer in consequence of them; the Epsom escapade where Etherege played the prudent hero to Rochester's blustering villain occurred after the *Allusion* had gone into circulation. Etherege was a sensitive man with his fair share of personal vanity, but he clearly felt that he could live with Rochester's critical pronouncements.

The reason may have been that he was not really in a position to dispute them. His first play, *The Comical Revenge; or, Love in a Tub* was a great success, despite its rambling construction.[64] *She Would If She Could*, while more concentrated with regard to plot, was also more than anything else a 'talking *Play*'. It was recognised from the first that Etherege's strongest points were his witty, realistic dialogue and entertainingly developed characters, and Rochester never calls that into question. Besides, Etherege himself was forever insisting that he was an idle fellow whose libertine existence had given him 'little time to turn over bookes'.[65] As for his 'originality', *The Comical Revenge* had a freshness which the Restoration audience seems to have felt and appreciated, especially – as is generally recognised by Etherege critics – in the presentation of Sir Frederick Frollick. In view of such circumstances, Etherege may well have shrugged his shoulders and thought his friend's lines fair comment.

If so, he was not the only poet exposed to criticism in the *Allusion* who still appreciated Rochester afterwards. Thomas Otway, for

---

[63] Huseboe, for example, looks on line 33 in Rochester's *Allusion* and line 125 in *Timon* as expressions of recognition.

[64] Underwood argues that the structure of this play actually reveals a palpable unity of concern; see *Etherege*, pp. 43ff.

[65] A quotation from one of Etherege's letters; see Huseboe, *Sir George Etherege*, p. 33.

instance, dedicated both *Don Carlos* and *Titus and Berenice* to him, in terms of fervent gratitude.[66] Nat Lee included an elegant tribute to Rochester's qualities as a wit in *The Princess of Cleve*, after Rochester's death.[67] Flatman celebrated Rochester's conversion in a pastoral.[68] Of course, these men could only have suffered as a consequence of attacking Rochester, to whom they were greatly inferior in terms of social status. In respect of the latter two, *de mortuis* considerations – and especially after such a *mors* – may have been pertinent, too. Even so, these eulogies imply that some Restoration writers were able to swallow justified criticism.

It has to be remembered that this was a time of jibing and flyting, and that a certain ability to tolerate a joke at your own expense was required.[69] Many people – Dryden and Rochester among them – anticipated the jests and censure of others, or blunted their edge, by making fun of themselves. The furious vituperations of combatants such as Dryden and Shadwell may make posterity regard the Restoration writers as exceedingly disputatious, but this was a coarse and combative age, and quite a few 'bobs' could be exchanged without bones being broken. Reproaches against Rochester for being rude to protégés should, I think, be regarded in that light. Excepting the attacks on Dryden, the critical observations on the works of contemporary writers in the *Allusion* are not informed by personal malice. Also, they are, in essence, just. Even Dryden, understandably hurt, did not allow personal affront to prevent him from improving his writing in ways that can be related to Rochester's criticisms. In addition, his later poetry shows traces of Rochester's poetical influence.

Factions and conflicting loyalties did not, moreover, prevent both Etherege and Dorset from remaining on perfectly amicable terms with Dryden after he had fallen foul of their friend Rochester. Dorset, indeed, patronised both Dryden and Shadwell in subsequent years when their notorious feud was in full swing. Clearly, loyalty to one's friends did not necessarily entail cutting their enemies. If it had done, little in the way of friendly contacts between men of letters would have been possible.

---

[66] See Prinz, *John Wilmot*, p. 76. Prinz devoted a good deal of attention to Rochester's functions as a patron, and though some of his statements can now be challenged, his discussion makes several vital points.

[67] The passages on 'Count *Rosidore*' are easily accessible in Farley-Hills' *Critical Heritage* volume; see pp. 28–9. It should be borne in mind, though, that the character of Nemours may well, as Robert Hume has argued (*The Development of English Drama*, pp. 356–7), embody 'a mixed but profoundly hostile depiction' of Rochester.

[68] Printed in the *Critical Heritage* volume, p. 115.

[69] Shadwell, for example, had to put up with an unkind reference in *Timon*; see lines 15–16.

JUDGE AND JURY

In Rochester's *Allusion*, the poet's chief loyalty is to his literary ideals. By way of piecing together the vital points in his praise and criticism of other authors, a fairly clear picture of what constitutes good writing can be established. In addition, there are some sixteen lines of general instruction in the art.

Throughout the *Allusion*, two concerns are predominant: the creation of a proper poetic idiom; and the necessity of articulating meaningful matter. The two concerns are fused in the line 'Your Rethorick, with your Poetry, unite'. The seventeenth century used other terms than form and content, or tenor and vehicle; but the awareness of both dimensions, as well as of their essential inseparability, was there.

The major vice, looseness, can only be combated by restraint. 'Within due proportions, circumscribe' and 'Weigh ev'ry word, and ev'ry thought refine' are the first and last lines of Rochester's directives – both speak of the need to cut away everything that does not 'hit the thing home'. Rochester obviously agreed with Boileau that 'Qui ne sçait se borner ne sceut jamais écrire' (*L'Art poétique*, 1.63; cf. below).

Considerations of 'due proportions' and the exercise of 'Judgment' are not the only qualities required to make a good writer, though: natural talent is a prerequisite, too. Other phenomena associated with congenital aptitude are force, fire, spirit, grace and fancy; wit in the sense of brainpower belongs here, too. Waller, like Shadwell, is naturally gifted in this respect and could afford not to confine his fancy. Incidentally, Waller praised Roscommon's translation of Horace's *Art of Poetry* (London, 1680) in an introductory poem in which the nestor of Restoration verse implicitly subscribed to Rochester's views:

> He that proportion'd wonders can disclose,
> At once his Fancy and his Judgment shows.

Lines 88–92 of the *Allusion* imply that it is not clear whether Dryden's flaws are due to deficient intelligence ('Witt'), faulty workmanship ('want of Judgment') or lack of imagination and inspiration ('lumpish fancy'). Any one of these defects was obviously fatal.

At this point, it might be added that other sets of prescriptions on good writing than Horace's tenth satire may be related to Rochester's *Allusion*. In 1674, Boileau's *L'Art poétique* had been published; Rochester may have heard of – or indeed heard – it before that.[70] Partly indebted to Horace's *Ars Poetica*, *L'Art poétique* urged poets to apply their rhymes with skill and judgement (I.27–36 and 115–16); to eschew prolixity (I.59–63); to observe the need for a stylistically varied discourse (I.70–2); to steer clear of vulgarity and coarseness (I.79ff. and II.129–38; cf. lines 71–6 in the *Allusion*); to labour patiently and revise with diligence (I.171–4 and III.309–11); and to take the advice of discerning friends (I.185ff. and IV.71ff.), distrusting the easy raptures of flatterers (IV.41–3). Like Rochester in *Timon*, Boileau maliciously quoted the efforts of inferior writers (III.265–6 and 272), and he recommended the writers of comedy to study Nature (III.359–72).

Some of the precepts articulated by Rochester in the *Allusion* may well have been coloured by *L'Art poétique*.[71] (At another level, the glorification of Louis XIV and the Franche-Comté campaign (IV.211–14) offers interesting sidelights on *Timon*.) The idea that 'the rakish Earl' could have studied a treatise on correct authorship which has been synonymous with boredom for subsequent generations might seem odd to some. Still, *L'Art poétique* caused a furore when it appeared; Rochester must have heard of this new, celebrated – and highly controversial – work by an admired colleague who loathed a 'loose, slatterne Muse' as warmly as he did. Although *L'Art poétique* contains much matter of little or no relevance to the *Allusion*, I have found nothing in the former that contradicts the literary ideals voiced in Rochester's poem.

Horace's tenth satire mentioned five literary categories in which some of his contemporaries – and he himself – had proved their worth: comedy, eulogies on great men, the epic, the pastoral and satire. Rochester makes the love lyric take the place of the epic and pastoral and devotes considerable space to it. It cannot have been due to those two genres being obsolete in late-seventeenth-century England, because they were not, or rather not yet – it is more likely to be a reflection of Rochester's own tastes. It might seem incongruous that he should in that case have included 'Panigericks'. Everybody was doing it, though, not least Dryden, and panegyric verse balances satire. It is significant that the

---

[70] Before its publication, Boileau prepared for the great success of the printed poem by reciting it among the *literati* of Paris; see, for instance, Antoine Albalat, *L'Art poétique de Boileau* (Paris, 1929), p. 35.

[71] The fact that 'la raison' is consistently held up as a supreme virtue in the latter work does not make such indebtedness unlikely; Boileau's *raison* has more in common with Rochester's sense, wit and judgement than with the '*Reason*' he detested. A résumé of scholarly investigations of Boileau's *raison* concept is supplied by August Buck in his edition, with commentary, of the poem, *Nicolas Boileau: L'Art poétique* (Munich, 1970), pp. 35–6. See also Gordon Pocock, *Boileau and the Nature of Neo-Classicism* (Cambridge, 1980), pp. 42–6 and 87–8.

tragic play is omitted: Rochester had dealt heroic tragedy a body blow in *Timon*; but it was a genre he would attempt towards the end of his life, in adapting Fletcher's *Valentinian*. In the course of that unfinished project, he 'circumscribed' Fletcher's language, cutting out a good deal of somewhat melodramatic verse which apparently seemed superfluous to him and sharpening the essential conflicts inherent in the sombre theme.

Does a review of Rochester's poetical works afford reasons for thinking that he seriously believed in the precepts articulated in the *Allusion*, and that he attempted to practise them himself? Such a matter is difficult to prove. Anyone who sets out to do so is easily caught up in specious or circular argumentation. Nevertheless, one simple question might be asked: does Rochester's *œuvre* contain any appreciable amounts of stylistically monotonous discourse, 'uselesse Words', turgid, inflated language, indiscriminate invective and obscure ideas? Leaving the occasional verses and the juvenilia aside, I think one may fairly answer 'no'. The libels on Sir Carr Scroope contain quite a few lines that are mere rant; but they cannot be equated, in terms of artistry, with such poems as *Artemiza to Chloe*, *The Mistress* and the *Satyr*. Even haphazard-seeming poems like *Tunbridge Wells* and *A Ramble in Saint James's Parke*, when closely investigated, show signs of structural deliberation, and superfluous verbiage is not a feature in them. True, the latter poem – and some others – contain more of '[morose] Satyr' than of 'Jeast(s) in Scorne'; but as I have tried to show, those torrents of abuse are part of a design and generally well controlled. Besides, there to balance them are the austere *Satyr* and the delicious paradoxical encomia *Upon Nothing* and *Signior Dildo*.

What these questions ultimately produce is yet another, and fundamental, query: was Rochester a prodigiously talented literary dilettante or a serious artist?

In a Restoration context, the distinction between 'professional' and 'amateur' is not relevant when attempting to answer such a question. In the introductory passage in *Timon*, the speaker/poet tries to belittle his poetic achievements, ascribing a uniform ulterior motive to his (scant, he implies) writing. This should be taken for what it is, the disclaimer of – as Peter Porter has rightly said – a 'gentleman who must be seen to eschew professionalism'.[72] Professional writers, however successful,

---

[72] P. 72 in 'The Professional Amateur'. Cf. Suckling's light dismissal of literary ambition in his *A Session of the Poets*: ' ... of all Men living he [i.e., Suckling himself] car'd not for't, / He lov'd not the Muses so well as his Sport ... ' Cf. also Brice Harris' Introduction to his edition of

were dependent on the approval of those who would pay to enjoy their work. Hack writing was not a thing to which an aristocrat could possibly stoop, and it was good manners for him to make light of any literary pursuits he might indulge in. John Lough has described how utterly ruinous it could be for a French nobleman to be identified as the author of a book. It was rare for such a writer to publish anything, and if he did, he would take care that his name did not appear on the title-page. Plebeian professionals whose work happened to displease an aristocrat were quite frequently beaten up, and even mutilated, by hired bullies.[73] The same thing, of course, happened in England, and a more graphic illustration of the poor esteem in which the professional writer was held is scarcely imaginable. No wonder the members of the aristocracy were keen to distance themselves from these men. Rochester's own representation of them is characterised by appropriate disdain:

> Shou'd I be troubled ...
> ... when the poor-fed Poets of the Towne
> For Scrapps, and Coach roome cry my Verses downe?

Consequently, it cannot be argued that Rochester did not care about his writing because he never bothered to have texts properly printed, or because his extant letters do not speak of literary labours. The latter were addressed to people with whom he had other things to discuss. It is significant that the only letter in Treglown's edition that deals with literary matters in some detail is Dryden's to Rochester – the professional writer's to his patron. Regardless of what licensing acts might have allowed, Rochester would never have written for the public. His readership was the Court of Charles II and people of consequence to members of that Court. When, in the *Allusion*, he spoke of being content to please a small number of good judges, I think he meant exactly what he said. Taking his word for it disposes of another question that might well be asked: if Rochester took his writing seriously enough to devote much time and effort to it, why did he apparently never take steps to ensure that his texts survived in a reliable canon? He would have seen to it that the people who mattered had decent copies; beyond that, he simply would not care. He had, I believe, suffered the kind of indignity recounted in lines 5–32 of *Timon* often enough to endure misrepresentation and misinterpretation in resigned silence. This would

Dorset's poetry, p. xi: 'No one would have been more surprised than Charles Sackville, sixth Earl of Dorset, to know that three hundred years after he began to write, a twentieth-century press would issue an edition of his poems with all the scholarly paraphernalia.'

[73] *An Introduction to Seventeenth Century France* (London, 1954), pp. 194–6.

be consistent with the Rochesterian quality, characteristic of the man and the poet, which was – apart from his conversion – his best claim to exemption from that hellfire for which so many of his contemporaries believed him bound: his abomination of pride.

Excluded from the adulation of large audiences and from any success as a poet other than a *succès d'estime*, too inured against personal vanity to exult in his achievements merely on the basis of his own appreciation of them, Rochester must indeed have come to rely heavily on the panel of arbitrators he presented in lines 120–4 of the *Allusion*. He may have been confident of his ability to judge others, but his own work was for others to judge. All he could do was appoint a body of eight-plus good men and true and hope that what he had tried to say – his 'Sense' – would find favour with them.

12

The poems on Mulgrave and Scroope

There is ample precedent for considering Rochester's attacks on Mulgrave and Scroope in a lump.[1] Placing such a discussion in a context where matters of craftsmanship form the main issue calls for an *apologia*, though. Of the five poems reviewed below – *An Epistolary Essay, A very Heroicall Epistle in Answer to Ephelia, On the suppos'd Authour of a late Poem in defence of Satyr, On Poet Ninny* and *My Lord All-Pride* – only the first is predominantly concerned with writing, and the second does not mention literary matters at all.

Still, the grouping adopted here seems defensible on two grounds: first, difficulties of tone, stance and identity have bedevilled analyses of these poems (especially the first two) for decades, and these issues should be subjected to a joint consideration. Second, the inferior quality of the poetical works produced by Rochester's enemies John Sheffield, Earl of Mulgrave, and Sir Carr Scroope is one of the two main charges against them. The other is their inadequacy as lovers. Both accusations are examined in this chapter, along with the special problems involved in each of the five satires. The *Epistolary Essay* and the *Heroicall Epistle* are far more complex than the other three, which is why they are given considerably greater space. The *Epistolary Essay* may be the last of the five to be written, but it is best contemplated against the background of the analysis of *An Allusion to Horace* in the preceding chapter.

---

[1] Three of them are members of a linked group of five satires which are found together in several manuscript collections (see Vieth, *Attribution*, ch. 13.) Walker prints the 'Poems to Mulgrave and Scroope' together; see pp. 107–17 in his edition.

AN EPISTOLARY ESSAY

The poem which was first printed as *An Epistolary Essay from M. G. to O. B. upon their Mutual Poems* has been regarded in very different ways by Rochester critics. Before David Vieth's *Attribution in Restoration Poetry* appeared, it was generally believed to be – and even praised as being – a frank declaration of personal uninhibitedness on Rochester's part.[2] Vieth, however, effected an about-turn: he contended that the *Epistolary Essay* is in fact a satire on Mulgrave, the latter being set up as a *persona* speaker. Subsequent scholars tended to accept his argumentation, with more or less strong reservations (see below). Only one of the more recent Rochester experts has flatly refused to agree with it: David Brooks maintains that there is 'no evidence' for Vieth's belief that the poem is a 'satirical self-exposé' of Mulgrave's, adding that 'Vieth's contention that M. G. stands for Mulgrave, and O. B. for "Old Bays", meaning Dryden, is pure speculation.'[3]

It is true that Vieth's argumentation is speculative, but speculation can be more or less persuasive. The last word remains to be said on the subject, but one thing seems irrefutable to me: by no means can it be convincingly argued that the *Epistolary Essay* expresses Rochester's personal views.

A recapitulation of the points made in Rochester's *Allusion to Horace* should suffice to dispel such a notion. My assumption that the speaker of that poem is Rochester himself is not one for which hard evidence could be adduced, but a comparison between it and the *Epistolary Essay* shows that the latter is a much less ambitious effort. The *Allusion* lashes the lack of substance and self-discipline, arguing that natural aptitude and painstaking craftsmanship make a good writer. The poem's speaker refrains from venturing to hold any sort of opinion regarding his own work; he submits it to a select 'jury' whose members pay him a compliment merely by considering it.

The contrast between this stern, but in respect of his own poetry decidedly modest, judge and the complacent 'M. G.' could not have been more striking. The latter knows that his verses are inferior to those of his addressee, but – as David Farley-Hills has said – he justifies his writing 'on the egotistical grounds that he likes doing it, he thinks it is

---

[2] Vieth provides an account of these views on pp. 119–29 in *Attribution*.

[3] See p. 107 in the annotation to Brooks' edition of Rochester's lyrics and satires. (It was perhaps to be expected that Vieth's predecessor as Rochester editor, Vivian de Sola Pinto, should express his disapproval of Vieth's theory in terms of the strongest censure; see his bibliographical note in *Philological Quarterly* 43.3 (July 1964), 383–4.)

good and that no-one else need read it if they do not wish to' (*Rochester's Poetry*, p. 128). In fact, he even aligns it with the physical need to defecate. On point after point, he contradicts the speaker of the *Allusion*: his guiding principle is to 'avoyd... all sort of self denyall'; he writes to please himself; he aspires to originality; he raises his own judgement above that of everybody else; and he does not care whether his admiration of his own output is due to true 'merit' or merely to 'Arrogance'. Like Samuel Butler's 'Small Poet' *Character*,[4] he 'gives his Genius all Freedom', 'writes for his Pleasure', will not be 'confined to any Thing', 'has no Respect to Decorum and Propriety of Circumstance', and dislikes 'Restraint' being imposed on 'poetical Licence'.

Those critics who more or less grudgingly conclude that quite a few of the sentiments expressed by the speaker of the *Epistolary Essay* '[do] sound like Rochester himself'[5] forget that there is a vital distinction between the advocacy of sensual pleasure in, for instance, the *Satyr* and literary self-indulgence. Dustin Griffin's suggestion that debasing poetry by comparing it to excrement 'is just the sort of thing the poet of the "Satyr against Mankind" (and of the Huysmans portrait)[6] would do' (*Satires Against Man*, p. 73) is a fatal misconception, rare in this sensitive critic.

Around 1960, Vieth was not alone in feeling that the speaker in the *Epistolary Essay* was a satirical creation. Justly emphasising Rochester's hatred of pride, Melvin Delmar Palmer enumerated cogent reasons against believing the poem to be a confessional piece.[7] Palmer, however, argued that the initials should be read as 'M. C.' and 'D. B.' – as they appear in a note in the Bodleian copy of 1691 – and that they refer to Martin Clifford and the Duke of Buckingham. This suggestion has been

---

[4] The pertinence of this portrait of a miserable scribbler was first indicated by Griffin (*Satires Against Man*, p. 71). The text of 'A Small Poet' is found on pp. 82–94 in Daves' edition of Butler's *Characters*.

[5] *Rochester's Poetry*, p. 129. Farley-Hills claims that 'Rochester is by no means modest in his poetic self-confidence', which seems totally erroneous to me.

[6] An intriguing account of that portrait and its relevance to Rochester's life and works – including his dealings with Dryden – is provided by Hans-Joachim Zimmermann in 'Simia Laureatus: Lord Rochester Crowning a Monkey', in Ulrich Broich, Theo Stemmler and Gerd Stratmann, eds., *Functions of Literature: Essays presented to Erwin Wolff on his sixtieth birthday* (Tübingen, 1984), pp. 147–72.

[7] See 'The Identity of "M. G." and "O. B." in Rochester's "An Epistolary Essay from M. G. to O. B. Upon Their Mutual Poems"', *Modern Language Notes* 75.8 (December 1960), 644–7. Recently, D. K. Alsop has restated the case against an identification of author and speaker in this poem, drawing attention to the discrepancy between the attitudes to writing expressed by the *Allusion* on the one hand and by 'M. G.' on the other ('"An Epistolary Essay"', 62–3).

turned down by subsequent scholars; as Keith Walker says, the evidence is very slight.[8]

What of Vieth's identification, then? Even those scholars who have accepted it have been less than whole-hearted in subscribing to it.[9] Farley-Hills, who is one of them, attributes the difficulty in deciding which attitude to adopt towards M. G. to Rochester's 'lack of clarity'.[10] Did Rochester intend his readers to feel some sympathy for M. G., and if so, can he really be equated with the obnoxious Mulgrave who is so thoroughly reviled in *My Lord All-Pride*?

As the reasons against believing in Vieth's theory are less weighty than those which speak for it, they might be disposed of first. The most important one is found in lines 60–8 of the *Epistolary Essay*:

> Just soe seemes Providence, as poor and vaine,
> Keeping more Creatures, than it can maintaine.
> Here 'tis profuse, and there it meanly saves,
> And for One Prince, it makes Ten Thousand Slaves:
> In Witt alone, it has beene Magnificent,
> Of which, soe just a share, to each is sent
> That the most Avaricious are content.
> For none e're thought, (the due Division's such),
> His owne too little, or his Friends too much.

These lines have amused a great many readers, who have sensed Rochester's own wicked humour behind them. While they certainly serve to ridicule mankind in general rather than the speaker, they do not make the latter a very profound critic of men's ways, especially as the concluding sting may be borrowed from Descartes.[11] Besides, he goes on to exalt himself in the most shameless manner:

> But I, who am of sprightly Vigour full
> Looke on Mankind, as Envious, and dull.
> Borne to my self, my self I like alone,
> And must conclude my Judgment good, or none.

The contemptuous dismissal of what 'the World' will say (lines 81ff.) has also been taken to suggest a degree of identification between Rochester and his speaker. Still, I think one should bear in mind that this passage follows, and is related to, that speaker's exaltation of his own literary judgement – a completely un-Rochesterian notion.

---

[8] P. 294 in his edition of Rochester's poems. On Clifford and Dryden, see p. 315n. above.

[9] Cf. Griffin, *Satires Against Man*, pp. 68–9, and Erskine-Hill, 'Rochester: Augustan or Explorer?', pp. 62–3.   [10] *Rochester's Poetry*, p. 131.

[11] See p. 146 in Vieth's edition of Rochester's poems.

Other objections to Vieth's identification may be made. For instance, why should Rochester's Mulgrave character declare his indifference to true quality in writing, when both Mulgrave's *Essay upon Satire* and his subsequent *Essay upon Poetry* (first published in 1682) stress the importance of writing well? Regardless of the possibility that Rochester's poem antedated both *Essays* (cf. below), there is a distinction between theory and practice, and Rochester may well have felt that the latter discredited the former where Mulgrave was concerned. Another question mark is set up by the humility of the speaker in relation to his addressee. Would the Earl of Mulgrave refer to the commoner Dryden as a 'Civet-Catt' (line 43) greatly superior to himself in *any* respect? That sounds more like the sort of flattery Dryden would himself dispense. And what about the 'deserved Bays'? Was Mulgrave respected for his poetical achievements at any point in the late 1670s; did he, in other words, have any bays to be divested of? We know that his standing around the turn of the century, long after Rochester's death, was as high as any dilettante could ever aspire to;[12] but during the last years of Rochester's life evidence of recognition for his sparse literary output is not easy to find. Indeed, it could well be argued that the reference to the 'Bays' and the carelessness in writing which M. G. cheerfully admits to, along with his inflated belief in his own judgement, are more easily applied to Dryden than to Mulgrave.

Against these reservations, however, speaks a string of persuasive arguments. John Sheffield, Earl of Mulgrave, was 'notoriously vain'.[13] Besides, one of the traits for which Dryden professed to admire him was his indifference to the adulation of the multitude, and Rochester seems to allude to that admiration in the *Epistolary Essay*.[14] Dryden's dedication of *Aureng-Zebe* to Mulgrave (early in 1676) praises the latter for being 'above the wretched affectation of popularity':

A popular man is, in truth, no better than a prostitute to common fame and to the people ... How much more great and manly in your Lordship is your contempt of popular applause and your retired virtue, which shines only to a few ...[15]

---

[12] Mulgrave was the subject of many eulogies; one of Pope's may be quoted by way of illustration: 'Muse! 'tis enough; at length thy labour ends, / And thou shalt live, for Buckingham commends.' (Quoted from the Introduction to Cooke's edition of *The Poetical Works of John Sheffield, Duke of Buckinghamshire* (London, 1800), p. ix.)

[13] George deF. Lord, pp. 401 and 410n. in *Poems on Affairs of State*. Lord goes so far as to call Sheffield 'the unspeakable Mulgrave' (p. 400). See also Wilson's account of Mulgrave in *Court Wits*, pp. 7, 30 and 119.   [14] See p. 348 in *Poems on Affairs of State*.

[15] Lines 65–84, p. 5 in the Regents Restoration Drama Series edition by Frederick Link (London, 1971). Such praise, of course, lends weight to Rochester's nasty remarks on the general scorn

The verbal resemblances between this passage and lines 85 and 90 are strong indications in favour of an allusion on Rochester's part. The dedication of _Aureng-Zebe_ also expatiates on the theme of retirement, Mulgrave serving as a model. The last line of Rochester's poem – 'keepe at home, and write' – suggests a deliberate reference, too. Mulgrave seems to have been anxious to project himself as a contented homebody; his _Essay upon Satire_, where he portrays himself as a successful cuckold-maker, mentions his 'boasted quiet'.[16]

Even the ambition to write 'soe ... as none ere writ before' (line 49 in the _Epistolary Essay_) can, I believe, be related to Mulgrave. While originality was in no way a late-seventeenth-century ideal (see p. 329 above), Mulgrave reportedly wrote the following lines about himself,

> Here a Poet you behold,
> Who with disadvantage wrote:
> For, of Authors new or old,
> I would never steal a thought.[17]

Rochester may never have seen or heard of this claim; but the attitude could have been displayed to – and disliked by – him.

Mulgrave was certainly Dryden's patron, and lines 7–8 in the _Epistolary Essay_ may – as several scholars have suggested – constitute a reference to that relationship. The meaning of the expression 'mutual poems' and the implications of lines 3–4 have been the focus of much discussion. They may, as Vieth and others have proposed, refer to the _Essay upon Satire_ which Mulgrave wrote with a little help from Dryden,[18] but which Rochester believed to be the latter's work.[19]

Small indications of an interrelationship between Mulgrave's _Essay_ and Rochester's _Epistolary Essay_ are supplied by the latter poem's title, as

with which Mulgrave was regarded by contemporary society. Another indication to that effect is – unwittingly – supplied by Nat Lee's admiring words on Mulgrave's '[daring to] be alone'; see Ham, _Otway and Lee_, p. 51.

16 Line 209; see p. 411 in Lord's _Poems on Affairs of State_. It has been suggested that Wycherley's Manly, the Plain Dealer, was modelled on Mulgrave. See J. M. Auffret, '_The Man of Mode_ & _The Plain Dealer_: Common Origin & Parallels', _Etudes anglaises_ 19.3 (July–September 1966), 209–22.

17 Quoted by Wilson; see p. 119n. in _Court Wits_. Cf. Boileau's disapprobation of those who would be original at any price, 'Ils croiroient s'abaisser, dans leurs vers monstrueux, / S'ils pensoient ce qu'un autre a pû penser comme eux' (_L'Art poétique_, 1.41–2).

18 It was subsequently revised by Pope. 'Never has an indifferent poem had two such godfathers as this', says Lord (p. 401 in _Poems on Affairs of State_); before him, George Rapall Noyes and Herman Ralph Mead expressed a similar sentiment in 'An Essay upon Satyr/London/Dring/1680', _University of California Publications in English_, VII (Berkeley and Los Angeles, 1948), p. 154 ('Surely no mediocre squib ever had two more distinguished revisers').

19 According to a letter dated 21 November 1679. He may, of course, have been informed of Mulgrave's authorship after that date. See _Letters_, pp. 232–3.

well as by the former's glance at Howard's *British Princes* (lines 192–3), its reference to the 'world's nonsense' (line 274) and its lines on Sedley's 'skillful nose',

> Which from all stinks can with peculiar art
> Extract perfume, and essence from a fart.[20]

If Mulgrave's poem antedated Rochester's, lines 11, 30–6 and 81–4 of the latter may constitute echoes of these passages. Even if Rochester believed Dryden to have written the *Essay upon Satire*, he regarded both men as being connected with it. This, then, could be taken to imply further support of Vieth's view with regard to the respective identities of M. G. and O. B.

Such links are pretty tenuous, though; abuse of *The British Princes*, for instance, was a Restoration cliché. It is more fruitful to contemplate M. G. against the background of biographical accounts of Mulgrave.

Dr Johnson's *Life* of 'Sheffield/Buckinghamshire' is a fairly straight-forward outline of Mulgrave's life and career. His loose morals are regretted and his verse not highly recommended (he had 'not the fire and fancy of a poet', according to Johnson's final sentence; these, incidentally, were two of Waller's praiseworthy characteristics in Rochester's *Allusion to Horace*). However, Johnson is impressed by Mulgrave the autodidact; other sources agree that he 'kept at home and read' on a regular basis to make up for an early lack of education. A more interesting record of Mulgrave's personality is found in *A Character of John Sheffield Late Duke of Buckinghamshire* (London, 1729), published eight years after Mulgrave's death and written by one 'AN'. The *Character* purports to be commendatory; but to a modern reader at least, many of its attempts at *Ehrenrettung* are tinged with faint damns.[21]

According to this writer, Mulgrave's poems were 'composed meerly for Amusement, and sometimes even with negligence' (p. 2), a description which fits M. G. perfectly. Against the general view of Mulgrave as 'haughty', 'AN' counters that he was so good-natured as to have tears in his eyes when 'seeing in the Streets any real object of compassion' (p. 18), another backhanded compliment. Not even this

---

[20] Pp. 410–13 in Lord's *Poems on Affairs of State*.

[21] Mulgrave is, for instance, freed from the imputation of meanness in money matters by references to his regularity in giving his third wife 'her Pin-money to a day' (p. 22) and to his 'having lost a great part of his fortune meerly through an indolence and unwillingness to visit his Estates at some distance from *London*' (p. 23). Another biographical sketch of Mulgrave introduces Cooke's 1800 edition of *The Poetical Works of John Sheffield*. It was subsequently reprinted in the Haworth Press edition, published in 1933, of *Miscellanea from the Works of John Sheffield Earl of Mulgrave Marquis of Normanby and Duke of Buckingham*.

biographer disputes his subject's choleric temper, and his discourse on Mulgrave the lover seems highly relevant to *A very Heroicall Epistle*:

The liberties which he had allow'd himself in relation to ladies, are too well known, to be omitted ... But this ought to be remarked as a proof of his good sense, that none of his mistresses could ever prevail upon him to marry foolishly, or ever gain'd too great an ascendant over him.[22]

A VERY HEROICALL EPISTLE IN ANSWER TO EPHELIA

'AN' may have been in earnest when complimenting the late Duke of Buckinghamshire on being obdurate to the wiles and charms of women, and deaf to their pleas. The quoted eulogy on his 'good sense' does have a hollow ring, though; Mulgrave clearly was not a man of feeling. His self-portrait in the *Essay upon Satire* reinforces that impression. Its main point is that he managed to '"scape the snare', and he is expressly said to be unmoved by 'soft thoughts' and 'gratitude' (line 204).

It was John Harold Wilson who first noticed the reference to the Mall Kirke affair in the concluding lines of the *Heroicall Epistle*. Realising that its speaker must be Mulgrave,[23] he prevented subsequent misguided 'confessional' analyses of the poem.

The fact that the *Heroicall Epistle* answers Etherege's[24] *Ephelia to Bajazet* has been acknowledged as such for years. In addition to the obvious echoes in Rochester's *Epistle*,[25] there is the simple circumstance that the two poems are of exactly the same length (56 lines). Hence, Walker's decision to print them together is well grounded. The *Epistle* – the designation '*very Heroicall*' is a piece of unveiled cynicism as well as a nod to Ovid's *Heroides*[26] – is a reply to accusations summarised in its first half: the speaker[27] has been charged with deceit, inconstancy and ingratitude. The charges exactly match those put forward in the first 34 lines of *Ephelia to Bajazet*.

Rochester's Bajazet character deals with each of them in turn. He is

---

[22] Pp. 20–1 of the *Character*, which also paint a dismal picture of Mulgrave's attitude to illegitimate fatherhood.   [23] See *Court Wits*, pp. 117–19.

[24] Etherege's authorship has not been established beyond doubt, but few would challenge Walker's statement, 'Probably by Sir George Etherege' (p. 295 in his edition of Rochester's poems).

[25] Griffin enumerates some; see p. 59 n. 61 in *Satires Against Man*. The very different uses of the word 'Mute' (line 13 in *Ephelia to Bajazet* and line 51 in the *Heroicall Epistle*) form another example.   [26] See, for instance, Vieth's headnote to the poem on p. 113 in his edition.

[27] As Etherege's addressee was called Bajazet (possibly a loan from Marlowe's *Tamburlaine*; see p. 296 in Walker's edition), that name is often given to the speaker in the *Heroicall Epistle*. As it is a convenient appellation, I have made use of it, too. (Incidentally, Cowley maintained that the raving of Bajazet on stage had nothing to do with wit; see stanza 7 in his *Ode*, 'Of Wit'.)

above dissembling; he never pretended to give a moment's consideration to anyone but himself; his alleged inconstancy is merely the result of his being true to his own nature, and to Nature; and he is under no obligation for favours received, as they were adequately repaid. Ephelia's emotional vocabulary ('Passions', 'tender', 'Love', 'Charmes', 'cruell', 'Rage', 'hate', etc.) is answered by coolly businesslike discourse ('Maxim', 'favour', 'changeing of my Gold', 'paid you back', 'Obligation').

In *Ephelia to Bajazet*, line 35 marks a shift from a description (Bajazet is 'he', and the account is addressed to an undefined audience) to a solicitation directed at the faithless one. Similarly, there is a break in the middle of the *Heroicall Epistle*. The addressee Ephelia ('you', a pronoun which agrees with the invocation 'Madam') is replaced by the imagined 'happy Sultan' ('thou', as if the speaker, too, regards him 'like some God').

One may well wonder what effect the second half (lines 32–56) would have on Ephelia. Polemically, it could not but damage the speaker's case. Having claimed supreme indifference to the lady's pathetic pleas, he compromises his would-be Olympian inviolability by conceding vulnerability in the end. Worse, he indirectly admits to not being the amorous sovereign he set himself up as being. He certainly has no pity for Ephelia, who said that she did not want any in any case; but there is more than a hint of larmoyant self-pity in the concluding lines of the *Epistle*.

This is, it seems to me, the heart of the inconsistency that has bothered so many readers of the *Heroicall Epistle*.[28] Can it be argued that Rochester somehow lost sight of his satirical purpose here and gave Bajazet/Mulgrave a touch of genuine pathos?[29] Does the Sultan passage reflect Rochester's own wishful thinking? Did he, in other words, fail to retain his perspective to the detriment of his poem and the confusion of its readers? An attempt to answer such questions calls for a look at the argumentation of the entire *Epistle* against the background of Rochester's *œuvre* as a whole.

[28] Cf., for instance, Erskine-Hill, 'Rochester: Augustan or Explorer?', pp. 59–60, and Griffin, *Satires Against Man*, pp. 58–67.
[29] Erskine-Hill spoke for many when maintaining that 'the irony is not consistent' in the *Heroicall Epistle* ('Rochester: Augustan or Explorer?', p. 60) and that 'the speaker's protestations are not entirely ridiculous'. To this, Paul C. Davies replied that 'Bajazet may be an egoist, but he is not a complete idiot; his brand of special pleading contains the same admixture of truth and specious argument as we find in Butler's *Hudibras*.' See 'Rochester: Augustan and Explorer', *The Durham University Journal* 61.2 (n.s. 30.2; March 1969), 61.

David Vieth claimed that Bajazet is satirised 'because his self-centered attitudes implicitly violate traditional standards of conduct and morality'.[30] Various Rochester readers have been doubtful about that claim, feeling that the idea of Rochester as a champion of 'traditional standards of conduct' defies credibility. Still, Vieth is surely right in pointing to the gross violation of seventeenth-century notions of 'degree' in lines 8–9.[31] Rochester's letters, especially the ones to Savile, do not afford any reason to suppose that he would place self-interest before friendship. Nor is he ever on record as defending loutish manners (cf. line 10 in the *Heroicall Epistle*); it is noticeable that all three satires on Mulgrave charge him with being socially offensive.

But the quality that forms the focus of the satire in the poems on Mulgrave is – once again – pride. Whenever other Rochester speakers have acknowledged inconstancy, they have evaded responsibility by claiming to be impelled by forces beyond their control. By contrast, Bajazet claims to be subject to no other influences than those he has brought into and adjusted to the sphere of his own ego. It is an attitude of the most stupendous vanity and would as such have been especially abhorrent to Rochester.

A man who hated self-glorification as much as Rochester did could never even for an instant have envisaged the 'happy Sultan's' existence, described in lines 32–52, as an ideal. Many commentators have argued that Bajazet identifies with this potentate in a kind of waking reverie, and the words 'sexual/sensual fantasy' are often applied to these lines:[32]

> Oh happy Sultan! whom wee Barb'rous call!
> How much refin'd art thou above us all?
> Who Envys not the joys of thy Seraill?
> Thee, like some God, the trembling Crowd adore,
> Each Man's thy Slave, and Woman-kind, thy Whore.
> Methinkes I see thee underneath the shade,
> Of Golden Cannopies, supinely laid:
> Thy crowching Slaves, all silent as the Night,
> But at the Nod, all Active as the Light!
> Secure in Solid Sloth, thou there dost Reigne,
> And feel'st the joys of Love, without the paine:
> Each Female Courts thee with a wishing Eye,

[30] The headnote to the *Heroicall Epistle* in Vieth's edition; p. 113. A more detailed and qualified presentation of Vieth's line of thought in this respect is found in *Attribution*, pp. 109–18.

[31] *Ibid.*, p. 109. Many subsequent scholars have echoed, and elaborated on, these views; see, for example, Whitley, 'Rochester', 182–3.

[32] Farley-Hills repeatedly uses the term 'sexual fantasy' to describe them; see pp. 124–5 in *Rochester's Poetry*.

Whilst thou with Awfull Pride, walkst carelesse by,
Till thy kind Pledge at last markes out the Dame,
Thou fancy'st most to quench thy present flame:
Then from thy Bed, submissive she retires,
And thankfull for the Grace, noe more requires.
Noe lowd reproach, nor fond unwelcome sound
Of Womens Tongues, thy sacred Eare dares wound;
If any doe, a nimble Mute strait tyes,
The True-Love-Knot, and stops her foolish cryes.

While there is mention of 'joys of Love' and 'present flame', the quality of sensual experience is not an issue here at all. What Bajazet envies the Sultan – a circumstance which clashes with his vaunting utterances in the first half of the poem – is that he can gratify his every desire without suffering from a vile aftertaste. The Sultan is in control; his admirer indirectly admits that he himself, for all his blustering, is not.

Hence, Bajazet is ridiculous because he is not the regal figure he pretended to be; but the Sultan passage entails yet another satirical dimension.

Dreaming of being able to command the instant compliance, sexual and otherwise, of slaves is not an occupation for the discerning Restoration gentleman. Rochester's poems, his *Valentinian*, his letters and other records of his life suggest that he would find such an attitude repellent as well as stupid. Whenever hints of bliss – betrayed, threatened or as-yet-unrealised – are articulated, they involve an interaction of lover and lady at some level, and finding unbroken rest, security and peace in the arms of the beloved is the never-fulfilled aim. Rochester's verse often speaks of suffering in connexion with love, and a wish to surmount it is certainly a feature in these poems; but that wish can only be gratified by way of a harmony of wills and bodies. The idea of 'security' represented by the sultan pipe-dream is entirely foreign to every utterance that can with some degree of credibility be related to Rochester's own views.

This is not to say that he was in any sense a supporter of the equality of the sexes, or that he never spoke of, or treated, women in a cavalier manner. Rochester could be callous, condescending, even brutal; but he has not deserved having the notion of the Godlike potentate 'with Awfull Pride' ascribed to him as an ideal solution to the pains of love. Such a solution, to him, would always entail an element of reciprocity. The *problem* – tasting earthly joys with an aching heart – was one he knew better than most, but his *answer* – in poems like 'Absent from thee', *The Fall* and *The Mistress* – could hardly be more different from Bajazet's.

Mulgrave/Bajazet, then, is mocked because the falseness of his initial boasts is revealed by his sultan ambitions and because those ambitions are silly in themselves. The author of *The Character of a Town-Gallant* (1675), whose comments on Restoration hectors sometimes recall passages in Rochester's social satire, would have agreed. A town gallant, 'a bundle of Vanity',

vows *Mahomet* was a brave Bully and deserves to be *Worshipped*, because he had the wit to make his *Paradice* a *Seraglio*.[33]

Bajazet's alignment of Damocles' sword with the blades of jealous rivals and offended male relatives is a ridiculous one in itself:

> Thou fearst noe injur'd Kinsmans threatning Blade,
> Nor Midnight Ambushes, by Rivalls laid;
> While here with Akeing Heart, our joys wee taste,
> Disturb'd by Swords, like Democles his Feast.

The Damocles'-sword image was something of a cliché among commentators on the Restoration social scene. To quote just one example, Richard Graham's *Angliae Speculum Morale* referred to 'the Gallant or Hector' as

he who maketh Vice his business; who recreates himself with dangerous follies; who feedeth upon his greatest enjoyments with Heaven's sword of justice hanging over his head by a very slender hair of Mercy. (p. 31)

By all accounts, Mulgrave's and Rochester's contemporaries regarded the *Heroicall Epistle* as an efficient attack on the former; 'Bajazet' soon became one of his soubriquets. One of the poem's most insidious stabs at his vanity is the four-line passage on the 'Blazeing Starr':

> Noe glorious thing, was ever made to stay,
> My Blazeing Starr, but visits, and away:
> As fatall too, it shines, as those i' th' Skyes,
> Tis never seene, but some great Lady dyes.

The reference is, as many commentators have pointed out, to the Order of the Garter; Mulgrave received it in the spring of 1674,[34] only twenty-

---

[33] P. 2. References to Oriental monarchs and the like seem to have been Restoration commonplaces. John Hayman has noted a pertinent passage from Waller; see 'An Image of the Sultan in Waller's "Of Love" and "A Very Heroical Epistle in Answer to Ephelia"', *Notes and Queries* 15.10 (vol. 213 in the continuous series; October 1968), 380–1. Another instance is found in Aphra Behn's *On Mr. J. H. in a Fit of Sickness* (stanza III).

[34] On 23 April, according to all modern scholars; but the quoted *Character* of Mulgrave gives the date as 29 May. (29 May was, of course, the anniversary of Charles II's entering London on the Restoration.)

five years old. He is said to have been extremely proud of it. A 'blazing star' is, as editors have noted, also a designation for a comet. Fusing the Garter emblem, erotic conquest and the portentous implications of comets results in a truly funny conceit, and contemporary readers must have relished it. Thomas Rawlins'(?) *Tunbridge-Wells*, probably written a year or two after the *Heroicall Epistle*, may embody an allusion to this jest. In that play, one 'Poet Witless' proposes a toast to 'the blazing Star of perfection'. His companions do not quite know what to make of this, supposing it to be a reference to a lady, but Witless replies, 'I say the Blazing Star, th' Epithet's my own, and I'le mantain it' (p. 25). The suspicion that Witless is meant to recall Mulgrave is not perhaps too far-fetched.

There seems to be little reason to doubt that the *Epistolary Essay* and the *Heroicall Epistle* are bona fide satires on Rochester's enemy John Sheffield, Earl of Mulgrave, and it is difficult to find any appreciable amount of ambiguity or insincerity[35] in either of them. The *Heroicall Epistle* is no hedonist fantasy. Bajazet actually perverts the true Epicurean's attitude to life with his maxim 'to avoyd all paine'. In line 13 of the *Heroicall Epistle*, pain clearly means 'effort' as well as 'suffering'. No intelligent person who pursued mental satisfaction and peace through sensory experience could allow such a principle to guide his/her life. It is certainly far from the sober realisation, in one of Rochester's finest poems, that 'pain can ne're deceive'.[36]

MY LORD ALL-PRIDE

There is a radical difference between having an enemy condemn himself out of his own mouth and simply piling abuse on him. Rochester does the latter in the thirty-line lampoon *My Lord All-Pride*. It is no wonder that the virulence of this attack has struck readers as inconsistent with the carefully wrought ironies of the two 'epistles'. In the latter poems, a fool praises his own folly, like Erasmus' Stultitia.[37] The result may not

---

[35] According to Whitley, 'the question of [Rochester's] sincerity is bound to loom large in his readers' minds' ('Rochester', 185).

[36] Farley-Hills, calling that sentence to mind, concluded that 'we are meant to reject Bajazet's point of view' (*Rochester's Poetry*, p. 125).

[37] In Vieth's recent essay on the influence of Erasmus' *Moriae Encomium*, he suggests (p. 20) that the application of such a perspective could resolve the uncertainties which readers have felt in respect of the speaker's status in the Mulgrave satires. It was not a new idea; Erskine-Hill had

be a paradoxical kind of wisdom, as is the case in Erasmus' long and entertaining monologue; but the whole undertaking is coloured by an intent to amuse as well as abuse.

In *My Lord All-Pride*, however, no tonal and structural subtleties temper the loathing of the attacker, whom I see no reason for not referring to as Rochester. Mulgrave and he were personal enemies, and there is no hint of a *persona* speaker in this record of what is obviously personal malice and disgust.

For all the difference in perspective and idiom, the thematic links between the *Epistolary Essay* and the *Heroicall Epistle* on the one hand and *My Lord All-Pride* on the other are considerable. In addition to the excremental parallel between the *Epistolary Essay* and *My Lord All-Pride*, and the stellar imagery common to the *Heroicall Epistle* and *My Lord All-Pride* (two features often noted by critics), the latter poem contains several instances of an outsider's view of M. G./Bajazet's self-confessed, or self-proclaimed, characteristics. That composite Mulgrave *persona* makes no bones about admitting that he collaborates with a superior poet; will not submit himself to any kind of restraint; is generally disapproved of as having regrettable manners but refuses to contemplate mending them; is consequently indifferent to his unpopularity; esteems his own judgement above that of 'this sawcy World'[38] and hence *a priori* disallows any criticism; is impervious to any female claims which do not agree with his own fancy; and has self-interest as his sole ideal. *My Lord All-Pride* takes up these features from a different angle. The benefits drawn from better men's efforts are compared to feeding off their faeces; the absence of self-criticism renders the proud lord incapable of perceiving his own inadequacies; far from behaving 'naturally', he actually offends against Nature by aspiring to purposes and pursuits she did not equip him for; he is hence hopeless in the role of ladies' man; he is blind to his own bungling awkwardness; and as a result, he does not have a single friend in the world. The pride of M. G. and Bajazet is thus turned to 'Shame, and derision' in *My Lord All-Pride* ('Baffl'd', incidentally, means 'disgraced, dishonoured', according to *OED* 1). What may seem to be dissimilarities are merely due to a difference in outlook.

Some features in *My Lord All-Pride* fall outside this pattern of

expressed it in 'Rochester: Augustan or Explorer?', pp. 57 and 63. The relevance of Erasmus' work to Restoration poetry in general was first brought up by Richard Quaintance in 'Passion and Reason', pp. 51–3.

[38] Line 83 in the *Epistolary Essay*, where 'sawcy' probably means 'wanton, lascivious' (*OED* 2b).

correspondence, though. For one thing, Mulgrave's military career comes in for a withering blast in lines 19–22. Biographical accounts of Mulgrave do not suggest that he lacked military aptitude or valour;[39] in fact, he won recognition for his warlike exploits on land and sea. One circumstance that could have prompted Rochester's contention that Mulgrave was a parody of a soldier is that his career under Turenne, under whom he served at the time of the Third Dutch War, was short and attended by rivalry with Monmouth, who enjoyed the reputation of being a good soldier. Their contretemps took place in 1674, and the brevity of Mulgrave's martial stint in France may well have looked like, and been, a discreditable performance. In any case, Rochester was not the only contemporary satirist who saw Mulgrave as a military and amorous failure.[40]

Mulgrave's deficiencies as a lover are hinted at in lines 15–18, where his physical attributes are said to render him ridiculous in the part.[41] Much more extensive and explicit abuse with regard to erotic ineptitude is heaped on Sir Carr Scroope, but Mulgrave's lack of appeal to women is clear from this passage. The contrast with the braggart in the *Heroicall Epistle* could hardly be greater.

Three references to Restoration theatre emphasise the ridicule with which Mulgrave is regarded 'abroad, at home, i' th' Camp, and Court'. The comparisons between him and two figures from the *commedia dell'arte* testify to the popularity of the Italian comedy in England at this time.[42] Both Punchinello and Harlequin were clownish types; Dryden's epilogue to *The Man of Mode* mentions 'those nauseous Harlequins', who 'in Farce may pass' (line 3). The 'knight of the burning pestle', Ralph in Beaumont and Fletcher's play, was, of course, also a figure of fun. A parody of knight-errantry and an absurd intrusion on the actual plot, he is an apt metaphor for the preposterous Lord All-Pride.[43]

It is only marginally a kinder one than the initial equation of

[39] In the *Heroicall Epistle*, Bajazet claims not to have the slightest ambition to appear 'stout', that is, physically brave. [40] Cf. Vieth, *Attribution*, p. 337.

[41] The only physical imperfection allowed in the *Character* of Mulgrave is that he was 'a little too long-waisted, and rather too narrow in his chest and shoulders' (p. 2).

[42] See, for instance, Nicoll, *Restoration Drama*, pp. 192–3, 249–53 and 255. Italian companies visited London in 1675 and again in 1678. The dating of *My Lord All-Pride* is uncertain. As it seems to allude to a poisonous poem of Mulgrave's, it is most naturally associated with the *Essay upon Satire*; but as Vieth shows, there are problems connected with such a dating (*Attribution*, p. 341).

[43] *The Knight of the Burning Pestle* seems to have been revived between 1665 and 1671; see Van Lennep et al., *The London Stage*, p. 95. Walker suggested a bawdy secondary meaning in the 'burning pestle'; see p. 300 in his edition.

Mulgrave with a purulent swelling or cyst[44] and the swine simile. Even the Restoration offers few examples of one nobleman vilifying another which could be said to match *My Lord All-Pride* for sheer acrimony.

THE LAMPOONS ON SCROOPE

One thing that immediately strikes a reader who turns to Rochester's satirical portraits of Scroope after studying the ones on Mulgrave is how similar the charges against these two men are: they are bungling, awkward writers, deficient in intellect as well as in skill; they are conceited and vain; and they are friendless butts of general ridicule. To make matters worse, sneers the most attractive man at the Court of Charles II, their ugliness makes their social and amorous ambitions revolting as well as ludicrous. Both men are Nature's failures; Scroope's existence is even claimed to be an offence against her.

Vieth mapped out the following chronological outline with regard to the Scroope poems: first, Rochester attacked Scroope in the 'Purblind Knight' lines of *An Allusion to Horace* (115–17); Scroope paid him back with *In Defence of Satyr*, in which lines 48–59 portray Rochester; Rochester's reaction was *On the suppos'd Authour of a late* Poem *in defence of* Satyr, to which Scroope replied in the six-line *Answer* ('Raile on poor feeble Scribbler'); Rochester retorted by means of *On Poet Ninny*. This literary quarrel seems to have taken place between the winter of 1675–6 (the *Allusion*) and 1678.[45] One amusing feature in it is Rochester's highly indecent burlesque of Scroope's love lyric 'I cannot change as others do'. That is not a bad poem – even Rochester champions have praised it –; but Rochester's brutally hyperbolic make-over slashes its gracefulness to shreds.

This history of the Rochester–Scroope quarrel places Rochester in the invidious position of having started it; but the *Allusion* passage is itself a reaction to Scroope's criticism:

> Shou'd I be troubled when the Purblind Knight
> Who squints more in his Judgment, than his sight,
> Picks silly faults, and Censures what I write?

---

[44] 'Impostume' means 'abscess' (*OED* 1). I cannot find the toad image advanced by Kristoffer Paulson as a source of inspiration for Pope in *My Lord All-Pride*; see Paulson's 'Rochester and Milton: The Sound, Sense, and Sources of Pope's Portraits of Bufo, Atticus, and Sporus in *An Epistle to Dr. Arbuthnot*', *Papers on Language and Literature* 12.3 (Summer 1976), 300–1.

[45] See Vieth, *Attribution*, pp. 160–3, and Lord, *Poems on Affairs of State*, pp. 357–75.

The nature of the respective attacks is far more interesting than the genesis of the conflict, though. Rochester's charges against Scroope have already been reviewed; Scroope's accusations against Rochester are far less heated. Wondering at Rochester's popularity (and thus implicitly conceding a point to his adversary), the author of *In Defence of Satyr* finds it unfair that he himself should be regarded as a 'railer'. After a string of inherently unlikely events resembling lines 143–50 in Rochester's *Ramble*, Scroope pronounces that they will all happen before he will resort to 'black malice' 'That wrongs a worthy man or hurts his friend'.[46] His main accusation against Rochester is that the latter is capable of maltreating and betraying his friends for the sake of salvaging a joke, or his hide.

It is not an unfounded accusation, and it is one which a man who valued friendship would not take in good part (see below). Stung, Rochester resorts to invective; the greater part of his reply is devoted to Scroope's appearance and its deleterious effects on the baronet's attempts to woo the ladies:

> A lump deform'd, and shapeless wert thou born,
> Begot in *Loves* despight, and *Natures* scorn;
> And art grown up, the most ungraceful *Wight*,
> Harsh to the *Ear*, and hideous to the sight,
> Yet *Love's* thy bus'ness, *Beauty* thy delight.
> Curse on that silly hour, that first inspir'd,
> Thy madness, to pretend to be admir'd;
> To paint thy grizly *Face*, to dance, to dress,
> And all those Awkward *Follies* that express,
> Thy loathsome Love, and filthy daintiness.
> Who needs will be an Ugly *Beau-Garcon*,
> Spit at, and shun'd, by ev'ry *Girl* in *Town*;
> Where dreadfully *Loves Scare-Crow*, thou art plac'd
> To fright the tender *Flock*, that long to taste:
> While ev'ry coming *Maid*, when you appear,
> Starts back for shame, and strait turns chaste for fear.
> For none so poor, or *Prostitute* have prov'd,
> Where you made love, t'endure to be belov'd.

The expression '*Beau-Garcon*' is lifted from Scroope's portrait of Mulgrave in the *Defence*:

---

[46] Lines 72–3 in Scroope's *Defence*; p. 368 in Lord's *Poems on Affairs of State* edition and p. 138 in Walker's edition of Rochester's poems, where Scroope's *In defence of Satyr* has well-advisedly been included in its entirety.

> Grandio thinks himself a beau garçon,
> Goggles his eyes, writes letters up and down,
> And with his saucy love plagues all the town,
> Whilst pleas'd to have his vanity thus fed,
> He's caught with Gosnell, that old hag, abed.[47]

Paradoxically enough, Rochester's attack on Scroope in *On the suppos'd Authour* thus takes place in the arena where Scroope attacked Mulgrave.

When Scroope replies to *On the suppos'd Authour*, he voices his pitying contempt of Rochester's fulminations. The alleged inefficacy of Rochester's abuse is not so much imputed to inability to write well as to Rochester's personal infamy:

> Raile on poor feeble Scribbler, speake of me,
> In as bad Terms as the World speakes of thee;
> Sit swelling in thy hole, like a vext Toad,
> And full of Pox, and Mallice spit abroad.
> Thou canst blast noe Mans Fame with thy ill word,
> Thy Pen, is full as harmlesse as thy Sword.

This is a neat rejoinder, and by and large, Scroope proved a deadlier enemy than Mulgrave. Rochester's *On Poet Ninny*, to which no reply from Scroope is known, is not a very impressive piece of bluster. There is a note of impotent rage in it:

> All Pride, and Uglinesse! Oh how wee loath,
> A nauseous Creature soe compos'd of both!
> ...
> For of all Folly, sure the very topp,
> Is a conceited Ninny, and a Fopp.

With the exception of 'Mela[n]cholly', implying mental derangement,[48] the actual charges against Scroope (pride, ugliness, incompetence in writing, low standing among men of wit) were made, and rather better made, before. Perhaps the end of the lampoon was in part dictated by such a realisation:

> But 'tis too much, on soe despis'd a Theame;
> Noe Man, wou'd dabble in a dirty Streame:
> The worst that I cou'd write, wou'd be noe more,
> Then what thy very Friends have said before.

---

[47] Lines 96–100 of Scroope's *Defence*; p. 369 in Lord's volume.

[48] Melancholy was occasionally aligned with madness, denoting what later ages would refer to as monomania. To quote just one Restoration example, a handbill of 1673 advertised an asylum for the *Madd and Melancholy* (see John F. Sena, *A Bibliography of Melancholy* (London, 1970), p. 16, item 55).

The concluding couplet has a sting lacking in the remainder of *On Poet Ninny*; but it does not quite manage to destroy the impression that Rochester came out of this tussle rather the worse for wear.[49]

Several critics have asked themselves what Scroope did to deserve all he got from Rochester. Scholarly studies of the late seventeenth century present the 'Purblind Knight' as a person of very little consequence. He was below Rochester and Mulgrave in social status, having been made a baronet in 1667. His short stature and ditto sight were ridiculed in a number of satires, and in love he seems to have been as unsuccessful as Rochester implies.[50] *In Defence of Satyr* was an indifferent work, and Scroope never reaped any laurels as a poet. Rochester, whose handsome appearance, poetic skill and devastating charm were generally acknowledged, surely had no need to take a man like Scroope seriously.

My Lord All-Pride, *On the suppos'd Authour* and *On Poet Ninny* all seem to have been actuated by pieces of satirical verse directed against Rochester. While the first of them is violent enough, it is not uncontrolled; the metaphors (abscess, excretions, swine, stars, Punchinello/Harlequin, elephant, knight of the burning pestle) have a certain sadistic force, and the piece is not wholly devoid of humour. The same may be said of the beginning and end of the first satire on Scroope:

> To rack, and torture thy unmeaning *Brain*,
> In *Satyrs* praise, to a low untun'd strain,
> In thee was most impertinent and vain.
> When in thy *Person*, we more clearly see,
> That *Satyr's* of Divine Authority,
> For *God*, made one on *Man*, when he made thee.
>
> ...
>
> Half-witty, and half-mad, and scarce half-brave,
> Half-honest (which is very much a *Knave*.)
> Made up of all these Halfs, thou can'st not pass,
> For any thing intirely, but an *Asse*.

But for all its elaborate oxymora,[51] the middle of that lampoon, and virtually all of *On Poet Ninny*, is little more than rant. Another contemporary lampoon on Scroope, *A Familiar Epistle to Mr. Julian, Secretary to the Muses*,[52] is much more wickedly amusing; its barbed

---

49 Robinson, conversely, thinks Scroope had the worst of it ('The Art of Violence', p. 102). I wish I could agree.
50 Cf. Vieth's *Attribution*, pp. 235–8, and p. 210 in Wilson's *Nell Gwyn*.
51 Kristoffer Paulson has drawn attention to the oxymoronic images 'loathsome Love', 'filthy daintiness' and so on; see 'Rochester and Milton', 308.
52 Believed to be by Buckingham; see Lord, *Poems on Affairs of State*, pp. 387–91, and Vieth, *Attribution*, pp. 350–2.

mock-compliments merely serve to sharpen the attack on Scroope's execrable verse, unimpressive exterior and lack of success in love and in society.

Did Scroope's words on Rochester's unreliability as a friend hit him on the funny-bone at a time when friendship, and his inability to make and keep friends, were evidently much on his mind?[53] The conclusion of *On Poet Ninny* could be viewed as an attempt to pay Scroope back in kind. Whatever the reason, the satires on Scroope show Rochester losing his grasp of 'Epethets' and 'Jeast[s] in Scorne', slipping into 'uselesse Words' and forgetting all about 'circumscrib[ing]'. This failure to live up to precepts and ideals in an area of activity which was patently important to him indicates that not even the realm of writing afforded him complete contentment and control. That a nobody like Scroope should have caused Rochester to offend against his own high literary standards is a bitter joke and arguably a better one than any he himself made at Scroope's expense.

---

[53] Cf. pp. 92–3, 106–9, 113, 114, 117 and 158 in Treglown's edition of Rochester's *Letters*.

Epilogue

If Sir Carr Scroope's lampoons on Rochester penetrated his defences to some degree, they were preceded by a portrait of him which none of his enemies could match for sheer savagery and hyperbole:

> Son of A whore God dam you can you tell
> A Peerless Peer the Readyest way to Hell?
> Ive out swilld Baccus sworn of my own make
> Oaths wod fright furies and make Pluto quake.
> Ive swived more whores more ways than Sodoms walls
> Ere knew or the College of Romes Cardinalls.
> Witness Heroick scars, look here nere go
> Sear cloaths and ulcers from the top to toe.
> Frighted at my own mischeifes I have fled
> And bravely left my lifes defender dead.
> Broke houses to break chastity and died
> That floor with murder which my lust denyed.
> Pox on it why do I speak of these poor things?
> I have blasphemed my god and libelld Kings;
> The readyest way to Hell come quick –
> Boy   nere stirr
> The readyest way my Lords by Rochester.

These lines have been regarded as a piece of exultant, Don Juanesque bragging;[1] but other and more subtle characteristics have been observed in them, too.[2]

---

[1] See, for example, Wilcoxon, 'Sexual Politics', 138. An interesting parallel between this poem and Shadwell's contemporary play *The Libertine* was noted by Griffin, p. 56 in *Satires Against Man*: 'I cannot but admire, since you are resolv'd to go to the Devil, that you cannot be content with the common way of travelling, but must ride post to him.'

[2] See, for instance, Vieth, *Attribution*, p. 203, and Righter, 'John Wilmot', 53. Patterson suggests that the crimes of which the peerless peer boasts 'might be the ten commandments of the

One of the most intriguing features of *To the Post Boy* is the mixture of braggadocio and literal truth. Drinking more than the god of wine, frightening Hades and the Furies with home-made oaths, and out-performing Sodom in respect of diversity as well as numbers can hardly be credited to one person, however notorious. These monstrosities are simply ludicrous. The standard sodomy accusation against priests of the Catholic Church is included for good measure. But in line 8, the details of the description move uncomfortably close to home. The second half of the self-characterisation alludes to the torments of venereal disease, and of contemporary VD therapy, with which Rochester was thoroughly acquainted. It goes on to mention the disgraceful incident at Epsom, where his behaviour was not only foolish but cowardly. The word 'bravely' carries the fiercest sting in the lash of lines 9–10. Lines 11–12 may form a reference to the same incident.[3] If so, it lacks the veracity of the preceding lines; neither at Epsom nor anywhere else is Rochester known to have murdered anyone who placed obstacles in the way of his lust. Libelled kings he certainly did, though, and repeatedly – not only his own monarch, but Louis XIV as well.

The issue of blasphemy is one that will be given separate treatment, but one point might be briefly considered before leaving *To the Post Boy*. Why should Rochester turn against himself in this manner? Is the poem a strange act of contrition, as Vieth suggests?[4]

The view, put forward by several critics, that Rochester is taking the wind out of his opponents' sails by reviling himself is surely pertinent. He poses hyperbolic charges which his contemporaries would recognise, and laugh at, as being ridiculous exaggerations of the ones often levelled at him by his adversaries in various camps. In lines 8–9, conversely and audaciously, he sails as close to the wind as possible without losing his steerageway. Nobody could render his shameful part in the Epsom brawl more viciously than he did himself. In consequence, Scroope's subsequent criticism of Rochester in that regard (lines 52–4 of *In Defence of Satyr*) failed to augment Rochester's infamy where the actual event was concerned. The only fresh element was Scroope's indignation over Rochester's having made a 'buffoon conceit' (line 55) of his disgrace.

Prophylactic self-preservatory measures are only one aspect of *To the Post Boy*, though. It should not be forgotten that this was a time when

---

Disabled Debauchee's religion: drinking, swearing, fornication, buggery, cowardice, violence, rape, murder, blasphemy and libel'; see 'Rochester's Second Bottle', 13.

[3] Vieth points out that it is in that case 'a lurid exaggeration'; p. 201 in *Attribution*.

[4] *Ibid.*

vice was all the rage, whether actually practised or not. Butler's *Satire upon the Licentious Age of Charles II* provides a sardonic representation of substance and pretence:

> For those who heretofore sought private holes,
> Securely in the dark to damn their souls,
> Wore vizards of hypocrisy, to steal
> And slink away in masquerade to hell,
> Now bring their crimes into the open sun,
> For all mankind to gaze their worst upon ...
> Call heav'n and earth to witness how they've aim'd,
> With all their utmost vigour, to be damn'd,
> And by their own examples, in the view
> Of all the world, striv'd to damn others too;
> ...
> For men have now made vice so great an art,
> The matter of fact's become the slightest part;
> And the debauched'st actions they can do,
> Mere trifles to the circumstance and show.
> For 'tis not what they do that's now the sin,
> But what they lewdly' affect and glory in,
> As if prepost'rously they would profess
> A forc'd hypocrisy of wickedness ...
> For vices for themselves may find excuse,
> But never for their complement and shows ...[5]

To the Post Boy starts with a specimen of run-of-the-mill town-gallant swearing (see pp. 256 and 283 above), and Butler had caustic things to say about that kind of language:

> How copious is our language lately grown,
> To make blaspheming wit, and a jargon!
> And yet how expressive and significant,
> In *damme* at once to curse, and swear, and rant!
> As if no way express'd men's souls so well,
> As damning of them to the pit of hell;
> Nor any asseveration were so civil,
> As mortgaging salvation to the devil;
> Or that his name did add a charming grace,
> And blasphemy a purity to our phrase.

Blasphemy is one of the allegations that Rochester directs against himself, and rightly, as was pointed out above. During the reign of

---

[5] *The Poetical Works of Samuel Butler*, vol. II (London, 1866), pp. 191–3, lines 35–40, 43–6, 53–60 and 63–4; the subsequent quotation is made up of lines 101–10.

Charles II, it was not a mere *Kavaliersdelikt*; it was an offence at common law, and people were punished for it. An interesting feature of blasphemy at the time of the Restoration was its association with attacks on the worldly power. In the eyes of contemporary lawyers, an attack on Christianity was an attack on the law of the realm, and attacking the law was criminal. The section on the Restoration years in G. D. Nokes' *A History of the Crime of Blasphemy*[6] makes that connexion very clear. It was, for instance, an offence 'maliciously and advisedly to affirm that the King was a heretic or papist, or ... by words or writing to "stir up the people to hatred or dislike of the Person of his Majestie or the established Government"' (Nokes, *History*, p. 42).

When Rochester placed blasphemy and libel against God and King respectively side by side, and indicated that these were worse crimes than violence against persons, he was thus to some extent reflecting Restoration notions. One may wonder why, if such a grave view was taken of these related offences, he should himself have escaped retribution. Other men lost money and employment after being tried for such seditious behaviour. Rochester, however, was a peer and as such exempt from the legal provisions that applied to ordinary people; besides, nothing overtly blasphemous was published under his name in his lifetime. Still, *Upon Nothing*, good-humoured and subtle as it is, is definitely blasphemous (cf. p. 148) as well as containing defamatory sniping at the monarch (who is, of course, very thoroughly libelled in the *Satire on Charles II*).

Rochester's attitudes to matters associated with religion have been touched on here and there in this book, but no close definition of his stance in respect of the Christian faith has so far been attempted. It is hard to name any one school of thought, in any field, of which he may confidently be said to have been an adherent; 'isms' have a way of slipping off him. He articulated views associated with Epicureanism, scepticism, libertinism and so on,[7] but identifying him with one or several of these concepts is a difficult business. For one thing, defining the concepts themselves is no easy matter. A fairly wide net has to be thrown, and the job of subsequently locating Rochester in it does not seem to be a very fruitful endeavour. Sensationalism and empiricism

---

[6] London, 1928; the Restoration section is found on pp. 42–64, but there are many other references to this period in the book.

[7] James G. Turner has contributed a clearsighted consideration of the concept of libertinism as related to Rochester; see his 'The Properties of Libertinism' in Maccubbin, ed., *Unauthorized Sexual Behaviour*, 76–81.

may be quoted as designations for key elements in Rochester's way of thinking, and yet they do not always seem applicable.[8]

It is tempting to look for similar excuses for not going into the question of Rochester's faith, including the most spectacular aspect of it, his deathbed conversion. A student of his poetry could, for instance, argue that his making his peace with the Church of England has no bearing on the poems and is hence irrelevant to a critical investigation. Still, sidestepping the event that has played such a vital part in shaping the various attitudes to Rochester adopted by subsequent generations would be pusillanimous. Any consideration of it must be speculative – the following pages certainly cannot claim to be anything else –; but no Rochester scholar should, in decency, shirk that issue.

In the eyes of many of his contemporaries, Rochester was an atheist, and in the sense that his views on religion were unorthodox, he was.[9] He is on record as having denied the charge, though (see p. 147 above). Whatever else he might have been, Rochester was not a hypocrite, and I think he deserves to be believed on this score. His conception of God seems to have been far removed from that of the Established Church – Burnet's account provides plenty of evidence –, amounting to a *deus-absconditus* Creator whose indifference to the fates of men parallels that of the deities in the passage from Lucretius which Rochester translated:

> The *Gods*, by right of Nature, must possess
> An Everlasting Age, of perfect Peace:
> Far off, remov'd from us, and our Affairs:
> Neither approach'd by *Dangers*, or by *Cares*:
> Rich in themselves, to whom we cannot add:
> Not pleas'd by *Good* Deeds; nor provok'd by *Bad*.

These lines have often been quoted as being relevant to Rochester's own notion of the Christian God. Although they are a translation, people who translate epigrammatic poetry for pleasure are hardly likely to pick passages they disagree with.

---

[8] As Whitley points out, Rochester found the sensationalist universe inadequate ('Rochester', 179; I find it hard to believe that this was the outcome of 'traditional habits of thought', though).

[9] See p. 174 above on the meaning of the term 'atheism' in Rochester's day. With regard to Rochester's religion, Larry Carver has maintained that his poetry supplies evidence 'of an excessive preoccupation with *and acceptance of* Christian orthodoxy' (italics added), suggesting ways in which 'rejection signalizes affirmation' (pp. 90 and 98 in Vieth's *Critical Essays* collection). The argumentation is a little too complicated for me. There are certainly many instances of Christian idiom in Rochester's writings – Treglown's edition of the *Letters* shows, with great knowledge and skill, how chunks from the Christian literature he was brought up on had stayed imprinted on his memory –, but they need not signal any adherence to Christian values.

Another translation of Rochester's is interesting in this context, and many critics have dwelt on it. His rendering of the *Post mortem nihil est* lines from Seneca's *Troades* includes a kick at the clergy ('Rogues') who attempt to frighten mankind with insubstantial tales of infernal torment.[10] The attitude to Heaven and Hell articulated in the *Troades* translation was common enough for seventeenth-century *bienséance* writers to express urgent warnings against it.

Not only did many late-seventeenth-century men and women disbelieve the idea of hell as a place of eternal punishment;[11] Seneca's lines themselves were apparently popular. Rochester's translation was preceded by a more ambitious one of the whole Chorus from 'Verum est?' to 'par sollicito fabula somnio'. It was composed by Jean Dehénault, a poet whose work Rochester may well have known.[12] Dehénault, like many of his contemporaries, was fond of paraphrasing purple passages from the classics, and Rochester may have picked up the idea of translating the *Troades* lines from him.

Be that as it may, Rochester's version is terse and effective, perhaps somewhat overburdened with alliteration ('grim griezly Dogg') but clearly carefully wrought. Again, there is reason to believe that he sympathised with the content of the Latin text. The date of this translation is uncertain.[13] Regardless of whether it was a contemporary of the major satires or made in the last year or two of Rochester's life, it constitutes a very determined denial of resurrection as well as of damnation.

In his last illness, though, both eventualities became very much alive to him. A letter to Burnet, dated 25 June 1680,[14] is a painful record of his apprehension:

bestow your prayers upon mee that God would spare mee, (if itt bee his Good Will) to shew a true repentance, & amendment of life for the Time to come, or els if the Lord Pleaseth to put an end to my Worldly being now, that hee would mercifully except of my death bed repentance, & performe that promise hee hath binn pleased to make, that att what time soever a sinner doth repent hee would receiue him ...

---

[10] See p. 146 above.

[11] Cf. *Leviathan*, part 3, ch. 38, where Hobbes explains his view of the Second Death, after which there is no other. See also pp. 79–80 above.

[12] Dehénault was the mentor of Madame Deshoulières; his Seneca translation appeared in his *Oeuvres diverses* of 1670. See Lachèvre, ed., *Les Oeuvres de Jean Dehénault*, pp. 6–8.

[13] See p. 254 in Walker's edition of Rochester's poems.

[14] See p. 244 in Treglown's edition of the *Letters*.

When Burnet finally came to see him, Rochester allegedly told him that '*Horrour had given him his first awaking, yet that was now grown up into a settled Faith and Conversion*'.[15] The question of whether Rochester's repentance really deserves to be called a conversion depends on the truth of that statement. Did faith replace horror, and did Rochester die a devout Christian believer, as Burnet insists?

The circumstance which, more than any other, makes me believe that Rochester's conversion was indeed genuine is the impact which Isaiah's fifty-third chapter is said to have had on him. All the dying man's alleged pious utterances could have been touched up by those who – like his mother and her chaplain Parsons – may have felt that some embellishment would serve godly purposes. Some of his alleged deathbed utterances make embarrassing reading. His old crony Fanshaw, who called on him while he was dying, thought he was mad, and he was occasionally delirious. But there is no reason why anyone should have invented such a detail as the overwhelming impact of Isaiah 53. There was no need to supply a Biblical passage to which the sick man responded with particular warmth, and if there had been, there are plenty of rather more likely candidates to choose from in both Testaments. Pinto, who also believed that Burnet's description of the way in which Rochester was affected by these verses 'is the record of a genuine and memorable religious experience',[16] emphasised the importance of the poetic/mystic qualities of the text. This is surely a pertinent observation; but I think the actual words mattered a great deal, too.

The suffering redeemer is not presented as a being enveloped in celestial glory; 'there is no beauty that we should desire him'. Rochester himself is said (by Burnet) to have given special thought to the Saviour's lack of 'form' and 'comeliness'. Isaiah certainly stresses the external repulsiveness of the despised 'man of sorrows'. He was treated as an outcast by those whose souls he saved, but he bore their rejection as mutely as their griefs and iniquities. 'He had done no violence, neither was any deceit in his mouth.'

In Rochester's short life, he had experienced a fair amount of violence

---

[15] P. 84 in Farley-Hills' *Critical Heritage* reproduction of Burnet's *Some Passages*.

[16] See *Enthusiast in Wit*, p. 217; see also pp. 218–19 and 222–5. Another firm believer in Rochester's conversion is Don Cameron Allen, who devotes a long and thoughtful discussion to the matter in his *Doubt's Boundless Sea: Skepticism and Faith in the Renaissance* (Baltimore, 1964); see especially pp. 210–23. Both Graham Greene and Charles Williams dwell on the Isaiah passage in their discussions of Rochester's death; see especially the latter's *Rochester*, pp. 250–2 and 260.

and deceit, and his mature poetry bespeaks great weariness of both. He had seen as much of personal beauty and worldly splendour as anybody else in England at that time, and little good had it done him. Before hearing the Isaiah passage, he was allegedly in great distress and anxiety of mind, which is not surprising (Parsons said that 'his conscience [was] full of terrors'). To someone in that condition, the words 'Surely he hath borne our griefs, and carried our sorrows ... the chastisement of our peace was upon him' may well have conveyed a profound message of security and rest.

Isaiah's scruffy pariah, who sought out sinners even in death and humbly shouldered the burden of their wickedness, is a negation of that pride and vanity which Rochester had always loathed. At the same time, the contempt with which his inglorious figure must be regarded by people who trust to the evidence of their eyes only is a crushing condemnation of those who rely on their senses. As this Biblical locus took possession of Rochester's mind – he is said to have learnt it by heart and lain repeating it to himself –, I believe a reversal took place which formed a crucial factor in his conversion. The senses had ultimately proved incapable of satisfying Rochester's search for peace in the perfect experience, the harmony of mind and body. Wasting away, and often enough in physical as well as mental agony, he cannot have found it so very hard to renounce his commitment to their testimonies. If all his life he had been in the wrong about the possibility of finding lasting contentment by way of his senses, his error paralleled that of the misguided spectators who did not see the Saviour in the outcast. Their outward sense treacherously blinded them to the inner essence; his had done the same to him.

Many readers throughout the ages who have been attracted to Rochester precisely because of his earthiness, irreverence and impudence have found his repentance hard to take. Others have been bothered by the hackneyed piety with which it was exploited by zealous churchmen. Anne Righter, ever acute, vented her unhappiness in the following terms:

Rochester's old companion and fellow-reveller Fanshaw fled from the obsessive pieties of the death-bed at Woodstock convinced that his friend had gone mad. He hadn't, but he had effectively ceased to be Rochester. The very anonymity of the last letters, and of the recantation and apology for his past life which he dictated and signed on 19 June 1680 is startling. They could have been written by anyone. A whole personality has collapsed simultaneously with the doubts and contradictions at its centre.[17]

It is true that the documents signed by Rochester *in extremis* 'could have been written by anyone'. The poor man was surrounded by well-meaning if narrow-minded people who would not have shied away from wrapping his sentiments in veils of conventional religiousness. Deathbed conversions were commonplace,[18] and dead men disprove no pretty stories. The only evidence of a true spiritual conversion that seems wholly credible to me is Isaiah 53. The man who took comfort in that vision of a redeemer may not have taken leave of his personality, but he seems to have abandoned something that had made up a vital part of it: his conviction that the senses were the sole conveyors of reliable insights. The moment that conviction lost its force, 'Misterious truths, which no *Man* can conceive' could rush in and swamp Rochester's 'Fantastick mind'. Of that experience, alas, the poet's pen could leave us no record.

[17] 'John Wilmot', 69.
[18] For instance, the old libertine Des Barreaux allegedly summoned a priest as soon as he feared that he was mortally ill but forgot his new-found religious fervour once he was cured; see Dulong, *L'Amour au XVIIème siècle*, pp. 84 and 90–2.

Select bibliography

————◆◆◆◆————

Allen, Don Cameron, *Doubt's Boundless Sea: Skepticism and Faith in the Renaissance* (Baltimore, 1964).

Alsop, D. K., '"An Epistolary Essay from M. G. to O. B. upon Their Mutual Poems" and the Problem of the Persona in Rochester's Poetry', *Restoration: Studies in English Literary Culture 1660–1700* 12.2 (Fall 1988).

Atkinson, C. T., 'Charles II's Regiments in France', *Journal of the Society for Army Historical Research* 24 (1946).

Bredvold, Louis I., *The Intellectual Milieu of John Dryden: Studies in Some Aspects of Seventeenth-Century Thought* (Ann Arbor, 1934; reprinted 1956).

Brooks, David, ed., *Lyrics and Satires of John Wilmot Earl of Rochester* (Sydney, 1980).

Brooks, Harold F., 'The "Imitation" in English Poetry, Especially in Formal Satire, before the Age of Pope', *The Review of English Studies* 25 (1949).

Brooks, Harold F., and Raman Selden, eds., *The Poems of John Oldham* (Oxford, 1987).

Carroll, Robert Todd, *The Common-Sense Philosophy of Religion of Bishop Edward Stillingfleet* (The Hague, 1975).

Childs, John, *The Army of Charles II* (London, 1976).

Clark, A. F. B., *Boileau and the French Classical Critics in England (1660–1830)* (Paris, 1925).

Clay, Christopher, 'Marriage, Inheritance, and the Rise of Large Estates in England, 1660–1815', *The Economic History Review* second series, 21.3 (December 1968).

Cope, Jackson I., *Joseph Glanvill: Anglican Apologist* (St Louis, 1956).

Cragg, G. R., *From Puritanism to the Age of Reason* (Cambridge, 1950).
Puritanism in the Period of the Great Persecution: 1660–1688 (Cambridge, 1957; reprinted in 1971).

Crocker, S. F., 'Rochester's *Satire against Mankind*: A Study of Certain Aspects of the Background', *West Virginia University Bulletin* 3, Philological Papers, vol. 2 (May 1937).

Daves, Charles W., ed., *Samuel Butler 1612–1680 Characters* (Cleveland and London, 1970).

Davies, Paul C., 'Rochester: Augustan and Explorer', *The Durham University Journal* 61.2 (n.s. 30.2; March 1969).

'Rochester and Boileau: A Reconsideration', *Comparative Literature* 21 (Fall 1969).

Doody, Margaret Anne, *The Daring Muse: Augustan Poetry Reconsidered* (Cambridge, 1985).

Dulong, Claude, *L'Amour au XVIIème siècle* (Paris, 1969).

Erskine-Hill, Howard, 'Rochester: Augustan or Explorer?' in G. R. Hibbard, ed., *Renaissance and Modern Essays Presented to Vivian de Sola Pinto in Celebration of his 70th Birthday* (London, 1966).

Everett, Barbara, 'The Sense of Nothing', in Treglown, ed., *Spirit of Wit*.

Fabricant, Carole, 'Rochester's World of Imperfect Enjoyment', *Journal of English and Germanic Philology* 73 (1974).

Farley-Hills, David, ed., *Rochester: The Critical Heritage* (New York, 1972).

Rochester's Poetry (London, 1978).

Fea, Allan, *Some Beauties of the Seventeenth Century* (London, 1906).

Forbes, Thomas Rogers, *The Midwife and the Witch* (New Haven and London, 1966).

Fraser, Lady Antonia, *King Charles II* (London, 1979; reprinted as a Futura paperback, 1988).

The Weaker Vessel (New York, 1984).

Fujimura, Thomas J., 'Rochester's "Satyr against Mankind": An Analysis', *Studies in Philology* 55.4 (October 1958).

Gagen, Jean Elisabeth, *The New Woman: Her Emergence in English Drama 1600–1730* (New York, 1954).

Gill, James E., 'Mind against Itself: Theme and Structure in Rochester's *Satyr against Reason and Mankind*', *Texas Studies in Literature and Language* 23 (Winter 1981).

Grant, Douglas, *Margaret the First: A Biography of Margaret Cavendish Duchess of Newcastle 1623–1673* (London, 1957).

Greene, Graham, *Lord Rochester's Monkey: Being the Life of John Wilmot, Second Earl of Rochester* (London and New York, 1974).

Griffin, Dustin H., *Satires Against Man: The Poems of Rochester* (Berkeley, Los Angeles and London, 1973).

'Rochester and the "Holiday Writers"', in Griffin and Vieth, eds., *Rochester and Court Poetry*.

Griffin, Dustin H., and David M. Vieth, eds., *Rochester and Court Poetry: Papers Presented at a Clark Library Seminar 11 May 1985* (Los Angeles, 1988).

Hagstrum, Jean, *Sex and Sensibility: Ideal and Erotic Love from Milton to Mozart* (Chicago, 1980).

Ham, Roswell Gray, *Otway and Lee: Biography from a Baroque Age* (New Haven, 1931).

Hammond, Paul, ed., *John Wilmot Earl of Rochester: Selected Poems* (Bristol, 1982).

Harris, Brice, ed., *The Poems of Charles Sackville Sixth Earl of Dorset* (New York and London, 1979).

Harth, Phillip, *Contexts of Dryden's Thought* (Chicago and London, 1968).

Heinrich, Joachim, *Die Frauenfrage bei Steele und Addison: Eine Untersuchung zur englischen Literatur- und Kulturgeschichte im 17./18. Jahrhundert* (Leipzig, 1930); no. 168 in the Palaestra series.

Hewison, P. E., 'Rochester, the "Imitation", and "An Allusion to Horace"', *The Seventeenth Century* 2 (1987).

Hill, Christopher, *The Collected Essays of Christopher Hill*, vol. 1 (Brighton, 1985).

Hume, Robert D., *The Development of English Drama in the Late Seventeenth Century* (Oxford, 1976).

Huseboe, Arthur R., *Sir George Etherege* (Boston, 1987).

Hutton, Ronald, *The Restoration: A Political and Religious History of England and Wales 1658–1667* (Oxford, 1985).

Hutton, William Holden, *The English Church: From the Accession of Charles I to the Death of Anne (1625–1714)* (London, 1903).

Johnson, Jos. A. Jr, '"An Allusion to Horace": The Poetics of John Wilmot, Earl of Rochester', *The Durham University Journal* 66.1 (n.s. 35.1; December 1973).

Johnson, Ronald W., 'Rhetoric and Drama in Rochester's "Satyr against Reason and Mankind"', *Studies in English Literature 1500–1900* 15.3 (Summer 1975).

Jones, J. R., *Country and Court: England 1658–1714* (London, 1978), vol. v in Edward Arnold's *The New History of England*.

Jones, Richard Foster, *Ancients and Moderns: A Study of the Rise of the Scientific Movement in Seventeenth-Century England* (St Louis, 1961).

Kearns, Edward John, *Ideas in Seventeenth-Century France: The most important thinkers and the climate of ideas in which they worked* (Manchester, 1979).

Knight, Charles A., 'The Paradox of Reason: Argument in Rochester's "Satyr against Mankind"', *The Modern Language Review* 65 (1970).

Lord, George deF., ed., *Poems on Affairs of State: Augustan Satirical Verse, 1660–1714*, vol. 1 (New Haven and London, 1963).

Lough, John, *An Introduction to Seventeenth Century France* (London, 1954).

Love, Harold, 'Rochester and the Traditions of Satire', in Love, ed., *Restoration Literature: Critical Approaches* (London, 1972), pp. 145–75.

Maccubbin, Robert P., ed., *Unauthorized Sexual Behaviour during the Enlightenment*, special issue of *Eighteenth-Century Life* 9 (n.s., May 1985).

Macfarlane, Alan, *Marriage and Love in England*: *Modes of Reproduction 1300–1840* (Oxford, 1986).

Main, C. F., 'The Right Vein of Rochester's *Satyr*', in R. Kirk and C. F. Main, eds., *Essays in Literary History Presented to J. M. French* (New Brunswick, 1960, and New York, 1965).

Manning, Gillian, 'Rochester and *Much A-Do about Nothing*', in *Notes and Queries* 33 (n.s., December 1986).

McNeilly, F. S., *The Anatomy of Leviathan* (London and New York, 1968).

Mendelson, Sara Heller, *The Mental World of Stuart Women*: *Three Studies* (Brighton, 1987).

Michel, Robert H., 'English Attitudes towards Women, 1640–1700', *Canadian Journal of History* 13.1 (April 1978).

Mignon, Elisabeth, *Crabbed Age and Youth*: *The Old Men and Women in the Restoration Comedy of Manners* (Durham, N. C., 1947).

Mintz, Samuel I., *The Hunting of Leviathan*: *Seventeenth-Century Reactions to the Materialism and Moral Philosophy of Thomas Hobbes* (Cambridge, 1962).

Moore, John F., 'The Originality of Rochester's *Satyr against Mankind*', *PMLA* 58.2 (June 1943).

Nadelhaft, Jerome, 'The Englishwoman's Sexual Civil War: Feminist Attitudes towards Men, Women, and Marriage 1650–1740', *Journal of the History of Ideas* 43.4 (1982).

Nicoll, Allardyce, *Restoration Drama 1660–1700*, vol. I in *A History of English Drama 1660–1900* (Cambridge 1923).

Nicolson, Marjorie Hope, *The Breaking of the Circle*: *Studies in the Effect of the 'New Science' upon Seventeenth-Century Poetry* (Evanston, Ill., 1950; rev. ed. 1960).

Nussbaum, Felicity A., *The Brink of All We Hate*: *English Satires on Women*, 1660–1750 (Lexington, Ky., 1984).

Ogg, David, *England in the Reign of Charles II* (Oxford, 1934; reprinted in paperback, 1963).

Ollard, Richard, *The Image of the King*: *Charles I and Charles II* (London, 1979).

O'Neill, John H., 'Sexuality, Deviance, and Moral Character in the Personal Satire of the Restoration', *Eighteenth-Century Life* 2 (1975).

'Rochester's "Imperfect Enjoyment": "The True Veine of Satyre" in Sexual Poetry', *Tennessee Studies in Literature* 25 (1980).

Overton, J. H., *Life in the English Church (1660–1714)* (London, 1885).

Patterson, John D., 'Rochester's Second Bottle: Attitudes to Drink and Drinking in the Works of John Wilmot, Earl of Rochester', *Restoration* 5.1 (Spring 1981).

Paulson, Kristoffer F., 'The Reverend Edward Stillingfleet and the Epilogue to Rochester's *A Satyr against Reason and Mankind*', *Philological Quarterly* 50 (1971).

Paulson, Ronald, 'Rochester: The Body Politic and the Body Private', in Louis

L. Martz and Aubrey Williams, eds., *The Author in His Work*: *Essays on a Problem in Criticism* (New Haven and London, 1978).

Pearson, Jacqueline, *The Prostituted Muse*: *Images of Women & Women Dramatists 1642–1737* (London and New York, 1988).

Pelous, Jean-Michel, *Amour précieux*: *Amour galant (1654–1675)* (Paris 1980).

Picavet, Camille-Georges, *Les dernières années de Turenne*: *1660–1675* (Paris, 1918).

Pinto, Vivian de Sola, *Enthusiast in Wit*: *A Portrait of John Wilmot Earl of Rochester, 1647–1680* (Lincoln and London, 1962).

Pinto, Vivian de Sola, ed., *The Poetical and Dramatic Works of Sir Charles Sedley*, 2 vols. (London, 1928).

Porter, Peter, 'The Professional Amateur', in Treglown, ed., *Spirit of Wit*.

Prinz, Johannes, *John Wilmot Earl of Rochester*: *His Life and Writings* (Leipzig, 1927); no. 154 in the Palaestra series.

Quaintance, Richard E., Jr., 'Passion and Reason in Restoration Love Poetry', dissertation, Yale University, 1962.

Quehen, Hugh de, ed., *Samuel Butler*: *Prose Observations* (Oxford, 1979).

Raphael, D. D., *Hobbes*: *Morals and Politics* (London, 1977).

Reynolds, Myra, *The Learned Lady in England, 1650–1760* (New York, 1920).

Richmond, H. M., *The School of Love*: *The Evolution of the Stuart Love Lyric* (Princeton, 1964).

Righter, Anne (now Anne Barton), 'John Wilmot, Earl of Rochester', *Proceedings of the British Academy* 53, 1967 (1968).

Robinson, K. E., 'Rochester and Hobbes and the Irony of *A Satyr against Reason and Mankind*', *The Yearbook of English Studies* 3 (1973).

'Rochester's Dilemma', *The Durham University Journal* 71.2 (n.s. 40.2, June 1979).

'The Art of Violence in Rochester's Satire', in Claude Rawson and Jenny Mecziems, eds., *English Satire and the Satiric Tradition* (Oxford, 1984).

Rogers, Katharine M., *The Troublesome Helpmate*: *A History of Misogyny in Literature* (Seattle and London, 1966).

Rogers, Pat, '*An Allusion to Horace*', in Treglown, ed., *Spirit of Wit*.

Rothstein, Eric, *Restoration and Early Eighteenth-Century Poetry*, vol. III of *The Routledge History of English Poetry* (Boston, London and Henley, 1981).

Selden, Raman, *English Verse Satire (1590–1765)* (London, 1978).

'Rochester and Shadwell', in Treglown, ed., *Spirit of Wit*.

Shapiro, Barbara J., *Probability and Certainty in Seventeenth-Century England* (Princeton, 1983).

Sitter, John, 'Rochester's Reader and the Problem of Satiric Audience', *Papers on Language and Literature* 12.3 (Summer 1976).

Smith, Hilda L., *Reason's Disciples*: *Seventeenth-Century English Feminists* (Urbana, Ill., 1982).

Spink, F. S., *French Free-Thought from Gassendi to Voltaire* (London, 1960).

Stenton, Doris Mary, *The English Woman in History* (London and New York, 1957).

Stone, Lawrence, *The Family, Sex and Marriage in England 1500–1800* (London, 1977).

Sutch, Victor D., *Gilbert Sheldon: Architect of Anglican Survival, 1640–1675* (The Hague, 1973).

Thomas, Keith, *Religion and the Decline of Magic* (London, 1971).

Man and the Natural World: A History of the Modern Sensibility (New York, 1983).

Thompson, Roger, *Unfit for Modest Ears: A Study of Pornographic, Obscene and Bawdy Works Written and Published in England in the Second Half of the Seventeenth Century* (London, 1979).

Thormählen, Marianne, 'Rochester and Jealousy: Consistent Inconsistencies', *The Durham University Journal* 80.2 (n.s. 49.2, June 1988).

'Rochester and *The Fall*: The Roots of Discontent', *English Studies* 69.5 (October 1988).

Thorpe, James, ed., *The Poems of Sir George Etherege* (Princeton, 1963).

Treglown, Jeremy, 'The Satirical Inversion of Some English Sources in Rochester's Poetry', *The Review of English Studies* 24 (1973).

'He knew my style, he swore', in Treglown, ed., *Spirit of Wit*.

Treglown, Jeremy, ed., *The Letters of John Wilmot Earl of Rochester* (Oxford, 1980).

Spirit of Wit: Reconsiderations of Rochester (Oxford, 1982).

Trotter, David, 'Wanton Expressions', in Treglown, ed., *Spirit of Wit*.

Underwood, Dale, *Etherege and the Seventeenth-Century Comedy of Manners* (New Haven and London, 1957).

Van Lennep, William, ed., *The London Stage 1660–1800*, part 1, with an introd. by Emmett L. Avery and Arthur H. Scouten (Carbondale, 1963–4).

Vieth, David M., *Attribution in Restoration Poetry: A Study of Rochester's Poems of 1680* (New Haven and London, 1963).

'Toward an Anti-Aristotelian Poetic: Rochester's *Satyr against Mankind* and *Artemisia to Chloe*, with Notes on Swift's *Tale of a Tub* and *Gulliver's Travels*', *Language and Style* 5 (1972).

'"Pleased with the Contradiction and the Sin"': The Perverse Artistry of Rochester's Lyrics', *Tennessee Studies in Literature* 25 (1980).

Rochester Studies 1925–1982: An Annotated Bibliography (New York, 1984).

Vieth, David M., ed., *The Complete Poems of John Wilmot, Earl of Rochester* (New Haven and London, 1968).

John Wilmot, Earl of Rochester: Critical Essays (New York and London, 1988).

Vieth, David M., and Dustin H. Griffin, eds., *Rochester and Court Poetry: Papers Presented at a Clark Library Seminar 11 May 1985* (Los Angeles, 1988).

Walker, Keith, ed., *The Poems of John Wilmot Earl of Rochester* (Oxford, 1984).

Weinbrot, Howard D., 'The "Allusion to Horace": Rochester's Imitative Mode', *Studies in Philology* 69.3 (July 1972).
'The Swelling Volume: The Apocalyptic Satire of Rochester's *Letter from Artemisia in the Town to Chloe in the Country*', *Studies in the Literary Imagination* 5 (1972).
Westfall, Richard S., *Science and Religion in Seventeenth-Century England* (New Haven, 1958).
White, Isabelle, '"So Great a Disproportion": Paradox and Structure in Rochester's *A Satyr against Reason and Mankind*', *Kentucky Philological Association Bulletin* (1976; repr. in Vieth, ed., *Critical Essays*).
Whitley, Raymond K., 'Rochester: A Cosmological Pessimist', *English Studies in Canada* 4 (Summer 1978).
Wilcoxon, Reba, 'Rochester's Philosophical Premises: A Case for Consistency', *Eighteenth-Century Studies* 8 (Winter 1974–5).
'Pornography, Obscenity, and Rochester's "The Imperfect Enjoyment"', *Studies in English Literature 1500–1900* 15 (Summer 1975).
'Rochester's Sexual Politics', *Studies in Eighteenth-Century Culture* 8 (1979; ed. Roseann Runte).
Wilders, John, 'Rochester and the Metaphysicals', in Treglown, ed., *Spirit of Wit*.
Wilders, John, ed., *Samuel Butler Hudibras* (Oxford, 1967).
Wilkinson, D. R. M., *The Comedy of Habit: An Essay on the Use of Courtesy Literature in a Study of Restoration Comic Drama* (Leyden, 1964).
Willey, Basil, *The Seventeenth-Century Background: Studies in the Thought of the Age in Relation to Poetry and Religion* (London, 1934).
Williams, Charles, *Rochester* (London, 1935).
Wilson, John Harold, *The Court Wits of the Restoration: An Introduction* (Princeton, 1948).
Nell Gwyn: Royal Mistress (New York, 1952).
A Rake and His Times: George Villiers 2nd Duke of Buckingham (London, 1954).
Wilson, John Harold, ed., *Court Satires of the Restoration* (Columbus, 1976).
Winn, James Anderson, *John Dryden and His World* (New Haven and London, 1987).
Wintle, Sarah, 'Libertinism and Sexual Politics', in Treglown, ed., *Spirit of Wit*.
Witcombe, D. T., *Charles II and the Cavalier House of Commons 1663–1674* (Manchester and New York, 1966).
Wrigley, E. A., 'A Simple Model of London's Importance in Changing English Society and Economy 1650–1750', *Past and Present* 77 (July 1967).
Younger, William, *Gods, Men, and Wine* (London, 1966).

Index

Editors [ed.] whose names are quoted in that capacity only are represented by a reference to the first mention of their volumes. With regard to editions of seventeenth-century texts, the name of the author is also included (e.g. [Butler ed.]).

Accius, 313
Adrian, Judith, 243
Albalat, Antoine, 333n.
Albemarle, George Monck, 1st Duke of, 14, 16, 290n.
Allen, Don Cameron, 363n.
Allestree, Richard, *The Ladies Calling*, 129; *The Whole Duty of Man*, 11n.
Alsace, 267–8
Alsop, D. K., 4n., 339n.
Anacreontea and Anacreontic verse, 10, 11, 16–19, 20, 23n, 26
'Ancients' vs 'Moderns' in philosophy and science, 211–12, 239, 249–50
Anglican church and clergy, 151, 152, 158, 163, 167, 168, 170, 171–2, 173, 174, 194, 198, 201, 206, 213, 228–35, 239, 248–9, 361
Anne, Duchess of York (*née* Hyde), 259–60
Anne, Princess [future Queen Anne], 322
anti-fruition, convention, 56–8
Aristotles Master-piece, 258
Arlington, Henry Bennet, 1st Earl of, 128n., 156–7, 160n., 246, 301
Art of Complaisance, The, 116, 282n.
Ashley, Anthony Cooper, *see* Shaftesbury
Ashley, Maurice, 244n., 296n.
Astell, Mary, 124
astrology, 18, 19
atheism, 101, 147, 148, 149, 174–5, 214, 248, 361
Atkinson, C. T., 270n., 273n.

Auffret, J. M., 342n.
Augustine, St, 170
Avery, Emmett L., 322n.

Baader, Renate, 31n.
Bacon, Francis, 177, 184
Bagwell, Mrs, 53
Balfour, Sir Andrew, 159, 303, 308
Barlow, Thomas, 233n.
Barnett, Correlli, 261n.
Barre, Poulain de la, *De l'égalité des deux sexes*, 124
Barry, Elizabeth, 36–7, 41n., 76, 136n., 322n.
Barton, Anne, *see* Righter
Baumann, Michael, 17n., 18n.
Baumrin, B. H. [ed.], 221n.
Baxter, Richard, 169, 214n.
Beaumont, Francis, 314; *The Knight of the Burning Pestle*, 351
Behn, Aphra, 45, 134–5; *The Disappointment*, 85; *The Forc'd Marriage*, 134n.; *The Golden Age*, 47n., 135; *On a Juniper Tree*, 54–5; *On Mr J. H. in a Fit of Sickness*, 348n.; *To Lysander*, 78n.
Belleau, Rémy, Anacreontic translations, 17, 18; *Impuissance*, 85, 87, 93, 94
Bend, J. G. van der [ed.], 177n.
'Bendo, Alexander', 2, 154–5, 249, 250, 258
Bennet, Henry, *see* Arlington
Bentley, Richard, 149
Beys, Charles, *La Iovissance Imparfaite*, 85, 86, 88

Bilson, Thomas, 80n.
blasphemy, 33, 147, 148, 209, 359–60
Bliss, Alan, 254n.
Bloomfield, Morton W., 229n.
Blot l'Eglise, Claude de Chouvigny, baron de, 91, 170
Blount, Charles, *Anima Mundi*, 169
Boas, George, 216n.
Boase, Alan M., 183n.
Boileau (Despréaux), Nicolas, 162, 180, 184–9; *L'Art poétique*, 184–5, 332, 333, 342n.; *Epistles*, 159; *Satires*, 185–9, 198, 200–1, 202, 272n., 274–5, 276, 281, 312
Bolnest, Edward, 250n.
Bossuet, Jacques Bénigne, 183
Boswell, Eleanore, 322n.
Boudhors, C.-H. [Boileau ed.], 185n.
Bournonville, Imperial general, 168
Boyle, the Hon. Robert, 149, 169, 172n., 214
Boyle, Roger, *see* Orrery
Bracher, Frederick [Etherege ed.], 305n.
Bray, René, 185n.
Bredvold, Louis I., 165n., 169n., 171n., 210n.
Broich, Ulrich [ed.], 339n.
Brongersma, Edward, 20n.
Brooks, David, 65, 75n., 116n., 153, 163, 246, 249, 280n., 338
Brooks, Harold F., 16, 125, 266, 267, 311n.
Brown, Frank C., 316n., 323n.
Browne, Sir Thomas, 4, 101n., 184; *Religio Medici*, 101n., 168, 216n., 221
Browning, Andrew [ed.], 296n.
Bruser, Fredelle, 5n., 95n.
Buck, August, 333n.
Buckhurst, Charles Sackville, *see* Dorset
Buckingham, George Villiers, 2nd Duke of, 156–7, 160n., 228, 250, 262–3n., 270, 288, 290–1, 292, 293–4, 305, 324, 339–40, 355n.; *The Rehearsal*, 251, 324
Büff, Renate, 30–1n.
Bulstrode papers, 270
Bunyan, John, *The Pilgrim's Progress*, 212n.
Burnet, Gilbert, 2, 3, 4, 10n., 12, 13, 41n., 125, 147n., 151n., 154n., 160, 168n., 169, 172, 183, 184, 216, 228, 232n., 235, 252, 266, 294, 296n., 361, 362, 363
Burr, Thomas Benge, 250n.
Bush, Douglas, 19n.
Butler, James, *see* Ormonde
Butler, Samuel, 158, 198, 312n., 323; *Characters*, 113n., 155, 193, 196, 206n., 227n., 231, 235, 280n., 283n., 339; other miscellaneous prose, 80, 144, 207, 209, 214n., 225, 234–5; *Dildoides* [attrib.], 287; *Hudibras*, 4n., 18n., 19, 151, 192n., 197–8,

204, 213n., 244n.; *Satire upon the Licentious Age of Charles II*, 359; *Satire upon the Weakness and Misery of Man*, 77, 222
Byrne, F. J. [ed.], 254n.
Byron, George Gordon, Lord, *So We'll Go No More A-Roving*, 24

'Cabal', the, 156–7, 160, 247
Cambridge Platonists, 79, 169, 173, 194, 204n.
Cantenac, Benech (?) de, *L'Occasion perdue recouverte*, 85
Caprara, Aeneas Sylvius, Graf v., 268
Care, Henry, *The Female Secretary*, 105
Carew, Thomas, *The Rapture*, 89n.
Carman, W. Y., 261n.
Carroll, Robert Todd, 164n., 230n.
Carver, Larry, 33n., 361n.
Caryll, John, 322, 323, 324; *Sir Salamon Single*, 324n.
Castlemaine, Countess of, *see* Cleveland
Catherine, Queen, 233, 244, 257, 259, 328
Catholicism and Catholics, 4, 101, 164, 171, 173, 183, 230, 233, 247, 289, 293–4, 295
Cavendish, Margaret, *see* Newcastle
Champagne [the province], 268, 270
champagne [the wine], *see* drinking
Charles II, 49, 123, 152, 154, 156, 157, 158, 159, 160, 164, 215, 218–19, 227, 229, 230, 231, 232–3, 238, 243, 247, 250, 251, 254–5, 259, 261, 273, 289n., 291, 292, 295–303, 348n., 358, 360
Charleton, Walter, 4, 168, 169; *Epicurus' Morals*, 168, 169n.; *The Immortality of the Human Soul*, 168
Charleval, Charles Faucon de Ris, seigneur de, 45
Charron, Pierre, 210
Chernaik, Warren L., 251n.
Childs, John, 261n., 262, 263n.
Choisy, l'abbé de, 217–18
Chouvigny, Claude de, *see* Blot l'Eglise
Churchill, John [future Duke of Marlborough], 270, 290n., 292
citizens of London, 293
Clanbrassil, Alice, 305
Clarendon, Edward Hyde, 1st Earl of, 154, 227–8, 233n.
Clark, A. F. B., 186
Clark, John R., 49n.
Clay, Christopher, 136n.
Cleveland, Barbara (*née* Villiers) Palmer, Countess of Castlemaine, Duchess of, 289, 291, 292, 293, 301n.
Clifford, Martin, 195, 315n., 339–40; *A Treatise of Humane Reason*, 195

Clifford of Chudleigh, Thomas, Lord, 154, 160n., 227–8, 247
Colbert, Jean Baptiste, 185, 271
Coleman, Antony [ed.], 311n.
Colie, Rosalie L., 141–2n.
Collinson, Patrick, 255n.
commedia dell'arte, 351
Conaghan, John [Etherege ed.], 114n.
conventicles, 254–5
Cooper, Anthony Ashley, *see* Shaftesbury
'Cootes, the' [Irish ladies], 305
Cope, Jackson I., 169n., 173n., 194n., 212n., 214n., 231n., 234n.
Corneille, Pierre, 50n.
Corvisier, André, 274n.
Cotton, Charles, 17
Cousins, A. D., 192n.
Cowley, Abraham, 148, 194, 196, 323; Anacreontic verse, 17, 18, 19, 20; *The Country Mouse*, 244n.; *Davideis*, 143; *Essays*, 184, 218, 222–3, 225; *Hymn to Light*, 143; imitations of Horace, 137n.; *Life and Fame*, 144; *Mistress* poems [love lyrics], 42n., 45, 46, 48–9, 56–7, 79, 128; *Odes*, 134n., 207, 344n.; *The Tree of Knowledge*, 207
Cox, David N., 20n.
Cragg, G. R., 160, 168n., 169n., 211n.
Crashaw, Richard, *Steps to the Temple*, 34, 147–8
Crawford, Patricia, 259n.
Crisp, Sir Nicholas, 242–3
Crocker, S. F., 180, 181, 182, 184, 186
Cromwell, Oliver, 326
Crowne, John, 310, 316, 317, 322–3, 324, 330; *Calisto*, 322; *The Country Wit*, 324n.

Danby, Thomas Osborne, 1st Earl of, 247
Danielsson, Bror [Gyldenstolpe ed.], 286n.
Dasent, Arthur Irwin, 290n.
Davenant, Sir William, 221n.; *Against Womens pride*, 47; *Gondibert*, 14; *To Mr. W. M. Against Absence*, 74
Daves, Charles W. [Butler ed.], 113n.
Davies, Paul C., 186, 188, 345n.
Davis, 'Moll', 244
Dearing, Vinton A. [Dryden ed.], 48n.
Dehénault, Jean, 52n., 362
Denmark, 158
Des Barreaux, Jacques Vallée, 198–201, 365n.
Descartes, Catherine, 204
Descartes, René, and Cartesians, 4, 194, 203–5, 340
Deshoulières, Mme Antoinette du Ligier de la Garde, 200, 362n.
Digby, Sir Kenelm, 168n.

Diogenes of Sinope, 215–16
Dissenters, *see* Puritans
Dobson, Austin [Evelyn ed.], 131n.
Döderlein, Ludwig, 329n.
Donaldson, Ian, 15n.
Donne, John, *Elegies*, 32; *The Extasie*, 34, 57
Doody, Margaret Anne, 7, 25n., 111n.
Dorchester, Countess of, Dorset's poems on, 35
Dorrell (Dayrell), Sir Francis, 242–3
Dorset, Charles Sackville, Lord Buckhurst, Earl of [and of Middlesex], 15, 81, 278, 289n., 290, 305, 310, 322n., 324, 327, 328, 331, 332; *The Advice*, 53, 128; *Advice to Lovers*, 53; *Colon*, 289n.; poems on the Countess of Dorchester, 35; *The Fire of Love*, 50
Dover, K. J., 20, 23n.
Doyle, Anne T., 316n.
drinking, 10–16, 25–7, 96, 271–2
Drummond, J. C., 272n.
Dryden, John, 14, 45, 81, 109–10, 112n., 159n., 168, 184, 270, 295n., 310, 311–19, 320–1, 323, 324, 325, 326, 327, 328, 330, 331, 332, 334, 335, 338, 339n., 340n., 341, 342, 343; *Absalom and Achitophel*, 250; *Annus Mirabilis*, 14, 312; *The Assignation*, 50n., 318; *Astraea Redux*, 312; *Aureng-Zebe*, dedication of, 341–2, epilogue to, 317; *The Conquest of Granada*, 52n., 110; *The Hind and the Panther*, 196, 220; *The Indian Emperour*, 280, 319; *The Indian Queen*, 132; *MacFlecknoe*, 131n., 243; *Marriage A-la-Mode*, 48, 57, 78n., 112n., 113n., 120n., 129–30, 133, 137–8, 139, 140n.; *Religio Laici*, 196, 210–11; *The State of Innocence*, 318; *Tyrannick Love*, prologue to, 316; translation from Lucretius, 89–90; epilogue to Etherege's *The Man of Mode*, 119n., 351; prologue and epilogue to Jonson's *The Silent Woman*, 319; prose writings on literary matters, 312, 314–15, 316, 319, 321n.
Duffy, Maureen, 47n., 134n.
Dulong, Claude, 30n., 50n., 53n., 365n.
Duncan Jones, Mrs E., 292n.
Dutch, the, *see* Netherlands
Dyce, Revd Alexander [Bentley ed.], 149

Eachard, John, 235n.
eating habits and food in the Restoration, 271–2, 279–80
Ellis, Frank H., 157n., 303n.
Ennius, 313, 321
Epaminondas, 182

Epicurean notions, 70, 76–7, 168, 169n., 180, 193, 198, 212, 217, 349, 360

Erasmus, Desiderius, 279; *The Praise of Folly*, 279, 349–50

Erskine-Hill, Howard, 148–9n., 300n., 340n., 345n., 349–50n.

Estienne, Henri, 17n., 20n.

Etherege, Sir George, 45, 112n., 117, 243, 305, 310, 322n., 324, 325, 328–31; *The Comical Revenge*, 81n., 245, 330–1; *Ephelia to Bajazet*, 344–5; *The Imperfect Enjoyment*, 85–6, 88; *The Man of Mode*, 12n., 15, 114, 119, 128, 137n., 295n., 324, 326; 'See how fair Corinna lies', 54n.; *She Would if She Could*, 47n., 122, 330; 'Tell me no more you love', 48n.; *To Her Excellency the Marchioness of Newcastle*, 134; *Upon Love in Imitation of Cowley*, 68

Evelyn, John, 131, 154n., 244n., 247, 288n., 296n., 297n., 307n., 322

Evelyn, Mary, 105, 131

Everett, Barbara, 7, 11n., 69n., 107n., 108n., 141n.

Exclamation from Tunbridge and Epsom, An, 255n., 257–8

Fabian, Bernhard [Glanvill ed.], 170n., 213n.

Fabricant, Carole, 22n., 82, 92, 111n., 281n.

Falmouth, Mary Bagot, Dowager Countess of, 288, 289–90

Familiar Epistle to Mr. Julian, Secretary to the Muses, A, 355–6

Fane, Sir Francis, 293n., 301

Fanshaw, W., 363, 364

Farley-Hills, David, 2n., 3n., 13n., 30, 38n., 44n., 49n., 52n., 54, 65n., 70n., 76–7, 82, 92, 96, 98n., 103, 112n., 117, 141, 147n., 161, 190, 198n., 224, 245n., 274, 275, 276, 277, 278, 281, 292, 294n., 299n., 303n., 310n., 312n., 320, 321n., 338–9, 340, 346n., 349n.

Fea, Allan, 288n., 290n., 300n., 306n.

Felton, Lady Betty, 135, 289

Fielding, Henry, 272

Flatman, Thomas, 316, 322, 323, 329, 331

Flecknoe, Richard, *Characters*, 75, 129, 259, 262

Fletcher, John, 314, 315, 321, 334; *The Knight of the Burning Pestle*, 351

Florio, John, 183

Forbes, Thomas Rogers, 260n.

Forgues, Emile D., 198n.

Fox, Mrs, 305

Fox, Stephen, 261

Foxcroft, H. C., 125n.

Frame, Donald M., 181n.

Frampton, Robert, 230

France, 4, 38, 45, 158, 183, 184, 198–9, 203–4, 266–74, 275

Franche-Comté, 266–7, 268, 270, 333

Fraser, Lady Antonia, 124n., 140n., 259n., 300n.

Frazier, Sir Alexander, 306, 307n.

Frazier, Cary, 291, 306–7

Frazier, Lady, 306

Freke, John [?], *The History of Insipids*, 157, 303

Fujimura, Thomas H., 175, 177n., 178, 179

Gagen, Jean Elisabeth, 110n., 124n., 130

Garrison, Fielding H., 258n.

Gassendi, Pierre, 4, 168, 169n., 198, 203–4

Genesis, 169–70

Gibbs, A. M., 74

Gert, Bernard, 221n.

Giffard, Francis, 147n.

Gill, James E., 191n., 219n., 224

Glanvill, Joseph, 4, 130, 165n., 168n., 169, 211–12, 213–15, 231n., 234; 'Anti-Fanatical Religion', 173; *An Apology and Advice*, 234; *Saducismus Triumphatus*, 213–15; *Vanity of Dogmatizing*, 169n., 170n.

Godolphin, Sidney, 324

Goodman, Godfrey, *The Fall of Man*, 34n., 220–1.

Goreau, Angeline, 64n.

Gould, Robert, 121–2, 134

Graham, Richard, *Angliae Speculum Morale*, 98n., 348

Gramont, Philibert, comte de, 288, 293n.

Grant, Douglas, 131n., 132, 280n.

Greene, Graham, 5n., 363n.

Greenslade, Basil, 154

Grew, Nehemjah, 149, 150

Griffin, Dustin H., 1n., 2n., 3n., 7, 14, 24, 52n., 62, 69, 76, 85n., 88, 92n., 99n., 100n., 104n., 105, 107n., 117–18, 141, 142–3, 144, 151, 152n., 161, 162, 165, 166, 167, 169n., 175n., 191, 194, 198n., 203n., 204n., 212, 217n., 223–4, 236n., 238n., 272, 274, 276, 277, 278, 281, 285n., 310n., 311n., 321n., 328n., 339, 340n., 344n., 345n., 357n.

Grosart, Alexander [Sibbes ed.], 165n., 166n.

Gwyn, Nell, 244, 294, 298, 299, 300–1

Hagstrum, Jean H., 30, 41n., 81, 313n.

Hale, Sir Matthew, *Light of Nature and Natural Reason*, 194n.

Haley, K. H. D., 273n., 299

Halifax, George Savile, 1st Marquess of, 125, 128, 129, 227n.

Ham, Roswell Gray, 323n., 342n.
Hammond, Antony [ed.], 311n.
Hammond, Paul, 6n., 7, 49n., 150, 153n., 154, 163, 247n., 262n., 278, 319n.
'happy/lucky minute, the', convention, 54–5
Harris, Brice, 53n., 290, 306, 335
Harth, Phillip, 168n., 169n.
Hartmann, Cyril Hughes, 227n., 230n., 244n.
Hayman, John, 348n.
Hayward, John, 163, 213
Head, Richard, 109, 247n.; *The English Rogue*, 86, 96; *Proteus Redivivus*, 109, 247n., 264n.
Hearne, Thomas, 10n.
Heinrich, Joachim, 124–5
Hell, seventeenth-century ideas on, 79–80
Henning, Basil Duke, 218n.
Henrietta Anne ['Minette'], Duchess of Orléans ['Madame'], 259
Henrietta Maria, Queen [Dowager], 155n., 250, 293
Henty, G. A., 273
Herbert of Cherbury, Edward Herbert, Lord, 194n.
Hermogenes, 329
Herostratus, 16
Herrick, Robert, Anacreontic verse, 18, 19, 20; *His fare-well to Sack*, 10–11; *The Invitation*, 276
Hewison, P. E., 311n., 321n.
Hibbard, G. R. [ed.], 149n.
Hill, Christopher, 168n., 300n.
Hilton, Michael, 17n.
History of Insipids, The, see Freke
Hobbes, Thomas, 67, 162, 174–9, 180, 183, 237; *The Elements of Law*, 67; *Leviathan*, 69, 128n., 144–5, 155, 168, 176–7, 178, 179, 214, 221, 225, 226–7, 362
homosexuality, 20–1, 23, 101
Hood, F. C., 175n.
Hoopes, Robert, 201n.
Horace, 10, 137, 185, 310, 320–1, 327; *Ars Poetica*, 332, 333; *Epistles*, 10, 11; *Odes*, 10, 282n.; *Satires*, 21n., 241, 274, 276, 280n., 281, 311–12, 313, 315, 320–2, 327, 329, 333
Howard, Dorothy, 288
Howard, Edward, *The British Princes*, 327n., 343
Howard, Sir Robert, *The Indian Queen*, 132
Hoyles, John, 212n.
Huart, Suzanne d'[Turenne ed.], 270n.
Hughes, Leo [Wycherley ed.], 329n.
Huizinga, Johan, 159n.
Hume, Robert D., 326n., 331n.
Humiliata, Sister Mary, 105n.

Hunt, John Dixon, 255n.
Hunt, Morton, 122
Huseboe, Arthur R., 329n., 330n.
Hutton, Ronald, 246, 251n., 255n., 305n.
Hutton, William Holden, 230n., 232n.
Huysmans, Jacob, portrait of Rochester, 339 and n.
Hyde, Edward, see Clarendon

illegitimacy, 136, 259–60
immortality, doctrine of, 167–9, 174, 214
imperfect-enjoyment genre, 85–7, 90, 94–5
Ingelo, Nathaniel, 167, 211–13; *Bentivolio and Urania*, 212
inheritance of estates, 136, 259–60
Ireland and the Irish, 158, 253–4, 303–5
Isaiah, 148n., 363–5

James, Duke of York [future James II], 251, 259–60, 270, 288–9, 294, 295, 297
Jermyn, Henry, Earl of St Albans, 290n., 292–3
Jermyn, Henry ['the younger'], 290
Johnson, Jos. A., Jr, 310–11, 315n., 325n.
Johnson, Paul J., 177n.
Johnson, Reginald Brimley, 77n.
Johnson, Ronald W., 13n., 192n., 201n.
Johnson, Dr Samuel, 141, 161, 184, 185–6, 319, 343; *Dictionary*, 149–50, 194, 211, 254, 264, 323, 329
Joly, Claude, 200n.
Jones, J. R., 153, 156n., 232n., 255n., 301n., 304n.
Jones, Richard Foster, 250
Jonson, Ben, 314–15, 321, 328; 'Doing a filthy pleasure is', 56; *Epicoene, or The Silent Woman*, 129, 319; *Ode to Himselfe*, 37
Juvenal, *Satires*, 24–5, 117, 121, 125, 132, 137, 138

Kearns, Edward John, 193n., 204n., 205n.
Keast, William R. [ed.], 13n.
Ken, Thomas, 230
Ker, W. P. [Dryden ed.], 314n.
Kéroualle, Louise de, see Portsmouth
Killigrew, Charlotte, 289
Killigrew, Thomas, 289
King, Bruce, 264n.
King's Vows, The, 156n.
Kirk, R. [ed.], 205n.
Kirke, Mall, 344
Knight, Charles A., 192n., 196n.
Knight, Mary, 291–2, 294n., 307
Kunz, Don R., 243n.

Lachèvre, Frédéric, *Libertinage* ed., 52n.
[Dehénault], 91n. [Blot l'Eglise], 199n.
[Des Barreaux], 200n. [Mme Deshoulières]
La Fontaine, Jean de, 204
Lair, J., 269n.
'Lane, Jane' [pseud. for Elaine Dakers], 302–3
Langlois, Marcel, 269n.
La Rochefoucauld, François, 53
Laslett, Peter, 124n., 136n.
Latitudinarians, 168, 169n., 172, 173, 211, 213
Lauderdale, John Maitland, Duke of, 159, 160n.
La Vallière, Louise Françoise de Labaume Leblanc, Duchesse de, 269–70
Lee, Nathaniel, 322, 323, 331, 342n.; *The Princess of Cleve*, 331; *Sophonisba*, 323; *Theodosius*, 87
Legouis, Pierre, 251n.
L'Enclos, Ninon, 53, 55
Leopold I, 273
L'Estrange, Sir Roger, 195, 322n.
libertinage in France [*see also* Viau, Théophile de], 198–201
'libertine', implications of the term, 61–2, 64, 67, 96, 216, 217, 360
Link, Frederick [Dryden ed.], 341n.
Loftis, John [Dryden ed.], 48n., 280n.
Lord, George deF., 2, 14n., 156n., 270n., 293n., 297, 303n., 341n., 342n., 352n., 355n.
Lorraine, Duke of, 268
Loudon, Irvine, 258n.
Lough, John, 296n., 335
Louis XIV, 4, 152, 155, 230n., 266–71, 282, 296, 297, 299, 300, 304, 333, 358
Louvois, François Michel Le Tellier, marquis de, 268, 271
love, Restoration notions concerning, 41, 57–8, 106–7, 109, 122–3, 135, 138–40, 255–7, 278, 281–2
Love, Harold, 86n., 87n., 89n., 157, 159n., 264, 272n., 274, 277n., 311n.
Lovejoy, Arthur O., 216n.
Lovelace, Richard, 31, 45; *Dialogue. Lucasta, Alexis*, 68; *A loose Saraband*, 12n.
Lucian, *Timon the Misanthrope*, 279
Lucilius, 313, 320, 321, 327
Lucretius, *De Rerum Natura*, 89–90, 146, 150, 193n., 198, 311, 319
Lynch, Kathleen M., 324n.
Lyttelton, Sir Charles, 131

Maastricht, siege of, 18
McCarthy, B. Eugene, 325n.
Maccubbin, Robert P. [ed.], 258n.

McFadden, George, 327n.
Macfarlane, Alan, 41n., 124n., 136n., 259n.; Josselin ed., 244n.
MacGregor-Hastie, Roy, 290n.
MacLysaght, Edward, 254n.
Macmillan, Dougald, 132n.
McNeilly, F. S., 177–8
Main, C. F., 205–6
Maintenon, Françoise d'Aubigné, marquise de, 269–70
Maitland, John, *see* Lauderdale
Makin, Bathsua, 124
Malebranche, Nicolas, 184
Malherbe, François de, 33, 34; 'Victoire de la constance: Stances', 80; 'Quoi donc c'est un arrêt', 81
Mancini, Hortense, *see* Mazarin
Manning, Gillian, 142n., 157
Marlowe, Christopher, *Tamburlaine*, 344n.
Marmier, Jean, 312n.
Martial, 20–1, 222n.
Martin, F. X. [ed.], 254n.
Martin, L. C. [Crashaw ed.], 148n.
Martz, Louis L. [ed.], 296n.
Marvell, Andrew, 45, 52, 195n., 203n., 234, 255, 300; *Bill-borow*, 202; *The Character of Holland*, 159; *Last Instructions to a Painter*, 289n.; *The Rehearsal Transpros'd*, 247, 251–3; *To His Coy Mistress*, 63
Mary of Modena, Duchess of York, 288–9
Mary, Princess [future Mary II], 322
Mason, John E., 24n.
Matthew, Gospel acc. to St, 148
Mavidal, J., 267n.
Mazarin, Hortense Mancini, Duchess of, 300–1
Mead, Herman Ralph, 342n.
Mecziems, Jenny [ed.], 86n.
medicine and illness in the Restoration, 249–50, 253, 257–9, 306, 358
melancholy, 354 and n.
Melville, Lewis, 247n.
Mendelson, Sara Heller, 124n., 132n., 134n.
Meres, Sir Thomas, 218–19
Michel, Robert H., 65n., 124n., 258n., 259n.
midwives, status and practices of, 260
Mignon, Elisabeth, 35, 50n.
Milhous, Judith, 326n.
military matters in the Restoration, 159, 260–3, 270, 273
Miller, Clarence H. [Erasmus trans.], 279n.
Miller, H. K., 141n.
Miller, John, 293n.
Millett, Kate, 123–4

Milton, John, 41; *Paradise Lost*, 81, 168, 318
Mintz, Samuel I., 174, 175, 214n.
Mitchell, W. Fraser, 231n.
Modena, Laura d'Este, Duchess of, 288–9
Molière (Jean Baptiste Poquelin), *L'Amour médecin*, 258; *Les Femmes savantes*, 130
Monck, George, *see* Albemarle
Mongrédien, Georges, 57n.
Monmouth, James, Duke of, 270, 351
Montagu, Lady Mary Wortley, 125
Montague, Elizabeth, 287, 288, 292n.
Montague, Ralph, 128n., 287, 288, 292n.
Montaigne, Michel Eyquem, seigneur de, 88, 162, 179–84, 210
Montespan, Françoise A., marquise de, 269–70
Moody, T. W. [ed.], 254n.
Moore, John F., 182, 184, 186
Morangle, Payot de, *L'Occasion perdue*, 85
Mordaunt, Charles, Viscount, 307
More, Henry, 4, 169, 204n.
Moreau, Pierre, 180n.
morophilia, 99, 138–9, 291
Moseley, Mrs, 306
Mulgrave, John Sheffield, Earl of [future Marquess of Normanby and Duke of Buckingham], 76, 185, 263n., 292, 307, 318, 337, 338–52, 353–4, 355; *Essay upon Poetry*, 341; *Essay upon Satire*, 341, 342, 344; [?] *The Perfect Enjoyment*, 87

Nadelhaft, Jerome, 129n.
Nankivell, James, 233n.
Nero, 16
Netherlands, the, and the Dutch, 158–9, 267, 273, 289
Newcastle, Margaret Cavendish, Duchess of, 50, 66, 130–3, 134, 280n.
Newcastle, William Cavendish, Duke of, 50, 130, 131n.
Newton, Isaac, 149, 194
Nicoll, Allardyce, 323n., 325
Nicolson, Marjorie Hope, 202n., 249n.
Nokes, G. D., 360
North's Plutarch, 279
Noyes, George Rapall, 342n.
Nussbaum, Felicity A., 111n., 134n., 140n.

Ober, William, 85n.
O'Donovan, John, 305n.
Ogg, David, 227n., 234, 235, 243n., 249n., 254n., 256n.
Oldham, John, *Aude aliquid. Ode*, 16; *The Cup*, 17n.; *Satyrs upon the Jesuits*, 16, 101n.
Ollard, Richard, 53n., 230, 232n.

O'Neill, John, 84n., 85n., 86, 92, 287n., 296n., 298, 299n.
Oosterveen, K. [ed.], 136n.
Orinda, *see* Philips, Katherine
Orlich, Leopold von [ed.], 270n.
Ormonde, James Butler, 1st Duke of, 254, 304
Orrery, Roger Boyle, 1st Earl of, 322, 323, 324, 330; *Mustapha*, 322n., 326n.
Osborne, Dorothy, 105, 132–3
Osborne, Francis, *Advice to a Son*, 24
Osborne, Sir Thomas, *see* Danby
Otway, Thomas, 310, 322, 323, 331; *Alcibiades*, 323; *The Soldier's Fortune*, 255n.
Overton, J. H., 215n., 229n., 231, 232n.
Ovid, 23, 311; *Amores*, 12n., 23n., 32, 38, 85, 87n., 90–1, 93, 94, 95, 101n.; *Ars Amatoria*, 21n., 34, 37; *Heroides*, 344

Packe, Capt. Edmund, 261n., 262
paedophilia, 9–10, 20–3
Palatinate, the, 268, 270n.
Palmer, Melvin Delmar, 339–40
Park, Thomas [Waller ed.], 56n.
Parker, Samuel, 234, 245, 247n., 250–3, 255
Parsons, Robert, 363, 364
Pascal, Blaise, 165n., 183, 193
Pasch, Thomas K., 100n.
pastoral verse, 45–6, 52, 59, 333–4
Patrick, Simon, 167, 168n., 172, 211–13; *Parable of the Pilgrim*, 212
Patrides, C. A., 79–80n.
Patterson, Annabel M., 255n.
Patterson, John D., 10n., 19n., 22, 100n., 357–8n.
Paulson, Kristoffer F., 146, 163n., 164, 165, 230n., 352n., 355n.
Paulson, Ronald, 296n., 298n., 300
Pearson, Jacqueline, 53
pederasty, *see* paedophilia
Pelous, Jean-Michel, 30n., 38n., 45, 53n.
Pepys, Samuel, 53, 130, 192n., 233n., 244, 247, 306
Peter, Heinrich, 267n., 268
Petrarchism, 38
Petronius, 56; *Satyricon*, 85, 87n.
Philips, Katherine ('Orinda'), 58, 134
Picavet, Camille-Georges, 267n.
Pineau, Joseph, 185n.
Pinto, Vivian de Sola, 5, 10, 13, 15n., 35n., 81n., 119n., 127n., 128n., 131n., 143n., 155n., 160n., 163, 166, 167, 175n., 212n., 233n., 236n., 287n., 289n., 295n., 300n., 302n., 318n., 338n., 363
Plutarch, 182

Pocock, Gordon, 333n.
politics in Restoration England, 152–7, 159,
  227–8, 237, 239, 247, 251, 254–5, 295,
  297–8, 303–5
Pomponne, Simon Arnauld, marquis de, 267
Pope, Alexander, *Imitations of Horace*, 311n.;
  imitations of Dorset, 108n; eulogy on
  Mulgrave, 341n.; revises Mulgrave's *Essay
  upon Satire*, 342n.; *To Miss Blount*, 137n.
Popkin, Richard A., 210n.
Porter, Peter, 61n., 77, 91, 334
Porter, Roy, 258n.
Portsmouth, Louise de Kéroualle, Duchess of,
  289, 291, 293, 298, 299, 300–1, 302
Portsmouth's Looking-Glass, 299n.
Prinz, Johannes, 5, 331n.
Prior, Matthew, *A Better Answer*, 71
Privy Council, the, 156
Propertius, *Elegies*, 11
Puritans and Protestant dissent generally, 151,
  167, 168, 170, 171, 192n., 194, 251, 254–5
Pyrrhonism, 210

Quack-Doctor, The Character of a, 245n., 250n.
Quaintance, Richard E., Jr, 18n., 56n., 85, 86,
  87, 88, 93n., 99n., 108, 350n.
Quehen, Hugh de [Butler ed.], 80n.

Raleigh, Sir Walter, 212n.
Ram(e)sey, William, *The Gentlemans
  Companion*, 4n., 101n., 124n.
Randolph, Mary Claire, 163n.
Ranters, the, 79
Raphael, D. D., 174n., 175n., 177n.
Rawlins, Thomas, 246n., 260n.
Rawson, Claude [ed.], 86n.
Redwood, John, 168–9n.
Refin'd Courtier, The, 256n., 263
Régnier, Mathurin, 198, 274; *Impuissance*, 85,
  87n., 88; *Satires*, 275–6, 281, 312n.
Reynolds, Myra, 124n., 130, 134n., 202n.
Rhys, Hedley Howell [ed.], 19n.
Richmond, Frances (*née* Stuart), Duchess of,
  289n.
Richmond, H. M., 51n., 62n., 74n.
Righter, Anne [now Anne Barton], 4, 30n.,
  60, 69, 79n., 111n., 113, 161n., 357n.,
  364–5
Roberts, James Deotis, Sr, 171n.
Robinson, Ken (K. E.), 6, 7, 19, 70, 86, 92n.,
  101n., 175n., 177n., 211, 306, 355n.
Rochester, Anne (*née* St John) Wilmot,
  Dowager Countess of, 136, 166, 363
Rochester, Elizabeth (*née* Malet) Wilmot,
  Countess of, 4, 39–41, 76, 183, 222n., 234,

294; *The Answer* ('Nothing adds to your
  fond fire'), 39–41
Rochester, Henry Wilmot, 1st Earl of, 160,
  302
ROCHESTER, John Wilmot, 2nd Earl of.
  Works: 'Absent from thee', 29, 38, 42,
  70–9, 82, 309n., 347–8; *The Advice*, 31–3,
  37; *Against Constancy*, 61–4; *An Allusion to
  Horace*, 3, 65, 291n., 309–36, 337, 338–9,
  352; 'As *Chloris* full of harmless thought',
  22, 52, 54–5, 82–3; 'Att Last you'l force
  mee to confess', 48–9; 'By all *Loves* soft,
  yet mighty *Pow'rs*', 285, 307–8; 'Could I
  but make my wishes insolent', 38–9; *A
  Dialogue between Strephon and Daphne*,
  59–61, 68; *The Disabled Debauchee*, 9, 12,
  13–16, 21–2, 23, 63, 95, 152; *The Discovery*,
  38, 44; *The Earl of Rochester's Answer ...
  L. B. Felton*, etc., 135; *An Epistolary Essay*,
  337, 338–43, 349, 350; 'Fair *Cloris* in a
  Piggsty lay', 51–2, 54, 55, 286; *The Fall*,
  29, 37, 51, 70, 79–82, 95, 107, 123, 124,
  309n., 318, 348; 'Give me leave to raile at
  you', 39–41; *Grecian Kindness*, 9, 11–12;
  'Her father gave her Dildoes six' (*Upon
  Cary Frazer*), 285; *The Imperfect Enjoyment*,
  21, 30, 43, 51, 55, 84–96, 98, 100, 102, 103,
  249, 308; 'Injurious Charmer of my
  vanquisht Heart', 67–8; 'Insulting *Beauty*,
  you mispend', 38–9; 'I' th' Isle of
  Britaine', *see Satire on Charles II*; *A
  Lampoon upon the English Grandees*
  ('Monmouth the wittiest!'), 154; 'Leave
  this gawdy guilded Stage', 36–7, 78, 82; *A
  Letter from Artemiza in the Towne to Chloe
  in the Countrey*, 4, 42, 99, 104–140, 152,
  282, 284, 309n., 334; 'Lorrain he stole',
  300n.; 'Love a *Woman*! y'are an *Ass*', 9,
  10, 21, 22, 23–5, 26, 27, 121, 122, 124; *Love
  and Life*, 29, 43, 67, 68–70, 72, 309n.; *The
  Mistress*, 29, 37, 41, 70, 73–9, 82, 309n.,
  334, 348; *Mistress Knights Advice*, 285, 289,
  290n., 292; 'My dear Mistris has a heart',
  66–7; *My Lord All-Pride*, 337, 340, 349–52,
  355; *On Mistress Willis*, 285, 305–6; *On
  Poet Ninny*, 337, 352, 354–5, 356; *On the
  suppos'd Author of a late Poem in defence of
  Satyr*, 337, 352, 353–4; *A Pastoral Dialogue
  between Alexis and Strephon*, 38, 44–6;
  '*Phillis*, be gentler I advice', 32, 34–5, 43,
  46, 49; *The Platonick Lady*, 55–9; *A Ramble
  in Saint James's Parke*, 30, 42, 51, 55, 62, 84,
  95–103, 107, 110, 234, 242, 279, 286, 308,
  353; *Satire on Charles II*, 156, 160, 285,
  295–301, 360; *A Satyr against Reason and*

Mankind, 3, 108, 111, 118, 119, 162–239, 264, 283, 284, 287, 309n., 334; *Signior Dildo*, 2, 52, 99, 285–95, 307, 308, 334; *A Song of a Young Lady to her Ancient Lover*, 4, 49–51, 95, 309n.; *The submission*, 38, 41–3, 107; *Timon*, 2, 98, 126, 208, 243, 266–84, 285, 311, 319, 322–3, 330, 331n., 333, 334, 336; *To A Lady, in A Letter*, 9, 10, 12, 25–7, 99; *To His Sacred Majesty* ('Vertues triumphant Shrine!'), 303; 'To longe the Wise Commons' (*Lampoone*), 253n., 285, 303–5; *To the Post Boy*, 160, 208, 357–60; *Tunbridge Wells*, 2, 117, 136, 192, 207, 241–65, 266, 277, 278, 284, 285; 'T'was a dispute', 38, 43; *Upon his Drinking a Bowl*, 9, 11, 12, 16–19, 20, 22, 311; *Upon his leaving his Mistriss*, 64–6; *Upon Nothing*, 119, 141–61, 162, 190, 226, 227, 253n., 284, 287, 304, 309n., 334, 360; *Valentinian*, 68, 334, 347; *Verses put into a Lady's Prayer-book*, 32, 33–4; *A very Heroicall Epistle in Answer to Ephelia*, 76–7, 337, 344–9, 350, 351; 'What Cruel pains Corinna takes', 47–8, 49, 51; 'What vaine unnecessary things are men' (*Fragment of a Satire on Men*), 122, 126–7, 132; 'When to the King I bid good Morrow' (*Dialogue*), 245n., 285, 292, 300–1; 'While on those lovely looks I gaze', 38, 43–4; *Womans Honor*, 46–7; translations from: Lucretius, 361; Ovid, 311n.; Seneca, 80, 146, 152, 362; prologue to *The Empress of Morocco*, 114; epilogue to *Love in the Dark*, 207; *Letters*, 2, 10, 12–13, 25, 51, 76, 159, 160, 192, 222n., 238, 269, 288n., 301–2, 317, 318, 342n., 356, 362, 364–5

Rodes, David Stuart [Dryden ed.], 48n.
Rogers, Katharine M., 24
Rogers, Pat, 310n., 312n., 313n., 327n., 328n., 329n.
Ronsard, Pierre de, Anacreontic verse, 17, 18, 19
Roscommon, Wentworth Dillon, 4th Earl of, trans. of Horace's *Ars Poetica*, 332
Rosenfield, Leonora Cohen, 203n., 204n.
Ross, Alexander, 168n.
Røstvig, Maren-Sofie, 222n.
Rothstein, Eric, 4–5n., 13n., 108n.
Rowzee, Dr Lodwick, 247n., 250
Ruggiero, Guido, 259n.
Rules of Civility, 253n.
Runte, Roseann [ed.], 22n.
Russell family, 249n.
Russell, Ford, 175n.
Rymer, Thomas, 14n., 185, 329

Sackville, Charles, Lord Buckhurst, *see* Dorset
St Evremond, Charles M. St Denis, seigneur de, 87n., 271n., 272
Salmon, Nathaniel, 232n.
Sandys, Lady Lucy Hamilton, 294
Sargeaunt, John [Dryden ed.], 210n.
Savile, George, *see* Halifax
Savile, Henry, 2, 10, 12–13, 20n., 25, 51, 160, 227n., 238, 263n., 278, 287, 292n., 301–2
Sayers, Dorothy L., 272n.
Scargill, Daniel, 175
Scarron, Françoise, *see* Maintenon
scepticism, 210, 360
Schurman, Anna Maria van, *The Learned Maid*, 130
Schwerin, Otto von, d.J., 270n.
Scotland and the Scots, 158, 159, 273
Scouten, Arthur H., 322n.
Scrivener, Matthew, *A Treatise Against Drunkennesse*, 11n., 136n., 220n.
Scroope, Sir Carr, 185, 307, 323, 334, 337, 351, 352–6, 357, 358; *Answer* [to Rochester], 352, 354; 'I cannot change as others do', 352; *In Defence of Satyr*, 261n., 352, 353–4, 355, 358; prologue to *The Man of Mode*, 133
Scudéry, Mlle Madeleine de, 38, 58, 204; *Le Grand Cyrus*, 57
Sedley, Sir Charles, 45, 243, 278, 312, 318, 324, 327–8, 343; *Advice to the Old Beaux*, 50n.; 'Fair Aminta, art thou mad', 35–6; 'Not, Celia, that I juster am', 63–4, 66, 70; *A Pastoral Dialogue*, 45; *Songs*, 328 and n.; *The Submission*, 41; *To a Devout Young Gentlewoman*, 33; 'To Flavia', 235; trans. from Martial, 21
Seidel, Michael A., 124n.
Selden, Raman, 16n., 167, 243n., 257n., 324
Sells, A. Lytton, 203–4n.
Sena, John F., 354n.
Seneca, *Troades*, 80, 146, 362
Settle, Elkanah, 310, 316, 317, 321, 323, 330; *The Empress of Morocco*, 316, 323
Sévigné, Mme Marie de, 204, 269
Shadwell, Thomas, 66, 131n., 312n., 316, 317, 322n., 324–5, 326, 331, 332; *Elegy* on the Duchess of Newcastle, 66; *Epsom Wells*, 26–7, 46, 57, 67, 131n., 138–140, 243–4, 247, 248–9, 250, 255, 256, 257, 272; *Letter... to Mr. Wicherley*, 137, 306; *The Libertine*, 357n.; adaptation of *Timon of Athens*, 278n.
Shaftesbury, Anthony Ashley Cooper, 1st Earl of, 156–7, 160n., 254

Shakespeare, William, 314–15, 321, 328; *Timon of Athens*, 277, 278–9
Shapiro, Barbara J., 169n., 171n., 174, 214
Shaw, William Arthur, 243n.
Sheehan, David, 104n., 120n.
Sheffield, John, *see* Mulgrave
Sheldon, Gilbert, Archbishop, 232–3, 255
Shepherd, Sir Fleetwood, 323
Shrewsbury, Anna Maria Talbot (*née* Brudenell), Countess of, 290–1, 293
Shugg, Wallace, 204n.
Sibbes, Richard, 151, 164–7, 170–1, 213, 221
Sillery, Marquis of, 272n.
Sillery wine, *see* drinking
Simon, Irène, 196n.
Sintzheim, battle of, 268
Sitter, John E., 197n.
Sloane, Eugene Hulse, 121n.
Smith, G.C. Moore [Dorothy Osborne ed.], 132n.
Smith, Hilda L., 50n., 124n., 134n.
Smith, John Harrington, 132n.
Smith, R. M. [ed.], 136n.
Sodom [authorship uncertain], 285
'Song of Nothing' [*anon.*, in *Merry Drollery Compleat*], 142
Souches, Ludwig Raduit de, 267–8
Souers, Philip, 58n., 134n.
Southesk, Anne (*née* Hamilton) Carnegie, Countess of, 288
Spain and Spaniards, 158, 246
Spenser, Edmund, *The Faerie Queene*, 92
Spink, J. S., 169n., 218n.
Stanley, Thomas, 18n.; Anacreontic translations, 18, 20; *History of Philosophy*, 18n.
Stemmler, Theo [ed.], 339n.
Stenton, Doris Mary, 124n., 132n.
Stephanus, Henricus, *see* Estienne
Stillingfleet, Edward, 149, 164–5, 168n., 171, 172, 229–31, 233; *Origines Sacrae*, 4, 194n.
Stone, Lawrence, 124n., 136n., 307
'Stop of the Exchequer', 157, 297
Stratmann, Gerd [ed.], 339n.
Stuart, Frances, *see* Richmond
Suckling, Sir John, 31, 56; *A Session of the Poets*, 335n.
Summers, Montague, 243n.; Shadwell ed., 27n.; Behn ed., 54
Sutch, Victor D., 232, 233, 235
Sutherland, James, 3
Switzerland and the Swiss, 270, 273–4
Sydenham, Thomas, 258

Tailhard, Jean, 159n.
Temple, Philippa, 289n.
Temple, Sir William, 132, 170n., 305n.
textual issues, 5–7, 21, 75n., 162–7, 246, 247n., 287
theriophily, 203–5
Third Dutch War, 18, 19, 219, 262, 270, 273, 297, 305, 351
Thomas, Keith, 80n., 124n., 192n., 204n., 214n.
Thompson, Roger, 10n., 101n., 285n., 286, 293n.
Thomson, Gladys Scott, 244n., 249n.
Thormählen, Marianne, 48n., 73n., 75n., 79n., 97n., 200n., 207n.
Thorn-Drury, G., 87n.
Thorpe, James [Etherege ed.], 47n.
Tillotson, John, 168n., 171
Timon of Phlius, 278
Tonson, Jacob, 185n.
town vs country, 135–8
Town-Gallant, The Character of a, 98n., 256, 348
Treglown, Jeremy, 2n., 20n., 34, 36–7, 54n., 61n., 62n., 68n., 69, 76, 118, 182n., 183n., 221n., 241n., 269, 283, 287, 302n., 317, 318, 361n.
Trickett, Rachel, 8n., 137n.
Trotter, David, 165, 168n., 234n.
Tunbridge-Wells; Or a Days Courtship [by Th. Rawlins?], 246n., 260n., 349
Turenne, Henri de la Tour d'Auvergne, vicomte de, Marshal of France, 267–8, 270, 273, 351
Turner, Edward Raymond, 156n.
Turner, James Grantham, 23n., 360n.

Underwood, Dale, 210n., 216, 330n.
Urfé, Honoré d', 38

Van Leeuwen, Henry G., 169n.
Van Lennep, William, 322n., 351n.
Varro of the Atax, 327
Vaughan, Henry, *A Rhapsodie*, 11
Verity, Arthur Wilson [Etherege ed.], 47n.
Verney, family, 140n.
Viau, Théophile de, 18n., 31, 198, 217, 312n.
Vieth, David M., 2n., 3, 5–7, 9n., 13n., 15, 17, 21, 30, 32n., 33n., 44, 49n., 50, 65n., 66, 68n., 69n., 73, 76, 78, 84, 104, 110n., 111, 112n., 117n., 124n., 127, 147, 148, 151n., 154, 157n., 158, 161, 162, 163, 165, 167, 190, 195, 205n., 208n., 215–16, 224, 231, 233n., 244, 245, 246, 248, 251, 266, 277–8, 280n., 286n., 288n., 291n., 294n., 295n., 296, 297,

299n., 302–3n., 306n., 311n., 313n., 327n., 337n., 338, 339, 340, 341, 342, 343, 344n., 346, 349n., 351n., 352, 355n., 357n., 358

Villiers, George *see* Buckingham

Voltaire, François Marie Arouet de, 185

Waker, Nathaniel, 256n.

Walker, D. P., 79n.

Walker, Keith, 6–7, 9, 17, 21, 26, 30, 32n., 33n., 44, 58n., 68n., 84, 86, 109n., 124n., 126, 128n., 135, 144, 157, 158–9, 163, 165, 195, 213, 233n., 245, 246, 247n., 248n., 254, 257n., 260, 261n., 279, 287n., 288n., 292n., 295n., 296, 297, 337n., 340, 344, 351n., 353n., 362n.

Walker, Obadiah, 207–8

Waller, A. R. [Cowley ed.], 42n., 137n.

Waller, Edmund, 45, 322n., 324, 326, 332, 343, 348; *Divine Poems*, 109, 220–1; *In Answer of Sir John Suckling's Verses*, 56; *Instructions to a Painter*, 159n.; *The Self-Banished*, 74n.; *The Triple Combat*, 300–1

Walpole, Horace, 185

Walton, Clifford, 261n., 262

Warren, Albertus, 195n.

Warton, Joseph, 186

Weber, Harold, 1n.

Weinbrot, Howard D., 104–5, 106, 111, 163n., 310n., 311n., 313n., 321, 329n.

Welwood, James, 296n., 297n.

Westfall, Richard S., 172n.

Whichcote, Benjamin, 171n.

White, Arthur Franklin, 323n.

White, Isabelle, 192n., 235n.

Whitley, Raymond K., 177n., 346n., 349n., 361n.

Wilbraham, Anne, 272n.

Wilcoxon, Reba, 1, 22n., 24, 49, 50, 61, 69n., 84n., 85n., 90n., 92, 100n., 107n., 120n., 123–4, 126, 148–9, 286n., 287n., 357n.

Wilde, Oscar, *The Importance of Being Earnest*, 112n.

Wilders, John, 62n., 71, 197n., 204n., 213n.

Wilkinson, D. R. M., 23n., 24, 126n., 256n.

Willey, Basil, 165n., 168n., 214n.

William III, 230, 273

Williams, Aubrey [ed.], 296n.

Williams, Charles, 5n., 363n.

Williams, George Walton, 148n.

Willis, Sue, 59, 91, 305–6

Wilmot family, *see* Rochester

Wilson, Glenn D., 20n.

Wilson, John Harold, 29n., 33, 86, 92–3, 111, 122n., 140n., 154n., 215n., 262n., 270n., 286n., 288n., 289n., 290, 291n., 292n., 299n., 300n., 301n., 306n., 307n., 309n., 322n., 341n., 342n., 344, 355n.

wine, *see* drinking

Winn, James Anderson, 159n., 288n., 295n., 309, 312n., 316n.

Wintle, Sarah, 25n., 66n., 125, 126, 286n.

Wise, James N., 168n.

wit, in Rochester's poems and implications of concept generally, 26, 118–20, 207–9, 332

witchcraft, 213–15

Witcombe, D. T., 218n., 219n.

women, presentation of in Rochester's poetry, 10, 23–7, 29–140, 258–60

women, situation of in Restoration society, 23–4, 25, 35–6, 52–3, 65, 124–6, 129, 130, 132, 136, 258–60

Womersley, D. J., 58n.

Wood, Anthony, 175

Wood, Stephen, 273n.

Woolley, Hannah, *The Gentlewoman's Companion*, 113n., 124

Wordsworth, William, *Ode*, 206

Wrigley, E. A., 138n.

Wycherley, William, 47, 117, 243, 306, 310, 312n., 324, 325–6; *Answer* to Shadwell, 137; *The Country Wife*, 47, 63, 325–6; *The Plain Dealer*, 325, 329, 342n.

Young Gallant's Academy, 244n., 293n.

Younger, William, 271n., 272

Youth's Behaviour, or Decency in Conversation Amongst Women, 36, 257n., 293n.

Zimansky, Curt A., 17

Zimmermann, Hans-Joachim, 339n.